Tests

A Comprehensive Reference for Assessments in Psychology, Education, and Business

Sixth Edition

Edited by
Taddy Maddox

8700 Shoal Creek Boulevard
Austin, Texas 78757-6897
800/897-3202   Fax 800/397-7633
www.proedinc.com

An International Publisher

© 1983, 1984, 1986, 1991, 1997, 2003, 2008 by PRO-ED, Inc.
8700 Shoal Creek Boulevard
Austin, Texas 78757-6897
800/897-3202   Fax 800/397-7633
www.proedinc.com

Library of Congress Cataloging-in-Publication Data

Tests : a comprehensive reference for assessments in psychology, education,
and business / edited by Taddy Maddox. — 6th ed.
          p. cm.
     Includes bibliographical references and indexes.
     ISBN-13: 978-1-4164-0340-1 (hardcover)
     ISBN-10: 1-4164-0340-X (hardcover)
     ISBN-13: 978-1-4164-0341-8 (softcover)
     ISBN-10: 1-4164-0341-8 (softcover)
     1. Psychological tests.   2. Educational tests and measurements.
  3. Occupational aptitude tests.   I. Maddox, Taddy.

  BF176 .T43   2007
  150.28'7—dc22

                                                                2007004170

Art Director: Jason Crosier
Designer: Vicki DePountis
This book is designed in Lucida Sans.

Printed in the United States of America

1 2 3 4 5 6 7 8 9 10   11 10 09 08 07

Contents

Preface

As this sixth edition of *Tests* is published, it is appropriate to comment on the project's development and background and to recognize the contributions of people who made the task possible. Richard C. Sweetland and Daniel J. Keyser prepared the first edition of *Tests* in response to the need for a resource containing consistent codified information describing and cataloging tests available for use by psychologists, educators, and human resources personnel. The professional community received *Tests,* published in 1983, enthusiastically. Within 1 year of publication, the first edition was in its third printing, indicating to the editors that thousands of professionals had come to rely on its quick-scanning, easy-to-read format. Committed to providing readers with the most current information possible on assessment instruments, Sweetland and Keyser launched a "search and find" effort that resulted in the 1984 publication of *Tests: Supplement,* a complement to the first edition that contained information on more than 500 new tests. The supplement was followed by the second edition of *Tests* in 1986.

Sweetland and Keyser's ongoing search-and-find efforts—which uncovered information on hundreds of new tests; rapid developments in areas such as substance abuse, eating disorders, and chronic illness; the increasing role of technology in assessment; and Sweetland and Keyser's continued firm commitment to providing users with quick access to current test information—resulted in the third edition, published in 1991. In the fourth edition, PRO-ED continued this commitment to providing a reference that can be used by professionals in the fields of psychology, education, and business to obtain information about testing instruments.

In this sixth edition, I have attempted to improve the usability of the reference guide. Web addresses are included for the publishers, as most provide the capability of purchasing tests through the Internet. Tests and publishers that were in the fifth edition but are not included in the sixth edition are again listed in indexes.

I thank the readers for the numerous suggestions they have offered, particularly for providing the names of assessment instruments not referenced in the previous edition. Special thanks are extended to the many test publishers and authors who generously and graciously contributed staff time, information, and support for this book.

How to Use This Book

Tests, a reference guide containing information on thousands of assessment instruments, is designed especially for psychologists, educators, and human resources personnel who search for tests to satisfy their assessment needs. In addition, students, librarians, and other nonspecialists who need to familiarize themselves with the broad range of available tests will find the contents and format helpful. *Tests* does not attempt to review or evaluate tests; its purpose is to present concise descriptions in a quick-scanning, easy-to-read format. This sixth edition, which presents the tests of 164 publishers, updates the information contained in the fifth edition and presents descriptions of new and revised tests.

How *Tests* Is Organized

The assessments described herein are organized according to a system of primary classification intended to make information as accessible to the reader as possible. Each of the book's three main sections — Psychology, Education, and Business—is divided into subsections. Psychology Instruments contains 21 subsections, Education Instruments contains 47 subsections, and Business Instruments contains 22 subsections. Each test has been given a primary classification in one of the Psychology, Education, or Business subsections and is described in detail in that subsection. The tests within each subsection are listed alphabetically by title.

To establish subsections that would be practical and functional for the reader, the editor sought considerable consultation from professionals who use tests on a daily basis. Based on feedback from these sources, the editor reorganized the subsections in this sixth edition both to facilitate the reader's search for assessments and to reflect contemporary terminology.

Format and Content of Descriptions

The format and content of each test entry are designed to provide the basic information necessary to decide whether a particular test is appropriate to consider for a given assessment need. Each test entry is structured as follows: (a) test title, (b) copyright date, (c) primary publisher, (d) authors' names, (e) population for which the test is intended, (f) a purpose statement, (g) a brief description highlighting the test's major features, (h) format information, (i) scoring method, and (j) relevant cost and availability information. Each of these components is explained in detail.

The **test title** is presented exactly as it appears in the test publisher's materials but without any articles (e.g., *a, an, the*). For example, one would find the description of *The Wonderlic Personnel Test* listed as *Wonderlic Personnel Test.*

The **copyright date** appears next. This date reflects the date the instrument or its revision was published.

Next to the copyright date is the name of the **primary publisher.** The Index of Test Publishers contains complete address, telephone, fax, and Web site information. The editor attempted to confirm the accuracy of every test entry through direct correspondence with the test publisher. Despite repeated contact attempts, however, some publishers did not respond to queries. Those publishers who did not respond are listed in the Index of Publishers Not in the Sixth Edition.

The test **author names** appear below the test title. Corporate authors are not listed, only individuals.

A description of the intended consumers of the test is listed in the **population** entry. For children, the target age or grade of the examinee may be provided.

The **purpose** statement offers a succinct overview of the test's intended application and what it purports to measure, assess, diagnose, evaluate, or identify.

The **description** presents the number of test items, test format (paper–pencil, true–false, projective, oral, observational, etc.), factors or variables measured, materials used, manner in which the test is administered, foreign language availability, and special features.

The **format** section describes how the test is administered (individual, group, or both), estimated time of administration, and whether the instrument is timed (when the information has been provided by the publisher).

The **scoring** description provides information about the method used to score the test: hand key, examiner evaluated, machine scored, or computer scored. Hand key indicates that the test is scored using an answer key or template provided by the test publisher. An examiner-evaluated test is scored using an examiner's opinion, skills, and knowledge. A computer- or machine-scored test uses answer sheets that are scored by computer or machine. When a combination of these terms appears in the scoring section, the first listed is the primary method employed.

The **cost** section contains price information that is as accurate as the editor could establish at the time of the book's publication. Because the pricing structure for some tests (covering the various forms, kits, options, etc.) is extensive, only representative costs are included here. The editor encourages readers to contact the publisher for complete cost information.

Indexes

Tests (6th ed.) contains five indexes that were compiled to make this reference book user friendly. The following listing does not show the indexes in the order in which they appear at the end of this book, but rather in the order in which they are most frequently used. For example, the Index of Test Titles is used most frequently, and so that index is the last (and most accessible to the reader) in the book. The other indexes have also been rearranged based on anticipated use.

The **Index of Test Titles** lists each test described in this book. As explained previously, the title of each test is presented exactly as it appears in the test publisher's materials, but without any articles (e.g., *a, an, the*) to allow for true alphabetical listing. British spelling has been retained in proper titles.

The **Index of Test Authors** lists all test authors except corporate and institutional staffs. This listing is in alphabetical order and includes all authors of each instrument, not only the first author.

The **Index of Test Publishers** provides addresses, telephone numbers, fax numbers, and Web site addresses for publishers whose tests are listed in this book.

The **Index of Tests Not in the Sixth Edition** lists those instruments that were in the fifth edition but are not included in the sixth edition. There are a variety of reasons for the exclusion of an instrument, including lack of response from the publisher, the publisher's going out of business, or the test's going out of print.

The **Index of Publishers Not in the Sixth Edition** lists those publishers who had tests listed in the fifth edition but not in this edition. For example, this listing includes those publishers who did not reply to the initial request for information and those publishers for whom current address and phone information is available but who did not return information on their instruments. A brief statement indicates why the publisher was not included.

The purpose of *Tests* from the outset has been to provide a quick reference for tests available in the English language. Some Spanish language tests are now included due to the growth of that population in the schools.

When the first edition of this volume was published, the editors decided to omit detailed reliability, validity, and normative data—aspects considered too complex to reduce to the quick-scanning desk-reference format. The current editor has continued to leave out this information.

Use of the Book

The system classification used in *Tests* and the inclusion of the indexes just described accommodate readers who need information about a particular test, as well as those conducting a general search for appropriate assessment instruments. The following suggestions for using *Tests* are intended to minimize the reader's efforts to locate information.

- Readers who are unable to locate a test using the Index of Test Titles should consult the Index of Test Authors or the Index of Test Publishers if either of these elements is known.

- Tests that cannot be located in the previously mentioned sections may be found in the Index of Tests Not in the Sixth Edition. Be aware that these instruments may or may not be out of print, but the editor was unable to determine current information about availability, price, or revisions.

PRO-ED fully supports the ethical and professional standards established by national and state professional organizations. The inclusion of specific restrictions on test accessibility noted in some descriptions in this book usually has been requested by the publisher or author; the fact that a test description does not list restrictions does not imply that such restrictions do not exist. *When ordering tests, ask each publisher for the standards or requirements for purchasing.*

Order forms, catalogs, and further information regarding tests may be obtained from each publisher. Anyone interested in ordering a specific test should contact the publisher by using the Index of Test Publishers, which provides mailing addresses, telephone and fax numbers, and Web site addresses.

Although the information in this book was obtained from primary sources, the editor is aware of possibilities for error. Each test entry has been researched, screened, written, edited, and read by professional test administrators; however, the editor emphasizes that the job of checking and ensuring the accuracy of a book such as this is a process that will continue throughout the publication of subsequent editions. The editor invites the submission of information about new tests and encourages test publishers and authors to apprise PRO-ED of errors in the test descriptions or of test revisions made available since publication of this edition by contacting PRO-ED at editorial@proedinc.com.

Psychology Instruments

The tests presented and described in the Psychology Instruments section have been selected on the basis of their appropriate usage in a clinical or counseling setting. In general, tests found in this section might be used by a mental health professional, rather than by an educator or a human resources specialist. The classification of tests on the basis of typical usage or function is, of course, arbitrary, and the reader is encouraged to review both the Education Instruments and the Business Instruments sections for additional tests that may be helpful in meeting assessment needs.

Attention Deficit

ACTeRS™ Parent Form

1996	MetriTech, Inc.

Rina K. Ullmann, Esther K. Sleator, Robert L. Sprague

Population: Grades Pre-K to 12

Purpose: Aids in diagnosis of attention-deficit disorder with or without hyperactivity; used as a screening device to differentiate between children with ADD and those who may be otherwise learning disabled; useful for monitoring medication levels of children with ADD

Description: Paper–pencil or computer-administered 25-item multiple-choice test assessing behavior relevant to attention-deficit disorder. Provides separate scores for five factors: Attention, Hyperactivity, Social Skills, Oppositional Behavior, and Early Childhood. The computer version for IBM PC and compatible systems supports both the *ACTeRS: Parent Form* and the *ADD-H: Comprehensive Teacher's Rating Scale* (ACTeRS).

Format: Examiner required; individual administration; untimed: 10 minutes

Scoring: Computer scoring available; hand key; examiner evaluated

Cost: Examiner Kit (50 rating/profile forms, manual) $64.00

ACTeRS™ Self-Report

1998	MetriTech, Inc.

Population: Ages 12 years and older

Purpose: Diagnoses attention-deficit/hyperactivity disorder

Description: Total of 35 items in three categories: Attention (10), Hyperactivity/Impulsivity (15), and Social Adjustment (10). Scores provided for all three categories.

Format: Rating scale; untimed: 10 to 15 minutes

Scoring: Examiner evaluated

Cost: Examiner Kit (50 rating/profile forms, manual) $69.00

ACTeRS™ Teacher Form– Second Edition

1991	MetriTech, Inc.

Rina K. Ullmann, Esther K. Sleator, Robert L. Sprague

Population: Grades K to 8

Purpose: Aids in diagnosis of attention-deficit disorder with or without hyperactivity; used as a screening device to differentiate between children with ADD and those who may be otherwise learning disabled. Useful in monitoring medication levels of children with ADD

Description: Paper–pencil or computer-administered 24-item multiple-choice test assessing behavior relevant to the diagnosis of attention-deficit disorder. Provides separate scores for four factors: Attention, Hyperactivity, Social Skills, and Oppositional Behavior. The classroom teacher rates items on a 5-point scale ranging from *al-*

most *never* to *almost always*. An ACTeRS Profile (Boys' and Girls' forms) is generated. The computer version for IBM PC and compatible systems supports both the teachers' form and the *ACTeRS: Parent Form*. APA purchase restrictions apply.

Format: Rating scale; untimed: 10 minutes

Scoring: Computer scoring available; hand key; examiner evaluated

Cost: Examiner Kit (50 rating/profile forms, manual) $64.00

ADHD Rating Scale–IV

1998	Guilford Publications, Inc.

George J. DuPaul, Thomas J. Power, Arthur D. Anastopoulos, Robert Reid

Population: Ages 5 to 17 years

Purpose: Used for diagnosing ADHD and assessing treatment response

Description: The test contains 18 items and is linked to DSM-IV diagnostic criteria. There are three versions of the scale: a parent questionnaire on home behaviors (one in English and one in Spanish) and a teacher questionnaire on classroom behaviors. Permission to reproduce the scale is provided. Scoring profiles are provided for boys and girls.

Format: Rating scale; untimed

Scoring: Examiner evaluated

Cost: $44.00

ADHD School Observation Code (ADHD-SOC)

1996	Checkmate Plus, Ltd.

Kenneth D. Gadow, Joyce Sprafkin, Edith E. Nolan

Population: Grades K to 6

Purpose: Assesses behavioral symptoms of ADHD, oppositional-defiant disorder, and conduct problems; used in treatment planning and for monitoring response to intervention

Description: There are five classroom behavior categories (Interference, Motor Movement, Non-compliance, Nonphysical Aggression, and Off Task) and five lunchroom/playground behavior categories (Appropriate Social Behavior, Non-compliance, Nonphysical Aggression, Physical Aggression, and Verbal Aggression). Measures percentage of (15-second) intervals during which behavior occurs. Classroom code sheet and lunchroom/playground code sheet.

Format: Requires observer; untimed

Scoring: Examiner evaluated

Cost: Complete Kit (manual, 25 each of classroom and lunchroom/playground code sheets) $25.00

ADHD Symptom Checklist–4 (ADHD-SC4)

1997	Checkmate Plus, Ltd.

Kenneth D. Gadow, Joyce Sprafkin

Population: Ages 3 to 18 years

Purpose: Screens for attention-deficit/hyperactivity disorder and oppositional-defiant disorder and monitors response to treatment

Description: Contains a total of 50 items in four categories: ADHD (18), Oppositional Defiant Disorder (8), Peer Conflict Scale (10), and Stimulant Side Effects Checklist (14). Symptom count scores (DSM-IV criteria) and symptom severity scores (norms-based) are provided. Same form for parent and teacher. Also available in Spanish.

Format: Rating scale; untimed: 5 minutes

Scoring: Examiner evaluated

Cost: Deluxe Kit (manual, 50 each of checklists and profiles) $52.00

Adult Attention Deficit Disorders Evaluation Scale (A-ADDES)

1996	Hawthorne Educational Services, Inc.

Stephen B. McCarney, Paul D. Anderson

Population: Ages 18 to 65+ years

Purpose: Aids in the diagnosis of ADHD

Description: Self-Report Version: 58 items (31 inattentive and 27 hyperactive–impulsive); Home Version: 46 items (24 inattentive and 22 hyperactive–impulsive); Work Version: 54 items (28 inattentive and 26 hyperactive–impulsive). Individual raw scores are converted to subscale standard scores, and then subscale standard scores are converted to a percentile score. Self-Report rating form is completed by the patient; Home Version rating form is completed by a spouse, parent, roommate, or someone who knows the person well; Work Version rating form is completed by a coworker or supervisor.

Format: Rating scale; untimed: 20 minutes

Scoring: Examiner evaluated

Cost: Complete Kit (3 technical manuals, intervention manual, 50 each of 4 forms) $175.00

Attention Deficit Disorders Evaluation Scale: Secondary-Age Student (ADDES-S)

1996   **Hawthorne Educational Services, Inc.**

Stephen B. McCarney

Population: Ages 11 years 6 months to 18 years

Purpose: Aids in the diagnosis of ADHD

Description: School Version includes 60 items in two subscales: Inattentive and Hyperactive–Impulsive. Home version has 46 items in two subscales: Inattentive and Hyperactive–Impulsive. Individual raw scores are converted to subscale standard scores, and then subscale standard scores are converted to a percentile score. The School Form is completed by an educator; the Home Form is completed by a parent or guardian. A Windows Quick Score is available. The Pre-Referral Checklist provides a means of calling attention to the behavior for the purpose of early intervention before formal assessment.

Format: Rating scale; untimed: 12 to 15 minutes

Scoring: Examiner evaluated; computer scoring available

Cost: Complete Kit (2 technical manuals, intervention manual, parent's guide, 50 each of all forms) $232.00

Attention Deficit Disorders Evaluation Scale–Third Edition (ADDES-3)

2004   **Hawthorne Educational Services, Inc.**

Stephen B. McCarney

Population: Ages 4 to 18 years

Purpose: Aids in the diagnosis of ADHD

Description: The scale is based on the APA definition of attention-deficit/hyperactivity disorder (DSM-IV). The ADDES-3 uses frequency-referenced quantifiers. Each item is rated on a 6-point scale from 0 (*not developmentally appropriate for age*) to 5 (*one to several times per hour*). Following administration, four types of scores may be obtained: frequency rating for individual items (reflecting the frequency and severity of the behavior), subscale standard score, quotient, and percentile rank. From the subscale standard scores, a profile of the student's behavior across the subscales (Inattentive and Hyperactive–Impulsive) is constructed. A scoring system for Windows-based PCs is available. Home (46 items) and School (60 items) versions are included in the kit. Spanish rating forms for home and school are available.

Format: Rating scale; untimed: 20 minutes

Scoring: Examiner evaluated; computer scoring available

Cost: Complete Kit (2 technical manuals, intervention manual, parent's guide, 50 each of 5 forms) $232.00

Attention-Deficit/Hyperactivity Disorder Test (ADHDT)

1995   **PRO-ED, Inc.**

James E. Gilliam

Population: Ages 3 to 23 years

Purpose: Identifies and evaluates attention-deficit/hyperactivity disorders

Description: Multiple-item checklist that is completed by teachers, parents, or others who are knowledgeable about a referred individual. Based on the diagnostic criteria for attention-deficit/hyperactivity disorder of the DSM-IV, the instrument contains 36 items that describe characteristic behaviors of persons with ADHD. These items comprise three subtests representing the core symptoms necessary for the diagnosis of ADHD: hyperactivity, impulsivity, and inattention. Results are reported in standard scores and percentiles that are interpreted related to degree of severity and probability for males and females.

Format: Rating scale; untimed: 10 minutes

Scoring: Examiner evaluated

Cost: Complete Kit (manual, 50 protocols, storage box) $110.00

Auditory Continuous Performance Test (ACPT)

1994   **Harcourt Assessment, Inc.**

Robert W. Keith

Population: Ages 6 to 11 years

Purpose: Screens for auditory attention deficits

Description: Pass/Fail criterion scores for each age helps the examiner to identify whether a child's performance matches that of children identified as having ADD or ADHD. The child listens to single words and raises his or her thumb when hearing the targeted word.

Format: Examiner required; individual administration; untimed: 10 minutes

Scoring: Examiner evaluated

Cost: Complete Kit (manual, cassette, 12 record forms) $125.00

Behavioral Inattention Test (BIT)

1987	Harcourt Assessment, Inc.

Barbara A. Wilson, Janet Cockburn, Peter Halligan

Population: Adults

Purpose: Measures unilateral visual neglect

Description: The BIT is an objective behavioral test of everyday skills relevant to visual neglect, aimed at increasing our understanding of specific difficulties that patients experience. There are two parallel versions with six conventional subtests and no behavioral subtests.

Format: Examiner required; individual administration; untimed: 25 minutes

Scoring: Examiner evaluated

Cost: $375.00

Brief Test of Attention (BTA)

1997	Psychological Assessment Resources, Inc.

David Schretlen

Population: Ages 17 to 84 years

Purpose: Assesses severity of attentional impairment in hearing individuals without aphasia

Description: Two parallel forms, numbers and letters, presented via audiocassette. Respondent must count the numbers or letters read aloud and disregard the others.

Format: Examiner required; individual administration; untimed: 10 minutes

Scoring: Examiner evaluated

Cost: Introductory Kit (manual, audiotape, 50 forms) $82.00

Brown Attention-Deficit Disorder Scales

2001	Harcourt Assessment, Inc.

Thomas E. Brown

Population: Ages 3 years to adult

Purpose: Evaluates cognitive and affective indications of ADD in adolescents and adults

Description: Self-report instrument that allows for screening of ADD by examining a wide variety of factors believed to be associated with ADD. The addition of a children's scale (ages 3 to 7) and a school-age scale (ages 8 to 12) is in this new edition. An adolescent (ages 12 to 18) and an adult form are still available. Ready Score Form gives an immediate summary score indicating overall impairment. Diagnostic Form includes guidelines and worksheets for conducting a clini-cal interview, scoring summary, multirater evaluation form, analysis of IQ subtest data relevant to ADD, screener for comorbid disorders, and an overall diagnostic summary form.

Format: Examiner required; individual administration; untimed: 10 to 20 minutes

Scoring: Examiner evaluated; computer scoring available

Cost: Complete Kit for Adolescents and Adults (manual, 25 of each form, scoring materials) $210.00; Starter Kit for Children and Adolescents (manual, 5 of each form, scoring materials) $195.00

Children's Attention and Adjustment Survey (CAAS)

1990	AGS Publishing/Pearson Assessments

Nadine Lambert, Carolyn Hartsough, Jonathan Sandoval

Population: Ages 5 to 13 years

Purpose: Evaluates behaviors related to hyperactivity and attention deficit in children

Description: A survey that identifies behavior problems associated with ADD and ADHD. Four scales are provided to provide more precise intervention planning: Inattentiveness, Impulsivity, Hyperactivity, and Conduct Problems/Aggressiveness. Since children's behavior often varies with their environment, CAAS uses an interactive systems model. The survey assesses behaviors observed both at home and at school through two 31-item forms: the Home Form (completed by the parent or primary caregiver) and the School Form (completed by the teacher or other school professional). Behaviors are classified according to criteria determined by DSM.

Format: Survey format; 5 to 10 minutes

Scoring: Examiner evaluated

Cost: Starter Set (manual, Home and School protocols, Scoring Profile) $154.99

Clinical Assessment of Attention Deficit–Adult™ (CAT-A)

2005	Psychological Assessment Resources, Inc.

Bruce A. Bracken, Barbara S. Boatwright

Population: Ages 10 to 79 years

Purpose: Measures attentional deficits both with and without hyperactivity

Description: The CAT-A is a 108-item self-report instrument that consists of two parts: Childhood

Memories and Current Symptoms. Clinical Index scores are provided for both scales. In addition, three validity scales are embedded with the instrument: Negative Impression, Infrequency, and Positive Impression. Links to DSM-IV diagnostic criteria.

Format: Rating scale; untimed: 20 to 25 minutes

Scoring: Examiner evaluated; computer scoring available

Cost: Introductory Kit (manual, CD, 25 of each form) $152.00

Clinical Assessment of Attention Deficit–Child™ (CAT-C)

| 2005 | Psychological Assessment Resources, Inc. |

Bruce A. Bracken, Barbara S. Boatwright

Population: Ages 8 to 18 years

Purpose: Measures attentional deficits both with and without hyperactivity

Description: The CAT-C is a 42-item self-report instrument that consists of three parallel forms: Self-Rating Form, Parent Rating Form, and Teacher Rating Form. Clinical Index scores are provided for both scales. In addition, three validity scales are embedded with the instrument: Negative Impression, Infrequency, and Positive Impression. Links to DSM-IV diagnostic criteria.

Format: Rating scale; untimed: 20 to 25 minutes

Scoring: Examiner evaluated; computer scoring available

Cost: Introductory Kit (manual, CD, 25 of each form) $265.00

Comprehensive Attention Battery (CAB)

| 2003 | NeuropsychWorks, Inc. |

John R. Rodenbough

Population: Ages 7 to 70 years

Purpose: Measures multiple factors of attention

Description: The CAB is a computer-based assessment tool developed to objectively assess attention/concentration through a battery with 15 tests. Assess the four primary factors of encoding, shifting, sustaining, and focus-execute abilities. Direct comparisons can be made between such factors as pure reaction times and discriminate reaction time measures. The software

requires Windows 95 or higher. Also available in Hebrew.

Format: Examiner required; individual administration; timed: 60 minutes

Scoring: Scoring service available

Cost: $700.00

Conners' Adult ADHD Diagnostic Interview for DSM-IV (CAADID)

| 2001 | Multi-Health Systems, Inc. |

Jeff Epstein, Diane Johnson, C. Keith Conners

Population: Adults

Purpose: Aids the process of diagnosing adult ADHD

Description: Empirically based structured interview in two parts that are administered separately. Part I, Patient History, is a self report questionnaire or may be administered as a clinical interview. It contains questions about the client's demographic history, developmental course of attention problems, and associated risk factors and comorbidity screen. Part II, Diagnostic Criteria Interview, assesses the client against DSM-IV criteria for ADHD, including age of onset, pervasiveness, and level of impairment.

Format: Examiner required; individually administered; untimed: 90 minutes each part

Scoring: QuikScore™ forms

Cost: Complete Kit (manual, 10 of each part) $112.00

Conners' Adult ADHD Rating Scales (CAARS)

| 1998 | Multi-Health Systems, Inc. |

C. Keith Conners, Drew Erhardt, Elizabeth Sparrow

Population: Ages 18 years and older

Purpose: Assists in the diagnosis of attention-deficit disorder in adults

Description: A set of comprehensive instruments for use as an extensive part of a multimodal assessment of symptoms and behaviors associated with ADHD in adults. The CAARS elicit self-report and observer ratings. Both self-report and observer forms are available in long (66 items), short (26 items), and screening (30 items) versions. A 4-point Likert format is used and is written at a sixth-grade reading level. The long and short versions contain factor-derived subscales, symptom subscales, and an ADHD Index.

Also available in Spanish, French, Portuguese, Hebrew, German, and more languages.

Format: Self-administered; untimed: 10 to 15 minutes

Scoring: QuikScore™ forms; computer scored; online scoring

Cost: Hand-Scored Complete Kit (manual, 25 of each form) $262.00

Conners' Continuous Performance Test II Version 5 for Windows (CPT II™ V.5)

2000   Multi-Health Systems, Inc.

C. Keith Conners

Population: Ages 6 years and older

Purpose: Identifies attention problems and monitors treatment effectiveness

Description: Computer-administered test requiring subject responses and inhibition to stimuli (letters) that appear on a computer screen. The test measures error rates, reaction time, and variability of reaction time. Statistics measure aspects of attention. Six blocks with three subblocks, each containing 20 trials. The CPT II program contains larger normative samples, new ADHD clinical data and data on neurologically impaired adults, better psychometric properties, newly designed reports, an easier to use interface, a more comprehensive software manual, and timing verification to confirm the validity of the administration.

Format: Self-administered; untimed: 14½ minutes

Scoring: Computer scored

Cost: $645.00 (unlimited use)

Conners' Kiddie Continuous Performance Test for Windows (K-CPT™)

2001   Multi-Health Systems, Inc.

C. Keith Conners

Population: Ages 4 to 5 years

Purpose: Identification of attention problems and monitoring of treatment effectiveness

Description: Assesses response and inhibition to stimuli (objects) that appear on a computer screen. The test measures response times and errors. The instrument yields raw scores, *t*-scores, percentiles, Confidence Index, and tim-

ing verification in single- and multi-administration reports.

Format: Self-administered on computer; timed: 7½ minutes

Scoring: Computer scored

Cost: $215.00 (unlimited use)

Conners' Rating Scales–Revised (CRS-R™)

1997   Multi-Health Systems, Inc.

C. Keith Conners

Population: Ages 3 to 17 years

Purpose: Assesses psychopathology and problem behavior

Description: This revision adds a number of enhancements to a set of measures that have long been the standard instruments for the measurement of ADHD in children and adolescents. The language has been updated with items that are simpler and clearer. Items have also been added that match the DSM-IV. CRS-R evaluates problem behaviors as reported by the teacher or parents (or alternative caregivers). Norms are based on more than 11,000 ratings. Separate norms are available for boys and girls. Available in a short or long version, self-report for ages 12 to 17 years, and in other languages (French and Spanish).

Format: Self-administered; untimed: long, 15 minutes; short, 5 minutes

Scoring: QuikScore™ forms; may be computer scored; online scoring

Cost: Hand-Scored Complete Starter Kit (manual, 25 of each form) $267.00

Early Childhood Attention Deficit Disorders Evaluation Scale (ECADDES)

1995   Hawthorne Educational Services, Inc.

Stephen B. McCarney

Population: Ages 24 to 83 months for females; Ages 24 to 78 months for males

Purpose: Aids in the diagnosis of ADHD

Description: The School Version of the scale includes 56 items easily observed and documented by educational personnel. The Home Version includes 50 items representing behavior exhibited in and around the home environment and is completed by the parent or guardian. Gender-based norms are provided. Also available in Spanish. A Windows Quick Score is available. Currently being renormed and will be published in 2007.

Format: Rating scale; untimed: 12 to 15 minutes

Scoring: Examiner evaluated; computer scoring available

Cost: Complete Kit (2 technical manuals, intervention manual, parent's guide, 50 each of 3 forms) $162.00

Gordon Diagnostic System (GDS)

1984	Gordon Systems, Inc.

Michael Gordon

Population: Ages 4 years to adult

Purpose: Assesses attention and impulse control used in evaluation of ADHD and illnesses and injuries associated with attentional problems

Description: The device has three subtests for Delay, Vigilance, and Distractibility. Measures ability to control impulses with immediate feedback and ability to attend with or without distractions. Attention is measured with visual stimuli. This is a self-contained microprocessor unit; no software is required. The device weighs 9 pounds and is portable. An auditory module is available from the publisher that can be added to any GDS. It allows the GDS to "speak" the digits that appear on the front display. Two tasks are administered: Auditory Vigilance and Auditory Interference.

Format: Examiner required; individual administration; timed: total 30 minutes

Scoring: Machine scored

Cost: System (unit, manual, interpretive guide, 50 record forms, 4 issues of newsletter, 1-year warranty) $1,595.00; customized units available for foreign use

Integrated Visual & Auditory Continuous Performance Test (IVA+Plus)

2006	BrainTrain

Joseph A. Sandford, Ann Turner

Population: Ages 6 to 96 years

Purpose: Measures impulsivity, inattention, and hyperactivity to help diagnose and differentiate ADD/ADHD

Description: A combined auditory and visual continuous performance test. Follows the diagnostic criteria outlined in the DSM-IV. The main test task presents 500 trials of 1s and 2s in a pseudo-random pattern requiring the shifting of sets between the visual and auditory modalities. The individual is required to click the mouse only when a 1 is seen or heard and inhibit clicking the mouse when a 2 is seen or heard. Available in a multitude of languages. A computer-generated narrative Interpretive Report Writer is available. This does all of the interpretive work and provides a choice of six types of reports for each testing session.

Format: Examiner required; individually computer administered; untimed: 13 minutes

Scoring: Computer scored

Cost: Unlimited Use Testing Kit $1,795.00

Scales for Diagnosing Attention Deficit/Hyperactivity Disorder (SCALES)

2002	PRO-ED, Inc.

Gail Ryser, Kathleen McConnell

Population: Ages 5 to 18 years

Purpose: Identifies and evaluates attention deficit/hyperactivity disorder

Description: The SCALES has two separate forms, one for the home environment and one for the school setting. In depth information is gathered from both parents and teachers, rather than gathering behavioral data from isolated clinical examinations. The Instrument was standardized using more than 3,000 children and is designed with two sets of norms: persons not identified with or suspected of having ADHD and individuals already diagnosed with ADHD. The SCALES employs a 4-point Likert scale to measure the extent to which the child's behavior interferes with his or her functioning.

Format: Rating scale; untimed: 15 to 20 minutes

Scoring: Examiner evaluated

Cost: Complete Kit (manual, 25 each of school and home forms, storage box) $95.00

Spadafore ADHD Rating Scale

1997	Academic Therapy Publications

Gerald J. Spadafore, Sharon J. Spadafore

Population: Ages 5 to 19 years

Purpose: Indicates both presence and severity of ADHD symptoms

Description: A 50-item questionnaire assesses three behavioral clusters in the classroom setting: Impulsivity/Hyperactivity, Attention, and Social Adjustment. A separate Likert-type scale is used to quantify the behavioral observations and to derive an overall ADHD Index. Observations and ratings are completed by the classroom teacher. Age- and gender-based norms are provided. Appropriate intervention strategies are included in the manual. Raw scores are converted to percentiles and severity levels.

Format: Observation and rating scale; untimed: 20 minutes

Scoring: Examiner evaluated

Cost: Test Kit (manual, test plates, 25 scoring protocols, 25 observational tracking forms, 25 medication tracking forms, in vinyl folder) $80.00

Test of Everyday Attention (TEA)

1994	Harcourt Assessment, Inc.

Ian H. Robertson, Tony Ward, Valerie Ridgeway, Ian Nimmo-Smith

Population: Adults

Purpose: Measures selective, sustained, and switching attention

Description: The TEA gives a broad-based measure of the most important clinical and theoretical aspects of attention. It can be used analytically to identify different patterns of attentional breakdown with a wide range of application, ranging from patients with Alzheimer's disease to young normal individuals. There are eight subtests: Map Search, Elevator Counting, Elevator Counting With Distraction, Visual Elevator, Auditory Elevator With Reversal, Telephone Search, Telephone Search Dual Task, and Lottery.

Format: Examiner required; individual administration; untimed: 35 minutes

Scoring: Examiner evaluated

Cost: $475.00

Test of Everyday Attention for Children (TEA-Ch)

1998	Harcourt Assessment, Inc.

Tom Manly, Ian H. Robertson, Vicki Anderson, Ian Nimmo-Smith

Population: Ages 6 to 16 years

Purpose: Measures abilities to selectively attend, to sustain attention, to divide attention between two tasks, to switch attention from one to another, and to inhibit verbal and motor responses

Description: Using attractive graphics and sound, the subtests are designed to be appealing. The nine subtests are Sky Search; Score; Sky Search DT; Creature Counting; Map Mission; Score DT; Opposite Worlds; Walk, Don't Walk; and Code Transmission. The subtests have been designed

to be as conceptually simple as possible so that children with a wide range of abilities may be tested. The test package is light and portable and can be easily used in many different settings. Two parallel forms of the test are provided that allow for confidence in retesting of the same child.

Format: Examiner required; individual or group administration; untimed: 35 minutes

Scoring: Examiner evaluated

Cost: $530.00

Test of Variables of Attention (TOVA®)

2000	Universal Attention Disorders, Inc.

Population: All ages

Purpose: Used for diagnosing and monitoring treatment of children and adults with attention disorders

Description: The TOVA is a computerized continuous performance test for use with IBM compatibles running MS-DOS and Macintosh with System 6.7 and 7.X computers. Highly reliable, cost-effective, and easy-to-administer tests provide relevant screening and diagnostic information about attention and impulsivity that is not otherwise available. Both tests (visual and auditory) have non-language-based stimuli that discriminate ADD from learning disabilities and minimize cultural differences. The visual test has two simple geometric stimuli, and the auditory test has two simple audible tones. The TOVA test is deliberately long, simple, and boring to effectively test attentional variables. Each TOVA kit includes software, hardware, manuals, and five administrations.

Format: Computer administered; untimed

Scoring: Immediate computer-generated interpretations

Cost: Visual (trigger, score box, manuals, clinical guide, 5 tests/interpretations, video) $375.00; Auditory/Visual (trigger, score box, manuals, clinical guide, 5 tests/interpretations, speakers, A/V hardware, video) $395.00

Vigil Continuous Performance Test

1996	Harcourt Assessment, Inc.

Population: Ages 6 to 90 years

Purpose: Explores attention, concentration, sustained attention, and complex sequential stimulus tracking

Description: A computer-administered and scored measure with each test consisting of several modules, including the onscreen presentation of verbal and nonverbal targets. The built-in database manager allows examination of previous test results or presentation of a test with previously defined display characteristics. Because specific test combinations are prepackaged, clinicians and researchers can modify over 52 parameters or construct their own test combinations.

Format: Computer administered; untimed: 8 minutes

Scoring: Computer scored

Cost: Complete Kit (Windows® disks, binder) $645.00

Family

Ackerman-Schoendorf Scales for Parent Evaluation of Custody (ASPECT)

1992	Western Psychological Services

Marc J. Ackerman, Kathleen Schoendorf

Population: Adults

Purpose: Evaluates parent effectiveness in child custody evaluations

Description: ASPECT offers a practical, standardized, and defensible approach to child custody evaluations. It draws information from a variety of sources, reducing the likelihood of examiner bias. It yields three scale scores: Observational (a measure of the parent's appearance and presentation), Social (a measure of the parent's interaction with others, including the child), and Cognitive-Emotional (a measure of the parent's psychological and mental functioning). Research has shown 90% agreement between ASPECT recommendations and custody decisions made by judges. ASPECT has also proven effective in identifying those parents who will need supervision during child visitations. The clinician must answer 56 yes-no questions, based on information drawn from the parent questionnaire, interviews with and observations of each parent with and without the child, and test data.

Format: Examiner required; individual administration; untimed

Scoring: Examiner evaluated; hand key; scoring service available

Cost: Kit (20 parent questionnaires, 10 Auto Score™ answer forms, 5 AutoScore Forms, manual, manual supplement, 2 test report prepaid mail-in answer sheets for computer scoring and interpretation) $152.00

Assessment of Parenting Skills: Infant and Preschooler (APSIP)

Date not provided	Village Publishing

Barry Bricklin, Gail Elliot

Population: Parents

Purpose: Evaluates a parent's genuine interest in a child

Description: Assesses the mother's or father's knowledge of the details of the child's development, routines, special needs, fears, health history, school history, and personal hygiene. A special section of 26 items is used to compare one parent with the other or to assess one parent alone with respect to parental attunement to the child, strengths in parenting skills, and weaknesses in parenting skills.

Format: Examiner required; individual administration; untimed: 30 to 35 minutes

Scoring: Hand key

Cost: Kit (manual, 8 booklets, 8 summaries, updates) $198.00

Borromean Family Index: For Married Persons

1988	Donna Bardis

Panos D. Bardis

Population: Adolescents, adults

Purpose: Measures a married person's attitudes and feelings toward his or her immediate family; used for clinical assessment, family and marriage counseling, family attitude research, and discussions in family education

Description: Paper-pencil assessment in which the subject rates nine statements about "forces that attract you to your family" on a scale from 0 (*absent*) to 4 (*very strong*) and nine statements about "forces that pull you away from your family" on a scale from 0 (*does not pull you away at all*) to 4 (*very strong*). Suitable for individuals with physical and hearing impairments.

Format: Examiner/Self-administered; suitable for group use; untimed: 10 minutes

Scoring: Examiner evaluated

Cost: $1.00

Borromean Family Index: For Single Persons

1988	Donna Bardis

Panos D. Bardis

Population: Adolescents, adults

Purpose: Measures an individual's attitudes and feelings toward his or her family; used for clinical assessment, family counseling, family attitude research, and discussion in family education

Description: Paper–pencil test in which the subject rates nine statements about "forces that attract you to your family" from 0 (absent) to 4 (very strong) and nine statements about "forces that pull you away from your family" from 0 (does not pull you away at all) to 4 (very strong). Suitable for use with individuals with physical and hearing impairments.

Format: Examiner/Self-administered; suitable for group use; untimed: 10 minutes

Scoring: Examiner evaluated

Cost: $1.00

Bricklin Perceptual Scales (BPS)

1984	Village Publishing

Barry Bricklin

Population: Children

Purpose: Measures the child's perception of parents

Description: The BPS has been successfully used with children as young as 4, but was designed primarily for children who are at least 6 years old. Perception is measured in four major areas: Competence, Follow-Up Consistency, Supportiveness, and Possession of Admirable Personality Traits. The BPS is made up of 64 cards.

Format: Examiner required; individual administration; untimed: 30 to 35 minutes

Scoring: Hand key; computer scoring available

Cost: Kit (manual, 8 sets of cards, 8 scoring summaries, stylus pen, placement dots, test box with foam insert, updates) $198.00

Checklist for Child Abuse Evaluation (CCAE)

1990	Psychological Assessment Resources, Inc.

Joseph Petty

Population: Children, adolescents

Purpose: Investigates and evaluates subjects who may have been abused or neglected

Description: Multiple-choice evaluation with 264 items in the following categories: Emotional Abuse, Sexual Abuse, Physical Abuse, Neglect, Child's Psychological Status, Credibility/Competence of Child, Conclusions of Six Categories. Treatment recommendations are yielded. A manual and checklist are used. Examiner must be trained in the evaluation of child abuse.

Format: Examiner required; individual administration; untimed

Scoring: Examiner evaluated

Cost: Introductory Kit (manual, 25 checklists) $140.00

Child Sexual Behavior Inventory (CSBI)

1997	Psychological Assessment Resources, Inc.

William N. Friedrich

Population: Ages 2 to 12 years

Purpose: Evaluates children who have been or may have been sexually abused

Description: A total of 38 items, in nine major content domains, are completed by mothers or primary female caregivers. Items are written on a fifth-grade reading level. Scores are reported in *t*-scores by gender and age.

Format: Self-administered; untimed: 10 to 13 minutes

Scoring: Examiner evaluated

Cost: Introductory Kit (manual, 50 booklets) $160.00

Clinical Rating Scale (CRS)

1993	Life Innovations, Inc.

David H. Olson

Population: All ages (families and couples)

Purpose: Assesses communication, cohesion, and flexibility within couples and families; used in clinical work and research

Description: Includes 21 interview questions: 13 assessing cohesion and 8 assessing flexibility. Yields scores on cohesion, flexibility, communication, and family type. The scores are used to plot the family or couple on the Circumplex Model.

Format: Ratings completed about interviews or by observing the couple and family

Scoring: Examiner evaluated

Cost: $30.00

Coping and Stress Profile

1995   Life Innovations, Inc.

David H. Olson

Population: Adults (individuals, couples, and families)

Purpose: Assesses coping, stress, resources, and satisfaction

Description: Paper-pencil assessment with a total of 311 items to aid in counseling individuals, couples, and families. The items represent four profiles: Personal Profile (97 items), Work Profile (74 items), Couple Profile (70 items), and Family Profile (70 items). Responses are given to a 5-point Likert scale. Scores are calculated for stress, problem solving, communication closeness, flexibility, and satisfaction in each profile.

Format: Self-administered; untimed

Scoring: Self-scored

Cost: $20.00

Custody Evaluation Questionnaire Kit

Date not provided   Village Publishing

Barry Bricklin, Gail Elliot

Population: Children and parents

Purpose: Helps to gather information for custody evaluations

Description: Six questionnaires are available: Child Access to Parental Strength, Parent Self-Report Data, Child Data, "Would," Child Self-Report Data, and Child Sexual Abuse. The questionnaires are completed by the child or the parent. The manual describes how to integrate the questionnaires into the framework of the comprehensive custody evaluation.

Format: Examiner required; individual administration; untimed

Scoring: Hand key

Cost: Kit (manual, 8 of each questionnaire) $198.00

Discipline Index (DI)

Date not provided   Village Publishing

Anita K. Lampel, Barry Bricklin, Gail Elliot

Population: Children

Purpose: Obtains information from a child about overall perceptions of each parent's discipline style and practices

Description: Nonverbal responses spare the child both loyalty conflicts and the need to verbalize directly negative statements about either parent. This makes the instrument suitable for use in cases covering an exceptionally broad range of issues. The DI has 64 questions, 32 each for the mother and the father. The child has available a continuum of response choices because he or she responds by punching a hole somewhere along a horizontal black line anchored on the right end by the words *very often* (or *very well*) and on the left end by *not so often* (or *not so well*). The DI yields answers about parental disciplinary practices in six categories: Clear Expectations, Effectively Monitors, Consistent Enforcement, Fairness, Attunement, and Moderates Anger.

Format: Examiner required; individual administration; untimed: 35 minutes

Scoring: Hand key; examiner evaluated; computer scoring available

Cost: Kit (handbook, 8 sets of cards, 8 scoring summaries, stylus pen, placement dots, test box with foam insert, 3 years update service) $198.00

ENRICH: Enriching Relationship Issues, Communication and Happiness

1996   Life Innovations, Inc.

David H. Olson, David G. Fournier, Joan M. Druckman

Population: Adults, married couples, and couples cohabiting 2 or more years

Purpose: Used in marital counseling and marriage enrichment

Description: Total of 195 items in 20 categories: Idealistic Distortion (7), Marriage Satisfaction (10), Personality Issues (10), Communication (10), Conflict Resolution (10), Financial Management (10), Leisure Activities (10), Sexual Expectations (10), Children and Parenting (10), Family and Friends (10), Role Relationship (10), Spiritual Beliefs (10), Couple Closeness (10), Couple Flexibility (10), Family Closeness (10), Family Flexibility (10), Self Confidence (8), Assertiveness (8), Avoidance (8), and Partner Dominance (8). Computer report (18 pages) contains revised Individual Scores, Couple Type, Personality Assessment Idealistic Distortion Scores, and Positive Couple Agreement Scores. Test available in Spanish. A separate version called the MATE is available for married couples over 50.

Format: Self-administered; untimed

Scoring: Computer scored; test scoring service available

Cost: $30.00 for scoring; $175.00 for training

FACES IV–Family Adaptability and Cohesion Scales

2006   **Life Innovations, Inc.**

David H. Olson, Dean M. Gorall, Judy W. Tiesel

Population: Ages 12 to adult

Purpose: Measures cohesion and flexibility; used for family therapy and family research

Description: This 62-item self-report instrument assesses the two major dimensions of the Circumplex Model, that is, family cohesion and family adaptability (flexibility). It is designed to be administered to families across the life cycle. There are six scales: two measure balanced cohesion and balanced flexibility, and four measure the unbalanced extremes of the cohesion (disengaged and enmeshed) and flexibility (rigid and chaotic). FACES IV has the added scales of Parent–Adolescent Communication and Family Satisfaction. Parent–Adolescent Communication assesses the third dimension of the Circumplex Model (Communication), and Family Satisfaction assesses how happy family members are with their family system. Ratio scores of balanced to unbalanced scales provide a way of assessing the functionality of the family system. Requires a seventh-grade reading level.

Format: Self-administered; untimed: 15 to 20 minutes

Scoring: Examiner evaluated; computer scoring with Excel available

Cost: Complete Package $95.00

Familism Scale

1988   **Donna Bardis**

Panos D. Bardis

Population: Adolescents, adults

Purpose: Assesses individual attitudes toward both nuclear and extended families; used for clinical evaluation, marriage and family counseling, research on the family, and discussion in family life education

Description: Paper–pencil test in which the subject reads 10 statements about nuclear family relationships and 6 statements about extended family relationships and rates them according to his or her personal beliefs on a scale from 0 (*strongly disagree*) to 4 (*strongly agree*). The Familism score equals the sum of the 16 numerical responses. The theoretical range of scores extends from 0 (*least familistic*) to 64 (*most*

familistic). Separate scores may be obtained for nuclear family integration and extended family integration. Suitable for use with individuals with physical or hearing impairments.

Format: Self-administered; untimed: 10 minutes

Scoring: Examiner evaluated

Cost: $1.00

Familism Scale: Extended Family Integration

1988   **Donna Bardis**

Panos D. Bardis

Population: Adolescents, adults

Purpose: Measures attitudes toward the extended family (beyond the nuclear family, but within the kinship group); used for clinical assessment, marriage and family counseling, family attitude research, and discussions in family education

Description: Paper–pencil test in which the subject reads a list of statements concerning extended family relationships and rates them according to personal beliefs on a scale from 0 (*strongly disagree*) to 4 (*strongly agree*). The Familism score is the sum of the six numerical responses. The theoretical range of scores extends from 0 (*least familistic*) to 24 (*most familistic*). Suitable for use with individuals who have physical and hearing disabilities.

Format: Examiner/Self-administered; suitable for group use; untimed: 5 minutes

Scoring: Examiner evaluated

Cost: $1.00

Familism Scale: Nuclear Family Integration

1988   **Donna Bardis**

Panos D. Bardis

Population: Adolescents, adults

Purpose: Measures attitudes toward the solidarity of the nuclear family; used for clinical assessment, marriage and family counseling, family attitude research, and discussion in family education

Description: Paper–pencil test in which the subject rates 10 statements about family relationships from 0 (*strongly disagree*) to 4 (*strongly agree*). The Familism score equals the sum of the 10 numerical responses. The theoretical range of scores extends from 0 (*least familistic*) to 40 (*most familistic*). Suitable for use with individuals who have physical and hearing disabilities.

Format: Self-administered; untimed: 5 minutes

Scoring: Hand key

Cost: $1.00

Family Assessment Measure (FAM-III™)

1992	Multi-Health Systems, Inc.

Harvey A. Skinner, Paul D. Steinhauer, Jack Santa-Barbara

Population: Ages 10 years and older

Purpose: Assesses family functioning; used in family counseling

Description: Paper-pencil test with General, Dyadic, and Self-Report Scales. Categories include Task Accomplishment, Communication, Involvement, Values and Norms, Role Performance, Affective Expression, Control, Social Desirability, and Defensiveness Control. Scores are yielded for each subscale and a total score. These scores can be converted to standard scores and plotted on a color-coded profile sheet. A fifth-grade reading level is required. The brief form consists of the same three categories, with 14 items each for screening and monitoring over time.

Format: Self-administered; untimed: 20 minutes per form

Scoring: QuikScore™ forms; may be computer scored

Cost: Kit (manual, 25 forms for each category, 15 profile forms) $209.00

Family Environment Scale (FES)

2002	Mind Garden, Inc.

Rudolf H. Moos

Population: Ages 11 to adult

Purpose: Examines each family member's perceptions of the family

Description: The 90 items of the FES are grouped into 10 subscales with three dimensions: Relationship, Personal Growth, and System Maintenance. The instrument has been used in clinical settings to facilitate family counseling and psychotherapy, to teach clinicians and program evaluators about family systems, and for program evaluation. Requires a sixth-grade reading level.

Format: Rating scale; untimed

Scoring: Examiner evaluated

Cost: Sampler Set $40.00; Permission for 200 Uses $150.00

Family Relationship Inventory (FRI)

1982	Psychological Publications, Inc.

Ruth B. Michaelson, Harry L. Bascom

Population: Ages 5 years to adult

Purpose: Evaluates family relationships along positive and negative lines; used as an aid in individual child–adult counseling, family therapy, youth groups, high school instruction, and marriage and family enrichment programs

Description: Paper–pencil 50-item test measuring self-esteem, positive or negative perception of self and significant others, most and least esteemed family members, and closest and most distant relationships within the family. One numbered item is printed on each of 50 cards. Items 1 through 25 have positive valence, and items 26 through 50 have negative valence. The subject lists "self" and "family members" across the top of a tabulating form and assigns each item to self, significant other, or the wastebasket column and tallies the data on scoring forms with the help of a counselor.

Format: Examiner required; suitable for group use; untimed: 30 to 45 minutes

Scoring: Examiner evaluated

Cost: Complete Kit (manual, 50 reusable item cards, 50 tabulating forms, 25 scoring forms, 50 individual relationship sheets, 25 Family-grams) $169.00

Family Satisfaction Scale

1982	Life Innovations, Inc.

David H. Olson, Marc Wilson

Population: Ages 12 years and older

Purpose: Measures level of satisfaction within families

Description: A paper–pencil instrument with a total of 14 items on two scales: Family Cohesion (8 items) and Family Adaptability (6 items). Items are rated on a 5-point Likert scale. The instrument, which is used in family counseling and research of families, to determine levels of cohesion and adaptability, yields a total score, a cohesion score, and an adaptability score. One form is available for all family members. Included as part of the FACES IV package.

Format: Self-administered; untimed

Scoring: Hand key

Cost: $30.00

Family System Test (FAST)

| 1998 | Hogrefe & Huber Publishers |

Thomas M. Gehring

Population: Ages 6 years and older

Purpose: Measures family structures to plan and evaluate preventive and therapeutic interventions

Description: The FAST is a figural technique that can be used quantitatively or qualitatively. It is based on the structural-systemic theory of families that provides for analysis of family structure, diagnosis of biopsychosocial problems, and planning and evaluation of preventive and therapeutic intervention. Test materials include a board and various schematic figures. The test is language independent and highly effective. Depending on the issue, the standard test procedure can be modified to include different phases of current conflicts, as well as past and anticipated events.

Format: Examiner required; individual and group administration; untimed: 5 to 10 minutes for individuals, 10 to 30 minutes for groups

Scoring: Examiner evaluated

Cost: Complete Test (manual, 20 recording blanks, materials) $348.00

Family Violence Scale

| 1988 | Donna Bardis |

Panos D. Bardis

Population: Adolescents, adults

Purpose: Measures the degree of verbal and physical violence in an individual's family during childhood; used for clinical assessment, marriage and family counseling, research on attitudes toward family and violence, and classroom discussion

Description: Paper-pencil test in which the subject rates 25 statements about family violence on a scale from 0 (*never*) to 4 (*very often*). The Family Violence score equals the sum of the 25 numerical responses. The theoretical range of scores extends from 0 (*least violent*) to 100 (*most violent*). Suitable for use with individuals with physical and hearing disabilities.

Format: Self-administered; untimed: 10 minutes

Scoring: Examiner evaluated

Cost: $1.00

Grandparent Strengths and Needs Inventory (GSNI)

| 1993 | Scholastic Testing Service, Inc. |

Robert D. Strom, Shirley K. Strom

Population: Adults

Purpose: Identifies favorable qualities of grandparents

Description: Multiple-choice test with 60 items in six subscales: Satisfaction, Success, Teaching, Difficulty, Frustration, and Information Needs. Scores yielded are 4 (*always*), 3 (*often*), 2 (*seldom*), and 1 (*never*). Three versions (grandparent, parent, and grandchild) are available.

Format: Self-administered; untimed

Scoring: Examiner evaluated

Cost: Starter Set (manual, 20 of each inventory, 20 profiles) $78.75

Hilson Caregivers Questionnaire (HCQ)

| 1995 | Institute for Personality and Ability Testing, Inc. |

Robin E. Inwald

Population: Adolescents, adults

Purpose: Measures suitability for a job that involves caregiving/parenting

Description: The HCQ includes 136 true–false questions from which both raw scores and *t*-scores are derived. A fifth-grade reading level is required. Online administration is available. Also available in Spanish.

Format: Self-administered; untimed: 15 minutes

Scoring: Examiner evaluated; computer scoring available

Cost: $16.00 to $20.00 depending on scoring method

Hilson Couples Compatibility Questionnaire (HCCQ)

| 2005 | Institute for Personality and Ability Testing, Inc. |

Robin E. Inwald

Population: Adults

Purpose: Assesses compatibility issues; used for marital/couples counseling

Description: The HCCQ includes 148 true–false questions from which both raw and *t*-scores are derived. A fifth-grade reading level is required. Online administration is available. Also available in Spanish.

Format: Self-administered; untimed: 30 minutes

Scoring: Examiner evaluated; computer scoring available

Cost: $16.00 to $20.00 depending on scoring method

Hilson Parent/Guardian Inventory (HPGI)

| 1992 | Institute for Personality and Ability Testing, Inc. |

Robin E. Inwald

Population: Ages 18 years and older

Purpose: Assesses custody determinations of parent or guardian of children

Description: A total of 156 items is administered to parents or guardians of children to determine custody, treatment, and child assessment. Test measures Parent Self-Worth, Family Patterns, and Coping Patterns. Also available in Spanish.

Format: Examiner required; individually administered; untimed: 20 minutes

Scoring: Computer scored; scoring service available

Cost: $16.00 to $20.00 depending on scoring method

Home Observation for Measurement of the Environment (HOME)

| 1994 | Home Inventory LLC |

Bettye M. Caldwell, Robert H. Bradley

Population: Ages birth to 15 years

Purpose: Measures the quality and quantity of stimulation and support available in the home environment

Description: There are four versions of the inventory: Infant/Toddler (birth to 3), Early Childhood (ages 3 to 6), Middle Childhood (ages 6 to 10), and Early Adolescent (ages 10 to 15). The Infant/Toddler has 45 items in six subscales: Parental Responsivity, Acceptance of Child, Organization of the Environment, Learning Materials, Parental Involvement, and Variety in Experience. The Early Childhood has 55 items clustered into eight subscales: Learning Materials, Language Stimulation, Physical Environment, Parental Responsivity, Learning Stimulation, Modeling of Social Maturity, Variety in Experience, and Acceptance of Child. Middle Childhood has 59 items in eight subscales: Parental Responsivity, Physical Environment, Learning Materials, Active Stimulation, Encouraging Maturity, Emotional Climate, Parental Involvement, and Family Participation. The Early Adolescent contains 60 items in seven subscales: Physical Environment, Learning Materials, Modeling, Instructional Activities, Regulatory Activities, Variety of Experience, and Acceptance and Responsivity. Information is obtained during a 45- to 90-minute home visit when the parent and child are present. A yes-no format is used to score the items in the inventory. Included in the Comprehensive Manual are a Disability Adapted HOME for all versions for four disability areas: Auditory, Visual, Orthopedic, and Developmental Delay. A Child Care HOME observation is available for Infant/Toddler and Early Childhood.

Format: Examiner required; observation; untimed: 45 to 90 minutes

Scoring: Examiner evaluated

Cost: Comprehensive Manual $50.00

Home Screening Questionnaire (HSQ)

| 1981 | Denver Developmental Materials, Inc. |

C. Cooms, E. Gay, A. Vandal, C. Ker, William F. Franenberg

Population: Ages birth to 6 years

Purpose: Evaluates the quality of a child's home environment; used to indicate need for further evaluation

Description: Paper-pencil questionnaire filled out by the parents and scored by an examiner. Suspect results must be followed by an evaluation of the home by a trained professional to see if intervention is needed. A 30-item blue form is available for children up to age 3, and a 34-item white form is available for ages 3 through 6. Both forms have toy checklists. The questionnaires are written at third- and fourth-grade reading levels. Also available in Spanish.

Format: Self-administered; untimed: 15 to 20 minutes

Scoring: Hand key

Cost: 25 Test Forms $17.00; Manual $18.00

Infant-Toddler and Family Instrument (ITFI)

| 2001 | Brookes Publishing Co., Inc. |

Sally Provence, Nancy H. Apfel

Population: Ages 6 months to 3 years

Purpose: Measures family function and child development

Description: The caregiver/parent interview has 36 questions concerned with home and family life; child characteristics, daily activities, and health, growth, and development; and family supports, issues, and concerns. The developmental map has 72 items in four categories: Gross and Fine Motor Development, Social and Emotional Development, Language Development, and Coping and Self-Help Development. The checklist for evaluating concern has 38 items about home and family environment and child health, development and safety, and stressors. May be used for persons with visual, physical, hearing, and mental impairments.

Format: Examiner required; individual interview; untimed

Scoring: Examiner evaluated

Cost: Manual and 15 forms $45.00

Inwald Partners Personality Inventory (IPPI)

| 2006 | Institute for Personality and Ability Testing, Inc. |

Robin E. Inwald

Population: Adults

Purpose: Couples assess each other on behavior patterns

Description: The IPPI includes 128 true–false questions from which both raw scores and *t*-scores are derived. A fifth-grade reading level is required. Online administration is available. Also available in Spanish.

Format: Self-administered; untimed: 30 minutes

Scoring: Examiner evaluated; computer scoring available

Cost: $16.00 to $20.00 depending on scoring method

Life Interpersonal History Enquiry (LIPHE)

| 1989 | Mind Garden, Inc. |

Will Schutz

Population: Adults

Purpose: Evaluates an individual's retrospective account of relationship to parents before age 6; used for counseling and therapy

Description: Paper–pencil report of an individual's early relationship with parents in the areas of inclusion, control, and affection at both the behavioral and the feeling levels. Separate scores are obtained for the father, the mother, and the respondent's perception of the relationship between the parents.

Format: Self-administered; untimed

Scoring: Examiner evaluated

Cost: Sampler Set $30.00; Permission for 200 Uses $150.00

Marital Satisfaction Inventory– Revised (MSI-R)

| 1997 | Western Psychological Services |

Douglas K. Snyder

Population: Adults

Purpose: Identifies the nature and extent of marital distress; used in marital and family counseling

Description: Multiple-item paper–pencil or computer-administered true–false test providing information concerning nine basic measured dimensions of marriage: Affective Communication, Problem-Solving Communication, Time Together, Disagreement About Finances, Sexual Dissatisfaction, Role Orientation, Family History of Distress, Dissatisfaction With Children, and Conflict Over Child Rearing. In addition, a validity scale and a global distress scale measure each spouse's overall dissatisfaction with the marriage. The test is available in two forms: a 280-item version for couples with children and a 239-item version for couples without children. The results for both spouses are recorded on the same profile form, graphically identifying the areas of marital distress. Each spouse's scores can be individually evaluated, as well as directly compared, thereby facilitating diagnostic and intervention procedures. Group mean profiles for each gender are provided for couples seeking general marital therapy.

Format: Self-administered; untimed: 30 to 40 minutes

Scoring: Hand key; may be computer scored; scoring service available

Cost: Kit (40 AutoScore™ answer forms, manual) $121.00

Parent–Adolescent Communication Scale

| 1982 | Life Innovations, Inc. |

Howard Barnes, David H. Olson

Population: Ages 12 years and older

Purpose: Used in family counseling, for parents and adolescents

Description: Paper–pencil test to aid in communication of families. Twenty 5-point Likert items on two scales: Open Family Communication (10 items) and Problems in Family Communication

(10 items). Yields Open Family Communication score, Problems in Family Communication score, and totals score. Three forms available: Adolescent and Mother form, Adolescent and Father form, and Parent form. Included as part of the FACES IV package.

Format: Self-administered; untimed

Scoring: Hand key

Cost: $30.00

Parent as a Teacher Inventory (PAAT)

1995   Scholastic Testing Service, Inc.

Robert D. Strom

Population: Parents of children ages 3 to 9 years

Purpose: Assesses parents' attitudes toward their parent–child relationship

Description: Multiple-choice inventory measuring parental attitudes in the following areas: feelings toward the parent–child interactive system, standards for assessing the importance of certain aspects of child behavior, and value preferences and frustrations concerning child behavior. Also available in Spanish.

Format: Self-administered; untimed: 30 to 45 minutes

Scoring: Examiner evaluated

Cost: Starter Set (inventory manual, 20 inventory booklets/identification questionnaires, 20 profiles) $58.95

Parent Awareness Skills Survey (PASS)

1990   Village Publishing

Barry Bricklin

Population: Parents

Purpose: Reflects the sensitivity and effectiveness with which a parent responds to typical childcare situations

Description: PASS targets skills that reflect a parent's awareness of just what makes a given child unique, thus following the principle that the meaning of parental behavior is best understood in terms of a child's ability to be positively influenced by it. The scores pinpoint parental awareness of the following: the critical issues in a given situation; adequate solutions; the need to communicate in terms understandable to a child; the desirability of acknowledging a child's feelings; the importance of the child's own past history in the present circumstances; and the need to pay attention to how the child is responding in order to fine-tune one's own response. A completed

PASS-BOOK provides a permanent record of each PASS that is administered.

Format: Examiner required; individual administration; untimed

Scoring: Hand key

Cost: Kit (manual, 8 PASS-BOOKS, 8 scoring summaries, answer pen, updates) $198.00

Parent–Child Relationship Inventory (PCRI)

1994   Western Psychological Services

Anthony B. Gerard

Population: Parents of 3- to 15-year-old children

Purpose: Evaluates parenting skills and attitudes, child custody arrangements, family interaction, and physical or sexual abuse of children

Description: Self-report inventory with 78 items covering seven scales: Parental Support, Involvement, Limit Setting, Role Orientation, Satisfaction With Parenting, Communication, and Autonomy. Includes two validity scales and separate norms for mothers and fathers.

Format: Self-administered; untimed: 15 minutes

Scoring: Examiner evaluated; computer scored

Cost: Kit (25 AutoScore™ answer sheets, manual) $99.00

Parent Perception of Child Profile (PPCP)

1991   Village Publishing

Barry Bricklin, Gail Elliot

Population: Parents

Purpose: Elicits an extensive portrait of a parent's knowledge and understanding of a specific child

Description: Responses are gathered from the parent in a wide variety of important life areas to assess the degree to which a parent's perceptions are accurate, compare to other sources, and reflect genuine interest in a child. The PPCP also assesses the irritability potential of a parent.

Format: Examiner required; individual administration; untimed: less than an hour

Scoring: Hand key

Cost: Kit (manual, 8 Q-books, 8 recall worksheets, 8 summary sheets, pens, updates) $198.00

Parent Success Indicator (PSI)

1998   Scholastic Testing Service, Inc.

Robert D. Strom, Shirley K. Strom

Population: Ages 10 to 14 years and their parents

Purpose: Provides parents with self-reports of their perception of their children

Description: Family counseling applications. Total of 61 items, yielding PSI profile. Materials used: PSI manual, parent inventory booklets, child inventory booklets, PSI profiles. Scales are available in Spanish. Allows parents to make better decisions about self-improvement.

Format: Self-administered; untimed: 15 to 20 minutes

Scoring: Self-scored

Cost: Starter Set (manual, 20 of each inventory, 20 profiles) $73.90

Parental Acceptance–Rejection Questionnaire (PARQ)

2004	Rohner Research Publications

Ronald P. Rohner

Population: Children and adults

Purpose: Assesses perceived parental acceptance and rejection

Description: Paper–pencil questionnaire measuring perceived parental acceptance and rejection in four scales: Warmth/Affection (20 items), Hostility/Aggression (15 items), Indifference/Neglect (15 items), and Undifferentiated Rejection (10 items). The test, designed to cut across social classes and available in more than 30 languages, can be combined with the formal interview (Parental Acceptance–Rejection Interview Schedule) and behavior observations. It is scored on a 4-point scale (*almost always* to *almost never*), with some items having reversed scoring to reduce response bias. Scores range from 60 (*maximum acceptance, minimum rejection*) to 240 (*maximum rejection, minimum acceptance*). Now 12 versions of instruments, including infant/toddler.

Format: Examiner/Self-administered; suitable for group use; untimed

Scoring: Hand key; may be computer scored

Cost: Handbook with All Instruments $35.00

Parenting Alliance Measure (PAM)

1999	Psychological Assessment Resources, Inc.

Richard R. Abidin, Timothy R. Konold

Population: Adults

Purpose: Measures the strength of the child-rearing alliance between parents

Description: PAM is a 20-item measure. Materials include manual and 50 hand-scorable test forms. Requires a third-grade reading level.

Format: Self-administered; untimed: 10 to 15 minutes

Scoring: Self-scored

Cost: Introductory Kit (manual, 50 forms) $126.00

Parenting Satisfaction Scale (PSS)

1994	Harcourt Assessment, Inc.

John Guidubaldi, Helen K. Cleminshaw

Population: Parents of elementary children

Purpose: Identifies troubled parent–child relationships

Description: A 45-item standardized assessment of parents' attitudes toward parenting. Defines, compares, and communicates levels of parenting satisfaction in three domains: Satisfaction with the Spouse/Ex-Spouse Parenting Performance, Satisfaction with the Parent-Child Relationship, and Satisfaction with Parenting Performance. PSS can be useful in making child custody decisions and conducting family therapy.

Format: Self-administered; untimed: 30 minutes

Scoring: Examiner evaluated

Cost: Complete Kit (manual, 25 answer documents) $150.00

Parenting Stress Index–Third Edition (PSI)

1995	Psychological Assessment Resources, Inc.

Richard R. Abidin

Population: Parents of children ages 1 month to 12 years

Purpose: Used in family counseling, stress management, and forensic evaluation to identify parent–child problem areas

Description: Paper–pencil yes–no Likert scale index with four short form scales: Total Stress, Parental Distress, Parent–Child Dysfunctional Interaction, and Difficult Child. Long form domains and subscales include the following: Total Stress, Child Domain (distractibility/hyperactivity, attachment, reinforcement of parent, depression, mood, acceptability), and Parent Domain (competence, isolation, adaptability, health, role restriction, demandingness, spouse). A computer version using a PC is available.

Format: Examiner required; individual administration; untimed: long, 20 to 30 minutes; short, 10 minutes

Scoring: Examiner evaluated; computer scoring available

Cost: Short Form Kit (manual, 25 forms) $115.00; Long Form Kit (manual, 10 reusable booklets, 25 forms) $165.00

Parents Preference Test (PPT)

2003	Dansk psykologisk Forlag

Finn Westh

Population: Adults

Purpose: Measures preferences of parenting role and child-rearing style for parent counseling

Description: The test consists of 24 pictures depicting typical parent–child situations. To each source picture four target pictures are presented. The parent is to select the target picture that best represents his or her form of parent–child interaction shown in the source picture. Parents then elaborate why they have chosen this response. The responses can be entered either directly into the scoring system on the computer or on a manual scoring sheet and then transferred. The scoring system generates a numerical and descriptive report. Four major dimensions are addressed: (1) is the parent active or passive; (2) is the parent attentive toward the child or himself/herself; (3) is the parent's perception of the interaction primarily emotional or cognitive based; (4) is the parent's regulation of the child's behavior based on predefined rules or determined by the situations. Also available in Danish. May be purchased only by psychologists.

Format: Examiner required; individual administration; untimed: 30 minutes

Scoring: Computer scoring

Cost: $850.00 (DKR 5100)

Perception-of-Relationships Test (PORT)

1989	Village Publishing

Barry Bricklin

Population: Children

Purpose: Measures how close a child feels to each parent

Description: The PORT is made up of seven tasks (mostly drawings) that measure the degree to which a child seems to be psychologically close to each parent, and the strengths and weaknesses developed as a result of interacting with

each parent. One spiral-bound booklet contains everything necessary to administer, record, and score the test.

Format: Examiner required; individual administration; untimed: 30 minutes

Scoring: Hand key; computer scoring available

Cost: Kit (handbook, 8 booklets, pen, eraser, updates) $198.00

Physical Punishment Questionnaire (PPQ)

2004	Rohner Research Publications

Ronald P. Rohner

Population: Grades 3 and above

Purpose: Assesses experiences of children and adults with physical punishment received; parents report use of physical punishment; used for research on antecedents and consequences of physical punishment

Description: Paper–pencil oral-response verbal test consisting of 59 items on the child and adult forms and 29 items on the parent form. Three versions of test: child, adult, and parent. Measures major variables: frequency, severity, consistency, predictability, incidence, deservedness, timing, and explanation of punishment; 13 specific forms of punishment; four write-in forms of punishment experienced; sum of different forms of punishment experienced from major caregiver; sum of different forms of punishment experienced from major disciplinarian; harshness of punishment received; and justness of punishment received. Third-grade reading level is required. Soon available in Spanish, Arabic, and other languages.

Format: Examiner/Self-administered; suitable for group use, untimed. 10 to 15 minutes

Scoring: Hand key

Cost: Handbook with All Instruments $35.00

Religion Scale

1961	Donna Bardis

Panos D. Bardis

Population: Adolescents, adults

Purpose: Measures attitudes toward religion; used for clinical assessment, family and marriage counseling, research on attitudes toward religion, and discussion in religion and social science classes

Description: Paper–pencil test in which the subject reads 25 statements about religious issues and rates them according to his or her beliefs on a scale from 0 (*strongly disagree*) to 4 (*strongly agree*). The score is the sum of the 25 numerical responses. The theoretical range of scores extends from 0 (*least religious*) to 100 (*most religious*). Suitable for individuals with physical and hearing disabilities.

Format: Self-administered; untimed: 10 minutes

Scoring: Examiner evaluated

Cost: $1.00

Stress Index for Parents of Adolescents (SIPA)

1998	Psychological Assessment Resources, Inc.

Peter L. Sheras, Richard R. Abidin

Population: Parents of adolescents ages 11 to 19 years

Purpose: Identify stressful areas in parent-adolescent interactions

Description: The 112-item SIPA is an upward extension of the *Parenting Stress Index* with four subscales for Adolescent Characteristics and four subscales for Parent Characteristics. A fifth-grade reading level is required. Materials include the SIPA manual, 25 reusable item booklets, and 25 hand-scorable answer sheet/profile forms.

Format: Self-administered; untimed: 20 minutes

Scoring: Examiner evaluated

Cost: Introductory Kit (manual, 25 reusable booklets, 25 forms) $125.00

Uniform Child Custody Evaluation System (UCCES)

1994	Psychological Assessment Resources, Inc.

Harry L. Munsinger, Kevin W. Karlson

Population: Individuals involved in child custody litigation

Purpose: Provides a comprehensive and uniform custody evaluation procedure

Description: Paper–pencil short-answer test. Twenty-five forms are organized into three categories: general data and administration forms, parent forms, and child forms. Materials used include a manual and 25 different forms used to document and organize data for report writing and court testimony.

Format: Examiner required; individual administration; untimed

Scoring: Examiner evaluated

Cost: Introductory Kit (manual, 2 sets of parent forms, 2 sets of child forms, 1 set of administrative/data forms) $180.00

Geropsychology

Arizona Battery for Communication Disorders of Dementia (ABCD)

1993	PRO-ED, Inc.

Kathryn A. Bayles, Cheryl K. Tomeda

Population: Ages 15 years and older w/TBI

Purpose: Useful for the comprehensive assessment and screening of communication, memory, mental status, and visuospatial functioning of Alzheimer's and other dementia patients

Description: Fourteen subtests evaluate functional linguistic expression, functional linguistic comprehension, verbal episodic memory, visuospatial functions, and cognitive status. The test provides raw scores, summary scores for intertask comparisons, construct scores, and an overall score. The Mental Status subtest is an efficient, valid, and reliable measure of cognitive status for all types of patients. Standardized on patients with Alzheimer's and Parkinson's disease and young and older normal individuals. Provides norms for patients with dementia of varying severity.

Format: Examiner required; individual administration; untimed: 45 to 90 minutes

Scoring: Examiner evaluated

Cost: Complete Kit (manual, scoring and interpretation card, 25 response/record forms, screening test, 2 stimulus books, storage box) $225.00

Clinical Assessment Scales for the Elderly (CASE)

2001	Psychological Assessment Resources, Inc.

Cecil R. Reynolds, Erin D. Bigler

Population: Ages 55 to 90 years

Purpose: Assesses acute psychopathology

Description: Designed to assist the clinician in the diagnosis of selected DSM-IV Axis I clinical disorders, the CASE has 199 items on Form S and 190 items on Form R. These categories are included: Anxiety, Cognitive Competence, Depression, Fear of Aging, Obsessive–Compulsive, Paranoia, Psychoticism, Somatization, Mania, and Substance Abuse. The CASE yields 10 clinical scale scores and three validity scales. A fourth-grade reading level is required. A Fear of Aging scale assesses an individual's level of apprehension about the aging process.

Format: Self-administered; untimed: 20 to 40 minutes

Scoring: Examiner evaluated

Cost: Introductory Kit (manual, 25 of each form, 50 profile forms) $218.00

Clinical Assessment Scales for the Elderly–Short Form (CASE-SF)

2001	Psychological Assessment Resources, Inc.

Cecil R. Reynolds, Erin D. Bigler

Population: Ages 55 to 90 years

Purpose: Assesses acute psychopathology

Description: CASE-SF has 100 items on Form S and 88 items on Form R. These categories are included: Anxiety, Cognitive Competence, Depression, Fear of Aging, Obsessive Compulsive, Paranoia, Psychoticism, Somatization, Mania, and Substance Abuse. CASE-SF yields 10 clinical scale scores and three validity scales. A fourth-grade reading level is required.

Format: Self-administered; untimed: 10 to 20 minutes

Scoring: Examiner evaluated

Cost: Introductory Kit (manual, 25 of each form, 50 profile forms) $166.00

Clock Test

1995	Multi-Health Systems, Inc.

H. Tuokko, T. Hadjistavropoulos, J. A. Miller, A. Horton, B. L. Beattie

Population: Ages 65 years and older

Purpose: Screens for dementia; used for neurology and geriatric counseling

Description: Paper–pencil drawn response test comprised of three subtests: Clock Drawing (one clock must be drawn), Clock Setting (five clocks must be set), and Clock Reading (five times must be read). A score is obtained for each of the

subtests, then the scores are plotted on a profile sheet and the pattern is used to screen for dementia.

Format: Examiner required; individual administration; untimed: 5 to 10 minutes per component

Scoring: QuikScore™ forms

Cost: Kit (manual, administration tent, forms, profile sheets) $215.00

Dementia Rating Scale–Second Edition (DRS-2)

2001	Psychological Assessment Resources, Inc.

Steven Mattis

Population: Ages 55 to 89+ years

Purpose: Provides a brief, comprehensive measure of cortical status in individuals with cognitive impairment, particularly of the degenerative type

Description: An extension of the original DRS, the DRS-2 can be used to track changes in behavioral, neuropathological, and cognitive status over time. The DRS-2 has improved user-friendliness, demographically corrected normative data for a wider age range, additional validity information, and a comprehensive review of the literature. An alternate form is available to reduce the practice effects that occur with serial administrations.

Format: Examiner required; individual administration; untimed: 15 to 30 minutes

Scoring: Examiner evaluated; software scoring available

Cost: Introductory Kit (manual, 50 booklets, 50 forms, cards) $248.00

Fuld Object-Memory Evaluation

1977	Stoelting Company

Paula Altman Fuld

Population: Ages 70 to 90 years

Purpose: Measures memory and learning in adults regardless of vision, hearing, or language disabilities; cultural differences; or inattention problems

Description: Ten common objects in a bag are presented to the patient to determine whether he or she can identify them by touch. The patient names the item and then pulls it out of the bag to see if he or she was right. After being distracted, the patient is asked to recall the items from the bag. The patient is given four additional chances to learn and recall the objects. The test provides separate scores for long-term storage, retrieval, consistency of retrieval, and failure to recall items even after being reminded. The test also provides a chance to observe naming ability, left–right orientation, stereognosis, and verbal fluency. Separate norms are provided for total recall, storage, consistency of retrieval, ability to benefit from reminding, and ability to say words in categories.

Format: Examiner required; individual administration; timed: each first trial, 60 seconds; each second trial, 30 seconds

Scoring: Examiner evaluated

Cost: Complete Kit (testing materials, manual, 30 record forms) $75.00

Functional Linguistic Communication Inventory

1994	PRO-ED, Inc.

Kathryn A. Bayles, Cheryl K. Tomeda

Population: Adults

Purpose: Evaluates functional communication in patients with moderate and severe dementia

Description: Helps clinicians to determine status of greeting and naming, question answering, writing, sign comprehension and object-to-picture matching, word reading and comprehension, ability to reminisce, following commands, pantomime, gesture, and conversation. The examiner determines baseline level of function, dementia severity, and preserved functional skills. Comparison can be made of examinee's performance to performance profiles of other patients at different levels of severity. Information provided by test results is crucial for reports, treatment goals and functional management plans, discharge summaries, and counseling caregivers.

Format: Examiner required; individual administration; untimed: 30 minutes

Scoring: Examiner evaluated

Cost: Complete Kit (manual, 25 response/record forms, 25 score forms, stimulus book, objects, storage box) $200.00

Independent Living Scales™ (ILS™)

1996	Harcourt Assessment, Inc.

Patricia Anderten Loeb

Population: Adults 65+ years

Purpose: Assesses competency in instrumental activities of daily living

Description: Provides a standardized approach for identifying areas of competence in forensic cases and for determining the most appropriate living setting for adults who are experiencing a decline in cognitive functioning. The ILS is composed of five scales: Memory/Orientation, Managing Money, Managing Home and Transportation, Health and Safety, and Social Adjustment. The performance-based results from the 68 items are more objective and reliable than third-party observations or examinees' self-reports. Performance data are also provided on samples of individuals, 17 years of age and older, who have a psychiatric diagnosis, dementia, mental retardation, or traumatic brain injury.

Format: Examiner required; individual administration; untimed: 45 minutes

Scoring: Examiner evaluated

Cost: Complete Kit (manual, 25 record forms, stimulus booklet, manipulatives) $299.00

Older Persons Counseling Needs Survey (OPCNS)

1993	Mind Garden, Inc.

Jane E. Myers

Population: Ages 60 years and older

Purpose: Assesses an elderly person's needs and desires for counseling

Description: Likert-type scale with 56 items measuring personal, social, activity, and environment concerns. A fifth-grade reading level is required.

Format: Examiner required; individual administration; suitable for group use; untimed: 10 to 15 minutes

Scoring: Examiner evaluated

Cost: Sampler Set $30.00; Permission for 200 Uses $150.00

Ross Information Processing Assessment–Geriatric (RIPA-G)

1996	PRO-ED, Inc.

Deborah G. Ross-Swain, Paul Fogle

Population: Ages 55 years and older

Purpose: Assesses cognitive–linguistic deficits in geriatric patients who are residents in skilled nursing facilities, hospitals, and clinics

Description: Multiple-item paper–pencil instrument that incorporates questions from the Minimum Data Set used by nursing staffs to provide correlational data with nursing staff's assessments of patients' cognitive-linguistic abilities. Enables examiner to quantify deficits, determine severity levels for the skill areas (Immediate Memory, Recent Memory, Temporal Orientation, Spatial Orientation, Orientation to Environment, Recall of General Information, Problem Solving and Abstract Reasoning, Organization of Information, Auditory Processing and Comprehension, and Problem Solving and Concrete Reasoning), and develop rehabilitation goals and objectives.

Format: Examiner required; individual administration; untimed: 45 to 60 minutes

Scoring: Examiner evaluated

Cost: Complete Kit (manual, 25 response forms, 25 profile/summary forms, picture book, storage box) $235.00

Illness

Coping with Health Injuries and Problems (CHIP)

2000   Multi-Health Systems, Inc.

Norman S. Endler, James D. A. Parker

Population: Ages 18 years and older

Purpose: Measures ability to cope with a broad range of health problems

Description: A 32-item multidimensional measure that examines four basic coping dimensions for responding to health problems: Distraction, Palliative, Instrumental, and Emotional Preoccupation Coping. Used with patients having chronic pain, sports injuries, cancer, asthma, diabetes, and other health problems, the CHIP is administered as a self report over the course of the specific health problem to help determine the coping strategies utilized at different times in the development and/or treatment of the problem.

Format: Self-administered; untimed: 10 to 15 minutes

Scoring: QuikScore™ forms

Cost: Complete Kit (manual, 25 forms) $68.00

Health Attribution Test (HAT)

1990   Institute for Personality and Ability Testing, Inc.

Jeanne Achterberg, G. Frank Lawlis

Population: Ages 14 years and older

Purpose: Measures patient attitudes toward health responsibility regarding their own health maintenance or treatment program; used in rehab therapy and for chronic illness treatments

Description: Paper-pencil test containing 22 items that provide scores for three scales. The Internal Scale assesses the degree to which a patient will assume responsibility for, and actively participate in, the maintenance of his or her health program. The Powerful Others Scale predicts how much the patient can be expected to rely on others for health management. The Chance Score measures the patient's tendency to attribute health problems to luck or to other forces beyond his or her control. A sixth-grade reading level is required. Also available in Spanish

Format: Self-administered; untimed: 10 minutes

Scoring: Hand key

Cost: Testing Kit (10 test/answer sheet/scoring key booklets, user's guide) $27.00

Intelligence

Arlin Test of Formal Reasoning (ATFR)

1984   Slosson Educational Publications, Inc.

Patricia Kennedy Arlin

Population: Grades 6 to 12

Purpose: Assesses students' cognitive abilities; used by teachers to plan curriculum, to modify teaching techniques, and to identify gifted students

Description: Paper-pencil 32-item multiple-choice test assessing students' cognitive abilities at one of five levels: concrete, high concrete, transitional, low formal, and high formal reasoning in the application of Piaget's developmental theory. The interpretation of both the total test score and the subtest scores is based on Inhelder and Piaget's description of formal operational thought and the eight schemata associated with that thought (multiplicative compensation, probability, correlations, combinational reasoning, proportional reasoning, forms of conservation beyond direct verification, mechanical equilibrium, and coordination of two or more systems or frames of reference). The computer-scoring package provides an alphabetical pupil list indicating subtest scores, total test scores, and cognitive level designation. A sixth-grade reading level is required.

Format: Examiner required; individual or group administration; untimed: 45 minutes

Scoring: Hand key; may be computer scored

Cost: Complete Kit (manual, 35 test booklets, 35 answer sheets, template, Teaching for Thinking) $95.50

Beta III

1999	Harcourt Assessment, Inc.

C. E. Kellogg, N. W. Morton

Population: Ages 16 to 89 years

Purpose: Measures nonverbal intellectual abilities

Description: Beta III is easy to administer and score and is useful for screening large numbers of people for whom administering comprehensive test batteries would be time consuming and costly. It is the latest revision of an instrument with a long and distinguished history. The original version was developed by the U.S. Army during World War I to assess the intellectual ability of illiterate recruits. Four subtests have been retained from Beta II: Coding, Picture Completion, Clerical Checking, and Picture Absurdities. Matrix Reasoning is new to Beta III.

Format: Examiner required; individual or group administration; untimed: 30 minutes

Scoring: Examiner evaluated

Cost: Complete Kit (manual, 25 response booklets, scoring key) $189.00

Canadian Cognitive Abilities Test (CCAT)

1998	Thomson Nelson

Robert L. Thorndike, Elizabeth P. Hagen

Population: Grades K to 12

Purpose: Assesses students' abilities in three

parallel batteries: Verbal, Nonverbal, and Quantitative

Description: Series of multiple-choice paper-pencil subtests. Primary Battery is for Grades K to 2, and Levels A-H are for Grades 3 to 12. This test is a Canadian adaptation of the *Cognitive Abilities Test*, published by Riverside Publishing Company. Examiner must have a teaching certificate.

Format: Examiner required; suitable for group use; timed: 90 minutes

Scoring: Hand key; scoring service available; computer scoring available

Cost: Contact publisher

CHIPS–Children's Problem Solving

1996	Dansk psykologisk Forlag

Mogens Hansen, Svend Kreiner, Carsten Rosenberg Hansen

Population: Ages 5 to 13 years

Purpose: Assesses the child's actual problem-solving strategies when faced with tasks of different cognitive complexity; used in the teacher's planning of classroom learning (global cognition, analytic/synthetic cognition, comprehensive cognition)

Description: Multiple-choice test requiring global cognition (12 items) and categorical (12 items). Profiles depict the child's development through the stages of cognitive development. One group version and one individual version is used along with a test booklet with one item per page. Examiner must be a teacher or psychologist. Available in Danish only.

Format: Examiner required; individual or group administration; untimed: 6 to 15 minutes

Scoring: Hand key

Cost: Set $33.00 (DDK 195)

CHIPS–Young Children's Problem Solving

1996	Dansk psykologisk Forlag

Mogens Hansen, Svend Kreiner, Carsten Rosenberg Hansen

Population: Ages 3 to 7 years

Purpose: Assesses the child's actual problem-solving strategies when faced with tasks of different cognitive complexity; used in the teacher's planning of classroom learning (global cognition, analytic/synthetic cognition, comprehensive cognition)

Description: Multiple-choice test requiring global

cognition (12 items) and categorical (12 items). Profiles depict the child's development through the stages of cognitive development. One group version and one individual version is used along with a test booklet with one item per page. Examiner must be a teacher or psychologist. Available in Danish only.

Format: Examiner required; individual or group administration; untimed: 6 to 15 minutes

Scoring: Hand key

Cost: Set $59.00 (DDK 355)

Cognitive (Intelligence) Test: Nonverbal (C(I)T: nv)

2000	Academic Therapy Publications

Morrison F. Gardner

Population: Ages 4 to 14 years

Purpose: Measures nonverbal reasoning

Description: Two types of visual tasks are used to estimate a child's aptitude and potential for academic achievement. Two subtests use discrimination tasks and visual analogies. No verbal response is necessary.

Format: Examiner required; individual administration; untimed: 10 to 20 minutes

Scoring: Examiner evaluated

Cost: Test Kit (manual, test plates, 25 forms) $71.00

Columbia Mental Maturity Scale (CMMS)

1972	Harcourt Assessment, Inc.

Bessie B. Burgemeister, Lucille Hollander Blum, Irving Lorge

Population: Ages 3 years 6 months to 9 years

Purpose: Assesses mental ability

Description: Test of general reasoning abilities with 92 items arranged in a series of eight overlapping levels. The level administered is determined by the child's chronological age. Items are printed on 95 (6 × 9 in.) cards. The child responds by selecting from each series of drawings the one that does not belong. Guide for Administration and Interpretation includes directions in Spanish.

Format: Examiner required; individual administration; untimed: 15 to 20 minutes

Scoring: Examiner evaluated

Cost: Complete Kit (95 item cards, guide for administering and interpreting, 35 record forms) $799.00

Comprehensive Test of Nonverbal Intelligence (CTONI)

1996	PRO-ED, Inc.

Donald D. Hammill, Nils A. Pearson, J. Lee Wiederholt

Population: Ages 6 years to 90 years

Purpose: Measures nonverbal reasoning abilities of individuals for whom most other mental ability tests are either inappropriate or biased

Description: Six subtests (Pictorial Analogies, Geometric Analogies, Pictorial Categories, Geometric Categories, Pictorial Sequences, and Geometric Sequences) require students to look at a group of pictures or designs to solve problems. Individuals indicate their answer by pointing to alternative choices. Three composite scores are computed: Nonverbal Intelligence Quotient, Pictorial Nonverbal Intelligence Quotient, and Geometric Nonverbal Intelligence Quotient. No oral responses, reading, writing, or object manipulation are required to take the test. Instructions for administration include pantomime and oral delivery.

Format: Individual administration; computer administration available; untimed: 60 minutes

Scoring: Examiner Interpretation

Cost: Complete Kit (manual, picture books, 25 protocols, storage box) $350.00

Culture Fair Intelligence Tests

1963	Institute for Personality and Ability Testing, Inc.

Raymond B. Cattell, A. Karen Cattell

Population: Ages 4 years and older

Purpose: Measures individual intelligence for a wide range of ages without, as much as possible, the influence of verbal fluency, cultural climate, and educational level; aids in the identification of learning and emotional problems

Description: Nonverbal paper-pencil tests with three scales. Test items require only that the individual be able to perceive relationships in shapes and figures. Scale 1 contains one form with eight subtests. Scales 2 and 3 contain two forms each with four subtests. Scale 1 is designed for ages 4 to 8 years and individuals with developmental delay. Scale 2 is designed for ages 8 to 14 years and adults. Scale 3 is designed for adults.

Format: Examiner required; suitable for group

use; Scale 1 untimed: 22 minutes; Scale 2 and Scale 3; timed: 12.5 minutes each

Scoring: Hand key

Cost: Scale 1: Introductory Kit $64.00; Scales 2 and 3 Introductory Kit $51.00

Das-Naglieri Cognitive Assessment System (CAS)

1997	PRO-ED, Inc.

Jack A. Naglieri, J. P. Das

Population: Ages 5 years to 17 years 11 months

Purpose: Provides a cognitive-processing measure of ability that is fair to minority children, effective for differential diagnosis, and related to intervention

Description: A norm-referenced measure of ability developed according to a well-researched and supported theory known as PASS. The Planning, Attention, Simultaneous, Successive theory is based on cognitive and neuropsychological research. CAS provides practitioners with a tool to evaluate children's strengths and weaknesses in important areas of cognitive processing. The Standard Battery is composed of three subtests in each of the four PASS scales. The Basic Battery includes two subtests from each of the four scales.

Format: Examiner required; individual administration; time varies depending on battery administered

Scoring: Examiner evaluated; computer scored

Cost: Complete Kit (stimulus book, manual, interpretive handbook, 10 record forms, 5 response books for two age groups, 10-figure memory response books, scoring templates, red pencil, carrying case) $800.50

Differential Ability Scales™–Second Edition (DAS™-II)

2006	Harcourt Assessment, Inc.

Colin D. Elliott

Population: Ages 2 years 5 months to 17 years 11 months

Purpose: Provides in-depth analysis of children's learning abilities

Description: The second edition offers a comprehensive understanding of a child's cognitive ability and contains subtests that assess narrowly defined processing areas and provide a measure of expressive and receptive language comprehension. The instrument includes decision points,

which provide the flexibility to customize the assessment based on the child's needs. Expands its assessment of children with lower functioning, for increased confidence when evaluating children with severe disabilities and incorporates an engaging format appropriate for young children. A Spanish translation of nonverbal subtests and signed nonverbal subtest administration instructions are available.

Format: Examiner required; individual administration; core battery, 45 to 60 minutes; diagnostic subtests, 30 minutes

Scoring: Examiner evaluated; computer scoring available

Cost: Complete Kit (manuals, stimulus books, record forms, manipulatives) $875.00

Draw A Person: A Quantitative Scoring System (Draw A Person: QSS)

1988	Harcourt Assessment, Inc.

Jack A. Naglieri

Population: Ages 5 to 17 years

Purpose: Provides a measure of intellectual ability through human figure drawing

Description: Used as a part of a comprehensive assessment, as a screening device, or as a supplement to other intelligence tests. Clear scoring guidelines reflect the many possible ways a child can respond.

Format: Examiner required; individual or group administration; untimed: 15 minutes

Scoring: Examiner evaluated

Cost: Complete Kit (manual, scoring chart, 25 each of record forms and response forms) $175.00

Draw-A-Person Intellectual Ability Test for Children, Adolescents, and Adults (DAP:IQ)

2004	PRO-ED, Inc.

Cecil R. Reynolds, Julia A. Hickman

Population: Ages 4 to 89 years

Purpose: Estimates IQ using draw-a-person format

Description: The DAP:IQ provides a common set of scoring criteria to estimate intellectual ability from a human figure drawing. This instrument includes adults, as well as children and adolescents. The scoring is standardized with a set of simple, easily understood instructions, requiring a short administration time. Scoring criteria have less cultural specificity than most intelligence tests.

Format: Examiner required, individual or group administration; untimed: 10 to 12 minutes

Scoring: Examiner evaluated

Cost: Complete Kit (manual, 50 scoring forms, 50 drawing forms, storage box) $99.00

General Ability Measure for Adults (GAMA®)

1996	Pearson Assessments

Jack A. Naglieri, Achilles N. Bardos

Population: Adults

Purpose: Measures intelligence

Description: A total of 65 nonverbal items measure matching, analogies, sequences, and construction.

Format: Self-administered; timed: 25 minutes

Scoring: Self-scored; machine scored; scoring service available

Cost: Starter Kit (manual, test booklet, 3 mail in answer documents) $84.00

Goodenough-Harris Drawing Test

1963	Harcourt Assessment, Inc.

Florence L. Goodenough, Dale B. Harris

Population: Ages 3 to 15 years

Purpose: Assesses mental ability without requiring verbal skills

Description: Measures intelligence through three drawing tasks in three tests: Goodenough Draw-a-Man Test, Draw-a-Woman Test, and the experimental Self-Drawing Scale. The man and woman drawings may be scored for the presence of up to 73 characteristics. Materials include Quality Scale Cards, which are required for the short-scoring method. Separate norms are available for males and females.

Format: Examiner required; suitable for group use; untimed: 10 to 15 minutes

Scoring: Hand key

Cost: Complete Kit (test booklet, manual, quality scale cards) $159.00

Haptic Intelligence Scale

1925	Stoelting Company

Harriet C. Shurrager, Phil S. Shurrager

Population: Adults

Purpose: Measures the intelligence of adults who are blind or visually impaired; used as a substitute for or supplement to the *Wechsler Adult Intelligence Scale*

Description: Seven nonverbal (except for instructions) task assessments measure the intelligence of adults who are blind and partially sighted. The subtests are Digit Symbol, Object Assembly, Block Design, Plan-of-Search, Object Completion, Pattern Board, and Bead Arithmetic. Wechsler's procedures were followed in establishing age categories and statistical treatment of the data.

Format: Examiner required; individual administration; timed: 90 minutes

Scoring: Examiner evaluated

Cost: Complete Kit (25 record blanks, testing materials, manual, carrying case) $850.00

Kaplan Baycrest Neurocognitive Assessment™ (KBNA™)

2000	Harcourt Assessment, Inc.

Larry Leach, Edith Kaplan, Dmytro Rawilak, Brian Richards, Guy B. Proulx

Population: Ages 20 to 89 years

Purpose: Assesses cognitive abilities

Description: Seven areas of cognition are measured: Attention/Concentration, Immediate Memory-Recall, Delayed Memory-Recall, Delayed Memory-Recognition, Verbal Fluency, Spatial Processing, and Reasoning/Conceptual Shifting. The KBNA allows examiners to choose among a general overview of cognition by calculating Index Scores only, a detailed analysis of neurocognitive functioning by also calculating Process Scores, or a combination of both.

Format: Examiner required; individual administration; untimed: 60 minutes

Scoring: Examiner evaluated

Cost: Complete Kit (manual, stimulus book, chips, cassette, 25 each of response booklets and record forms, response grid, box) $275.00

Kasanin-Hanfmann Concept Formation Test (Vygotsky Test) and Modified Vygotsky Concept Formation Test

1983	Stoelting Company

Paul L. Wang

Population: All ages

Purpose: Measures an individual's ability to

think in abstract concepts; used with uneducated adults, children, and special groups such as patients with severe emotional problems

Description: Task-assessment test consisting of 22 blocks that the subject analyzes and sorts. The blocks are of different colors, shapes, and sizes but are alike in some way. The subject must determine the common factor and sort the blocks according to that factor. The *Modified Vygotsky Concept Formation Test* provides a new method of administering and scoring. The modification standardizes and simplifies the observation of the subject and adds a divergent thinking test. The modification is particularly useful in the study of mental retardation, schizophrenia, and cerebral organicity (e.g., frontal lobe pathology).

Format: Examiner required; individual administration; untimed: 30 minutes

Scoring: Examiner evaluated

Cost: Test Materials $195.00; Modified Vygotsky Concept Formation Manual $35.00; 30 Record Forms $28.00

Kaufman Adolescent and Adult Intelligence Test (KAIT)

1993 AGS Publishing/Pearson Assessments

Alan S. Kaufman, Nadeen L. Kaufman

Population: Ages 11 to 85+ years

Purpose: Comprehensive measure of intelligence

Description: The KAIT is a comprehensive measure of general intelligence. It includes separate Crystallized and Fluid Scales. Subtests are Auditory Comprehension, Double Meanings, Definitions, Rebus Learning, Mystery Codes, Logical Steps, Memory for Block Designs, Famous Faces, Rebus Delayed Recall, and Auditory Delayed Recall. Includes a well-standardized measure of Mental Status. The KAIT's high-level, adult-oriented tasks require reasoning and planning ability. Because fine motor coordination and motor speed are not emphasized, the KAIT yields a more meaningful and pure measure of intelligence of older adults.

Format: Examiner required; individual administration; timed and untimed: Core Battery, 1 hour; Expanded Battery, 90 minutes

Scoring: Examiner evaluated; DOS scoring available

Cost: Complete Kit (2 test easels, manual, 25 individual test records, 25 response booklets,

audiocassette, blocks with holder, carrying case) $709.99

Kaufman Assessment Battery for Children–Second Edition (KABC-II)

2004 AGS Publishing/Pearson Assessments

Alan S. Kaufman, Nadeen L. Kaufman

Population: Ages 3 to 18 years

Purpose: Measures cognitive ability

Description: A dual theoretical foundation using the Luria neuropsychological model and the Cattell-Horn-Carrol approach. Composite scores can be based on either model. Either approach provides a global score. The test was co-normed with the *Kaufman Test of Educational Achievement–Second Edition.*

Format: Examiner required; individual administration; timed and untimed: Luria model, 25 to 55 minutes; CHC model, 35 to 70 minutes

Scoring: Examiner evaluated; computer scoring available

Cost: Complete Kit (4 test easels, manual, 25 individual test records, manipulatives) $749.99

Kaufman Brief Intelligence Test–Second Edition (KBIT-2)

2004 AGS Publishing/Pearson Assessments

Alan S. Kaufman, Nadeen L. Kaufman

Population: Ages 4 to 90 years

Purpose: Used to obtain an estimate of intelligence

Description: Measures two distinct cognitive abilities through two scales: Crystallized and Fluid. The Crystallized (Verbal) Scale contains two item types: Verbal Knowledge and Riddles. The Fluid (Nonverbal) Scale is a Matrices subtest.

Format: Examiner required; individual administration; untimed: 20 minutes

Scoring: Examiner evaluated

Cost: Complete Kit (easel, manual, 25 individual test records, carrying bag) $204.99

Knox's Cube Test–Revised (KCT-R)

2002 Stoelting Company

Mark Stone

Population: Ages 3 years and older

Purpose: Measures short-term memory and attention span, which together constitute the most elementary stage of mental activity; used to evaluate persons who are deaf, language impaired, and foreign speaking

Description: Multiple-task assessment of attention span and short-term memory measuring how accurately an individual can repeat simple rhythmic figures tapped out for him or her by the examiner. Test materials include four cubes attached to a wooden base and a separate tapping block. Directions can be delivered in pantomime. The manual provides procedures and rationale for administering, scoring, and interpreting a comprehensive version of the KCT, which incorporates all previous versions. This revision utilizes Rasch measurement procedures to develop an objective psychometric variable, along which both items and persons can be positioned. Two versions are available: KCT JR (ages 2 to 8) and KCT SR (ages 8 and older).

Format: Examiner required; individual administration; untimed: 10 to 15 minutes

Scoring: Examiner evaluated

Cost: Complete Kit (testing materials, manual, record forms) $105.00 each version

Kohs Block Design Test

1919	Stoelting Company

S. C. Kohs

Population: Ages 3 to 19 years

Purpose: Measures performance Intelligence

Description: Multiple-item task-assessment test consisting of 17 cards containing colored designs and 16 colored blocks that the subject uses to duplicate the designs on the cards. Performance is evaluated for attention, adaptation, and auto-criticism. This test also is included in the *Merrill-Palmer V* and *Arthur* performance scales.

Format: Examiner required; individual administration; timed: 40 minutes or less

Scoring: Examiner evaluated

Cost: Complete Kit (manual, cubes, cards, 50 record blanks) $140.00

Leiter Adult Intelligence Scale (LAIS)

1972	Stoelting Company

Russell G. Leiter

Population: Adults

Purpose: Measures general intelligence in adults; used with individuals from the upper and lower

levels of the socioeconomic hierarchy and with individuals who are psychologically disabled

Description: Six oral-response and task-performance tests assessing verbal and nonverbal intelligence. The verbal tests are Similarities–Differences, Digits Forward and Backward, and Free Recall–Controlled Recall. The nonverbal tests are Pathways (following a prescribed sequence), Stencil Designs (reproduction of designs), and Painted Cube Test (duplication of designs). Test results identify deficits in cognitive, psychophysical, or social areas and provide a measure of functional efficiency for psychologically disabled and superior individuals.

Format: Examiner required; individual administration; untimed: 40 minutes

Scoring: Examiner evaluated

Cost: Test Kit (all test materials, manual, 100 record blanks) $225.00

Leiter International Performance Scale-Revised (Leiter-R)

1997	Stoelting Company

Gale H. Roid, Lucy J. Miller

Population: Ages 2 to 21 years

Purpose: Assesses intelligence in a totally nonverbal format

Description: This revision of the original Leiter consists of two nationally standardized batteries: A revision of the original Visualization and Reasoning domains for measuring intelligence and the new Attention and Memory domains. Included in both batteries are unique "growth" scores, which measure small, but important, improvement in children with significant cognitive disabilities. The Leiter-R emphasizes fluid intelligence. Validity information is provided for psychometric studies with many groups to establish fairness for all cultural and ethnic backgrounds. The four social-emotional rating scales (Examiner, Parent, Self Rating, and Teacher) provide essential information about the child's activity level, attention, impulse control, and other emotional characteristics. There are 20 subtests standardized on 1,719 typical children and adolescents and 692 children with atypical development.

Format: Examiner required; individual administration; untimed: 25 to 40 minutes

Scoring: Examiner evaluated; scoring software available

Cost: Complete Kit (manual; 3 easels; response

cards; manipulatives; 20 each VR and AM forms, attention and rating booklets, growth profile; rolling case) $895.00

Matrix Analogies Test–Expanded Form (MAT-Expanded Form)

| 1985 | Harcourt Assessment, Inc. |

Population: Ages 5 to 17 years

Purpose: Measures nonverbal reasoning ability

Description: Paper–pencil multiple-choice 64-item test consisting of abstract designs or matrices from which an element in progression is missing. The child chooses the missing element from six alternatives. Items are organized in four groups: Pattern Completion, Reasoning by Analogy, Serial Reasoning, and Spatial Visualization. The test yields standard scores, percentile ranks, age equivalents for the total score, and item group scores. Since minimal verbal comprehension and response are required, the test can be used for assessment of persons with limited response capabilities who are bilingual, gifted, learning disabled, mentally retarded, hearing and/or language impaired, and physically disabled. The test can be administered by psychologists, counselors, school psychologists and diagnosticians, rehabilitation psychologists, and other professionals with proper training and experience in testing.

Format: Examiner required; individual administration; untimed: 20 to 25 minutes

Scoring: Hand key

Cost: Complete Kit (manual, stimulus manual, 50 answer sheets, carrying case) $273.00

McCarthy Scales of Children's Abilities

| 1972 | Harcourt Assessment, Inc. |

Dorothea McCarthy

Population: Ages 2 years 6 months to 8 years 6 months

Purpose: Assesses cognitive and motor development of children

Description: Measure of five aspects of children's thinking, motor, and mental abilities. The subtests are Verbal Ability, Short-Term Memory, Numerical Ability, Perceptual Performance, and Motor Coordination. The verbal, numerical, and perceptual performance scales are combined to yield the General Cognitive Index. Items involve puzzles, toylike materials, and gamelike tasks. Six of the 18 task components that predict the child's ability to cope with schoolwork in the early grades form the *McCarthy Screening Test.*

Format: Examiner required; individual administration; untimed: 45 to 60 minutes, 20 minutes for Screening Test

Scoring: Examiner evaluated

Cost: Complete Set (stimulus, manipulatives, manual, 25 record forms, 25 drawing booklets, carrying case) $599.00

Moray House Tests

| 1994 | Hodder Murray |

Population: Ages 8 to 17 years

Purpose: Measures verbal reasoning ability

Description: Used as part of the procedure for entry to selective secondary education. Ideal for comparing pupils on intake with their subsequent performance. Uses objective scoring. Provides a choice of equivalent tests to ensure a different suite of tests is available for use each year. Purchase is restricted to schools and must be ordered on letterhead.

Format: Examiner required; group administration; untimed: 45 minutes

Scoring: Examiner evaluated; computer scoring available

Cost: Evaluation Pack (manual, 1 of each of 11 tests, sample answer key/conversion table) £35.00

Multidimensional Aptitude Battery–II

| 1998 | Sigma Assessment Systems, Inc. |

Douglas N. Jackson

Population: Ages 16 years to adult

Purpose: Assesses aptitudes and intelligence; used for clinical and research purposes with normal and deviant populations

Description: Multiple-item paper–pencil multiple-choice test consisting of two batteries of five subtests each. The Verbal Battery includes the following subtests: Information, Comprehension, Arithmetic, Similarities, and Vocabulary. The Performance Battery subtests include Digit Symbol, Picture Completion, Spatial, Picture Arrangement, and Object Assembly. Verbal, Performance, and Full Scale IQs and standard scores for the 10 subtests have been calibrated to those of another popular IQ test and permit appraisal of intellectual functioning at nine different age levels, ranging from ages 16 to 74. Separate test booklets and answer sheets are provided for the two batteries. One battery of five subtests (7 minutes per test) can be administered in one sitting. An optional tape recording of instruction and timing may be used to administer all subtests. Scoring templates are available for hand scoring. Also available in French.

Format: Examiner required; suitable for group use; timed: 7 minutes per subtest

Scoring: Hand scored; computer scored; scoring service available

Cost: Contact publisher

Naglieri Nonverbal Ability Test®–Individual Administration (NNAT®-Individual)

2003	Harcourt Assessment, Inc.

Jack A. Naglieri

Population: Ages 5 to 17 years

Purpose: Assesses general nonverbal ability

Description: The test uses progressive matrices that allow for a fair evaluation of nonverbal reasoning and general problem-solving ability. Four item types are utilized: Pattern Completion, Reasoning by Analogy, Serial Reasoning, and Spatial Visualization. Two parallel forms are available.

Format: Examiner required; individual administration; untimed: 20 to 30 minutes

Scoring: Examiner evaluated

Cost: Complete Kit (manual, stimulus booklet, 50 each of Form A and Form B) $265.00

Non-Reading Intelligence Tests

1989	Hodder Murray

Dennis Young

Population: Ages 6 to 10 years

Purpose: Measures aspects of language and thinking to counterbalance assessments based solely on attainments

Description: Three overlapping tests comprise four verbal subtests, presented orally to ensure that the abilities of pupils who may have difficulty in reading questions are not underestimated.

Format: Examiner required; group administration; untimed: 45 minutes

Scoring: Examiner evaluated

Cost: Specimen Set (manual, 1 of each test) £15.99

Nonverbal Abilities Tests

2002	Hodder Murray

Denis Vincent, Mary Crumpler

Population: Ages 6 to 13 years

Purpose: Measures cognitive ability to provide objective indicators of pupil potential

Description: These *Nonverbal Abilities Tests* give a standardized measure of cognitive abilities that is largely independent of pupils' language skills, and provide an objective indicator of individual pupil potential, which can help to establish appropriate expectations. The tests also help to identify underachievers and pupils needing learning support, while allowing teachers to "benchmark" new intakes, review value added, and evaluate school performance. There are two test forms, one for ages 6 to 10 years and one for ages 8 to 13 years.

Format: Examiner required; group administration; untimed: 50 minutes

Scoring: Examiner evaluated

Cost: Specimen Set (manual, 1 of each test) £15.99

Pictorial Test of Intelligence–Second Edition (PTI-2)

2001	PRO-ED, Inc.

Joseph L. French

Population: Ages 3 to 8 years

Purpose: Measures general intelligence

Description: The PTI-2, a revision of the 1964 PTI, is an objectively scored, individually administered test of general intelligence for both normal children and children with disabilities. Administer three subtests and combine the scores to get the Pictorial Intelligence Quotient, a global index of performance to provide a multidimensional measure of *g*. The subtests are Verbal Abstractions, Form Discrimination, and Quantitative Concepts. The PTI-2 is helpful when used with children who have difficulty with fine motor skills and/or a speech-language problem. Respondents do not need to use expressive language, but they do need to have near normal vision and hearing.

Format: Examiner required; individual administration; untimed: 15 to 30 minutes

Scoring: Examiner evaluated

Cost: Complete Kit (manual, picture book, 25 protocols, storage box) $143.00

Porteus Mazes

| 1965 | Harcourt Assessment, Inc. |

S. D. Porteus

Population: All ages

Purpose: Assesses mental ability

Description: Nonlanguage test of mental ability in which the items are mazes. Materials include the Vineland Revision, Porteus Maze Extension, and Porteus Maze Supplement. The Vineland Revision, consisting of 12 mazes, is the basic test. The Porteus Maze Extension is a series of eight mazes designed for retesting and is not intended for use as an initial test. The Porteus Maze Supplement is designed for a third testing in clinical and research settings.

Format: Examiner required; individual administration; untimed: 25 minutes per scale

Scoring: Examiner evaluated

Cost: Basic Set (mazes, 100 score sheets) $264.00; Manual $65.00

Raven's Progressive Matrices

| 1998 | Harcourt Assessment, Inc. |

J. C. Raven

Population: Ages 5 to 17+ years

Purpose: Assesses nonverbal abilities at three levels

Description: Three levels—Coloured Progressive Matrices (CPM), Standard Progressive Matrices (SPM), and Advanced Progressive Matrices (APM)—are designed to measure eductive ability, a component of Spearman's *g*, related to the ability to educe relationships. Many new features enhance assessment, including alternative forms of the CPM and SPM and an extended version of the SPM. CPM is printed in several colors. It is considered an easy level test that spreads the scores of the bottom 20% of the population. SPM is an average level test for the general population. The SPM consists of five sets of 12 problems each. The new extended version contains more difficult items while retaining the 60-item format. The AM is the difficult level test, spreading the scores of the top 20% of the population. It is divided into two tests: Set I, with 12 problems, and Set II, with 36 problems.

Format: Examiner required; individual or group administration; untimed: 15 to 60 minutes

Scoring: Examiner evaluated

Cost: Complete Kit (manual, 2 each of each level booklets, 50 answer documents for each level, supplement, carrying case) $749.00

Reasoning Progress Tests

| 2002 | Hodder Murray |

Denis Vincent, Mary Crumpler

Population: Ages 4 to 12 years

Purpose: Compares actual performance with underlying ability and identifies able underachievers and those most likely to benefit from learning support

Description: Tests are available as verbal or nonverbal. There is a picture reasoning test for the youngest. Measure verbal and/or nonverbal ability; these tend to correlate highly, but are most informative when at variance. Choose one or both measures according to pupil background, special needs, and degree of any social/language disadvantage. *Reasoning Progress Tests* can be used with *Reading Progress Tests* and with *Numeracy Progress Tests*.

Format: Examiner required; group administration; untimed: 40 to 45 minutes

Scoring: Examiner evaluated; computer scoring available

Cost: Varies by level

Schaie-Thurstone Adult Mental Abilities Test (STAMAT)

| 1985 | Penn State Gerontology Center |

K. Warner Schaie

Population: Ages 22 to 84 years

Purpose: Measures five separate factors of intelligence

Description: Multiple-item paper–pencil test in two forms measuring verbal, spatial, reasoning, number, and word fluency abilities of adults. Form A (adult) is the original *Thurstone Primary Mental Abilities Test,* Form 11-17, with new adult norms. Form OA (older adult) is a large-type version of the original test, plus two additional scales relevant for adults ages 55 and older. The test was used by Schaie for assessing the development of adult intelligence longitudinally and cross-sectionally. New normative data are based on 4,500 people from ages 22 to 84. Instructions have been written to enhance performance by older adults.

Format: Examiner required; suitable for group use; timed: 45 minutes

Scoring: Hand key

Cost: $5.00

Schubert General Ability Battery (GAB)

1979   Slosson Educational Publications, Inc.

Herman J. P. Schubert

Population: Adolescents, adults

Purpose: Measures general mental abilities; used for scholastic and industrial placement and guidance in high school, college, and industry

Description: Multiple-item paper–pencil battery of tests assessing general mental abilities in order to predict educational and employment success. The battery yields scores for verbal skills, precise thinking, arithmetic reasoning, and logical analysis.

Format: Examiner required; Individual or group administration; untimed: 45 minutes

Scoring: Examiner evaluated

Cost: Complete Kit (manual, 25 protocols) $79.75

Slosson Full-Range Intelligence Test (S-FRIT)

1993   Slosson Educational Publications, Inc.

Bob Algozzine, Ronald C. Eaves, Lester Mann, H. Robert Vance

Population: Ages 5 to 21 years

Purpose: Provides a balanced measure of Verbal/Performance/Memory cognitive abilities

Description: The S-FRIT is intended to supplement the use of more extensive cognitive assessment instruments to facilitate screening in charting cognitive progress. The test can be given by regular or special education teachers, psychologists, counselors, or other personnel who have taken basic courses in statistics and/or tests and measurements. Items are arranged according to levels of difficulty, and the examiner presents items at suggested starting points by chronological age. When the examinee fails eight items in a row, testing is completed and the examiner very quickly gets a picture of the individual's mental abilities in the following areas: Verbal Skills, Quantitative, Recall Memory, and Abstract Performance Reasoning.

Format: Examiner required; individual administration; untimed: 25 to 45 minutes

Scoring: Examiner evaluated; computer scoring available

Cost: Complete Kit $144.50

Slosson Intelligence Test–Primary (SIT-P)

1999   Slosson Educational Publications, Inc.

Bradley T. Erford, Gary J. Vitali, Steven W. Slosson

Population: Ages 2 to 7 years

Purpose: Measures cognitive ability in verbal and performance areas

Description: Designed to facilitate the screening identification of children at risk for educational failure, to provide a quick estimate of mental ability, and to identify children who may be appropriate candidates for deeper testing services. Items are ordered with an approximate ascending degree of difficulty. The test yields Verbal and Performance subscale scores and a Total Stand Score. Scoring is simple; one point is awarded for each acceptable response. There are two separate scoring forms: Lower Level (ages 2 to 3-11) and Upper Level (ages 4 to 7-11).

Format: Examiner required; individual administration; untimed: 10 to 25 minutes

Scoring: Examiner evaluated

Cost: Complete Kit $138.75

Slosson Intelligence Test–Revised (SIT-R3:P)

2004   Slosson Educational Publications, Inc.

Richard L. Slosson, Charles L. Nicholson, Terry L. Hibpshman

Population: Ages 4 to 65 years

Purpose: Measures mental age and intelligence

Description: This 187-item verbal screening instrument consists of questions arranged on a scale of chronological age. The administrator finds the basal, then adds the questions passed after the basal to find the raw score. Test scores range from 36 (*moderate M/H*) to 164 (*very superior*). The national restandardization creates a Total Standard Score (TSS), establishes a 95% or 99% confidence interval, Mean Age Equivalent, *t*-score, stanine, Normal Curve Equivalent, and percentiles, based on the TSS. Norms include regular and special populations, as well as individuals who are visually impaired and blind. Quantitative reasoning questions were designed to be administered to populations who use metric or standard references, using language common to both. Six cognitive areas of measurement include Vocabulary, General Information, Similarities and Differences, Comprehension, Quantitative, and Auditory Memory. New supplementary manual is available to assess individuals who are visually impaired. Includes a Profiling Kit that allows strengths and weaknesses to be plotted.

Format: Examiner required; individual administration; untimed: 10 to 20 minutes

Scoring: Examiner evaluated

Cost: Complete Kit $85.00

Standard Progressive Matrices–New Zealand Standardization (SPM)

1985   New Zealand Council for Educational Research

Population: Ages 8 to 15 years and adults

Purpose: Measures nonverbal reasoning skills; used in educational and psychological assessment

Description: Total of 60 items, yielding totals, percentile rank, and stanine. The SPM is a measure of nonverbal reasoning skills, particularly useful when reading or linguistic difficulties exist. It contains five sets of 12 problems, in which the client is required to select from a number of alternatives the patterned figure that correctly completes the presented matrix.

Format: Examiner required; group administration; untimed: 30 minutes

Scoring: Examiner evaluated

Cost: Specimen Kit (test booklet, norms, answer sheet, key) $55.35

Stanford-Binet Intelligence Scale–Fifth Edition (SB5)

2003   Riverside Publishing Company

Gale H. Roid

Population: Ages 2 to 85+ years

Purpose: Assesses intelligence and cognitive abilities

Description: SB5 blends many of the important features of earlier editions with significant improvements in psychometric design. It incorporates the use of two routing subtests in the point-scale format of the 1986 edition, with the functional-level design of the 1926 and 1960 editions for the remaining subtests. It provides comprehensive coverage of five factors of cognitive ability: Fluid Reasoning, Knowledge, Quantitative Reasoning, Visual-Spatial Processing, and Working Memory. There are two domain scales: Non-

verbal IQ (combines the five nonverbal subtests) and Verbal IQ (combines the five verbal subtests). The Full Scale IQ combines all 10 subtests. Two routing subtests (Nonverbal Fluid Reasoning and Verbal Knowledge) combine to form the Abbreviated Battery IQ.

Format: Examiner required; individual administration; timed and untimed: varies, approximately 5 minutes per subtest

Scoring: Examiner evaluated; computer scoring available

Cost: Complete Kit (3 item books, 2 manuals, 25 record booklets, manipulatives, briefcase) $937.00

Stoelting Brief Nonverbal Intelligence Test (S-BIT)

1999   Stoelting Company

Gale H. Roid, Lucy J. Miller

Population: Ages 6 years to adult

Purpose: Measures nonverbal intelligence, memory, and attention

Description: Provides norm-referenced and criterion-referenced scores for IQ, Fluid Reasoning, and four subtests related to academic skills. The examiner pantomimes the instructions, and the individual responds by pointing or placing a card in the appropriate position. Test items include a variety of problem-solving tasks increasing in complexity and difficulty. The range of IQ scores is 30 to 170. The test is ideal for individuals who are cognitively impaired, disadvantaged, nonverbal, non-English speaking, or hearing or speech impaired, and for speakers of English as a second language. It is a good measure of fluid intelligence and is highly correlated with other intelligence tests.

Format: Examiner required; individual administration; timed: 15 to 20 minutes

Scoring: Examiner evaluated

Cost: Complete Kit (manual, easel, cards, 20 record forms, bag) $295.00

Swanson Cognitive Processing Test (S-CPT)

1996   PRO-ED, Inc.

H. Lee Swanson

Population: Ages 4 years 5 months to 78 years 6 months

Purpose: Measures different aspects of intellectual abilities and information-processing potential

Description: Battery of 11 subtests that can be administered in an abbreviated form (5 subtests) or in a complete form under traditional, or interactive, testing conditions. Information is drawn from the work on information-processing theory and dynamic assessment. Normative data for the S-CPT were gathered between 1987 and 1994. The test was individually administered to 1,611 children and adults in 10 U.S. states and 2 Canadian provinces. The sample closely matches the 1990 U.S. Census figures. The S-CPT includes test–teach–test conditions that required measures of internal reliability. The total coefficient alpha score for the S-CPT is highly reliable. The results on composite and component scores indicate that the majority of scores range from .82 to .95, with 64% (16 of 25) of the reliabilities at .90 or greater. High construct and criterion-related validity coefficients are reported.

Format: Examiner required; individual administration; timed: 2 hours

Scoring: Examiner evaluated

Cost: Complete Kit (manual, 25 profile/examiner record booklets, picture book, card decks, strategy cards, storage box) $215.00

Test of Behavioral Rigidity (TBR)

| 1997 | Penn State Gerontology Center |

K. Warner Schaie

Population: Adults

Purpose: Measures cognitive flexibility and motor speed

Description: A paper–pencil short-answer true-false instrument that yields scores on Attitudinal Flexibility, Motor-Cognitive Flexibility, and Psycho-Motor Speed.

Format: Self-administered; timed: 30 minutes

Scoring: Examiner evaluated; computer scoring available

Cost: $2.75

Test of Nonverbal Intelligence–Third Edition (TONI-3)

| 1997 | PRO-ED, Inc. |

Linda Brown, Rita J. Sherbenou, Susan K. Johnsen

Population: Ages 6 to 89 years

Purpose: Measures intelligence, aptitude, abstract reasoning, and problem solving; requires no reading, writing, speaking, or listening on the part of the test participant

Description: This unique language-free format makes the TONI-3 ideal for evaluating subjects who have been difficult to test with any degree of confidence or precision. It is particularly well suited for individuals who are known or believed to have disorders of communication or thinking, such as aphasia, dyslexia, language disabilities, learning disabilities, speech problems, specific academic deficits, and similar conditions. The format also accommodates the needs of subjects who do not read or write English well, due to disability or lack of exposure to the English language and U.S. culture.

Format: Examiner required; individual administration; untimed: 15 to 20 minutes

Scoring: Examiner evaluated

Cost: Complete Kit (manual, picture book, 50 of each form A and B record forms, storage box) $275.00

Universal Nonverbal Intelligence Test™ (UNIT™)

| 1998 | Riverside Publishing Company |

Bruce A. Bracken, R. Steve McCallum

Population: Ages 5 to 17 years

Purpose: Provides a fair assessment of general intelligence, measured nonverbally

Description: Unlike many nonverbal tests that include only matrices, the UNIT subtests require multiple response modes, including use of manipulatives, paper–pencil, and pointing. The materials and test stimuli are designed to be relatively universal and cross-cultural. The tasks are engaging to children across races, ethnicities, and cultures. A broad range of complex memory and reasoning abilities are measured. There are six subtests (Symbolic Memory, Analogic Reasoning, Object Memory, Spatial Memory, Cube Design, and Mazes) organized into four quotients (Symbolic, Nonsymbolic, Memory, and Reasoning), and a full-scale quotient. The UNIT may be administered in three forms: abbreviated, standard, or extended batteries.

Format: Examiner required; individual administration; time varies depending on battery administered

Scoring: Examiner evaluated; computer scoring available

Cost: Complete Test (manual, 2 stimulus books,

manipulatives, 25 record forms, 25 mazes booklets, canvas carrying case) $536.00

Verbal Abilities Tests

2002   **Hodder Murray**

Denis Vincent, Mary Crumpler

Population: Ages 6 to 13 years

Purpose: Measures cognitive ability to provide objective indicators of pupil potential

Description: These *Verbal Abilities Tests* provide a reliable tool for assessing academic ability, particularly in verbally based subjects and among pupils for whom English is the first language. As such, they give an objective indicator of individual pupil potential, which can help to establish appropriate teaching and learning expectations. The tests also help to identify underachievers and pupils needing learning support, while allowing teachers to "benchmark" new intakes, review value added, and evaluate school performance. There are two test forms, one for ages 6 to 10 years and one for ages 8 to 13 years.

Format: Examiner required; group administration; untimed: 50 minutes

Scoring: Examiner evaluated

Cost: Specimen Set (manual, 1 of each test) £15.99

Visual Gestalt Test

1989   **Dansk psykologisk Forlag**

Ruth Andersen

Population: Adults

Purpose: Assesses cognitive dysfunction related to cerebral deficits applicable for research with patients who have right-hemisphere dysfunctions

Description: Four-item paper–pencil test measuring quantitative and qualitative assessment of visual gestalts using these figures: circle, triangle, rectangle, and semicircle. Materials include four stimulus cards, four pads with figure outlines, a scoring key, and a scoring sheet. Examiner must be a qualified neuropsychologist. Available in Danish only.

Format: Examiner required; individual administration; untimed

Scoring: Hand key

Cost: Set $66.00 (DDK 395)

Wechsler Abbreviated Scale of Intelligence™ (WASI™)

1999   **Harcourt Assessment, Inc.**

Population: Ages 6 to 89 years

Purpose: Measures intelligence

Description: Consists of four subtests—Vocabulary, Similarities, Block Design, and Matrix Reasoning—resulting in Verbal, Performance, and Full Scale scores. All WASI items are new and parallel to their full Wechsler counterparts. Another new feature is the oral and visual presentation of words in the Vocabulary subtest.

Format: Examiner required; individual administration; timed and untimed: 30 minutes

Scoring: Examiner evaluated; may be computer scored

Cost: Complete Kit (manual, stimulus booklet, 25 record forms, blocks, carrying bag) $250.00

Wechsler Adult Intelligence Scale®–Third Edition (WAIS®-III)

1997   **Harcourt Assessment, Inc.**

David Wechsler

Population: Ages 16 to 89 years

Purpose: Measures intellectual ability

Description: One of the primary goals of the revision was to develop new norms on a contemporary sample. The focus was on improvements to the well known features of this scale rather than on redesign. Item content, artwork, and materials have been improved and updated. Administration time was reduced, and supplementary subtests were added to increase diagnostic utility. The Verbal subtests are Vocabulary, Similarities, Arithmetic, Digit Span, Information, Comprehension, and Letter–Number Sequencing. The Performance subtests are Picture Completion, Digit Symbol, Block Design, Matrix Reasoning, Picture Arrangement, Symbol Search, and Object Assembly. Four index scores are available.

Format: Examiner required; individual administration; timed and untimed: 75 minutes

Scoring: Examiner evaluated; computer scoring available

Cost: Complete Set (2 manuals, stimulus booklet, 25 each of record forms and response booklets, manipulatives, carrying case) $925.00

Wechsler Intelligence Scale for Children®–Fourth Edition (WISC-IV®)

2003	Harcourt Assessment, Inc.

David Wechsler

Population: Ages 6 to 16 years

Purpose: Assesses intellectual ability in children

Description: Understanding of learning disabilities and attentional disorders has greatly expanded since the publication of the WISC-III. The WISC-IV makes important advances from the WISC-III in order to provide the most effective clinical tool representing cutting-edge research and thinking. The WISC-IV is designed to meet several goals: expand and strengthen clinical utility to support decision making; develop the four Index Scores as the primary interpretive structure; and improve the assessment of fluid reasoning, working memory, and processing speed. Three WISC-III subtests have been eliminated from WISC-IV: Object Assembly, Mazes, and Picture Arrangement. The WISC-III subtests that are now supplemental include Picture Completion, Arithmetic, and Information.

Format: Examiner required; individual administration; timed and untimed

Scoring: Examiner evaluated; computer scoring available

Cost: Complete Kit (manual, stimulus booklet, manipulatives, 25 record forms, carrying case) $925.00

Wechsler Preschool and Primary Scale of Intelligence™– Third Edition (WPPSI-III®)

2002	Harcourt Assessment, Inc.

David Wechsler

Population: Ages 2 years 6 months to 7 years 3 months

Purpose: Measures intellectual abilities in young children

Description: The WPPSI-III incorporates the same outstanding technical features as the WPPSI-R, plus new features such as a lower age range (down to 2-6 years); more engaging, child-friendly stimulus materials, with colorful and playlike tasks; modified testing materials and easier administration and scoring procedures requiring minimal retraining; simplified instructions to the child; the ability to test by age group (2-6 to 3-11 and 4-0 to 7-3); reduced testing time, especially for youngest children; age-appropriate start, reverse, and discontinue rules; deemphasis on speeded performance; new factor index scores; and new subtests (e.g., Picture Naming, Receptive Vocabulary, Matrix Reasoning, Picture Concepts, Symbol Search, and Coding) designed to measure abilities such as verbal and nonverbal fluid reasoning, receptive versus expressive vocabulary, and processing speed.

Format: Examiner required; individual administration; ages 2-6 to 3-11, 30 to 45 minutes; ages 4 to 7-3, 45 to 60 minutes

Scoring: Examiner evaluated; computer scoring available

Cost: Complete Set (manual, manipulatives, 25 each of record forms and maze booklets, carrying case) $899.00

Wide Range Intelligence Test (WRIT)

1999	Psychological Assessment Resources, Inc.

Joseph Gluttina, Wayne Adams, David Sheslow

Population: Ages 4 to 80 years

Purpose: Measures cognitive abilities

Description: The WRIT yields a Verbal IQ and a Visual IQ, which generate a General IQ when combined. The Vocabulary and Verbal Analogies form the Verbal Scale, and the Matrices and Diamonds form the Visual Scale. Standardized on more than 2,500 individuals, WRIT IQs are highly correlated with those from traditional and much lengthier cognitive measures. The WRIT was co-normed with the *Wide Range Achievement Test,* allowing sound and efficient determination of an intelligence/achievement discrepancy.

Format: Examiner required; individual administration; untimed: 20 to 30 minutes

Scoring: Examiner evaluated

Cost: Introductory Kit (Diamonds/Matrices easel, diamonds in case, manual, 25 forms, briefcase) $275.00

Woodcock-Johnson® III (WJ III®) Tests of Cognitive Abilities

2001	Riverside Publishing Company

Richard W. Woodcock, Kevin S. McGrew, Nancy Mather

Population: Ages 2 to 90+ years

Purpose: Assesses general intellectual ability, cognitive abilities, and scholastic aptitudes

Description: Based on the Cattell-Horn-Carroll theory of cognitive abilities with two batteries. The Standard Battery and the Extended Battery each consist of 10 tests. New features of the third edition are eight new tests that measure information-processing abilities; five new cognitive clusters; a modified organization and interpretation plan that increases depth and breadth of coverage; expanded cognitive factor structure so that two to three tests clearly measure different narrow aspects of a broader ability; three broad cognitive areas—verbal, thinking, and cognitive efficiency; and expanded procedures for evaluating ability–achievement discrepancies. Co-normed with the *WJ III Tests of Achievement* to provide ability–achievement discrepancies and an intraindividual discrepancy.

Format: Examiner required; individual administration; timed and untimed: 5 minutes per subtest

Scoring: Computer scored; examiner evaluated

Cost: Complete Battery (standard and extended test books, 2 manuals, cassette, 25 each of test records and response booklets, 5 BIA test records, scoring software, scoring guides, leather case) $690.00

Neuropsychology

Auditory Verbal Learning Test (AVLT)

2000	Australian Council for Educational Research Limited

Gina Geffen, Laurie Geffen

Population: Ages 7 to 70 years

Purpose: Measures several indices of learning and memory

Description: Originally developed in France by André Rey, the test has been adapted by Taylor and Lezak for use with English-speaking clients. The primary appeal of this test is that it is brief and easy to administer and score. The test is administered on a computer. The program produces a summary of the client's test performance and compares these with a relevant normative group matched on the basis of age and sex. The manual is included in electronic format on the CD-ROM and can be printed out if required. There are 15 items across five consecutive trials, then four further trials.

Format: Examiner required; computer administered; timed and untimed

Scoring: Computer scored

Cost: Contact publisher

Autobiographical Memory Interview (AMI)

1990	Harcourt Assessment, Inc.

Michael Kopelman, Barbara A. Wilson, Alan Baddeley

Population: Adults

Purpose: Investigates retrograde amnesia

Description: Retrograde amnesia often leads to an impairment of autobiographical memory, the capacity to recollect the facts and incidents of one's earlier life. Although this is not measured by standard memory tests, it is valuable to assess autobiographical memory for at least three reasons: to understand the nature of any memory deficit observed, to allow more adequate counseling, and to provide an individual focus for subsequent treatment. An assessment of personal remote memory is provided.

Format: Examiner required; individually administered; untimed: 25 minutes

Scoring: Examiner evaluated

Cost: $125.00

Balloons Test

1998	Harcourt Assessment, Inc.

Jennifer Edgeworth, Ian Robertson, Tom McMillan

Population: Adolescents, adults

Purpose: Measures visual inattention in individuals with neurological impairments

Description: The test has been designed as a screening test and has a number of potential advantages over existing screening tests. It is quick and simple to administer, can be used as a bedside test, and detects a higher proportion of visual inattention in patients with right-brain injury than other commonly used tests do. The test consists of two sheets, each containing 202 items. In Subtest A, the control test, 22 of the 202 items are targets to be canceled. Targets are circles with a line adjoining; other items in the array are circles. Patients are required to locate and put a line through each balloon in a fixed time limit. In Subtest B, the number and position of balloons and circles are exactly the reverse of those of Subtest A.

Format: Examiner required; individual administration; timed: 6 minutes

Scoring: Examiner evaluated

Cost: $185.00

Barry Rehabilitation Inpatient Screening of Cognition (BRISC)

1995	Valpar International Corporation

Philip Barry

Population: Grade 2 to adult

Purpose: Assesses eight categories of cognitive function for patients with severe brain injuries

Description: Paper-pencil oral response short-answer verbal test. Scores on the individual subtests may be compared to norms provided for adults and for children in separately normed Grades 2 through 12. The total score provides a reliable index of the relative severity of dysfunction and progress in the early stages of recovery. The subtests are Reading, Design Copy, Verbal Concepts, Orientation, Mental Imagery, Mental Control, Initiation, and Memory. A total score of less than 120 points is indicative of impaired function in persons between the ages of 12 and 39. Scores between 110 and 120 should be interpreted cautiously in older adults.

Format: Examiner required; individual administration; untimed

Scoring: Examiner evaluated

Cost: Set (1 manual, pad of 5 protocols) $74.95

Bayley Infant Neurodevelopmental Screener® (BINS™)

1995	Harcourt Assessment, Inc.

Glen P. Aylward

Population: Ages 3 to 24 months

Purpose: Screens infants at risk for neurological impairment or developmental delay

Description: Reliably assesses basic neurological functions, auditory and visual receptive functions, verbal and motor expressive functions, and

cognitive processes. Item sets contain 11 to 13 items selected from the *Bayley Scales of Infant Development–Second Edition* and neurological assessment. Three classifications of risk status are delimited by two cutoff scores, allowing selection of the cut score. A training video covers item administration and scoring for all item sets.

Format: Examiner required; individual administration; untimed: 10 to 15 minutes

Scoring: Examiner evaluated

Cost: Complete Kit (manual, 25 record forms, stimulus card, manipulatives, carrying case) $315.00

Behavior Rating Inventory of Executive Function (BRIEF)

2000	Psychological Assessment Resources, Inc.

Gerald A. Gioia, Peter K. Isquith, Steven C. Guy, Lauren Kenworthy

Population: Ages 5 to 18 years

Purpose: Assesses impairment of executive function

Description: A total of 86 items within eight non-overlapping theoretically and empirically clinical scales, as well as two validity scales. These scales form two broader indexes: Behavioral Regulation (three scales) and Metacognition (five scales), as well as a Global Executive Composite. Materials used: Professional Manual, Parent Form, Teacher Form, and two-sided Scoring Summary/Profile Form.

Format: Self-administered; untimed: 10 to 15 minutes

Scoring: Examiner evaluated

Cost: Introductory Kit (manual, 25 of each form) $205.00

Behavior Rating Inventory of Executive Function–Adult Version (BRIEF-A)

2005	Psychological Assessment Resources, Inc.

Robert M. Roth, Peter K. Isquith, Gerard A. Gioia

Population: Ages 18 to 90 years

Purpose: Assesses adult executive functioning/self-regulation

Description: Two formats are used—a self-report and an informant report. The Self-Report Form is designed to be completed by adults 18 to 90 years of age, including adults with a wide variety of developmental, systemic, neurological, and psychiatric disorders such as attention disorders, learning disabilities, autism spectrum disorders, traumatic brain injury, multiple sclerosis, depression, mild cognitive impairment, dementia, and schizophrenia. The Informant Report Form is administered to an adult informant who is familiar with the rated individual's everyday functioning. It can be used alone when the rated individual is unable to complete the Self-Report Form or has limited awareness of his or her own difficulties, or with the Self-Report Form to gain multiple perspectives on the individual's functioning. When administered in conjunction with the Self-Report Form, the BRIEF-A Informant Report Form provides a more clinically comprehensive picture of the individual being rated. The BRIEF-A is composed of 75 items within nine nonoverlapping theoretically and empirically derived clinical scales that measure various aspects of executive functioning.

Format: Examiner required for informant; self-report; untimed: 10 to 15 minutes

Scoring: Examiner evaluated

Cost: Introductory Kit (manual, 25 of each form) $189.00

Behavior Rating Inventory of Executive Function–Preschool Version (BRIEF-P)

2003   Psychological Assessment Resources, Inc.

Gerard A. Gioia, Kimberly Andrews Espy, Peter K. Isquith

Population: Ages 2 years 5 months to 5 years

Purpose: Assesses executive functioning

Description: The BRIEF-P consists of a single Rating Form used by parents, teachers, and day care providers to rate a child's executive functions within the context of his or her everyday environments—home and preschool. The original *Behavior Rating Inventory of Executive Function™* (BRIEF™) was the basis for the development of the BRIEF-P. Consequently, the BRIEF-P is an ecologically valid and efficient tool for screening, assessing, and monitoring a young child's executive functioning and development. The hand-scorable BRIEF-P Rating Form consists of 63 items that measure various aspects of executive functioning: Inhibit, Shift, Emotional Control, Working Memory, and Plan/Organize. The clinical scales form three broad indexes (Inhibitory Self-Control, Flexibility, and Emergent Metacognition) and one composite score (Global Executive Composite). The BRIEF-P also provides two validity scales (Inconsistency and Negativity).

Format: Rating scale; untimed: 10 to 15 minutes

Scoring: Examiner evaluated

Cost: Introductory Kit (manual, 25 of each form) $128.00

Behavior Rating Inventory of Executive Function– Self-Report Version (BRIEF-SR)

2004   Psychological Assessment Resources, Inc.

Steven C. Guy, Peter K. Isquith, Gerard A. Gioia

Population: Ages 11 to 18 years

Purpose: Assesses an adolescent's view of his or her own ability to guide, direct, and manage cognitive, emotional, and behavioral functions

Description: The BRIEF-SR is a standardized 80-item self-report behavior rating scale that can serve as an important tool in the clinical evaluation and treatment of children and adolescents who have problems involving the executive control functions. The BRIEF-SR was designed to complement the *Behavior Rating Inventory of Executive Function™* (BRIEF™) Parent and Teacher Forms by capturing a child or adolescent's view of his or her own purposeful, goal-directed, problem-solving behavior. The development of executive control functions varies in terms of age of onset, rate of development, level of proficiency, and pattern of skill acquisition. During adolescence (ages 11 to 18 years), important executive functions emerge and develop: increased reasoning, self-awareness, flexibility, organization, and self-monitoring; greater memory capacity; better behavioral regulation; and the ability to multitask. Understanding an adolescent's level of awareness of his or her own difficulties with self-regulation is a critical element in focused treatment and educational planning. It can help the clinician to estimate how much external support the adolescent will need and facilitate the intervention by building rapport and a collaborative working relationship with the adolescent.

Format: Rating scale; untimed: 10 to 15 minutes

Scoring: Examiner evaluated

Cost: Introductory Kit (manual, 25 rating forms, 50 summary forms) $140.00

Behavioral Assessment for the Dysexecutive Syndrome for Children (BADS-C)

2003   Harcourt Assessment, Inc.

Hazel Emslie, F. Colin Wilson, Vivian Burden,
Ian Nimmo-Smith, Barbara A. Wilson

Population: Ages 8 to 16 years

Purpose: Assists in early identification of deficits in executive functioning in children

Description: BADS-C examines inflexibility and perseveration, novel problem solving, impulsivity, planning, and the ability to utilize feedback and moderate one's behavior accordingly. Subtests are brief, varied, and fun to do. The tests are not influenced by practiced subskills or motor control. BADS-C scoring methodology captures the qualitative richness of the observational data since it is important to look at the level of competence, as well as how the task was attempted.

Format: Requires examiner; individual administration; untimed: 35 to 45 minutes

Scoring: Examiner evaluated

Cost: Complete Kit (manual, 25 record forms, stimulus cards, materials, timer, manipulatives) $475.00

Behavioral Assessment of the Dysexecutive Syndrome (BADS)

1996	Harcourt Assessment, Inc.

Barbara A. Wilson, Nick Alderman,
Paul Burgess, Hazel Emslie, Jonathan I. Evans

Population: Ages 16 to 87 years

Purpose: Measures executive functioning

Description: The test battery includes items that are specifically sensitive to those skills involved in problem solving, planning, and organizing behavior over an extended period of time. There are six tests in BADS: Temporal Judgment, Rule Shift Cards, Action Program, Key Search, Zoo Map, and Modified Six Elements. The battery also includes a 20-item "Dysexecutive Questionnaire" with items that are constructed in order to sample the range of problems commonly associated with the syndrome in four broad areas of likely changes: Personality, Motivational, Behavioral, and Cognitive.

Format: Examiner required; individual administration; untimed: 35 minutes

Scoring: Examiner evaluated

Cost: $425.00

Booklet Category Test–Second Edition (BCT-2)

1997	Psychological Assessment Resources, Inc.

Nick A. DeFilippis, Elizabeth McCampbell

Population: Ages 15 years and older

Purpose: Diagnoses brain dysfunction; used for clinical assessment of brain damage

Description: This is a 208-item test of concept formation and abstract reasoning. Figures are presented one at a time to the subject, who responds with a number between 1 and 4. This is the booklet version of the *Halstead Category Test*. The first four subtests may be used to predict total error scores if time limitations do not allow administration of the entire BCT. Cutoff scores are used.

Format: Examiner required; individual administration; untimed: 30 to 60 minutes

Scoring: Examiner evaluated

Cost: Introductory Kit (manual, stimulus books, 50 response forms) $480.00

Boston Qualitative Scoring System for the Rey-Osterrieth Complex Figure (BQSS)

1999	Psychological Assessment Resources, Inc.

Robert A. Stern, Debbie J. Javorsky,
Elizabeth A. Singer, Naomi C. Singer-Harris,
Jessica A. Somerville, Lisa M. Duke,
Jodi A. Thompson, Edith Kaplan

Population: Ages 18 to 94 years

Purpose: Provides a quantitative approach to rating the qualitative features of ROCF productions

Description: Evaluates Copy Condition, Immediate Recall, and Delayed Recall. Scoring criteria include presence, accuracy, and fragmentation.

Format: Examiner required; individual administration; untimed: 45 minutes

Scoring: Examiner evaluated

Cost: Introductory Kit (manual, 50 scoring booklets, 50 response sheets, stimulus card, reference guide, scoring templates, metric ruler) $209.00

Brief Neuropsychological Cognitive Examination (BNCE)

1997	Western Psychological Services

Joseph M. Tonkonogy

Population: Ages 18 years and older

Purpose: Assesses the cognitive functions targeted in a typical neuropsychological exam

Description: A general cognitive profile is provided that can be used for screening, diagnosis, or follow-up. More efficient than a neuropsychological battery and more thorough than a screener, the BNCE is an ideal way to evaluate the cognitive status of patients with psychiatric disorders or psychiatric manifestations of neurological diseases. Composed of 10 subtests, it assesses working memory, gnosis, praxis, language, orientation attention, and executive functions. The test focuses on processing skills needed for everyday functioning and is sensitive to mild impairment often missed by other brief cognitive screeners. The BNCE manual provides extensive guidance in interpreting the test results.

Format: Examiner required; individual administration; untimed: 30 minutes

Scoring: Examiner evaluated

Cost: Complete Kit (manual, stimulus booklet, 20 response booklets, 20 forms) $137.50

Brief Test of Head Injury (BTHI)

1991	PRO-ED, Inc.

Nancy Helm-Estabrooks, Gillian Hotz

Population: Adolescents and adults w/TBI

Purpose: Used to quickly probe cognitive, linguistic, and communicative abilities of patients with severe head trauma

Description: The BTHI can be given to an individual in one or more short sessions. Results can be used in advising other team members on the best approaches for communicating with a patient and structuring individualized treatment. Item clusters include Orientation and Attention, Following Commands, Linguistic Organization, Reading Comprehension, Naming, Memory, and Visual-Spatial Skills. The test yields cluster raw and standard scores and a total. The total raw score can be converted to a percentile rank, standard score, or normative severity score.

Format: Examiner required; individual administration; untimed: 25 to 30 minutes

Scoring: Examiner evaluated

Cost: Complete Kit (manual, 25 record forms, stimulus cards, manipulatives) $180.00

Brief Visuospatial Memory Test–Revised (BVMT-R)

1997	Psychological Assessment Resources, Inc.

Ralph H. B. Benedict

Population: Ages 18 to 79 years

Purpose: Measures visuospatial memory

Description: The BVMT-R has six alternate,

equivalent forms. Each form consists of six geometric figures and 12 recognition items.

Format: Examiner required; individual administration; timed: 45 minutes

Scoring: Examiner evaluated

Cost: Introductory Kit (manual, recognition stimulus booklet, reusable booklet, 25 forms) $268.00

Burns Brief Inventory of Communication and Cognition (Burns Inventory)

1997	Harcourt Assessment, Inc.

Martha S. Burns

Population: Ages 18 to 80 years

Purpose: Evaluates clients who have communication or cognitive deficits as a result of a neurological injury

Description: Three inventories (Right Hemisphere, Left Hemisphere, and Complex Neuropathology) are included to help determine which skills are impaired and may be appropriate for intervention. Results are plotted on the Record Form's treatment grid to determine a starting point and to set goals for intervention. A goal bank is provided to develop treatment plans.

Format: Examiner required; individual administration; untimed: 30 minutes

Scoring: Examiner evaluated

Cost: Complete Kit (manual, 15 record forms for each inventory, stimulus plates, audiocassette) $179.00

California Verbal Learning Test®– Children's Version (CVLT®-C)

1994	Harcourt Assessment, Inc.

Dean C. Delis, Joel H. Kramer, Edith Kaplan, Beth A. Ober

Population: Ages 5 to 16 years

Purpose: Measures verbal learning and memory within the context of an everyday memory task

Description: Multitrial verbal-learning task consisting of a 15-word shopping list used in immediate and delayed free-recall, cued-recall, and recognition trials. Aged-based norms available on 27 key indices.

Format: Examiner required; individual administration; untimed: 15 to 20 minutes, plus a 20-minute delay period

Scoring: Examiner evaluated; may be computer scored

Cost: Set (manual, 25 record forms) $168.00

California Verbal Learning Test®– Second Edition (CVLT®-II)

2000	Harcourt Assessment, Inc.

Dean C. Delis, Joel H. Kramer, Edith Kaplan, Beth A. Ober

Population: Ages 16 to 89 years

Purpose: Measures verbal learning and memory

Description: A revision of the classic test that includes more comprehensive information provided by new items, flexible administration with new Short and Alternate Forms, expanded age range, correlation with the *Wechsler Abbreviated Scale of Intelligence,* and technologically advanced scoring system. The CLVT-II measures encoding strategies, learning rates, error types, and other process data. The test includes forced choice items useful for detecting malingering, thereby helping to reduce false results.

Format: Examiner required; individual administration; untimed: standard and alternate forms, 30 minutes, plus a 30-minute delay period; short form, 15 minutes, plus a 15-minute delay period

Scoring: Examiner evaluated; may be computer scored

Cost: Complete Kit (manual, 25 record forms, 1 alternate record form, 25 short record forms, scoring software) $525.00

Canter Background Interference Procedure (BIP) for the Bender Gestalt Test

1975	Western Psychological Services

Arthur Canter

Population: Ages 15 years and older

Purpose: Assesses the probability of organic brain damage; used for diagnosis and to plan rehabilitation programs

Description: Paper-pencil 10-item test comparing the subject's results on the standard *Bender Gestalt Test* (in which the subject is presented with stimulus cards and asked to copy the designs onto a blank sheet of paper) with the results of a *Bender Gestalt Test* in which the subject reproduces the designs on a special sheet with intersecting sinusoidal lines that provide background noise or interference during the copying

task. The difference between the standard and the BIP results provides the basis for defining the subject's level of impairment. Specific ranges of adequacy and inadequacy of performance are defined to permit a measure of impairment having a high probability of association with organic brain damage or disease. Scoring is a modification of the standard Pascal-Suttell system.

Format: Examiner required; individual administration; untimed: 20 to 30 minutes

Scoring: Examiner evaluated

Cost: Kit (25 tests, manual) $82.50

Category Test: Computer Version (CAT:CV)

1993	Psychological Assessment Resources, Inc.

Nick A. DeFilippis

Population: Ages 15 years and older

Purpose: Measures concept formation and abstract thinking; distinguishes normal individuals from those with brain damage

Description: Allows the examiner to select and administer onscreen any of three versions of the test: the standard 208-item version, the 120-item version, or the 108-item version. Produces a report that includes total errors for subtests and total test. Intended for research purposes.

Format: Self-administered; untimed

Scoring: Computer scored

Cost: Unlimited Use Software $525.00

Children's Auditory Verbal Learning Test-2 (CAVLT-2)

1993	Psychological Assessment Resources, Inc.

Jack L. Talley

Population: Ages 6 years 6 months to 17 years

Purpose: Measures auditory verbal learning and memory abilities; used for psychoeducational or neuropsychological assessment

Description: Oral response verbal test with the following seven scales: Immediate Memory Span, Level of Learning, Interference Trial, Immediate Recall, Delayed Recall, Recognition Accuracy, and Total Intrusions.

Format: Examiner required; individual administration; untimed

Scoring: Examiner evaluated

Cost: Introduction Kit (manual, 25 booklets) $112.00

Children's Category Test® (CCT®)

1993   Harcourt Assessment, Inc.

Thomas Boll

Population: Ages 5 to 16 years

Purpose: Measures higher order cognitive abilities nonverbally

Description: Appropriate for use in combination with intellectual and academic achievement tests. Appropriate for the identification of traumatic brain injury. The test accommodates the needs of children with color acuity problems. Two levels are available: colors for ages 5 to 8 and numbers for ages 9 to 16. It was co-normed with the *California Verbal Learning Test.*

Format: Examiner required; individual administration; untimed: 15 to 20 minutes

Scoring: Examiner evaluated

Cost: Complete Kit (manual, 25 of each level record forms, 2 stimulus booklets, response cards) $399.00

Children's Color Trails Test (CCTT)

2003   Psychological Assessment Resources, Inc.

Antolin M. Llorente, Jane Williams, Paul Satz, Louis F. D'Elia

Population: Ages 8 to 16 years

Purpose: Measures sustained attention and sequencing

Description: The CCTT substitutes the use of color for the use of letters from the English alphabet, thereby increasing the suitability of the test within cross-cultural contexts and with other special needs populations. The test can be administered using nonverbal instructions.

Format: Examiner required; individual administration; timed: 5 to 7 minutes

Scoring: Examiner evaluated

Cost: Introductory Kit (manual, 50 record forms, 50 administrations) $148.00

Children's Memory Scale™ (CMS)

1997   Harcourt Assessment, Inc.

Morris Cohen

Population: Ages 5 to 16 years

Purpose: Assesses children's memory abilities

Description: Provides comparison between memory and learning to ability, attention, and achievement. Identifies deficits in learning and memory, deficient recall strategies, and underlying processing disorders. The information can be used

to design remedial programs based on the child's strengths and compensatory strategies. Can be used as a screening or diagnostic instrument in the following dimensions: attention and working memory, verbal and visual memory, short-delay and long-delay memory, recall and recognition, and learning characteristics. Two forms are available: ages 5 to 8 and ages 9 to 16.

Format: Examiner required; individual administration; untimed: 30 minutes

Scoring: Examiner evaluated; computer scoring available

Cost: Complete Kit (manual, 2 stimulus booklets, 25 of each record form for both levels, manipulatives, carrying case) $549.00

Closed Head Injury Screener (CHIS)

1994   Mind Garden, Inc.

Michael Ivan Friedman

Population: Patients with head injuries

Purpose: Determines a basis for evaluation and rehabilitation; used for clinicians evaluating post-concussion syndrome.

Description: Oral-response yes–no test reporting the day-to-day manifestations of cortical functions. The CHIS is a systematic interview procedure based on neurobehavioral symptoms.

Format: Examiner required; individual administration; untimed: 30 minutes

Scoring: Examiner evaluated

Cost: Sampler Set $30.00; Permission Set $150.00

Cognitive Assessment of Minnesota

1993   Harcourt Assessment, Inc.

Ruth A. Rustad, Terry L. DeGroot, Margaret L. Jungkunz, Daren S. Freeberg, Laureen G. Borowick, Ann M. Wanttie

Population: Adults

Purpose: Measures the cognitive abilities of adults with neurological impairments

Description: General problem areas are identified and presented in a concise hierarchal approach. Subtests measure attention span, memory orientation, visual neglect, temporal awareness, safety and judgment, recall/recognition, auditory memory and sequencing, and simple math skills.

Format: Examiner required; individual administration; untimed: less than 1 hour

Scoring: Examiner evaluated

Cost: Complete Kit (manual, test cards, 25 score booklets, carrying case) $132.00

Cognitive Behavior Rating Scales-Research Edition (CBRS)

1987	Psychological Assessment Resources, Inc.

J. Michael Williams

Population: Adults

Purpose: Determines the presence and assesses the severity of cognitive impairment, behavioral deficits, and observable neurological signs in individuals with possible brain impairment; also used to assess dementia

Description: Paper-pencil instrument consisting of 116 items on nine scales intended to elicit information about the examinee's daily behaviors: Language Deficit, Agitation, Need for Routine, Depression, High Cognitive Deficits, Memory Disorder, Dementia, Apraxia, and Disorientation. The items on the scales are rated by the examinee's family or significant other. Percentiles and *t*-scores are reported for each of the nine scale scores.

Format: Examiner required; individual administration; untimed: 15 to 20 minutes

Scoring: Examiner evaluated

Cost: Introductory Kit (manual, 25 reusable item booklets, 50 rating booklets) $132.00

Cognitive Linguistic Quick Test (CLQT)

2001	Harcourt Assessment, Inc.

Nancy Helm-Estabrooks

Population: Ages 18 to 89 years

Purpose: Measures cognitive strengths and weaknesses

Description: Tests in five cognitive domains (Attention, Memory, Executive Functions, Language, and Visuospatial Skills) of individuals with neurological impairment due to strokes, head injury, or dementia. The CLQT can be administered at a table or bedside, as long as the patient can sit up and use a pen. Also available in Spanish.

Format: Examiner required; individual administration; untimed: 15 to 30 minutes

Scoring: Examiner evaluated

Cost: Complete Kit (manual, stimulus manual, 15 each of record forms and response forms) $185.00

Cognitive Symptom Checklist (CSC)

1993	Psychological Assessment Resources, Inc.

Christine O'Hara, Minnie Harrell, Eileen Bellingrath, Katherine Lisicia

Population: Ages 16 years and older

Purpose: Evaluates areas of impaired cognitive functioning; used in rehabilitation counseling and occupational therapy

Description: Paper-pencil short-answer checklists in five cognitive areas: Visual Processes, Attention/Concentration, Memory, Language, and Executive Functions. A clinician guide for each of the five checklists is used. A seventh-grade reading level is required. Examiner must be trained in therapeutic approaches to rehabilitation of cognition.

Format: Self-administered; untimed: 10 to 20 minutes each

Scoring: Examiner evaluated

Cost: Introductory Kit (clinician's guide, 25 of each checklist) $180.00

Color Trails Test (CTT)

1996	Psychological Assessment Resources, Inc.

Louis F. D'Elia, Paul Satz, Craig Lyons Uchiyama, Travis White

Population: Ages 18 years and older

Purpose: Measures sustained attention and sequencing

Description: The CTT uses numbered, colored circles, and universal sign language symbols. The circles are printed with vivid pink or yellow backgrounds that are perceptible to color-blind individuals. On Color Trails 1, the examinee connects circles by following circles numbered 1 through 25. On Color Trails 2, the examinee connects circles by following circles numbered 1 through 25, but alternates between pink and yellow circles.

Format: Examiner required; individual administration; timed: 3 to 8 minutes

Scoring: Examiner evaluated

Cost: Introductory Kit (manual, 25 record forms, 25 administrations) $112.00

Comprehensive Trail-Making Test (CTMT)

2002	PRO-ED, Inc.

Cecil R. Reynolds

Population: Ages 11 to 74 years

Purpose: Used to evaluate and diagnose brain injury and other forms of central nervous system compromise

Description: The CTMT is a standardized set of five visual search and sequencing tasks that are heavily influenced by attention, concentration, resistance to distraction, and cognitive flexibility. Scoring typically requires less than 5 minutes. Normative scores are provided in the form of *t*-scores, having a mean of 50 and standard deviation of 10, and percentiles. The basic task of trail-making is to connect a series of stimuli in a specified order as fast as possible.

Format: Examiner required; individual administration; untimed: 5 to 12 minutes

Scoring: Examiner evaluated

Cost: Complete Kit (manual, 10 record booklets, storage box) $90.00

Contextual Memory Test (CMT)

| 1993 | Harcourt Assessment, Inc. |

Joan P. Toglia

Population: Adults

Purpose: Assesses awareness of memory capacity, strategy of memory use, and recall

Description: Effective treatment plans can be designed by using the CMT at bedside or in clinical settings. Used with a variety of diagnoses, including head trauma, cerebral vascular disorders, multiple sclerosis, depression, schizophrenia, and chronic alcohol abuse.

Format: Examiner required; individual administration; untimed: 10 to 20 minutes

Scoring: Examiner evaluated

Cost: Complete Kit (manual, 2 test cards, picture cards, 25 score sheets, carrying case) $125.00

Continuous Visual Memory Test (CVMT)

| 1997 | Psychological Assessment Resources, Inc. |

Donald E. Trahan, Glenn J. Larrabee

Population: Ages 7 to 80+ years

Purpose: Assesses the visual memory of individuals with neurological impairments

Description: Multiple-item verbally administered oral-response visual memory test in three parts. The Acquisition Task (recognition memory) requires the individual to discriminate between new and old repeated stimuli from among 112 designs presented at 2-second intervals. The Delayed Recognition Task measures retrieval from long-term storage and is administered after a 30-minute delay. The Visual Discrimination Task assesses the individual's ability to perceive and discriminate stimuli, thus distinguishing visual discrimination deficits from visual memory problems.

Format: Examiner required; individual administration; untimed: 45 to 50 minutes (includes 30-minute delay)

Scoring: Examiner evaluated

Cost: Introductory Kit (manual, supplement, cards, 50 scoring forms) $175.00

Cortical Vision Screening Test (CORVIST)

| 2001 | Harcourt Assessment–UK |

Merle J. James, Gordon T. Plant, Elizabeth K. Warrington

Population: Adults

Purpose: Measures visual loss due to neurological disease

Description: The test is designed to allow vision specialists without any detailed knowledge of neuropsychology to probe the higher visual areas of the brain. Cerebral lesions affecting the occipital or parietal lobes result in problems with the perception of faces, pictures, colors, and the ability to read fluently. Each of the 10 tests focuses on a different aspect of early visual processing by cortical centers. They are simple to administer and make minimal demands on the examinee. An individual who has any difficulty with any of these tests should undergo appropriate neurological and neuropsychological testing.

Format: Examiner required; individual administration; untimed: 15 minutes

Scoring: Examiner evaluated

Cost: Complete Kit (manual, stimulus book, 25 record forms) £119.00

DCS-A Visual Learning and Memory Test for Neuropsychological Assessment

| 1998 | Hogrefe & Huber Publishers |

Georg Lamberti, Sigrid Weidlich

Population: Ages 6 to 70 years

Purpose: Detects memory deficits resulting from acquired brain damage

Description: This third edition contains nine symmetrical geometrical drawings in succession, which, after being removed, all have to be reproduced with five short sticks. Six trials are allowed, although the goal of reproducing all drawings in one trial can be reached well before then by some patients. Test performance is dependent on several factors, such as directing one's attention and perceiving, storing, and reproducing forms. The results of the test give an immediate indication of the probability that brain damage has or has not occurred and also how extensive it may be.

Format: Examiner required; individual administration; timed: 20 to 60 minutes

Scoring: Examiner evaluated

Cost: Complete Test (manual, 50 sheets, cards, sticks, folder) $93.00

Delis-Kaplan Executive Function System™ (D-KEFS™)

2001   Harcourt Assessment, Inc.

Dean C. Delis, Edith Kaplan, Joel H. Kramer

Population: Ages 8 to 89 years

Purpose: Assesses key components of executive functions within verbal and spatial modalities

Description: This unique instrument incorporates principles from cognitive science to evaluate the component processes of tasks thought to be especially sensitive to frontal-lobe dysfunction. The gamelike format is designed to be interesting and engaging for examinees, encouraging optimal performance without providing right-wrong feedback that can create frustration. There are 9 stand-alone tests: Card Sorting, Train Making, Verbal Fluency, Design Fluency, Color Word Interference, Tower, 20 Questions, Word Context, and Proverb.

Format: Examiner required; individual administration; untimed: 90 minutes

Scoring: Examiner evaluated

Cost: Complete Kit (manual, stimulus booklet, cards, tower and disks, 25 each of record forms and 2 response booklets, carrying case) $599.00

Digit Vigilance Test (DVT)

1995   Psychological Assessment Resources, Inc.

Ronald F. Lewis

Population: Ages 20 to 80 years

Purpose: Assesses attention during rapid visual tracking

Description: The DVT has 59 rows of digits printed in red on the first stimulus page and blue on the second stimulus page. Respondents are asked to find and cross out either 6s or 9s

to measure vigilance and accurate selection of target stimuli.

Format: Self-administered; timed: 10 minutes

Scoring: Examiner evaluated

Cost: Introductory Kit (user's guide, 50 test booklets, set of 4 scoring templates) $136.00

Doors and People

1994   Harcourt Assessment, Inc.

Alan Baddeley, Hazel Emslie, Ian Nimmo-Smith

Population: Adults

Purpose: Measures visual and verbal recall and recognition

Description: The test is a broadly based instrument of long-term memory. It yields a single age-scaled overall score that can be unpacked to give separate measures of visual and verbal memory, recall and recognition, and forgetting. It is designed for use both as a clinical tool and as a research instrument. It provides a more analytic overview of long-term explicit memory. There are four subcomponents. Visual Recognition, Visual Recall, Verbal Recognition, and Verbal Recall

Format: Examiner required; individual administration; untimed: 25 minutes

Scoring: Examiner evaluated

Cost: Doors Book $149.00; Names Book $95.00; People Book $75.00; Manual $55.00; 25 Record Forms $50.00

Frontal Systems Behavior Scale™ (FrBe)

2002   Psychological Assessment Resources, Inc.

Janet Grace, Paul F. Malloy

Population: Ages 18 to 95 years

Purpose: Assesses behavior related to frontal systems damage

Description: Research has demonstrated that many individuals with frontal-lobe damage are capable of normal performance on traditional neuropsychological measures. However, their behavior in natural settings is often disordered, resulting in severe impairment in social and occupational functioning. Three behavioral syndromes are measured: apathy, disinhibition, and executive functioning. It is a 46-item, paper–pencil behavior rating scale.

Format: Examiner required; group administration; untimed: 10 minutes

Scoring: Examiner evaluated

Cost: Introductory Kit (manual, 25 of each form) $204.00

Halstead Russell Neuropsychological Evaluation System–Revised (HRNES-R)

| 2001 | Western Psychological Services |

Elbert W. Russell, Regina I. Starkey

Population: All ages

Purpose: Provides a complete neuropsychological evaluation, generating age- and education-corrected scores for a full range of cognitive functions

Description: Uses a scaling system based on 10 index tests. The program takes raw scores from the tests administered, corrects them for age and education, and converts them to scaled scores. The HRNES-R generates three overall indexes of brain function: Percent Score, Average Index Score, and Lateralization Key. Tests are chosen from both the *Halstead-Reitan Battery* and clinical practice.

Format: Examiner required; individual administration; untimed

Scoring: Computer scored

Cost: Kit (manual, 10 recording booklets, unlimited use disk or CD) $495.00

Hayling and Brixton Tests

| 1997 | Harcourt Assessment, Inc. |

Paul W. Burgess, Tim Shallice

Population: Ages 18 to 80 years

Purpose: Measures deficits in executive functions

Description: People with deficits in executive functions present special difficulties for the practicing clinician because the problems they experience are often quite difficult to detect even though their effects on everyday life are devastating. The Hayling Sentence Completion Test yields three measures that can be considered separately or combined into an overall score. The test consists of two sets of 15 sentences, each having the last word missing. During the first section, the examiner reads each sentence aloud and the examinee completes the sentence. During the second section, the examinee is asked to provide a word that does not fit. The Brixton Spatial Anticipation Test is perceptually simple and does not require a verbal response.

Format: Examiner required; individual administration; timed: 15 minutes

Scoring: Examiner evaluated

Cost: Complete Kit (manual, stimulus book, 25 record forms) $175.00

Hooper Visual Organization Test (VOT)

| 1985 | Western Psychological Services |

H. Elston Hooper

Population: Adolescents, adults

Purpose: Assesses organic brain pathology of both hemispheres; used for clinical diagnosis

Description: Thirty-item pictorial test differentiating between functional and motivational disorders. The subject is presented with drawings of simple objects cut into several parts and rearranged and is asked to name the objects.

Format: Examiner required; suitable for group use; untimed: 15 minutes

Scoring: Examiner evaluated

Cost: Kit (4 test booklets, manual, 25 test booklets, 100 answer sheets, scoring key) $207.00

Hopkins Verbal Learning Test–Revised™ (HVLT-R)

| 2001 | Psychological Assessment Resources, Inc. |

Jason Brandt, Ralph H. B. Benedict

Population: Ages 16 years and older

Purpose: Assesses verbal learning and memory (immediate recall, delayed recall, delayed recognition)

Description: This is a brief assessment that is easy to administer and score. It is well tolerated even by significantly impaired individuals. Its use has been validated with individuals with brain disorders (e.g., Alzheimer's disease, Huntington's disease, amnesic disorders). Six distinct forms are available, eliminating practice effects on repeated administrations. Each form consists of a list of 12 nouns with four words drawn from each of three semantic categories. Each form is printed in a different color. Raw scores are derived for Total Recall, Delayed Recall, Retention, and a Recognition Discrimination Index.

Format: Examiner required; individual administration; untimed: 5 to 10 minutes, with a 25-minute delay

Scoring: Examiner evaluated

Cost: Introductory Kit (manual, 25 of each form) $265.00

Human Figure Drawing Test (HFDT): An Illustrated Handbook for Clinical Interpretation and Standardized Assessment of Cognitive Impairment

1993	Western Psychological Services

Jerry Mitchell, Richard Trent, Roland McArthur

Population: Ages 15 years to adult

Purpose: Evaluates cognitive deterioration in adults

Description: A complete scoring and interpretation system for human figure drawings that provides adult norms for cognitive impairment. Using the handbook and the AutoScore™ form, a complete qualitative evaluation can be made. The HFDT provides four measures of cognitive status: Impairment Score, Distortion Score, Simplification Score, and Organic Factors Index. These scores are helpful in discriminating cognitive impairment caused by thought disorders from that caused by organic conditions. Norms are based on a sample of 800 individuals (over age 15), including the following groups: nonclinical, depressed, antisocial, manic, paranoid, schizophrenic, organic, and mentally retarded.

Format: Examiner required; individual administration; untimed: 15 minutes

Scoring: Examiner evaluated

Cost: Kit (handbook, 25 AutoScore™ forms, 25 drawing forms) $86.50

Human Information Processing Survey® (HIP Survey)

1984	Scholastic Testing Service, Inc.

E. Paul Torrance, Barbara Taggart, William Taggart

Population: Adults

Purpose: Used in human resource development to assess learning styles and brain hemisphere dominance

Description: Forty-item paper–pencil survey with left-brain, right-brain, or integrated categories. Raw scores, standard scores, and percentiles are yielded. Research and Professional Forms are available. Booklets, profiles, and pencils are used. Examiner must be certified for assessment.

Format: Self-administered; untimed: 20 to 30 minutes

Scoring: Self-scored

Cost: Starter Set (manual, 10 survey forms, 10 strategy and tactics forms) $56.90

Infant/Toddler Sensory Profile™ (Clinical Edition)

2000	Harcourt Assessment, Inc.

Winnie Dunn

Population: Ages birth to 36 months

Purpose: Evaluates sensory information processing

Description: Caregivers complete a questionnaire to provide a profile of how well a child with sensory-processing issues functions in daily life. The six sections are General Processing, Auditory Processing, Visual Processing, Tactile Processing, Vestibular Processing, and Oral Sensory Processing. Results help to provide a method for linking performance strengths and barriers with sensory-processing patterns, but must be combined with other evaluation data to create a complete picture of a child's status for intervention planning.

Format: Examiner required; individual administration; untimed: 15 minutes

Scoring: Examiner evaluated

Cost: Complete Kit (manual, 25 questionnaires, 25 scoring sheets) $155.00

Kaufman Short Neuropsychological Assessment Procedure (K-SNAP)

1994	AGS Publishing/Pearson Assessments

Alan S. Kaufman, Nadeen L. Kaufman

Population: Ages 11 to 85+ years

Purpose: Measures cognitive functioning

Description: Four subtests are organized in three levels of cognitive complexity: attention-orientation (Mental Status), simple memory and perceptual skills (Number Recall and Gestalt Closure), and complex intellectual functioning and planning ability (Four-Letter Words). An 8-point Impairment Index can be used to identify examinees who are likely to need further diagnostic testing.

Format: Examiner required; individual administration; untimed: 20 to 30 minutes

Scoring: Examiner evaluated

Cost: Complete Kit (manual, easel, 25 record forms) $219.99

Learning and Memory Battery (LAMB)

1995   Multi-Health Systems, Inc.

James P. Schmidt, Tom N. Tombaugh

Population: Ages 20 to 80 years

Purpose: Assesses specificity of and sensitivity to diverse memory problems

Description: Paper–pencil oral response test with seven subtests: Paragraph Learning, Word List Learning, Word Pairs, Digit Span, Supraspan, Simple Figure, and Complex Figure. All subtests contribute to an overall assessment of learning and memory abilities. All components of memory are considered, including storage and retrieval. Scores are yielded for each of the subtests. These scores are plotted on a profile sheet for easy comparison to norms. A Windows-based computer version is available.

Format: Examiner required; individual administration; untimed: 1 hour or less

Scoring: Examiner evaluated; computer scored

Cost: Complete Kit (manual, stimulus cards tent, 25 record forms, 25 profile/summary sheets, score conversion booklet, 100 drawing forms) $370.00

Luria-Nebraska Neuropsychological Battery (LNNB)

1984   Western Psychological Services

Charles J. Golden, Arnold D. Purisch, Thomas A Hammeke

Population: Ages 15 years and older

Purpose: Assesses a broad range of neuropsychological functions; used to diagnose specific cerebral dysfunction and to select and assess rehabilitation programs

Description: Multiple-item verbal, observational test available in two forms: Form I (269 items) and Form II (279 items). The discrete, scored items produce a profile for the following scales: Motor, Rhythm, Tactile, Visual, Receptive Speech, Expressive Speech, Writing, Reading, Arithmetic, Memory, Intellectual, Pathognomonic, Left Hemisphere, Right Hemisphere, Impairment, and Profile Evaluation. Form II also assesses intermediate memory. The battery diagnoses the presence of cerebral dysfunction and determines lateralization and localization. Test materials include six stimulus cards, a tape cassette, comb, quarter, and stopwatch. The Administration and Scoring Booklet includes the Profile Form and Computation of Critical Level Tables. It is used to record all scores during administration.

Format: Examiner required; individual administration; untimed: 90 to 150 minutes

Scoring: Examiner evaluated; Form I may be computer scored, Form II is only computer scored

Cost: Kit (set of test materials, 10 administration/scoring booklets, 10 patient response booklets, manual, 2-use disk, carrying case) $549.50

Luria-Nebraska Neuropsychological Battery: Children's Revision (LNNB-C)

1987   Western Psychological Services

Charles J. Golden

Population: Ages 8 to 12 years

Purpose: Measures cognitive strengths and weaknesses; used to diagnose cerebral dysfunction and to select and assess rehabilitation programs

Description: Verbal, observational adaptation of the *Luria-Nebraska Neuropsychological Battery*, with 149 items assessing cognitive functioning. The clinical scales are Motor Functions, Tactile Functions, Receptive Speech, Writing, Arithmetic, Intellectual Processes, Rhythm, Visual Functions, Expressive Speech, Reading, and Memory. The summary scales are Pathognomonic, Left Sensorimotor, and Right Sensorimotor. Two optional scales, Spelling and Motor Writing, are available.

Format: Examiner required; individual administration; untimed: 150 minutes

Scoring: Examiner evaluated; computer scored

Cost: Kit (set of test materials, 10 administration/scoring booklets, 10 patient response booklets, manual, 2-use disk, carrying case) $549.50

Memory Assessment Scales (MAS)

1991   Psychological Assessment Resources, Inc.

J. Michael Williams

Population: Ages 18 to 90 years

Purpose: Used in clinical rehabilitation and neuropsychology to assess memory functioning

Description: Contains the following subtests: List Learning, Prose Memory, List Recall, Verbal Span, Visual Span, Visual Recognition, Visual Reproduction, Names–Faces, Delayed List Recall, Delayed Prose Memory, Delayed Visual Recognition, and Delayed Names–Faces Recall. Materials used include a manual, stimulus card set, 25 record forms, and attaché case. Examiner must be Level C qualified.

Format: Examiner required; individual administration; untimed: 40 to 45 minutes

Scoring: Examiner evaluated

Cost: Introductory Kit (manual, card set, 25 record forms, carrying case) $296.00

MicroCog2: Assessment of Cognitive Functioning Version 2.4 (MicroCog™)

1996   **Harcourt Assessment, Inc.**

Douglas Powell, Edith Kaplan, Dean Whitla, Sandra Weintaub, Randolph Catlin, Harris Funkenstein

Population: Ages 18 to 89 years

Purpose: Assesses adults with cognitive impairment

Description: The user-friendly software allows most examinees to complete the test with minimal assistance; computer literacy is not required. The instrument covers a broad range of cognitive functioning, including both the accuracy and speed of cognitive processing. The updated version allows the examiner to choose only those subtests wanted. Nine interrelated areas are measured: attention/mental control, memory, reasoning/calculation, spatial processing, reaction time, information-processing accuracy, information-processing speed, cognitive functioning, and cognitive proficiency. Standard scores are automatically computed for all indexes and subtests.

Format: Computer administered: untimed: 30 to 60 minutes

Scoring: Computer scored

Cost: Complete Kit (user's guide, manual, disks, 10 report credits—5 for each form) $195.00

Middlesex Elderly Assessment of Mental State (MEAMS)

1989   **Harcourt Assessment, Inc.**

Evelyn Golding

Population: Adults

Purpose: Detects gross impairment of specific cognitive skills in elderly individuals

Description: The test is designed to assist examiners in differentiating between functional illnesses and organically based cognitive impairments. The test items are sensitive to the func-

tioning of different areas of the brain. The test will determine if parts of the brain are working less efficiently than they should, and consequently, whether it is necessary to recommend that more investigation is necessary. The 12 subtests are Orientation, Memory, New Learning, Naming, Comprehension, Arithmetic, Visuospatial Skills, Perception, Fluency, and Motor Perseveration.

Format: Examiner required; individually administered; untimed: 20 minutes

Scoring: Examiner evaluated

Cost: Complete Kit (manual, 25 record forms, 2 stimulus books) $185.00

Mini Inventory of Right Brain Injury–Second Edition (MIRBI-2)

2000   **PRO-ED, Inc.**

Patricia A. Pimental, Jeffrey A. Knight

Population: Ages 20 to 80 years

Purpose: Identifies severity of right-brain injury

Description: The examiner can quickly screen clients for neurocognitive deficits associated with right-hemisphere lesions. Its development meets the need for a brief, standardized, right-brain injury screening instrument that yields severity levels for deficit areas. New features include more data collected on an increased number of cases. Many new validity studies have been conducted with particular emphasis on the relationships of MIRBI-2 scores to other measures of neurocognitive impairment. Principal components factor analysis was performed. Each item was reevaluated. A revised Right Left Differential Scale was created. A table was added for converting raw scores. The rationale has been updated to reflect current trends. The test booklet was revised to include more user-friendly areas for recording patient information, as well as revised criteria for scoring patient responses.

Format: Examiner required; individual administration; untimed: 25 to 30 minutes

Scoring: Examiner evaluated

Cost: Complete Kit (manual, 25 examiner record booklets, 25 report forms, 25 response sheets, caliper, storage box) $163.00

Mini-Mental™ State Examination (MMSE)

1975   **Psychological Assessment Resources, Inc.**

Marshal F. Folstein, Susan E. Folstein, Paul R. McHugh

Population: Adults

Purpose: Screens for cognitive impairment, estimates the severity of cognitive impairment at a given point in time; ideal for routine and serial assessment of cognitive function

Description: The MMSE is one of the most widely used clinical instruments for quickly detecting and assessing the severity of cognitive impairment and for monitoring cognitive changes over time. Standard form with demonstrated validity and reliability in psychiatric, neurological, geriatric, and other medical populations. The convenient new "all-in-one" test form includes a detachable sheet with stimuli for the Comprehension, Reading, Writing, and Drawing tasks. The form also includes alternative item substitutions for administrations in special circumstances. Pocket-size user's guide provides valuable clinical information (population-based norms) and detailed instructions for standard administration and scoring. Available in multiple languages.

Format: Examiner required; individual administration; untimed: 5 to 10 minutes

Scoring: Examiner evaluated

Cost: Introductory Kit (clinical guide, pocket norms card, user's guide, 50 test forms) $125.00

NEPSY®

| 1997 | Harcourt Assessment, Inc. |

Marit Korkman, Ursula Kirk, Sally Kemp

Population: Ages 3 to 12 years

Purpose: Assesses neuropsychological development

Description: A child-friendly test that provides a wealth of clinical data useful for planning treatment. Strengths and subtle deficiencies are detected in five functional domains that facilitate or interfere with learning. The test provides a thorough means of assessing the neuropsychological status of children with congenital or acquired brain dysfunction, damage, or disease and is invaluable as a basis for planning treatment, special education, and long-term care. The domains measured are Attention and Executive Functions, Language, Sensorimotor Functions, Visuospatial Processing, and Memory and Learning. Each domain has a core set of subtests.

Format: Examiner required; individual administration; untimed: 45 to 65 minutes depending on age

Scoring: Examiner evaluated; computer scoring available

Cost: Complete Set (manual, stimulus booklet, 10 each of record forms for ages 3 to 4 and ages 5 to 12, 10 each of both response booklets, scoring templates, manipulatives, carrying case) $599.00

Neurobehavioral Functioning Inventory (NFI™)

| 1999 | Harcourt Assessment, Inc. |

Jeffrey S. Kreutzer, Ronald T. Seel, Jennifer H. Marwitz

Population: Ages 17 to 80 years

Purpose: Allows the development of an effective treatment plan and measures change for patients with traumatic brain injury

Description: The NFI is a brief self-report inventory that is completed by the patient or family member. There are 76 items organized into six independent scales reflecting symptoms and problems commonly encountered following the onset of neurological disability. The two forms (Patient Record Form and Family Record Form) allow comparison between two perspectives. The behaviors and symptoms are written at a sixth-grade reading level. Both scales use a 5-point Likert scale.

Format: Rating scale; untimed: 30 minutes

Scoring: Examiner evaluated

Cost: Complete Kit (manual, 25 each of family and patient record forms) $175.00

Neuropsychological Assessment Battery® (NAB)

| 2003 | Psychological Assessment Resources, Inc. |

Robert A. Stern, Travis White

Population: Ages 18 to 97 years

Purpose: Assesses a wide array of cognitive skills and functions in individuals with a known or suspected disorder of the central nervous system

Description: Provides a common set of core tests that serve as a comprehensive reference base for most routine clinical applications. The NAB consists of six modules: Screening, Attention, Language, Memory, Spatial, and Executive Functions. Each of the modules may be administered independently of the other modules. Each module has two equivalent, parallel forms. Each of the five domain-specific NAB modules includes a Daily Living test designed to be multifactorial in nature and related to real-world tasks of everyday living. The NAB provides both quantitative summary scores and standardized measures of qualitative features.

Format: Examiner required; individual administration; untimed: less than 4 hours for complete battery

Scoring: Examiner evaluated; computer scoring included

Cost: Complete Kit (3 manuals, 2 sets of manipulatives, 6 sets of Form 1 materials, 6 sets of Form 2 materials, scoring software, carrying case) $2,995.00

Neuropsychological Status Examination (NSE)

1983   Psychological Assessment Resources, Inc.

John A. Schinka

Population: Adults

Purpose: Evaluates and collects data pertaining to an individual's neuropsychological functioning; used for a variety of neuropsychological assessments, ranging from screening procedures to extensive work-ups and preparation for expert-witness testimony

Description: Paper-pencil 10 page multiple item assessment evaluating neuropsychological information, such as patient data, observational findings, test administration parameters, neuroanatomical correlates, reports of test findings, clinical impressions, and recommendations for treatment. The instrument consists of 13 sections, including patient and referral data; neuropsychological symptom checklist (NSC); premorbid status; physical, emotional, and cognitive status; results of neuropsychological testing; diagnostic comments and follow-up and treatment recommendations. The NSC is a two-page screening instrument used to assess the status of potential neurological/neuropsychological signs and symptoms. Each section was designed with consideration of base rate data for common findings in neuropsychological evaluations. The manual includes a discussion of the rationale of the logic underlying the structure of the instrument and provides suggestions for its most efficient use.

Format: Examiner required; individual administration; untimed

Scoring: Examiner evaluated

Cost: Introductory Kit (manual, 25 of each form) $62.00

NeuroPsychology Behavior and Affect Profile (NBAP)

1994   Mind Garden, Inc.

Linda Nelson, Paul Satz, Louis F. D'Elia

Population: Individuals with brain injuries

Purpose: Assesses affective change used for clinical evaluation; intended for stroke patients, outpatients with dementia, and individuals with closed head injuries

Description: This is a 106-item agree–disagree test measuring reliability and validity data for indifference, inappropriateness, prognosia, depression, and mania.

Format: Self-administered; untimed: 20 to 30 minutes

Scoring: Examiner evaluated

Cost: Sampler Set $30.00; Permission for 200 Uses $150.00

Pediatric Early Elementary Examination (PEEX2)

1996   Educators Publishing Service, Inc.

Melvin D. Levine

Population: Grades 2 to 4

Purpose: Assesses neurological development, behaviors, and health of children; used by clinicians in health-care and other settings for educational planning, counseling, use of medication, and general programming

Description: Multiple-item response test providing standardized observation procedures for characterizing children's functional health and its relationship to neurodevelopmental and physical status. The test enables clinicians to integrate medical, developmental, and neurological findings while making observations of behavioral adjustment and style.

Format: Examiner required; individual administration; untimed: 45 to 60 minutes

Scoring: Examiner evaluated

Cost: Complete Set (manual, stimulus book, 12 forms) $111.30

Pediatric Examination of Educational Readiness at Middle Childhood (PEERAMID2)

1995   Educators Publishing Service, Inc.

Melvin D. Levine

Population: Grades 4 to 10

Purpose: Assesses children's and adolescents' neurological development, behaviors, and health; used by clinicians in health-care and other settings

Description: Multiple-item response test providing standardized observation procedures for characterizing children's and adolescents' functional health and its relationship to neurodevelopmental and physical status. The test assesses a wide range of functions, including neuromaturation, attention, many aspects of memory, motor efficiency, language, and other areas critical to the academic and social adjustment of older children. It is particularly sensitive to the often subtle developmental dysfunctions of junior high school students.

Format: Examiner required; individual administration; untimed: 45 to 60 minutes

Scoring: Examiner evaluated

Cost: Complete Set (manual, stimulus book, 12 forms) $131.80

Pediatric Extended Examination at Three (PEET)

1986	Educators Publishing Service, Inc.

Melvin D. Levine

Population: Ages 3 and 4 years

Purpose: Enables clinicians to integrate medical, developmental, and neurological findings and make observations of behavioral adjustment and style to assist them in identifying specific interventions

Description: Verbal paper–pencil, show-and-tell performance measure of five developmental areas: Gross Motor, Language, Visual–Fine Motor, Memory, and Intersensory Integration. The child is asked to perform gross motor tasks (jumping, throwing and kicking a small ball), identify pictures, name objects, follow directions, and copy figures with a pencil. Tasks are presented using numerous miscellaneous items (sticks, crayon, doll) contained in kit. Words and sentences are provided for language assessment. The examination produces an empirically derived profile of the child in the developmental areas, based on his or her performance of age-appropriate tasks, which can be used to clarify concerns, determine need for further evaluation in specific areas, and initiate services or continued surveillance.

Format: Examiner required; individual administration; untimed: 45 to 60 minutes

Scoring: Examiner evaluated

Cost: Complete Set (manual, stimulus book, 12 forms) $151.80

Portable Tactual Performance Test (P-TPT)

1984	Psychological Assessment Resources, Inc.

Population: Ages 5 years to adult

Purpose: Measures tactile perception and problem-solving ability

Description: Multiple-task examination measuring spatial perception, discrimination of forms, manual or construction ability, motor coordination, and the ability to meet new situations. This portable version features a wooden carrying case, which can be set up for standardized administration.

Format: Examiner required; individual administration; untimed: 10 to 15 minutes per trial

Scoring: Examiner evaluated

Cost: Kit (manual, 50 record forms, carrying case) $420.00

Quick Neurological Screening Test–II (QNST-II)

1998	Academic Therapy Publications

Margaret Mutti, Harold M. Sterling, Nancy A. Martin, Norma V. Spalding

Population: Ages 5 to 18 years

Purpose: Assesses neurological integration as it relates to learning disabilities

Description: A nonverbal test of 15 functions, each involving a motor task similar to those observed in neurological pediatric examinations. The areas measured include maturity of motor development, skill in controlling large and small muscles, motor planning and sequencing, sense of rate and rhythm, spatial organization, visual and auditory perceptual skills, balance and cerebellar–vestibular function, and disorders of attention. Materials include geometric form reproduction sheets and filmcards printed with directions for administration and scoring. Scoring occurs simultaneously and neurodevelopmental difficulties result in increasingly larger numerical scores. The test is interpreted in terms of three functional categories.

Format: Examiner required; individual administration; untimed: 20 minutes

Scoring: Examiner evaluated

Cost: Test Kit (manual, 25 scoring forms, 25 geometric form reproduction sheets, 25 remedial guideline forms, filmcards, in vinyl folder) $95.00

Repeatable Battery for the Assessment of Neuropsychological Status (RBANS™)

| 1998 | Harcourt Assessment, Inc. |

Christopher Randolph

Population: Ages 20 to 89 years

Purpose: Measures cognitive decline in adults who have neurological injury or disease such as dementia, head injury, or stroke

Description: A quick sampling of five cognitive areas (immediate memory, visuospatial/constructional, attention, language, and delayed memory) is obtained. Two parallel forms are available to measure status over time. There are 12 subtests.

Format: Examiner required; individual administration; untimed: 30 minutes

Scoring: Examiner evaluated

Cost: Primary Form Kit (manual, 25 record forms, stimulus book, coding scoring template) $190.00

Revised Comprehensive Norms for an Expanded Halstead-Reitan Battery: Demographically Adjusted Neuropsychological Norms for African American and Caucasian Adults (HRB)

| 2004 | Psychological Assessment Resources, Inc. |

Robert K. Heaton, Walden Miller, Michael J. Taylor, Igor Grant

Population: Ages 20 to 85 years

Purpose: Provides a normative system that assists in interpreting test data

Description: The instrument provides test score corrections based on age, gender, education, and race/ethnicity for more than 50 test measures, including core Halstead-Reitan measures; lateralized sensorimotor and psychomotor Halstead-Reitan measures; as well as additional tests of executive functions, attention, memory, spatial, verbal/academic, and motor skills. A major purpose of the system is to improve neurodiagnostic accuracy by providing simultaneous corrections for demographic variables. Another purpose is to

convert raw scores on diverse tests to a common score metric.

Format: Examiner required; individual administration

Scoring: Examiner evaluated; computer scoring available

Cost: Introductory Kit (manual, 50 record forms) $184.00

Rey Complex Figure Test and Recognition Trail (RCFT)

| 1996 | Psychological Assessment Resources, Inc. |

John E. Meyers, Kelly R. Meyers

Population: Ages 6 to 89 years

Purpose: Measures visuospatial ability and visuospatial memory

Description: The RCFT consists of four separate tasks that measure Visuospatial Constructional Ability (Copy Trial) and Visuospatial Memory (Immediate Recall Trial, Delayed Recall Trial, and Recognition Trial).

Format: Examiner required; individually administered; untimed: 45 minutes, including 30-minute delay interval

Scoring: Examiner evaluated

Cost: Introductory Kit (professional manual, manual supplement, 50 test booklets, stimulus card) $262.00

Rivermead Assessment of Somatosensory Performance (RASP)

| 2000 | Harcourt Assessment, Inc. |

Charlotte E. Winward, Peter W. Halligan, Derick T. Wade

Population: Adults

Purpose: Measures somatosensory functioning after stroke or other neurological disorders

Description: The RASP consists of seven subtests covering a wide and representative range of clinical assessments traditionally considered important for somatosensory assessment. The battery is short, easy to administer, and simple to score. The seven quantifiable tests are divided into primary (surface pressure touch, surface localization, temperature discrimination, proprioception, sharp/dull discrimination) and secondary tests (extinction and two-point discrimination).

Format: Examiner required; individual administration; untimed: 20 to 30 minutes

Scoring: Examiner evaluated

Cost: Complete Kit (manual, 25 record forms, materials) $264.00

Rivermead Behavioural Memory Test-Extended Version (RBMT-E)

1998	Harcourt Assessment, Inc.

Barbara A. Wilson, Linda Clare, Alan Baddeley, Janet Cockburn, Peter Watson, Robyn Tate

Population: Ages 5 to 65 years

Purpose: Predicts everyday memory problems in people with acquired, nonprogressive brain injury and monitors change over time

Description: The RBMT-E comprises tasks analogous to situations found in daily living that often appear troublesome for people with memory impairments. The intention of the authors of the RBMT was to design a set of simple subtests that could be passed by the majority of normal controls. Two parallel versions have been developed.

Format: Examiner required; individual administration; untimed: 25 to 30 minutes

Scoring: Examiner evaluated

Cost: Complete Kit (manual, 25 record forms, stimulus books, cards, timer) $528.00

Rivermead Behavioural Memory Test for Children (RBMT-C)

1991	Harcourt Assessment, Inc.

Barbara A. Wilson, Rebecca Ivani-Chalian, Frances Aldrich

Population: Ages 5 to 11 years

Purpose: Measures memory impairment

Description: Applications include neuropsychology. There are a number of subtests, each attempting to provide an objective measure of one of a range of everyday memory problems reported and observed in subjects with memory difficulties. It has been validated using the observations of houseparents of children with severe epilepsy. Each of the nine subtests yields screening and profile scores.

Format: Examiner required; individual administration; untimed: 25 to 30 minutes

Scoring: Examiner evaluated

Cost: Complete Kit (manual, 25 record forms,

supplement, stimulus books, materials, audiotape, timer) $370.00

Rivermead Behavioural Memory Test-Second Edition (RBMT-2)

2003	Harcourt Assessment, Inc.

Barbara A. Wilson, Janet Cockburn, Alan Baddeley

Population: Ages 16 to 96 years

Purpose: Measures memory impairment

Description: The RBMT-2 is an internationally renowned, highly sensitive, ecological test of gross memory impairment. It allows for repeated assessments using everyday examples to monitor stability, improvement, or deterioration over time. Subtests measure many of the everyday memory problems reported and observed in patients with memory difficulties. Kit includes four parallel versions for minimized practice effects in retesting. For each subtest, two scores are produced: a simple pass–fail or screening score and a standardized profile score. The second edition includes a set of photographs of faces that are representative of the multiracial nature of most societies around the world.

Format: Examiner required; individual administration; untimed: 25 minutes

Scoring: Examiner evaluated

Cost: Complete Kit (manual, 25 record forms, supplements, stimulus books, audiotape/CD, timer) $375.00

Ross Information Processing Assessment-Primary (RIPA-P)

1999	PRO-ED, Inc.

Deborah G. Ross-Swain

Population: Ages 5 to 12 years

Purpose: Identifies information-processing skill impairments

Description: Eight subtests (Immediate Memory, Recent Memory, Recall of General Information, Spatial Orientation, Temporal Orientation, Organization, Problem Solving, Abstract Reasoning) allow assessment of a wide range of information-processing skills in children who have had a traumatic brain injury, have experienced other neuropathologies such as seizure disorders and anoxia, or exhibit learning disabilities.

Format: Examiner required; individual administration; untimed: 30 minutes

Scoring: Examiner evaluated

Cost: Complete Kit (manual, 25 record forms, 25 profile/summary forms, storage box) $130.00

Ross Information Processing Assessment–Second Edition (RIPA-2)

| 1996 | PRO-ED, Inc. |

Deborah G. Ross-Swain

Population: Ages 15 to 90 years

Purpose: Enables the examiner to quantify cognitive-linguistic deficits, determine severity levels for each skill area, and develop rehabilitation goals and objectives

Description: The RIPA-2 provides quantifiable data for profiling 10 key areas basic to communicative and cognitive functioning: Intermediate Memory, Recent Memory, Temporal Orientation (Recent Memory), Temporal Orientation (Remote Memory), Spatial Orientation, Orientation to Environment, Recall of General Information, Problem Solving and Abstract Reasoning, Organization, and Auditory Processing and Retention. The study sample included 126 individuals with traumatic brain injury (TBI) in 17 states. The sample was representative of TBI demographics for gender, ethnicity, and socioeconomic status. Internal consistency reliability was investigated, and the mean reliability coefficient for the RIPA-2 subtests was .85, with a range of .67 to .91.

Format: Examiner required; individual administration; untimed: 45 to 60 minutes

Scoring: Examiner evaluated

Cost: Complete Kit (examiner's manual, 25 record forms, 25 profile/summary forms, storage box) $150.00

Ruff Figural Fluency Test (RFFT)

| 1997 | Psychological Assessment Resources, Inc. |

Ronald M. Ruff

Population: Ages 16 to 70 years

Purpose: Provides information about nonverbal capacity for initiation, planning, and divergent reasoning

Description: The test consists of 36 identical stimulus items containing five dots. The respondent is asked to connect two or more dots to make as many different patterns as possible. The test is given in five parts timed at 60 seconds each.

Format: Examiner required; individual administration; timed: 5 minutes total

Scoring: Examiner evaluated

Cost: Introductory Kit (manual, 25 booklets) $122.00

Ruff-Light Trail Learning Test (RULIT)

| 1999 | Psychological Assessment Resources, Inc. |

Ronald M. Ruff, C. Christopher Allen

Population: Ages 16 to 70 years

Purpose: Assesses visuospatial learning and memory

Description: Two stimulus cards provide alternate versions of the 15-step trail. Successive trials are administered until the trail is recalled without error on two consecutive trials.

Format: Requires examiner; individually administered; untimed: 5 to 15 minutes, with 60-minute delay

Scoring: Examiner evaluated

Cost: Introductory Kit (manual, 50 test booklets, 2 stimulus cards) $145.00

Ruff 2 and 7 Selective Attention Test

| 1996 | Psychological Assessment Resources, Inc. |

Ronald M. Ruff, C. Christopher Allen

Population: Ages 16 to 70 years

Purpose: Measures sustained attention and selective attention

Description: Consists of 20 trials of a visual search and cancellation task, with 10 automatic detection trials and 10 controlled search trials.

Format: Examiner required; individual administration; untimed: 5 minutes

Scoring: Examiner evaluated

Cost: Introductory Kit (manual, 50 test booklets) $160.00

Scales of Cognitive Ability for Traumatic Brain Injury (SCATBI)

| 1992 | PRO-ED, Inc. |

Brenda B. Adamovich, Jennifer Henderson

Population: Adolescents, adults

Purpose: Assesses cognitive and linguistic abilities of patients with head injuries

Description: The SCATBI consists of five subtests: Perception/Discrimination, Orientation, Organization, Recall, and Reasoning. Unlike other tests for this population, the SCATBI progresses in difficulty to levels that even some noninjured adults do not typically master. This permits patients who functioned at very high levels prior to injury to be measured with the same instrument as they regain the use of higher level abilities. Administer only those scales that are useful for evaluating a particular patient. The test was standardized on a sample of head-injured patients and a sample of matched adults with no history of head injury.

Format: Individual administration; untimed: 30 minutes to 2 hours

Scoring: Examiner evaluated

Cost: Complete Kit (manual, stimulus book, 25 record forms, audiocassette, card set, storage box) $277.00

Screening Test for the Luria-Nebraska Neuropsychological Battery: Adult and Children's Forms (ST-LNNB)

1987	Western Psychological Services

Charles J. Golden

Population: Ages 8 years to adult

Purpose: Assesses cognitive functioning; used to identify individuals who will show a significant degree of impairment when administered the complete battery; also used for neuropsychological screening in schools and for alcohol abuse programs

Description: Fifteen-item screening test predicting overall performance on the *Luria-Nebraska Neuropsychological Battery*. Testing is discontinued when the client reaches the critical score. Forms are available for children ages 8 to 12 and adolescents and adults ages 13 and older.

Format: Examiner required; individual administration; untimed: 20 minutes

Scoring: Examiner evaluated

Cost: Kit (stimulus cards, 25 adult administration and scoring booklets, 25 children administration scoring booklets, manual) $157.00

Sensory Profile

1999	Harcourt Assessment, Inc.

Winnie Dunn

Population: Ages 3 to 10 years

Purpose: Evaluates sensory information processing

Description: Helps to determine how well children process sensory information in everyday situations. The examiner can combine the information with other evaluation data to create a com-

plete picture of the child's status for diagnostic and intervention planning. Caregivers complete the 125-question profile. The summary score sheet provides a profile of the child's sensory responses. The Short Sensory Profile is a 38-item caregiver questionnaire and score sheet designed for screening. The items are grouped into three major sections: Sensory Processing, Modulation, and Behavioral and Emotional.

Format: Examiner required; individual administration; untimed: 30 minutes

Scoring: Examiner evaluated

Cost: Complete Kit (manual, 25 caregiver questionnaires, 25 summary score sheets) $155.00

Severe Cognitive Impairment Profile (SCIP)

1998	Psychological Assessment Resources, Inc.

Guerry M. Peavy

Population: Ages 42 to 90+ years

Purpose: Measures and tracks impairment of cognitive abilities in adults with primary progressive dementia

Description: Total of eight subtests: Comportment, Language, Motor Functioning, Conceptual Reasoning Abilities, Attention, Memory, Arithmetic, and Visuospatial. Identifies four levels of impairment: moderately severe, severe, very severe, and profound.

Format: Requires examiner; individually administered; untimed: 30 to 45 minutes

Scoring: Examiner evaluated

Cost: Introductory Kit (manual, manipulatives, 25 record forms, briefcase) $399.00

Severe Impairment Battery (SIB)

1993	Harcourt Assessment, Inc.

Judith Saxton, K. L. McGonigle, A. A. Swihart, F. Boller

Population: Ages 51 to 91 years

Purpose: Assesses a range of cognitive functioning in individuals too impaired to complete standard neuropsychological tests

Description: The instrument is designed to assist therapists in the assessment of elderly individuals with severe dementia. Direct performance-based data are gathered on a wide variety of low-level tasks that take into account the specific behavioral and cognitive deficits associated with severe dementia. The test enhances understanding of the disease process and provides clinical information regarding the later stages of dementia. It is composed of very simple one-step commands that are presented in conjunction with gestural cues, and it allows for nonverbal and partially correct responses, as well as for simpler response modes such as matching. The six major subscales are Attention, Orientation, Language, Memory, Visuospatial Ability, and Construction.

Format: Examiner required; individually administered; untimed: 30 minutes

Scoring: Examiner evaluated

Cost: Complete Kit (manual, 25 record forms, cards, materials) $299.00

Shipley Institute of Living Scale

1991	Western Psychological Services

Walter C. Shipley

Population: Ages 14 years to adult

Purpose: Used as a measure of intellectual ability and impairment

Description: The Shipley measures cognitive impairment and is composed of two brief subtests: a 40-item vocabulary test and a 20-item abstract thinking test. The scale produces six summary scores: Vocabulary, Abstraction, Total, Conceptual Quotient (an index of impairment), Abstraction Quotient (the conceptual quotient adjusted for age), and Estimated Full Scale WAIS or WAIS-R IQ scores.

Format: Self administered; timed: 20 minutes

Scoring: Hand key; computer scored

Cost: Kit (100 test forms, manual, hand-scoring key, 2 AutoScore™ test forms) $126.50

Short Category Test, Booklet Format

1987	Western Psychological Services

Linda C. Wetzel, Thomas J. Boll

Population: Ages 15 years and older

Purpose: Assesses brain dysfunction; used for clinical diagnosis of brain damage

Description: Multiple-item paper–pencil test assessing adaptability, abstract concept formation, capacity to learn from experience, and cognitive flexibility. This booklet format reduces the length and complexity of the Category Test of the *Halstead-Reitan Neuropsychological Battery* by using only half the items of the original and eliminating the equipment necessary for administering it. The test may be administered at bedside.

Format: Examiner required; individual administration; timed: 20 minutes

Scoring: Examiner evaluated

Cost: Kit (1 set of stimulus cards, 100 answer sheets, manual) $192.50

Speed and Capacity of Language Processing Test (SCOLP)

1992	Harcourt Assessment, Inc.

Alan Baddeley, Hazel Emslie, Ian Nimmo-Smith

Population: Ages 16 to 65 years

Purpose: Measures the rate of information processing

Description: The test enables differentiation between a subject who has always been slow and a subject whose performance has been impaired as a result of brain damage or some other stressor. The Speed of Comprehension Test requires the subject to verify as many sentences as possible in 2 minutes. The sentences are all obviously true or false. In the Spot-the-Word Vocabulary Test, the subject is given pairs of items, each comprising one real word and one nonword, and is required to indicate the real word. Words range from common to very obscure.

Format: Examiner required; individually administered; timed and untimed: 6 minutes

Scoring: Examiner evaluated

Cost: Complete Kit (manual, 6 packages of 25 record forms, scoring acetates) $135.00

Stroop Color and Word Test

2002	Stoelting Company

Charles J. Golden

Population: Grade 2 to adult

Purpose: Evaluates personality, cognition, stress response, psychiatric disorders, and other psychological phenomena

Description: Multiple-item response test of an individual's ability to separate word and color stimuli and react to them independently. The test consists of three pages: a Word Page containing color words printed in black ink; a Color Page with a series of Xs printed in colored inks; and a Word-Color page on which the words on the first page are printed in the colors of the second page except that the word and color do not match. The subject is given all three pages and asked to read the Word Page. The individual then names the colors of the Xs on the Color Page. Next he or she must name the color of the ink in which the words on the Word-Color Page are printed, ignoring the semantic meaning of the words. The test requires a second-grade grade reading level. Also available in Spanish.

Format: Examiner required; individual administration; timed: 5 minutes

Scoring: Examiner evaluated

Cost: Complete Kit (manual, 25 sets of 3 sheets, mail-in form for technical manual) Specify Child or Adult $85.00

Stroop Neuropsychological Screening Test (SNST)

1989	Psychological Assessment Resources, Inc.

Max. R. Trenerry, Bruce Crosson, James DeBoe, William R. Leber

Population: Ages 18 to 79 years

Purpose: Screens neuropsychological functioning

Description: A two-part (Color Task, Color–Word Task) oral-response short-answer test measuring neuropsychological functioning. Scores yield percentile and probability values for Color Score and Color–Word Score.

Format: Examiner required; individual administration; timed: 4 minutes

Scoring: Hand scored

Cost: Introductory Kit (Form C Stimulus Sheets, Form C-W Stimulus Sheets, record form, manual) $132.00

Symbol Digit Modalities Test (SDMT)

1982	Western Psychological Services

Aaron Smith

Population: Ages 8 to 75 years

Purpose: Measures brain damage; used to screen and predict learning disorders and to identify children with potential reading problems

Description: Multiple-item test in which the subject is given 90 seconds to convert as many meaningless geometric designs as possible into their appropriate numbers according to the key provided. When group-administered, the test may be used as a screening device. The test may be administered orally to individuals who cannot take written tests. Since geometric figures and numbers are nearly universal, the test is virtually culture-free.

Format: Examiner required; individual or group administration; untimed: 90 seconds

Scoring: Hand key

Cost: Complete Kit (25 WPS AutoScore™ test forms, manual) $91.00

Test of Memory and Learning–Second Edition (TOMAL-2)

2007	PRO-ED, Inc.

Cecil R. Reynolds, Judith K. Voress

Population: Ages 5 to 59 years

Purpose: Provides comprehensive assessment of memory

Description: The TOMAL-2 includes eight core subtests, six supplementary subtests, and two delayed recall tasks that evaluate general and specific memory functions; features composite memory scores for Verbal Memory, Nonverbal Memory, and a Composite Memory Index. The supplementary composite scores include Verbal Delayed Recall Index, Learning Index, Attention and Concentration Index, Sequential Memory Index, Free Recall Index, and an Associate Recall Index. The Record Booklet has been redesigned to be more convenient for the examiner. In addition, the scoring and administration rules are clearer.

Format: Examiner required; individual administration; timed and untimed: Core, 30 minutes; Supplementary, 30 minutes

Scoring: Examiner evaluated

Cost: Complete Kit (manual, 2 picture books, 25 record forms, 25 supplementary analysis forms, chips, visual selective reminding test board, delayed recall cue cards, storage box) $363.00

Test of Memory Malingering (TOMM)

1996	Multi-Health Systems, Inc.

Tom N. Tombaugh

Population: Ages 16 to 84 years

Purpose: Helps to distinguish between malingerers and true memory impairment in cognitively intact normal individuals and clinical samples that include no cognitive impairment, cognitive impairment, aphasia, traumatic brain injury, or dementia

Description: The TOMM consists of two learning trials and an optional retention trial. On each learning trial, 50 pictures (line drawings) are presented at the rate of 1 every 4 seconds. The same 50 pictures are used on each trial. Then, 50 two-choice recognition panels are presented individually. Each panel contains one of the previously presented pictures and a picture not previously shown. From each panel, the examinee is required to select the correct picture. Designed to appear more difficult than they actually are, some TOMM tasks are mistaken as difficult when, in fact, they are quite easy. Almost everyone who takes the TOMM does well except for patients who are malingering. Research has found the TOMM to be insensitive to a wide variety of neurological impairments. Two cutoff scores are included: below chance and criteria based on patients with head injuries and cognitive impairments. Available in computer-administered format.

Format: Examiner required; individual administration: untimed: 30 to 40 minutes

Scoring: Examiner evaluated, computer scored

Cost: Kit (manual, stimulus booklets, 25 forms) $144.00

Tower of London^dx-2nd Edition (TOL^dx™ 2nd Edition)

Multi-Health Systems, Inc.

William C. Culbertson, Eric A. Zillmer

Population: Ages 7 years and older

Purpose: Assesses higher order problem solving, specifically executive-planning abilities

Description: Although similar to the original *Tower of London*, developed for assessing adult patients with frontal lobe damage, the TOL^dx presents a number of modifications in administration and scoring, including elimination of repeated trials for failed problems; introduction of six- and seven-move test problem configurations, which increases the sensitivity of the measure to executive functioning across age levels; and an empirical selection of test problem configurations. Uses of the test include attention-deficit/hyperactivity diagnosis.

Format: Examiner required; individually administered; untimed: 10 to 15 minutes

Scoring: Examiner evaluated

Cost: Complete Kit (manual, 25 adult forms, 25 child forms, 2 peg boards) $278.00

Victoria Symptom Validity Test (VSVT)

1997   Psychological Assessment Resources, Inc.

Daniel Slick, Grace Hopp, Esther Strauss, Carrie B. Thompson

Population: Ages 18 years and older

Purpose: Assesses possible exaggeration or feigning of cognitive impairments

Description: The VSVT's 48 items are presented onscreen in three blocks of 16 items. A single five-digit study number is presented on the screen for five seconds followed by the Recognition Trial in which the study number (the correct choice) and a five-digit foil are displayed. The respondent is then asked to choose the correct response.

Format: Computer administered; untimed: 18 to 25 minutes

Scoring: Computer scored

Cost: CD; Manual $525.00

Visual Analog Mood Scales (VAMS)

1997   Psychological Assessment Resources, Inc.

Robert A. Stern

Population: Ages 18 to 94 years

Purpose: Assesses internal mood states in adults with neurological impairments and in patients in medical and psychiatric settings

Description: Eight individual scales that require minimal cognitive or linguistic demands on the patient measure these specific mood states: Afraid, Sad, Energetic, Happy, Confused, Angry, Tired, and Tense. Materials used: manual, 25 response booklets, and metric ruler.

Format: Self administered; untimed: 5 minutes

Scoring: Examiner evaluated

Cost: Introductory Kit (manual, 25 booklets, metric ruler) $124.00

Visual Object and Space Perception Battery (VOSP)

1991   Harcourt Assessment, Inc.

Elizabeth Warrington, Merle James

Population: Adults

Purpose: Assesses object or space perception while minimizing the involvement of other cognitive skills

Description: The VOSP consists of eight tests that enable an examiner to compare the scores of an individual with those of a normal control sample and those obtained by patients with right- and left-cerebral lesions.

Format: Examiner required; individual or group administration; untimed: 20 minutes

Scoring: Examiner evaluated

Cost: Complete Kit (manual, 25 record forms, 3 stimulus books) $238.00

Visual Search and Attention Test (VSAT)

1990	Psychological Assessment Resources, Inc.

Max R. Trenerry, Bruce Crosson, James DeBoe, William R. Leber

Population: Adults

Purpose: Measures attentional processes in individuals with neuropsychological impairments

Description: Four paper–pencil visual cancellation tasks yield the following scores: overall attention score, and left- and right-side performance.

Format: Examiner required; individual administration; timed: 6 minutes

Scoring: Examiner evaluated

Cost: Introductory Kit (manual, 50 test booklets) $162.00

Wechsler Memory Scale®– Third Edition (WMS®-III)

1997	Harcourt Assessment, Inc.

David Wechsler

Population: Ages 16 to 89 years

Purpose: Assesses adult memory abilities

Description: A primary purpose for developing the WMS-III was to expand its clinical utility. The revision includes five subtests from the WMS® and four new subtests. Subtests are organized into summary index scores. The Primary Indices are Auditory Immediate, Visual Immediate, Immediate Memory, Auditory Delayed, Visual Delayed, Auditory Recognition Delayed, General Memory, and Working Memory. In addition, four Auditory Process Composites have been added to help evaluate clinically meaningful aspects of memory functioning. The WMS-III and WAIS-III can be used together to evaluate the discrepancy between IQ and memory. Also available in Spanish and an abbreviated form.

Format: Examiner required; individual administration; untimed: 30 to 35 minutes

Scoring: Examiner evaluated; computer scoring available

Cost: Complete Kit (manual, 25 each of record forms and visual reproduction response book-

lets, 2 stimulus booklets, board, carrying case) $549.00

Wechsler Test of Adult Reading™ (WTAR™)

2001	Harcourt Assessment, Inc.

Population: Ages 16 to 89 years

Purpose: Estimates premorbid intellectual functioning

Description: This new assessment tool for older adolescents was normed with the *Wechsler Adult Intelligence Scale-Third Edition* and *Wechsler Memory Scale-Third Edition.* The test is comprised of a list of 50 words that have atypical grapheme-to-phoneme translations. The intent in using words with irregular pronunciations is to minimize the current ability of the client to apply standard pronunciation rules and to assess previous learning of the word. Reading recognition is relatively stable in the presence of cognitive declines associated with normal aging or brain injury. United Kingdom norms are also available.

Format: Examiner required; individual administration; untimed: 5 to 10 minutes

Scoring: Examiner evaluated

Cost: Complete Kit (manual, 25 record forms, word card, cassette) $125.00

Wessex Head Injury Matrix (WHIM)

2000	Harcourt Assessment, Inc.

Agnes Shiel, Barbara A. Wilson, Lindsay McLellan, Sandra Horn, Martin Watson

Population: Ages 16 years and older

Purpose: Assesses and monitors recovery of cognitive function

Description: The 62-item observational matrix can be used by a multidisciplinary team to assess the patient and to set goals for rehabilitation from the outset of coma. With a patient who is slow to recover, it is not unusual to believe mistakenly that no recovery is occurring even though subtle progress is being made over weeks and months. The WHIM has been designed to pick up minute indices demonstrating recovery and provide objective evidence so that prediction is neither overoptimistic nor too pessimistic.

Format: Examiner required; individual administration; untimed

Scoring: Examiner evaluated

Cost: Complete Kit (manual, 25 record forms, carrying case) $105.00

Wide Range Assessment of Memory and Learning, Second Edition (WRAML2)

2005	Psychological Assessment Resources, Inc.

David Sheslow, Wayne Adams

Population: Ages 5 to 90 years

Purpose: Measures an individual's verbal and visual memory ability; helpful in measuring memory-related learning ability and problems within the psychological, educational, and medical communities

Description: The WRAML2 Core Battery is composed of two Verbal, two Visual, and two Attention/Concentration subtests, yielding a Verbal Memory Index, a Visual Memory Index, and an Attention/Concentration Index. Together, these subtests yield a General Memory Index. A new Working Memory Index has been added, which is comprised of the Symbolic Working Memory and Verbal Working Memory subtests. Four new recognition subtests have been added: Design Recognition, Picture Recognition, Verbal Recognition, and Story Memory Recognition. The Story Memory subtest includes new stories, and the Picture Memory subtest provides new full-color scenes. The designs on the Design Memory Cards have been changed, and an additional Design Card has been added.

Format: Examiner required; individual administration; untimed: Core, less than 1 hour

Scoring: Examiner evaluated; scoring software available

Cost: Introductory Kit (manual, 25 each of examiner and response forms, briefcase, materials) $475.00

Wisconsin Card Sorting Test (WCST)

1993	Psychological Assessment Resources, Inc.

David A. Grant, Esta A. Berg

Population: Ages 6 years 6 months to 89 years

Purpose: Assesses perseveration and abstract thinking; used for neuropsychological assessment of individuals suspected of having brain lesions involving the frontal lobes; can help discriminate frontal from nonfrontal lobe dysfunction

Description: Multiple-task nonverbal test in which the respondent matches cards in two response decks to one of four stimulus cards for color, form, or number. Responses are recorded on a form for later scoring. The test provides measures of overall success and particular sources of difficulty. A CD-ROM version for onscreen administration and scoring and a scoring program are available.

Format: Examiner required; computer or individual administration; untimed: 20 to 30 minutes

Scoring: Examiner evaluated; may be computer scored

Cost: Introductory Kit (manual, card decks, 50 record booklets) $340.00

Wisconsin Card Sorting Test®– 64 Card Version (WCST-64®)

2000	Psychological Assessment Resources, Inc.

Robert K. Heaton

Population: Ages 6 years 5 months to 89 years

Purpose: Assesses perseveration and abstract thinking, as well as executive functioning

Description: The WCST-64 uses only the first 64 WCST cards, thereby shortening the administration time for most individuals while retaining the task requirements of the standard version. The WCST-64 also eliminates variability in the number of cards administered, facilitating straightforward comparisons of test–retest stability and comparisons of individual test results with normative and validity data.

Format: Examiner required; individual administration; untimed: 10 to 15 minutes

Scoring: Examiner evaluated; computer scoring available

Cost: Introductory Kit (manual, 50 record booklets, card deck) $260.00

Pain

Behavioral Assessment of Pain–Medical Stability Quick Screen (BAP-MSQS)

2000	Pain Assessment Resources

Michael J. Lewandowski

Population: Adults, patients with pain

Purpose: Screens pain beliefs, mood, and perception of pain

Description: This paper–pencil or computer-administered multiple-choice test was developed to provide a brief screening of information relevant to persons suffering from subacute and chronic pain-related problems. The BAP-MSQS can be useful in identifying patient assets and potential obstacles for recovery in terms of behavioral, cognitive, and psychosocial areas frequently seen in pain patients. In addition, the BAP-MSQS can identify problem areas in which more comprehensive assessment might be needed and to assess patient progress in functional restorations/pain/work hardening programs. The clinical report is intended to be used by professionals who are trained or supervised in the appropriate uses and limitations of self-report questionnaires and who have experience working with patients with subacute and chronic benign pain. Also available in Spanish. Used with Windows 95, 98, 2000, NT.

Format: Self-administered; timed: 5 minutes

Scoring: Computer scored; test scoring service available

Cost: $7.50 per test

Behavioral Assessment of Pain Questionnaire (BAP)

1989	Pain Assessment Resources

Michael J. Lewandowski, Blake H. Tearnan

Population: Adults, patients with pain

Purpose: Pain management; diagnoses factors maintaining and exacerbating pain

Description: Paper–pencil or computer-administered test has 10 subscales with a total of 312 items: Pain Behavior (10 items), Activity Interference (34 items), Avoidance (34 items), Spouse/Partner Influence (27 items), Physician Influence (25 items), Physician Qualities (13 items), Pain Beliefs (52 items), Perceived Consequences (24 items), Coping (57 items), and Mood (36 items).

Works with Windows 95, 98, 2000, NT. Also available in Spanish and French.

Format: Self-administered; untimed: 45 minutes

Scoring: Computer scored or machine scored; test scoring service available

Cost: $21.00 per test

Pain Patient Profile™ (P-3™)

1996	Pearson Assessments

C. David Tollison, Jerry C. Langley

Population: Ages 17 to 76 years

Purpose: Assesses psychological factors that can influence the severity and persistence of pain

Description: Multiple-choice 44-item computer or paper–pencil test measuring psychological factors that influence patient pain. Scales include the following: Depression, Anxiety, and Somatization. Includes a validity index. An eighth-grade reading level is required.

Format: Self-administered; untimed: 15 minutes

Scoring: Hand key; computer scored; test scoring service available from publisher

Cost: Starter Kit (manual, 10 prepaid fax-in answer sheets) $150.00

Psychosocial Pain Inventory (PSPI)

1985	Psychological Assessment Resources, Inc.

Robert K. Heaton, Ralph A. W. Lehman, Carl J. Getto

Population: Adults

Purpose: Evaluates psychosocial factors related to chronic pain problems; used in the treatment of chronic pain patients

Description: Eight-page multiple-item paper–pencil inventory assessing the following psychosocial factors considered important in maintaining and exacerbating chronic pain problems: several forms of secondary gain, the effects of pain behavior on interpersonal relationships, the existence of stressful life events that may contribute to subjective distress or promote avoidance learning, and components of past history that familiarize the patient with the chronic invalid role and with its personal and social consequences. Ratings take into account that patients differ in the degree to which they are likely to be influenced by potential sources of secondary gain.

The inventory yields a total score. High scores predict poor response to medical treatment for pain.

Format: Examiner required; individual adminis-

tration; untimed: 1 to 2 hours

Scoring: Examiner evaluated

Cost: Introductory Kit (50 forms, manual) $120.00

Pathology

General

ACDI-Corrections Version II

1997	Behavior Data Systems, Ltd.

Herman H. Linderman

Population: Ages 12 to 17 years

Purpose: Measures six areas of concern for troubled juveniles

Description: Designed for troubled youth assessment for juvenile courts and probation, the test contains six scales: Truthfulness, Alcohol, Drugs, Violence, Distress, and Adjustment. Each scale provides specific recommendations for intervention, supervision, and treatment. There are 143 multiple choice/true false items. Measures juveniles' truthfulness, evaluates their overall adjustment, and assesses their anxiety and depression level, as well as violence proneness. Truth-corrected scores. Computer-generated report summarizes risk range and recommendations. Standardized and normed on the juvenile population. Available in English or Spanish. Online administration is available at www.online-testing .com.

Format: Self-administered; untimed: 20 to 25 minutes

Scoring: Computer scored; online

Cost: $8.00 each administration; $9.95 each online

Adolescent & Child Urgent Threat Evaluation™ (ACUTE)

2005	Psychological Assessment Resources, Inc.

Russell I. Copelan, David Ashley

Population: Ages 8 to 18 years

Purpose: Assesses risk of violence (both homicidal and suicidal)

Description: The ACUTE is a 27-item structured

assessment that is based on information obtained through various sources, including, but not limited to, patient interview, chart review, and family interview. The instrument is designed to assist in determining the associated level of risk for near-future (e.g., hours to days) violence. An overall Threat Classification is provided, as well as additional cluster scores.

Format: Examiner completed rating scale; untimed: 10 to 20 minutes

Scoring: Examiner evaluated

Cost: Introductory Kit (manual, 50 rating forms) $115.00

Adolescent Psychopathology Scale™ (APS)

1998	Psychological Assessment Resources, Inc.

William M. Reynolds

Population: Ages 12 to 19 years

Purpose: Evaluates the presence and severity of symptoms of psychological disorders and distress

Description: It empirically assesses the severity of symptoms associated with specific DSM-IV clinical and personality disorders. The APS also assesses other psychological problems and behaviors that may interfere with an adolescent's psychological adaptation and personal competence. A multiple-response format is used to measure six distinct anxiety disorders. There are 346 items.

Format: Self-report; untimed: 45 to 60 minutes

Scoring: Examiner evaluated; computer scoring included

Cost: Introductory Kit (manual, CD, 25 test booklets) $378.00

Adolescent Psychopathology Scale-Short Form™ (APS-SF)

1998	Psychological Assessment Resources, Inc.

William M. Reynolds

Population: Ages 12 to 19 years

Purpose: Evaluates the presence and severity of symptoms of psychological disorders and distress

Description: It empirically assesses the severity of symptoms associated with specific DSM-IV clinical and personality disorders. The APS also assesses other psychological problems and behaviors that may interfere with an adolescent's psychological adaptation and personal competence. A multiple-response format is used to measure six distinct anxiety disorders. There are 115 items.

Format: Self-report; untimed: 15 to 20 minutes

Scoring: Examiner evaluated; computer scoring included

Cost: Introductory Kit (manual, CD, 25 test booklets) $238.00

Adolescent Symptom Inventory-4 (ASI-4)

1999	Checkmate Plus, Ltd.

Kenneth D. Gadow, Joyce Sprafkin

Population: Ages 12 to 18 years

Purpose: Screens for DSM-IV emotional and behavioral disorders

Description: The ASI-4 has 120 items on the Parent checklist that screen for emotional and behavioral disorders: attention-deficit/hyperactivity disorder, oppositional-defiant disorder, conduct disorder, depressive disorders, bipolar disorder, anxiety disorders, and eating disorders. The Teacher checklist contains 79 items that screen for 15 disorders. Provides symptom count scores (DSM-IV criteria) and symptom severity profiles (norms-based). Also available in Spanish.

Format: Rating scale; can be computer-administered; untimed: 10 to 15 minutes

Scoring: Examiner evaluated; computer scored

Cost: Deluxe Kit (screening and norms manuals, 25 parent checklists, 25 teacher checklists, 50 symptom count score sheets) $102.00

Adult Inventories-4

Date not provided	Checkmate Plus, Ltd.

Kenneth D. Gadow, Joyce Sprafkin, Margaret Weiss

Population: Adults

Purpose: Screens for DSM-IV psychiatric disorders

Description: The self-report 135-item scale is completed by the patient, and the Adult Inventory is filled out by someone who knows the patient well. When clinicians obtain ratings prior to the patient interview, they can review the answers and ask more detailed questions about specific problem areas. The self-report inventory can be scored according to symptom count criteria (diagnostic model) or symptom severity model (normative data model). Also available in Spanish.

Format: Rating scale; can be computer administered; untimed: 15 to 20 minutes

Scoring: Examiner evaluated; computer scored

Cost: Deluxe Kit (manual, 50 self-report checklists, 5 adult inventories, 50 symptom count score sheets, 50 symptom severity profiles) $102.00

Adult Treatment Outcome (ATO)

Date not provided	Behavior Data Systems, Ltd.

Herman H. Linderman

Population: Ages 18 to 75 years

Purpose: Provides test–retest comparison at stages of treatment intervention (intake, change of status, completion, and outcome)

Description: The ATO has 153 items in 12 scales: Truthfulness, Self-Esteem, Outlook, Distress, Depression, Anxiety, Suicide, Control, Violence, Alcohol, Drugs, and Stress Coping Abilities. Requires a high fifth-grade reading level. Also available in Spanish.

Format: Self-administered; untimed: 35 to 40 minutes

Scoring: Computer scored

Cost: $8.00 per administration

Beck Youth Inventories™–Second Edition for Children and Adolescents

2005	Harcourt Assessment, Inc.

Judith S. Beck, Aaron T. Beck, John Jolly

Population: Ages 7 to 18 years

Purpose: Assesses depression, anxiety, anger disruptive behavior, and self-concept

Description: Five self-report inventories with 20 statements each can be used separately or in combination to assess symptoms of depression, anxiety, anger, disruptive behavior, and self-concept. Children describe how frequently the statement has been true for them during the past 2 weeks, including today. Items are written at a second-grade reading level, with language that is easy to understand for self-reporting. They may also be administered orally.

Format: Self-report; untimed: 5 minutes per inventory

Scoring: Examiner evaluated

Cost: Starter Kit (manual, 25 combination booklets) $150.00

Brief Symptom Inventory (BSI)

1975	Pearson Assessments

Leonard R. Derogatis

Population: Ages 13 years and older

Purpose: Screens for psychological problems and measures progress

Description: Multiple-choice 53-item computer-administered or paper-pencil test with a 5 point rating scale of 0 to 4. The nine primary dimensions are Somatization, Obsessive–Compulsive, Interpersonal Sensitivity, Depression, Anxiety, Hostility, Phobic Anxiety, Paranoid Ideation, and Psychoticism. A sixth-grade reading level is required. Examiner must be M-level qualified. A computer version using an IBM-compatible 486 PC or higher is available. The test is available on audiocassette and in 23 foreign languages; 13 additional languages are available for research purposes only.

Format: Self-administered; untimed: 8 to 10 minutes

Scoring: Hand key; computer scored

Cost: Starter Kit with Interpretative Report (manual, 3 answer sheets, 3 reports) $57.25

Butcher Treatment Planning Inventory (BTPI™)

1998	Multi-Health, Inc.

James N. Butcher

Population: Ages 18 years and older

Purpose: Assesses client characteristics that facilitate or interfere with treatment progress

Description: The BTPI Full Form consists of 210 items on 14 scales that fall within three clusters. It is useful early in the treatment process and serves as a baseline for evaluating symptom reduction during treatment using the Symptom Monitoring Form. The 80 items on that form are from Cluster 3 scales (Assessment of Symptoms).

The Treatment Issues Form has 174 items from Clusters 1 (Assessment of Validity of Self-Report) and 2 (Assessment of Treatment Issues). This form was created as an alternative to the Full Form for appraising treatment accessibility, not symptomatology. The Treatment Process/Symptom Form has 171 items from Clusters 2 and 3.

Format: Self-administered; untimed: 12 to 30 minutes

Scoring: QuikScore™ forms

Cost: Hand-Scoring Starter Kit (manual, 10 Full Form question booklets, 25 answer/profile sheets, scoring templates, 1 Symptom Monitoring Form booklet and scoring document) $160.00

Child Symptom Inventory–4 (CSI-4)

1994	Checkmate Plus, Ltd.

Kenneth D. Gadow, Joyce Sprafkin

Population: Ages 5 to 12 years

Purpose: Screens for DSM-IV emotional and behavioral disorders; provides behavioral ratings of child psychopathology

Description: The Parent Checklist contains 97 items that screen for 15 emotional and behavioral disorders: ADHD, ODD, Conduct Disorder, Depressive Disorders, Anxiety Disorders, and Pervasive Developmental Disorders. The Teacher Checklist contains 77 items that screen for 13 disorders. Symptom count scores (DSM-IV criteria) and symptom severity profiles (norms-based) are provided. Also available in Spanish.

Format: Rating scale; can be computer administered; untimed: 10 to 15 minutes

Scoring: Examiner evaluated; computer scored

Cost: Deluxe Kit (manual, 25 parent checklists, 25 teacher checklists, 50 symptom count sheets, 50 symptom severity profiles) $98.00

Childhood Trauma Questionnaire: A Retrospective Self-Report (CTQ)

1997	Harcourt Assessment, Inc.

David P. Bernstein, Laura Fink

Population: Ages 12 years and older

Purpose: Identifies clients with histories of trauma

Description: This is a 28-item self-report. The CTQ is useful with individuals referred for a broad range of psychiatric symptoms and problems. The examiner can determine whether traumatic childhood conditions are a factor to determine appropriate treatment. The CTQ is comprised of five scales: Physical, Sexual, and Emotional Abuse, and Physical and Emotional Neglect. A minimization/denial scale is included.

Format: Self-report; untimed: 5 minutes

Scoring: Examiner evaluated

Cost: Complete Kit (manual, 25 answer documents) $125.00

ChIPS–Children's Interview for Psychiatric Syndromes

American Psychiatric Publishing, Inc.

Elizabeth B. Weller, Ronald A. Weller, Mary A. Fristad, Marijo Teare Rooney

Population: Children, adolescents

Purpose: Helps clinicians make standardized, reliable, and accurate diagnoses

Description: The interview is based on strict DSM-IV criteria and has been validated in 12 years of studies. The questions are brief and simple to administer. There is a parent version (P-ChIPS) that contains essentially the same interview test, altered from second to third person to address the parent. The instrument screens for attention-deficit/hyperactivity disorder, conduct disorder, substance abuse, phobias, anxiety disorders, stress disorders, eating disorders, mood disorders, elimination disorders, and schizophrenia.

Format: Examiner required; individual administration; untimed: varies

Scoring: Examiner evaluated

Cost: Guide $59.00; 20 Report Forms for Child and Parent $28.50 each; 20 Scoring Forms for Child and Parent $33.95 each; Administration Manual $34.95

Classification of Violence Risk™ (COVR)

2005   Psychological Assessment Resources, Inc.

John Monahan, Henry J. Steadman, Paul S. Applebaum, Thomas Grisso, Edward P. Mulvey, Loren H. Roth, Pamela Clark Robbins, Steven Banks, Eric Silver

Population: Inpatients ages 18 to 60 years

Purpose: Estimates violence risk after discharge

Description: The COVR is an interactive software program designed to estimate the risk of an acute civil psychiatric patient becoming violent to others over the next several months after discharge into the community. The program guides the evaluator through a brief chart review and a 10-minute interview with the patient. The COVR then generates a report that contains a statistically valid estimate of the patient's violence risk. The instrument is based on a "classification tree" method.

Format: Computer administered; examiner required; untimed: 10 minutes

Scoring: Computer scored

Cost: Introductory Kit (CD, manual, 10 uses) $299.00

Clinical Analysis Questionnaire (CAQ)

1978   Institute for Personality and Ability Testing, Inc.

Raymond B. Cattell, Samuel Krug

Population: Ages 16 years and older

Purpose: Evaluates personality and psychiatric/psychological difficulties; used as a measure of primary behavioral dimensions; used for clinical diagnosis, evaluation of therapeutic progress, and vocational and rehabilitation guidance

Description: Multiple-choice test with 331 items measuring 16 personality factors (the 16PF factors), as well as hypochondriasis, agitation, suicidal depression, anxious depression, guilt and resentment, low energy depression, boredom, paranoia, psychopathic deviation, schizophrenia, psychasthenia, and psychological inadequacy. General population adult norms are provided. A seventh-grade reading level is required. Completed using computer or paper–pencil format. Also available as a short form with 272 items. The scoring report contains narrative concerning the clinical scales and specific intervention suggestions, normal personality vocational observations and occupational comparisons, and item responses.

Format: Self-administered; untimed: 2 hours

Scoring: Hand key; scoring service available from publisher

Cost: 25 Answer Sheets $18.00; Manual $30.00; 25 Reusable Test Booklets $40.00

Clinical Assessment of Behavior™ (CAB)

2004   Psychological Assessment Resources, Inc.

Bruce A. Bracken, Lori K. Keith

Population: Ages 2 to 18 years (parent rating); Ages 5 to 18 years (teacher rating)

Purpose: Assesses adjustment, psychosocial strengths and weaknesses, and problem behaviors

Description: Three rating forms are provided: Parent Extended Rating Form (170 items), Parent Rating Form (70 items), and Teacher Rating Form (70 items). The parent and teacher forms have corresponding items. Requires an eighth-grade reading level.

Format: Rating scale; untimed: 15 to 20 minutes, extended 30 minutes

Scoring: Examiner evaluated; computer scoring included

Cost: Introductory Kit (manual, CD, 25 of each form) $235.00

Coddington Life Events Scales (CLES)

1999	Multi-Health Systems, Inc.

R. Dean Coddington

Population: Ages 5 to 19 years

Purpose: Measures the impact of life events and change in development

Description: The three scales (primary, child, adolescent) measure significant events in terms of Life Change Units. The scale can be easily completed in the waiting room prior to client consultation and then quickly scored. The scales are written at a fourth-grade reading level. The importance of evaluating life change is demonstrated by a large body of research indicating that a high degree of change is associated with increased susceptibility to medical and emotional problems.

Format: Self-administered; untimed: 10 to 15 minutes

Scoring: QuikScore™ forms

Cost: Complete Kit (manual, 25 of each form) $157.00

Cognitive Distortion Scales (CDS)

2000	Psychological Assessment Resources, Inc.

John Briere

Population: Ages 18 years and older

Purpose: Assesses negative thinking patterns that interfere with optimal functioning

Description: The CDS scales reflect five types of cognitive distortion: Self-Criticism, Self-Blame, Helplessness, Hopelessness, and Preoccupation with Danger. Requires a fifth-grade reading level.

Format: Self-administered; untimed: 10 to 15 minutes

Scoring: Hand key

Cost: Introductory Kit (manual, 25 test booklets, 25 profile forms) $70.00

Comprehensive Addictions and Psychological Evaluation (CAAPE™)

2000	Change Companies

Norman G. Hoffman

Population: Adults

Purpose: Identifies co-occurring conditions

Description: The instrument covers seven Axis I conditions and six Axis II conditions, in addition to detailed documentation of substance dependence and abuse for each substance category of the DSM-IV-TR. The pragmatic clinical approach of the CAAPE focuses on the most common conditions and those likely to complicate recovery from additions. The interview provides key information compatible with the ASAM PPC-2R for treatment planning and placement.

Format: Examiner required; individual administration; untimed. 10 minutes

Scoring: Examiner evaluated

Cost: Manual $20.00; 25 Forms $67.50

Computer-Assisted SCID– Clinician Version (CAS-CV)

1998	Multi-Health Systems, Inc.

Michael B. First, Robert L. Spitzer, Miriam Gibbon, Janet B. W. Williams

Population: Ages 18 years and older

Purpose: A computer-assisted version of the SCID-CV for Axis I disorders

Description: Thirty-seven DSM-IV Axis I diagnoses are included. Key areas measured are Mood Disorders, Substance Use Disorders, Anxiety Disorders, Somatoform Disorders, Eating Disorders, Adjustment Disorders, Schizophrenic and Other Psychotic Disorders. Yields Diagnostic Summary Report, Detailed Diagnostic Report, Unknown Items Report, and Overview Report.

Format: Examiner required; individually administered; untimed

Scoring: Computer scored

Cost: $3.50 per administration

Computer-Assisted SCID II Expert System (CAS II ES)

1997   Multi-Health Systems, Inc.

Michael B. First, Miriam Gibbon, Janet B. W. Williams, Robert L. Spitzer, Lorna Smith Benjamin

Population: Ages 18 years and older

Purpose: Guides the clinician through the AXIS II personality disorders

Description: Depends on branching mechanism DSM-IV AXIS II disorders. Yields Categorical Summary Report, Dimensional Score Report, Overview Questions Report, and Unknown/Missing Items Report.

Format: Examiner required; individually administered; untimed: 30 to 45 minutes

Scoring: Computer scored

Cost: $216.00 (unlimited use)

Conners' Global Index

1997   Multi-Health Systems, Inc.

C. Keith Conners

Population: Ages 3 to 17 years

Purpose: Screens for general psychopathology and monitors treatment effectiveness and change

Description: Ten items per form (parent and teacher) measure two empirically derived factors: Restless–Impulsive and Emotional Lability. Available in paper–pencil, computer-administered, and online format. Available in multiple formats. Requires a 9th- to 10th-grade reading level.

Format: Self-administered; untimed: 5 minutes

Scoring: QuikScore™; computer scored; online scoring

Cost: Hand-Scored Complete Kit (manual, 25 of each form, 15 treatment progress forms) $100.00

Davidson Trauma Scale (DTS)

1996   Multi-Health Systems, Inc.

Jonathan Davidson

Population: Ages 18 years and older

Purpose: Measures post traumatic stress disorder (PTSD) symptoms that correspond to the DSM-IV

Description: A total of 17 items are rated in terms of both frequency and severity in the areas of Intrusion, Avoidance/Numbing, and Hyper-

arousal. Yields *t*-scores and percentage of PTSD and non-PTSD individuals that obtain each DTS score. Available in French and Spanish.

Format: Self-administered; untimed: 10 minutes

Scoring: QuikScore™

Cost: Kit (test manual, 25 QuikScore™ forms) $76.00

Depression and Anxiety in Youth Scale (DAYS)

1994   PRO-ED, Inc.

Phyllis L. Newcomer, Edna M. Barenbaum, Brian R. Bryant

Population: Ages 6 to 18 years

Purpose: Useful in identifying major depressive and overanxious disorders

Description: A battery of three norm-referenced scales: Student Rating Scale, Teacher Rating Scale, and Parent Rating Scale. The primary theoretical frame of reference for the scales is the DSM-III-R. The norming sample included 5,000 typical learners living in 25 states. Norms are available for identified populations.

Format: Rating scales completed by student, teacher, or parent; untimed: 10 minutes

Scoring: Examiner evaluated

Cost: Complete Kit (manual, 50 each of student, teacher, parent scales, 50 profile/record forms, scoring keys, storage box) $150.00

Detailed Assessment of Posttraumatic Stress

2001   Psychological Assessment Resources, Inc.

John Briere

Population: Ages 18 years and older

Purpose: Assesses trauma exposure and symptoms of post traumatic stress

Description: The DAPS is a 104-item, detailed, and comprehensive clinical measure. The instrument assesses peri- and posttraumatic symptoms (e.g., intrusion, avoidance, hyperarousal) and associated features related to a specific traumatic event and generates a tentative diagnosis of Posttraumatic Stress Disorder or Acute Stress Disorder. The diagnosis can then be confirmed by a clinical interview.

Format: Self-administered; untimed: 20 to 30 minutes

Scoring: Examiner evaluated; computer scoring available

Cost: Introductory Kit (manual, 10 reusable booklets, 50 answer sheets, 50 profile forms) $196.00

Devereux Scales of Mental Disorders (DSMD™)

1994	Harcourt Assessment, Inc.

Jack A. Naglieri, Paul A. LeBuffe, Steven I. Pfeiffer

Population: Ages 5 to 18 years

Purpose: Identifies behavioral or emotional problems

Description: Indicates whether an individual is experiencing or is at risk for an emotional or behavioral disorder. The instrument is designed for treatment planning and outcome evaluation. The 111-item child form and the 110-item adolescent form cover a full range of psychopathology and are based on DSM-IV categories. Behavior is evaluated in a variety of settings. Any adult who has known the child for 4 weeks may serve as a rater. The same form is used for parent and teacher raters, with separate norms provided for each.

Format: Rating scale; untimed: 15 minutes

Scoring: Examiner evaluated; computer scoring available

Cost: Complete Kit (manual, 25 of each child and adolescent answer documents) $245.00

Diagnostic Interview for Children and Adolescents IV (DICA IV™)

1997	Multi-Health Systems, Inc.

Zila Welner, Wendy Reich, Barbara Herjanic

Population: Ages 6 to 17 years

Purpose: Identifies a broad range of behavioral problems

Description: Covers 28 categories, each of which can take about 5 to 20 minutes to complete due to automatic branching of questions. Both the Child/Adolescent and Parent versions yield three reports: Concise Report of Possible Diagnoses, Summary of Responses Report, and the Possible Diagnoses and Criteria Report.

Format: Examiner required; individual administration; untimed

Scoring: Computer scored

Cost: $535.00 each for either Child/Adolescent or Parent Version; $859.00 for both (unlimited use)

Dimensional Assessment for Patient Placement Engagement & Recovery (DAPPER™)

2004	Change Companies

Norman G. Hoffman, David Mee-Lee, Gerald D. Shulman

Population: Adolescents, adults

Purpose: Provides quantifiable measures of current status

Description: Consists of ratings covering the content of the ASAM PPC-2R. Up to six ratings can also document progress or changes over time. The ratings form subscales to pinpoint problems and strengths. Flowcharts provide assistance in determining the appropriate level of care. This instrument can be used as a semistructured interview for routine clinical work or staff training.

Format: Examiner evaluated; individual administration; untimed

Scoring: Examiner evaluated

Cost: Manual $25.00; 25 Forms $78.75

Domestic Violence Inventory (DVI)

1991	Behavior Data Systems, Ltd.

Herman H. Linderman

Population: Adult domestic violence offenders

Purpose: Evaluates domestic violence offenders

Description: Designed for domestic violence risk and needs assessment, the test contains six scales: Truthfulness, Violence, Alcohol, Drugs, Aggressivity, and Stress Coping Ability. Each scale provides specific recommendations for intervention, supervision, and treatment. There are 157 multiple-choice and true–false items. Truth-corrected scores are yielded. A computer-generated report summarizes risk range and recommendations; on-site reports within 4 minutes of test completion. Designed specifically for assessing domestic violence. Also available in Spanish. Online administration is available at www.online-testing.com. A short form is also available with 76 items.

Format: Self-administered; untimed: 30 minutes

Scoring: Computer scored; online

Cost: $8.00 each administration; $9.95 each online

Domestic Violence Inventory–Juvenile (DVI-Juvenile)

Date not provided   Behavior Data Systems, Ltd.

Herman H. Linderman

Population: Ages 12 to 18 years

Purpose: Evaluates juveniles accused or convicted of domestic violence

Description: The inventory has 156 items with six scales: Truthfulness, Violence, Control, Alcohol, Drugs, and Stress Coping Abilities. Online administration is available at www.online-testing.com.

Format: Self-administered; untimed: 30 minutes

Scoring: Computer scored; online

Cost: $8.00 each administration; $9.95 each online

DTREE: The DSM-IV Expert for Windows

1997   Multi-Health Systems, Inc.

Michael B. First, Janet B. W. Williams, Robert L. Spitzer

Population: Ages 18 years and older

Purpose: Assists in diagnosing DSM-IV adult Axis I disorders

Description: Uses SCID Screen Patient Questionnaire or Screen PQ Extended results, or the DTREE Screener can be used to identify decision trees to explore. It rules out diagnoses to produce a differential diagnosis. Provides Case Summary Report and Positive Diagnosis Report.

Format: Clinician completed; untimed

Scoring: Computer scored

Cost: $319.00 (unlimited use)

DVI Pre-Post

Date not provided   Behavior Data Systems, Ltd.

Herman H. Linderman

Population: Adults

Purpose: Measures domestic violence treatment outcome

Description: The same test is given before and after treatment and upon posttest, results are compared. There are 147 items with six scales: Truthfulness, Violence, Control, Alcohol, Drugs, and Stress Coping Abilities. Although this test evolved from the DVI, it objectively compares pretest and posttest scores.

Format: Self-administered; untimed: 30 minutes

Scoring: Computer scored

Cost: $8.00 each administration

Early Childhood Inventory–4 (ECI-4)

1996   Checkmate Plus, Ltd.

Kenneth D. Gadow, Joyce Sprafkin

Population: Ages 3 to 5 years

Purpose: Screens for DSM-IV emotional and behavioral disorders; provides behavioral ratings of child psychopathology

Description: The Parent checklist contains 108 items that screen for emotional and behavioral disorders, including attention-deficit/hyperactivity disorder, oppositional-defiant disorder, conduct disorder, depressive disorders, anxiety disorders, and pervasive developmental disorders. The Teacher checklist contains 87 items that screen for 13 disorders. Scores yield Symptom Count scores (DSM-IV criteria) and Symptom Severity Profiles (norms-based). Also available in Spanish.

Format: Rating scale; can be computer administered; untimed: 10 to 15 minutes

Scoring: Examiner evaluated; computer scored

Cost: Deluxe Kit (manual, 25 parent checklists, 25 teacher checklists, 50 symptom count score sheets, 50 symptom severity profiles) $102.00

Evaluation of Competency to Stand Trial™–Revised (ECST-R)

2004   Psychological Assessment Resources, Inc.

Richard Rogers, Chad E. Tillbrook, Kenneth W. Sewell

Population: Ages 18 years and older

Purpose: Evaluates an individual's competency to stand trial

Description: The ECST-R is designed for specialized forensic evaluations related to competency to stand trial. It also can be used to evaluate important elements of competency to plead and competency for pro se. The instrument is a semi-structured interview.

Format: Examiner required; individual administration; untimed

Scoring: Examiner evaluated

Cost: Introductory Kit (manual, binder with interview booklet, 25 record forms, 25 summary forms, carrying case) $228.00

Feelings, Attitudes, and Behaviors Scale for Children (FAB-C™)

1996	Multi-Health Systems, Inc.

Joseph H. Beitchman

Population: Ages 6 to 13 years

Purpose: Assesses emotional and behavior problems

Description: Self-report scale consisting of 48 yes–no items that produces five factors that assess the following areas: Self-Image, Negative Peer Relations, Conduct Problems, Antisocial Behavior, and Worry. Also includes a Problem Index and a Lie Scale.

Format: Examiner required; individual or group administration; untimed: 10 minutes

Scoring: QuikScore™ forms

Cost: Complete Kit (manual, 25 forms) $85.00

Gambler Addiction Index (GAI)

Date not provided	Behavior Data Systems, Ltd.

Herman H. Linderman

Population: Adults

Purpose: Designed for gambler assessment

Description: The instrument has 166 items with seven scales: Truthfulness, Gambling, Suicide, Attitude, Alcohol, Drugs, and Stress Coping Abilities. The GAI assesses important gambler attitudes and behaviors. Online administration is available at www.online-testing.com.

Format: Self administered; untimed: 35 minutes

Scoring: Computer scored; online

Cost: $8.00 each administration; $9.95 each online

G-MAP: The Maroondah Assessment Profile for Problem Gambling

1998	Australian Council for Educational Research Limited

Tim Loughnan, Mark Pierce, Anastasia Sagris-Desmond

Population: Adults

Purpose: Provides an individualized profiling of problem gamblers

Description: This 85-item questionnaire gathers information on 17 factors associated with problem gambling. The manual contains analysis and interpretation information and individual Action Sheets for clients, with information about each of the 17 factors. A reproducible Response Report is provided showing the 17 factors divided into five broad groups. This grouping allows the counselor to pinpoint more accurately why someone gambles and can assist with finding the best way to work toward resolving problems. A computer-administered format is available.

Format: Examiner required; individual administration; untimed: 25 minutes

Scoring: Examiner evaluated; computer scoring available

Cost: Contact publisher

Hare Psychopathy Checklist–Revised (PCL-R™) 2nd Edition

1991	Multi-Health Systems, Inc.

Robert D. Hare

Population: Ages 18 years and older

Purpose: Assesses psychopathic (antisocial) personality disorders

Description: Used in forensic assessment with a total of 20 items. Two major facets of psychopathy: callous, selfish, remorseless use of others (Factor 1) and a chronically unstable and antisocial lifestyle (Factor 2). Yields a total score indicating the degree to which the individual matches a prototypical individual with psychopathic personality disorder.

Format: Examiner required; structured interview and expert rating; untimed: 90 to 120 minutes, 60 minutes for collateral review

Scoring: QuikScore™ forms

Cost: Complete Kit (manual, 25 forms, 25 interview guides) $295.00

Hare Psychopathy Checklist: Screening Version (PCL:SV™)

1995	Multi-Health Systems, Inc.

Stephen Hart, David N. Cox, Robert D. Hare

Population: Ages 18 years and older

Purpose: Screens for psychopathic (antisocial) personality disorders

Description: Consists of 12 items yielding a total score and two factor scores. These factor scores are analogous to the two factors of the *Hare Psychopathy Checklist–Revised.*

Format: Examiner required; structured interview and expert rating; untimed: 45 minutes, 30 minutes for collateral review

Scoring: QuikScore™ forms

Cost: Kit (manual, 25 each Interview guide and forms) $153.00

Hare Psychopathy–Scan Research Version (P-Scan™ RV)

| 1998 | Multi-Health Systems, Inc. |

Robert D. Hare, Hugues F. Hervé

Population: Ages 13 years and older

Purpose: Assesses risk for antisocial, criminal, and violent behavior

Description: Has forensic applications with a total of 90 items: Lifestyle (30 items), Affective (30 items), and Interpersonal (30 items).

Format: Evaluator rated; untimed: 10 to 15 minutes

Scoring: QuikScore™ forms

Cost: Kit (manual, 25 forms) $65.00

Hilson Career Satisfaction Index (HCSI)

| 1988 | Institute for Personality and Ability Testing, Inc. |

Robin E. Inwald

Population: Adults

Purpose: Identifies and predicts stress-related behavior patterns and career satisfaction

Description: Paper–pencil 161-item true–false instrument consisting of four scales: Stress Patterns, Anger/Hostility, Dissatisfaction with Career, and Defensiveness. Designed for individuals on the job who have been referred for evaluation. Total score measures overall level of stress and dissatisfaction related to current work-oriented activities. This score should be used only as a general indicator, and individual scale elevations should be reviewed whenever conclusions are drawn about test results. The teleprocessing software allows input of test responses. Also available in Spanish.

Format: Self-administered; untimed: 25 to 35 minutes

Scoring: Computer scored

Cost: $16.00 to $20.00 depending on scoring method

Hilson Trauma Recovery Inventory (HTRI)

| 2001 | Institute for Personality and Ability Testing, Inc. |

Robin E. Inwald

Population: Children through adults

Purpose: Assesses symptoms and level of trauma

Description: The HTRI includes 111 true–false questions from which both raw scores and *t*-scores are derived. A fifth-grade reading level is required. Online administration is available. Also available in Spanish.

Format: Self-administered; untimed: 20 minutes

Scoring: Examiner evaluated; computer scoring available

Cost: $16.00 to $20.00 depending on scoring method

Holden Psychological Screening Inventory (HPSI™)

| 1996 | Multi-Health Systems, Inc. |

Ronald R. Holden

Population: Ages 14 years and older

Purpose: Assesses psychiatric and social symptomatology and depression

Description: Provides an efficient, concise, and practical method of exploring psychopathology and is a valuable screening tool for assessing the need for lengthier clinical measures. Comprises 36 items, each of which is rated on a 5-point Likert scale. The HPSI is designed to be a component of a comprehensive psychological assessment procedure to be used with nonclinical, psychiatric, and forensic populations. Online administration is available.

Format: Self-administered; untimed: 5 to 7 minutes

Scoring: QuikScore™ forms, online scoring, computer scored

Cost: Hand-Scored Complete Kit (manual, 25 forms) $75.00

House Tree Person and Draw a Person (HTP/DAP)

| 1994 | Psychological Assessment Resources, Inc. |

Valerie Van Hutton

Population: Ages 7 to 11 years

Purpose: Used in outpatient counseling and school psychology to screen for sexual abuse

Description: Paper–pencil projective four-drawing test with the following categories: Preoccupation with Sexually Relevant Concepts; Aggression and Hostility; Withdrawal and Guarded Accessibility; and Alertness for Danger, Suspiciousness, and Lack of Trust.

Format: Examiner required; individual administration; untimed

Scoring: Examiner evaluated

Cost: Introductory Kit (book, 25 scoring booklets) $108.00

Internalized Shame Scale (ISS™)

2001	Multi-Health Systems, Inc.

David R. Cook

Population: Ages 13 years and older

Purpose: Measures an individual's feeling of shame

Description: Focuses on evaluating the extent to which the negative affect of shame becomes magnified and internalized. The ISS items reflect feelings of inferiority, worthlessness, inadequacy, and alienation and help the practitioner to isolate a client's specific feelings of shame that are involved in the presenting problem. Lends itself to repeated administration, which can be helpful in monitoring treatment progress.

Format: Self-administered; untimed: 15 minutes

Scoring: QuikScore™ forms, computer scored

Cost: Kit (manual, 25 forms, 25 handouts) $92.00

Interpersonal Behavior Survey (IBS)

1980	Western Psychological Services

Paul A. Mauger, David R. Adkinson, Suzanne K. Zoss, Gregory Firestone, J. David Hook

Population: Grades 9 and above

Purpose: Measures and distinguishes assertive and aggressive behaviors among adolescents and adults; used for assertiveness training, marriage counseling, and in a variety of clinical settings

Description: Paper–pencil test in which the subject responds to 272 statements written in the present tense to provide sensitivity to ongoing changes. The test yields eight aggressiveness scales (including one that measures general aggressiveness over a broad range of item content, including aggressive behaviors, feelings, and attitudes), nine assertiveness scales (including one that measures general assertiveness over a broad range of behaviors), three validity scales, and three relationship scales (Conflict Avoidance, Dependency, and Shyness). Two shorter forms are available: a 38-item form providing a general

sampling of behaviors and a 133-item form providing information on all scales. The Profile Form provides a display of raw scores, t-scores, and percentiles. Norms are provided for adult males, adult females, high school students, college students, and African Americans. The manual presents validity and reliability data, interpretive guidelines, and a number of illustrated cases.

Format: Self-administered; untimed: 10 to 45 minutes depending on form

Scoring: Examiner evaluated

Cost: Kit (5 booklets, 50 profile forms, 50 answer sheets, key, 25 short forms, manual) $143.00

Interview for the Retrospective Assessment of the Onset and Course of Schizophrenia and Other Psychoses (IRAOS)

2003	Hogrefe & Huber Publishers

H. Hafner, W. Loffler, A. Riecher-Rossler, A. Stein

Population: All ages

Purpose: Allows systematic research on the onset of schizophrenia

Description: The social course, symptoms, disability, and treatment from the first sign or indicators of illness until the time of interview are assessed. In addition to studying the onset and early course of schizophrenia and other nonorganic psychotic disorders, the present revised version of the IRAOS can be used in research on affective psychoses. In the socio-demographic part of the instrument, the entire life of the patient is thoroughly recorded with the help of the so-called continuity items. With these items, based on six key social roles, breaks in social development and their causes can be assessed. The episodes part provides information on the current, as well as earlier, episodes of illness and the relevant treatments. The part on indicators deals with a retrospective recording of symptoms that might be indicators of a beginning psychiatric illness or are relevant to diagnosing the disorder in question. The aim is to determine onset, end, and course for each indicator and each illness episode.

Format: Examiner required; individual administration; untimed

Scoring: Examiner evaluated

Cost: Complete Kit (manual, 5 interview booklets, 50 score sheets, 50 IND forms, 50 TREAT forms, 50 EPIS forms, 50 time schedules, 50 calendars of episodes) $238.00

Inventory of Suicide Orientation–30 (ISO-30™)

Date not provided	Pearson Assessments

John D. King, Brian Kowalchuk

Population: Ages 13 to 18 years

Purpose: Provides an overall suicide risk classification based on measurements of both hopelessness and suicide ideation

Description: This is a brief screening tool to help identify adolescents at risk for suicide. It is appropriate for use by psychologists, social workers, and counselors in school settings, juvenile justice evaluations, and inpatient and outpatient mental health facilities. The test's brevity helps minimize test-taking resistance. Results help alert psychologists and counselors to the early signs of an adolescent's suicidal tendencies. Clinical data were collected on 366 adolescents. The test is written at a sixth-grade level.

Format: Self-administered; untimed: 10 minutes

Scoring: Hand key; software scoring available

Cost: Hand Scoring Starter Kit (manual, 3 carbonless answer sheets) $40.00

Inwald Survey 2– Adolescent Version (IS2-A)

1995	Institute for Personality and Ability Testing, Inc.

Robin E. Inwald

Population: Ages 9 to 19 years

Purpose: Measures risk taking, temper control, violence/antisocial behavior patterns

Description: Contains a total of 119 items. Also available in Spanish.

Format: Requires examiner; suitable for group use; untimed: 20 minutes

Scoring: Computer scored; scoring service available

Cost: $16.00 to $20.00 depending on scoring method

Jesness Behavior Checklist (JBC™)

1996	Multi-Health Systems, Inc.

Carl F. Jesness

Population: Ages 13 to 20 years

Purpose: Measures risk for antisocial behavior

Description: An 80-item scale measuring 14

bipolar behavioral tendencies and consisting of two parallel forms: an Observer Form and a Self-Appraisal Form. The scales measured are Unobtrusiveness, Friendliness, Responsibility, Consideration, Independence, Rapport, Enthusiasm, Sociability, Conformity, Calmness, Communication, Insight, Social Control, and Anger Control.

Format: Self-administered; untimed: 20 minutes

Scoring: QuikScore™; computer scored

Cost: Complete Kit (manual, 10 each observer and self booklets, 25 each observer and self forms) $156.00

Jesness Inventory–Revised (JI-R™)

1996	Multi-Health Systems, Inc.

Carl F. Jesness

Population: Ages 8 years to adult

Purpose: Provides a personality classification system for youths who are delinquent and who have conduct disorders

Description: A restandardized version. The JI-R provides a subtype evaluation using nine distinct subtype areas. This helps with understanding and leads to specific suggestions about treatment and risk. The revision introduces scales that relate directly to the relevant DSM-IV diagnostic categories. May be administered online. Requires a fourth-grade reading level.

Format: Self-administered; untimed: 20 to 30 minutes

Scoring: QuikScore™ forms; computer scored; online scoring

Cost: Kit (manual, 10 item booklets, 25 forms, scoring template) $182.00

Juvenile Presentence Evaluation (JPE)

2006	Behavior Data Systems, Ltd.

Herman H. Linderman

Population: Ages 13 to 17 years

Purpose: Measures behaviors to help determine appropriate sentencing

Description: The JPE has 159 items with nine scales: Truthfulness, Suicide, Resistance, Self-Esteem, Violence (Lethality), Alcohol, Drugs, Distress, and Stress Coping Abilities. This type of information helps in deciding on probation, alternatives to incarceration, and treatment. Requires a high fifth-grade reading level. Also available in Spanish.

Format: Self-administered; untimed: 35 minutes

Scoring: Computer scored

Cost: $8.00 per administration

Juvenile Pretrial Test (JPT)

2006   Behavior Data Systems, Ltd.

Herman H. Linderman

Population: Ages 13 to 17 years

Purpose: Establishes juvenile risk and needs at the pretrial stage of the juvenile justice system

Description: The JPT identifies criminogenic needs, authenticates their severity, and recommends graduated sanctions according to problem severity. The instrument has 140 items with seven scales: Truthfulness, Alcohol, Drugs, Violence (Lethality), Distress, Adjustment, and Stress Quotient. Information acquired includes attitudes, substance abuse involvement, acting out propensity, perceived distress, and coping behaviors. Requires a high fifth-grade reading level. Also available in Spanish.

Format: Self-administered; untimed: 35 minutes

Scoring: Computer scored

Cost: $8.00 per administration

Juvenile Treatment Outcomes (JTO)

2006   Behavior Data Systems, Ltd.

Herman H. Linderman

Population: Ages 13 to 17 years

Purpose: Evaluates attitudes and behaviors important to counseling and treatment outcomes

Description: The JTO has 163 items with 12 scales: Truthfulness, Self-Esteem, Outlook, Adjustment, Depression, Anxiety, Suicide, Control, Violence, Alcohol, Drugs, and Stress Coping Abilities. Pretest and posttest comparison report automatically scored. Requires a high fifth-grade reading level. Also available in Spanish.

Format: Self-administered; untimed: 35 minutes

Scoring: Computer scored

Cost: $8.00 per administration

Level of Care Index–2R (LOCI-2R™)

2001   Change Companies

Norman G. Hoffman, David Mee-Lee, Gerald D. Shulman

Population: Adolescents, adults

Purpose: Decision support instrument for treatment planning and placement

Description: This comprehensive tool based on the ASAM DDC-2R is designed for use at admis-

sion, subsequent continued service reassessment, and at transfer or discharge. It provides documentation for up to six assessments per case to record treatment progress. Offers adolescent and adult versions.

Format: Examiner completed

Scoring: Examiner evaluated

Cost: Package of 25 Forms (specify adolescent or adult) $78.75

Level of Service Inventory–Revised (LSI-R™)

1995   Multi-Health Systems, Inc.

Don A. Andrews, James L. Bonta

Population: Ages 16 years and older

Purpose: Assesses risk and needs in criminal offenders; used for criminal corrections and probation decisions

Description: Test with 54 items in these categories: Criminal History (10 items), Education/Employment (12 items), Family/Marital (4 items), Accumulation (3 items), Leisure/Recreation (2 items), Companions (5 items), Alcohol/Drug Problem (9 items), Emotional/Personal (5 items), Attitudes/Orientation (4 items). The total score indicates the level of risk/needs. Also available in Spanish.

Format: Examiner required; individual administration; untimed: 30 to 45 minutes

Scoring: QuikScore™; computer scored

Cost: Kit (manual, 25 each of interview guides, forms, profiles) $182.00

MacArthur Competence Assessment Tool–Criminal Adjudication (MacCAT-CA)

1999   Psychological Assessment Resources, Inc.

Steven K. Hoge, Richard J. Bonnie, Norman G. Poythress, John Monahan

Population: Ages 18 years and older

Purpose: Evaluates adult's capacity to proceed to adjudication

Description: Structured interview with 22 items measures three competence-related abilities: Understanding (8 items), Reasoning (8 items), and Appreciation (6 items).

Format: Examiner required; individual administration; untimed: 25 to 55 minutes

Scoring: Hand key; examiner evaluated

Cost: Introductory Kit (manual, 20 interview booklets) $170.00

Miller Forensic Assessment of Symptoms Test (M-FAST)

| 2001 | Psychological Assessment Resources, Inc. |

Holly A. Miller

Population: Ages 18 to 80 years

Purpose: Provides a screening assessment of malingered psychiatric illness

Description: Used for inpatient and outpatient, forensic, and correctional evaluations. The M-FAST has 25 items with seven scales that assess response styles and interview strategies useful for differentiating malingers from honest responses.

Format: Examiner required; individual administration; untimed: 5 to 10 minutes

Scoring: Examiner evaluated

Cost: Introductory Kit (manual, 25 interview booklets) $142.00

Millon™ Behavioral Medicine Diagnostic (MBMD™)

| 2001 | Pearson Assessments |

Theodore Millon, Michael Antoni, Carrie Millon, Sarah Meagher, Seth Grossman

Population: Adults

Purpose: Measures psychosocial assets and liabilities that may support or interfere with a patient's course of medical treatment

Description: The test was designed to help increase the probability of positive health-care treatment outcomes that may reduce medical utilization and the overall costs of care. Results of the MBMD can be used in a number of medical settings to help identify patients who may have significant psychiatric problems and recommend specific interventions, pinpoint personal and social assets that may facilitate adjustment to physical limitations or lifestyle changes, identify individuals who may need more communication and support in order to comply with prescribed medical regimens, and structure posttreatment plans and self-care responsibilities in the context of the patient's social network. Written at a sixth-grade reading level. Also available in Spanish.

Format: Examiner required; individual administration; untimed: 20 to 25 minutes

Scoring: Hand key; scoring service available; software available

Cost: Starter Kit (manual, user's guide, 10 test booklets, 50 answer sheets, worksheets, profile forms and keys) $337.00

Millon Clinical Multiaxial Inventory–II (MCMI-II)

| 1987 | Pearson Assessments |

Theodore Millon

Population: Adults

Purpose: Diagnoses adults with personality disorders; used in private or group practice, mental health centers, outpatient clinics, and general and psychiatric hospitals and clinics with individuals in assessment or treatment programs

Description: True–false test evaluating adults with emotional or interpersonal problems. The inventory has 175 items that form scales measuring both the state and the trait features of personality. The Clinical Personality Pattern scales are Schizoid, Avoidant, Dependent, Histrionic, Narcissistic, Antisocial, Aggressive/Sadistic, Compulsive, Passive/Aggressive, and Self-Defeating. There are three Modifier Indices—Disclosure, Desirability, and Debasement—and three Severe Pathology scales—Schizotypal, Borderline, and Paranoid. The Clinical Syndrome scales are Anxiety Disorder, Somatoform Disorder, Hypomanic Disorder, Dysthymic Disorder, Alcohol Dependence, and Drug Dependence. There are three Severe Syndrome Scales: Thought Disorder, Major Depression, and Delusional Disorder. A validity index is included also. The MCM-II is intended to reflect DSM-III-R diagnoses.

Format: Self-administered; untimed: 20 to 30 minutes

Scoring: Computer scored

Cost: Starter Kit (manual, hand-scoring user's guide, 10 test booklets, 50 answer sheets, 50 worksheets, 50 profile forms and answer keys) $335.00

Multiphasic Sex Inventory I (MSI I)

| 1984 | Nichols and Molinder Assessments |

H. R. Nichols, Ilene Molinder

Population: Adolescent and adult male sex offenders

Purpose: Measures the sexual characteristics of adolescent and adult sexual offenders; used to evaluate sexual deviance and assess progress in the treatment of sexual deviance

Description: Paper-pencil 300-item true-false test of psychosexual characteristics from which 20 scales and a 50-item sexual history are derived. Six of the 20 scales are validity scales. The inventory also contains a Treatment Attitudes Scale. The sex deviance scales include the Child Molest Scale, Rape Scale, and Exhibitionism Scale. There are five atypical sexual outlet scales: Fetish, Voyeurism, Obscene Call, Bondage and Discipline, and Sado-Masochism. The four sexual dysfunction scales include Sexual Inadequacy, Premature Ejaculation, Impotence, and Physical Disabilities. There is also a Sexual Knowledge and Beliefs Scale. The 50-item Sexual History includes a sex deviance development section, marriage development section, gender identity section, gender orientation development section, and a sexual assault behavior section. Scores are yielded for all 20 scales and are recorded on the profile form.

Format: Self-administered; untimed: 45 minutes

Scoring: Hand key

Cost: Kit (all forms, manual) $450.00

Multiphasic Sex Inventory II (MSI II)

2000	Nichols and Molinder Assessments

H. R. Nichols, Ilene Molinder

Population: Adult and adolescent sex offenders

Purpose: Evaluates clients who have been alleged to have engaged in sexual misconduct but who deny any such behavior

Description: The MSI II is an expanded version of the MSI I. The core scales remain basically intact, but some of the wording of the questions has been revised for the sake of clarity. This is a paper-pencil test with true-false questions. It requires approximately a seventh-grade reading level; however, cassette tapes of the questions are available. The scoring information is placed on a profile form designed for ease in interpretation.

Format: Self-administered; untimed: 90 minutes

Scoring: Examiner evaluated; scoring service available

Cost: Kit (5 interpretive reports, 1 test booklet) $165.00

Outcome Assessment and Reporting System (OAARS™)

2005	Change Companies

Norman G. Hoffmann, Gerald D. Shulman, David Mee-Lee

Population: Adults

Purpose: Documents the effectiveness of treatment programs

Description: Compatible with the DSM-IV-TR and the ASAM PPC-2, OAARS is a brief, practical outcome assessment tool. It provides relevant longitudinal data that documents improvements or progress throughout the treatment episode. Key measures of initial outcomes, including completion status for the initial phase of the program and engagement and recovery status during three and six months of aftercare or maintenance services, are documented.

Format: Examiner completed

Scoring: Examiner evaluated

Cost: Kit (manual, 50 tools, reporting tables, tabulation sheets, electronic version of tables and sheets) $99.00

Panic and Somatization Scales

1994	Albert Mehrabian, PhD

Albert Mehrabian

Population: Ages 14 years and older

Purpose: Assesses panic disorder and somatization or hypochondria. Used for research and counseling

Description: Paper-pencil test with 18 items on two subtests: Panic and Somatization. A 10th-grade reading level is required.

Format: Self-administered; untimed: 10 minutes

Scoring: Hand key, test scoring service available

Cost: Test Kit $33.00

Parolee Inventory (PI)

1997	Behavior Data Systems, Ltd.

Herman H. Linderman

Population: Adults

Purpose: Designed specifically for parole department use

Description: The PI has 155 items and seven scales: Truthfulness, Violence, Antisocial, Resistance, Alcohol, Drugs, and Stress Coping Abilities. The PI is an objective, comprehensive, and standardized screening instrument that examines important attitudes and behaviors. The PI provides an on-site, objective second opinion, in a timely manner.

Format: Self-administered; untimed: 30 to 35 minutes

Scoring: Computer scored

Cost: $8.00 per administration

Paulhus Deception Scales (PDS™)

| 1998 | Multi-Health Systems, Inc. |

Delroy L. Paulhus

Population: Ages 16 years and older

Purpose: Measures one's tendency to give socially desirable responses

Description: Total of 40 items with two subscales: Self Deceptive Enhancement and Impression Management.

Format: Self-administered; untimed: 5 to 7 minutes

Scoring: QuikScore™, computer scored

Cost: Kit (manual, 25 forms) $67.00

Personal Problems Checklist–Adolescent

| 1985 | Psychological Assessment Resources, Inc. |

John A. Schinka

Population: Ages 13 to 17 years

Purpose: Assesses personal problems of adolescents; used as a survey instrument in clinical and counseling settings to initiate the consultation process and to introduce the client to formal diagnostic testing

Description: Paper–pencil or computer-administered 240-item test identifying common problems cited by adolescents in 13 areas: Social, Appearance, Job, Family, Home, School, Money, Religion, Emotions, Dating, Health, Attitude, and Crises.

Format: Self-administered; untimed: 10 to 20 minutes

Scoring: Examiner evaluated

Cost: 50 Checklists $52.00

Personal Problems Checklist–Adult

| 1985 | Psychological Assessment Resources, Inc. |

John A. Schinka

Population: Adults

Purpose: Assesses the personal problems of adults; used as a survey instrument in clinical

and counseling settings to initiate the consultation process and to introduce the client to formal diagnostic testing

Description: Paper–pencil 211-item test identifying problems in 13 areas: Social, Appearance, Vocational, Family and Home, School, Finances, Religion, Emotions, Sex, Legal, Health and Habits, Attitude, and Crises.

Format: Self-administered; untimed: 10 to 20 minutes

Scoring: Examiner evaluated

Cost: 50 Checklists $52.00

Personality Assessment Screener (PAS)

| 1997 | Psychological Assessment Resources, Inc. |

Leslie C. Morey

Population: Ages 18 years and older

Purpose: Screens for a broad range of emotional and behavioral problems

Description: The PAS is a 22-item screener, in which 10 distinct clinical problem domains are represented: Negative Affect, Hostile Control, Acting Out, Suicidal Thinking, Health Problems, Alienation, Psychotic Features, Alcohol Problems, Social Withdrawal, and Anger Control.

Format: Self-administered; untimed: 5 minutes

Scoring: Examiner evaluated

Cost: Introductory Kit (manual, 25 response forms) $85.00

Personality Disorder Interview–IV (PDI-IV)

| 1994 | Psychological Assessment Resources, Inc. |

Thomas A. Widiger, Steve Mangine, Elizabeth M. Corbitt, Cynthia G. Ellis, Glenn V. Thomas

Population: Ages 18 years and older

Purpose: Assists in the diagnosis of DSM-IV personality disorders

Description: Oral response semistructured interview with the following booklets: Thematic Content Areas Interview Booklet (attitudes toward self, attitudes toward others, security of comfort of others, friendships and relationships, conflicts and disagreements, work and leisure, social norms, mood, and appearance and perception) and Personality Disorders Interview Booklet (antisocial personality disorder, avoidant personality disorder, borderline personality disorder, dependent personality disorder, histrionic personality disorder, narcissistic personality disorder, obsessive-compulsive personality disorder, paranoid personality disorder, schizoid personality disorder, schizotypal personality disorder, depressive personality disorder, and passive-aggressive personality disorder). Materials include PDI-IV book, 2 each of thematic content booklet and personality disorders booklet, 10 each of summary and profile booklets.

Format: Examiner required; individual administration; untimed: 2 hours

Scoring: Examiner evaluated

Cost: Introductory Kit (book, 2 of each interview booklet, 10 summary booklets) $152.00

Positive and Negative Syndrome Scale (PANSS™)

1992	Multi-Health Systems, Inc.

Stanley R. Kay, Lewis A. Opler, Abraham Fiszbein

Population: Ages 18 years and older

Purpose: Assesses positive and negative symptomology in schizophrenics

Description: The 33 item scale is broken up into eight scales and one composite score. The scales are Positive Symptoms, Negative Symptoms, General, Anergia, Thought Disturbance, Activation, Paranoid, and Depression. Scores for all subscales are obtained, plus a composite and General Psychopathology score. A profile form is used to convert raw scores into standard scores. Includes a structured clinical interview and an informant questionnaire. Available in multiple languages.

Format: Examiner required; individually administered; untimed: 30 to 40 minutes

Scoring: QuikScore™

Cost: Kit (manual, 25 forms, 25 interview forms, 25 questionnaire forms) $207.00

Practical Adolescent Dual Diagnostic Interview (PADDI™)

2001	Change Companies

Norman G. Hoffman, Todd W. Estroff

Population: Adolescents

Purpose: Identifies co-occurring mental health and substance use disorders

Description: This interview enables both addiction and mental health professionals to docu-

ment problems within their areas of expertise and make focused referrals for conditions outside their domain of practice. This instrument provides key information compatible with the ASAM PPC-2R for treatment planning and placement. The PADDI covers symptoms of common affective and anxiety disorders including indications of major depression, mania, posttraumatic stress disorder, panic attacks, and phobias. It also explores dangerousness to self or others, including history of suicide attempts/gestures and examines physical, sexual, and emotional victimization.

Format: Examiner required; individual administration; untimed: 20 to 40 minutes

Scoring: Examiner evaluated

Cost: Manual $20.00; 25 Forms $67.50

Pre-Post Inventory

Date not provided	Behavior Data Systems, Ltd.

Herman H. Linderman

Population: Adolescents, adults

Purpose: Designed for objective pretest-posttest outcome comparison

Description: This is a counseling or treatment outcome measure. It has 148 items with seven scales: Truthfulness, Self-Esteem, Resistance, Distress, Alcohol, Drugs, and Stress Coping Abilities. It is suitable for evaluating intervention, counseling, or treatment effectiveness.

Format: Self-administered; untimed: 30 minutes

Scoring: Computer scored

Cost: $8.00 per administration

Prison Inmate Inventory (PII)

2000	Behavior Data Systems, Ltd.

Herman H. Linderman

Population: Adult prison inmates

Purpose: Designed for inmate risk assessment and needs identification; reports help to determine risk and to establish supervision levels and readiness for classification or status changes

Description: Designed for prison inmate risk and needs assessment, the test contains 10 scales: Validity, Violence, Antisocial, Risk, Self-Esteem, Alcohol, Drugs, Judgment, Distress, and Stress Coping Abilities. There are 161 multiple-choice/true-false items. Truth-corrected scores. Computer-generated report summarizes risk range and recommendations for each scale; on-site reports within four minutes of test completion. Available in English or Spanish.

Format: Self-administered; untimed: 35 to 40 minutes

Scoring: Computer scored

Cost: $8.00 per administration

Psychopathic Personality Inventory™–Revised (PPI-R)

2005	Psychological Assessment Resources, Inc.

Scott O. Lilenfield

Population: Ages 18 to 86 years

Purpose: Assesses psychopathic personality traits

Description: A 154-item self-report of both global psychopathy and the component traits of psychopathy. The PPI-R measures the continuum of psychopathic personality traits present in a range of individuals and can be used in both clinical and nonclinical settings. The measures require a fourth-grade reading level. Provides both offender and community/college normative samples.

Format: Rating scale; untimed: 15 to 25 minutes

Scoring: Examiner evaluated

Cost: Introductory Kit (manual, 25 item booklets, 25 response forms, 25 summary forms) $210.00

Psychosexual Life History (PSLH)

1995, 2000	Nichols and Molinder Assessments

H. R. Nichols, Ilene Molinder

Population: Adult and adolescent sex offenders

Purpose: Used for clinical interview and assessment of behavior patterns, emotional states, attitudes, and personal history of sex offenders

Description: Short-answer 16-page questionnaire detailing experiences, thoughts, and feelings from childhood through adult life. Categories are Sexual History, Health, Parental and Family, Childhood and Adolescent Development and Behaviors, Education, Work, Substance Abuse, Marital, Adult Behaviors, and Treatment. A sixth-grade reading level is required.

Format: Interview; can be self-administered; untimed

Scoring: Examiner evaluated

Cost: Contact publisher

Recovery Attitude and Treatment Evaluator (RAATE™)

1992	Change Companies

David Mee-Lee, Norman G. Hoffmann, Maurice B. Smith

Population: Adults

Purpose: Provides both clinician and client impressions

Description: The instrument covers five areas: resistance/acceptance of treatment, resistance/acceptance of recovery as an ongoing effort, biomedical problems, emotional problems, and the recovery environment. Provides quantitative documentation for reimbursement.

Format: Self-administered rating scale; untimed

Scoring: Examiner evaluated

Cost: Package of 25 Forms (specify clinician or client) $78.75

Reynolds Adolescent Adjustment Screening Inventory (RAASI)

2001	Psychological Assessment Resources, Inc.

William M. Reynolds

Population: Ages 12 to 19 years

Purpose: Screens psychological adjustment

Description: The RAASI has 32 self-report items with four scales: Antisocial Behavior, Anger Control Problems, Emotional Distress, and Positive Self. A third-grade reading level is required.

Format: Self-administered; untimed: 5 minutes

Scoring: Hand key

Cost: Introductory Kit (manual, 50 test booklets) $150.00

Roberts–2

2005	Western Psychological Services

Glen E. Roberts, Dorothea S. McArthur

Population: Ages 6 to 18 years

Purpose: Identifies children with emotional disturbance; used for clinical diagnosis, particularly with children just entering counseling or therapy

Description: Oral-response 16-item test in which the child is shown cards containing realistic line illustrations and is asked to make up stories about each. The illustrations depict adults and children in up-to-date clothing and emphasize the everyday, interpersonal events of contemporary life, including (in addition to the standard situations of the TAT and CAT) such situations as parental disagreement, parental affection, observation of nudity, and school and peer interpersonal events. Stimuli are chosen to elicit psychologically meaningful responses. The clinical areas measured and reported on the Interpersonal Chart are conflict, anxiety, aggression, depression, rejection, punishment, dependency, support, closure, resolution, unresolved indicator, maladaptive outcome, and deviation response. Other measures include the Ego Functioning Index, the Aggression Index, and the Levels of Projection Scale. The manual includes a number of case studies and examples.

Format: Examiner required; individual administration; untimed: 20 to 30 minutes

Scoring: Examiner evaluated

Cost: Kit (set of test pictures, 25 record booklets, manual) $140.00

Rogers Criminal Responsibility Assessment Scales (R-CRAS)

1984	Psychological Assessment Resources, Inc.

Richard Rogers

Population: Adults

Purpose: Evaluates the criminal responsibility of individuals who may or may not, depending on their sanity or insanity at the time they committed a crime, be held legally accountable for their actions

Description: Paper-pencil inventory evaluating criminal responsibility. The instrument quantifies essential psychological and situational variables at the time of the crime that are to be used in a criterion-based decision model. This allows the clinician to quantify the impairment at the time of the crime, conceptualize the impairment with respect to the appropriate legal standards, and render an expert opinion with respect to those standards. Descriptive criteria are provided on scales measuring the individual's reliability, organicity, psychopathology, cognitive control, and behavioral control at the time of the alleged crime. Part I establishes the degree of impairment on psychological variables significant to the determination of insanity. Part II articulates the decision process toward rendering an accurate opinion on criminal responsibility with the ALI standard and includes experimental criteria and decision models for guilty but mentally ill and M'Naughten standards.

Format: Examiner required; individual administration; untimed

Scoring: Examiner evaluated

Cost: Introductory Kit (manual, 50 booklets) $110.00

Ruff Neurobehavioral Inventory™ (RNBI)

2003	Psychological Assessment Resources, Inc.

Ronald M. Ruff, Kristin M. Hibbard

Population: Ages 18 years and older

Purpose: Assesses cognitive, emotional, physical, and psychosocial functioning and general quality of life

Description: The RNBI is a 243-item self-report questionnaire that provides diagnostic insights and assesses treatment outcomes. During the recovery phase, the instrument can track the rate of improvement based on the patient's self-perceptions of daily problems. The RNBI consists of 17 Premorbid Basic scales and 18 Postmorbid Basic scales. Scale scores are combined to create four Premorbid and four Postmorbid Composite scale scores that provide global information. Four Validity scales are included.

Format: Rating scale; untimed: 30 to 45 minutes

Scoring: Examiner evaluated

Cost: Introductory Kit (manual, 25 reusable item booklets, 25 answer booklets, 25 profile booklets) $162.00

SAQ-Adult Probation III

Updated yearly	Behavior Data Systems, Ltd.

Herman H. Linderman

Population: Adults on probation

Purpose: Measures eight areas of concern with adults on probation

Description: Version II contains eight scales: Truthfulness, Alcohol, Drugs, Resistance, Aggressivity, Violence, Antisocial, and Stress Coping Abilities. The instrument has 181 multiple-choice and true-false items and is computer or paper-pencil administered. Computer-generated results are available within 4 minutes of test completion. Truth-corrected scores are provided. Computer-generated report includes summary reports on each scale. Standardized and normed on probationers and parolees. Available in English or Spanish. Online administration is available at www.online-testing.com.

Format: Self-administered; untimed: 30 minutes

Scoring: Computer scored; online

Cost: Contact publisher; $9.95 each online

SCID II Patient Questionnaire for Windows (SCID II PQ™)

| 1997 | Multi-Health Systems, Inc. |

Miriam Gibbon, Janet B. W. Williams, Robert L. Spitzer, Lorna Smith Benjamin

Population: Ages 18 years and older

Purpose: Provides information for DSM-IV Axis II

Description: Total of 119 items for DSM-IV Axis II Disorders. Provides Dimensional Score Report and Question-by-Question Report.

Format: Self-administered; untimed: 30 to 45 minutes

Scoring: Computer scored

Cost: $319.00 (unlimited use)

SCID Screen Patient Questionnaire for Windows (SSPQ™) and SCID Screen Patient Questionnaire–Extended for Windows (SSPQ-X™)

| 2001 | Multi-Health Systems, Inc. |

Michael B. First, Miriam Gibbon, Janet B. W. Williams, Robert L. Spitzer

Population: Ages 18 years and older

Purpose: Probes for DSM-IV Axis I symptoms

Description: Screens patients using questions dealing with mood, anxiety, somatoform, psychotic, substance use, eating disorders, and psychotic symptoms. Yields Complete Summary of Patient Responses, Concise Summary of Possible Diagnoses, and Long Summary of Diagnoses Reports. The extended version provides more detail and reduces the number of false positives. It distinguishes between substance abuse and dependency and includes questions for each type of drug.

Format: Self-administered; untimed: short, 20 minutes; long, 30 to 45 minutes

Scoring: Computer scored

Cost: SSPQ $427.00; SSPQ-X $535.00 (unlimited use)

Self-Assessment Index

| 2000 | Behavior Data Systems, Ltd. |

Herman H. Linderman

Population: Ages 15 to 80 years

Purpose: Screens attitudes and behaviors for understanding welfare-to-work participants

Description: The index has 103 items in five scales: Truthfulness, Work Index, Alcohol, Drugs, and Stress Coping Abilities. Test results can be used to coordinate intervention, treatment, and vocational rehabilitation services. Requires a high fifth-grade reading level. Also available in Spanish.

Format: Self-administered; untimed: 20 minutes

Scoring: Computer scored

Cost: $8.00 per administration

Self-Audit (SA)

| 2006 | Behavior Data Systems, Ltd. |

Herman H. Linderman

Population: Ages 17 to 80 years

Purpose: Helps clients to understand their life situation, pressures, coping abilities, and stressors

Description: Designed for counseling and treatment program intake, the SA has 160 items in nine scales: Truthfulness, Distress, Resistance, Morale, Violence, Alcohol, Drugs, Self-Esteem, and Stress Coping Abilities. The SA differs from the Victim Index in that it contains Violence, Alcohol, and Drugs scales. The instrument can be used in HMOs, EAP programs, courts, probation, and community corrections. Requires a high fifth-grade reading level. Also available in Spanish.

Format: Self-administered; untimed: 25 to 35 minutes

Scoring: Computer scored

Cost: $8.00 per administration

Sexual Adjustment Inventory (SAI)

| 1997 | Behavior Data Systems, Ltd. |

Herman H. Linderman

Population: Sex offenders

Purpose: Identifies sexually deviant and paraphiliac behavior in people accused or convicted of sexual offenses

Description: Screens sexual offenders and measures degree of severity of sexually deviant and paraphiliac behavior. The test contains 13 scales: Test Item Truthfulness, Sex Item Truthfulness, Sexual Adjustment, Child Molest, Sexual Assault, Exhibitionism, Incest, Alcohol, Drugs, Violence, Antisocial, Distress, and Judgment. There are 214 multiple-choice/true–false items. Computer-generated report summarizes risk range and recommendations for each scale; on-site reports within

4 minutes of test completion. Two separate truthfulness scales permit comparison of client's test-taking attitude to sex-related and non-sex-related questions, which provides insight into client's attitude, motivation, and assessment-related behavior. Truth-corrected scores. Online administration is available at www.online-testing.com.

Format: Self-administered; untimed: 45 to 60 minutes

Scoring: Computer scored; online

Cost: Contact publisher; $9.95 each online

Sexual Adjustment Inventory–Juvenile

Date not provided	Behavior Data Systems, Ltd.

Herman H. Linderman

Population: Ages 12 to 18 years

Purpose: Evaluates juveniles accused or convicted of sexual offenses

Description: The SAI-Juvenile has 195 items with 13 scales: Test Item Truthfulness, Sex Item Truthfulness, Child Molest, Sexual (Rape) Assault, Incest, Exhibitionism, Sexual Adjustment, Violence, Antisocial, Distress, Alcohol, Drugs, and Judgment. Online administration is available at www.online-testing.com.

Format: Self-administered; untimed: 60 minutes

Scoring: Computer scored; online

Cost: $8.00 each administration; $9.95 each online

Shoplifting Inventory

2000	Behavior Data Systems, Ltd.

Herman H. Linderman

Population: Adolescent and adult shoplifters

Purpose: Designed for shoplifter evaluation

Description: This assessment inventory contains nine scales—Truthfulness, Entitlement, Shoplifting, Antisocial, Peer Pressure, Self-Esteem, Impulsiveness, Alcohol, and Drugs—and evaluates people charged or convicted of shoplifting. There are 185 multiple-choice/true–false items. Computer-generated report summarizes risk range and recommendations for each scale; Truth-corrected scores; on-site reports within 4 minutes of test completion. Available in English or Spanish.

Format: Self-administered; untimed: 45 minutes

Scoring: Computer scored

Cost: $8.00 each administration

Structured Clinical Interview for DSM-IV® Axis I Disorders (SCID-I), Clinician Version

1998	American Psychiatric Publishing, Inc.

Michael B. First, Robert L. Spitzer, Miriam Gibbon, Janet B. W. Williams

Population: Ages 18 years and older

Purpose: Helps clinicians make standardized, reliable, and accurate diagnoses

Description: Covers those DSM-IV diagnoses most commonly seen by clinicians and includes the diagnostic criteria for these disorders with corresponding interview questions. Divided into six self-contained modules that can be administered in sequence: Mood Episodes; Psychotic Symptoms; Psychotic Disorders; Mood Disorders; Substance Use Disorders; and Anxiety, Adjustment, and Other Disorders

Format: Examiner required; individual administration; untimed: varies

Scoring: Examiner evaluated

Cost: Complete Set (administration booklet, 5 score sheets, user's guide) $116.00

Structured Clinical Interview for DSM-IV® Axis II Disorders (SCID-II)

1998	American Psychiatric Publishing, Inc.

Michael B. First, Robert L. Spitzer, Miriam Gibbon, Janet B. W. Williams

Population: Ages 18 years and older

Purpose: Helps clinicians make standardized, reliable, and accurate diagnoses

Description: Analyses the 10 DSM-IV Axis II personality disorders, as well as depressive personality disorder, passive-aggressive personality disorder, and personality disorder not otherwise specified.

Format: Examiner required; individual administration; untimed: varies

Scoring: Examiner evaluated

Cost: Set (user's guide, 5 questionnaires) $84.00

Structured Clinical Interview for DSM-IV® Dissociative Disorders (SCID-D-R)

Date not provided	American Psychiatric Publishing, Inc.

Marlene Steinberg

Population: Ages 18 years and older

Purpose: Helps clinicians make standardized, reliable, and accurate diagnoses

Description: This diagnostic interview is specific to the assessment of DSM-IV dissociative disorders and acute stress disorder. The interview documents posttraumatic dissociative symptoms for psychological reports and medical records and makes DSM-IV diagnosis of dissociative amnesia, depersonalization disorder, dissociative disorder not otherwise specified, and also the new DSM-IV categories of acute stress disorder and dissociative trance disorder.

Format: Examiner required; individual administration; untimed: varies

Scoring: Examiner evaluated

Cost: Set (interviewer's guide, 5 questionnaires) $97.00

Structured Interview of Reported Symptoms (SIRS)

| 1992 | Psychological Assessment Resources, Inc. |

Richard Rogers, R. Michael Bagby, Susan E. Dickens

Population: Adults

Purpose: Used for forensic assessment to detect malingering and feigning of psychiatric symptoms

Description: Oral response short-answer interview with 172 items and the following scales: Rare Symptoms, Symptom Combinations, Improbable and Absurd Symptoms, Blatant Symptoms, Subtle Symptoms, Severity of Symptoms, Selectivity of Symptoms, and Reported vs. Observed Symptoms. Supplementary Scales include Direct Appraisal of Honesty, Defensive Symptoms, Symptom Onset and Resolution, Overly Specified Symptoms, and Inconsistency of Symptoms.

Format: Examiner required; individual administration; untimed: under 1 hour

Scoring: Examiner evaluated

Cost: Introductory Kit (manual, 25 booklets) $250.00

Structured Inventory of Malingered Symptomatology™ (SIMS)

| 2005 | Psychological Assessment Resources, Inc. |

Glenn P. Smith

Population: Ages 18 years and older

Purpose: Screens for malingered psychopathology and cognitive symptoms

Description: The SIMS is a 75-item, true-false screening instrument that reduces clinician burden and increases assessment efficiency. The SIMS can be used as part of a battery of tests providing convergent evidence of malingering, rather than relying on a single instrument for diagnosis. The SIMS is written at a fifth-grade reading level. Five scale domains (Psychosis, Neurologic Impairment, Amnestic Disorders, Low Intelligence, and Affective Disorders) and an overall score are provided.

Format: Rating scale; untimed 10 to 15 minutes

Scoring: Examiner evaluated

Cost: Introductory Kit (manual, 25 response forms) $120.00

Symptom Assessment-45 Questionnaire (SA-45™)

| 2000 | Multi-Health Systems, Inc. |

Population: Ages 13 years and older

Purpose: Measures symptomatology across nine psychiatric domains

Description: Contains a total of 45 items to assess Anxiety, Interpersonal Sensitivity, Paranoid Ideation, Hostility, Obsessive-Compulsivity, Phobic Anxiety, Somatization, Depression, and Psychoticism.

Format: Self-administered; untimed: 10 minutes

Scoring: QuikScore™; computer scored

Cost: Kit (manual, 25 forms) $75.00

Symptom Checklist-90 Revised (SCL-90-R)

| 1975 | Pearson Assessments |

Leonard R. Derogatis

Population: Ages 13 years and older

Purpose: Screens for psychological problems and measures progress

Description: Computer-administered or paper-pencil 90-item multiple-choice test with a 5-point rating scale from 0 to 4. The nine primary dimensions are Somatization, Obsessive-Compulsive, Interpersonal Sensitivity, Depression, Anxiety, Hostility, Phobic Anxiety, Paranoid Ideation, and Psychoticism. A sixth-grade reading level is required. Examiner must be M-level qualified. A computer version using an IBM-compatible 486 PC or higher is available. The test is available on audiocassette and in 23 foreign languages. Twenty-four additional languages are available for research purposes only.

Format: Self-administered; untimed: 12 to 15 minutes

Scoring: Hand key; computer scored

Cost: Starter Kit with Interpretative Report (manual, 3 answer sheets, 3 reports) $65.00

Temperament and Atypical Behavior Scale (TABS)

1999	Brookes Publishing Co., Inc.

Stephen J. Bagnato, John T. Neisworth, John Salvia, Frances M. Hunt

Population: Ages 11 to 71 months

Purpose: Measures critical temperament and self-regulation problems that may indicate a child's risk for atypical development, including attention and activity, social behavior, sleeping, play, senses, movement, and vocal and oral behavior

Description: The TABS is an assessment tool with four categories (55 items): Detached (20 items) measures aloof, withdrawn behavior that may be indicative of autism; Hypersensitive/Active (17 items) measures impulsive, nightly active, defiant behavior; Underreactive (11 items) measures passivity and lethargy that may be indicative of a variety of severe neurodevelopmental problems; Dysregulated (7 items) measures sleeping, crying, self-comforting, and jitteriness. May be used for persons with visual, hearing, physical, and mental impairments. The TABS screener yields raw score, and assessment yields raw score, percentile, and standard score for each of the four categories, plus overall score.

Format: Examiner required; individual administration; untimed

Scoring: Examiner evaluated

Cost: Specimen Kit (screener, assessment tools, manual) $85.00

Trauma Symptom Checklist for Children™ (TSCC™)

2001	Psychological Assessment Resources, Inc.

John Briere

Population: Ages 8 to 16 years

Purpose: Measures posttraumatic stress and related psychological symptomatology

Description: Item responses on a 4-point scale are entered on the top page of the carbonless booklet; item responses are automatically transferred to the scoring page underneath. Raw scores are converted to *t*-scores. The 54 items have two validity scales (Underresponse and Hyperresponse), six clinical scales (Anxiety, Depression, Anger, Posttraumatic Stress, Dissociation, and Sexual Concerns), and eight critical items. The alternate 44-item version is identical except that it makes no reference to sexual issues and includes seven critical items.

Format: Rating scale; untimed: 15 to 20 minutes

Scoring: Examiner evaluated; computer scoring available

Cost: Introductory Kit (manual 25 test booklets, 25 of each scoring form) $148.00

Trauma Symptom Inventory (TSI)

1995	Psychological Assessment Resources, Inc.

John Briere

Population: Adults

Purpose: Evaluates acute and chronic posttraumatic symptomology

Description: Paper–pencil 4-point scale with 100 items addressing the following: Anxious Arousal, Dissociation, Depression, Sexual Concerns, Anger/Irritability, Dysfunctional Sexual Behavior, Intrusive Experiences, Impaired Self-Reference, Defensive Avoidance, and Tension Reduction Behavior. A fifth- to seventh-grade reading level is required. An alternate 86-item version (TSI-A) contains no sexual content.

Format: Examiner required; individual or group administration; untimed: 20 minutes

Scoring: Examiner evaluated; computer scoring available

Cost: Introductory Kit (manual, item booklet, hand-scorable answer sheet, male/female profile forms) $195.00

Treatment Intervention Inventory (TII)

Date not provided	Behavior Data Systems, Ltd.

Herman H. Linderman

Population: Adults

Purpose: Designed for treatment intake assessment

Description: The TII has 162 items with nine scales: Truthfulness, Anxiety, Depression, Distress, Self-Esteem, Family Issues, Alcohol, Drugs, and Stress Coping Abilities. The TII is appropriate for HMO's EAP Programs and chemical dependency treatment settings. The scales identify problems that warrant referral, intervention, or treatment. Online administration is available at www.online-testing.com.

Format: Self-administered; untimed: 35 minutes

Scoring: Computer scored; online

Cost: $8.00 per administration; $9.95 online

Treatment Intervention Inventory–Juvenile (TII-Juvenile)

Date not provided	Behavior Data Systems, Ltd.

Herman H. Linderman

Population: Adolescents

Purpose: Designed for juvenile inpatient or outpatient and counseling intake screening

Description: The TII-Juvenile has 143 items with nine scales: Truthfulness, Self-Esteem, Family Issues, Anxiety, Depression, Distress, Alcohol, Drugs, and Stress Coping Abilities.

Format: Self-administered; untimed: 25 to 30 minutes

Scoring: Computer scored

Cost: $8.00 each administration

Triage Assessment for Psychiatric Disorders (TAPD™)

1995	Change Companies

Norman G. Hoffman

Population: Adults

Purpose: Measures psychiatric disorders to determine if further assessment or services are needed

Description: Covers nine AXIS I and five AXIS II conditions. Offers quick documentation of both positive and negative findings. The TAPD documents both current conditions and past history and is DSM-IV-TR compatible.

Format: Examiner required; individual administration; untimed: 15 to 20 minutes

Scoring: Examiner evaluated

Cost: Manual $15.00; 25 Forms $52.50

Victim Index (VI)

2000	Behavior Data Systems, Ltd.

Herman H. Linderman

Population: Ages 14 to 80 years

Purpose: Screens victims of physical and/or mental abuse

Description: The VI has 147 items and contains eight scales: Truthfulness, Distress, Morale, Self-Esteem, Resistance, Substance Abuse, Stress Coping Abilities, and Suicide Ideation. The instrument is appropriate for male and female victims. Also available in Spanish. Online administration is available at www.online-testing.com.

Format: Self-administered; untimed: 25 to 30 minutes

Scoring: Computer scored

Cost: $8.00 per administration

Violence Scale

1973	Donna Bardis

Panos D. Bardis

Population: Adolescents, adults

Purpose: Measures attitudes toward violence (words and actions aimed at property damage and personal injury); used for clinical assessment, marriage and family counseling, research on violence, and discussions in social science classes

Description: Paper–pencil test in which the subject rates 25 statements concerning various aspects of violence on a scale from 0 (*strongly disagree*) to 4 (*strongly agree*). The violence score equals the sum of the 25 numerical responses. The theoretical range of scores extends from 0 (lowest approval of violence) to 100 (highest approval). Suitable for use with individuals who are physically or hearing impaired.

Format: Examiner/Self-administered; suitable for group use; untimed: 10 minutes

Scoring: Examiner evaluated

Cost: $1.00

Ways of Coping Questionnaire

1988	Mind Garden, Inc.

Susan Folkman, Richard S. Lazarus

Population: Adults

Purpose: Helps counselors work with clients to develop practical coping skills

Description: The *Ways of Coping Questionnaire* measures the style of the respondent's coping. The instrument is excellent for research on coping. Scales include Confrontative Coping, Distancing, Self-Controlling, Seeking Social Support, Accepting Responsibility, Escape–Avoidance, Playful Problem Solving, and Positive Reappraisal.

Format: Self-administered; untimed: 10 minutes

Scoring: Examiner evaluated

Cost: Sampler Set $30.00; Permission Set for Up to 200 Uses $150.00

Youth Inventory–4 (YI-4)

1997	Checkmate Plus, Ltd.

Kenneth D. Gadow, Joyce Sprafkin

Population: Ages 12 to 18 years

Purpose: Screens for DSM-IV emotional and behavioral disorders and applies behavioral ratings of child psychopathology

Description: In 120 items, symptoms of multiple disorders are measured. This is a self-report instrument that corresponds item by item to the ASI-4. The scale can be scored to derive Symptom Count scores (diagnostic model) or Symptom Severity scores (normative data mode.). Also available in Spanish.

Format: Rating scale; can be computer administered; untimed: 10 to 15 minutes

Scoring: Examiner evaluated; computer scored

Cost: Deluxe Kit (manual, 50 checklists, 50 symptom count score sheets, 50 symptom severity profiles) $75.00

Anger

Aggression Questionnaire (AQ)

2000	Western Psychological Services

Arnold H. Buss, W. L. Warren

Population: Ages 9 to 88 years

Purpose: Measures aggressive responses

Description: The AQ measures an individual's aggressive responses and his or her ability to channel those responses in a safe, constructive manner. Because it takes just 10 minutes to complete, the AQ can be administered quickly to large numbers of people. The AQ is a full revision of the *Buss-Durkee Hostility Inventory*, a longtime standard for assessing anger and aggression. It consists of just 34 items, scored on the following scales: Physical Aggression, Hostility, Verbal Aggression, Indirect Aggression, and Anger. A total score is also provided, along with an Inconsistent Responding Index. Standardization is based on a sample of 2,138 individuals, and norms are presented in three age sets: 9 to 18, 19 to 39, and 40 to 88.

Format: Self-administered; untimed

Scoring: Hand key; computer scored; scoring service available

Cost: Complete Kit (manual, 25 AutoScore™ forms) $99.00

Attitudes Toward Guns and Violence Questionnaire (AGVQ)

2000	Western Psychological Services

Jeremy P. Shapiro

Population: Ages 6 to 29 years

Purpose: Measures attitudes of young people toward guns, physical aggression, and interpersonal conflict

Description: Composed of 26 items, this is a unique self-report inventory. AGVQ items focus on violence-related issues relevant to young people, with an emphasis on guns. The test form asks individuals to choose one of three response options to indicate the extent of agreement with each item. The test yields a Total Score, plus scores for the following subscales: Aggressive Response to Shame, Comfort With Aggression, Excitement, and Power/Safety. Norms are based on a nationally representative, age-stratified sample of 1,745 individuals in school and community settings. The AGVQ kit includes the Aggressive Behavior Checklist (ABC), which provides student and teacher ratings of violent behavior. By assessing attitudes, the examiner can determine what kind of cognitive and behavioral training should be implemented.

Format: Self-administered; untimed: 5 to 10 minutes

Scoring: Computer scored; test scoring service available

Cost: Complete Kit (manual, 25 answer forms, 25 each aggressive behavior checklists) $99.00

Children's Inventory of Anger (ChIA)

2000	Western Psychological Services

W. M. Nelson, III, A. J. Finch

Population: Ages 6 to 16 years

Purpose: Identifies situations that provoke anger and anger intensity in children

Description: This self-report inventory identifies the kinds of situations that provoke anger in particular children, as well as the intensity of their anger response. The ChIA contains 39 items, produces a Total Score, an Inconsistent Responding Index, and four subscale scores: Frustration, Physical Aggression, Peer Relationships, and

Authority Relations. Response options are keyed to drawings of four faces, with expressions ranging from happy to furious. The child simply marks the option that shows how angry he or she would be in the circumstances described. The ChIA is ideal any time you need a quick assessment of children's anger. The ChIA is helpful in treatment planning and in program evaluation.

Format: Examiner required; individual and group administration; untimed

Scoring: Examiner evaluated; computer scored; test scoring service available

Cost: Complete Kit (manual, 25 AutoScore™ forms) $93.50

Novaco Anger Scale and Provocation Inventory (NAS-PI)

2003	Western Psychological Services

Raymond W. Novaco

Population: Ages 9 to 84 years

Purpose: Tells how individuals experience anger and what kind of situations provoke anger

Description: The NAS-PI is composed of two parts: The Novaco Anger Scale (60 items), which tells you how an individual experiences anger, and the Provocation Inventory (25 items), which identifies the kind of situations that induce anger in particular individuals. The following scores are provided for the Anger Scale: Total (general inclination toward anger reactions, based on Cognitive, Arousal, and Behavior subscales); Cognitive (anger justification, rumination, hostile attitude, and suspicion); Arousal (anger intensity, duration, somatic tension, and irritability); Behavior (impulsive reaction, verbal aggression, physical confrontation, and indirect expression); and Anger Regulation (ability to regulate anger-engendering thoughts, effect self-calming, and engage in constructive behavior when provoked). For the Provocation Inventory, a Total Score is obtained.

Format: Self-administered; untimed: 25 minutes

Scoring: Examiner evaluated

Cost: Kit (manual, 25 AutoScore™ forms) $92.00

State-Trait Anger Expression Inventory-2 (PTI-2)

1999	Psychological Assessment Resources, Inc.

Charles D. Spielberger

Population: Ages 16 years and older

Purpose: Measures type and expression of an-

ger; used as a screening and outcome measure in psychotherapy and stress management programs, with particular application in behavioral medicine

Description: Paper–pencil 44-item Likert-type test assessing anger along six scales: State Anger, Trait Anger, Anger Expression (In and Out), Anger Control (In and Out), and an Anger Expression Index.

Format: Self-administered; untimed: 5 to 10 minutes

Scoring: Examiner evaluated; computer scoring available

Cost: Kit (manual, 25 reusable booklets, 50 item booklets, 50 rating sheets) $232.00

Tiffany Control Scales (TCS)

2006	Psychological Growth Associates, Inc.

Donald W. Tiffany, Phyllis G. Tiffany

Population: Ages 10 to 99 years

Purpose: Assesses control problems anywhere anger and loss of control is involved

Description: The standard scales include eight situations: work, school (or learning), opposite sex, same sex, community, home, other people (other than peers), and self-in-general. Questionnaire items ask four questions for each of the eight situations, making up the 32-item instrument. All variables are measured in terms of standard situations, and all variable and situation interactions are normed. The TCS is written on a fifth-grade reading level. The TCS can be customized to evaluate any user-chosen situation.

Format: Self-administered; untimed: 10 to 20 minutes

Scoring: Examiner evaluated; computer, machine, and scoring service available

Cost: Unlimited Uses $349.00

Anxiety

Anxiety Scales for Children and Adults (ASCA)

1993	James Battle and Associates, Ltd.

James Battle

Population: Ages 5 years to adult

Purpose: Measures anxiety; is applicable for

psychotherapy and anxiety therapy; is suitable for most populations

Description: The form for children (Form Q) has 25 items and the form for adults (Form M) has 40 items. Scores yielded: Classifications, percentile ranks, and t-scores. Criterion-referenced response format. Available in large print, on audiocassette, and in French and Spanish. May be used for those with visual, physical, hearing, or mental impairments.

Format: Self-administered; untimed: less than 15 minutes

Scoring: Hand key, computer scored, test scoring service

Cost: Complete Battery $120.00

Beck Anxiety Inventory® (BAI®)

1993	Harcourt Assessment, Inc.

Aaron T. Beck

Population: Ages 17 to 80 years

Purpose: Measures anxiety levels

Description: Patients respond to 21 items rated on a scale from 0 to 3. Each item is descriptive of subjective, somatic, or panic-related symptoms of anxiety.

Format: Self-administered; untimed: 5 to 10 minutes

Scoring: Examiner evaluated; can be computer scored

Cost: Complete Kit (manual, 25 record forms) $77.00

Endler Multidimensional Anxiety Scales (EMAS)

1991	Western Psychological Services

Norman S. Endler, Jean M. Edwards, Romeo Vitelli

Population: Adolescents, adults

Purpose: Evaluates phobias, panic attacks, generalized anxiety disorder, test anxiety, posttraumatic stress disorder, and treatment outcome

Description: Three related self-report measures assess and predict anxiety across situations and measure treatment response. The first scale measures state anxiety—the individual's actual transitory anxiety response. It assesses both physiological and cognitive responses. The second scale measures the individual's predisposition to experience anxiety in four types of situations. The third scale evaluates the individual's perception of the type and intensity of threat in the immediate situation. The scales can be given separately or as a set.

Format: Examiner required; individual and group administration; untimed: 25 minutes

Scoring: Examiner evaluated; computer scoring available

Cost: Kit (25 AutoScore™ test forms for each scale, manual) $109.00

Multidimensional Anxiety Questionnaire (MAQ)

1999	Psychological Assessment Resources, Inc.

William M. Reynolds

Population: Ages 18 to 89 years

Purpose: Quickly screens for symptoms of anxiety

Description: The MAQ has 40 items to screen for presence and severity of anxiety symptoms.

Format: Self-administered; untimed: 10 minutes

Scoring: Examiner evaluated

Cost: Introductory Kit (manual, 25 hand-scorable booklets, 50 profile forms) $122.00

Multidimensional Anxiety Scale for Children (MASC)

1997	Multi-Health Systems, Inc.

John. S. March

Population: Ages 8 to 19 years

Purpose: Assesses the major dimensions of anxiety

Description: The MASC consists of 39 items; a 10-item screener is also available. Scales are Physical Symptoms, Social Anxiety, Harm Avoidance, Separation/Panic, Anxiety Disorders, Total Anxiety, and Inconsistency index. Yields t-scores. Available in many languages.

Format: Self-administered; untimed: 5 to 15 minutes

Scoring: QuikScore™ forms

Cost: Complete Kit (manual, 25 forms) $119.00

Panic and Agoraphobia Scale (PAS)

1999	Hogrefe & Huber Publishers

Borwin Bandelow

Population: Adults

Purpose: Assesses the severity of panic disorder with or without agoraphobia

Description: Compatible with both DSM-IV and

ICD-10 classifications, and available in both self-rated and observer-rated versions, the PAS was specially developed for monitoring the efficacy of both drug and psychotherapy treatments. In addition to the English scale, translations are available in 16 languages. The PAS has excellent psychometric properties and is quick to use. It has been successfully applied in both double-blind placebo-controlled studies and open treatment trials.

Format: Rating scale; untimed

Scoring: Examiner evaluated

Cost: Complete Test (folder, manual, 50 of each patient questionnaires and observer-rated scales) $79.00

Revised Children's Manifest Anxiety Scale (RCMAS)

1985	Western Psychological Services

Cecil R. Reynolds, Bert O. Richmond

Population: Ages 6 to 19 years

Purpose: Measures the level and nature of anxiety in children

Description: The RCMAS helps to pinpoint the problems in a child's life. A brief self-report inventory provides scores for Total Anxiety and four subscales: Worry/Oversensitivity, Social Concerns/Concentration, Physiological Anxiety, and Lie Scale. It is composed of 37 yes-no items. The scale is useful to clinicians who are treating children for academic stress, test anxiety, peer and family conflicts, or drug problems. It provides objective data on anxiety that can inform and guide treatment.

Format: Self-administered; untimed: 15 minutes

Scoring: Hand key

Cost: Kit (50 AutoScore™ forms, manual) $126.50

Social Phobia and Anxiety Inventory (SPAI)

1996	Multi-Health Systems, Inc.

Samuel M. Turner, Deborah C. Beidel, Constance V. Dancu

Population: Ages 14 years and older

Purpose: Assesses social anxiety and fear

Description: The 45-item scale measures specific somatic symptoms, cognition, and behaviors across a wide range of potentially fear-producing situations. The SPAI consists of two subscales: Social Phobia and Agoraphobia.

Format: Self-administered; untimed: 20 to 30 minutes

Scoring: QuikScore™ forms

Cost: Complete Kit (manual, 25 forms) $85.00

Social Phobia and Anxiety Inventory for Children (SPAI-C)

2000	Multi-Health Systems, Inc.

Samuel M. Turner, Deborah C. Beidel, Tracy L. Morris

Population: Ages 8 to 14 years

Purpose: Assesses social anxiety and phobia

Description: The 26-item questionnaire evaluates the somatic, cognitive, and behavioral aspects of social phobia unique to childhood situations.

Format: Self-administered; untimed: 10 to 15 minutes

Scoring: QuikScore™ forms

Cost: Complete Kit (manual, 25 forms) $85.00

State–Trait Anxiety Inventory (STAI™)

1999	Multi-Health Systems, Inc.

Charles D. Spielberger

Population: Ages 16 years and older

Purpose: Measures two distinct anxiety concepts

Description: The STAIC contains two 20-item scales measuring long-standing (trait) and temporary (state) anxiety. A separate score is produced for each scale to determine which type of anxiety is dominant

Format: Self-administered on computer; untimed: 20 minutes

Scoring: Examiner evaluated, computer scored

Cost: Complete Kit (manual, 25 questionnaires) $70.00

State–Trait Anxiety Inventory for Adults (STAI)

1983	Mind Garden, Inc.

Charles D. Spielberger

Population: Adolescents, adults

Purpose: Differentiates between long-standing

(trait) and temporary (state) anxiety; used for research and clinical practice

Description: The essential qualities evaluated by the score are feelings of apprehension, tension, nervousness, and worry. Scores increase in response to physical danger and psychological stress, and decrease as a result of relaxation training. Items are ranked on a 4-point Likert scale.

Format: Self-administered; untimed: 5 to 20 minutes

Scoring: Examiner evaluated

Cost: Sample Set $30.00; Permission for Up to 200 Uses $150.00

State-Trait Anxiety Inventory for Children

1973	Mind Garden, Inc.

Charles D. Spielberger, C. D. Edwards, J. Montuori, R. Lushene

Population: Grades 4 to 6

Purpose: Assesses anxiety in children; used for research screening and treatment evaluation

Description: Two 20-item scales measuring two types of anxiety: state anxiety (current level of anxiety, or S-Anxiety) and trait anxiety (anxiety proneness, or T-Anxiety). The S-Anxiety scales ask how the child feels at a particular moment in time, and the T-Anxiety scales ask how he or she generally feels. The inventory is based on the same concept as the *State-Trait Anxiety Inventory*.

Format: Self-administered, untimed: 10 to 20 minutes

Scoring: Examiner evaluated

Cost: Sample Set $30.00; Permission Set for Up to 200 Uses $150

State-Trait Anxiety Inventory for Children (STAIC™)

1999	Multi-Health Systems, Inc.

Charles D. Spielberger

Population: Ages 6 to 14 years

Purpose: Measures two distinct anxiety concepts

Description: The STAIC contains two 20-item scales measuring long-standing (trait) and temporary (state) anxiety. A separate score is produced for each scale to determine which type of anxiety is dominant.

Format: Self-administered; untimed: 20 minutes

Scoring: Examiner evaluated; computer scoring available

Cost: Complete Kit (manual, 25 questionnaires) $75.00

Test Anxiety Inventory (TAI)

1980	Mind Garden, Inc.

Charles D. Spielberger

Population: Grades 10 and above

Purpose: Measures individual differences in test-taking anxiety; used for research

Description: Paper–pencil 20-item test of two major components of test anxiety: worry and emotionality. Respondents report how frequently they experience specific anxiety symptoms in examination situations. Similar in structure and concept to the T-Anxiety scale of the *State-Trait Anxiety Inventory*.

Format: Self-administered; untimed: 10 to 20 minutes

Scoring: Examiner evaluated

Cost: Sample Set $30.00; Permission for Up to 200 Uses $150.00

Depression

BDI® FastScreen for Medical Patients

2000	Harcourt Assessment, Inc.

Aaron T. Beck, Robert A. Steer, Gregory K. Brown

Population: Ages 13 to 80 years

Purpose: Screens for depression

Description: This new version of the *Beck Depression Inventory* is designed specifically for medical patients. The seven-item self-report instrument measures the severity of depressive symptoms corresponding to the psychological, nonsomatic criteria for diagnosing major Depressive Disorders in DSM-IV.

Format: Self-report; untimed: less than 5 minutes

Scoring: Examiner evaluated

Cost: Complete Kit (manual, 50 record forms) $78.00

Beck Depression Inventory®–II (BDI®-II)

| 1996 | Harcourt Assessment, Inc. |

Aaron T. Beck, Robert A. Steer, Gregory K. Brown

Population: Ages 13 to 80 years

Purpose: Assesses depression

Description: This revision consists of 21 items to assess the intensity of depression. Each item is a list of four statements arranged in increasing severity about a particular symptom of depression. These new items bring the BDI-II into alignment with DSM-IV criteria.

Format: Self-administered; untimed: 5 minutes

Scoring: Examiner evaluated; computer scoring available

Cost: Complete Kit (manual, 25 record forms) $79.00

Beck Hopelessness Scale® (BHS®)

| 1993 | Harcourt Assessment, Inc. |

Aaron T. Beck

Population: Ages 17 to 80 years

Purpose: Measures negative attitudes about the future

Description: Allows prediction of eventual suicide by measuring three aspects of hopelessness: feelings about the future, loss of motivation, and expectations. Responding to 20 true–false statements, patients either endorse a pessimistic statement or deny an optimistic statement.

Format: Self-administered; untimed: 5 to 10 minutes

Scoring: Examiner evaluated; can be computer scored

Cost: Complete Kit (manual, 25 record forms) $79.00

Beck Scale for Suicide Ideation® (BSS®)

| 1991 | Harcourt Assessment, Inc. |

Aaron T. Beck

Population: Ages 17 years and older

Purpose: Evaluates suicidal thinking

Description: The scale is made up of 21 items. Five screening items reduce the length and the intrusiveness of the questionnaire for patients who are nonsuicidal.

Format: Self-administered; untimed: 5 to 10 minutes

Scoring: Examiner evaluated; can be computer scored

Cost: Complete Kit (manual, 25 record forms) $79.00

Carroll Depression Scales (CDS-R™)

| 1999 | Multi-Health Systems, Inc. |

Bernard Carroll

Population: Ages 18 years and older

Purpose: Measures severity of depressive symptoms

Description: A total of 61 items measure Major Depression, Dysthymic Disorder, Melancholic Features, and Atypical Features. A brief CDS contains 12 items to be used as a screener. Linked directly to DSM-IV criteria.

Format: Self-administered; untimed: full, 20 minutes; brief, 5 minutes

Scoring: QuikScore™ forms; computer scored

Cost: Hand-Scored Complete Kit (manual, 25 of each form) $138.00

Children's Depression Inventory (CDI)

| 1992 | Multi-Health Systems, Inc. |

Maria Kovacs

Population: Ages 7 to 17 years

Purpose: Measures depressive symptoms

Description: The CDI has 27 items. A 10-item screener (CDI-S) is also available. The CDI yields the following scales: Total CDI score, Negative Mood, Interpersonal Problems, Ineffectiveness, and Negative Self-Esteem. Yields t-scores. Also available in Spanish, French-Canadian, Dutch, Hebrew, Hungarian, and more.

Format: Self-administered; untimed: 15 minutes

Scoring: QuikScore™ forms; computer scored

Cost: Hand-Scored Complete Kit (manual, 25 of each form) $187.00

Children's Depression Rating Scale–Revised (CDRS-R)

| 1996 | Western Psychological Services |

Elva O. Poznanski, Hartmut B. Mokros

Population: Ages 6 to 12 years

Purpose: Used to diagnose depression and determine its severity

Description: In clinical contexts, the CDRS-R can be used to diagnose depression and to monitor treatment response. In nonclinical contexts, such as schools and pediatric clinics, it serves as screening tool, identifying children who need professional intervention. This is a brief rating scale based on a semistructured interview with the child. The scale requires the interviewer to rate 17 symptom areas (including those that serve as DSM-IV criteria for a diagnosis of depression): School Work, Capacity to Have Fun, Social Withdrawal, Eating Patterns, Sleep Patterns, Excessive Fatigue, Physical Complaints, Irritability, Guilt, Self-Esteem, Depressed Feelings, Morbid Ideation, Suicidal Ideation, Weeping, Facial Expressions of Affect, Tempo of Speech, and Hyperactivity. The majority of these symptom areas are rated on an expanded 7-point scale. The CDRS-R gives a single Summary Score, along with a clear interpretation of, and recommendations for, six different score ranges.

Format: Examiner required; individual administration; untimed: 15 to 20 minutes

Scoring: Examiner evaluated

Cost: Kit (25 administration booklets, manual) $90.75

Children's Depression Scale–Third Edition

2004	Australian Council for Educational Research Limited

Moshe Lange, Miriam Tisher

Population: Ages 7 to 18 years

Purpose: Measures depression in children; identifies depressed children in need of further evaluation

Description: This revised edition includes a shortened scale of 50 items to use with children and their parents and two new 10-item questionnaires for teachers and health practitioners. The CDS covers two scales: Depression and Pleasure. The revised report form provides an excellent means of gathering information from multiple informants, allowing users to summarize and compare responses of children and a variety of adult respondents. The use is restricted to suitably qualified professionals.

Format: Examiner required; individual administration; untimed: 20 to 50 minutes

Scoring: Examiner evaluated

Cost: Specimen Set $149.95

Hamilton Depression Inventory (HDI)

1995	Psychological Assessment Resources, Inc.

William M. Reynolds, Kenneth A. Kobak

Population: Adults

Purpose: Used as a comprehensive screening for symptoms of depression in private practice, hospitals, and correctional institutions

Description: Paper–pencil 23-item 3- to 5-point scale with the following categories: Depressed Mood, Loss of Interest/Pleasure, Weight Loss, Insomnia/Hypersomnity, Psychomotor Retardation/Agitation, Fatigue, Worthlessness, Indecisiveness, and Suicide Ideation. Materials used include a manual, item booklet, summary sheet, answer sheet, and short form test booklet. A fifth-grade reading level is required. Available in PC-administered format. Short form with nine items available.

Format: Self-administered; untimed

Scoring: Examiner evaluated; software scoring available

Cost: Comprehensive Kit (manual, 5 reusable booklets, 25 each of summary and answer sheets, 5 short form booklets, PC scoring) $268.00

Multiscore Depression Inventory for Adolescents and Adults (MDI)

1983	Western Psychological Services

David J. Berndt

Population: Ages 13 years and older

Purpose: Measures the severity and specific aspects of depression and detects subtle variations in mild forms of depression

Description: Paper–pencil or computer-administered true–false questionnaire containing 118 items and 10 subscales: Low Energy Level, Cognitive Difficulty, Guilt, Low Self-Esteem, Social Introversion, Pessimism, Irritability, Sad Mood, Instrumental Helplessness, and Learned Helplessness. An interpretive report that provides a general score, as well as scores for each subscale, is available. In addition, one section of the report indicates the probability that the examinee is depressed, conduct disordered, psychotic, suicidal, bulimic, anorexic, or nondepressed; has a mixed diagnoses; has endogenous depression; or is a chronic pain sufferer. A short form consists of the first 47 items of the full-length inventory.

Format: Self-administered; untimed: 20 minutes

Scoring: Examiner evaluated; computer scored

Cost: Kit (manual, 25 forms, 25 profile forms, scoring key) $132.00

Multiscore Depression Inventory for Children (MDI-C)

1996	Western Psychological Services

David J. Berndt, Charles F. Kaiser

Population: Ages 8 to 17 years

Purpose: Measures the severity and specific aspects of depression and detects subtle variations in mild forms of depression

Description: Paper–pencil or computer-administered inventory containing 79 items on eight scales: Anxiety, Self-Esteem, Social Introversion, Instrumental Helplessness, Sad Mood, Pessimism, Low Energy, and Defiance. The inventory yields scores for each of these scales, plus a total score, and several validity indicators. This inventory is a downward extension of the *Multiscore Depression Inventory for Adolescents and Adults.*

Format: Self-administered; untimed: 10 to 20 minutes

Scoring: Examiner evaluated; computer scored

Cost: Kit (manual, 25 AutoScore™ forms, 25 profile forms) $115.50

North American Depression Inventories (NADI)

1988	James Battle and Associates, Ltd.

James Battle

Population: Ages 6 years to adult

Purpose: Assesses depression, is applicable for psychotherapy and depression counseling, and is suitable for most populations

Description: Form A for adults has 40 items; Form C for children has 25 items. The following scores are yielded: classifications, percentile ranks, and *t*-scores. The inventories are available in large print, on audiocassette, and in French and Spanish. The NADI may be used for persons with visual, physical, hearing, or mental impairments.

Format: Examiner required; individual or group administration; untimed: 15 minutes

Scoring: Hand key and computer scored

Cost: Complete Battery $120.00

Revised Hamilton Rating Scale for Depression (RHRSD)

1997	Western Psychological Services

W. L. Warren

Population: Adults

Purpose: Used to evaluate depression in adult clinical populations in medical or mental health settings

Description: The RHRSD was developed in a medical setting and used concurrently with antidepressant medication to evaluate treatment response. The instrument covers both psychoaffective and somatic symptoms. It gives three levels of interpretation: Overall Symptom Severity, Groups of Symptoms, and Specific Symptom Areas. Can be used to quickly evaluate symptom severity, to confirm a diagnosis of depression, to explore depressive symptoms, and to measure treatment outcome. The revision includes several new features: a self-report version (can be completed in the waiting room by the client), a WPS AutoScore™ Form, and eight new critical items that help confirm diagnoses of depression.

Format: Self-administered; untimed: 5 to 10 minutes

Scoring: Auto scored; computer scored; scoring service available

Cost: Kit (10 AutoScore™ Clinician Forms, 10 AutoScore™ Self-Report Problem Inventories, manual) $115.50

Reynolds Adolescent Depression Scale–Second Edition (RADS-2)

2002	Psychological Assessment Resources, Inc.

William M. Reynolds

Population: Ages 11 to 20 years

Purpose: Evaluates the current level of an adolescent's depressive symptomatology

Description: Measures four basic dimensions of depression: Dysphoric Mood, Anhedonia/Negative Affect, Negative Self-Evaluation, and Somatic Complaints. The RADS-2 provides *t*-scores and clinical cutoff scores. A Depression total score represents overall severity of depressive symptomatology.

Format: Self-administered; untimed: 5 to 10 minutes

Scoring: Examiner evaluated

Cost: Introductory Kit (manual, 25 booklets, 25 summary forms) $140.00

Reynolds Child Depression Scale (RCDS)

1989	Psychological Assessment Resources, Inc.

William M. Reynolds

Population: Grades 3 to 6

Purpose: Assesses and screens for depressive symptomatology

Description: Paper–pencil 30-item multiple-choice test. Percentiles by grade and sex are provided for the total score. A second-grade reading level is required. This is one test in the *Reynolds Depression Scale* series.

Format: Self-administered; untimed: 10 minutes

Scoring: Examiner evaluated

Cost: Introductory Kit (manual, 50 answer sheets, scoring key) $138.00

Suicidal Ideation Questionnaire (SIQ)

1988	Psychological Assessment Resources, Inc.

William M. Reynolds

Population: Ages 13 to 18 years

Purpose: Assesses suicidal ideation in adolescents

Description: Paper-pencil 30-item test utilizing a 7-point Likert-type response format. It was designed as a companion instrument to the *Reynolds Adolescent Depression Scale.* The 15-item SIQ-JR version is appropriate for students in Grades 7 to 9.

Format: Self administered; untimed: 10 minutes

Scoring: Examiner evaluated

Cost: Introductory Kit (manual, 25 of each form) $152.00

Suicide Probability Scale (SPS)

1982	Western Psychological Services

John G. Cull, Wayne S. Gill

Population: Ages 14 to 65 years

Purpose: Predicts the probability of suicidal behavior; used by clinicians to assess the probability that individuals may harm themselves; may be used for screening, monitoring changes in suicide potential over time, clinical exploration, and research

Description: Paper-pencil or computer-administered 36-item test in which the subject uses a 4-point scale ranging from *none or little of the time* to *most or all of the time* to indicate how often the behavior described in the statements would be descriptive of his or her behavior or feelings. The test itself does not mention suicide. Items are broken down into four subscales: Hopelessness, Suicide Ideation, Negative Self-Evaluation, and Hostility. Scoring yields a total weighted score, a normalized *t*-score, and a Suicide Probability Score. The manual presents cutoff scores

indicating the level of probable suicide behavior, interpretive guidelines, and clinical strategies for each level. The computer version is available for PC systems.

Format: Examiner required; individual or group administration; untimed: 5 to 10 minutes

Scoring: Hand key; computer scored

Cost: Kit (25 tests, manual, 25 profile sheets) $121.00

Trait Anxiety and Depression Scales

1994	Albert Mehrabian, PhD

Albert Mehrabian

Population: Ages 14 and older

Purpose: Assesses trait anxiety and depression; used for research and in counseling

Description: Paper–pencil test with two subtests: Trait Anxiety (6 Items) and Depression (20 items). A 10th-grade reading level is required.

Format: Self-administered; untimed: 10 minutes

Scoring: Hand key; test scoring service available

Cost: Test Kit $33.00

Eating Disorders

Eating Disorder Inventory–Third Edition (EDI-3)

2004	Psychological Assessment Resources, Inc.

David M. Garner

Population: Females ages 13 to 53 years

Purpose: Provides a standardized clinical evaluation of symptomatology associated with eating disorders

Description: An independent and structured self-report form that is easy to complete and provides data regarding frequency of symptoms. The EDI-3 consists of 91 items organized onto 12 primary scales, consisting of three eating-disorder-specific scales and nine general psychological scales. A Symptom Checklist contains detailed information regarding the symptom areas necessary for determining whether patients meet the formal diagnostic criteria for an eating disorder. A Referral Form is an abbreviated form.

Format: Self-administered; untimed: 20 minutes

Scoring: Examiner evaluated

Cost: Introductory Kit (manual, 25 of each form) $246.00

Eating Inventory

| 1988 | Harcourt Assessment, Inc. |

Albert J. Stunkard, Samuel Messick

Population: Ages 17 years and older

Purpose: Measures behavior important to the understanding and treatment of eating-related disorders such as anorexia and bulimia; also used to predict response to weight-loss programs, weight gain after quitting smoking, and weight change during depression

Description: Paper–pencil 51-item questionnaire measuring three dimensions of eating behavior: cognitive restraint of eating, disinhibition, and hunger. This test is for use only by persons with at least a master's degree in psychology or a related discipline. Registration is required.

Format: Self-administered; untimed: 15 minutes

Scoring: Hand key

Cost: Examination Kit (manual, 25 questionnaires, 25 answer sheets) $199.00

Substance Abuse

Adolescent Chemical Dependency Inventory (ACDI)

| 1989 | Behavior Data Systems, Ltd. |

Herman H. Linderman

Population: Ages 12 to 18 years

Purpose: Screens for and evaluates adolescent substance abuse; used in intake/referral settings, adolescent chemical dependency treatment programs, and juvenile court/probation systems

Description: Paper–pencil or computer-administered multiple-choice and true–false inventory containing 104 items and five scales: Truthfulness, Alcohol, Drugs, Adjustment, and Distress. The Truthfulness scale measures how truthfully the examinee responded to ACDI items. The Alcohol scale measures alcohol-related problems. The Drugs scale measures drug use or abuse-related problems. The Adjustment scale measures overall level of adjustment (personal, home, school, authority, relationship). The Distress scale measures anxiety and depression levels. Results are reported as percentiles, corrected raw scores,

and risk-level classifications (low, low-medium, high-medium, high). Narrative explanations and recommendations are presented in automated reports. The computer version operates on PC-compatible systems. Diskettes containing 50, 100, 150 ACDS test applications provided; computer scoring on-site. A sixth-grade reading level is required. Also available in Spanish.

Format: Self-administered; untimed: 20 minutes

Scoring: Computer scored

Cost: $8.00 each administration

Adolescent Diagnostic Interview

| 1993 | Western Psychological Services |

Ken C. Winters, George H. Henly

Population: Ages 12 to 18 years

Purpose: Systematically assesses psychoactive substance use disorders and evaluates psychosocial stressors, school and interpersonal functioning, and cognitive impairment

Description: Used by chemical dependency practitioners, clinical psychologists, and social workers, the ADI consists of a series of questions about behaviors, events, and attitudes related to DSM-III-R and DSM-IV diagnostic criteria for psychoactive substance use disorders. The interviewer reads the questions from the Administration Booklet and enters the client's responses. When the ADI is scored, it yields the following information: presence or absence of a DSM-III-R or DSM-IV diagnosis, level of functioning, severity of psychosocial stressors, and a rating of memory and orientation.

Format: Examiner required; individually administered; untimed: 45 minutes

Scoring: Examiner evaluated

Cost: Kit (manual, 5 administration booklets) $91.00

Adolescent Drinking Index (ADI)

| 1989 | Psychological Assessment Resources, Inc. |

Adele V. Harrell, Philip W. Wirtz

Population: Ages 12 to 17 years

Purpose: Assesses alcohol abuse in adolescents with emotional or behavioral problems; used for screening and treatment planning

Description: Rating scale with 24 items. Requires a fifth-grade reading level.

Format: Self-administration; untimed: 5 minutes

Scoring: Examiner evaluated

Cost: Introductory Kit (manual, 25 booklets) $88.00

Adult Presentence Evaluation (APE)

2006	Behavior Data Systems, Ltd.

Herman H. Linderman

Population: Ages 18 to 75 years

Purpose: Classifies substance abuse and dependency in terms of DSM-IV criteria, while measuring alcohol and drug use severity

Description: The APE evolved from the *Offender Assessment Index* (OAI). The instrument has 158 items in seven scales: Truthfulness, Resistance, Violence (Lethality), Substance Abuse/Dependency, Alcohol, Drugs, and Stress Coping Abilities. It is appropriate for misdemeanor and felony offender assessment. Requires a high fifth-grade reading level. Also available in Spanish.

Format: Self-administered; untimed: 35 minutes

Scoring: Computer scored

Cost: $8.00 per administration

Adult Pretrial Test (APT)

2006	Behavior Data Systems, Ltd.

Herman H. Linderman

Population: Ages 18 to 80 years

Purpose: Measures severity of alcohol and drug use

Description: Designed for male and female pretrial defendants and appropriate for misdemeanor and felony cases, the instrument has 162 items in seven scales: Truthfulness, Alcohol, Drugs, Substance Abuse/Dependency, Violence (Lethality), Antisocial, and Stress Coping. Requires a high fifth-grade reading level. Standardized on the adult defendant population. Empirically demonstrated reliability and validity. Also available in Spanish.

Format: Self-administered; untimed: 35 minutes

Scoring: Computer scored

Cost: $8.00 per administration

Alcadd Test–Revised (AT)

1988	Western Psychological Services

Morse P. Manson, Lisa A. Melchior

Population: Ages 18 years and older

Purpose: Assesses the extent of alcohol addiction; used for diagnosis, treatment, and alcoholism research

Description: Multiple-choice paper–pencil test consisting of 65 items on five subscales measuring regularity of drinking, preference for drinking over other activities, lack of controlled drinking, rationalization of drinking, and excessive emotionality. Fourth-grade reading level is required. This test is suitable for individuals with visual, hearing, or physical impairments. Can be read to individuals with visual impairments. This is a revision of the 1978 test.

Format: Self-administered; untimed: 5 to 15 minutes

Scoring: Hand key; computer scored

Cost: Kit (25 AutoScore™ forms, manual) $82.50

Alcohol and Drug Use Scales

1994	Albert Mehrabian, PhD

Albert Mehrabian

Population: Ages 14 years and older

Purpose: Measures alcohol/drug abuse; used for research and counseling

Description: Paper–pencil test with 18 items and two subscales: Extent of Alcohol Use/Abuse (11 items), and Extent of Drug Use/Abuse (7 items). A 10th-grade reading level is required.

Format: Self-administered; untimed: 10 minutes

Scoring: Hand key

Cost: Test Kit $33.00

Alcohol Use Inventory (AUI)

1987	Pearson Assessments

J. L. Horn, K. W. Wanberg, F. M. Foster

Population: Adults

Purpose: Identifies patterns of behavior, attitudes, and symptoms associated with the use and abuse of alcohol; used for planning treatments

Description: Self-report 228-item inventory measuring the alcohol-related problems of addicted, dependent, binge, and violent drinkers along four domains: benefits, styles, consequences, and concerns associated with alcohol use. The test contains 24 scales (17 primary, 6 second-order, and 1 general) covering drinking for social or mental improvement, drinking to manage moods, gregarious versus solo drinking, compulsive obsession about drinking, sustained versus periodic drinking, social role maladaptation, loss of control over behavior when drinking, perceptual and somatic withdrawal symptoms, relationship of marital problems and drinking, quantity of alcohol consumed when drinking, guilt and worry associated with drinking, prior attempts to deal with drinking, and awareness of drinking problems and readiness for help. A profile report is included. Items are written at a sixth-grade reading level.

Format: Self-administered; untimed: 35 to 60 minutes

Scoring: Computer scored; hand scoring materials available

Cost: Starter Kit (manual, 10 test booklets, 50 answer sheets, 50 profile forms, answer keys) $145.00

American Drug and Alcohol Survey™ (ADAS)

1999, 2005	Rocky Mountain Behavioral Science Institute, Inc.

E. R. Oetting, F. Beauvais, R. Edwards

Population: Grades 4 to 12

Purpose: Assesses substance abuse experience and attitudes; used for prevention program planning and evaluation

Description: Multiple-choice paper–pencil survey. Adolescent Form has 58 questions; Children Form has 51 questions. The ADAS is not an instrument for clinical use with individuals; it is an anonymous survey to be administered to a group. Reports present percentages of respondents who answer in certain ways. RMSBI scans surveys, runs analysis, and produces comprehensive reports on the student population surveyed. Forms are optical scan forms processed by the publisher. Adolescent Form is available in Spanish.

Format: Self-administered; untimed: 30 minutes.

Scoring: Test scoring service

Cost: Contact publisher

American Tobacco Survey (ATS)

1999	Rocky Mountain Behavioral Science Institute, Inc.

E. R. Oetting, F. Beauvais, R. Edwards

Population: Grades 4 to 12

Purpose: Measures the rate of use and attitudes regarding tobacco

Description: A 32-item, school-based survey used in assessment needs and program planning and evaluation.

Format: Self-administered; untimed: 15 minutes

Scoring: Test scoring service

Cost: Contact publisher

Behaviors and Experiences Inventory

1999	Change Companies

Norman G. Hoffman, David Mee-Lee, Gerald D. Shulman

Population: Adolescents, adults

Purpose: Identifies commonly occurring disorders found in addiction treatment and correctional populations

Description: This questionnaire covers history of physical, sexual, and emotional victimization, as well as behavioral problems. Ideal for identifying behavioral tendencies likely to be disruptive in group treatment settings. Useful in identifying individuals who may have residual posttraumatic stress disorder symptoms from traumatic backgrounds.

Format: Rating scale; untimed: 15 to 20 minutes

Scoring: Examiner evaluated

Cost: Manual $15.00; 25 Forms $52.50

Defendant Questionnaire (DQ)

2000	Behavior Data Systems, Ltd.

Herman H. Linderman

Population: Ages 17 to 80 years

Purpose: Measures severity of alcohol and drug use; used for court-related defendant assessment

Description: This instrument is appropriate for drug courts and general court populations in misdemeanor and felony cases. The DQ has 162 items with seven scales: Truthfulness, Violence (Lethality), Antisocial, Alcohol, Drugs, Substance Abuse/Dependency, and Stress Coping Abilities. Dependency is classified in terms of DSM-IV criteria and incorporates ASAM-compatible treatment recommendations. Also available in Spanish. Online administration is available at www.online-testing.com.

Format: Self-administered; untimed: 35 minutes

Scoring: Computer scored; online

Cost: $8.00 per administration; $9.95 online

Driver Risk Inventory–II (DRI-II)

2000	Behavior Data Systems, Ltd.

Herman H. Linderman

Population: Ages 14 years and older

Purpose: Measures the driving risk of DWI (driving while intoxicated) or DUI (driving under the influence) offenders; used to identify problem drinkers, substance abusers, and high-risk drivers

Description: Paper–pencil or computer-administered multiple-choice and true–false screening inventory contains 130 items on five scales. The Validity, or Truthfulness, scale measures how truthfully the examinee responded to DRI items. The Alcohol Scale measures the examinee's alcohol proneness and related problems. The Drugs Scale measures the examinee's drug use or abuse proneness and related problems and distinguishes between alcohol and drug abuse. The Driver Risk Scale measures driver risk potential, identifying the problem-prone driver independent of the respondent's substance abuse history. The Stress Coping Abilities Scale is a measure of the examinee's ability to cope with stress. Results are presented in the DRI Profile and as percentiles. Risk ranges low, low–medium, high–medium, high) for each scale, as well as scores for all five scales, are reported. Available in Spanish. Online administration is available at www.online testing.com. A 73-item short form also available.

Format: Self administered; untimed: 25 minutes

Scoring: Computer scored; online

Cost: $8.00 each administration; $9.95 each online

Juvenile Automated Substance Abuse Evaluation (JASAE)

2000 — ADE Incorporated

Bryan R. Ellis

Population: Adolescents

Purpose: Measures alcohol use, drug use, attitude, and life stress

Description: This is a 107-item survey which generates a report that provides DSM-IV classifications for alcohol and drug use and offers suggestions for patient placement in treatment. A fifth-grade reading level is required, but audiotapes are available in English and Spanish.

Format: Rating scale; untimed: 20 minutes

Scoring: Computer scored

Cost: Software $40.00; Each Evaluation $4.50; Audiotape $10.00

Juvenile Substance Abuse Profile (JSAP)

2006 — Behavior Data Systems, Ltd.

Herman H. Linderman

Population: Ages 12 to 17 years

Purpose: Screen in a nonintrusive manner

Description: The instrument is designed for school systems, juvenile screen programs, and troubled youth treatment agencies. The JSAP has 116 items with five scales: Truthfulness, Aggressiveness, Alcohol, Drugs, and Stress Coping Abilities. Extreme aggressiveness can spill over into violence. Greatly impaired stress coping abilities identify existing emotional and mental health problems. A high fifth-grade reading level is required. Also available in Spanish.

Format: Self-administered; untimed: 25 minutes

Scoring: Computer scored

Cost: $8.00 per administration

Manson Evaluation–Revised (ME)

1987 — Western Psychological Services

Morse P. Manson, George J. Huba

Population: Adults

Purpose: Assesses alcohol abuse proneness and eight related personality characteristics

Description: Paper–pencil true–false computer-administered test with 72 items on seven subscales measuring anxiety, depressive fluctuations, emotional sensitivity, resentfulness, incompleteness, aloneness, and interpersonal relations. Raw scores, t-scores, and percentiles are yielded. This revised version provides 1985 norms, as well as a new, easy-to-use test form featuring the WPS AutoScore™ system. This makes it possible for the administrator to score, profile, and interpret the test in just a minute or two. It can be used for personnel screening, diagnosis, therapy, research, and alcohol abuse programs.

Format: Examiner required; group administration; untimed: 5 to 10 minutes

Scoring: Hand key; computer scored; test scoring service available

Cost: Kit (25 AutoScore™ Test/Profile forms, manual) $82.50

Maryland Addictions Questionnaire (MAQ)

2000 — Western Psychological Services

William E. O'Donnell, Clinton B. DeSoto, Janet L. DeSoto

Population: Ages 16 years and older

Purpose: Used for patients entering an addiction treatment program to tell how severe the addiction is, how motivated the patient is, and which treatment approach is most likely to work

Description: A self-report inventory composed of 111 items on the following scales: Substance Abuse Scales, Summary Scores, Treatment Scales, and Validity Scales. The test provides standard scores and percentiles for each of these scales. Based on the relative elevation of the Summary Scores, it also assigns the patient one of six Summary Codes, indicating his or her ability to benefit from treatment. The MAQ is brief yet multidimensional; the items are easy to complete; the scales are easy to interpret; and the results facilitate treatment planning. Norms are based on a large sample of people receiving substance abuse treatment at clinics. A 30-item short form with six scales can be completed in only 5 minutes. A fifth-grade reading level is required.

Format: Self-administered; untimed: 15 to 20 minutes

Scoring: Examiner evaluated; computer scored

Cost: Complete Kit (manual, 25 AutoScore™ answer sheets) $99.00

NEEDS

2000	ADE Incorporated

Bryan R. Ellis

Population: Adults

Purpose: Used in all situations where substance use/abuse needs to be evaluated

Description: This is a 130-item survey which generates a report that provides DSM-IV classifications for alcohol and drug use and offers suggestions for patient placement in treatment. Ten areas are measured: Respondent Attitude, Substance Abuse, Problem Solving and Reading Assessment, Physical Health Assessment, Criminal History, Emotional Stability, Personal Relationship and Support System, Employment, Educational, Risk Assessment and Suggested Supervision Level. A fifth-grade reading level is required, but audiotapes are available in English and Spanish.

Format: Rating scale; untimed: 30 minutes

Scoring: Computer scored

Cost: Software $40.00; Each Evaluation $6.00; Audiotape $10.00

Personal Experience Inventory (PEI)

1989	Western Psychological Services

Ken C. Winters, George H. Henly

Population: Ages 12 to 18 years

Purpose: Assesses chemical dependency of adolescents

Description: Paper–pencil or computer administered multiple-choice two-part test. Part I contains 129 items relating to personal involvement with chemicals, effects of drug use, social benefits of drug use, consequences of drug use, poly drug use, social-recreational use, psychological benefits of drug use, transitional use, preoccupation with drugs, and loss of control. In addition to documenting the degree, duration, and onset of drug use, this section also provides several clinical scales, validity indexes, and a problem severity section. Part II consists of 147 items that measure aspects of psychosocial functioning related to patterns of drug use and treatment responsiveness. Eight personal risk factor scales and four environmental risk factor scales are included in this section. Scores are used to generate a PEI computer report and PEI chromagraph. A sixth-grade reading level is required.

Format: Self-administered; untimed: 40 to 50 minutes

Scoring: Computer scored; test scoring service available

Cost: Mail-In Kit (manual, 5 test report prepaid mail-in answer booklets) $165.00; On-Site CD Kit (manual, 5 answer booklets, 5-use CD) $132.00

Personal Experience Inventory for Adults (PEI-A)

1996	Western Psychological Services

Ken C. Winters

Population: Ages 19 years or older

Purpose: Used to identify alcohol and drug problems, make referrals, and plan treatment

Description: Self-report inventory provides comprehensive information about substance abuse patterns in adults. It is designed to address the broad scope of problems associated with substance abuse. The PEI-A has two parts: the Problem Severity Section (120 items) and the Psychosocial Section (150 items). The interpretive report for the PEI-A presents results for each validity indicator; a graphic profile of all scale scores; the raw score, drug clinic *t*-score, and nonclinical *t*-score for each scale; results of the drug use frequency and duration items; and a narrative interpretation, including analysis of the Treatment Receptiveness scale score.

Format: Examiner required; suitable for group use; untimed: 45 to 60 minutes

Scoring: Computer scored; test scoring service available

Cost: Mail-In Kit (manual, 5 test report prepaid mail-in answer booklets) $165.00; On-Site CD Kit (manual, 5 answer booklets, 5-use CD) $132.00

Personal Experience Screening Questionnaire (PESQ)

1991	Western Psychological Services

Ken C. Winters

Population: Ages 12 to 18 years

Purpose: Used to identify and refer teenagers who may be chemically dependent

Description: This self-report questionnaire identifies teenagers who should be referred for a complete chemical dependency evaluation. The questionnaire includes 40 items divided into three sections: Problem Severity, Psychosocial Items, and Drug Use History. Two validity scales measure response distortion.

Format: Examiner required; suitable for group use; untimed: 10 minutes

Scoring: Hand key

Cost: Kit (25 AutoScore™ test forms, manual) $91.00

Prevention Planning Survey (PPS)

1999, 2005	Rocky Mountain Behavioral Science Institute, Inc.

E. R. Oetting, R. Edwards, F. Beauvais

Population: Grades 8 to 12

Purpose: Screens for risk and protective factors for substance use and violence

Description: A school-based survey with a total of 57 questions with applications for needs assessment and program planning/evaluation. Available only in booklets combined with the American Drug and Alcohol Survey.

Format: Self-administered; untimed: 45 minutes

Scoring: Test scoring service available

Cost: Contact publisher

Reinstatement Review Inventory (RRI)

Date not provided	Behavior Data Systems, Ltd.

Herman H. Linderman

Population: Adults

Purpose: Screens applicants before driver's license reinstatement

Description: The RRI has 124 items with six scales: Truthfulness, Road Rage, Alcohol, Drugs, Comparative Change, and Intervention Checklist.

It was designed to answer the question, Has the applicant changed since his or her driver's license was suspended or revoked?

Format: Self-administered; untimed: 25 minutes

Scoring: Computer scored

Cost: $8.00 per administration

Reinstatement Review Inventory–II (RRI-II)

Date not provided	Behavior Data Systems, Ltd.

Herman H. Linderman

Population: Adults

Purpose: Screens applicants before driver's license reinstatement

Description: The RRI-II has 128 items with six scales: Truthfulness, Stress Coping Abilities, Alcohol, Drugs, Comparative Change, and Intervention Checklist. It was designed to answer the question, Has the applicant changed since his or her driver's license was suspended or revoked? The RRI-II differs from the RRI in that it has replaced the Road Rage Scale with the Stress Coping Abilities Scale. Also available in Spanish.

Format: Self-administered; untimed: 25 minutes

Scoring: Computer scored

Cost: $8.00 each administration

Smoker Anchored Withdrawal Grid

1984	Nina G. Schneider, PhD

Nina G. Schneider

Population: Adults

Purpose: Measures nicotine or tobacco craving and withdrawal symptoms

Description: A 7-point Likert-type scale with 21 items designed to measure changes in physiological, emotional, and craving states as a function of smoking cessation.

Format: Self-administered; untimed: 5 to 7 minutes

Scoring: Examiner evaluated

Cost: Free

Smoker Complaint Scale (SCS)

1984	Nina G. Schneider, PhD

Nina G. Schneider

Population: Adults

Purpose: Assesses withdrawal symptoms of individuals during smoking cessation

Description: A 7-point Likert-type scale with 20 items designed to measure changes in physiological, emotional, and craving states as a function of smoking cessation.

Format: Self-administered; untimed: 5 to 7 minutes

Scoring: Examiner evaluated

Cost: Free

Substance Abuse Life Circumstance Evaluation (SALCE)

2000	ADE Incorporated

Bryan R. Ellis

Population: Adults

Purpose: Measures alcohol use, drug use, attitude, and life stress

Description: This is a 98-item survey which generates a report that provides DSM-IV classifications for alcohol and drug use and offers suggestions for patient placement in treatment. A fifth-grade reading level is required, but audiotapes are available in English and Spanish.

Format: Rating scale; untimed: 20 minutes

Scoring: Computer scored

Cost: Software $40.00; Each Evaluation $4.50; Audiotape $10.00

Substance Abuse Questionnaire (SAQ)

1985	Behavior Data Systems, Ltd.

Herman H. Linderman

Population: Ages 18 years and older

Purpose: Screens and evaluates adult chemical dependency. Used as an intake/referral device, in chemical dependency treatment settings, and in the criminal justice system

Description: Paper–pencil or computer-administered 153-item multiple-choice and true–false test designed to screen for and evaluate chemical dependency. The Truthfulness Scale measures how truthfully the examinee responded to the SAQ items. The Alcohol Scale measures the examinee's alcohol-related problems and proneness. The Drugs Scale measures drug use or abuse-related problems and proneness. The Aggressivity Scale measures the examinee's risk-taking behavior and aggressiveness. The Resistance Scale measures uncooperativeness and resistance to assistance. The Stress Coping Abilities Scale measures the examinee's ability to cope with stress, tension, and anxiety. The SAQ Profile reports scores, percentiles, and risk levels (low, low–medium, high–medium, high) for all six scales. The computer version operates on PC-compatible systems. A sixth-grade reading level is required. Also available in Spanish. Also available as a Short Form with 64 items.

Format: Self-administered; untimed: 30 minutes

Scoring: Computer scored

Cost: $8.00 each administration

Substance Abuse Relapse Assessment (SARA)

1993	Psychological Assessment Resources, Inc.

Lawrence Schonfeld, Roger Peters, Addis Dolente

Population: Adolescents, adults

Purpose: Used in substance abuse counseling and treatment to assess and monitor relapse causes and coping skills

Description: Oral response interview with 39 items in the following categories: Substance Abuse Behavior, Antecedents of Substance Abuse, Consequences of Substance Abuse, and Responses to Slips.

Format: Examiner required; individual administration; untimed: 1 hour

Scoring: Examiner evaluated

Cost: Introductory Kit (manual, stimulus card, interview record form, relapse prevention planning forms) $136.00

Substance Abuse Screening Test (SAST)

1993	Slosson Educational Publications, Inc.

Terry L. Hibpshman, Sue Larson

Population: Ages 13 years to adult

Purpose: Facilitates early identification and reliable referral of individuals who are abusing substances or are at risk

Description: The SAST elicits simple yes–no responses to questions that target critical areas of an individual's daily functioning. Responses may be written or verbal. The SAST may be administered by teachers, nurses, counselors, social workers, psychologists, and by well-informed adults who are under the supervision of a professional. The respondent's score can be interpreted by the use of a simple pass–fail table or by the use of a traditional standard score table. A comprehensive and user-friendly manual addresses critical sections, such as administration, scoring and interpretation, and statistics.

Format: Examiner required; group administration; untimed: 5 minutes

Scoring: Examiner evaluated

Cost: Complete $65.25

Substance Abuse Subtle Screening Inventory (SASSI)

1988	SASSI Institute

Glenn A. Miller

Population: Adolescent form: ages 14 to 17 years; Adult form: ages 18 years and older

Purpose: Identifies likelihood of substance use disorders to assist individuals in getting treatment

Description: Computer-administered or paper–pencil test. The substance abuse classification is based on subscale scores. A third-grade reading level is required. Examiner must meet APA guideline qualifications, be alcohol/drug certified, and be SASSI trained. Suitable for individuals with visual and hearing impairments. Clinical support is provided by a toll-free consultation.

Format: Examiner required; suitable for group administration; online administration; untimed: 10 to 15 minutes

Scoring: Examiner evaluated; computer scoring available; online available

Cost: Contact publisher

Substance Use Disorder Diagnostic Schedule–IV (SUDDS-IV™)

1995	Change Companies

Patricia A. Harrison

Population: Adults

Purpose: Documents substance-specific dependence and abuse diagnoses

Description: Structured comprehensive interview covers both current and lifetime indications based on the DSM-IV-TR. This instrument provides information compatible with the ASAM PPC-2R for treatment planning and placement.

Format: Examiner required; individual administration; untimed: 35 to 45 minutes

Scoring: Examiner evaluated

Cost: Manual $20.00; 25 forms $67.50

Triage Assessment for Addictive Disorders (TAAD™)

1995	Change Companies

Norman G. Hoffman

Population: Adults

Purpose: Identifies current alcohol and drug problems

Description: A brief structured interview that produces alcohol and drug dependence profiles similar to those of more time-intensive instruments. Covers all DSM-IV-TR criteria. A technician or paraprofessional can administer the TAAD for interpretation by a qualified professional.

Format: Examiner required; individual administration; untimed: 10 minutes

Scoring: Examiner evaluated

Cost: Manual $15.00; 25 Forms $52.50

Western Personality Inventory (WPI)

1963	Western Psychological Services

Morse P. Manson

Population: Adults

Purpose: Diagnoses the presence and degree of alcoholism; useful in alcohol rehabilitation programs

Description: Paper–pencil or computer-administered test that combines the Manson Evaluation, which identifies the potential alcoholic personality, and the Alcadd Test, which measures the extent of alcohol addiction, into one booklet. The computer version is available on PC-compatible systems. Computer scoring is available via mail-in services or on-site.

Format: Examiner required; suitable for group use; untimed: 15 to 20 minutes

Scoring: Hand key; computer scored

Cost: Kit (5 AutoScore™ Test Forms, Manson Evaluation Manual, Alcadd Manual, 2-use PC disk) $104.50

Personality

Multiage

Achievement Motivation Inventory (AMI)

2004	Hogrefe & Huber Publishers

H. Schuler, G. C. Thornton, A. Frintrup, R. Mueller-Hanson

Population: Adults

Purpose: Measures work-related achievement motivation

Description: A personality inventory that enables users to test candidates for 17 areas of achievement motivation. The AMI is based on the acceptor theories of the construct, but uniquely it also integrates relevant social motives. Scores are provided for Confidence in Success or Persistence, Dominance, or Status Orientation. The AMI consists of 170 items to be responded to on a 7-point Likert scale. Used for personnel selection, potential analysis, professional counseling, personnel development, profiling, psychology of sports, and personality research.

Format: Self-administered; untimed: 30 minutes

Scoring: Examiner evaluated

Cost: Complete Kit (manual, booklet, 20 response sheets, 20 score profiles, carrying case) $188.00

Adjustment Scales for Children and Adolescents (ASCA)

1994	Ed & Psych Associates

Paul A. McDermott, Neville C. Marston, Denis H. Stott

Population: Ages 5 to 17 years

Purpose: Assesses social and behavioral adjustment for use in educational and psychological diagnosis and intervention

Description: Paper–pencil teacher behavioral rating test for special education. An adult reading level is required. Examiners must be qualified educational and psychological specialists.

Format: Rating scale; untimed: 10 to 20 minutes

Scoring: Examiner evaluated

Cost: Kit (user's manual, male/female self-scoring forms) $87.00

Blue Pearl

1992	Dansk psykologisk Forlag

Lotte Boeggild, Sonja Overby

Population: Ages 7 to 14 years

Purpose: Evaluates the well-being of immigrant children

Description: Seven-picture projective verbal test measuring everyday life situations common in the classroom, the schoolyard, and at home. Used in child guidance for children with a background in the Muslim farming culture, primarily Turkey. Only one form is used, but the material contains specific gender-related items. Must be supervised by a psychologist. Available in Danish only.

Format: Examiner required; individual administration; untimed

Scoring: Examiner evaluated

Cost: $69.00 (DDK 415)

d2 Test of Attention

1998	Hogrefe & Huber Publishers

R. Brickenkamp, E. Zillmer

Population: Ages 9 to 59 years

Purpose: Psychodiagnostic instrument used for measuring concentration, particularly visual attention; used for personnel selection and for clinical, educational, and developmental psychology assessment

Description: Detail-discrimination paper–pencil test used to assess individuals' visual attention and concentration. Giving the test is virtually language independent since the test taker is intensively engaged in simply crossing out certain items on a sheet of many possibilities. Also available in German.

Format: Self-administered; timed: 8 minutes

Scoring: Examiner evaluated

Cost: Complete Test $78.00

Early Memories Procedure (EMP)

1989	Arnold R. Bruhn and Associates

Arnold R. Bruhn

Population: Adults

Purpose: Exploring personality reorganization

Description: Paper–pencil instrument with short-answer, projective, essay, and verbal response questions about 21 specific, one time memories. A fourth-grade reading level is required. Suitable for individuals with visual, physical, or hearing impairments. The EMP is useful for identifying the major unresolved issue in an individual's life.

Format: Examiner required; individual or group administration; untimed: 1½ to 2¼ hours

Scoring: Examiner evaluated

Cost: 25 Tests $140.00

Emotional Quotient Inventory (Bar-On EQ-i®)

1997	Multi-Health Systems, Inc.

Reuven Bar-On

Population: Ages 16 years and older

Purpose: Measures self-reported emotional intelligence

Description: Consists of 52-item QuikScore™ and 133-item mail-in, fax-in, computer-scored versions. Results include EQ score, five composite scale scores (Intrapersonal EQ, Interpersonal EQ, Adaptability EQ, Stress Management EQ, and General Mood EQ), and 15 subscale scores. The subscales are Self-Regard, Emotional Self-Awareness, Assertiveness, Independence, Self-Actualization, Empathy, Social Responsibility, Interpersonal Relationship, Reality Testing, Flexibility, Problem Solving, Stress Management, Impulse Control, Optimism, and Happiness. There are several manuals available. Available in many languages, including French, Spanish, Chinese, Czech, and Danish. Has application for clinical, educational, forensic, medical, corporate, human resources, and research uses. Online administration is available.

Format: Self-administered; untimed: 30 minutes

Scoring: Scoring service available; computer scored; online scoring

Cost: Preview Kit (manual, booklet, response sheet, development report) $77.50

Emotional Quotient Inventory: Youth Version (EQ-i:YV™)

2000	Multi-Health Systems, Inc.

Reuven Bar-On, James D. A. Parker

Population: Ages 7 to 18 years

Purpose: Measures emotional intelligence

Description: Applications of this 60-item inventory include counseling and development. Scales are Intrapersonal Abilities, Interpersonal Abilities, Stress Management, Adaptability, and General Mood. A 30-item screener version and a French-Canadian edition are also available.

Format: Self-administered; untimed: short, 10 minutes; long, 30 minutes

Scoring: QuikScore™

Cost: Complete Kit (manual, 25 of each form) $124.00

Five-Factor Personality Inventory–Children (FFPI-C)

2007	PRO-ED, Inc.

Ronnie L. McGhee, David J. Ehrler, Joseph A. Buckhalt

Population: Ages 9 through 18 years

Purpose: Measures personality traits and dispositions

Description: The FFPI-C is based on a five-factor personality theory, which concludes that five broad factors account for the majority of variance in personality descriptors: Agreeableness, Extraversion, Openness to Experience, Conscientiousness, and Emotional Regulation. The instrument is an efficient method of identifying, evaluating, and describing social adjustment and academic performance difficulties. The test contains 75 items, each of which has two opposing anchor statements. Respondents choose the statement that best represents their opinion and then make a qualitative decision on the degree of support for that choice by filing in one of five circles. Scores are reported as t-scores and percentiles.

Format: Self-administered; untimed: 15 to 40 minutes

Scoring: Examiner evaluated

Cost: Complete Kit (manual, 25 administration/scoring forms, storage box) $138.00

Hand Test

1983	Western Psychological Services

Edwin E. Wagner

Population: Ages 5 years to adult

Purpose: Used to measure action tendencies such as acting out and aggressive behavior

Description: Using pictures of hands as the projective medium, the Hand Test elicits responses that reflect behavioral tendencies. The client is shown 10 picture cards containing simple line drawings of a hand in various positions. The client's task is to explain what each hand is doing. It is scored by classifying responses according to clear-cut quantitative and qualitative scoring categories. The quantitative scores reflect the individual's overt behavior. The qualitative scores generally reflect feelings and motivations underlying the impaired action tendencies. The test also provides six summary scores, including an index of overall pathology and an acting-out ratio, which is used to predict aggressive behavior. Manual Supplement: Interpreting Child and Adolescent Responses.

Format: Examiner required; individual administration; untimed: 10 minutes

Scoring: Examiner evaluated

Cost: Kit (25 scoring booklets, picture cards, manual, manual supplement) $164.50

Hilson Personality Screening Survey (HPSS)

2006	Institute for Personality and Ability Testing, Inc.

Robin E. Inwald

Population: Adolescents and adults

Purpose: Measures areas of emotional IQ, drive, and social skills

Description: The HPSS includes 105 true–false questions from which both raw scores and *t*-scores are derived. A fifth-grade reading level is required. Online administration is available.

Format: Self-administered; untimed: 20 minutes

Scoring: Examiner evaluated; computer scoring available

Cost: $16.00 to $20.00 depending on scoring method

Holtzman Inkblot Technique (HIT)

1972	Harcourt Assessment, Inc.

W. H. Holtzman

Population: Ages 5 years to adult

Purpose: Assesses an individual's personality characteristics; used for diagnosis and therapy planning

Description: Projective measure of personality in which the examinee responds to 45 inkblots. Some inkblots are asymmetric, and some are in a color other than black. An objective scoring system has been developed. Materials include two alternate and equivalent forms, A and B, for a total of 90 stimulus cards.

Format: Examiner required; individual administration; untimed

Scoring: Examiner evaluated

Cost: Complete Kit Form A or B (inkblots, 25 record forms, manual) $325.00

House–Tree–Person (H-T-P) Projective Drawing Technique

1970	Western Psychological Services

John N. Buck

Population: Ages 3 years and older

Purpose: Assesses personality disturbances in psychotherapy, school, and research settings; may be used with individuals who are culturally disadvantaged, educationally deprived, mentally retarded, or elderly

Description: Multiple-item paper–pencil and oral-response test providing a projective study of personality. The test consists of two steps. The first, which is nonverbal, creative, and almost completely unstructured, requires the subject to make a freehand drawing of a house, a tree, and a person. The second step, which is verbal, apperceptive, and more formally structured, gives the subject an opportunity to describe, define, and interpret the drawings and their respective environments.

Format: Examiner required; individual administration; untimed: 15 minutes

Scoring: Examiner evaluated

Cost: Complete Set (manual, interpretive guide, 25 interpretation booklets, 25 drawing forms) $192.50

Kinetic Drawing System for Family and School

1985	Western Psychological Services

Howard M. Knoff, H. Thompson Prout

Population: Ages 5 to 20 years

Purpose: Provides personalized themes within school and family contexts; used for school psychology referrals

Description: Paper–pencil oral-response projective system integrating Kinetic Family Drawing and Kinetic School Drawing and therefore covering a broad range of the most frequent areas of child and adolescent distress. It consists of two drawings with a series of suggested projective questions in relation to the action between figures; figure characteristics; position, distance, and barriers style; and symbols. Each has a projective interpretation for family and school forms and a variable number of items subject to examiner discretion.

Format: Examiner required; individual administration; untimed

Scoring: Examiner evaluated

Cost: Kit (manual, 25 scoring booklets) $81.50

Personality Assessment Questionnaire (PAQ)

2004	Rohner Research Publications

Ronald P. Rohner

Population: Ages 4 to 16 years

Purpose: Predicts personality and mental health outcome of variations in perceived parental acceptance–rejection

Description: Multiple-item paper-pencil instrument measuring seven personality dimensions: Hostility/Aggression, Dependence/Independence, Self-Esteem, Self-Adequacy, Emotional (Un)Responsiveness, Emotional (In)Stability, and World View. Theoretically, these dispositions are linked to the acceptance–rejection process. The test is available in a child version and an adult version. The questionnaire yields seven scale scores in addition to the Total Test score, which is often used as a measure of overall mental health. A computer scoring program is available for PC systems. The examiner may read the items to individuals who are visually impaired and explain the meanings of words to those who are very young or are mentally impaired. The Handbook for the Study of Parental Acceptance and Rejection contains all versions of the PAQ and provides scoring instructions; descriptions of validity and reliability; and other information needed for administration, scoring, and interpretation.

Format: Self-administered; suitable for group use; untimed: 10 minutes

Scoring: Self-scored; may be computer scored

Cost: Handbook with All Instruments $35.00

Q-Tags Test of Personality

Date not provided	Institute of Psychological Research, Inc.

Arthur G. Storey, Louis I. Masson

Population: Ages 6 years and older

Purpose: Measures individual personality traits;

used for counseling, self-examination, and research

Description: Test measuring five factors of personality: Assertive, Effective, Hostile, Reverie, and Social. By sorting 54 cards, subjects are able to describe themselves both as they are and as they wish to be. The test was developed with norms for age, grade, occupation, and gender based on a wide range of subjects.

Format: Self-administered; untimed: 30 minutes

Scoring: Examiner evaluated

Cost: Contact publisher

Rorschach® Inkblot Test

1994	Western Psychological Services

Hermann Rorschach

Population: All ages

Purpose: Evaluates personality tendencies

Description: The classic projective technique contains 10 Rorschach color inkblot plates used for psychodiagnostic purposes. The examiner shows one at a time to the client and records responses.

Format: Examiner required; individual administration; untimed

Scoring: Examiner evaluated

Cost: Set (set of plates, 100 miniature inkblots in color/summary forms, 25 each record booklets and summary forms) $180.00

Rorschach® Psychodiagnostic Test–Rorschach Ink Blot Test

1951	Hogrefe & Huber Publishers

Hermann Rorschach

Population: Ages 3 years and older

Purpose: Evaluates personality through projective technique; used in clinical evaluation

Description: Oral-response projective personality test in which the subject is asked to interpret what he or she sees in 10 inkblots, based on the assumption that the individual's perceptions and associations are selected and organized in terms of his or her motivations, impulses, and other underlying aspects of personality. Extensive scoring systems have been developed. Although many variations are in use, this entry refers only to the Psychodiagnostic Plates first published in 1921. Materials include inquiry charts, tabulation sheets, and a set of 10 inkblots. A set of 10 Kodaslides of the inkblots may be imported on request. Trained examiner required.

Format: Individually administered; examiner required; untimed

Scoring: Examiner evaluated

Cost: Plates $75.00; Recording Blanks $17.00; Charts $32.00; Manual $54.00

Scenotest

| 1991 | Hogrefe & Huber Publishers |

G. von Staabs

Population: Children, adolescents

Purpose: Quickly assess emotional problems in children

Description: Specifically developed to evaluate children and adolescents' unconscious problems, the test is suited for working with adults and families. It permits accessing consciously denied or personally unknown relationships in the attitudes of the subjects to themselves and their social environment. Flexible dolls and a supply of additional material (selected according to psychological and dynamic considerations)—such as animals, trees, symbolic figures, and important objects from everyday life—are used as standard stimuli to prompt the subject easily to form and play out scenes that reveal real-life experiences, relations, fears, wishes, and coping strategies. Initial sessions reveal considerable matter that could not be tapped by direct questioning. In particular, neurotic disturbances can be revealed, and differential diagnosis is strongly supported. Used as part of an explicit therapy, it helps the patient see his or her problems at a distance and cope with them.

Format: Examiner required; individually administered; untimed

Scoring: Examiner evaluated

Cost: Complete Test Kit $980.00; Manual $36.95

TEMAS (Tell-Me-a-Story)

| 1986 | Western Psychological Services |

Giuseppe Costantino, Robert G. Malgady, Lloyd Rogler

Population: Ages 5 to 18 years

Purpose: Measures strengths and deficits in cognitive, affective, interpersonal, and intrapersonal functioning in children and adolescents

Description: Multicultural thematic apperception test designed for use with minority and nonminority children and adolescents. The test, which features 35 scales, uses 23 full-color stimulus cards to elicit stories from the examinee. Two parallel forms, minority and nonminority, are available. Separate norms are available for Blacks, Hispanics, and Whites.

Format: Examiner required; individual administration; untimed: short form, 1 hour; long form, 3 hours

Scoring: Examiner evaluated

Cost: Kit (set of stimulus cards, set of minority stimulus cards, 25 record booklets, administration instruction card, manual) $291.50

Test of Social Insight: Youth and Adult Editions

| 1959 | Martin M. Bruce, PhD |

Russell N. Cassel

Population: Ages 10 years to adult

Purpose: Measures the subject's understanding of and adaptation to acceptable patterns of culture in the United States

Description: Paper–pencil 60-item multiple-choice test involving five ways of responding to interpersonal problems: withdrawal, passivity, cooperation, competition, and aggression. The potential conflict areas covered include Home and Family, Authority Figures, Avocational Contacts, and Work Situations. The Youth Edition is appropriate for individuals ages 10 to 18; the Adult Edition is designed for individuals ages 18 and older. A fifth-grade reading level is required. Suitable for individuals with physical, hearing, or visual impairments.

Format: Self-administered; untimed: 30 to 40 minutes

Scoring: Hand key

Cost: Specimen Set $61.50 each edition

Welsh Figure Preference Test (WFPT)

| 1987 | Mind Garden, Inc. |

George S. Welsh

Population: Ages 6 years to adult

Purpose: Evaluates individual personality traits through figure identification; used for counseling and research

Description: Paper–pencil 400-item nonverbal test measuring an individual's personality traits by evaluating his or her preference for types of black-and-white figures. The subject responds by indicating "likes" or "dislikes" for each figure. Scales include Conformity Male–Female, Neuropsychiatric, Consensus, Origence, Intellectence,

Barron-Welsh Original Art Scale, Revised Art Scale, Repression, Anxiety, Children, Movement, Figure–Ground Reversal, Sex Symbol, and several measuring preferences for specific kinds of geometric figures. All scales need not be scored. The Barron-Welsh Art Scale (86 items) is available separately.

Format: Examiner required; suitable for group use; untimed: 50 minutes

Scoring: Hand key

Cost: Sampler Set $30.00; Permission Set for 200 Uses $150.00

Child

California Q-Sort (Child)

1980	Mind Garden, Inc.

Jeanne Block, Jack Block

Population: Children

Purpose: Describes individual behavior and personality in contemporary psychodynamic terms; used for research in child development

Description: A total of 100 descriptive personality statements are sorted from most to least applicable to the subject. Materials include individual cards.

Format: Examiner required; individual administration; untimed

Scoring: Examiner evaluated

Cost: Sampler Set $30.00; Permission Set for 200 Uses $150.00

Children's Personality Questionnaire (CPQ)

1973	Institute for Personality and Ability Testing, Inc.

Rutherford B. Porter, Raymond B. Cattell

Population: Ages 8 to 12 years

Purpose: Assesses personality development in children; used for clinical evaluations and educational and personal counseling

Description: Paper–pencil 140-item test measuring 14 primary personality traits useful in understanding and evaluating the course of personal, social, and academic development. The traits measured include emotional stability, self-concept level, excitability, and apprehension. Scores for extraversion, anxiety, and other broad trait patterns are obtained as combinations of the primary scales. Norms are available for both genders together and separately. The test is available in four forms: A, B, C, and D. Each form is divided into two parts for scheduling convenience in school settings. A third-grade reading level is required.

Format: Self-administered; untimed 30 to 60 minutes

Scoring: Computer scored; scoring service available

Cost: Hand-Scored Introductory Kit $40.00

Children's Problems Checklist

1985	Psychological Assessment Resources, Inc.

John A. Schinka

Population: Parents of children ages 5 to 12

Purpose: Assesses children's problems as reported by parents or guardians; used as a survey instrument in clinical and counseling settings to initiate the consultation process and to introduce the client to formal diagnostic testing

Description: Paper–pencil 190-item test completed by a parent or guardian and identifying problems in 11 areas: Emotions, Self-Concept, Peers/Play, School, Language/Thinking, Concentration/Organization, Activity Level/Motor Control, Behavior, Values, Habits, and Health. The test is a component of the *Clinical Checklist Series*

Format: Self-administered; untimed: 10 to 20 minutes

Scoring: Examiner evaluated

Cost: 50 Checklists $52.00

Early School Personality Questionnaire (ESPQ)

1966	Institute for Personality and Ability Testing, Inc.

Raymond B. Cattell, Richard W. Coan

Population: Ages 6 to 8 years

Purpose: Provides insights into the needs and predispositions of young children; used for clinical evaluation and educational and personal counseling

Description: Paper–pencil 160-item test measuring personality in children. Questions are read aloud by the administrator (an optional tape recording may be used instead), and the students mark their answers on the answer sheet. To use the answer sheet, children need only be able to discriminate the letters A and B and common objects. Percentiles and standard scores are provided for both genders separately. The test is divided into two equal parts of 80 items each for scheduling convenience.

Format: Examiner required; suitable for group use; untimed: 30 to 50 minutes each part

Scoring: Hand key

Cost: Introductory Kit $37.00

Measure of Child Stimulus Screening (Converse of Arousability)

1978	Albert Mehrabian, PhD

Albert Mehrabian, Carol Falender

Population: Ages 3 months to 7 years

Purpose: Measures major components of a child's arousability and stimulus screening; used for research, counseling, and education program selection purposes

Description: Multiple-item paper–pencil observational inventory measuring parents' descriptions of their children's arousability (responses of one parent are sufficient). Test results indicate the child's characteristic arousal response to complex, unexpected, or unfamiliar situations. Stimulus screening/arousability has been shown to be a major component of many important personality dimensions, such as anxiety, neuroticism, extroversion, or hostility. This test is based on the same conceptual framework used to develop the corresponding adult measure.

Format: Examiner required; suitable for group use; untimed: 10 minutes

Scoring: Hand key

Cost: Test Kit (scale, scoring directions, norms, descriptive material) $33.00 (price for students only)

Mental Status Checklist™–Children

1988	Psychological Assessment Resources, Inc.

Edward H. Dougherty, John A. Schinka

Population: Ages 5 to 12 years

Purpose: Surveys the mental status of children; used to identify problems and to establish rapport in order to prepare individuals for further diagnostic testing; also provides written documentation of presenting problems

Description: This 153-item paper–pencil test covers presenting problems, referral data, demographics, mental status, personality function and symptoms, diagnosis, and disposition.

Format: Self-administered; untimed: 10 to 20 minutes

Scoring: Examiner evaluated

Cost: 25 Checklists $52.00

Personality Inventory for Children–Second Edition (PIC-2)

2001	Western Psychological Services

David Lachar, Christian P. Gruber

Population: Ages 5 to 19 years

Purpose: Evaluates the personality attributes of children and adolescents; used by professionals for counseling and identification of psychopatholgy, developmental problems, and social disabilities

Description: Paper–pencil 275-item true–false inventory completed by one of the child's parents. Provides three Response Validity Scales: Inconsistency, Dissimulation, and Defensiveness and nine content categories: Cognitive Impairment, Impulsivity and Distractibility, Delinquency, Family Dysfunction, Reality Distortion, Somatic Concern, Psychological Discomfort, Social Withdrawal, and Social Skill Deficits. The PCI-2 also offers a Behavioral Summary that is comprised of the first 96 items.

Format: Examiner required; individual administration; untimed: full scale, 45 minutes; summary, 15 minutes

Scoring: Hand key; may be computer scored

Cost: Kit (manual, 2 reusable administration booklets, 50 answer sheets, scoring templates, 25 behavioral AutoScore™ forms, 50 standard profiles, 25 behavioral profiles, 50 critical items summary sheets) $203.50

Adolescent and Adult

Adolescent Dissociative Experiences Scale (A-DES)

	Sidran Foundation

Judith Armstrong, Frank W. Putnam, Eve Bernstein Carlson

Population: Ages 10 to 21 years

Purpose: Measures frequency of dissociative experiences

Description: The scale was developed to provide a reliable, valid, and convenient way to quantify dissociative experiences. A response scale that allows subjects to quantify their experiences for each item was used so that scores could reflect a wider range of dissociative symptomatology than possible using a dichotomous format. This version was developed especially for adolescents.

Format: Self-report; untimed

Scoring: Examiner evaluated

Cost: Packet (manual, 5 protocols, manual, reference list) $12.00

Association Adjustment Inventory (AAI)

1959	Martin M. Bruce, PhD

Martin M. Bruce

Population: Adults

Purpose: Evaluates the extent to which the subject is maladjusted, immature, and deviant in ideation; used as an aid to predicting potential deviant behavior and job tenure

Description: Inventory with 100 items in which the subject matches one of four words with a stimulus word, allowing the examiner to score for ideational deviation, general psychosis, depression, hysteria, withdrawal, paranoia, rigidity, schizophrenia, impulsiveness, psychosomapathia, and anxiety. The scores are compared to norms to measure deviation. Also available in Spanish and German. Suitable for individuals with physical, hearing, or visual impairments.

Format: Self-administered; untimed: 10 minutes

Scoring: Hand key

Cost: Specimen Set $76.50

Balanced Emotional Empathy Scale (BEES)

1996	Albert Mehrabian, PhD

Albert Mehrabian

Population: Ages 14 years and older

Purpose: Assesses emotional empathy (sensitivity) to others; used for research, job placement, and counseling

Description: Paper-pencil 30-item test yielding a single total score. A 10th-grade reading level is required.

Format: Self-administered; untimed: 10 minutes

Scoring: Hand key; test scoring service available

Cost: Test Kit $35.00 (price for students only)

Basic Personality Inventory (BPI)

1997	Sigma Assessment Systems, Inc.

Douglas N. Jackson

Population: Adolescents, adults

Purpose: Identifies personality dimensions indicating personal strengths, as well as psychopathological dimensions; used in psychiatric hospitals, in community mental health centers, and in psychological, psychiatric, and counseling practices

Description: Paper-pencil or computer-administered true-false multiphasic personality inventory used with both normal and clinical populations to identify personal strengths or sources of maladjustment. The test contains 240 items in 11 substantive clinical scales and one critical item scale: Hypochondriasis, Anxiety, Depression, Thinking Disorder, Denial, Impulse Expression, Interpersonal Problems, Social Introversion, Alienation, Self-Depreciation, Persecutory Ideas, and Deviation (critical item scale). The computer version, which operates on PC/AT/XT and compatible systems, yields scores, profiles, and reports.

Format: Examiner required; suitable for group use; untimed: 20 to 45 minutes

Scoring: Hand key, machine scored; scoring service available; computer scored

Cost: Contact publisher

Bell Object Relations and Reality Testing Inventory (BORRTI)

1995	Western Psychological Services

Morris D. Bell

Population: Adults

Purpose: Used by clinicians to evaluate adults with character disorders and psychoses

Description: Composed of 90 items, the inventory measures object relations and reality testing on seven scales: Object Relations (Alienation, Egocentricity, Insecure Attachment, Social Incompetence) and Reality Testing (Reality Distortion, Uncertainty of Perception, Hallucinations and Delusions). The test report profiles scores, describes client characteristics, makes diagnostic suggestions, and provides individualized treatment recommendations. Lists specific clinical themes that apply to the client in question.

Format: Examiner required; individual administration; untimed: 15 to 20 minutes

Scoring: Examiner evaluated; scoring service
available

Cost: Kit (20 AutoScore™ forms, 2 prepaid mail-
in answer sheets, manual) $126.50

Bem Sex-Role Inventory (BSRI)

1978, 1981	Mind Garden, Inc.

Sandra L. Bem

Population: Adults

Purpose: Measures masculinity and femininity;
used for research on psychological androgyny

Description: Paper-pencil 60-item measure of
integration of masculinity and femininity. Items
are three sets of 20 personality characteristics:
masculine, feminine, and neutral. The subject
indicates on a 7-point scale how well each characteristic describes himself or herself. Materials
include a 30-item short form.

Format: Self-administered; untimed: 10 minutes

Scoring: Examiner evaluated

Cost: Sampler Set $30.00; Permission Set for
Up to 200 Uses $150.00

Bloom Sentence Completion
Attitude Survey

1974	Stoelting Company

Wallace Bloom

Population: Adolescents, adults

Purpose: Assesses adult and student attitudes
toward self and important factors in everyday living; used to identify change in an individual over
time and to compare individuals and groups

Description: Paper-pencil 40-item free-response
test consisting of sentence stems that the subject completes in his or her own words. The responses measure attitudes toward age mates or
people, physical self, family, psychological self,
self-directedness, education or work (depending on which version is used), accomplishment,
and irritants. Two versions are available: one for
adults and one for unmarried students. The scoring system facilitates use of the test as both an
objective and a projective instrument.

Format: Examiner required; suitable for group
use; untimed: 25 minutes

Scoring: Examiner evaluated

Cost: Complete Kit (manual, 30 test forms, 30
analysis record forms) specify version $44.00

California Psychological Inventory™–
Third Edition (CPI™)

1987	CPP, Inc.

Harrison G. Gough

Population: Ages 14 years to adult

Purpose: Assesses personality characteristics
important for daily living; used in business, in
schools and colleges, in clinics and counseling
agencies, and for cross-cultural and other research

Description: Paper-pencil 434-item true-false
test measuring behavioral tendencies along 20
scales: Dominance, Capacity for Status, Sociability, Social Presence, Self-Acceptance, Independence, Empathy, Responsibility, Socialization,
Self-Control, Good Impression, Communality,
Well-Being, Tolerance, Achievement via Independence, Achievement via Conformance, Intellectual Efficiency, Psychological-Mindedness,
Flexibility, and Femininity/Masculinity. There are
three vector scales that define a theoretical model
of personality structure and 13 special purpose
scales, such as Managerial Potential, Work Orientation, Creative Temperament, and Anxiety.
Four personality types (Alphas, Betas, Gammas,
and Deltas) are described across seven levels.
Windows-based scoring and mail-in computer
scoring are available. Reports available are the
CPI Profile, CPI Narrative Report, CPI Configural
Analysis Supplement, and Police and Public Safety
Selection Report.

Format: Self-administered; untimed: 45 to
60 minutes

Scoring: Online; scoring service

Cost: Profile Preview Kit (prepaid answer sheet,
item booklet) $20.25; Manual $83.50; Narrative
Report Preview Kit (prepaid answer sheet, item
booklet) $39.00; Configural Analysis Preview Kit
(prepaid answer sheet, item booklet) $47.50

California Q-Sort for Adults

1961	Mind Garden, Inc.

Jack Block

Population: Adults

Purpose: Describes individual personality in
contemporary psychodynamic terms; used for
research

Description: Test used to formulate personality descriptions. Items are 100 descriptive personality statements on cards sorted from most
to least applicable to the subject's experience.
Materials include individual cards and a sorting

guide. Cards may be sorted by professionals or paraprofessionals.

Format: Examiner required; individual administration; untimed

Scoring: Examiner evaluated

Cost: Card Set, Manual $30.00; Duplication Set for 150 Uses $120.00

Carlson Psychological Survey (CPS)

1997	Sigma Assessment Systems, Inc.

Kenneth A. Carlson

Population: Adolescents, adults

Purpose: Assesses and classifies criminal offenders; used to evaluate persons presenting behavioral or substance-abuse problems and to analyze the effects of intervention programs

Description: Paper-pencil 50-item questionnaire in a five-category response format with space for the respondent's comments. The scales measured are Chemical Abuse, Thought Disturbance, Antisocial Tendencies, Self-Depreciation, and Validity. The test is designed for offenders, those charged with crimes, and others who have come to the attention of the criminal justice or social welfare systems. The results are classified into 18 offender types. A companion edition, the Psicologico Texto (PT), is designed for use with Spanish-literate offenders. A fourth-grade reading level is required. Also available in French.

Format: Examiner required; suitable for group use; untimed: 15 minutes

Scoring: Hand key; computer scored; scoring service available

Cost: Contact publisher

College Adjustment Scales (CAS)

1991	Psychological Assessment Resources, Inc.

William D. Anton, James R. Reed

Population: Ages 17 to 30 years

Purpose: Used by college counselors to identify psychological adjustment problems experienced by college students

Description: Paper-pencil 108-item 4-point Likert scale measuring anxiety, depression, suicidal ideation, substance abuse, self-esteem problems, interpersonal problems, family problems, academic problems, and career problems. A fifth-grade reading level is required.

Format: Individual administration; suitable for group use; examiner required; untimed

Scoring: Hand scored

Cost: Introductory Kit (manual, 25 reusable item booklets, 25 answer sheets) $132.00

Coping Operations Preference Enquiry (COPE)

1962	Mind Garden, Inc.

Will Schutz

Population: Adults

Purpose: Measures individual preference for certain types of coping or defense mechanisms; used for counseling and therapy

Description: Paper-pencil 6-item test measuring the characteristic use of five defense mechanisms: Denial, Isolation, Projection, Regression-Dependency, and Turning-Against-the-Self. Each item describes a person and his or her behavior in a particular situation. The respondent rank-orders five alternative ways he or she might feel; the alternatives represent the inventory's five coping mechanisms. Materials include separate forms for men and women.

Format: Examiner recommended; may be self-administered; suitable for group use; untimed

Scoring: Examiner evaluated

Cost: Sampler Set $30.00; Permission for Up to 200 Uses $150.00

Dissociative Experiences Scale (DES)

Date not provided	Sidran Foundation

Eve Bernstein Carlson, Frank W. Putnam

Population: Adults

Purpose: Measures frequency of dissociative experiences

Description: The scale was developed to provide a reliable, valid, and convenient way to quantify dissociative experiences. A response scale that allows subjects to quantify their experiences for each item was used so that scores could reflect a wider range of dissociative symptomatology than possible using a dichotomous format. The DES has been translated into over 20 languages other than English.

Format: Self-report; untimed

Scoring: Examiner evaluated

Cost: Packet (manual, 5 protocols, reference list) $12.00

Dissociative Features Profile (DFP)

Date not provided	Sidran Foundation

Joyanna Silberg

Population: Children, adolescents

Purpose: Identifies dissociative pathology

Description: The DFP was developed to be used with a typical psychological testing battery. The DFP may be used if at least two measures were administered.

Format: Examiner required to analyze testing information; untimed

Scoring: Examiner evaluated

Cost: Packet (manual, 5 protocols, reference list) $12.00

Dynamic Factors Survey

1993	Mind Garden, Inc.

J. P. Guilford, Paul R. Christensen, Nicholas A. Bond, Jr.

Population: Adolescents, adults

Purpose: Measures general motivational factors

Description: Used in personality and interest research, personnel selection, and vocational assessment, this 300-item inventory measures general motivational factors such as Need for Freedom, Cultural Conformity, Need for Precision, Need for Attention, Realistic Thinking, Need for Diversion, Adventure, and Security, Liking for Thinking, Self Reliance vs. Dependence, and Aesthetic Appreciation.

Format: Self-administered; untimed

Scoring: Hand key

Cost: Sampler Set $30.00; Permission Set for 200 Uses $150.00

Educational Values (VAL-ED)

1977	Mind Garden, Inc.

Will Schutz

Population: Adults

Purpose: Assesses an individual's attitudes toward education; used to evaluate the working relationships of students, teachers, administrators, and community members

Description: Multiple-item paper–pencil survey of values regarding interpersonal relationships in school settings. The factors included relate to inclusion, control, and affection at both the feeling and the behavioral levels and to the purpose and importance of education.

Format: Self-administered; untimed

Scoring: Examiner evaluated

Cost: Sampler Set $30.00; Permission Set for 200 Uses $150.00

Edwards Personal Preference Schedule (EPPS)

1959	Harcourt Assessment, Inc.

A. L. Edwards

Population: Ages 18 years and older

Purpose: Assesses an individual's personality

Description: Paper–pencil forced-choice test designed to show the relative importance of 15 needs and motives: Achievement, Deference, Order, Exhibition, Autonomy, Affiliation, Intraception, Succorance, Dominance, Abasement, Nurturance, Change, Endurance, Sexuality, and Aggression.

Format: Self-administered; untimed: 45 minutes

Scoring: Hand key; machine scoring

Cost: Examination Kit (manual, schedule booklet, hand-scorable answer sheet, machine-scored answer sheets) $56.00

Employee Assistance Program Inventory (EAPI)

1994	Psychological Assessment Resources, Inc.

William D. Anton, James R. Reed

Population: Adults

Purpose: Used in employee assistance programs and counseling to screen for identification of common psychological problems in 10 areas

Description: Four-point scale inventory with 120 items on the following 10 scales: Anxiety, Depression, Self-Esteem Problems, Marital Problems, Family Problems, External Stressors, Interpersonal Conflict, Work Adjustment, Problem Minimization, and Effects of Substance Abuse. A third-grade reading level is required.

Format: Self-administered; untimed

Scoring: Hand-scorable answer sheet

Cost: Introductory Kit (manual, 25 reusable item booklets, 25 answer profile sheets) $124.00

Friedman Well-Being Scale

1994	Mind Garden, Inc.

Philip Friedman

Population: Adults

Purpose: Can easily be used to track changes over time during psychotherapy or during other intervention modalities

Description: Consists of 20 bipopular adjectives. It is easy to administer, score, and interpret. It can be scored for an overall measure of well-being and for five subscales: Emotional Stability, Self-Esteem/Self-Confidence, Joviality, Sociability, and Happiness. Norms exist for a clinical, college, and community population, It correlates significantly in the expected directions with over 100 clinical, personality, attitudinal, stress, relational, marital, and interpersonal scales and subscales. It can easily be used to track changes and serves as an excellent outcome measure of change in the current health-care environment.

Format: Examiner or self-administered; untimed: 5 to 10 minutes

Scoring: Examiner evaluated

Cost: Sampler Set $30.00; Permission Set for 200 Uses $150.00

Fundamental Interpersonal Relations Orientation–Behavior® (FIRO-B®)

1989	CPP, Inc.

Will Schutz, Marilyn Wood

Population: Ages 13 years and older

Purpose: Measures characteristic behavior of children toward other people; used for counseling and therapy

Description: Paper–pencil 54-item test containing six Guttman-type scales measuring the characteristic behavior of children in the areas of Inclusion, Control, and Affection—the three dimensions of interpersonal behavior described by the author in his book *The Interpersonal Underworld*. The test measures the relative strength of the needs within the individual. Because it does not compare a person with a population, norms are not provided.

Format: Self-administered; untimed; 15 minutes

Scoring: Self-scored

Cost: Self-Scorable Preview Kit (booklet/answer sheet, introduction, explanation) $29.25

Fundamental Interpersonal Relations Orientation–Feelings® (FIRO-F®)

1989	CPP, Inc.

Will Schutz

Population: Adults

Purpose: Evaluates an individual's characteristic feelings toward others; used to assess both individual and interactional traits as an aid to counseling and therapy

Description: Paper–pencil 54-item test measuring six dimensions of an individual's feelings toward others: Expressed Significance, Expressed Competence, Expressed Lovability, Wanted Significance, Wanted Competence, and Wanted Lovability. Dimensions parallel the three dimensions of the FIRO-B. The FIRO-F is identical to the FIRO-B except that the questions are phrased to assess feelings rather than behaviors.

Format: Self-administered; untimed: 15 minutes

Scoring: Hand key

Cost: 25 Test Booklets $43.40; Scoring Key $61.60

Group Embedded Figures Test (GEFT)

2002	Mind Garden, Inc.

Herman A. Witkin, Philip K. Oltman, Evelyn Raskin, Stephen A. Karp

Population: Adolescents, adults

Purpose: Measures field dependence independence

Description: Test takers find common geometric shapes in a larger design. This simple assessment yields a wealth of information about field dependence–independence. The GEFT was developed for research into cognitive functioning, but it has become a recognized tool for exploring analytical ability, social behavior, body concept, preferred defense mechanism, and problem-solving style, as well as other areas. The GEFT is a 25-item assessment contained in a 32-page non-reusable booklet.

Format: Examiner required; suitable for group administration; timed: 12 minutes

Scoring: Examiner evaluated

Cost: Manual and Sampler Set $40.00; Package of 25 Booklets $50.00

Guilford-Zimmerman Temperament Survey (GZTS)

1978	CPP, Inc.

J. P. Guilford, Wayne S. Zimmerman

Population: Adults

Purpose: Identify nonclinical personality and temperament; can be used for crisis intervention, assertiveness training, and desensitization

Description: Records orientation on 10 scales (General Activity, Restraint, Ascendancy, Sociability, Emotional Stability, Objectivity, Friendliness, Thoughtfulness, Personal Relations, and Masculinity/Femininity) to identify positive and negative temperament.

Format: Individual administration; 45 minutes

Scoring: Hand key; scoring service

Cost: Preview Kit (manual, booklet, answer sheet) $52.00

Hassles and Uplifts Scale (HSUP)

1989   Mind Garden, Inc.

Richard S. Lazarus, Susan Folkman

Population: Adults

Purpose: Measures respondents' attitudes about daily situations; used in counseling and in clinical settings

Description: Likert scale measuring the frequency and severity of hassles and the frequency and intensity of uplifts. An eighth-grade reading level is required.

Format: Self-administered; untimed: 30 minutes

Scoring: Examiner evaluated

Cost: Sampler Set $30.00; Permission Set for 200 Uses $150.00

Health and Daily Living Form (HDL)

1990   Mind Garden, Inc.

Rudolph H. Moos, Ruth C. Cronkite, John W. Finney

Population: Adolescents, adults

Purpose: Assesses health-related factors, life stressors, social functioning, and resources; used by health psychologists and clinicians

Description: A structured yes–no test for patient and community groups. An eighth-grade reading level is required.

Format: Examiner required; individual administration; untimed

Scoring: Examiner evaluated

Cost: Sampler Set $30.00; Permission Set for 200 uses $150.00

Hilson Adolescent Profile (HAP)

1984   Institute for Personality and Ability Testing, Inc.

Robin E. Inwald

Population: Ages 10 to 18 years

Purpose: Identifies and predicts troubled and/or delinquent behavior in adolescents

Description: Behaviorally oriented 310-item paper-pencil true-false test consisting of a validity measure and 15 scales assessing specific external behaviors, attitudes and temperament, interpersonal adjustment measures, and internalized conflict measures: Guardedness, Alcohol/Drugs,

Educational Adjustment Difficulties, Law/Society Violations, Frustration Tolerance, Antisocial/Risk-Taking Attitudes, Rigidity/Obsessiveness, Interpersonal/Assertiveness Difficulties, Homelife Conflicts, Social/Sexual Adjustment, Health Concerns, Anxiety/Phobic Avoidance, Depression/Suicide Potential, Suspicious Temperament, and Unusual Responses. Raw scores and three sets of *t*-scores are provided for each scale. The *t*-scores are based on juvenile offender norms, clinical inpatient norms, and student norms. A fifth- to sixth-grade reading level is required. Also available in Spanish.

Format: Self-administered; untimed: 30 to 45 minutes

Scoring: Computer scored; scoring service available; online scoring available

Cost: $16.00 to $20.00 depending on scoring method

Hirsch Opinions about Psychological & Emotional Disorders in Children (HOPE)

1995   Joseph A. Hirsch, PhD, PsyD

Joseph A. Hirsch

Population: Adults

Purpose: Measures attitudes toward mental illness in children; used for adoption, daycare, teachers, pediatricians, and others who may work with children

Description: Paper–pencil 42-item survey using a Likert scale that measures two factors: Biases and Dynamic/Clinical. The Dynamic/Clinical assesses treatment efficacy and psychodynamic etiology. Scaled scores are provided for each factor, with separate norms for special populations. Requires a sixth-grade reading level.

Format: Examiner required; individual or group administration; untimed

Scoring: Examiner scoring and interpretation

Cost: 50 Surveys $100.00

Impact Message Inventory–Circumplex (IMI-C)

1991   Mind Garden, Inc.

Donald J. Kiesler, James A. Schmidt

Population: Adolescents, adults

Purpose: Measures the affective, behavioral, and cognitive reactions of one individual to another; helpful in clarifying interpersonal transactions in any dyad, including teacher–student, friends, employer–employee, and therapist–client

Description: Measures a target person's interpersonal behavior. It was constructed on the assumption that the interpersonal or evoking behavior of one person (A) can be validly defined and measured by assessing the covert responses or "impact messages" of another person (B) who has interacted with or observed A. Eight interpersonal styles are measured in a 4-point Likert format.

Format: Self-administered; untimed: 15 minutes

Scoring: Examiner evaluated

Cost: Sampler Set $30.00; Permission Set for 200 Uses $150.00

Interpersonal Adjective Scales (IAS)

1995	Psychological Assessment Resources, Inc.

Jerry S. Wiggins

Population: College students and other adults

Purpose: Used in personality assessment to measure the two most important dimensions of interpersonal behavior: dominance and nurturance

Description: Paper–pencil 64-item 8-point scale with the following categories: Cold Hearted, Aloof-Introverted, Unassured Submissive, Unassuming-Ingenious, Warm–Agreeable, Gregarious-Extroverted. A 10th-grade reading level is required. Examiner must be B-level qualified. A computer version using PC-compatible computers is available. Also available in Spanish.

Format: Self-administered; untimed: 15 minutes

Scoring: Hand score, computer scoring available

Cost: Introductory Kit (manual, test booklet, scoring booklet) $118.00

Interpersonal Style Inventory (ISI)

1985	Western Psychological Services

Maurice Lorr, Richard P. Youniss

Population: Ages 14 years and older

Purpose: Assesses an individual's manner of interacting with other people and style of impulse control. Used for self-understanding, counseling and therapy, personnel guidance, and research.

Description: Paper–pencil 300-item true–false inventory assessing an individual's style of interpersonal interactions along 15 primary scales: Directive, Sociable, Help-Seeking, Nurturant, Conscientious, Trusting, Tolerant, Sensitive, Deliber-

ate, Independent, Rule Free, Orderly, Persistent, Stable, and Approval Seeking. Each item is a statement describing ways in which people relate and respond to each other. The individual reads each statement and decides whether it is mostly true or not true for himself or herself. High school and college norms are provided by gender. The computer report includes a full-color WPS ChromaGraph profile of major scores.

Format: Self-administered; untimed: 30 minutes

Scoring: Computer scored

Cost: Test Kit (2 reusable administration booklets; 20 AutoScore™ forms) $99.00

Inventory of Altered Self-Capacities (IASC)

2000	Psychological Assessment Resources, Inc.

John Briere

Population: Ages 18 years and older

Purpose: Assess difficulties in relatedness, identity, and affect control

Description: The IASC is a 63-item self-report with seven scales with nine items each. Two of those scales have subscales.

Format: Self-administered; untimed: 10 to 15 minutes

Scoring: Examiner evaluated

Cost: Introductory Kit (manual, 25 reusable item booklets, 25 hand-scorable answer sheets, 50 profile forms) $180.00

Jackson Personality Inventory Revised (JPI-R)

1997	Sigma Assessment Systems, Inc.

Douglas N. Jackson

Population: Adolescents, adults

Purpose: Assesses personality characteristics of normal people who have average and above-average intelligence; used to evaluate behavior in a wide range of settings, including those involving work, education, organizations, interpersonal, and performance

Description: Paper–pencil 300-item true–false test covering 15 substantive scales and one validity scale. The scales measured are Complexity, Breadth of Interest, Innovation, Tolerance, Empathy, Anxiety, Cooperativeness, Sociability, Social Confidence, Energy Level, Social Astuteness, Risk Taking, Organization, Traditional Values, and Responsibility. To hand-score the test, materials needed include a manual, a reusable test booklet, a quick-scoring answer sheet, and a profile sheet; no template is required. Norms include updated college norms and new norms for blue- and white-collar workers. This test differs from the *Personality Research Form* (PRF) in terms of the nature of the variables measured and is a further refinement of substantive psychometric and computer-based strategies for scale development. Machine-readable answer sheets may be mailed to the publisher for a computer-generated report. Test booklets are also available in French.

Format: Examiner required; suitable for group use; untimed: 45 minutes

Scoring: Hand key; computer scored; scoring service available

Cost: Contact publisher

Make a Picture Story (MAPS)

1947	Western Psychological Services

Edwin S. Shneidman

Population: Adolescents, adults

Purpose: Measures fantasies, defenses, and impulses

Description: Projective oral-response test consisting of 22 stimulus cards and a set of 67 cut-out figures. Stimulus cards range from structured situations (bedroom, bathroom, schoolroom, baby's room) to more ambiguous presentations (a blank doorway, a cave, and a totally blank card). Figures include men, women, boys, girls, police officers, mythical characters, animals, people with disabilities, nudes, and a variety of frequently encountered individuals. The examiner asks the patient to select a stimulus card, place figures on the background stimulus card, and tell a story explaining those choices. He or she may also be asked to act out a story about the figures and their environment. The Location Sheet is used to record the placement of the figures on the stimulus card.

Format: Examiner required; individual administration; untimed

Scoring: Examiner evaluated

Cost: Kit (set of test materials, manual, 25 Location Sheets) 104.50

Mathematics Self-Efficacy Scale (MATHS)

1993	Mind Garden, Inc.

Nancy Betz, Gail Hacket

Population: Adults

Purpose: Measures degree of confidence in their ability to perform certain math tasks

Description: This scale is intended to measure beliefs regarding ability to perform various math-related tasks and behaviors. Subjects are asked to indicate their degree of confidence in their ability to perform the math task on a scale ranging from *not at all difficult* to *extremely difficult.*

Format: Examiner required; individual or group administration; untimed: 15 minutes

Scoring: Examiner evaluated

Cost: Sampler Set $30.00; Permission Set for 200 Uses $150.00

Measure of Achieving Tendency

1994	Albert Mehrabian, PhD

Albert Mehrabian

Population: Adults

Purpose: Assesses an individual's motivation to achieve; used for research, counseling, and employee selection and placement purposes

Description: Multiple-item verbal questionnaire assessing all major components of achievement. Test items are based on extensive factor-analytic investigation of most experimentally identified components of achievement.

Format: Self-administered; untimed: 10 minutes

Scoring: Hand key

Cost: Test Kit (scales, scoring directions, norms, test manual) $33.00 (price for students only)

Measure of Arousal Seeking Tendency

1994	Albert Mehrabian, PhD

Albert Mehrabian

Population: Adults

Purpose: Assesses an individual's desire for change, stimulation, and arousal; used for research, job placement, and counseling purposes

Description: Multiple-item verbal questionnaire measuring an individual's arousal-seeking tendencies. Test items are based on extensive factor-analytic and experimental studies of all aspects of change-seeking, sensation-seeking, variety-seeking, and, generally, desire to master high-uncertainty situations.

Format: Self-administered; untimed: 10 minutes

Scoring: Hand key

Cost: Test Kit (scale, scoring directions, norms, descriptive material) $33.00 (price for students only)

Measures of Affiliative Tendency and Sensitivity to Rejection

1994	Albert Mehrabian, PhD

Albert Mehrabian

Population: Adults

Purpose: Assesses an individual's friendliness, sociability, and general interpersonal and social approach–avoidance characteristics; used for research and counseling purposes

Description: Multiple-item verbal questionnaire consisting of two subscales: Affiliative Tendency and Sensitivity to Rejection. The standardized sum of the scores on both subscales also provides a reliable and valid measure of dependency.

Format: Self-administered; untimed: 10 minutes

Scoring: Hand key

Cost: Test Kit (scales, scoring directions, norms, descriptive material) $33.00 (price for students only)

Measures of Psychosocial Development (MPD)

1988	Psychological Assessment Resources, Inc.

Gwen A. Hawley

Population: Ages 13 years and older

Purpose: Provides an index of overall psychosocial health and personality development through the eight stages of the lifespan based on Erik Erikson's criteria

Description: Paper–pencil 112-item multiple-choice test that provides a measure of the positive and negative attitudes or attributes of personality associated with each developmental stage, the status of conflict resolution at each stage, and overall psychosocial health. The items are rated on a 5-point scale ranging from *very much like me* to *not at all like me*. Results are reported as *t*-scores or percentiles and can be plotted on profile forms, which are available separately for males and females by age groups from 13 to 50+ years. Interpretation of the MPD is consistent with Erikson's focus on healthy personality development and growth, rather than a pathology-oriented focus. A sixth-grade reading level is required.

Format: Examiner required; suitable for group use; untimed: 15 to 20 minutes

Scoring: Hand key

Cost: Introductory Kit (manual, 25 reusable item booklets, 50 answer sheets, 25 each male and female profile forms) $160.00

Memories of Father (MOF)

1993	Arnold R. Bruhn and Associates

Arnold R. Bruhn

Population: Adults

Purpose: Designed for individuals who have experienced a conflicted relationship

Description: A structured method of exploring the relationship and lifetime with father (or a paternal surrogate), based on the individual's memories of this relationship. It is recommended for individuals who have experienced a conflicted relationship with their father for some period in their lives and suspect that patterns arising from that relationship may be affecting their lives now.

Format: Examiner required; individual or group administration; untimed

Scoring: Examiner evaluated

Cost: 25 Tests $140.00

Memories of Mother (MOM)

1993	Arnold R. Bruhn and Associates

Arnold R. Bruhn

Population: Adults

Purpose: Designed for individuals who have experienced a conflicted relationship

Description: A structured method of exploring the relationship and lifetime with mother (or a maternal surrogate), based on the individual's memories of this relationship. It is recommended for individuals who have experienced a conflicted relationship with their mother for some period in their lives and suspect that patterns arising from that relationship may be affecting their lives now.

Format: Examiner required; individual or group administration; untimed

Scoring: Examiner evaluated

Cost: 25 Tests $140.00

Mental Status Checklist™–Adolescent

1988	Psychological Assessment Resources, Inc.

Edward H. Dougherty, John A. Schinka

Population: Ages 13 to 17 years

Purpose: Surveys the mental status of adolescents; used to identify problems and establish rapport in order to prepare individuals for further diagnostic testing; provides written documentation of presenting problems

Description: This 174-item paper–pencil checklist covers presenting problems, referral data, demographics, mental status, personality function and symptoms, diagnosis, and disposition.

Format: Self-administered; untimed: 10 to 20 minutes

Scoring: Examiner evaluated

Cost: 25 Checklists $52.00

Mental Status Checklist™–Adult

1988	Psychological Assessment Resources, Inc.

John A. Schinka

Population: Adults

Purpose: Surveys the mental status of adults; used to identify problems and to establish rapport in order to prepare individuals for further diagnostic testing; also provides written documentation of presenting problems

Description: Paper–pencil 174-item checklist covering presenting problems, referral data, demographics, mental status, personality function and symptoms, diagnosis, and disposition.

Format: Self-administered; untimed: 10 to 20 minutes

Scoring: Examiner evaluated

Cost: 25 Checklists $52.00

Millon Adolescent Personality Inventory (MAPI)

1982	Pearson Assessments

Theodore Millon, Catherine J. Green, Robert B. Meagher, Jr.

Population: Ages 13 to 18 years

Purpose: Evaluates adolescent personality; used as an aid to clinical assessment and academic and vocational guidance; identifies student behavioral and emotional problems

Description: True–false test with 150-items covering eight personality style scales, eight expressed concern scales (such as peer security), and four behavioral correlates scales (such as impulse control). The clinical version is coordinated with DSM-III-R and is available to those with experience in the use of self-administered clinical tests.

Format: Examiner required; suitable for group use; untimed: 20 to 30 minutes

Scoring: Computer scored; scoring service

Cost: Starter Kit with Interpretative Report (manual, test booklet, 3 mail-in answer sheets) $110.00

Millon Index of Personality Styles– Revised (MIPS® Revised)

2003	Pearson Assessments

Theodore Millon

Population: Ages 18 years and older

Purpose: Assesses normal-range personality

Description: The MIPS Revised instrument addresses three key dimensions of normal personalities: Motivating Styles (helps to assess the person's emotional style in dealing with his or her environment); Thinking Styles (helps to examine the person's mode of cognitive processing); and Behaving Styles (helps to assess the person's way of interrelating with others).

Format: Self-administered; can be administered on computer or online; untimed: 30 minutes

Scoring: Hand key; computer scoring; scoring service; online

Cost: Starter Kit (manual, 10 test booklets, 50 answer sheets, answer keys) $163.00

Minnesota Multiphasic Personality Inventory–Adolescent™ (MMPI-A™)

1992	Pearson Assessments

James N. Butcher, Carolyn L. Williams, John R. Graham, Robert P. Archer, Auke Tellegen, Yossef S. Ben-Porath, Beverly Kaemmer

Population: Ages 14 to 18 years

Purpose: Assists with the diagnosis of mental disorders and the selection of appropriate treatment methods

Description: The MMPI-A provides descriptive and diagnostic information pertinent to today's patients and clients. In addition, tailored reports present interpretive information for specific settings and applications to help meet a wide range of needs. The normative sample is nationally representative, consisting of 805 males and 815 females. Uniform *t*-scores are provided for eight of the clinical scales and the content scales, ensuring percentile equivalency across scales. New validity scales were developed to help refine the clinician's assessment of test-taking attitudes. The test is written at a sixth-grade reading level. Also available in Spanish.

Format: Self-administration; online administration; untimed: 60 to 90 minutes

Scoring: Hand key; software scoring available; scoring service available

Cost: Hand-Scoring Starter Kit (manual, 10 test

booklets, 50 each of answer and profile forms, answer key sets) $500.00

Minnesota Multiphasic Personality Inventory–Second Edition™ (MMPI-2™)

| 2001 | Pearson Assessments |

J. N. Butcher, W. G. Dahlstrom, J. R. Graham, A. Tellegen, B. Kaemmer

Population: Adults

Purpose: Assists with the diagnosis of mental disorders and the selection of appropriate treatment methods

Description: The MMPI-2 provides descriptive and diagnostic information pertinent to today's patients and clients. In addition, tailored reports present interpretive information for specific settings and applications to help meet a wide range of needs. The normative sample is nationally representative, consisting of 1,138 males and 1,462 females between the ages of 18 and 80. Uniform *t*-scores were developed because percentiles for the traditional linear *t*-scores are not strictly comparable from scale to scale. Written at a sixth grade reading level.

Format: Self-administration; online administration; untimed: 60 to 90 minutes

Scoring: Hand key, software scoring available, scoring service available

Cost: Starter Kit with Interpretative Report (manual, user's guide, 3 answer sheets) $165.00

Mooney Problem Check Lists

| 1950 | Harcourt Assessment, Inc. |

R. L. Mooney, L. V. Gordon

Population: Grades 7 and above

Purpose: Identifies individuals who want or need help with personal problems; used for individual counseling, increasing teacher understanding of students, and preparing students for counseling interviews

Description: Multiple-item paper–pencil self-assessment of personal problems. The subjects read examples of problems, underline those of some concern, circle those of most concern, and write a summary in their own words. The areas covered vary from form to form but include Health and Physical Development, Home and Family, Boy and Girl Relations, Morals and Religion, Courtship and Marriage, Economic Security, School or Occupation, and Social and Recreational. Materials include separate checklists for junior high students, high school students, college students, and adults.

Format: Self-administered; untimed: 30 minutes

Scoring: Hand key; may be machine scored

Cost: Examination Kit (checklist and manual) $15.00 per level

Myers-Briggs Type Indicator® (MBTI®)

| 1998 | CPP, Inc. |

Isabel Briggs Myers, Katharine C. Briggs

Population: Ages 14 years to adult

Purpose: Measures personality dispositions and interests based on Jung's theory of types; used in executive development programs, educational settings, personality research, and personal, vocational, and marital counseling

Description: Form M self-scorable has 93 items in a combined item booklet and answer sheet format with easy to understand interpretative information. The inventory is at the seventh-grade reading level. Other available reports are Profile, Interpretive, Organizational, Team, Work Styles, and Career. Form Q provides results graphically in four pages with the client's Step I four-letter type along with the results of the 20 Step II facet results. Includes an interpreter's summary.

Format: Self-administered; untimed: 15 to 25 minutes

Scoring: Self-scored; scoring service; online; hand score

Cost: Self-Score Preview Kit (form, explanation) $19.75; other reports vary

NEO Five-Factor Inventory (NEO-FFI)

| 1989 | Psychological Assessment Resources, Inc. |

Paul T. Costa, Jr., Robert R. McCrae

Population: Ages 17 years and older

Purpose: Assesses the five major personality domains; used in clinical psychology, psychiatry, behavioral medicine, vocational counseling, and industrial psychology

Description: Paper–pencil 60-item multiple-choice test providing a general description of an adult's personality. The NEO-FFI is a shortened version of the *NEO Personality Inventory–Revised*. Domains assessed are Neuroticism, Extraversion, Openness to Experience, Agreeableness, and Conscientiousness. The NEO-FFI is based on NEO-PI-R™ normative data and is interpreted in the same manner. Correlations with NEO-PI-R validimax factors range from .75 to .89. Examiner must meet APA Level B guidelines.

Format: Examiner required; suitable for group use; untimed

Scoring: Hand key

Cost: Kit (manual, 25 summary sheets, 25 test booklets) $140.00

NEO Personality Inventory–Revised (NEO-PI-R™)

| 1992 | Psychological Assessment Resources, Inc. |

Paul T. Costa, Jr., Robert R. McCrae

Population: Adults

Purpose: Measures five major personality domains of adults; used in clinical psychology, psychiatry, behavioral medicine, vocational counseling, and industrial psychology

Description: Paper–pencil 240-item test providing a general description of an adult's personality. Domains assessed are Neuroticism (N), Extraversion (E), Openness to Experience (O), Agreeableness (A), and Conscientiousness (C). Facet scales for all domains yield a more detailed analysis of personality structure. Domain N scales are Anxiety, Angry Hostility, Depression, Self-Consciousness, Impulsiveness, and Vulnerability. Domain E scales are Warmth, Gregariousness, Assertiveness, Activity, Excitement-Seeking, and Positive Emotions. Domain O scales are Fantasy, Aesthetics, Feelings, Actions, Ideas, and Values. Domain A facets are Trust, Straightforwardness, Altruism, Compliance, Modesty, and Tender-Mindedness. Domain C facets are Competence, Order, Dutifulness, Achievement Striving, Self-Discipline, and Deliberation. Two versions (self and other rating) of the inventory are available. Form S and Form R are appropriate for men and women. Answers are provided on a 5-point scale. Also available in French from the Institute of Psychological Research, Inc.

Format: Self-administered; untimed: 30 minutes

Scoring: Examiner evaluated; may be computer scored; scoring service available

Cost: Comprehensive Kit (manual, 10 each of reusable booklets, 25 each of hand-scorable answer sheets, 25 feedback sheets) $255.00

Offer Self-Image Questionnaire for Adolescents–Revised (OSIQ-R)

| 1992 | Western Psychological Services |

D. Offer, E. Ostrov, K. I. Howard, S. Dolan

Population: Ages 13 to 19 years

Purpose: Used to measure adjustment and self-image in adolescents

Description: Composed of 129 simple statements, the questionnaire measures adjustment in 12 areas—Impulse Control, Emotional Tone, Body Image, Social Functioning, Self-Reliance, Sexuality, Family Functioning, Self-Confidence, Vocational Attitudes, Ethical Values, Mental Health, and Idealism—using a 6-point response scale. The OSIQ-R yields conventional t-scores and validity checks.

Format: Examiner required; individual administration; untimed: 30 minutes

Scoring: Examiner evaluated; computer scored; scoring service available

Cost: Kit (manual, 2 reusable administration booklets, 5 test report prepaid mail-in answer sheets) $109.50

Personal Styles Inventory (PSI-120)

| 1999 | Educational & Psychological Consultants, Inc. |

Joseph T. Kunce, Corrine S. Cope, Russel M. Newton

Population: Ages 16 and older

Purpose: Measures dual aspects of personal styles; used for counseling

Description: Contains 120 items in terms of everyday, nonpathological behaviors. The findings relate to everyday behavior. Discrepancies between scores for basic and current behavior indicate level of stress. Twenty-four personal styles (eight each) for Emotion, Action, and Thinking. Provides six different types of reports for each scoring. Requires an eighth-grade reading level. Also available in Spanish. May be completed online.

Format: Self-administered; untimed: 25 to 30 minutes

Scoring: Computer scoring; online scoring

Cost: $150.00 for 25 administrations

Personality Assessment Inventory (PAI)

| 1991 | Psychological Assessment Resources, Inc. |

Leslie C. Morey

Population: Ages 18 years and older

Purpose: Used in forensic psychology and personality assessment to assess adult psychopathology

Description: Paper–pencil 4-point Likert scale with 344 items; four Validity Scales: Inconsistency, Infrequency, Negative Impression, and Positive Impression; 11 Clinical Scales and Subscales: Somatic Complaints, Anxiety, Anxiety-Related Disorders, Depression, Mania, Paranoia, Schizophrenia, Borderline Features, Antisocial Features, Alcohol Problems, Drug Problems; five Treatment Scales: Aggression, Suicidal Ideation, Stress, Nonsupport, and Treatment Rejection; and two Interpersonal Scales: Dominance and Warmth. A fourth-grade reading level is required. A computer version using PC is available. A Spanish version is also available.

Format: Examiner required; individual administration; untimed: 50 to 60 minutes

Scoring: Hand key; computer scoring available

Cost: Comprehensive Kit (manual, 2 reusable item books, 25 hand-scorable answer sheets, 25 profile forms, 25 critical items forms) $260.00

Personality Research Form (PRF)

1997	Sigma Assessment Systems, Inc.

Douglas N. Jackson

Population: Grades 6 and above

Purpose: Assesses personality traits relevant to the functioning of an individual in a variety of situations, used in self-improvement courses and guidance centers and for personnel selection

Description: True–false paper–pencil or computer-administered test in five forms. Forms AA and BB contain 440 items covering 22 areas of normal functioning. Form E has 352 items in 22 scales. Forms A and B have 300 items in 15 scales. The 22 scales measured are Abasement, Achievement, Affiliation, Aggression, Autonomy, Change, Cognitive Structure, Defendance, Dominance, Endurance, Exhibition, Harm–Avoidance, Impulsivity, Nurturance, Order, Play, Sentience, Social Recognition, Succorance, Understanding, Infrequency, and Desirability. A 90-minute cassette tape with simplified wording is available for use with those who have limited verbal skills or sight or reading problems. Materials include a manual, reusable test booklet, answer sheets, profiles, and a scoring template. The computer version operates on PC-compatible systems. Form E is also available in French and Spanish.

Format: Suitable for group use; Form E, 1 hour; Forms A and B, 45 minutes; Forms AA and BB, 1 hour, 15 minutes; audiocassette, 90 minutes

Scoring: Hand key; computer scored; scoring service available

Cost: Contact publisher

Polyfactorial Study of Personality

1959	Martin M. Bruce, PhD

Ronald Stark

Population: Adults

Purpose: Aids in the clinical evaluation of an individual's personality

Description: Paper–pencil 300-item true–false test measuring 11 aspects of psychopathology: Hypochondriasis, Sexual Identification, Anxiety, Social Distance, Sociopathy, Depression, Compulsivity, Repression, Paranoia, Schizophrenia, and Hyperaffectivity. Suitable for individuals with physical, hearing, or visual impairments.

Format: Self-administered; untimed: 45 minutes

Scoring: Hand key

Cost: Specimen Set $54.50

Problem Behavior Inventory– Adolescent Symptom Screening Form

Date not provided	Western Psychological Services

Leigh Silverton

Population: Adolescents

Purpose: Helps clinicians structure and focus diagnostic interviews

Description: This inventory lists more than 100 DSM-IV-R-related symptoms in clear, simple language. The adolescent checks those symptoms that he or she has experienced. This inventory identifies areas where personality testing might be helpful.

Format: Self-administered; untimed: 10 to 15 minutes

Scoring: Hand key

Cost: Package of 25 AutoScore™ Forms $42.50

Problem Behavior Inventory– Adult Symptom Screening Form

Date not provided	Western Psychological Services

Leigh Silverton

Population: Adults

Purpose: Helps clinicians structure and focus diagnostic interviews

Description: This inventory lists more than 100 DSM-III-R-related symptoms in clear, simple language. The client checks those symptoms that he or she has experienced. This inventory guides the initial interview, provides material for the intake report, and identifies areas in which personality testing might be helpful.

Format: Self-administered; untimed: 10 to 15 minutes

Scoring: Hand key

Cost: Package of 25 AutoScore™ Forms $42.50

Problem Experiences Checklist– Adolescent Version

Date not provided	Western Psychological Services

Leigh Silverton

Population: Adolescents

Purpose: Checklist used to pinpoint problems and to identify areas for discussion prior to the initial clinician interview

Description: This checklist gives the clinician a quick picture of the adolescent's life situation, indicating what kind of difficulties he or she is experiencing. More than 250 problems and troubling life events are listed under the following headings: School, Opposite Sex Concerns, Peers, Family, Goals, Crises, Emotions, Recreation, Habits, Neighborhood, Life Phase Transition, Beliefs and Attitudes, and Occupational and Financial Circumstances. The adolescent checks the problems that he or she is experiencing.

Format: Self-administered; untimed: 10 to 15 minutes

Scoring: Hand key

Cost: Package of 25 AutoScore™ Forms $27.50

Problem Experiences Checklist– Adult Version

Date not provided	Western Psychological Services

Leigh Silverton

Population: Adults

Purpose: Used to help clinicians structure and focus diagnostic interviews

Description: This checklist gives the clinician a quick picture of the client's life situation, indicating what kind of difficulties he or she is experiencing. More than 20 problems and troubling life events are listed under the following headings: Marital Relationship, Children–Parents, Financial–Legal, Bereavement, Personal Habits, Work Adjustment, Life Transition, Beliefs and Goals, Pain-

ful Memories, and Emotions. The client checks the problems that he or she is experiencing.

Format: Self-administered; untimed: 10 to 15 minutes

Scoring: Hand key

Cost: Package of 25 AutoScore™ Forms $27.50

PsychEval Personality Questionnaire (PEPQ)

2002	Institute for Personality and Ability Testing, Inc.

Raymond B. Cattell, A. Karen Cattell, Heather E. P. Cattell, Mary T. Russell, Scott Bedwell

Population: Ages 16 years and older

Purpose: Measures both normal personality and pathology-oriented traits to provide a multidimensional profile; used for intake screenings, general clinical assessments, clinical counseling strategy development, and the screening/selection and evaluation of protective services personnel

Description: The instrument has one form with two parts, for a total of 325 items. Part I contains the 16 primary factor normal personality scales and five global factor normal personality scales. Part II has 12 pathology-oriented scales and four pathology-oriented indices. Additional scores are available for response style and projected scores for the six Holland Occupational Interest Themes.

Format: Self-administered; may be administered online; untimed: 75 to 90 minutes

Scoring: Online scoring; scoring service available from publisher

Cost: Interpretation Introductory Kit $61.00

Psychological Screening Inventory (PSI)

1978	Sigma Assessment Systems, Inc.

Richard I. Lanyon

Population: Adolescents, adults

Purpose: Identifies adults and adolescents who may need a more extensive mental health examination or professional attention; used in clinics, hospitals, schools, courts, and reformatories

Description: True–false 130-item test covering five scales: Alienation, Social Nonconformity, Discomfort, Expression, and Defensiveness. Also available in Spanish.

Format: Examiner required; suitable for group use; untimed: 15 minutes

Scoring: Hand key

Cost: Contact publisher

Quality of Life Inventory (QOLI®)

1994　　　　　　　　　Pearson Assessments

Michael B. Frisch

Population: Adults

Purpose: Measures satisfaction/dissatisfaction with life; used for personal counseling, marriage counseling, and outcomes assessment

Description: Computer-administered or paper-pencil 32-item multiple-choice test with a 3-point rating scale for importance and a 6-point scale for satisfaction. A sixth-grade reading level is required. Examiner must have B-level qualification. A computer version is available using an IBM-compatible 486 PC or higher.

Format: Self-administered; untimed: 5 minutes

Scoring: Hand key; computer scored

Cost: Starter Kit (manual, 50 answer sheets, 50 worksheets) $98.00

Quickview® Social History

Date not provided　　　　　Pearson Assessments

Ronald A. Gianetti

Population: Ages 16 years to adult

Purpose: Provides the clinician with a complete psychosocial history in nine major areas

Description: This instrument enables the clinician or other staff to collect a standardized set of social and clinical data on every client with a minimal amount of administration time. The report format enables all individuals who require a client's information to receive a standardized history. The areas of inquiry are Demographics and Identifying Data, Developmental History, Family of Origin, Educational History, Marital History, Occupational History/Financial Status, Legal History, Military History, and Symptom Screen (physical and psychological). A computer-generated report provides a narrative description of client demographic and clinical information. Each area of inquiry includes a narrative explanation of results.

Format: Self-administered; online; untimed: 30 to 45 minutes

Scoring: Hand key; scoring service available; software scoring available

Cost: Starter Kit with Interpretative Report (manual, test booklet, 3 answer sheets) $89.00

Risk of Eruptive Violence Scale

1996　　　　　　　Albert Mehrabian, PhD

Albert Mehrabian

Population: Adults

Purpose: Identifies adolescents and adults who, although generally quiet and nonaggressive, have a tendency to become extremely violent and destructive

Description: Paper-pencil 35-item measure that deals with a wide range of fantasy, cognitive, emotional, and frustrated violent impulses. It has been shown to be a moderately strong negative correlate of emotional empathy, to be a positive correlate of other measures of aggressiveness and violence, and to clearly differentiate between violent incarcerated adolescents and adults versus controls.

Format: Self-administered; untimed: 10 minutes

Scoring: Hand key

Cost: Test Kit (scale, scoring directions, norms, descriptive material) $33.00 (price for students only)

Rotter Incomplete Sentences Blank–Second Edition (RISB™)

1992　　　　　　Harcourt Assessment, Inc.

Julian B. Rotter, Michael I. Lah, Janet E. Rafferty

Population: High school students through adults

Purpose: Assesses overall adjustment

Description: Paper-pencil 40-item test of personality. Items are stems of sentences to be completed by the subject. Responses may be classified into three categories: Conflict or Unhealthy Responses, Neutral Responses, and Positive or Healthy Responses. The test is available in high school, college, and adult forms.

Format: Self-administered; untimed: 20 to 40 minutes

Scoring: Examiner evaluated

Cost: Incomplete Sentences Blanks (high school, college, or adult) 25-Count $45.00, Manual $108.00

Sentence Completion Series (SCS)

1992　　Psychological Assessment Resources, Inc.

Larry H. Brown, Michael A. Unger

Population: Adolescents, adults

Purpose: Used in counseling to identify themes,

underlying concerns, and specifications of distress

Description: Paper–pencil projective, sentence-completion series with 50 items per form. The categories are as follows: Adult, Adolescence, Family, Marriage, Parenting, Work, Illness, and Aging. Materials include a professional user's guide and forms for each of the categories.

Format: Self-administered; untimed: 10 to 45 minutes

Scoring: Examiner evaluated

Cost: Introductory Kit (user's guide, 15 of each form) $88.00

Six Factor Personality Questionnaire (SFPQ)

| 2000 | Sigma Assessment Systems, Inc. |

Douglas N. Jackson, Sampo V. Paunonen, Paul F. Tremblay

Population: Adults

Purpose: Measures factors underlying basic traits of personality

Description: Assessment of normal adult personality in business and industrial settings, counseling and clinical settings, or for research requiring a broad coverage of personality dimensions. The SFPQ has 108 items, 6 scales, and 18 facet scales. The six scales are Extraversion, Agreeableness, Independence, Openness to Experience, Methodicalness, and Industriousness. SFPQ provides set scale scores that can be interpreted individually or in series of standardized scale scores. Profiles provided are Typical (percentile comparisons against norms) and Modal (pattern of personality attributes that is characteristic of a subset or cluster of persons in a particular population who share certain personality characteristics). Computer version is available.

Format: Examiner required; individual or group administration; computer administered; untimed

Scoring: Hand key; machine scored; test scoring service available

Cost: Contact publisher

16PF Adolescent Personality Questionnaire (APQ)

| 2001 | Institute for Personality and Ability Testing, Inc. |

James M. Schuerger

Population: Ages 11 to 22 years

Purpose: Provides a concise portrait of how an adolescent sees himself or herself

Description: The first three sections elicit valuable information regarding the youth's personal style (normal personality; 135 items), problem-solving abilities (12 items), and preferred work activities (15 items). The optional Life's Difficulties section (43 items) provides an opportunity for the individual to indicate particular problems in areas known to be problematic to adolescents, making the instrument appropriate for screening and for introducing sensitive topics in a counseling situation. Scores are provided for 16 primary personality factor scales, five global factor scales, a ranking on six work activity categories (Manual, Scientific, Artistic, Helping, Sales/Management, and Procedural), plus additional scores for Impression Management, Missing Responses, Central Responses, and Predicted Grade Point Average. Norms are based on over 1,000 normal adolescents from various parts of the United States. Two types of reports are available: Guidance and Psychological.

Format: Self-administered; untimed: 65 minutes

Scoring: Computer scoring; online scoring and administration

Cost: Guidance Report Introductory Kit $41.00; Psychological Report Introductory Kit $41.00

16PF Fifth Edition Questionnaire

| 1994 | Institute for Personality and Ability Testing, Inc. |

Raymond B. Cattell, A. Karen Cattell, Heather E. P. Cattell

Population: Ages 16 years and older

Purpose: Measures 16 personality factors and five global factors; used for personnel selection, individual and couples counseling, career counseling, and management development

Description: Multiple-choice computer-administered or paper–pencil test with 185 items yielding 16 Personality Factors: Warmth, Reasoning, Emotional Stability, Dominance, Liveliness, Rule-Consciousness, Social Boldness, Sensitivity, Vigilance, Abstractedness, Privateness, Apprehension, Openness to Change, Self-Reliance, Perfectionism, and Tension. Global Factors yielded: Extraversion, Anxiety, Tough-Mindedness, Independence, and Self-Control. Response Style Indices yielded: Impression Management, Infrequency, and Acquiescence. Eight unique interpretive reports can be generated from this questionnaire.

Format: Self-administered; untimed: paper–pencil, 35 to 50 minutes; computer, 25 minutes

Scoring: Hand key; machine scored; computer scored; test scoring service available; online scoring available

Cost: Complete Set (manual, 10 questionnaires, 25 answer sheets, 25 record forms, scoring keys, norm table, prepaid mail-in report processing certificate for a basic interpretive report) $120.00

16PF Select Questionnaire
1999   Institute for Personality and Ability Testing, Inc.

Raymond B. Cattell, A. Karen Cattell, Heather E.P. Cattell, Mary L. Kelly

Population: Ages 16 years and older

Purpose: Assesses the degree to which the test taker matches the personality dimensions pre-specified by the professional as necessary for effective performance in a particular job

Description: The 16PF Select Report yields an Overall Model Similarity Score, as well as scores for 12 primary personality factors (Warmth, Calmness, Dominance, Liveliness, Rule-Consciousness, Social Boldness, Trust, Imagination, Self-Assuredness, Openness, Self Reliance and Organization). Scores for three Response Style Indices (Impression Management, Infrequency, and Acquiescence) are also reported.

Format: Self-administered; untimed

Scoring: Computer scored; scoring service available

Cost: Introductory Kit $58.00

Social Insight Test (SIT)
1993   Mind Garden, Inc.

F. Stuart Chapin

Population: Adults

Purpose: Measures the ability to diagnose situations involving human interaction

Description: Test with 25 items to recognize the dynamics underlying behavior or to choose the wisest course of action to resolve a difficulty. It helps to measure social insight and appraisal of others and respondents' evaluations of interpersonal situations.

Format: Examiner required; individual administration; untimed: 20 to 30 minutes

Scoring: Examiner evaluated

Cost: Sampler Set $30.00; Permission Set for 200 Uses $150.00

Social Reticence Scale (SRS)
1986   Mind Garden, Inc.

Warren H. Jones, Stephen Briggs

Population: Adolescents, adults

Purpose: Assesses shyness and interpersonal problems in high school and college students and adults

Description: Paper-pencil 20-item measure of shyness. Items are answered using a 5-point Likert-type scale. Used to provide client feedback and to assess the effectiveness of therapeutic interventions. Also used in research of interpersonal relationships.

Format: Examiner required; suitable for group use; untimed: 5 to 10 minutes

Scoring: Hand key

Cost: Sampler Set $30.00; Permission Set for 200 Uses $150.00

Structured Interview for the Five-Factor Model of Personality (SIFFM)
1997   Psychological Assessment Resources, Inc.

Timothy J. Trull, Thomas A. Widiger

Population: Ages 18 years and older

Purpose: Semistructured interview to assess both normal and abnormal personality functioning in specific settings

Description: A total of 120 interview items are rated on a 3-point rating scale. The interview assesses personality using the Five Factor Model: Neuroticism (vs. Emotional Stability), Extraversion (vs. Introversion), Openness to Experience (vs. Closedness to Experience), Agreeableness (vs. Antagonism), and Conscientiousness (vs. Negligence).

Format: Examiner required; individual administration; untimed: 60 minutes

Scoring: Examiner evaluated

Cost: Kit (manual, 25 interview booklets) $130.00

Taylor-Johnson Temperament Analysis®
2006   Psychological Publications, Inc.

Robert M. Taylor, Lucille P. Morrison

Population: Ages 13 years to adult

Purpose: Provides a clinical assessment of personality; used for educational and vocational guidance, for substance abuse counseling, and for individual, premarital, marital, and family counseling

Description: Paper–pencil 180-item test measuring common personality traits to assist in assessing individual adjustment and formulation of an overall counseling plan. The regular edition, for ages 17 to adult, has a special feature allowing "crisscross" testing in which questions are answered as applied to self and again as applied to significant other, thereby adding the dimension of interpersonal perception to the counseling perspective. An eighth-grade reading level is required. The secondary edition, for ages 13 to 17 and adults who are poor readers, is presented in direct-question format with simplified vocabulary for lower level readers. A fifth-grade reading level is required. Evaluation is presented as bipolar graphs of trait pairs: Nervous/Composed, Depressive/Lighthearted, Active–Social/Quiet, Expressive–Responsive/Inhibited, Sympathetic/Indifferent, Subjective/Objective, Dominant/Submissive, Hostile/Tolerant, and Self-Disciplined/Impulsive.

Format: Examiner required; suitable for group use; untimed: 30 to 45 minutes

Scoring: Examiner evaluated; online administration and scoring; mail-in scoring service available; computer software scored

Cost: Computer Kit (manual, handbook, software, set of trait suggestion sheets) $249.00; Hand-Scoring Kit (manual, scoring stencils, 5 question booklets, 25 answer sheets, 25 profiles, 5 report booklets, set of trait suggestion sheets, pens, ruler) $279.00; Online Kit (manual, handbook, set of trait suggestion sheets, 10 report booklets) $149.00

Temperament Inventory Tests
1979   Andrews University Press

Peter Blitchington, Robert J. Cruise

Population: Adolescents, adults

Purpose: Assesses an individual's basic temperament traits according to the four-temperament theory; used by professionals and paraprofessionals in marital, vocational, social, moral, and spiritual counseling settings

Description: Paper–pencil 80-item test determining an individual's basic temperamental traits. The test is available in a self-report form and a group form. The self-report form consists of a 42-page booklet, *Understanding Your Temperament*, containing the test and instructions for self-administration, self-scoring, and interpreting

the scores from a Christian viewpoint. The group form, called the Temperament Inventory, is administered and scored with temperament templates by the examiner or group leader. Interpretive material is not included with the group form. Also available in French, German, and Spanish.

Format: Self-administered; untimed

Scoring: Examiner evaluated

Cost: Guide Book $3.99; Each Test $1.75, 4 Scoring Templates $7.99

Trait Arousability Scale (Converse of Stimulus Screening)
1994   Albert Mehrabian, PhD

Albert Mehrabian

Population: Ages 14 years and older

Purpose: Assesses general emotionality or emotional reactivity; used for clinical research and counseling

Description: Paper–pencil 34-item test yielding a single total score. A 10th-grade reading level is required.

Format: Self-administered; untimed: 10 minutes

Scoring: Hand key; test scoring service

Cost: Test Kit $33.00 (price for students only)

Trait Dominance–Submissiveness Scale
1994   Albert Mehrabian, PhD

Albert Mehrabian

Population: Adults

Purpose: Measures aspects of dominance and submissiveness in an individual's personality; used for research, counseling, job placement purposes, and matching of coworkers

Description: Multiple-item verbal questionnaire assessing personality characteristics related to dominance and submissiveness. Test items are based on extensive factor-analytic and experimental studies on aspects of dominance (controlling, taking charge) versus submissiveness characteristics. This measure has been shown to be a basic component of many important personality attributes, such as extroversion, dependency, anxiety, or depression.

Format: Self-administered; untimed: 10 minutes

Scoring: Hand key

Cost: Test Kit (scale, scoring directions, norms, descriptive material) $33.00 (price for students only)

Trait Pleasure–Displeasure Scale

1994	Albert Mehrabian, PhD

Albert Mehrabian

Population: Ages 14 years and older

Purpose: Measures general psychological adjustment–maladjustment; used with clinical work, counseling, and research

Description: Paper–pencil 22-item test with a single total score.

Format: Self-administered; untimed: 10 minutes

Scoring: Hand key; test scoring service available

Cost: Test Kit $33.00 (price for students only)

Relationships

Abortion Scale

1988	Donna Bardis

Panos D. Bardis

Population: Adolescents, adults

Purpose: Measures attitudes toward many aspects of abortion; used in clinical assessment, marriage and family counseling, research on attitudes toward abortion, and discussion in family education

Description: Paper–pencil 25-item test in which the subject reads statements about issues concerning abortion and rates them according to his or her personal beliefs on a scale from 0 (*strongly disagree*) to 4 (*strongly agree*). The score equals the sum of the 25 numerical responses. Theoretical range of scores extends from 0 (lowest approval of abortion) to 100 (highest approval). Suitable for use with individuals with physical or hearing impairments.

Format: Examiner/Self-administered; suitable for group use; untimed: 10 minutes

Scoring: Examiner evaluated

Cost: $1.00

Abuse Risk Inventory for Women (ARI)

1989	Mind Garden, Inc.

Bonnie L. Yegidis

Population: Adult women

Purpose: Identifies women who are abused or are at risk for abuse; used for marital or relationship counseling and by social service agencies, physicians, and health-care providers

Description: Inventory has 25 items rated using a 4-point Likert scale. Scores provide socio-demographic information.

Format: Self-administered; untimed: 10 to 15 minutes

Scoring: Hand key; examiner evaluated

Cost: Sampler Set $30.00; Permission Set for 200 Uses $150.00

Coitometer

1988	Donna Bardis

Panos D. Bardis

Population: Adolescents, adults

Purpose: Measures knowledge of the anatomical and physiological aspects of coitus; used for clinical assessment, marriage and family counseling, research on human sexuality, and discussion in family and human sexuality classes

Description: Paper–pencil 50-item true–false four page instrument consisting of the questionnaire and a measure key. Suitable for use with individuals who are physically or hearing impaired.

Format: Examiner/Self-administered; suitable for group use; untimed: 12 minutes

Scoring: Hand key

Cost: $1.00

Dating Scale

1988	Donna Bardis

Panos D. Bardis

Population: Adolescents, adults

Purpose: Measures attitudes toward various aspects of dating; used for clinical assessment, marriage and family counseling, research on attitudes toward dating, and discussion in family education

Description: Paper–pencil test in which the subject rates 25 statements about dating from 0 (*strongly disagree*) to 4 (*strongly agree*). The score equals the sum of the 25 numerical responses. Theoretical range of scores extends from 0 (least liberal) to 100 (most liberal). Suitable for use with individuals with physical or hearing impairments.

Format: Examiner/Self-administered; suitable for group use; untimed: 10 minutes

Scoring: Examiner evaluated

Cost: $1.00

Domestic Situation Inventory (DSI)

2004   JIST Publishing

Robert P. Brady

Population: Adults

Purpose: Measures the risk of being in a potentially abusive situation; used for domestic abuse counseling and prevention

Description: A counseling tool consisting of 155 items that ask women about the past and present nature of their relationships, feelings, and situations. Provides information to help them understand their potential risk and encourages and guides them to seek help, including offering valuable contact information.

Format: Self-administered; untimed: 15 minutes

Scoring: Self-scoring

Cost: 25 Forms and Administration Guide $37.95

Dyadic Adjustment Scale (DAS)

1989   Multi-Health Systems, Inc.

Graham Spanier

Population: Adults

Purpose: Measures relationship adjustment for use in marital counseling

Description: Paper–pencil or computer-administered 32-item self-report measure consisting of four factored subcomponents: Dyadic Satisfaction, Dyadic Cohesion, Dyadic Consensus, and Affectional Expression. Windows-based computer version generates interpretive statements.

Format: Self-administered; untimed: 5 to 10 minutes

Scoring: QuikScore™ forms; may be computer scored

Cost: Kit (manual, 20 forms) $62.00

Erotometer: A Technique for the Measurement of Heterosexual Love

1988   Donna Bardis

Panos D. Bardis

Population: Adolescents, adults

Purpose: Measures the intensity of an individual's love for a member of the opposite sex; used for clinical assessment, marriage and family counseling, research on love, and discussions in family and sex education

Description: Paper–pencil 50-item test in which the subject reads statements concerning actual feelings, attitudes, desires, and wishes regarding one specific member of the opposite sex and rates them on the following scale: 0 (*absent*), 1 (*weak*), 2 (*strong*). The score equals the sum of the 50 numerical responses. The theoretical range of scores extends from 0 (no love) to 100 (strongest love). Suitable for use with individuals who have physical or hearing impairments.

Format: Self-administered; untimed: 12 minutes

Scoring: Examiner evaluated

Cost: $1.00

Family History Analysis (FHA)

1989   Psychological Publications, Inc.

H. Norman Wright

Population: Adults

Purpose: A tool for premarital counseling

Description: Eight pages of significant questions designed to help engaged couples thoroughly evaluate their own marriage mode: their marital dreams, marital expectations, attitudes, and behaviors. The tool provides information about family history, parents' history, and personal history.

Format: Self-administered; untimed

Scoring: Examiner evaluated

Cost: $21.50 (counselor's guide, 10 booklets)

Gravidometer

1988   Donna Bardis

Panos D. Bardis

Population: Adolescents, adults

Purpose: Measures knowledge of the anatomical and physiological aspects of pregnancy; used in clinical assessments, marriage and family counseling, and research on human sexuality and family classes

Description: Paper–pencil 50-item true–false test measuring knowledge of human pregnancy. Suitable for use with individuals who are physically or hearing impaired.

Format: Self-administered; untimed: 12 minutes

Scoring: Hand key

Cost: $1.00

Intimate Adult Relationship Questionnaire (IARQ)

2004	Rohner Research Publications

Ronald P. Rohner

Population: Adults

Purpose: Assesses current and recent-past intimate adult relationships

Description: Contains 85 items measured on a 4-point Likert scale. This is an adaptation of the adult PARQ/Control instrument.

Format: Examiner/Self-administered; suitable for group use; untimed: 10 to 15 minutes

Scoring: Hand key; computer scoring available

Cost: Handbook with All Instruments $35.00

Intimate Partner Acceptance–Rejection/Control Questionnaire (IPAR/CQ)

2004	Rohner Research Publications

Ronald P. Rohner

Population: Adults

Purpose: Assesses the quality of the relationship with one's intimate partner In terms of perceived partner acceptance–rejection and partner behavioral control

Description: Paper pencil questionnaire with 60 items on four scales that comprise the acceptance-rejection component: Warmth/Affection, Hostility/Aggression, Indifference/Neglect, and Undifferentiated Rejection. The test, designed to cut across social classes, ethnicity, and cultural boundaries, is available in 26 languages. Responses are given on a 4-point scale, with some items reversed when scoring to reduce response bias. The control scale comprises 13 additional items measuring the dimension of partner permissiveness-strictness.

Format: Rating scale; untimed

Scoring: Hand key; computer scoring available

Cost: Handbook with All Instruments $35.00

Intimate Partner Attachment Questionnaire (IPAQ)

2004	Rohner Research Publications

Ronald P. Rohner

Population: Adolescents, adults

Purpose: Assesses the nature and quality of attachment with one's intimate partner

Description. Paper-pencil 15-item questionnaire. Results provide information about whether the intimate partner is a true attachment figure, a significant other, or neither. Also measures the quality of the intimate relationship in terms of nine attachment variables.

Format: Examiner/Self-administered; suitable for group use; untimed: 10 to 15 minutes

Scoring: Hand key; computer scoring available

Cost: Handbook with All Instruments $35.00

Marital Attitude Evaluation (MATE)

1989	Mind Garden, Inc.

Will Schutz

Population: Adults

Purpose: Explores the relationship between spouses or other closely related persons; measures the amount of satisfaction respondents feel toward someone close to them; used in marital, relationship, and family counseling

Description: The evaluation uses a 6-point Likert scale test. An eighth-grade reading level is required.

Format: Examiner required; suitable for group use; untimed. 10 to 15 minutes

Scoring: Hand key; examiner evaluated

Cost: Sampler Set $30.00; Permission Set for 200 Uses $150.00

Marital Evaluation Checklist

1984	Psychological Assessment Resources, Inc.

Leslie Navran

Population: Adults

Purpose: Assesses common characteristics and problem areas in a marital relationship; used as a survey instrument in clinical and counseling settings to initiate the consultation process and to introduce the client to formal diagnostic testing

Description: Paper-pencil test with 140 items organized in three sections: Reasons for Marrying, Current Problems, and Motivation for Counseling. Areas surveyed include Interpersonal/Emotional, Material/Economic, Social, Personal, Money and Work, Sex, Personal Characteristics, and Marital Relationships.

Format: Self-administered; untimed: 10 to 20 minutes

Scoring: Examiner evaluated

Cost: 50 Checklists $52.00

Marriage Assessment Inventory (MAI)

| 1988 | Psychological Publications, Inc. |

H. Norman Wright

Population: Adults

Purpose: Used prior to seeing a couple or during the process of marriage counseling

Description: The inventory provides the counselor with much of the data needed for planning prior to the first counseling session. It helps the couple to anticipate the kinds of concerns that will be discussed, and in that way helps to introduce them to the process of counseling. Answers to inventory questions also initiate changes in the ways in which spouses think about their objectives and can bring about some change before the first interview. Among others, the following topics are included: Family Structure and Background, Marital Preparation, Current Levels of Satisfaction, and Change and Commitment Level.

Format: Self-administered; untimed

Scoring: Examiner evaluated

Cost: $21.50 (counselor's guide, 10 booklets)

Memories of Spouse

| 1993 | Arnold R. Bruhn and Associates |

Arnold R. Bruhn

Population: Adults

Purpose: Explores the spousal relationship

Description: Recommended for individuals who are considering marital therapy and want to undertake a review of the relationship and reconnect with what attracted them in the first place. Helps to identify the nature of the experiences that have compromised the quality of the relationship.

Format: Examiner required; individual or group administration; untimed

Scoring: Examiner evaluated

Cost: 25 Tests $140.00

Menometer

| 1988 | Donna Bardis |

Panos D. Bardis

Population: Adolescents, adults

Purpose: Measures knowledge of the anatomical and physiological aspects of menstruation. Used for clinical assessment, marriage and family coun-

seling, research on human sexuality, and discussion in family and human sexuality classes

Description: Paper–pencil 50-item true–false test in which the subject marks the appropriate answers. Suitable for use with individuals who have physical and hearing impairments.

Format: Examiner/Self-administered; suitable for group use; untimed: 12 minutes

Scoring: Hand key

Cost: $1.00

Pill Scale

| 1988 | Donna Bardis |

Panos D. Bardis

Population: Adolescents, adults

Purpose: Measures attitudes toward oral contraceptives; used for clinical assessment, marriage and family counseling, family attitude research, and discussions in family and sex education

Description: Paper–pencil 25-item test in which the subject reads statements concerning moral, sexual, psychological, and physical aspects of "the pill" and rates them on a scale from 0 (*strongly disagree*) to 4 (*strongly agree*). The score equals the sum of the 25 numerical responses. The theoretical range of scores extends from 0 (least liberal) to 100 (most liberal). Suitable for use with individuals who have physical or hearing impairments.

Format: Examiner/Self-administered; suitable for group use; untimed: 10 minutes

Scoring: Examiner evaluated

Cost: $1.00

PREPARE–Premarital Personal and Relationship Evaluation (Version 2000)

| 1996 | Life Innovations, Inc. |

David H. Olson, David G. Fournier, Joan M. Druckman

Population: Adults

Purpose: Used in premarital counseling to assess areas of strength and growth

Description: A total of 195 items in 20 categories: Idealistic Distortion, Marriage Expectations, Personality Issues, Communication, Conflict Resolution, Financial Management, Leisure Activities, Sexual Expectations, Children and Parenting, Family and Friends, Role Relationship, Spiritual Beliefs, Couple Closeness, Couple Flexibility, Family Closeness, Family Flexibility, Self Confidence, Assertiveness, Avoidance, and Partner

Dominance. Computer report (18 pages) contains revised Individual Scores, Couple Type, Personality Assessment Idealistic Distortion Scores, and Positive Couple Agreement Scores. Test available in Spanish. Also available is PREPARE-MC for premarital couples with children.

Format: Self-administered; untimed

Scoring: Computer scored; test scoring service available

Cost: $30.00 for scoring; $175.00 for training

Romantic Relationships Procedure (RRP)

| 1989 | Arnold R. Bruhn and Associates |

Arnold R. Bruhn

Population: Adults

Purpose: Explores the most significant romantic relationships

Description: A structured method of exploring romantic relationships as a class, or type, of relationship. Measures autobiographical memory.

Format: Examiner required; individual or group administration; untimed

Scoring: Examiner evaluated

Cost: 25 Tests $140.00

Sexometer

| 1988 | Donna Bardis |

Panos D. Bardis

Population: Adolescents, adults

Purpose: Assesses knowledge of human reproductive anatomy and physiology; used for clinical assessment, marriage and family counseling, research on sex knowledge, and discussion in family and sex education

Description: Paper-pencil 50-item test consisting of short-answer and identification questions concerning human reproduction, anatomy, function, physiology, disease, birth control, and sexual behavior. Materials include the test form and answer key. Suitable for use with individuals who have physical or hearing impairments.

Format: Self-administered; untimed: 15 minutes

Scoring: Hand key

Cost: $1.00

Sex-Role Egalitarianism Scale (SRES)

| 1993 | Sigma Assessment Systems, Inc. |

Lynda A. King, Daniel W. King

Population: Ages 12 years and older

Purpose: Measures attitudes toward equality; used in marital counseling and prevention of sexual harassment

Description: Instrument with 95 items rated on a 5-point Likert scale with five subscales: Educational Roles, Marital Roles, Employment Roles, Social–Interpersonal–Heterosexual Roles, and Parental Roles. Alternate forms include 25 items. Requires a sixth- to seventh-grade reading level.

Format: Examiner required; individual and group administration; untimed: 25 minutes

Scoring: Examiner evaluated

Cost: Contact publisher

16PF Couple's Counseling Questionnaire

| 1995 | Institute for Personality and Ability Testing, Inc. |

Mary T. Russell

Population: Ages 16 years and older

Purpose: Identifies key relationship issues

Description: Enables the counselor to provide possible implications of similarities and differences between two people. The counselor can use the report to help the couple to see how their personal qualities may affect their relationship, identify areas that are causing dissatisfaction, and then establish a counseling framework that will result in increased relationship satisfaction for the couple. A valuable tool in relationship counseling that is appropriate for use with cohabitating, premarital, married, separated, divorcing, and same-sex couples. There is one form with 211 items. Items may be administered by computer or online.

Format: Self-administered; untimed

Scoring: Computer scored; scoring service available; online scoring

Cost: Introductory Kit $35.00

Socio-Sexual Knowledge and Attitudes Test-Revised (SSKAT-R)

| 2003 | Stoelting Company |

Dorothy Griffiths, Yona Lunsky

Population: Ages 15 years to adult

Purpose: Measures sexual knowledge and attitudes of individuals with developmental disabilities

Description: The predecessor test was developed in 1979 to obtain an idea of how individuals with special needs understood their own bodies, relationships, and sex. The new version of the test addresses most of the original topics (except substance issues), and it adds the topics of HIV/AIDS, sexual health, menopause, age discrimination, appropriate/inappropriate touch, and diversity in sexual activities. There are six subscales: Anatomy; Male and Female Bodies (individuals respond only to their own gender); Intimacy; Pregnancy, Childbirth, and Child Rearing; Birth Control and STDs; and Healthy Sexual Boundaries. An easy-to-use stimulus picture easel and picture cards present illustrations requiring a simple response to respond to questions. This full revision represents updated and changed materials based on extensive feedback from the field. Subjects must have some visual and verbal comprehension, but expressive language requirements are minimal.

Format: Examiner required; individual administration; untimed: 45 minutes

Scoring: Examiner evaluated

Cost: Complete Kit (manual, easel picture book, stimulus cards, 20 record forms) $295.00

Spousal Assault Risk Assessment Guide (SARA™)

1999	Multi-Health Systems, Inc.

P. Randall Kropp, Stephen D. Hart, Christopher D. Webster, Derek Eaves

Population: Adults

Purpose: Helps to predict the likelihood of domestic violence

Description: Has forensic applications with a total of 20 items: Alleged Most Recent Offense (3 items), Criminal History (3 items), Psychosocial Adjustment (7 items), and Spousal Assault History (7 items).

Format: Examiner required; individually administered; untimed: 15 to 20 minutes

Scoring: QuikScore™ forms

Cost: Kit (manual, 25 checklists, 25 scoring forms) $74.00

Vasectomy Scale: Attitudes

1988	Donna Bardis

Panos D. Bardis

Population: Adolescents, adults

Purpose: Measures attitudes toward the social and psychological aspects of vasectomy; used for clinical assessment, marriage and family counseling, research on human sexuality, and discussions in family and sex education

Description: Paper–pencil 25-item test in which the subject rates 25 statements concerning vasectomy on a scale from 0 (*strongly disagree*) to 4 (*strongly agree*). The score equals the sum of the 25 numerical responses. The theoretical range of scores extends from 0 (lowest approval of vasectomy) to 100 (highest approval). Suitable for use with individuals who have physical or hearing impairments.

Format: Self-administered; untimed: 10 minutes

Scoring: Examiner evaluated

Cost: $1.00

Self-Esteem

Adolescent Coping Scale

1993	Australian Council for Educational Research Limited

Erica Frydenberg, Ramon Lewis

Population: Adolescents

Purpose: Assesses a broad range of coping strategies, focusing on what an individual does

Description: Paper–pencil instrument in a general and specific long form (80 items, 18 scales) and short form (1 item from each scale). The focus is on psychological well-being and adaptive strategies for coping. It can be used for initiating self-directed and behavioral change and for stimulating group discussion. The long form can be computer or hand scored. Data can then be transferred to a Profile Chart. A Practitioner's Kit has been specially produced.

Format: Examiner required; individual or group administration; untimed: long form, 10 minutes; short form, 2 minutes

Scoring: Hand key; computer scoring; scoring service available

Cost: Contact publisher

Children's Inventory of Self-Esteem–Second Edition (CISE-2)

2001	Brougham Press

Richard A. Campbell

Population: Ages 5 to 12 years

Purpose: Provides a quick assessment of a child's inferred self-worth and furnishes strategies for improving self-esteem; used during parent and teacher consultations, for program evaluations, and as an aid in designing individual and group counseling goals and strategies

Description: This 64-item inventory compares the relative strengths and weaknesses of four self-esteem components: Belonging, Control, Purpose, and Self. Each category has 16 items that are divided into defensive and aggressive items to identify favored coping strategies. The scale is completed by counselors, school and clinical psychologists, social workers, and other helping professionals. Male and female forms are provided. The lifetime license entitles the holder to make unlimited copies of all inventory forms and pages. Examiner must have an advanced degree in mental health or testing field.

Format: Rating scale; untimed: 10 minutes

Scoring: Hand key; examiner evaluated

Cost: Lifetime Licenses: Individual $99.00, School and Agency $125.00; School District: $110.00 per building

Coopersmith Self Esteem Inventories (CSEI)

2002	Mind Garden, Inc.

Stanley Coopersmith

Population: Ages 8 years to adult

Purpose: Measures attitudes toward the self in social, academic, and personal contexts; used for individual diagnosis, classroom screening, pre- and posttreatment evaluations, and clinical and research studies

Description: Paper–pencil test of self-attitudes in four areas: Social–Self–Peers, Home–Parents, School–Academic, and General–Self. Materials include the 58-item School Form and 25-item Adult Form. The School Form is suitable for use with individuals ages 8 to 15, and the Adult Form is administered to individuals ages 16 and older.

Format: Self-administered; untimed: 15 minutes

Scoring: Examiner evaluated

Cost: Manual/Sampler Set $30.00; Permission Set of 200 Uses $150.00

Coping Scale for Adults (CSA)

1997	Australian Council for Educational Research Limited

Erica Frydenberg, Ramon Lewis

Population: Adults

Purpose: Measures how frequently 18 coping strategies are used

Description: The CSA can assist individuals and organizations that work with adults in clinical, counseling, and human resource contexts to consider issues surrounding coping and facilitate coping strategies. A self-report inventory with 74 items, including 70 structured items that reliably assess 18 conceptually and empirically distinct coping strategies. The Specific Form enables the measurement of responses to a particular concern. There is a 20-item Short Form, comprising 19 structured items and a final open-ended response question.

Format: Self-report; untimed

Scoring: Examiner evaluated

Cost: Contact publisher

Culture-Free Self-Esteem Inventories– Third Edition (CFSEI-3)

2002	PRO-ED, Inc.

James Battle

Population: Ages 6 to 18 years

Purpose: Assesses self-esteem

Description: There are three age-appropriate self-report versions: Primary, Intermediate, and Adolescent. All three versions of the inventory provide a Global Self-Esteem Quotient. The Intermediate and Adolescent Forms provide self-esteem scores in four areas: Academic, General, Parental/Home, and Social. The Adolescent Form provides an additional self-esteem score: Personal Self-Esteem. A defensiveness measure is also provided to assess the extent to which an examinee's responses are guarded. The CFSEI-3 was standardized on a sample of 1,727 persons from 17 states. Information is provided on an extensive Canadian sample in reliability and validity chapters of the manual.

Format: Rating scale; untimed: 10 to 15 minutes

Scoring: Examiner evaluated

Cost: Complete Kit (manual; 50 each of Primary, Intermediate, and Adolescent response and scoring forms, storage box) $184.00

Indiana Student Scale: A Measure of Self-Esteem

1998	Meryl E. Englander

Meryl E. Englander

Population: Ages 12 years and older

Purpose: Prepares a profile of individual self-esteem

Description: Used in counseling and serves as the basis for designing a learning environment to enhance individual self-esteem. This 63-item scale gives a profile for eight dimensions of self-esteem.

Format: Examiner required; group administration; untimed: 40 minutes

Scoring: Examiner scored

Cost: No charge

Multidimensional Self-Esteem Inventory (MSEI)

1988	Psychological Assessment Resources, Inc.

Edward J. O'Brien, Seymour Epstein

Population: College age and older

Purpose: Assesses global self-esteem and its components; used to evaluate job dissatisfaction, eating disorders, anxiety/depression, and treatment intake/outcome

Description: Paper–pencil 116-item multiple-choice test that measures global self-esteem and eight components of self-esteem: Competence, Lovability, Likability, Personal Power, Self-Control, Moral Self-Approval, Body Appearance, and Body Functioning. The MSEI uses a 5-point response format, reporting results as *t*-scores and percentiles. A 10th-grade reading level is required.

Format: Examiner required; suitable for group use; untimed: 15 to 30 minutes

Scoring: Hand key

Cost: Kit (manual, 25 reusable test booklets, 50 rating forms, 50 profile forms) $172.00

Self-Esteem Index (SEI)

1991	PRO-ED, Inc.

Linda Brown, Jacquelyn Alexander

Population: Ages 8 to 18 years

Purpose: Measures the way individuals perceive and value themselves

Description: Paper–pencil 120-item survey assessing self-esteem. Items are divided into four scales: Perception of Familial Acceptance, Perception of Academic Competence, Perception of Peer Popularity, and Perception of Personal Security. Results are reported as standard scores and percentiles.

Format: Rating scale; untimed: 30 minutes

Scoring: Examiner evaluated

Cost: Complete Kit (manual, 50 student response booklets, 50 profile/record forms, storage box) $128.00

Self Image Profile for Adults (SIP-Adult)

2004	Harcourt Assessment-UK

Richard J. Butler, Sarah L. Gasson

Population: Ages 17 to 65 years

Purpose: Assesses self-image and self-esteem

Description: Provides a visual display of self-image, enabling individuals, as they complete it, to reveal to themselves, as well as to the clinician, ways they construe themselves. Self-esteem is estimated by the discrepancy between ratings of "How I am" and "How I would like to be." Items are short well-known descriptions, based on frequently elicited accounts self-derived from a large sample of adults.

Format: Rating scale; untimed: 7 to 15 minutes

Scoring: Examiner evaluated

Cost: Complete Kit (manual, 25 record forms) £62.50

Self Image Profiles (SIP)

2001	Harcourt Assessment-UK

Richard J. Butler

Population: Ages 7 to 16 years

Purpose: Assesses self-esteem and self-image

Description: The SIP provides a visual display from two forms: one for children 7 to 11 years and another for ages 12 to 16 years. The discrepancy between self-image and self-esteem is obtained from ratings of "How I am" and "How I would like to be."

Format: Rating scale; untimed: 9 to 25 minutes

Scoring: Examiner evaluated

Cost: Complete Kit (manual, 25 of each age level form, in a bag) £73.50

Smell

Brief Smell Identification Test (B-SIT)

| 2001 | Sensonics, Inc. |

Richard L. Doty

Population: Ages 5 years and older

Purpose: Detects smell ability differential and early diagnosis of neurodegenerative disorders (e.g., Alzheimer's disease)

Description: Total of 12 items that measure abil- ity to smell. Profiles Anosmia and Normosmia. Provides percentile-ranked scores with age and gender adjustment. Materials used are microencapsulated odors. Also available in German.

Format: Examiner required; individually administered; untimed: 5 minutes

Scoring: Hand key

Cost: $19.50

Stress

Coping Inventory for Stressful Situations (CISS™)

| 1989 | Multi-Health Systems, Inc. |

Norman Endler, James Parker

Population: Ages 13 years to adult

Purpose: Measures coping styles in individuals

Description: Paper pencil 48-item instrument measuring three major types of coping styles: Task-Oriented, Emotion-Oriented, and Avoidance-Coping. The CISS also identifies two types of Avoidance Coping patterns: Distraction and Social Diversion. Scores provide a profile of an individual's coping strategy. Adult and adolescent forms are available. The CISS: Situation Specific Coping (CISS:SSC) is a 21-item measure for adults modified such that responses are given with a particular designated stressful situation in mind.

Format: Self-administered; untimed: 10 minutes

Scoring: QuikScore™ forms

Cost: Complete Kit (manual, 25 forms) $94.00

Coping Resources Inventory

| 2004 | Mind Garden, Inc. |

M. Susan Marting, Allen L. Hammer

Population: Adolescents, adults

Purpose: Measures five basic ways people handle stress

Description: The instrument measures stress reactions in Cognitive, Social, Emotional, Spiritual/Philosophical, and Physical domains. It is used in treatment planning for stress-related problems of individuals in counseling; in treatment planning for specific rehabilitation programs, such as those for cardiac patients; as a tool for designing stress workshops tailored for specific groups; as a tool for identifying individuals who might be at risk, in need of counseling, or in need of medical intervention; as a tool for program evaluation; as an educational planning and assessment device in high school health classes; and as a research instrument to investigate coping resources in various populations and to provide a standardized measure in coping research.

Format: Self-administered; untimed

Scoring: Examiner evaluated

Cost: Manual/Sampler Set $40.00; Permission Set of 200 Uses $150.00

Coping Resources Inventory (CRI)

| 1987 | CPP, Inc. |

M. Susan Marting, Allen L. Hammer

Population: Adults

Purpose: Measures an individual's resources for coping with stress; used in individual counseling, workshops, and health settings

Description: Paper–pencil 60-item inventory consisting of five scales measuring an individual's cognitive, social, physical, emotional, and values resources. The results identify the resources a person has developed for coping with stress and those that still must be developed. The manual includes scale descriptions, reliability and validity information, separate norms for males and females, and case illustrations for interpreting the profiles.

Format: Self-administered online; untimed: 15 minutes

Scoring: Online

Cost: 1 to 99 Inventory Administrations $8.40 each; Manual $29.00

Coping Responses Inventory (CRI)
| 1993 | Psychological Assessment Resources, Inc. |

Rudolf H. Moos

Population: Ages 12 years and older

Purpose: Used in counseling and stress management education to identify and monitor coping strategies

Description: Paper–pencil short-answer 4-point scale with the following categories: Logical Analysis, Positive Reappraisal, Seeking Guidance and Support, Problem Solving, Cognitive Avoidance, Acceptance or Resignation, Seeking Alternative Rewards, and Emotional Discharge. Two forms are available: youth and adult. Materials used include an adult manual, youth manual, adult actual and ideal test booklets, youth actual and ideal test booklets, and answer sheets. A sixth-grade reading level is required.

Format: Self-administered; untimed

Scoring: Hand-scored answer sheet; scoring software available

Cost: Youth or Adult Introductory Kit (manual, 10 reusable test booklets, 50 answer sheets, supplement) $164.00

Life Stressors and Social Resources Inventory (LISRES-Adult and LISRES-Youth)
| 1994 | Psychological Assessment Resources, Inc. |

Rudolf H. Moos

Population: Ages 12 years to adult

Purpose: Measures ongoing life stressors and social resources and their changes over time

Description: Can be used as a structured interview with individuals whose reading and comprehension skills are below a sixth-grade level. It can be administered and scored by those with no formal training in clinical or counseling psychology. Each version (adult and youth) has its own manual. The adult domains are Physical Health

Status, Housing and Neighborhood, Finances, Work, and Relationships. The youth domains are Physical Health, Home and Money, and Relationships.

Format: Examiner required; individual administration; untimed: 30 minutes

Scoring: Examiner evaluated

Cost: Adult or Youth Introductory Kit (manual, 10 reusable booklets, 50 hand-scorable forms) $170.00

Maslach Burnout Inventory (MBI)
| 1986, 1996 | CPP, Inc. |

Christina Maslach, Susan E. Jackson

Population: Adults

Purpose: Measures burnout among social and human service personnel; used in job counseling to reduce burnout symptoms and by school districts to detect potential problems among school staffs

Description: Paper–pencil 22-item inventory consisting of three subscales measuring various aspects of burnout: Emotional Exhaustion, Personal Accomplishment, and Depersonalization. Examinees answer each item on the basis of how frequently they experience the feeling described in the item. The Demographic Data Sheet may be used to obtain biographical information. The revised manual contains more research data and more extensive norms than the previous manual, future research suggestions, and a supplement on burnout in education. In addition, a new MBI Educators Survey and an Educators Demographic Data Sheet are available.

Format: Self-administered; untimed: 20 to 30 minutes

Scoring: Hand key

Cost: Preview Kit (Human Services booklet, Educators Survey booklet, General Survey booklet, scoring keys, manual) $75.75

Posttraumatic Stress Diagnostic Scale (PDS)
| Date not provided | Pearson Assessments |

Edna B. Foa

Population: Ages 17 to 65 years

Purpose: Aids in the detection and diagnosis of posttraumatic stress disorder (PTSD)

Description: This brief screening and diagnostic

tool parallels DSM-IV criteria. It may be administered repeatedly over time to help monitor changes in symptoms. It enables the examiner to screen for the presence of PTSD in large groups or with patients who have identified themselves as victims of a traumatic event and to gauge symptom severity and functioning in patients already identified as suffering from PTSD. The test helps to identify the source of a client's pain early on, helping to make treatment planning more effective. The PDS was normed on a group of 248 men and women who had experienced a traumatic event at least one month before they took the test. Written at an eighth-grade reading level.

Format: Self-administered; untimed: 10 to 15 minutes

Scoring: Hand key; software scoring available

Cost: Hand-Scoring Starter Kit (manual, 10 test booklets, 10 each of answer and scoring worksheets, scoring sheet) $57.00

School Situation Survey

1989	Mind Garden, Inc.

Barbara J. Helms, Robert K. Gable

Population: Ages 5 to 18 years

Purpose: Identifies the causes of stress that students feel at school

Description: This survey helps to identify causes of stress that students feel at school, as well as the ways in which stress is demonstrated. It is a valuable instrument for those investigating stress related problems experienced by children in grade school through high school. The 5-point Likert scales are under two categories: Sources of Stress (Teacher Interactions, Academic Stress, Peer Interactions, Academic Self-Concept) and Manifestations of Stress (Emotional, Behavioral, Physiological).

Format: Examiner required; individual or group administration; untimed: 10 to 15 minutes

Scoring: Hand key

Cost: Sampler Set $30.00; Permission Set for 200 Uses $150.00

Stress Profile

2000	Western Psychological Services

Kenneth M. Nowack

Population: Adults

Purpose: Identifies individual characteristics and behaviors that protect against or contribute to stress-related illness

Description: The Stress Profile measures all personal traits and lifestyle habits that have been shown to moderate the stress–illness relationship. This convenient self-report inventory provides scores in 15 areas related to stress and health risk. Norms are based on an ethnically diverse sample of 1,111 men and women, ages 20 to 68, from various working environments. Computer scoring gives you a complete interpretive report, which lists Health Risk Alerts and Health Resources for the individual assessed. This lets you see at a glance the areas in which an individual is vulnerable to stress-related illness.

Format: Self-administered; untimed: 20 to 30 minutes

Scoring: Hand key; computer scored

Cost: Kit (25 AutoScore™ forms, manual, reusable administration booklet) $110.00

Wellness

Five Factor Wellness Inventory

2005	Mind Garden, Inc.

Jane E. Meyers, Thomas J. Sweeney

Population: Grade 3 to adult

Purpose: Assesses characteristics of wellness

Description: Used as a basis for helping individuals make choices for healthier living. There are three forms: one for teens and adults with a ninth-grade reading level, one for adolescents with a sixth-grade reading level, and one for elementary-school-aged children with a third grade reading level. Three scales—Wellness, Context, and Overall Life Satisfaction—are measured using 74 scored items and a number of experimental items. The latter items include a six-item perceived safety scale, a three-item perceived wellness scale, and an eight-item context scale.

Format: Online rating scale; untimed

Scoring: Online scoring

Cost: Sampler Set $40.00; Online $10.00 each

Health Problems Checklist

| 1984 | Psychological Assessment Resources, Inc. |

John A. Schinka

Population: Adults

Purpose: Assesses the health problems of adults; used as a survey instrument in clinical and counseling settings to initiate the consultation process and to introduce the client to formal diagnostic testing

Description: Paper–pencil 200-item test identifying health problems that may affect overall psychological well-being. The test, which can be used as a screening tool for medical referrals, covers 13 areas: General Health, Cardiovascular/ Pulmonary, Endocrine/Hematology, Gastrointestinal, Dermatological, Visual, Auditory/Olfactory, Mouth/Throat/Nose, Orthopedic, Neurological, Genitourinary, Habits, and History. The test is a component of the Clinical Checklist Series.

Format: Self-administered; untimed: 10 to 20 minutes

Scoring: Examiner evaluated

Cost: 50 Checklists $52.00

Menstrual Distress Questionnaire (MDQ)

| 1991 | Western Psychological Services |

Rudolf H. Moos

Population: Ages 13 years and older

Purpose: Assesses the characteristics of a woman's menstrual cycle in order to diagnose and treat premenstrual symptoms

Description: Multiple-item paper–pencil or computer-administered questionnaire assessing the examinee on eight characteristics (Pain, Concentration, Behavior Change, Autonomic Reactions, Water Retention, Negative Affect, Arousal, and Control) during each of three phases of the menstrual cycle: premenstrual, menstrual, and intermenstrual. Form C (Cycle) is a retrospective screening tool. It asks about symptoms experienced during the most recent menstrual cycle. Because Form C takes only 10 to 15 minutes to fill out, it can easily be completed in the waiting room. Form T (Today) contains the same 47 items as Form C, but it is completed every day over two or more cycles to build an accurate profile of symptoms.

Format: Self-administered; untimed

Scoring: Scoring service

Cost: Manual $49.50; Form C $13.00; Form T $29.50

Quality of Life Questionnaire (QLQ™)

| 1989 | Multi-Health Systems, Inc. |

David Evans, Wendy Cope

Population: Adults

Purpose: Measures an individual's quality of life

Description: Paper–pencil 192-item self-report measure consisting of 15 content scales and a social desirability scale. The five major domains are General Well-Being, Interpersonal Relations, Organizational Activity, Occupational Activity, and Leisure and Recreational Activity. An overall Quality of Life score is obtained from the questionnaire.

Format: Self-administered; untimed: 30 minutes

Scoring: QuikScore™ forms

Cost: Kit (manual, 10 question booklets, 25 forms) $69.00

Social Adjustment Scale– Self Report (SAS-SR)

| | Multi-Health Systems, Inc. |

Myrna Weissman

Population: Ages 17 years and older

Purpose: Measures ability to adapt to and be satisfied with social roles

Description: Contains 54 items dealing with work, social and leisure, family unit, extended family, parental, and primary relations. Also available in French, Spanish, and 17 other languages. Available in short (24 items) and screener (14 items) forms.

Format: Self-administered; untimed: 15 to 20 minutes

Scoring: QuikScore™ forms

Cost: Complete Kit (manual, 10 question booklets, 25 forms) $142.00

Wellness Evaluation of Lifestyle (WEL)

| 2001 | Mind Garden, Inc. |

Jane E. Meyers, Thomas J. Sweeney, Melvin Witmer

Population: Adolescents, adults

Purpose: Helps respondents make healthy lifestyle choices

Description: Individuals respond to each of the

five life tasks and subtasks defined in the Wheel of Wellness. The Life Tasks Scales are Spirituality, Self-Regulation, Work and Leisure, Friendship, and Love. The instrument consists of 131 items generated as self-statements to which respondents reply using a 5-point Likert scale. Online version is available.

Format: Rating scale; untimed

Scoring: Examiner evaluated; online administration available

Cost: Sampler Set $30.00; Permission Set for 200 Uses $150.00

Education Instruments

Tests classified in the Education Instruments section generally are used in an educational or school setting to assess the cognitive and emotional growth and development of persons of all ages. Typically, professionals who use the tests listed in this section are school psychologists, diagnosticians, school counselors, and classroom teachers. Because the classifications of tests by function or usage is somewhat arbitrary, the reader is encouraged to check both the Psychology Instruments and the Business Instruments sections for additional tests that may be helpful in meeting assessment needs.

Academic Achievement

Academic Competence Evaluation Scales (ACES)

2000   Harcourt Assessment, Inc.

James C. DiPerna, Stephen N. Elliott

Population: Grades K to college

Purpose: Provides a standardized instrument to screen students who are having difficulty

Description: Facilitates prereferral assessment and identifies students at risk for academic failure. Both general and special educators can identify and prioritize skills that may need intervention. Based on these results, child study teams can identify students who could benefit from a comprehensive assessment or early intervention. The Teacher Record Form summarizes all areas necessary for academic competence: Academic Skills, Interpersonal Skills, Academic Motivation, Study Skills, and Classroom Engagement. Multiple teachers may evaluate the same student for a comprehensive view of student functioning. For Grades 6 to 12, a student self-report evaluates academic skills and strategic academic behaviors. College students can also complete a self-report.

Format: Rating scale; untimed: 10 to 15 minutes

Scoring: Examiner evaluated; computer scoring available

Cost: K-12 Complete Kit (manual, 25 each of student and teacher forms, scoring software, box) $230.00; College Complete Kit (manual, 25 forms, scoring software) $195.00

Academic Intervention Monitoring System (AIMS)

2000   Harcourt Assessment, Inc.

Stephen N. Elliott, James C. DiPerna, Edward Shapiro

Population: Grades K to 12

Purpose: Assists in designing interventions and pinpointing intervention goals

Description: The AIMS includes student, parent, and teacher forms for identification, implementation, and monitoring of strategies most likely to enhance student performance, including strategies for use at home. Also available in Spanish.

Format: Rating scale; untimed: 10 to 15 minutes

Scoring: Examiner evaluated

Cost: Complete Kit (manual; 25 each of teacher, parent, and student forms) $145.00

ACER Advanced Test B40 (Revised)

2003   Australian Council for Educational Research Limited

Population: Ages 15 years and older

Purpose: Measures intelligence

Description: Paper–pencil 77-item test measuring general mental abilities, including both verbal and numerical reasoning. The revised manual includes norms for adults and supplementary data for 15-year-olds and first-year college students.

Materials include an expandable booklet, score key, manual, and specimen set.

Format: Examiner required; suitable for group use; untimed: 1 hour

Scoring: Examiner evaluated

Cost: Contact publisher

ACER Higher Tests: WL-WQ, ML-MQ (Second Edition) and PL-PQ

2003	Australian Council for Educational Research Limited

Population: Ages 13 years and older

Purpose: Measures the intelligence of students

Description: Paper–pencil 72-item tests of general mental abilities available in three forms: WL-WQ for students ages 13 and older and parallel forms ML-MQ and PL-PQ for students ages 15 and older. The L section (36 items) on each form has a linguistic bias; the Q section (36 items) is quantitative. Australian norms are provided for both sections separately for a combined score.

Format: Examiner required; suitable for group use; timed: L section, 15 minutes; Q section, 20 minutes

Scoring: Examiner evaluated

Cost: Contact publisher

ACER Tests of Basic Skills– Orchid Series

2003	Australian Council for Educational Research Limited

Population: Years 3, 5, and 6

Purpose: Measures literacy and numeracy

Description: Tests contain Levels A, B, and C for Literacy and Numeracy. Literacy covers Reading, Proofreading, Listening, and Writing. Numeracy covers Numbers, Measurement, and Space. The instrument is paper–pencil, multiple-choice, short-answer, essay, and show-and-tell format.

Format: Examiner required; suitable for group use; timed: from 7 minutes to 55 minutes per section

Scoring: Scored with key; scoring service available

Cost: Contact publisher

ACT Assessment (ACT)

Yearly	ACT, Inc.

Population: Grades 11 and above

Purpose: Used for college admissions, course placement, and academic advising

Description: Paper–pencil multiple-choice test with the following categories: English Test (75 items, 45 minutes), Math Test (60 items, 60 minutes), Reading Test (40 items, 35 minutes), and Science Reasoning Test (40 items, 35 minutes). The following scores are reported: English Test total score and two subscores: Usage/Mechanics and Rhetorical Skills; Math Test total score and three subscores: Pre-Algebra/Elementary Algebra, Intermediate Algebra/Coordinate Geometry, Plane Geometry/Trigonometry; Reading Test total score and two subscores: Arts/Literature and Social Studies/Sciences; Science Reasoning Test total score. Raw scores are converted to scale scores; scale scores for the four tests and the composite range from a low of 1 to a high of 36. Subscores are reported on a scale score ranging from a low of 1 to a high of 18. Multiple forms are in use. Test booklets, answer folders, registration forms, and supplemental publications are used. The ACT Assessment Program also collects information about students' career interests, high school courses and grades, educational and career aspirations, extracurricular activities, and special education needs. May be used with individuals who have visual, physical, hearing, or mental impairments.

Format: Examiner required; suitable for group use; timed: 175 minutes

Scoring: Machine scored; test scoring service available

Cost: $24.00 to $27.00

Acuity™

2006	CTB/McGraw-Hill

Population: Grades 3 to 12

Purpose: Formative assessments for Math and English/Language Arts

Description: For Grades 3 to 10, Reading and Math are assessed. For Grades 7 to 12, Algebra is added. Acuity is an online/paper–pencil product that includes an integrated suite of diagnostic and predictive benchmark tests. Includes instructional exercises and robust reporting capabilities.

Format: Examiner required; suitable for group administration; online administration available; untimed

Scoring: Examiner evaluated; online scoring

Cost: Contact publisher

Adult Basic Learning Examination– Second Edition (ABLE)

| 1986 | Harcourt Assessment, Inc. |

Bjorn Karlsen, Eric F. Gardner

Population: Ages 17 years and older

Purpose: Measures adult achievement in basic learning

Description: Multiple-item paper–pencil measure of vocabulary knowledge, reading comprehension, spelling and arithmetic computation, and problem-solving skills. The test is divided into three levels. Level 1 is for adults with 1 to 4 years of formal education. Level 2 is for adults with 5 to 8 years of schooling. Level 3 is for those with at least 8 years of schooling and who may or may not have graduated from high school. Because the vocabulary test is dictated, no reading is required. The Arithmetic Problem-Solving test is dictated at Level 1. A short test, SelectABLE, is available for use in determining the appropriate level of ABLE for each applicant. The test is available in two alternate forms, E and F, at each level. SelectABLE is available in only one form. Also available in Spanish. Screening Battery can be used when testing time is limited for Level 2.

Format: Examiner required; suitable for group use; untimed: ABLE, 2 hours; screening, 1 hour

Scoring: Examiner and self-evaluated

Cost: ABLE Examination Kit $42.00; Screening Battery Examination Kit $22.00

AP Examination: Advanced Placement Program®

| Yearly | College Board |

Population: Grades 9 to 12

Purpose: Measures academic achievement in a wide range of fields; used by participating colleges to grant credit and placement in these fields to gifted/advanced students and to measure the effectiveness of a school's Advanced Placement Program

Description: The AP exams are a part of the AP Program, which provides course descriptions, exams, and curricular materials to high schools to allow those students who wish to pursue college-level studies while still in secondary school to receive advanced placement and/or credit upon entering college. The AP Program provides descriptions and exams on 35 introductory college courses in the following 20 fields: art, biology, chemistry, computer science, economics, English, French, German, government and politics, history, Latin, calculus, music, physics, environmental science, psychology, statistics, geography, and Spanish. No test is longer than 3 hours. All exams are paper–pencil tests (except the art portfolios) with an essay or problem-solving section and a multiple-choice section. Using the operational services provided by the Educational Testing Service, the AP Exams are administered in May by schools throughout the world. Any school may participate. Fee reductions are available for students with financial need. Also available in Braille and large print. Grades are sent to students, their schools, and colleges in July.

Format: Examiner required; suitable for group use; timed: 3 hours maximum

Scoring: Computer scored; examiner evaluated

Cost: $82.00 per exam

ASSET

| 1997, 2000, & 2001 | ACT, Inc. |

Population: Ages 18 years and older

Purpose: To assess writing, reading, numerical, and advanced math skills for course placement

Description: Multiple-choice 192-item paper-pencil test with the following categories. Writing (36 items); Reading (24 items); Numerical (32 items); Elementary Algebra (25 items); Intermediate Algebra (25 items); College Algebra (25 items), and Geometry (25 items). Scores yielded are Entering Student Descriptive Report, Returning Student Retention Report, Course Placement Service, and Underprepared Student Follow-Up. Forms B, B2, C1, and C2 are used. May be modified for students with disabilities.

Format: Examiner required; suitable for group use; timed: 25 minutes each subtest

Scoring: Hand key; machine scored; computer scored; scoring service available

Cost: 25 Test Booklets $30.00

Basic Achievement Skills Individual Screener (BASIS)

| 1983 | Harcourt Assessment, Inc. |

Population: Grades 1 and above

Purpose: Measures achievement in reading, mathematics, and spelling; assesses individual students' academic strengths and weaknesses with both norm-references and criterion-referenced information

Description: Three subtests assess academic achievement in reading, mathematics, and spelling. Test items are grouped in grade-referenced clusters, which constitute the basic unit of administration. Testing begins at a grade cluster with which the student is expected to have little difficulty and continues until the student fails to reach the criteria for a particular cluster. The clusters range from Readiness to Grade 8 for reading and mathematics and from Grades 1 to 8 for spelling. The reading test assesses comprehension of graded passages. The student is required to read the passages aloud and supply the missing words. Comprehension at the lower levels is assessed by word reading and sentence reading, and readiness is measured by letter identification and visual discrimination. The mathematics test consists of a readiness subtest and assesses computation and problem solving above that level. The student works on the computation items directly in the record form. Word problems are dictated by the teacher and require no reading on the part of the student. The spelling test for Grades 1 to 8 consists of clusters of words that are dictated in sentence contexts. The student writes the words on the record form.

Format: Examiner required; individual administration; untimed: 1 hour

Scoring: Hand key

Cost: Examiner's Kit (manual, content booklet, 2 record forms) $214.00

BRIGANCE® Comprehensive Inventory of Basic Scale–Revised (CIBS-R)

1999	Curriculum Associates®, Inc.

Albert H. Brigance

Population: Grades Pre-K to 9

Purpose: Measures attainment of basic academic skills; used to meet minimal competency requirements, develop IEPs, and determine academic placement

Description: A total of 154 skill sequences in the following 22 sections: Readiness, Speech, Word Recognition Grade Placement, Oral Reading, Reading Comprehension, Listening, Functional Word Recognition, Word Analysis, Reference Skills, Graphs and Maps, Spelling, Writing, Math Grade Placement, Numbers, Number Facts, Computation of Whole Numbers, Fractions and Mixed Numbers, Decimals, Percents, Word Problems, Metrics, and Math Vocabulary. Assessment is initiated at the skill level at which the student will be successful and continues until the student's level of achievement for that skill is attained. The following assessment methods may be used to ac-

commodate different situations: parent interview, teacher observation, group or individual, and informal appraisal of student performance in daily work. Two alternate forms, A and B, are available for pre- and posttesting for 51 skill sequences. All skill sequences are referenced to specific instructional objectives and grade-level expectations. The comprehensive book graphically indicates at each testing the level of competency the student has achieved. A videotape for in-service training of examiners is available. The revision includes normed assessments.

Format: Examiner required; many sections are suitable for group use; untimed

Scoring: Examiner evaluated; computer scoring available

Cost: Inventory with Standardization and Validation Manual $185.00; 10 Student Record Booklets $35.00

Canadian Achievement Survey Test for Adults (CAST)

1994	Canadian Test Centre

Population: Adults

Purpose: Measures achievement in reading, language, and mathematics

Description: Items were carefully screened and reviewed by Canadian adult educators and reflect language and content that are appropriate for adults. CAST scores can provide pre- and postinstruction information about an examinee's level of proficiency in the basic skills. Three levels are offered to accommodate the proficiency difference among adults: Level 1 for up to and including Grade 6, Level 2 for Grades 7 to 9, and Level 3 for Grade 10 and above. Each of the six CAST tests (two each in reading, language, and mathematics) were normed with a stratified random sample of over 16,000 senior high school students. Great care was taken to reduce bias from possible sources of greatest concern.

Format: Examiner required; individual or group administration; timed: 10 to 15 minutes for each test

Scoring: Hand key; machine scoring; scoring service available

Cost: Contact publisher

Canadian Achievement Tests– Third Edition (CAT-3)

2000	Canadian Test Centre

Population: Grades 1 to college

Purpose: Measures reading, language, writing, and mathematics

Description: The CAT-3 materials are easy to read while having a contemporary and attractive appearance. The format was finalized after much consultation with teachers, graphic artists, and publishing experts. The content was designed to reflect Canadian society and values. The tests are matched to four major Canadian curricula, those for Western Canada and the Territories, Ontario, Quebec, and Atlantic Canada. The assessments are in a modular and flexible format. The Basic Battery consists of a Reading/Language test that integrates comprehension, vocabulary, and language questions and a Mathematics test that includes questions from all strands as defined by each province. The Basic Battery can be comfortably administered within one morning of class time. Even more in-depth assessments of students' strengths and needs are provided through the Supplemental Tests: Word Analysis, Vocabulary, Spelling, Language/Writing Conventions, Computation, and Numerical Estimation. Norms are based on 11,000 students across Canada and are representative of the nation.

Format: Examiner required; individual or group administration; timed

Scoring: Hand key; machine scoring; scoring service available

Cost: Contact publisher

Canadian Tests of Basic Skills: High School Battery (CTBS), Levels 15-18, Form K

| 1998 | Thomson Nelson |

H. D. Hoover, A. Hieronymus, D. Frisbie

Population: Grades 9 to 12

Purpose: Assesses students' abilities in academic areas

Description: Four test levels (15 to 18) consist of a series of multiple-choice paper–pencil subtests: Vocabulary, Reading Comprehension, Quantitative Thinking, Written Expression, Using Sources of Information, and Science. This is an adaptation of the *Iowa Tests of Educational Development*, published by the Riverside Publishing Company.

Format: Examiner required; suitable for group use; timed: 195 minutes

Scoring: Hand key; machine scored; test scoring service available

Cost: Contact publisher

Canadian Tests of Basic Skills: Multilevel (CTBS), Levels 9-14, Forms K & L

| 1998 | Thomson Nelson |

E. King-Shaw, A. Hieronymus, H. D. Hoover

Population: Grades K 2 to 12

Purpose: Assesses students' abilities in vocabulary, reading comprehension, spelling, capitalization, punctuation, usage, visual materials, reference materials, mathematics concepts, mathematics problem solving, and mathematics computation

Description: A series of multiple-choice paper–pencil subtests: Vocabulary, Reading Comprehension, Spelling, Capitalization, Punctuation, Usage, Reference Materials, Maps and Diagrams, Mathematics Concepts, Mathematics Problem Solving, Mathematics Computation and Science. Materials include test booklets, answer sheets, scoring masks, teacher's guide, and supplementary materials as required. Form L is a shorter battery. This is an adaptation of the *Iowa Tests of Basic Skills*, published by the Riverside Publishing Company. Examiner must have a teaching certificate.

Format: Examiner required; suitable for group use; timed: Form K, 280 minutes; Form L, 100 minutes

Scoring: Hand key; machine scored; test scoring service available

Cost: Contact publisher

Canadian Tests of Basic Skills: Primary Battery (CTBS), Levels 5-8, Form K

| 1998 | Thomson Nelson |

E. King-Shaw, A. Hieronymus, H. D. Hoover

Population: Grades K 2 to 3.5

Purpose: Assesses students' abilities in listening, vocabulary, word analysis, language, reading, mathematics, and work study

Description: Four test levels (5 to 8) consist of a series of multiple-choice paper–pencil subtests: Listening, Vocabulary, Word Analysis, Language, Reading, Mathematics, and Work Study. Materials include test booklets, scoring masks, a teacher's guide, and supplementary materials as required. Examiner must have a teaching certificate. This test is a Canadian adaptation of the *Iowa Tests of Basic Skills,* published by the Riverside Publishing Company.

Format: Examiner required; suitable for group

use; untimed: 120 to 240 minutes (varies according to level)

Scoring: Hand key; machine scored; test scoring service available

Cost: Contact publisher

Career Programs Assessment Test (CPAt)

1997   **ACT, Inc.**

Population: Ages 18 years and older

Purpose: Used for career college admission and course placement to assess basic language, reading, and numerical skills

Description: Paper–pencil 115-item multiple-choice test with the following categories: Language Usage (60 items); Reading Skills (30 items); and Numerical Skills (25 items). These results are reported: scores for each content area and a composite; standard CPAt Summary Report; Customized CPAt Summary Report; and CPAt Retention Report. Forms B and C are available.

Format: Examiner required; individual and group administration; timed: 60 minutes

Scoring: Hand key; immediate results available

Cost: $165.00 per campus; $1.20 per test booklet; 50 Answer Sheets $125.00 (approximately $3.00 per student)

College Basic Academic Skills Examination (CBASE or College BASE)

2006   **Assessment Resource Center**

S. J. Osterlind

Population: College students

Purpose: Assesses knowledge of basic academic skills

Description: The instrument has 180 multiple-choice items that evaluate knowledge and skills in English, mathematics, science, and social studies. Each subject is further defined by clusters, skills, and subskills. CBASE has an optional essay prompt to evaluate students' writing abilities. Provides assessment of students' higher order thinking skills. Institutional and individual student report with composite score available. Test also available in large print and on audiocassette.

Format: Examiner required; group administration; untimed: 45 minutes per subject, 40 minutes for essay

Scoring: Machine scored, test scoring service available

Cost: Contact publisher

College-Level Examination Program (CLEP)

Yearly   **College Board**

Population: Grades 12 and above

Purpose: Enables any student to earn college credit by recognizing college-level achievement acquired outside the conventional college classroom; used by businesses to allow employees to earn required continuing education credits

Description: Thirty-four subject exams assessing college-level proficiency in a wide range of fields. The material tested is referred to as the general/liberal education requirement. The subject exams measure achievement in specific college courses and are used to grant exemption from and credit in specific college courses. The exams stress concepts, principles, relationships, and applications of course material. They contain questions of varying difficulty. Exams are administered each month via computer at more than 1,000 test centers located on college campuses throughout the country. Test scores are available immediately. Institutions honoring CLEP test scores for credit are listed in "CLEP Colleges," available free from the publisher.

Format: Examiner required; suitable for group use; timed: 90 minutes per test

Scoring: Computer scored; free response sections; examiner evaluated locally

Cost: $60.00 per exam + $15.00 administration fee

Comprehensive Testing Program– 4th Edition (CTP 4)

2002   **Educational Records Bureau**

Population: Grades 1 to 11

Purpose: Measures academic achievement

Description: This rigorous test battery designed to collect information about student achievement contains 10 levels, one for each grade from the spring of Grade 1 to the fall of Grade 11. Levels 1 to 3 allow students to place their answers directly in the test booklets. Depending on the grade of the student, the following areas are measured: Auditory Comprehension, Reading Comprehension, Word Analysis, Mathematics, Vocabulary, Writing Mechanics, and Writing Concepts and Skills. Verbal and Quantitative Reasoning is measured in Levels 3 to 10.

Format: Examiner required; group administration; timed: 300 minutes for full battery; partial battery an option

Scoring: Scoring service

Cost: Basic Scoring, Multiple-Choice Only $8.10 per student; other options available

Core Knowledge Curriculum-Referenced Tests

2000	Touchstone Applied Science Associates, Inc.

Population: Ages 6 to 10 years

Purpose: Assesses knowledge of core academic skills

Description: Paper–pencil multiple-choice criterion-referenced test with four subtests: Mathematics, Language Arts, History/Geography, and Science (35 to 50 items each, with a total of 140 to 200 items depending on grade). Individual scores for each subtest are obtained. Forms available: Grade 1: A1, Grade 2: A2, Grade 3: A3, Grade 4: A4, and Grade 5: A5.

Format: Requires examiner; suitable for group use; untimed: 45 to 55 minutes

Scoring: Machine scored; scoring service available

Cost: 25 Tests $131.00 (A1, A2), $99.00 (A3, A4, A5); 25 Answer Sheets (A3, A4, A5) $19.00

Criterion Test of Basic Skills (CTOBS)

2002	Academic Therapy Publications

James Evans, Kerth Lundell, William Brown

Population: Ages 6 to 11 years

Purpose: Assesses reading and arithmetic skills

Description: Paper–pencil multiple-item criterion-referenced test. The Reading subtest measures letter recognition, letter sounding, blending, sequencing, special sounds, and sight words. The Arithmetic subtest measures number and numerical recognition, addition, subtraction, multiplication, and division. Each part of the test offers optional objectives for evaluation. The manual contains over 200 teacher-directed, independent, and peer-tutoring activities correlated to the skill areas assessed and arranged according to increasing difficulty.

Format: Examiner required; individual or group administration; untimed: 15 to 20 minutes

Scoring: Examiner evaluated

Cost: Test Kit (manual, protocols, stimulus cards, in vinyl folder) $112.00

Diagnostic Achievement Battery–Third Edition (DAB-3)

2001	PRO-ED, Inc.

Phyllis L. Newcomer

Population: Ages 6 to 14 years

Purpose: Assesses a child's ability to listen, speak, read, write, and perform simple mathematics operations; diagnoses learning disabilities

Description: Multiple-item paper–pencil and oral-response subtests assess the following five components of a child's verbal and mathematical skills: Listening (Story Comprehension and Characteristics), Speaking (Synonyms and Grammatic Completion), Reading (Alphabet/Word Knowledge and Reading Comprehension), Written Language (Capitalization, Punctuation, Spelling, Contextual Language, and Story Construction), and Math (Math Reasoning and Math Calculation). Results, converted to standard scores, provide a profile of the child's strengths and weaknesses. The components of the test may be administered independently, depending on the needs of the child being tested.

Format: Examiner required; individual administration; untimed: 50 minutes

Scoring: Examiner evaluated; computer scoring available

Cost: Complete Kit (manual, student book, 25 record forms, 25 response forms, audiocassette, assessment probes, storage box) $285.00

Diagnostic Achievement Test for Adolescents–Second Edition (DATA-2)

1993	PRO-ED, Inc.

Phyllis L. Newcomer, Brian R. Bryant

Population: Ages 12 to 18 years

Purpose: Assesses a child's ability to listen, speak, read, write, and perform simple mathematics operations; diagnoses learning disabilities

Description: This multiple-item paper–pencil and oral-response test consists of 10 core subtests and 3 supplemental subtests. The core subtests are Receptive Vocabulary, Receptive Grammar, Expressive Grammar, Expressive Vocabulary, Word Identification, Reading Comprehension, Math Calculations, Math Problem Solving, Spelling, and Writing Composition. The supplemental subtests are Science, Social Studies, and Reference Skills. Nine composite standard scores are generated.

Format: Examiner required; individual administration; untimed: 50 minutes

Scoring: Examiner evaluated

Cost: Complete Kit (manual, student book, 25 protocols, 25 student response booklets, storage box) $175.00

Diagnostic Screening Test: Achievement (DSTA)

1977	Slosson Educational Publications, Inc.

Thomas D. Gnagey, Patricia A. Gnagey

Population: Grades K to 13

Purpose: Measures basic knowledge of science, social studies, literature, and the arts to help determine a course of study for special education students

Description: Paper–pencil 108-item multiple-choice test. Scores are obtained for practical knowledge and provide an estimated mental age. The manual discusses subtest pattern analysis of student motivation, cultural versus organic retardation, cultural deprivation, reading and study skill problems, and possession of practical versus formal knowledge. The examiner explains the procedure to individuals or groups and reads the test if the students have poor reading skills.

Format: Examiner required; suitable for group use; untimed: 5 to 10 minutes

Scoring: Hand key

Cost: Manual and 50 Test Forms $72.25

Einstein Evaluation of School-Related Skills (E = MC^2)

1996	Slosson Educational Publications, Inc.

Ruth L. Gottesman, Jo Ann Doino-Ingersoll, Frances M. Cerullo

Population: Grades K to 5

Purpose: Used to identify children who are at risk for or are experiencing school learning difficulties

Description: The test has six levels, one for each grade. Major skill areas underlying school

achievement are measured: Language/Cognition, Letter Recognition, Word Recognition, Oral Reading, Reading Comprehension, Auditory Memory, Arithmetic, and Visual-Motor Integration. The total score reflects the child's overall performance on a variety of tasks that assess school-related skills.

Format: Examiner required; individual administration; untimed: 7 to 10 minutes

Scoring: Hand key

Cost: Complete Multilevel Kit (manual, student booklets, 5 examiner forms for 5 levels) $96.25

Essential Skills Screener (ESS)

1995	Slosson Educational Publications, Inc.

Bradley T. Erford, Gary J. Vitali, RoseMary Haas, Rita R. Boykin

Population: Ages 3 to 11 years

Purpose: Identifies children at risk for school readiness or learning problems

Description: Reading, writing, and math skills are assessed for children in three age ranges: 3 to 5, 6 to 8, and 9 to 11. The ESS provides both grade and age norms. Interpretation is simplified through the use of percentile ranks, performance ranges, and standard scores. Age and grade scores are provided.

Format: Examiner required; individual or group administration; untimed: 10 minutes

Scoring: Hand key

Cost: Complete Multilevel Kit $237.25

Evaluation of Basic Skills (EBS)

1996	Trust Tutoring

Lee Havis

Population: Ages 3 to 18 years

Purpose: Measures basic skills in reading, writing, and math

Description: Provides a reliable measure of basic skill ability of students enrolled in a program of individualized in-home learning. The EBS is easy to administer and provides raw scores compared to age-level performance on easy-to-read charts. Areas of weakness and lack of concept understanding are revealed. Concepts in math are isolated for clear basic information. Specific rules of phonics are also isolated and sequenced in difficulty. Supplemental word test I and II included.

Format: Examiner required; individual or group administration; timed and untimed

Scoring: Hand key

Cost: Startup Kit (50 forms, manual, audiotape, 25 each of both word tests) $89.95

EXPLORE

1997	ACT, Inc.

Population: Grades 8 and 9

Purpose: Measures educational achievement for counseling and evaluation

Description: Paper–pencil 128-item multiple-choice test with the following categories: English Test (40 items, 30 minutes), Math Test (30 items, 30 minutes), Reading Test (30 items, 30 minutes), and Science Reasoning (28 items, 30 minutes). The results are reported are as follows: English Test total score and two subscores: Usage/Mechanics and Rhetorical Skills; a Mathematics Test total score; a Reading Test total score; a Science Reasoning Test total score; and a Composite score. Raw scores are converted to scale scores; scale scores for the four tests and the composite range from a low of 1 to a high of 12. The EXPLORE Program also collects information about students' career interests, educational plans, and special educational needs. Suitable for individuals with visual, physical, hearing, and mental impairments.

Format: Examiner required; suitable for group use; timed: 120 minutes

Scoring: Scoring service

Cost: 30 Reusable Test Booklets $52.50; 30 Consumable Student Assessment Sets $141.00

GOAL Formative Assessment

2002	Hodder Murray

Population: Ages 7 to 16

Purpose: Monitors individual and class progress and provides effective assessment for learning

Description: The assessment yields diagnostic feedback that supports effective teaching, learning, and target setting. As such, it provides a standardized basis for monitoring across the core curriculum in Literacy, Math, Science, and Information and Communications Technology. The tests allow all pupils to show their strengths. Each test is easy to administer. Pupils record their answers in the test booklet. A simple-to-use diagnostic mark scheme allows the teacher to profile strengths and weaknesses. Key Stage 2 tests have 50 items that cover national curriculum Levels 1 to 5, while Key Stage 3 tests have 60 items that cover Levels 2 to 7. For each pupil, each test gives

a national curriculum level, plus a standardized score and percentile.

Format: Examiner required; group administration, untimed: 45 minutes

Scoring: Examiner evaluated

Cost: Price varies

Graduate Record Examinations (GRE)

Updated yearly	Educational Testing Service

Population: Adults, college graduates

Purpose: Measures academic abilities and knowledge of graduate school applicants; used by graduate schools for screening the qualifications of applicants and by organizations for selecting fellowship recipients

Description: Multiple-item paper–pencil multiple-choice battery of advanced achievement and aptitude tests. The General Test measures verbal, quantitative, and analytical abilities. The Subject Tests are available for the following 17 subjects: biology, chemistry computer science, economics, education, engineering, French, geology, history, literature in English, mathematics, music, physics, political science, psychology, sociology, and Spanish. The tests are administered on specified dates at centers established by the publisher. The General Test is also offered on computer, taken at the examinee's convenience, at Sylvan Learning Centers.

Format: Examiner required; suitable for group use; timed: general test, 3 hours 30 minutes; subject tests, 2 hours 50 minutes each

Scoring: Computer scored; scoring service

Cost: Contact publisher

Hammill Multiability Achievement Test (HAMAT)

1998	PRO-ED, Inc.

Donald D. Hammill, Wayne P. Hresko, Jerome J. Ammer, Mary E. Cronin, Sally S. Quinby

Population: Ages 7 to 17 years

Purpose: Measures achievement in basic academic areas

Description: A content-driven achievement test that measures reading, writing, mathematics, and facts. The Reading subtest consists of a series of paragraphs, based on the cloze procedure. The Writing subtest requires the student to write sentences from dictation, stressing correctness. The Mathematics subtest measures the student's mastery of number facts and ability to complete mathematical calculations. The Facts subtest requires the student to answer questions that are based on the content of social studies, science, history, and literature curricula. Scores provided are standard scores (mean of 100, standard deviation 15), percentiles, and age and grade equivalents. The HAMAT was normed on 2,901 students. Alternate equivalent forms are available.

Format: Examiner required; individual or group administration; untimed: 30 to 60 minutes

Scoring: Examiner evaluated

Cost: Complete Kit (manual, 25 each of Form A and B student response and record booklets, storage box) $210.00

Hunter-Grundin Literacy Profiles

Date not provided   Hogrefe Limited

Elizabeth Hunter-Grundin, Hans U. Grundin

Population: Ages 6 years 6 months to 12+ years

Purpose: Assesses child's progress in reading and language development

Description: Battery of brief paper–pencil and oral tests measuring five components of literacy skills, including reading for meaning, attitude toward reading, spelling, free writing, and spoken language. The test is available on five levels: Level 1 (ages 6.5 to 8), Level 2 (ages 8 to 9), Level 3 (ages 9 to 10), Level 4 (ages 10 to 11+), and Level 5 (ages 11 to 12+). The Reading for Meaning passage is different at each level. The score correlates with the *Schonell Reading Test, Holborn Reading Scale,* and the *Neale Analysis of Reading Ability.* Only the Spoken Language subtest must be individually administered.

Format: Examiner required; individual or group administration; timed: 10 minutes

Scoring: Hand key

Cost: Contact publisher

Iowa Tests of Basic Skills® (ITBS®), Forms A and B

2001 (A), 2003 (B)   Riverside Publishing Company

H. D. Hoover, S. B. Dunbar, D. A. Frisbie

Population: Grades K to 9

Purpose: Provides a comprehensive assessment of student progress in the basic skills

Description: All-new test content aligned with the most current content standards, curriculum frameworks, and instructional materials measures critical-thinking skills across test levels, in every content area. Developed at the University of Iowa and backed by a tradition of more than 70 years of educational research and test development experience, the ITBS provides an in-depth assessment of students' achievement of important educational objectives. Tests in reading, language arts, mathematics, social studies, science, and information sources yield reliable and comprehensive information both about the development of students' skills and about their ability to think critically. The battery is available as a Complete Battery, a Core Battery (Reading, Language, and Mathematics tests only), and a Survey Battery (a shortened version of the Core Battery).

Format: Examiner required; suitable for group use; time varies according to battery

Scoring: Hand key; may be machine scored; scoring service available

Cost: Contact publisher

Iowa Tests of Educational Development® (ITED®), Forms A and B

2001 (A), 2003 (B)   Riverside Publishing Company

Robert A. Forsyth, Timothy N. Ansley, Leonard S. Feldt, Stephanie D. Alnot

Population: Grades 9 to 12

Purpose: Assesses academic skills that represent the long-term goals of secondary education; particularly the critical-thinking skills of analysis and evaluation

Description: The battery represents an upward extension of the *Iowa Tests of Basic Skills.* Available in either a Complete Battery booklet or a Core Battery booklet. The Complete Battery contains nine tests: Vocabulary, Reading Comprehension, Language: Revision Written Materials, Spelling, Mathematics: Concepts and Problem Solving, Computation, Analysis of Social Studies Materials, Analysis of Science Materials, and Sources of Information. The Core Battery contains the first six tests of the Complete.

Format: Examiner required; suitable for group use; time varies according to battery

Scoring: Hand key; may be machine scored; scoring service available

Cost: Contact publisher

Kaufman Functional Academic Skill Test (K-FAST)

| 1994 | AGS Publishing/Pearson Assessments |

Alan S. Kaufman, Nadeen L. Kaufman

Population: Ages 15 to 85+ years

Purpose: Measures reading and math functional skills

Description: Unlike adaptive behavior inventories that ask an informant to rate how a person functions, the K-FAST requires subjects to show they can perform the requested skill. K-FAST reading and arithmetic tasks relate to everyday activities, such as understanding labels on drug containers, following directions in a recipe, budgeting monthly expenses, and making price comparisons between products.

Format: Examiner required; individual administration; untimed: 15 to 25 minutes

Scoring: Examiner interpretation

Cost: Complete Kit (manual, easel, 25 forms) $144.95

Kaufman Test of Educational Achievement–Second Edition (KTEA-II)

| 2004 | AGS Publishing/Pearson Assessments |

Alan S. Kaufman, Nadeen L. Kaufman

Population: Ages 4 years 6 months to 25 years (Comprehensive Form); Ages 4 years 6 months to 90+ years (Brief Form)

Purpose: Diagnostic battery that measures reading, mathematics, written language, and oral language

Description: The battery covers achievement areas mandated by IDEA and Reading First for a comprehensive, research-based assessment. Alternate forms can be used to measure progress or response to intervention when using the Comprehensive Form. The Comprehensive Form provides composite scores for all examinees. Six additional subtests assess reading-related skills to give diagnostic information. The Brief Form (Reading, Math, and Written Expression) provides a short measure of achievement for screening and prereferral and yields norm-referenced subtest scores and a battery composite.

Format: Examiner required; individual administration; untimed: Comprehensive Form, 30 to 80 minutes; Brief Form, 15 to 45 minutes

Scoring: Examiner interpreted; computer scoring available for Windows and Mac formats

Cost: Complete Kit for Comprehensive (test easels, manuals, 25 of each protocol, stimulus material, tote bag) $564.99; Complete Kit for Brief (manuals, test easel, 25 of each protocol, briefcase) $154.99

Language Assessment System–LAS™ Links

| 2005 | CTB/McGraw-Hill |

Population: Grades K to 12

Purpose: Evaluates reading, writing, listening, speaking, and comprehension skills of English language learners

Description: Enables accurate placement and annual evaluation for bilingual or English as a second language instruction. The assessments are available in five grade bands: Primary (K to 1), Early Elementary (2 to 3), Elementary (4 to 5), Middle School (6 to 8), and High School (9 to 12). The test formats include multiple-choice and performance based questions.

Format: Examiner required; group administration; untimed; 95 to 115 minutes

Scoring: Examiner evaluated; scoring service available

Cost: Contact publisher

Metropolitan Achievement Test®– Eighth Edition (MAT-8)

| 2000 | Harcourt Assessment, Inc. |

Population: Grades K to 12

Purpose: Assesses school achievement; used for measuring performance of large groups of students

Description: Combining real-world content and design with cutting-edge reporting information that provides educators and parents with action strategies, this test is a smart choice for all children. Test questions range from measuring foundation skills to critical-thinking processes and strategies. This new edition reflects what is taught in today's classrooms. Subjects measured are Reading, Mathematics, Language, Writing, Science, and Social Studies. An interactive, online assessment is available for Grades 3 to 8 in Reading Comprehension, Mathematics Concepts and Problem Solving, and Mathematics Computation.

The battery can be easily customized to match local curriculum and testing requirements. Available in 13 levels based on grade.

Format: Examiner required; suitable for group use; timed: varies from 90 minutes to more than 4 hours

Scoring: Hand key; may be machine/computer scored; scoring service available; online scoring available

Cost: Examination Kit for Preview Only $42.00 per level

Mini-Battery of Achievement (MBA)

1994	Riverside Publishing Company

Richard W. Woodcock, Kevin S. McGrew, Judy Werder

Population: Ages 4 years to adult

Purpose: Provides a brief screening of achievement

Description: Designed to give broader coverage of the skills included in each achievement area, the MBA has four subtests: Reading, Mathematics, Writing, and Factual Knowledge. The Reading subtest measures a variety of aspects of reading, including sight recognition, comprehension, and vocabulary. The Mathematics subtest includes calculation, reasoning, and concepts. The Writing subtest includes spelling dictation, punctuation, usage, and proofing. The Factual Knowledge subtest helps assess general information in science, social studies, and the humanities. Each of the four subtests can be administered and scored independently of the others. Reading, writing, and mathematics scores can be combined to obtain a Basic Skills Cluster score. The MBA includes a computer program that will print a one-page narrative report summarizing all test results in a matter of seconds.

Format: Examiner required; individual administration; untimed: 20 minutes

Scoring: Computer scored; examiner evaluated

Cost: Complete Test (test book with manual, 25 test records with worksheets, software) $231.00

Monitoring Basic Skills Progress (MBSP)

Reading 1997; Math Computation 1998; Math Concepts and Applications 1999	PRO-ED, Inc.

Lynn S. Fuchs, Carol Hamlett, Douglas Fuchs

Population: Elementary and middle school grades

Purpose: Monitors progress in three academic areas: basic reading, basic math computation, and basic math concepts and applications

Description: Computers will automatically conduct curriculum-based measurement, provide students with immediate feedback on their progress, and provide teachers with individual and classwide reports that help them to plan more effective instruction. These programs automatically save students' scores and prepare graphs displaying the students' progress over time. The two math programs come with printed copies of tests for Grades 1 to 6. The child works the problem on the reproducible worksheet and inputs the answers for scoring.

Format: Self-administered; untimed

Scoring: Computer scored; Macintosh format only

Cost: Complete Program (one each of basic reading, basic math computation, and basic math concepts and applications, blackline masters for both math programs) $369.00

Multilevel Academic Survey Tests (MAST)

1985	Harcourt Assessment, Inc.

Kenneth W. Howell, Stanley H. Zucker, Mada K. Morehead

Population: Grades K to 12

Purpose: Assesses academic performance to ensure meaningful placement and curriculum decisions

Description: Multiple-item paper–pencil test using two methods: Grade Level and Curriculum Level. In the Grade Level tests, three levels are available: Primary, Short (reading and mathematics), and Extended (includes reading comprehension and problem solving). The Curriculum Level tests include comprehensive reading and mathematics.

Format: Examiner required; suitable for group use; untimed: 10 minutes to 30 minutes

Scoring: Examiner evaluated

Cost: Examination Kit (manual, grade-level test booklet, answer sheet, record form) $99.00

National Educational Development Test (NEDT)

1984	CTB/McGraw-Hill

Population: Grades 9 and 10

Purpose: Assesses students' strengths and weaknesses in English, math, social studies, reading, natural sciences, and educational ability

Description: Paper-pencil 209-item test measuring the ability to apply rules and principles of grammar and general English usage, understand mathematical concepts, and apply principles in solving quantitative problems, comprehend reading selections, and apply critical-reading skills. The test is semisecure (forms and keys are not released). The test is used only in schools that choose to serve as designated test centers.

Format: Examiner required; suitable for group use; timed: 2 hours 30 minutes

Scoring: Computer scored

Cost: Contact publisher

Norris Educational Achievement Test (NEAT)

1992	Western Psychological Services

Janet Switzer, Christian P. Gruber

Population: Ages 4 to 17 years

Purpose: Used as a standard assessment of basic educational abilities

Description: This diagnostic achievement battery features alternate forms, optional measures of written language and oral reading and comprehension, separate grade and age norms, tables identifying discrepancies between IQ and achievement, and a standardization sample. Readiness Tests are used to assess children between 4 and 6 years of age, and Achievement Tests are used to evaluate examinees ages 6 years and older.

Format: Examiner required; individually administered; untimed: 30 minutes

Scoring: Hand key

Cost: Kit (10 test booklets, administration and scoring manual, technical manual) $150.00

Peabody Individual Achievement Test-Revised/Normative Update (PIAT-R/NU)

1998	AGS Publishing/Pearson Assessments

Frederick C. Markwardt, Jr.

Population: Ages 5 to 22 years

Purpose: Measures academic achievement

Description: The PIAT-R/NU is an efficient individual measure of academic achievement. Reading, mathematics, and spelling are assessed in a simple, nonthreatening format that requires only a pointing response for most items. This multiple-choice format makes the instrument ideal for assessing individuals who are low functioning. There are six subtests: General Information, Reading Recognition, Reading Comprehension, Written Expression, Mathematics, and Spelling.

Format: Examiner required; individual administration; untimed: 60 minutes

Scoring: Examiner evaluated; computer scoring is available for Macintosh and Windows formats

Cost: Complete Kit (4 easels, 50 record forms, manual, carrying bag) $385.99

PLAN

Yearly	ACT, Inc.

Population: Grade 10

Purpose: Used in student guidance and program evaluation to assess educational achievement

Description: Paper-pencil 145-item multiple-choice test with the following categories: English (50 items, 30 minutes), Math (40 items, 40 minutes), Reading (25 items, 20 minutes), and Science Reasoning (30 items, 25 minutes). The following results are reported: English Test total score and two subscores: Usage/Mechanics and Rhetorical Skills; Math Test total score and two subscores: Pre-Algebra/Algebra and Geometry; Reading Test total score; and Science Reasoning Test total score. Raw scores are converted to scale scores; scale scores for the four tests and the composite range from a low of 1 to a high of 32. Subscores are reported on a scale score ranging from a low of 1 to a high of 16.

Format: Examiner required; suitable for group use; timed: 115 minutes

Scoring: Machine scored; test scoring service available

Cost: $8.25 per individual

Pre-Professional Skills Test (PPST)

Date not provided	Educational Testing Service

Population: College students

Purpose: Measures the basic academic skills and achievement of individuals preparing for careers as elementary or high school teachers

Description: Multiple-item paper-pencil multiple-choice and essay test assessing proficiency in reading, writing, and mathematics. The 50-minute Reading test (40 questions) assesses the ability to understand, analyze, and evaluate short passages (100 words), long passages (200

words), and short statements. The 50-minute Mathematics test (40 questions) evaluates the ability to judge mathematical relations. The two-part Writing test consists of a 45-item multiple-choice test of functional written English (30 minutes) and an essay (30 minutes). Each part is graded separately and combined for a single Writing score.

Format: Examiner required; suitable for group use; timed: 3 hours

Scoring: Computer scored; examiner evaluated

Cost: Contact publisher

Quic Tests

2005	Scholastic Testing Service, Inc.

Oliver Anderhalter

Population: Grades 2 to 12

Purpose: Used as an estimation of grade placement to assess achievement in communications and math

Description: Multiple-choice test with five to eight items per grade. Grade equivalent scores and competency-based grade equivalent scores are yielded. Alternate forms for both Communicative Arts and Mathematics are available.

Format: Examiner required; group administration; untimed: 35 minutes

Scoring: Examiner evaluated

Cost: Starter Set (manual, 20 test booklets, 20 response forms) specify which area and which form $68.90

SAT Subject Tests

Yearly	College Board

Population: Grades 9 to 12

Purpose: Used to predict college performance and by some schools for admissions selection and course placement in specific subject areas

Description: Paper–pencil multiple-choice tests in Writing, Literature, U.S. History and Social Studies, World History, Math (Levels I and II), Biology, Chemistry, Physics, French, German, Modern Hebrew, Italian, Latin, Korean, and Spanish. An individual may take up to three SAT Subject Tests on a single test date. The use of a calculator is allowed on Math Level I and Math Level II. They require a scientific calculator. Fee waivers are available for students with financial need. Available in a variety of formats if needed for students with disabilities.

Format: Examiner required; suitable for group use; timed: 1 hour

Scoring: Computer scored

Cost: $26.00 to $37.00 per exam

Scholastic Abilities Test for Adults (SATA)

1991	PRO-ED, Inc.

Brian R. Bryant, James R. Patton, Caroline Dunn

Population: Ages 16 years and older

Purpose: Measures an individual's scholastic aptitude and achievement; used to identify an individual's strengths and weaknesses and identify persons who may need special assistance in secondary and postsecondary training and educational settings

Description: Multiple-item paper–pencil assessment battery consisting of nine subtests: Verbal Reasoning—understanding verbal analogies; Nonverbal Reasoning—using geometric forms to assess nonverbal problem solving; Quantitative Reasoning—determining problem-solving abilities using numbers; Reading Vocabulary—recognizing synonyms and antonyms in print; Reading Comprehension—reading passages silently and responding to multiple-choice items; Math Calculation—computing arithmetic, geometry, and algebra problems; Math Application—reading and computing story problems; Writing Mechanics—writing sentences that require spelling, capitalization, and punctuation skills; and Writing Composition—writing a story that is checked for content maturity and vocabulary. Individual subtest raw scores are converted to estimated grade equivalents, standard scores ($M = 10$, $SD = 3$), and percentiles. Several composite scores are also generated: General Aptitude, Total Achievement, Reading, Mathematics, and Writing. Composite scores are reported as estimated grade equivalents, standard scores ($M = 100$, $SD = 15$), and percentiles. Norms are available as timed and untimed.

Format: Examiner required; suitable for group use; timed: 10 to 15 minutes each subtest

Scoring: Examiner evaluated

Cost: Complete Kit (manual, 10 test booklets, 25 response forms, 25 profile/summary forms, storage box) $159.00

Secondary Assessment Series

1991   CASAS

Population: Adults, adolescents; Native and nonnative speakers of English

Purpose: Measures a learner's reading comprehension, critical-thinking, and problem-solving capabilities in eight core academic subjects

Description: Multiple-choice tests include Mathematics, Economics, American Government, U.S. History, English/Language Arts, World History, Biological Science, and Physical Science. CASAS-scaled scores identify general skill level and enable comparison of performance across CASAS tests. Training required. Programs use the tests to award high school credit and for determining placement, monitoring progress, and targeting instruction.

Format: Examiner required; group administered; timed and untimed

Scoring: Self-/Computer scored

Cost: Testing Package (5 pretest booklets, 5 posttest booklets for each area) $220.00; Manual $15.00

Secondary School Admission Test (SSAT)

Updated yearly   Educational Testing Service

Population: Grades 5 to 10

Purpose: Measures the abilities of students applying for admission to selective schools; used by independent schools for student selection

Description: This multiple item paper pencil multiple-choice test measures verbal and quantitative abilities and reading comprehension. The test consists of four sections: one measuring verbal ability, two measuring mathematical ability, and one measuring reading comprehension. An upper level form is administered to students in Grades 8 to 10; a lower form is administered to students in Grades 5 to 7. Scores are normed on the student's grade level at the time of testing. Norms for each grade level are developed annually on the basis of the most recent 3-year sample of candidates tested. The test is administered on specific dates (six Saturdays during the school year and biweekly during the summer) at designated test centers. Students may designate six score recipients. Students with physical or visual disabilities are allowed up to double the amount of testing time per section.

Format: Examiner required; suitable for group use; timed: varies

Scoring: Computer scored; hand key

Cost: Domestic Test Fee (administration, parents' score report, six designated school reports) $25.00; Foreign Test Fee (including Canada, Puerto Rico, U.S. territories) $45.00

Secondary Screening Profiles

1995   Hodder Murray

Population: Ages 10 to 13 years

Purpose: Provides an objective assessment and profile of skills in reading, mathematics, and reasoning

Description: Identifies pupils' individual strengths and weaknesses on entry to secondary school. Generates a baseline against which to evaluate subsequent attainment. The Reading Test gives an objective measure of performance in comprehension, vocabulary, and understanding points of view. The Mathematics Test is designed to be independent of math teaching schemes and assesses number and algebra; shape; space and measures; and data-handling skills. The Reasoning Test includes a wide range of questions assessing both verbal and nonverbal (numerical and visual) skills and is a useful predictor of future school attainment. Parallel forms are available for all tests.

Format: Examiner required; group administration; untimed

Scoring: Examiner evaluated

Cost: Specimen Set (manual, 1 each of all tests) £25.00

Stanford Achievement Test™ Series– Tenth Edition (Stanford 10)

2002   Harcourt Assessment, Inc.

Population: Grades K to 12

Purpose: Assesses school achievement status of children in reading, mathematics, language, spelling, study skills, science, social studies, and listening

Description: Contains multiple-choice and open-ended assessment with a variety of battery configurations to meet individual schools' needs. A separate writing test is available either in paper–pencil format or online. Year 2000 norms are available from a norm group sample from more than 10 million students. The sample statistically represents the current U.S. student population. In addition, Stanford 10 offers separate sets of empirical normative information for the following subgroups: Catholic, Private, High Socioeconomic Status, and Urban.

Format: Examiner required; suitable for group use; timed: varies by subtest

Scoring: Hand key; scoring service available

Cost: Examination Kit (for preview only) $42.00 per level

TerraNova® (CTB5-5)

1996	CTB/McGraw-Hill

Population: Grades K to 12

Purpose: Assesses academic achievement in multiple measures format

Description: Multiple-item paper–pencil norm- and criterion-referenced multiple-choice/short-answer/essay assessment system with multiple components. Consists of Reading/Language Arts, Mathematics, Science, and Social Studies subtests. Available in Forms A or B. Spanish version available.

Format: Examiner required; suitable for group use; timed

Scoring: Hand key; machine scored; hand scored for constructed response

Cost: Contact publisher

TerraNova®, The Second Edition

2000	CTB/McGraw-Hill

Population: Grades K to 12

Purpose: Measures achievement in reading/language arts, math, science, and social studies

Description: The new edition offers a full range of testing options, from selected-response to open-ended tasks. Together, these assessments give students the best opportunity to show what they know and can do. Examiners can choose the combination that best meets their needs and customize the solution to reflect local and state standards. CTB offers custom options to complement any of the TerraNova assessments, or to serve as the basis for a local testing program. Two forms are available (C and D). The math subtest requires manipulatives that are included with booklets. Higher-order thinking skills, as well as basic and applied skills, are measured. It generates norm-referenced achievement scores, criterion-referenced objective mastery scores, and performance-level information.

Format: Examiner required; suitable for group use; timed and untimed

Scoring: Hand key; machine scored; scoring service available

Cost: Contact publisher

Test of Academic Achievement Scale–Revised (TAAS-R)

1999	Academic Therapy Publications

Morrison F. Gardner

Population: Ages 5 to 14 years

Purpose: Measures academic abilities

Description: The revised edition contains a new subtest: Oral Reading Stories and Comprehension. The revision measures how well a child has mastered various academic subjects. The subtests are Spelling, Letter and Word Reading, Listening Comprehension, and Arithmetic. Results are provided in standard scores.

Format: Examiner required; individual administration; untimed: 30 to 40 minutes

Scoring: Examiner evaluated

Cost: Complete Kit (manual, 25 test booklets, oral reading stories booklet, card) $100.00

Test of Academic Performance

1989	Harcourt Assessment, Inc.

Wayne Adams, Lynn Erb, David Sheslow

Population: Grades K to 12

Purpose: Assesses math, reading, writing, and spelling

Description: The test uses classroom-familiar formats. Spelling is assessed through dictation; mathematics is assessed through computation, and reading is assessed through decoding and comprehension of material read silently. There are two optional writing subtests.

Format: Examiner required; individual administration; untimed: 20 to 45 minutes

Scoring: Examiner evaluated

Cost: Complete Program (manual, 25 each of response forms and record forms, cards) $150.00

Tests of Adult Basic Education (TABE-PC™)

1994	CTB/McGraw-Hill

Population: Adults

Purpose: Provides automatic test administration,

scoring, and reporting of the TABE™ basic skills assessments

Description: Computerized version of the TABE™ basic skills assessments. Software is available for TABE Forms 9 and 10, TABE Forms 7 and 8, TABE Advanced Level Tests, TABE Work-Related Foundation Skills, and TABE Español.

Format: Examiner required; computer administered; complete battery, 2 hours 45 minutes; survey form, 1 hour 30 minutes

Scoring: Computer scored

Cost: Contact publisher

Tests of Adult Basic Education (TABE™), Forms 9 and 10

2003	CTB/McGraw-Hill

Population: Ages 16 years to adult

Purpose: Measures adult proficiency in reading, mathematics, and language; used to identify individual strengths and needs, establish appropriate level of instruction, and measure growth after instruction

Description: The TABE Forms 9 and 10 are used to measure achievement of basic skills commonly found in adult basic education curricula taught in high school and adult instructional programs. The program consists of a locator test for appropriate placement, and a pre- and posttest to measure growth. Two forms are available. Scores include scale scores, number correct, grade equivalents, and objectives mastery. Content covers material through Grade 12.9.

Format: Examiner required; suitable for group use; complete battery, 2 hours 8 minutes

Scoring: Examiner evaluated; computer scoring available; scoring service available

Cost: Contact publisher

Valpar Test of Essential Skills in English & Math (VTES)

1998	Valpar International Corporation

Bryan B. Christopherson, Alex Swartz

Population: Ages 15 years and older

Purpose: Measures basic English and math skills for adult basic education

Description: Math skills tested are computation (Grades 4 to 8, 20 items), usage (Grades 6 to 10, 21 items). English skills assessed are vocabulary (25 items), Spelling (5 items), usage (10 items), and reading (10 items). Items are presented in a multiple-choice format. Scores provided are

grade equivalents, percent correct by subarea, and GED Math and Language levels.

Format: Examiner required; suitable for group administration; untimed: 45 minutes

Scoring: Computer scored; machine scored; test scoring service available

Cost: $50.00 for Evaluation Kit (approximately $1.00 per complete test)

Wechsler Individual Achievement Test®-Second Edition (WIAT®-II)

2001	Harcourt Assessment, Inc.

Population: Ages 4 to 85 years

Purpose: Measures academic abilities to evaluate discrepancies between aptitude and achievement

Description: An expanded age range, more comprehensive items, and streamlined test materials are just a few of the benefits of the second edition. The subtests are Oral Language, Listening Comprehension, Written Expression, Spelling, Word Reading, Pseudoword Decoding, Reading Comprehension, Numerical Operations, and Mathematics Reasoning. The examiner can elect to administer the entire battery or select subtests for a more focused assessment. Age- and grade-based norms are available. An abbreviated version includes three subtests: Spelling, Word Reading, and Numerical Operations.

Format: Examiner required; individual administration; untimed: full, 45 to 120 minutes; abbreviated, 10 to 20 minutes

Scoring: Hand key; computer scoring available

Cost: Complete Kit (manual, stimulus booklets, 25 protocols, bag) $399.00; Abbreviated Kit (manual, 25 protocols, word cards, bag) $175.00

Wide Range Achievement Test– Expanded Edition (WRAT-Expanded)

2001	Psychological Assessment Resources, Inc.

Gary J. Robertson

Population: Ages 4 to 24 years

Purpose: Measures academic achievement and nonverbal reasoning

Description: Measures achievement in the areas of reading comprehension, mathematics, listening comprehension, oral expression, and written language. The test includes both group-administered and individually administered formats. Results on the group- and individually administered test forms can be compared resulting in a number of technical benefits to the user. The Group Form is available in five levels designed for Grades 2 to 12. Each level contains four subtests: Reading Comprehension, Mathematics, Written Language, and Nonverbal Reasoning. The Individual Form contains Pre-reading Skills, Beginning Reading, Reading Comprehension, Beginning Mathematics, Mathematics, Listening Comprehension, and Oral Expression. The same Written Language test is given in group and individual.

Format: Examiner required; suitable for group administration; untimed: 2 hours 30 minutes

Scoring: Hand key

Cost: Group Package (manual, 25 booklets) $158.00 per level; Individual Package (manual, flip books, 25 forms) $290.00

Wide Range Achievement Test–Fourth Edition (WRAT4™)

2006	Psychological Assessment Resources, Inc.

Gary S. Wilkinson, Gary J. Robertson

Population: Ages 5 to 94 years

Purpose: Measures basic academic skills of reading, sentence comprehension, spelling, and math computation

Description: Several new features have been added to the WRAT4. In addition to updated norms, the WRAT4 contains an entirely new measure of reading achievement—Sentence Comprehension—added to enhance the scope of the content measured and to meet a need often expressed by users of previous editions for a measure of reading comprehension. The other subtests are Word Reading, Spelling, and Math Computation. Alternate forms, designated the Blue Form and the Green Form, were developed and equated during standardization by use of a common-person research design. Derived scores were developed for both age- and grade-referenced groups. Standard scores, percentile ranks, stanines, normal curve equivalents, grade equivalents, and Rasch ability scaled scores are provided. The Blue Form and the Green Form can be used interchangeably with comparable results, thus permitting retesting within short periods of time without the potential practice effects that may occur from repeating the same items. The alternate forms also can be administered together (i.e., Combined Form) in a single examination. For those interested in a more qualitative assessment of academic skills, the Combined Form provides an additional opportunity for performance observance.

Format: Examiner required; portions suitable for group administration; untimed: 30 minutes

Scoring: Examiner evaluated; computer scoring available

Cost: Introductory Kit (manual, 25 of each form, cards) $235.00

Woodcock-Johnson® III (WJ III®) Tests of Achievement

2001	Riverside Publishing Company

Richard W. Woodcock, Kevin S. McGrew, Nancy Mather

Population: Ages 2 to 90+ years

Purpose: Provides a comprehensive assessment of oral language and achievement

Description: Comes in two forms that have parallel content. Each form is divided into Standard and Extended Batteries. The Standard Battery includes 12 tests that provide a broad set of scores. The Extended Battery contains 10 tests that provide more in-depth diagnostic information on specific academic strengths and weaknesses. With many new features, the WJ III provides broader coverage of key academic areas and more interpretive options than any other achievement battery. The new version includes seven new tests; eight new clusters; four oral language tests; expanded broad achievement clusters with three tests to measure basic skills, fluency, and application; revised procedure for evaluating intra-achievement discrepancies; an ability–achievement discrepancy using oral language; and expanded reading tests containing more items to measure early reading performance. Co-normed with the *WJ III Tests of Cognitive Abilities* to provide additional ability–achievement discrepancies and in intraindividual discrepancy.

Format: Examiner required; individual administration; untimed: 5 minutes per subtest

Scoring: Computer scored; examiner evaluated

Cost: Form A or Form B Complete Kit (standard and extended test books, 2 manuals, cassette, 25 each of test records and response booklets, scoring software, scoring guides, leather case) $509.50

Work Sampling System®

2001	Pearson Early Learning

Samuel J. Meisels, Judy R. Jablon, Margo L. Dichtelmiller, Dorothea B. Marsden, Aviva B. Dorfman

Population: Grades Pre-K to 5

Purpose: Documents children's skills, knowledge, behavior, and accomplishments

Description: Measures across a wide variety of curriculum areas on multiple occasions in order to enhance teaching and learning. The *Work Sampling System* consists of three complementary elements. Developmental Guidelines and Checklists provide a framework for observation that gives teachers a set of observational criteria that are based on national standards and knowledge of child development. Teachers' observations are recorded three times each year. Portfolios are purposeful collections of children's work that illustrate students' efforts, progress, and achievements. Summary Reports are completed three times a year and are intended to replace conventional reporting systems. Teachers combine information for the Developmental Checklists and Portfolios with their own knowledge of child development to assess students' performance and progress. Seven curriculum domains and eight age/grade levels are covered. The curriculum areas are Personal and Social Development, Language and Literacy, Mathematical Thinking, Scientific Thinking, Social Studies, The Arts, Physical Development, and Health. Spanish forms available.

Format: Examiner required; multiple methods of measurement; classroom embedded; untimed

Scoring: Examiner evaluated; online scoring

Cost: Annual price per child $19.95 (less than 100 children)

Young Children's Achievement Test (YCAT)

2000	PRO-ED, Inc.

Wayne P. Hresko, Pamela K. Peak, Shelley R. Herron, Deanna L. Bridges

Population: Ages 4 to 7 years

Purpose: Measures early academic achievement

Description: The YCAT represents a major improvement in the early identification of children at risk for school failure. It yields an overall Early Achievement standard score and individual subtest standard scores for General Information, Reading, Writing, Mathematics, and Spoken Language. The YCAT was designed with both the child and the examiner in mind. The individual subtests can be given independently of each other, leading to flexible testing sessions. The YCAT was normed on 1,224 children representing 32 states and Washington, D.C.

Format: Examiner required; individual administration, untimed; 25 to 45 minutes

Scoring: Examiner evaluated

Cost: Complete Kit (manual, picture book, 25 record booklets, 25 response forms, storage box) $210.00

Academic Aptitude

ACER Middle Years Ability Test (MYAT)

2005	Australian Council for Educational Research Limited

Population: Ages 10 to 15 years

Purpose: Measures general ability in numeracy, literacy, and nonverbal skills; can be used to identify students who are gifted or talented

Description: Two new parallel forms along the lines of Inter F and Inter G, called Form A and Form B. All questions are multiple-choice. Verbal, quantitative, and nonverbal reasoning items are presented in mixed order.

Format: Examiner required; suitable for group use; timed: 45 minutes

Scoring: Hand key

Cost: Specimen Set $99.95

ACER Word Knowledge Test: Form F

1990	Australian Council for Educational Research Limited

Marion de Lemos

Population: Years 9, 10, and 11

Purpose: Measures verbal skills and general reasoning ability

Description: Tests of word knowledge have been found to correlate highly with other measures of verbal skills and general reasoning ability. Because they are relatively quick and easy to administer, they have been widely used as screening tests. This test enables the user to assess quickly student knowledge of word meanings. Students are required to select, from a list of five alternatives, the word or phrase that most closely approximates the meaning of each of the 72 items.

Format: Examiner required; group administration; untimed: 10 minutes

Scoring: Hand key; scoring service available

Cost: Contact publisher

Ann Arbor Learning Inventory

1996 (Levels A and B); 1989 (Level C)	Academic Therapy Publications

Barbara Meister Vitale, Waneta Bullock

Population: Grades K to 8

Purpose: Evaluates the central-processing and perceptual skills necessary for reading, writing, and spelling to identify learning difficulties and deficits and to suggest appropriate remedial strategies

Description: Multiple-item task-performance oral-response paper–pencil test measuring the following central-processing skills: Visual Discrimination, Visual Memory, Auditory Discrimination, and Auditory Memory. Test items are presented in order of natural cognitive development, beginning with pictures; proceeding to objects and geometric forms; and finally to letters, words, and phrases. Tasks involve listening, manipulating, showing, matching, visualizing, telling, and writing. Results also provide objective data on developmental levels for prereading readiness, precomputational skills, kinesthetic and motor skills, and comprehension and critical thinking. Instrument is criterion referenced. Levels A and B are also available in Spanish.

Format: Examiner required; individual or group administration; untimed

Scoring: Examiner evaluated

Cost: Manuals (Levels A, B, or C) $20.00; Test Booklets (Levels A, B, or C) $15.00; Stimulus Cards (Level C) $10.00

Aptitude Profile Test Series (APTS)

2001	Australian Council for Educational Research Limited

George Morgan, Andrew Stephanou, Brian Simpson

Population: Years 9, 10, and 11

Purpose: Measures verbal, quantitative, abstract, and spatial-visual reasoning

Description: The Verbal Reasoning module tests two kinds of verbal analogy: semantic comprehension and vocabulary. The Quantitative Reasoning module tests three areas: abstract numeric; short word problems; and problems that require more extensive reading, comprehension, and processing of information to find the correct solution. The Abstract Reasoning module assesses a person's ability to reason in an abstract context in which one or more rules must be identified. The module challenges test takers to identify hidden rules that underlie patterns and sequences of patterns, presented in one or more dimensions. The Spatial-Visual module of the APTS involves three kinds of questions: two-dimensional objects/pattern flipping, three-dimensional objects involving maps and side views, and nets of cubes.

Format: Examiner required; suitable for group use; timed: from 30 minutes per section

Scoring: Scored with key; machine scored; computer scored; scoring service available from publisher

Cost: Contact publisher

California Critical Thinking Skills Test (CCTST)

1990 (Form A); 1992 (Form B); 2000 (Form 2000)	Insight Assessments

Peter A. Facione

Population: Adults; college and graduate levels

Purpose: Assesses core cognitive skills in critical thinking

Description: Electronic and paper–pencil 34-item multiple-choice test with five subtests. Categories include Analysis, Inference, Evaluation, Inductive Reasoning, and Deductive Reasoning. Three forms are available. CCTST test booklet (10 pages) is used; answer form is optional. Also available in Spanish, Arabic, Dutch, French, and Korean. Suitable for individuals with hearing impairments.

Format: Examiner required; group administration; timed and untimed

Scoring: Machine or electronic scored; scoring service available

Cost: Specimen Kit (manual, 1 protocol, 1 CapScore™ answer form) $45.00

Canadian Test of Cognitive Skills (CTCS)

1992	Canadian Test Centre

Population: Grades 2 to college

Purpose: Measures cognitive abilities important for scholastic success

Description: The CTCS provides the information needed to plan an educational program best suited to the learning and developmental needs of students. It measures selected abilities, such as understanding verbal and nonverbal concepts and comprehending relationships between ideas, so the teacher can screen students for placement in special programs and identify students in need of further diagnosis of learning problems. The CTCS is a thorough Canadian adaptation of CTB/McGraw-Hill's *Test of Cognitive Scale–Second Edition*. The subtests are Sequences, Analogies, Memory, and Verbal Reasoning. Norms were developed from a Canada-wide study involving 78 school jurisdictions. The stratified random sample of over 36,000 students ensured representativeness by region, district size, and degree of urbanization.

Format: Examiner required; individual or group administration; timed: 52 to 55 minutes

Scoring: Hand key; machine scoring, scoring service available

Cost: Contact publisher

Cognitive Abilities Test™ (CogAT®), Form 6

| 2001 | Riverside Publishing Company |

David F. Lohman, Elizabeth P. Hagen

Population: Grades K to 12

Purpose: Assess students' abilities in reasoning and problem solving using verbal, quantitative, and spatial (nonverbal) symbols

Description: This integrated series of tests provides information on the level of development In general and specific cognitive skills. These abilities have substantial correlations with learning and problem solving both in and out of school. The new edition was developed under the same rigorous standards as The Iowa Tests. Students who would benefit from enrichment or intervention can be easily identified. Individual reports describe the level and pattern of each student's abilities. Profile classifications are made dependable by a careful examination of the consistence of each student's responses to items within a subtest and across subtests within a battery. The following levels are available: K, 1, and 2 (Grades K to 2) and A to H (Grades 3 to 12). National norms are available for fall, midyear, and spring.

Format: Examiner required; suitable for group use; time varies depending on level

Scoring: Hand key; may be machine scored; scoring service available

Cost: Contact publisher

Collegiate Assessment of Academic Progress (CAAP) Critical Thinking Test

| 2001 | ACT, Inc. |

Population: Ages 17 years and older

Purpose: Assesses critical thinking

Description: Multiple-choice 32-item paper–pencil test. A test booklet, answer sheet, and pencil are used. Examiner must have experience with test administration at the college level. May be used for persons with visual, physical, hearing, or mental impairments.

Format: Examiner required; suitable for group use; timed: 40 minutes

Scoring: Machine scored; test scoring service available

Cost: $10.75

Detroit Tests of Learning Aptitude–Adult (DTLA-A)

| 1991 | PRO-ED, Inc. |

Donald D. Hammill, Brian R. Bryant

Population: Ages 16 to 79 years

Purpose: Measures general and specific aptitudes to identify deficiencies and to provide an index of optimal-level performance; permits interpretation in terms of current theories of intellect and behavior domains

Description: The battery's 12 subtests and 16 composites measure both general intelligence and discrete ability areas. The instrument was normed on more than 1,000 adults from more than 20 states. The overall composite is formed by combining the scores of all 12 subtests in the battery. Because of this, the overall composite is probably the best estimate of Spearman's g in that it reflects status on the widest array of different developed abilities. The DTLA-A includes a Verbal and Nonverbal Composite, an Attention-Enhanced and an Attention-Reduced Composite, and a Motor-Enhanced and a Motor-Reduced Composite.

Format: Examiner required; individual administration; timed and untimed: 90 minutes

Scoring: Examiner evaluated

Cost: Complete Kit (manual, picture books,

25 each of 3 types of protocol, manipulatives, storage box) $295.00

Detroit Tests of Learning Aptitude–Fourth Edition (DTLA-4)

| 1998 | PRO-ED, Inc. |

Donald D. Hammill

Population: Ages 6 to 17 years

Purpose: Measures general and specific aptitudes of children and identifies deficiencies

Description: Includes 10 subtests, the result of which can be combined to form 16 composites that measure both general intelligence and discrete ability areas. This test not only measures basic abilities, but also shows the effects of language, attention, and motor abilities on test performance. The subtests are Word Opposites, Design Sequences, Sentence Imitation, Reversed Letters, Story Construction, Design Reproduction, Basic Information, Symbolic Relations, Word Sequences, and Story Sequences. Subtests are assigned to composites that represent major popular theories. Thus, the subtests can be related to Horn and Cattell's fluid and crystallized intelligence, Jensen's associative and cognitive levels, Das's simultaneous and successive processes, and Wechsler's verbal and performance scales.

Format: Examiner required; individual administration; timed and untimed: 1 to 2 hours

Scoring: Examiner evaluated; computer scoring available

Cost: Complete Kit (manual, 2 picture books, 25 profile/summary forms, 25 record booklets, 25 response forms, story chips, design cubes, storage box) $367.00

Detroit Tests of Learning Aptitude–Primary: Third Edition (DTLA-P:2)

| 1991 | PRO-ED, Inc. |

Donald D. Hammill, Brian R. Bryant

Population: Ages 3 to 9 years

Purpose: Measures general and specific aptitudes of children and identifies deficiencies

Description: A quick, easily administered test for measuring the general aptitude of young children. It comprises six subtests, measuring cognitive ability in areas such as language, attention, and motor abilities. Six subtest scores (Verbal, Nonverbal, Attention-Enhanced, Attention-Reduced, Motor-Enhanced, and Motor-Reduced) and a General Mental Ability score provide a de-

tailed profile of a student's abilities and deficiencies. The test is useful with school-age children who are low functioning.

Format: Examiner required; individual administration; timed and untimed: 15 to 45 minutes

Scoring: Examiner evaluated

Cost: Complete Kit (examiner's manual, picture book, 25 record forms, 25 response forms, storage box) $200.00

Graduate Management Admissions Test (GMAT)

| Updated yearly | Educational Testing Service |

Population: College graduates

Purpose: Measures verbal and quantitative abilities related to success in graduate management schools; used for admission to graduate management school

Description: Paper–pencil multiple-choice test used by many graduate schools of business and management as one criterion for admission. In 1994, an analytical writing assessment was added to the GMAT. The test is administered four times annually at centers established by the publisher, and registration materials are available at no charge. The test is not available for institutional use.

Format: Examiner required; suitable for group use; timed: 4 hours

Scoring: Scoring service

Cost: Contact publisher

InView™

| 2000 and 2001 | CTB/McGraw-Hill |

Population: Grades 2 to 12

Purpose: Measures aptitude and cognitive ability for learning disabilities and gifted/talented identification

Description: There are five subtests with 20 items each: Verbal Reasoning—Context, Verbal Reasoning—Words, Sequences, Analogies, and Quantitative Reasoning. Scores provided are Anticipated Achievement, Cognitive Skills Index, percentiles, scale scores, stanines, and NCEs. Computer version is available for PC format. Web-enabled online for any platform.

Format: Examiner required; suitable for group use; timed: 15 to 20 minutes per subtest

Scoring: Hand key; machine scored; computer scored; scoring service available; online

Cost: Contact publisher

Kuhlmann-Anderson Tests (KA), 8th Edition

1982	Scholastic Testing Service, Inc.

Frederick Kuhlmann, Rose G. Anderson

Population: Grades K to 12

Purpose: Evaluates students' academic ability and potential; used for placement and diagnosing individual learning abilities

Description: Multiple-item multiple-choice test with eight subtests, four of which are nonverbal. The test is available in seven levels: K (Kindergarten), A (Grade 1), BC (Grades 2 to 3), CD (Grades 3 to 4), EF (Grades 5 to 6), G (Grades 7 to 8), and H (Grades 9 to 12). The test yields standard scores for verbal, nonverbal, and full battery; national and local percentiles; and stanines. Available in large print.

Format: Examiner required; group administration; timed: 50 to 75 minutes

Scoring: Examiner evaluated; machine scored; scoring service available from publisher

Cost: Level K, A, or BC Starter Set (directions, 20 machine-scorable test booklets) $44.35, Level CD, EF, G, or H Starter Set (directions, 20 reusable test booklets, class record sheet) $35.40; 50 Answer Sheets (specify level) $36.40

Measure of Questioning Skills

1993	Scholastic Testing Service, Inc.

Ralph Himsl, Garnet W. Miller

Population: Grades 3 to 10

Purpose: Assesses critical-thinking skills development

Description: Short-answer test shows four pictures to assess the quantity and quality of student questions. Four-minute time limit on each item. Forms A and B are available. A booklet and pencil are used. Examiner must be certified for assessment.

Format: Examiner required; group administration; timed: 20 minutes

Scoring: Examiner evaluated

Cost: Starter Set (guidebook, class record sheet, 20 activity booklets, 20 tally sheets, 20 results forms, 20 individual profile charts) Specify A or B $42.85

Naglieri Nonverbal Ability Test® Multilevel Form (NNAT®-Multilevel)

1996	Harcourt Assessment, Inc.

Jack A. Naglieri

Population: Grades K to 12

Purpose: Measures nonverbal reasoning and problem-solving abilities

Description: The test is independent of educational curricula, as well as students' cultural or language background. The test uses progressive matrices in seven grade-based levels with a wide range of items for each age group. The tests at each level contain 38 items, and the brief spoken instructions are available in several languages. All information needed to solve each task is presented with each diagram, so students do not have to depend on word or mathematical knowledge, or on reading skills, to answer the questions.

Format: Examiner required; suitable for group use; untimed: 30 minutes

Scoring: Hand key; scoring service available

Cost: Examination Kit $22.00 per level

Otis-Lennon School Ability Test®, Eighth Edition (OLSAT®8)

2002	Harcourt Assessment, Inc.

Arthur S. Otis, Roger T. Lennon

Population: Grades K to 12

Purpose: Assesses general mental ability or scholastic aptitude

Description: Assesses students' reasoning skills and provides an understanding of a student's relative strengths and weaknesses in performing a variety of reasoning tasks. The information allows educators to design programs that will enhance students' strengths while supporting their learning needs. Concepts measured are Verbal Comprehension, Verbal Reasoning, Pictorial Reasoning, Figural Reasoning, and Quantitative Reasoning.

Format: Examiner required; suitable for group use; timed: varies by level, 75 minutes maximum

Scoring: Hand key; may be machine scored; scoring service available

Cost: Machine-Scorable Test Packs $44.50 per level; Administration Directions $16.00 per level

Preliminary SAT/National Merit Scholarship Qualifying Test (PSAT/NMSQT™)

Yearly	College Board

Population: Grades 10 to 12 (Grade 11 score is

the only score considered by the National Merit Corporation)

Purpose: Assesses high school students' critical-reading, and math-reasoning abilities and writing to evaluate readiness for college-level study

Description: Five sections are included: two 25-minute critical-reading sections, two 25-minute math sections, and one 30-minute writing skills section. The reading section consists of sentence completions and critical-reading questions. The math section has multiple-choice questions and student-produced responses. The writing section consists of multiple-choice questions identifying sentence errors, improving sentences, and improving paragraphs. Individualized feedback is provided on score reports, and all examinees gain free access to an online college and career exploration program. Fee waivers are available to students with financial need. Available in a variety of formats if needed for students with disabilities.

Format: Examiner required; suitable for group use; timed: 2 hours 10 minutes

Scoring: Computer scored

Cost: $12.00 per exam

SAT Reasoning Test

Yearly	College Board

Population: Grades 11 and 12

Purpose: Measures developed critical reading, mathematic reasoning, and writing abilities that are related to successful performance in college

Description: The SAT includes a Critical Reading, Math, and Writing section, with a specific number of questions related to content. In addition, there is one 25-minute unscored section that may be from either section. This unscored section does not count toward the final score, but is used to try out new questions for future editions of the SAT. The 25-minute essay will always be the first section, and the 10-minute multiple-choice writing section will always be the final section. The remaining six 25-minute sections can appear in any order, as can the two 20-minute sections. Fee waivers are available for students with financial need. Available in a variety of formats if needed for students with disabilities.

Format: Examiner required; suitable for group use; timed: 3 hours 45 minutes

Scoring: Computer scored

Cost: $41.50 per exam

Structure of Intellect Learning Abilities Test (SOI-LA)

1975	Western Psychological Services

Mary Meeker, Robert Meeker

Population: Grades K to adult

Purpose: Measures an individual's learning abilities; used for cognitive clinical assessment, diagnosis, screening for giftedness, and identifying specific learning deficiencies

Description: Paper–pencil 430-item multiple-choice free-response test. The test measures 26 factors identified by Guilford's Structure-of-Intellect model. The operations of cognition, memory, evaluation, convergent production, and divergent production are applied to figural, symbolic, and semantic content. The test is available in two equivalent forms—A and B—and five shorter forms (gifted-screening, math, reading, primary screening, and reading readiness). The shorter forms use 10 to 12 subtest factors, printed test forms, and a manual with visual aids for group presentations. Training in administration and usage is required.

Format: Examiner required; suitable for group use in some situations; untimed: 2 hours 30 minutes

Scoring: Hand key

Cost: Kit (10 test booklets, 5 each of Form A and Form B, manual, set of scoring keys, set of stimulus cards, 10 worksheets and profile forms) $236.50

STS: High School Placement Test (HSPT) Closed Form

Updated annually	Scholastic Testing Service, Inc.

Population: Grades 8.3 to 9.3

Purpose: Assesses academic achievement and aptitude

Description: Multiple-choice test with 298 items on five subtests: Verbal Cognitive Skills, Quantitative Skills, Reading, Mathematics, and Language. Alphabetical lists, rank order lists, group summary reports, performance profiles, and item analysis reports are provided. Optional tests for Catholic religion, mechanical aptitude, and science are available. A booklet, answer sheet, and pencil are used. Examiner must be certified for assessment. Also available in large print.

Format: Examiner required; individual administration; untimed and timed portions: 2 hours 30 minutes

Scoring: Machine scored; test scoring service available

Cost: Sample Set $24.00

STS: High School Placement Test (HSPT) Open Form

2004	Scholastic Testing Service, Inc.

Population: Grades 8.3 to 9.3

Purpose: Assesses academic achievement and aptitude

Description: Multiple-choice test with 298 items on seven subtests: Verbal Cognitive Skills, Quantitative Skills, Language, Reading Comprehension, Reading Vocabulary, Math Concepts, and Math Problem Solving. Cognitive Skills Quotients, basic skills scores, and a composite score are yielded. Optional tests available are Catholic Religion, Mechanical Aptitude, and Science. A pencil, booklet, and answer sheet are used. Examiner must be certified for assessment. Also available in large print

Format: Examiner required; individual administration; untimed and timed portions: 2 hours 30 minutes

Scoring: Machine scored; test scoring service available

Cost: Sample Set $24.00

Test of Auditory Reasoning and Processing Skills (TARPS)

1993	Academic Therapy Publications

Morrison F. Gardner

Population: Ages 5 to 13 years

Purpose: Measures the quality and quantity of auditory thinking and reasoning

Description: While many of the questions and statements do reflect what a child has learned from home and formal education, the purpose of this test is to determine what the child does with what he or she has learned. This test will measure a child's ability to think logically, conceptually, and abstractly. Another purpose of the TARPS is to assess how well a child can pick out key words in a question or a statement and know that that key word holds the clue to the answer or is the answer. Spanish version is available.

Format: Examiner required; individual administration; untimed: 10 to 15 minutes

Scoring: Examiner evaluated

Cost: Complete Kit (manual, 25 test booklets) $64.00

Test of Cognitive Skills, Second Edition (TCS®/2)

1992	CTB/McGraw-Hill

Population: Grades 2 to 12

Purpose: Assesses skills important for success in school settings; used for predicting school achievement and screening students for further evaluation

Description: Multiple-item paper–pencil multiple-choice test consisting of four subtests (Sequences, Analogies, Memory, and Verbal Reasoning) assessing cognitive skills. The test is divided into six levels spanning Grades 2 to 12. The test yields the following scores: number of correct responses, age or grade percentile rank, scale score, and cognitive skills index.

Format: Examiner required; suitable for group use; timed: 1 hour

Scoring: Hand key; may be computer scored

Cost: Contact publisher

Test of Everyday Reasoning (TER)

2000	Insight Assessments

Peter A. Facione

Population: Ages 14 years and older

Purpose: Measures reasoning ability and critical thinking

Description: The TER is based on the Delphi consensus conceptualization of critical thinking and targets those core critical-thinking skills regarded to be essential elements for an individual's education. The items range from those requiring an analysis of the meaning of a given sentence to those requiring much more complex integration of critical-thinking skills. There are a total of 35 multiple-choice items that are scored in five categories: Analysis, Evaluation, Inference, Deductive Ability, and Inductive. Test is available in paper–pencil or electronic format. Also available in Greek and Russian.

Format: Examiner required; group administration; timed and untimed

Scoring: Machine or electronic scored; scoring service available

Cost: Specimen Kit (manual, 1 protocol, 1 CapScore™ answer form) $40.00

Assistive Technology

Functional Evaluation for Assistive Technology (FEAT)

| 2002 | Psycho-Educational Services |

Marshall H. Raskind, Brian R. Bryant

Population: Ages 5 to 65 years

Purpose: Measures the match between a person and technology; used in education and the workplace

Description: An easy-to-use, systematic, comprehensive, multidimensional, and ecologically based assessment protocol. The scale can be used to determine the most appropriate and effective assistive technology devices to help individuals with learning problems (e.g., learning disabilities, mental retardation) compensate for their difficulties and meet the demands of specific tasks and contexts. The FEAT has five scales: the Contextual Matching Inventory (which provides information about setting-specific demands), the Checklist of Strengths and Limitations (which is used to gather data regarding person-specific characteristics), the Checklist of Technology Experiences (which offers additional information about the person-specific characteristics with regard to his or her past/current use of technology), the Technology Characteristics Inventory (which examines device-specific characteristics such as dependability, product support), and the Individual-Technology Evaluation Scale (which is used to determine whether the proposed AT adaptation offers legitimate potential for compensatory effectiveness). The Summary and Recommendations Booklet is used to summarize the assessment information, make recommendations, and arrange for follow-ups to assess for effective implementation. The scales are completed by various members of the assistive technology assessment team and allow for an ecological assessment of assistive technology needs.

Format: Examiner required; individual administration; untimed

Scoring: Examiner evaluated

Cost: Complete Kit (manual, 25 each of forms, 25 summary forms, box) $149.00

Matching Person and Technology Assessment Process (MPT)

| 2005 | Institute for Matching Person & Technology, Inc. |

Marcia J. Scherer

Population: Ages birth to 90+ years

Purpose: Measures the degree of match between person and technology

Description: The MPT process contains a series of instruments that take into account the environments in which the person uses the technology, the individual's characteristics and preferences, and the technology's functions and features. Characteristics within these three components can each contribute either a positive or a negative influence on technology use. The Survey of Technology Use (SOTU) helps to identify technologies an individual feels comfortable or successful in using. Technology-specific forms are The Assistive Technology Device Predisposition Assessment (ATD PA), which helps people select assistive technologies; The Educational Technology Predisposition Assessment (ET PA), which helps students use technology to reach certain educational goals; The Workplace Technology Predisposition Assessment (WT PA), which is for employers or vocational counselors who introduce new technologies into the workplace and who train persons in their use; and The Health Care Technology Predisposition Assessment (HCT PA), which is for health-care providers who recommend or prescribe technologies for health maintenance, pain relief, and so on. The first four instruments have two forms: one for the provider and one for the technology user. Available in other languages.

Format: Rating scale; untimed: 15 minutes

Scoring: Computer scoring

Cost: CD $89.95 (5 assessments, manual, training video, sample scoring, case reports)

Auditory Skills

Auditory Processing Abilities Test (APAT)

| 2004 | Academic Therapy Publications |

Deborah Ross-Swain, Nancy Long

Population: Ages 5 to 12 years

Purpose: Measures auditory processing; used to determine patterns of strengths and weaknesses

Description: Understanding and use of linguistic information are measured by 10 subtests: Phonemic Awareness, Content Memory (Immediate and Delayed), Word Sequences, Complex Sentences, Cued Recall, Semantic Relationships, Sentence Absurdities, Sentence Memory, Following Directions, and Passage Comprehension. In each subtest, directions are spoken to the child, who then responds orally or by performing the task. It yields scaled scores for individual subtests and standard scores for composites (Global, Auditory Memory, Linguistic Processing).

Format: Examiner required; individual administration; untimed: 45 minutes

Scoring: Examiner evaluated

Cost: Test Kit (manual, 25 forms, 25 summary sheets, portfolio) $112.00

Children's Test of Nonword Repetition (CN REP)

| 1996 | Harcourt Assessment-UK |

Susan Gathercole, Alan Baddeley

Population: Ages 4 to 8 years

Purpose: Measures short-term memory

Description: The test contains 40 nonwords, each of which is presented on the accompanying audiocassette tape. The child listens to each nonword and is required to repeat it immediately. The single score calculated at the end corresponds to the total number of correct repetitions.

Format: Examiner required; individual administration; untimed: 15 minutes

Scoring: Examiner evaluated

Cost: Complete Kit (manual, 25 record forms, cassette) £74.00

Denver Audiometric Screening Test (DAST)

| 1973 | Denver Developmental Materials, Inc. |

William K. Frankenburg, Marion Dreris, Elinor Kuzuk

Population: Ages 3 years and older

Purpose: Detects children with hearing deficiencies; used to screen for 25dB loss; those who fail the test are referred for additional examination

Description: Function test in which a trained examiner creates a tone with an audiometer and checks the child's response. The child indicates whether the tone can be heard at different decibel levels.

Format: Examiner and audiometer required; individual administration; untimed: 5 to 10 minutes

Scoring: Examiner evaluated

Cost: 25 Tests $6.00; Manual/Workbook $28.00

Goldman-Fristoe-Woodcock Test of Auditory Discrimination

| 1974 | AGS Publishing/Pearson Assessments |

Ronald Goldman, Macalyne Fristoe, Richard W. Woodcock

Population: Ages 3 years 8 months to 70 years

Purpose: Measures the ability to discriminate speech sounds against two different backgrounds, quiet and noise

Description: Specifically designed to assess young children. Geared to children's vocabulary levels and limited attention spans. The individual responds by pointing to pictures of familiar objects. Writing and speaking are not required. In addition, the test can be used successfully with adults, particularly those with disabilities. Three parts—Training Procedure, Quiet Subtest, and Noise Subtest—provide practice in word–picture associations and provide two measures of speech-sound discrimination for maximum precision.

Format: Examiner required; individual administration; untimed: 20 to 30 minutes

Scoring: Examiner interpretation

Cost: Complete Kit (easel test plates, manual, 50 response forms, audiocassette) $139.99

Lindamood Auditory Conceptualization Test–Third Edition (LAC-3)

| 2004 | PRO-ED, Inc. |

Patricia C. Lindamood, Phyllis Lindamood

Population: Ages 5 through 18 years

Purpose: Measures an individual's ability to perceive and conceptualize speech sounds using a visual medium

Description: The LAC-3 has norm-referenced scores, as well as age and grade equivalents. The instrument is more complex by including 18 items in Category II and extending to five phonemes. Three new categories of items have been added that extend the test into the multisyllable level of processing. Reliability and validity studies are reported.

Format: Examiner required; individual administration; untimed: 10 minutes

Scoring: Examiner evaluated

Cost: Complete Kit (manual, 25 record booklets, 24 blocks, 6 felts, CD, storage box) $189.00

Listening Assessment for ITBS®

1994, 1987	Riverside Publishing Company

H. D. Hoover, A. N. Hieronymus,
Kathleen Oberley, Nancy Cantor

Population: Grades 3 to 9 (Levels 9 to 14)

Purpose: Monitors the effectiveness of listening instruction

Description: Provided as a supplement to the *Iowa Tests of Basic Skills,* Form K, L, and M. Emphasizes learning through reading, listening, and the use of visual materials. Consists of questions that measure Literal Meaning; Inferential Meaning; Following Directions; Visual Relationships; Numerical/Spatial/Temporal Relationships; and Speaker's Purpose, Point of View, or Style. There are a total of 95 questions on the test. Each test level is different, although questions that are included at the end of one test level also appear at the middle of the next level, and toward the beginning of the next higher level. This is because tasks that would be relatively difficult for a third-grade student would be somewhat easier for a fourth-grade student, and much easier for a fifth-grader.

Format: Examiner required; group administration; untimed: 35 minutes

Scoring: Scoring service

Cost: Mark Reflex® Listening Answer Folder (package of 50, directions for administration and score interpretation, materials needed for machine scoring) $76.50

Listening Assessment for TAP®/ITED®

1994, 1987	Riverside Publishing Company

Oscar M. Haugh, Dale P. Scannell

Population: Grades 9 to 12 (Levels 15 to 18)

Purpose: Assesses the developed listening skills of high school students

Description: Provided as a supplement to the Complete and Survey Batteries of *Tests of Achievement and Proficiency* (TAP) and the *Iowa Tests of Educational Development* (ITED). This assessment provides teachers and students with valuable insights into students' strengths and weaknesses in the important art of listening. The assessment consists of questions that measure the following content objectives: Literal Meaning, Inferential Meaning, and Speaker's Purpose or Point of View. In addition, questions are cross-classified according to four levels of cognition: knowledge/information, comprehension, application/analysis, and synthesis/evaluation. The test consists of 100 questions in four overlapping levels.

Format: Examiner required; group administration; untimed: 40 minutes

Scoring: Scoring service

Cost: Mark Reflex® Listening Answer Folder (package of 50, directions for administration and score interpretation, materials needed for machine scoring) $76.50

Listening Comprehension Test 2

2006	LinguiSystems, Inc.

Rosemary Huisingh, Linda Bowers,
Carolyn LoGiudice

Population: Ages 6 to 11 years

Purpose: Assesses ability to attend to, process, and respond to what is heard

Description: A diagnostic assessment of the integrated and complex process of listening in tasks that accurately mimic classroom listening situations. The student listens to a short passage and then answers questions. Provides standardized analyses for the tasks of Main Idea, Details, Reasoning, Vocabulary, and Understanding Messages. Clearly identifies student's listening strengths and weaknesses, making results easy to share with parents and other education professionals. Includes remediation suggestions for each skill area and a classroom rating scale completed by the teacher.

Format: Requires examiner; individual administration; untimed: 35 to 40 minutes

Scoring: Examiner evaluated

Cost: Manual and 20 Test Forms $129.95

Listening Inventory (TLI)

2006	Academic Therapy Publications

Donna Geffner, Deborah Ross-Swain

Population: Ages 3 to 17 years

Purpose: Quantifies behaviors to determine if an evaluation is necessary for auditory disorders

Description: An informal behavioral observation completed by parents and/or teachers. Six areas are assessed, and Index scores are derived for each: Linguistic Organization, Decoding/Language Mechanics, Attention/Organization, Sensory/Motor, Social/Behavioral, and Auditory Processes. Statements are rated on a 0- to 5-point Likert scale. The manual contains background information, as well as a guide for interpretation and use of the observations that were made. Index scores are compared to criterion-based cutoff scores to determine clinical significance.

Format: Examiner required; individual administration; untimed

Scoring: Examiner evaluated

Cost: Test Kit (manual, 25 forms, 25 profile sheets) $85.00

SCAN-A: Test for Auditory Processing Disorders in Adolescents and Adults

1994	Harcourt Assessment, Inc.

Robert W. Keith

Population: Ages 12 to 50 years

Purpose: Screens clients for auditory processing disorders

Description: This upward extension of the SCAN-C has four subtests: Filtered Words, Auditory Figure-Ground, Competing Words, and Competing Sentences. Requires a cassette player, two sets of stereo headphones, and a Y adapter. Used with individuals who have normal hearing acuity but poor understanding of speech when listening conditions are less than optimal.

Format: Examiner required; individual administration; untimed: 20 minutes

Scoring: Examiner evaluated

Cost: Complete Kit (manual, cassette, 12 record forms) $175.00

SCAN-C: Test for Auditory Processing Disorders in Children-Revised

1999	Harcourt Assessment, Inc.

Robert W. Keith

Population: Ages 5 to 11 years

Purpose: Detects auditory processing disorders

Description: Test is for children who have normal peripheral hearing but who appear to have poor listening skills, short auditory attention span, or difficulty understanding speech in the presence of background noise. Administered using a portable CD player. The child repeats the words and sentences heard.

Format: Examiner required; individual administration; untimed: 15 minutes

Scoring: Examiner evaluated

Cost: Complete Program (manual, CD, 25 record forms) $199.00

Screening for Central Auditory Processing Difficulties

2001	Academic Communication Associates

Dorothy A. Kelly

Population: Grades K to 2 for group; Grades K to 6 for individual

Purpose: Pinpoints a variety of auditory processing difficulties that may be affecting a child's functioning in the classroom

Description: Criterion-referenced instrument that allows recording observations or used as a schoolwide screening. Cutoff criteria are included for use in identifying children who should be tested further. The Quick-Checklist, completed by a speech-language pathologist, consists of 20 items assessing the student's ability to perform tasks such as repeating syllables, following oral directions, associating sounds with their source, and repeating digits. Reproducible checklists for the parent and teacher to complete are included in the manual.

Format: Examiner required; individual and group administration; untimed

Scoring: Hand key

Cost: Complete Kit $69.00

Slosson Auditory Perceptual Skill Screener

2005 Slosson Educational Publications, Inc.

Bradley T. Erford

Population: Ages 5 to 10 years

Purpose: Measures ability to perceive auditory information

Description: Three subtests: Auditory Word Discrimination, Auditory Figure–Ground, and Auditory Filtered Words. An Auditory Reception subtest is available to assess a child's basic auditory acuity. The subtests are administered using an audiotape and headphones.

Format: Examiner required; individual administration; untimed: 3 to 5 minutes

Scoring: Examiner evaluated

Cost: Complete Kit $89.25

Test of Auditory Processing Scale– Third Edition (TAPS-3)

2005 Academic Therapy Publications

Nancy Martin, Rick Brownell

Population: Ages 4 to 18 years

Purpose: Measures auditory processes

Description: The TAPS-3 is a revision of the *Test of Auditory Perceptual Skills, Revised.* There are no longer two levels; one instrument covers all ages. The instrument measures what one does with what is heard. The subtests are Word Discrimination, Phonological Segmentation (new), Phonological Blending (new), Numbers Forward, Numbers Reversed, Word Memory, Sentence Memory, Auditory Comprehension (new), and Auditory Reasoning (new). An optional Auditory Figure–Ground task flags possible attention problems. Individual subtests are reported as scaled scores; Indices (Phonological Skills, Memory, and Cohesion) and the Overall score are reported as standard scores. Percentile ranks and age equivalents are provided.

Format: Examiner required; individual administration; untimed: 60 minutes

Scoring: Examiner evaluated

Cost: Complete Kit (manual, 25 test booklets, CD) $120.00

Token Test for Children– Second Edition (TTFC-2)

2007 PRO-ED, Inc.

Ronnie L. McGhee, David J. Ehrler, Frank DiSimoni

Population: Ages 3 to 12 years

Purpose: Measures functional listening ability in children and identifies receptive language dysfunction

Description: The child is given three opportunities to practice with the 20 tokens varying in size, shape, and color. The administrator then gives the child 46 linguistic commands, to which he or she must respond by manipulating the tokens. The commands are arranged in four parts of increasing difficulty and must be administered in consecutive order. Scores provided are standard scores, percentile ranks, and age equivalents.

Format: Examiner required; individual administration; untimed: 10 to 15 minutes

Scoring: Examiner evaluated

Cost: Complete Kit (manual, 20 tokens, 50 scoring forms, storage box) $130.00

Wepman's Auditory Discrimination Test, Second Edition (ADT)

1987 Western Psychological Services

Joseph M. Wepman, William M. Reynolds

Population: Ages 4 to 8 years

Purpose: Measures the auditory discrimination ability; used to identify specific auditory learning disabilities for possible remediation

Description: Oral-response test in which children are verbally presented pairs of words and asked to discriminate between them. The test predicts articulatory speech defects and certain remedial reading problems. The second edition is identical to the original edition except for scoring. In the second edition, scoring is based on a correct score, rather than on the "error" basis of the original edition. The 1987 manual contains standardization tables for children ages 4 to 8, an interpretation section discussing how the test results may be used, reports on research using the test, and selected references.

Format: Examiner required; individual administration; untimed: 10 to 15 minutes

Scoring: Hand key

Cost: Complete Kit (100 each of Forms 1A and 2A, manual) $109.50

Behavior and Counseling

Attitudes

Achievement Identification Measure (AIM)

1985	Educational Assessment Service, Inc.

Sylvia B. Rimm

Population: Parents of students in Grades K to 12

Purpose: Identifies characteristics contributing to underachievement in students; used by teachers and parents for communication and intervention

Description: Paper–pencil 77-item inventory in which parents assess their child's characteristics in five areas (Competition, Responsibility, Independence/Dependence Achievement, Achievement Communication, and Respect/Dominance) by responding "no," "to a small extent," "average," "more than average," or "definitely" to each item. The test distinguishes between achievers and underachievers. Parents receive a computer-scored report with a manual that explains the meaning of the scores. Also available in Spanish.

Format: Self-administered; untimed: 20 minutes

Scoring: Computer scored

Cost: Class Set of 30 Tests $120.00; Specimen Set $15.00

Achievement Identification Measure–Teacher Observation (AIM-TO)

1988	Educational Assessment Service, Inc.

Sylvia B. Rimm

Population: Teachers in Grades K to 12

Purpose: Identifies characteristics contributing to achievement in students; used by teachers

Description: Paper–pencil 70-item inventory in which teachers assess students' achievement characteristics in five areas (Competition, Responsibility, Achievement Communication, Independence/Dependence, Respect, and Dominance). A computer scoring service is available. Also available in Spanish.

Format: Self-administered; untimed: 20 minutes

Scoring: Computer scored

Cost: Class Set of 30 Tests $120.00; Specimen Set $15.00

Achievement Motivation Profile (AMP)

1996	Western Psychological Services

Jotham Friedland, Harvey Mandel, Sander Marcus

Population: Ages 10 to 14 years (Junior form); Ages 14 years and older (High School and College form)

Purpose: Used to evaluate underachieving or unmotivated students

Description: This self-report inventory is composed of 140 brief, self-descriptive statements that produce scale scores in four areas: Motivation for Achievement, Interpersonal Strengths, Inner Resources, and Work Habits. Students respond to items using a 5-point scale. The AMP is designed specifically to measure motivation and is validated against objective measures of achievement.

Format: Self-administered; untimed: 20 to 30 minutes

Scoring: Hand key; computer scoring available for High School/College

Cost: Kit (25 AutoScore™ forms for each level, manuals) $150.00

Achieving Behavioral Competencies

1992	McCarron-Dial Systems

Lawrence T. McCarron, Kathleen M. Fad, Melody B. McCarron

Population: Ages 13 years and older

Purpose: Assesses coping skills, work habits, and peer relationships; used for the development of social and emotional skills

Description: Based on the results of the 80-item Teacher Rating Scale, a computer program generates individual and class profiles for 20 competencies within four skill areas. A comprehensive curriculum presents strategies for developing positive social-emotional skills through self-awareness, teacher instruction, teacher demonstration, student interaction, and self-management and generalization. Supplemental, ready-to-use instructor materials to facilitate class participation, generalization, and maintenance of skills are provided.

Format: Rating scale; untimed

Scoring: Computer scored

Cost: $150.00

Adolescent Anger Rating Scale (AARS)

| 2001 | Psychological Assessment Resources, Inc. |

DeAnna McKinnie Burney

Population: Ages 11 to 19 years

Purpose: Assesses anger intensity and frequency, as well as typical mode of anger expression and anger control

Description: Used as a screening measure for social maladjustment behavior. The AARS has 41 items. Instrumental Anger (IA) has 20 items and measures delayed or covert anger. Reactive Anger (RA) has eight items and measures angry responses immediately expressed. Anger Control (AC) has 13 items and measures proactive cognitive-behavioral responses. Profile chart provided in test booklet for plotting IA, RA, AC, and Total Anger *t*-scores.

Format: Self-administered; untimed: 5 to 10 minutes

Scoring: Examiner evaluated

Cost: Kit (manual, test booklets) $150.00

Children's Academic Intrinsic Motivation Inventory (CAIMI)

| 1986 | Psychological Assessment Resources, Inc. |

Adele E. Gottfried

Population: Grades 4 to 8

Purpose: Assesses academic motivation in children

Description: Paper–pencil measure of motivation for learning in both general and specific areas. The 44 questions comprise five scales: Reading, Math, Social Studies, Science, and General. Results are reported in *t*-scores or percentiles. Used to identify students with academic difficulties and to differentiate motivation from achievement and ability factors. Also used in course selection and individual and district-level program planning.

Format: Self-administered; untimed: 20 to 30 minutes

Scoring: Hand key

Cost: Intro Kit (manual, 50 test booklets, 50 profile forms) $168.00

Group Achievement Identification Measure (GAIM)

| 1986 | Educational Assessment Service, Inc. |

Sylvia B. Rimm

Population: Grades 5 to 12

Purpose: Identifies students with characteristics that may contribute to underachievement; used by classroom teachers to help underachieving students

Description: Paper–pencil 90-item inventory assessing achievement characteristics. The inventory directs both teachers and parents to the areas in which the child must change in order to achieve in school. The test yields a Total Score, as well as five dimension scores: Competition, Responsibility, Achievement Communication, Independence/Dependence, and Respect Dominance.

Format: Examiner required; suitable for group use; untimed

Scoring: Computer scored; scoring service available

Cost: Class Set of 30 Tests $120.00; Specimen Set $15.00

Inventory of Classroom Style and Skills (INCLASS)

| Date not provided | H & H Publishing Company, Inc. |

Curtis Miles, Phyllis Grummon

Population: High school and college students

Purpose: Assesses student attitudes and behaviors related to academic learning

Description: This is a self-assessment instrument designed to assess proficiency in seven competencies (Interest in Life-Long Learning, Having a Sense of Quality, Taking Responsibility, Persisting, Working in Teams, Solving Problems, and Adapting to Change) that affect student performance in the classroom. INCLASS is a diagnostic and prescriptive instrument that provides information to the student and gives teachers and others a framework to develop instructional and other interventions.

Format: Self-administered; untimed

Scoring: Hand key; also available online

Cost: $3.00 each (for 1 to 99 copies)

Learning Behavior Scale (LBS)

| 1999 | Ed & Psych Associates |

Paul A. McDermott, Leonard F. Green,
Jean M. Francis, Denis H. Stott

Population: Ages 5 to 17 years

Purpose: Measures classroom learning behavior in a standardized teacher observation

Description: Test contains 29 items measuring four factors: Competence Motivation, Attitude toward Learning, Attention/Persistence, and Strategy/Flexibility.

Format: Rating scale; untimed: 10 to 15 minutes

Scoring: Hand score

Cost: $26.95

Learning Process Questionnaire (LPQ)

1989	Australian Council for Educational Research Limited

J. Biggs

Population: Tertiary students

Purpose: Assesses a student's general orientation toward learning by identifying the motives and strategies that comprise an approach to learning; used by teachers and counselors

Description: Paper-pencil 36-item test identifying the motives and strategies that comprise a student's approach to learning. Items are rated in a Likert scale format. Stanine and percentile rank scores are yielded for total raw score conversion. Separate profiles are provided for motive and strategy subscales. One of two tests in a series (see entry for *Study Process Questionnaire*).

Format: Examiner required; suitable for group use; timed: 20 minutes

Scoring: Hand key; may be machine scored

Cost: Contact publisher

Occupational Self Assessment, Version 2.2 (OSA)

2006	Model of Human Occupation Clearinghouse

Kathi Baron, Gary Kielhofner, Anita Iyenger, Victoria Goldhammer, Julie Wolenski

Population: Adolescents, adults, and older adults

Purpose: Measures occupational competence in everyday activities and value for everyday activities

Description: A self-report form that is easily and quickly administered. It explores a client's performance, habits, roles, volition, interests, and environment. The OSA guides clinical practice by identifying clients' perceptions of their strengths and weaknesses, as well as their priority goal areas. The OSA 2.2 manual includes paper keyforms, which allow a therapist to generate an interval client measure, or score, based on the OSA ratings. Therapists and clients can compare measures to assess and document outcomes of intervention.

Format: Self-report; untimed: 15 to 35 minutes

Scoring: Examiner evaluated

Cost: $38.50

Occupational Therapy Psychosocial Assessment of Learning, Version 2.0 (OT PAL)

1999	Model of Human Occupation Clearinghouse

Sally C. Townsend, Paula D. Carey,
Nancy L. Hollins, Christine Helfrich,
Melinda Blondis, Amanda Hoffman,
Lara Collins, Julie Knudson, Angela Blackwell

Population: Ages 6 to 12 years

Purpose: Evaluates psychosocial impact on learning

Description: Observational and descriptive assessment tool evaluates a student's ability to make choices, habituation, and environmental fit within the classroom setting. The observational component has 21 items.

Format: Observation and interview; untimed: 45 to 60 minutes

Scoring: Examiner evaluated

Cost: $35.00

Pediatric Volitional Questionnaire, Version 2.0 (PVQ)

2002	Model of Human Occupation Clearinghouse

Semonti Basu, Ana Kafkes, Rebecca Geist,
Gary Kielhofner

Population: Children

Purpose: Provides information about a client's volition and how environment affects volition

Description: An observational assessment designed to evaluate motivation, values, and interests, and impact of the environment. The 36-page manual contains reproducible assessment and data summary forms.

Format: Observation and rating scale; untimed: 15 to 30 minutes per observation; 5 to 10 minutes for rating scale

Scoring: Examiner evaluated

Cost: $35.00

School Motivation and Learning Strategies Inventory (SMALSI)

| 2006 | Western Psychological Services |

Kathy Chatham Stroud, Cecil R. Reynolds

Population: Ages 8 to 18 years

Purpose: Identifies and targets poor learning strategies that affect academic performance

Description: Designed for both special and general education students, this new self-report inventory assesses 10 primary constructs associated with academic motivation, learning strategies, and study habits—7 focusing on student strengths and 3 focusing on student liabilities: Strengths (Study Strategies, Note-Taking/Listening Skills, Reading/Comprehension Strategies, Writing/Research Skills, Test-Taking Strategies, Organizational Techniques, Time Management); Liabilities (Low Academic Motivation, Test Anxiety, and Concentration/Attention Difficulties). Scores from these scales provide enough information to identify problems that interfere with academic development. An Inconsistent Responding index is also included as a validity measure. The SMALSI is available in two forms. The Child Form (147 items) is for students 8 to 12 years of age; the Teen Form (170 items) is for 13- to 18-year-olds. Both forms are written at a third-grade reading level.

Format: Self-administered; untimed 20 to 30 minutes

Scoring: Examiner evaluated; computer scoring available

Cost: Comprehensive Kit (manual, 25 of each form, 25 of each profile, scoring templates) $190.00

School Setting Interview, Version 3.0 (SSI)

| 2005 | Model of Human Occupation Clearinghouse |

Helena Hemmingsson, Snaefridur Egilson, Oshrat Regev Hoffman, Gary Kielhofner

Population: Children, adolescents

Purpose: Assesses student–environment fit and identifies the need for accommodations in the school setting

Description: The SSI includes 14 content areas that explore the student's functioning in the school setting. Provides suggested interview questions, which facilitate the investigation of the impact of the physical and social environment on the student's occupational performance, habits, meaning, and values. The SSI is a semistructured interview designed to assess student–environment fit and to identify the need for accommodations for students with disabilities in the school setting. This assessment is to be used collaboratively with the student and is therefore intended for students who are able to communicate their feelings. The assessment manual includes interview forms to facilitate this assessment with students, a goal-planning form, and a rating summary form.

Format: Interview; untimed: 40 to 60 minutes

Scoring: Examiner evaluated

Cost: $30.00

Study Process Questionnaire (SPQ)

| 1989 | Australian Council for Educational Research Limited |

J. Biggs

Population: Tertiary students

Purpose: Assesses a student's general orientation toward learning by identifying the motives and strategies that comprise an approach to learning; used by teachers or counselors

Description: Paper–pencil 42-item test identifying the motives and strategies that comprise the student's approach to learning. Items are rated on a Likert scale format. Stanine and percentile rank scores are presented for total raw score conversion. Separate profiles are presented for motive and strategy subscales. The test is one of two in a series (see entry for *Learning Process Questionnaire*).

Format: Examiner required; suitable for group use; timed: 20 minutes

Scoring: Hand key; may be machine scored

Cost: Contact publisher

Subsumed Abilities Test–A Measure of Learning Efficiency (SAT)

| 1963 | Martin M. Bruce, PhD |

Martin M. Bruce

Population: Grades 6 and above

Purpose: Nonverbally measures the subject's ability and willingness to learn; used for student placement, vocational counseling, and job selection

Description: Paper–pencil 60-item test consisting of 30 pairs of items, each of which is composed of four line drawings. The student analyzes one with three others, resulting in a Potential Abilities Score and a Demonstrated Abilities Score based on the student's ability to conceptualize, form abstractions, and recognize identicals. Designed for individuals with at least a sixth-grade education. Suitable for individuals with physical, hearing, or visual impairments.

Format: Examiner required; suitable for group use; timed: 30 minutes

Scoring: Hand key

Cost: Specimen Set $46.50

Test of Attitude Toward School (TAS)

1984　　　Institute of Psychological Research, Inc.

Guy Thibaudeau

Population: Grades 1 to 12

Purpose: Assesses an individual's attitude toward school

Description: Oral-response test assessing two principle components of scholastic attitude: emotional disposition toward school and tendencies to action. The administrator presents to the child drawings showing situations that arise at school and notes how the examinee interprets the situations depicted. The number of situations liked and hated is calculated. Available in English or in French.

Format: Examiner required; individual administration; untimed

Scoring: Examiner evaluated

Cost: Manual $15.00; Set of Drawings $12.00; 25 Questionnaires $18.00

Volitional Questionnaire, Version 4.0 (VQ)

2003　　　Model of Human Occupation Clearinghouse

Carmen Gloria de las Heras, Rebecca Geist, Gary Kielhofner

Population: Adolescents, adults, and older adults

Purpose: Provides information about a client's volition and how environment affects volition

Description: An observational assessment that evaluates motivation, values, and interests, and impact of the environment. The 42-page manual contains reproducible assessment forms, including multiple observation forms.

Format: Observation and rating scale; untimed: 15 to 30 minutes per observation; 5 to 10 minutes for rating scale

Scoring: Examiner evaluated

Cost: $35.00

Work Environment Impact Scale, Version 2.0 (WEIS)

1998　　　Model of Human Occupation Clearinghouse

Renee A. Moore-Corner, Gary Kielhofner, Linda Olson

Population: Adults

Purpose: Evaluates the impact of the work setting on a person with physical/psychosocial difficulties in performance, satisfaction, and well-being

Description: Semistructured interview that evaluates features in the work environment that support or impede occupational performance, and the impact on a person's performance, satisfaction, and well-being. The 82-page manual contains reproducible assessment and data summary forms.

Format: Interview; untimed: 30 to 60 minutes

Scoring: Examiner evaluated

Cost: Manual $35.00; Video $20.00

Worker Role Interview, Version 10.0 (WRI)

2005　　　Model of Human Occupation Clearinghouse

Brent Braveman, Mick Robson, Craig Velozo, Gary Kielhofner, Gail Fisher, Kirsty Forsyth, Jennifer Kerschbaum

Population: Adults

Purpose: Evaluates psychosocial factors that affect returning to work

Description: Used to evaluate injured workers in the areas of personal causation, values, interests, roles, habits, and perception of environmental supports. Looks at life outside work, past and present work experience, and plans for return to work. The WRI is a semistructured interview designed to be used as the psychosocial/environmental component of the initial rehabilitation assessment process for the injured worker or the worker with a long-term disability and poor/limited work history. The new WRI has three interview formats: one for workers with recent injuries/disabilities, one for clients with chronic disabilities, and a combined WRI and OCAIRS interview. There are a variety of reporting formats.

Format: Interview; untimed: 30 to 60 minutes

Scoring: Examiner evaluated

Cost: Manual $38.50; Video $20.00

Youth Risk and Resilience Inventory (YRRI)

2006	JIST Publishing

Robert P. Brady

Population: Ages 10 to 17 years

Purpose: Identifies youth at risk of abuse and measures coping skills

Description: This screening tool has 36 items that survey various risk factors associated with violence and abuse and an additional 18 items that assess internal and external resilience factors useful for early identification and intervention. The YRRI is research-based and statistically sound. It has been tested with abused children, general at-risk youth, children from violent homes in shelters, and youth in court-required drug-treatment programs.

Format: Requires examiner; suitable for group use; untimed 15 to 20 minutes

Scoring: Self-scoring

Cost: 25 Forms and Administration Guide $23.95

Learning Styles

Barsch Learning Style Inventory–Revised

1996	Academic Therapy Publications

Jeffrey Barsch

Population: Ages 14 to adult

Purpose: Measures learning style

Description: An informal, self-reporting instrument that provides an indication of the relative strengths and weaknesses in learning through different sensory channels: auditory, visual, tactile, and kinesthetic. It is useful for assessing the learning styles of students with learning disabilities. The Study Tips component gives guidelines on how to maximize individual learning styles.

Format: Rating scale; untimed: 5 to 10 minutes

Scoring: Examiner evaluated

Cost: Test Kit (10 forms, 10 study tips) $14.00

Eclectic Learning Profile

2005	Academic Therapy Publications

Erica Warren

Population: Grades 3 to adult

Purpose: Measures learning style

Description: An informal self-report checklist that describes the ways students learn best. Statements describe 12 ways to learn: visual, auditory, tactile, kinesthetic, sequential, simultaneous, reflective, verbal, interactive, direct experience, indirect experience, and through rhythm. When completing the questionnaire, individuals select those areas they feel are most descriptive of their way(s) of learning new material. Once the descriptors are selected, the information can be used to help develop compensatory strategies to use in the classroom, on the job, and in everyday tasks. The manual provides background information about various theories of learning styles. Two forms are available: one for use in Grades 3 to 6 and the other with Grades 7 to adult.

Format: Rating scale; untimed: 10 to 15 minutes

Scoring: Examiner evaluated

Cost: Test Kit (manual, 25 elementary/adult profiles, 15 summary forms) $50.00

Learning and Study Strategies Inventory (LASSI)

1987	H & H Publishing Company, Inc.

Claire E. Weinstein, David Palmer, Ann Schulte

Population: College freshmen

Purpose: Assesses learning, study practices, and attitudes; used as a counseling tool and a diagnostic measure

Description: Computer-administered or paper-pencil 10-scale 77-item multiple-choice test measuring attitude, motivation, time management, information processing, test strategies, anxiety, concentration, selecting main ideas, study aid, and self-testing. A chart yielding statistically valid and reliable percentile rankings is available. Computer version (PC and Macintosh) is available.

Format: Self-administered; untimed: 30 minutes

Scoring: Self- or computer scored; now available on the Web

Cost: $3.25 each (for 1 to 99 copies)

Learning and Study Strategies Inventory–High School (LASSI-HS)

1990	H & H Publishing Company, Inc.

Claire E. Weinstein, David R. Palmer, Ann Schulte

Population: Grades 9 to 12

Purpose: Measures learning, study practices, and attitudes; used as a counseling tool for diagnostic measure

Description: Paper–pencil multiple-choice test measuring attitude, motivation, time management, information processing, test strategies, anxiety, concentration, selecting main ideas, study aid, and self-testing. A chart yielding statistically valid and reliable percentile rankings is used as is a self-scored form or a scannable NCS form. A seven-page booklet and a pen or pencil is needed.

Format: Self-administered; untimed: 30 minutes

Scoring: Self- or computer scored; now available on the Web

Cost: $2.75 each (for 1 to 99 copies)

Learning and Working Styles Inventory

2005	Piney Mountain Press, Inc.

Halena Hendrix-Frye

Population: Ages 12 years and older

Purpose: Assesses individual learning styles

Description: Multiple-choice paper–pencil, video, or computer-administered test measuring cognitive learning style, social learning style, expressive learning style, and working (environmental) learning style. Computer printouts for individual and group profiles are provided, graphically indicating major and minor learning styles. Specific teaching and learning strategies are also outlined based on each individual's scores. All results are saved to disk and may be edited or printed at any time. Based on the *Hendrix-Frye Working Learning Styles* and the *CITE Academic Learning Styles*. Suitable for individuals with visual, hearing, physical, or mental impairments. Computer versions available for Windows.

Format: Examiner required; suitable for group use; timed: 14 minutes, untimed: 10 to 30 minutes

Scoring: Examiner interpretation; computer scored, hand key, or optical machine

Cost: Stand-Alone Version $195.00; Multistation Version $495.00; Network Version $995.00

Learning Style Inventory (LSI)

1975-2003	Price Systems, Inc.

Rita Dunn, Kenneth Dunn, Gary E. Price

Population: Grades 3 to 12

Purpose: Identifies students' preferred learning environments; used for designing instructional environments and counseling

Description: Paper–pencil or computer-administered 104-item Likert scale test assessing the conditions under which students prefer to learn. Individual preferences are measured in the following areas: Immediate Environment (sound, heat, light, and design), Emotionality (motivation, responsibility, persistence, and structure), Sociological Needs (self-oriented, peer-oriented, adult-oriented, or combined ways), and Physical Needs (perceptual preferences, time of day, food intake, and mobility). Test items consist of statements about how people like to learn. Students indicate whether they agree or disagree with each item. Results identify student preferences and indicate the degree to which a student's responses are consistent. Suggested strategies for instructional and environmental alternatives are provided to complement the student's revealed learning style. Computerized results are available in three forms: individual profile (raw scores for each of the 22 areas, standard scores and a plot for each score in each area), group summary (identifies students with significantly high or low scores and groups individuals with similar preferences), and a subscale summary. Available on two levels: Grades 3 and 4 and 5 to 12.

Format: Self-administered; untimed: 30 minutes

Scoring: Computer scored

Cost: Specimen Set (manual, research report, inventory booklet, answer sheet) $16.00; Diskette (100 administrations per licensing agreement) $395.00; Each Additional 100 Administrations $60.00; NCS Scanner Program $495.00; 100 Answer Sheets for NCS $60.00

Learning Styles Inventory (LSI)

1988	Western Psychological Services

Albert A. Canfield

Population: Adolescents, adults

Purpose: Identifies an individual's preferred learning methods; identifies individuals with little or no interest in independent or unstructured learning situations; used to maximize teaching and learning efficiency

Description: Paper–pencil 30-item forced-rank inventory measuring individual learning needs (interacting with others, goal setting, competition, friendly relations with instructor, independence in study, classroom authority), preferred mediums (listening, reading, viewing pictures, graphs, slides, or direct experience), and areas of interest (numeric concepts, qualitative concepts, and working with inanimate things and people). The inventory also indicates student perceptions as to how they will perform in the learning situation and identifies learning problems associated with either traditional or innovative teaching methods. The test is available in two forms: Form S-A for use with most adults and Form E for use with persons whose reading level is as low as the fifth grade. The test booklets are reusable. Separate norms are available for males and females.

Format: Self-administered; untimed: 15 to 20 minutes

Scoring: Self-scored

Cost: Kit (8 inventory booklets; 2 each of forms A, B, C, and E; manual; 2-use disk) $109.50

Student Styles Questionnaire

1996	Harcourt Assessment, Inc.

Thomas Oakland, Joseph Glutting, Connie Horton

Population: Ages 8 to 17 years

Purpose: Measures students' styles of learning, relating, and working

Description: Patterned after the original Jungian constructs in four scales: Extroverted/Introverted, Thinking/Feeling, Practical/Imaginative, and Organized/Flexible. Students respond to 69 forced-choice questions related to real-life situations to express their individual styles; each item is a brief description of an everyday event. Includes classroom applications booklet for activity ideas in specific subject areas appropriate for each student's style (personal, educational, and occupational). Optional scoring software generates a report for the child or adolescent and the professional.

Format: Examiner required; suitable for group use; untimed: 30 minutes

Scoring: Examiner evaluated; may be computer scored

Cost: Complete Kit (manual, classroom applications booklet, answer documents, question booklet) $115.00

Style of Learning and Thinking (SOLAT)

1988	Scholastic Testing Service, Inc.

E. Paul Torrance, Bernice McCarthy, Mary Kolesinski, Jamie Smith

Population: Grades K to 12

Purpose: Assesses learning styles

Description: Paper–pencil test with 25 to 28 items per questionnaire. Categories are Left-Brained, Right-Brained, or Whole-Brained. Raw scores, standard scores, and percentiles are yielded. A Youth Form and an Elementary Form are available. Examiner must be certified for assessment.

Format: Self-administered; untimed: 30 to 40 minutes

Scoring: Self-scored

Cost: Starter Set (manual, 35 questionnaires) specify which form $48.15

Behavior Problems

Adult Behavior Checklist for Ages 18–59 (ABCL)

2003	ASEBA® Research Center for Children, Youth, and Families

Thomas M. Achenbach

Population: Ages 18 to 59 years

Purpose: Used in mental health and special education applications to assess behavioral and emotional problems

Description: Paper–pencil short-answer rating scales with 126 problem items. The following scales are yielded: Adaptive Functioning, Empirically Based Syndromes, Substance Use, Internalizing, Externalizing, and Total Problems. In addition, the ABCL profiles feature new DSM-oriented scales. Choices are presented in a 3-point Likert scale. A Windows-based scoring program is available.

Format: Rating scale; untimed

Scoring: Hand key; computer scored; machine scored

Cost: Package of 50 Forms $25.00

Behavior Assessment System for Children–Second Edition (BASC-II)

| 2005 | AGS Publishing/Pearson Assessments |

Cecil R. Reynolds, Randy W. Kamphaus

Population: Ages 2 years 6 months to 21 years

Purpose: Facilitates differential diagnosis and educational classification of a variety of children's emotional and behavioral disorders and aids in the design of treatment plans

Description: The BASC is a multimethod, multidimensional approach to evaluating the behavior and self-perceptions of children. It has five components that can be used individually or in any combination. The three core components are Teacher Rating Scales (TRS), Parent Rating Scales (PRS), and Self-Report of Personality (SRP). Additional components include Structured Developmental History (SDH) and Student Observation System (SOS). The BASC measures positive (adaptive), as well as negative (clinical), dimensions of behavior and personality. Identifies behavior problems as required by IDEA and for developing FBAs, BIPs, and IEPs. Differentiates between hyperactivity and attention problems. Also available in Spanish.

Format: Examiner required; individual administration; untimed: TRS/PRS, 10 to 20 minutes; SRP, 30 minutes; SDH, varies from family to family; SOS, 15 minutes

Scoring: Computerized scoring available in the BASC Enhanced ASSIST and the BASC Plus software

Cost: Hand-Scored Forms Starter Set $359.99; Windows or Macintosh Starter Set $499.99

Behavior Dimensions Scale (BDS)

| 1995 | Hawthorne Educational Services, Inc. |

Stephen B. McCarney

Population: Ages 5 to 15 years (School Version); Ages 3 to 18 years (Home Version)

Purpose: Assesses dimensions of behavior of attention deficit/hyperactivity disorder, oppositional-defiant disorder, conduct disorder, avoidant personality, anxiety, and depression

Description: Each dimension of behavior is clarified by behavioral items that are observable overt descriptors of the behavior problems documented by primary observers of the child or adolescent's behavior (i.e., teachers and parents). Frequency-based quantifiers provide precise measures of the rate of problematic behavior. Available in both a School Version, completed by educators, and a Home Version, completed by the parent or guardian. A Windows Quick Score is available. Also available in Spanish. Currently being renormed and will be published in 2007.

Format: Rating scale; untimed

Scoring: Examiner evaluated; computer scoring available

Cost: Complete Kit (2 technical manuals, intervention manual, 50 each of 2 forms) $130.00

Behavior Disorders Identification Scale–Second Edition (BDIS-2)

| 2000 | Hawthorne Educational Services, Inc. |

Stephen B. McCarney, Tamara J. Arthaud

Population: Grades K to 12

Purpose: Identifies students with behavior disorders and emotional disturbance

Description: Includes both School and Home Versions to provide a comprehensive profile of student behavior problems. The scale relies on direct behavioral observations by educators and parents or guardians. The BDIS-2 focuses on both the overt indicators of behavior disorders, as well as the more subtle indicators of withdrawal, depression, and suicidal tendencies. The standardized sample represents all geographic regions of the United States, with particular attention given to the inclusion of racial and ethnic minorities in the creation of the national norms. Internal consistency, test-retest, interrater reliability, item analysis, factor analysis, content validity, criterion-related validity, diagnostic validity, and construct validity are all reported. A Windows Quick Score is available. Also available in Spanish.

Format: Rating scale; untimed

Scoring: Examiner evaluated; computer scoring available

Cost: Complete Kit (2 technical manuals, intervention guide, 50 of 3 forms) $190.00

Behavior Evaluation Scale– Third Edition (BES-3)

| 2005 | Hawthorne Educational Services, Inc. |

Stephen B. McCarney, Tamara J. Arthaud

Population: Ages 4 to 19 years

Purpose: Provides results that assist school personnel in making decisions about eligibility, placement, and programming for students with behavior problems who have been referred for evaluation

Description: The scale is based on the IDEA definition of behavior disorders and emotional disturbance and provides subscales for Learning Problems, Interpersonal Difficulties, Inappropriate Behavior, Unhappiness/Depression, and Physical Symptoms/Fears. There are two versions: a long and a short. The long school version includes 76 items; the short school version has 54 items. The home versions have 73 items for the long and 52 items for the short. There are also long and short prereferral checklists that provide a means of calling attention to the behavior for early intervention. The Intervention Manual includes IEP goals, objectives, and interventions for all items on each scale. The Parent's Guide provides parents with specific, practical strategies to use in helping the child in the home environment. A Spanish Home version is available. There is a Quick Score Program for Windows.

Format: Rating scale; untimed: 15 to 20 minutes

Scoring: Examiner evaluated; computer scoring available

Cost: Complete Kit–Long (2 technical manuals, intervention manual, parent's guide, 50 of 3 forms) $208.50; Complete Kit–Short (2 technical manuals, intervention manual, parent's guide, 50 of 3 forms) $206.50

Behavior Rating Profile–Second Edition (BRP-2)

1990	PRO-ED, Inc.

Linda L. Brown, Donald D. Hammill

Population: Ages 6 years 6 months to 18 years 6 months

Purpose: Identifies elementary and secondary students with behavior problems and the settings in which those problems seem prominent; also identifies individuals who have differing perceptions about the behavior of a student; may be used for identification of emotional disturbance

Description: Multiple-item paper–pencil battery consisting of six independent, individually normed measures: Student Rating Scales (Home, School, and Peer), Parent Rating Scale, Teacher Rating Scale, and the Sociogram.

Format: Rating scale; untimed

Scoring: Examiner evaluated

Cost: Complete Kit (manual; 50 each of student, parent, and teacher rating forms; 50 profile sheets; storage box) $204.00

Behavioral and Emotional Rating Scale–Second Edition (BERS-2)

2004	PRO-ED, Inc.

Michael H. Epstein

Population: Ages 5 to 18 years

Purpose: Measures personal strengths and competencies

Description: The BERS-2 measures interpersonal strength, involvement with family, intrapersonal strength, school functioning, affective strength, and career strength. The scale is a multimodal assessment system that measures the child's behavior from three perspectives: the child's (Youth Rating Scale), parent's (Parent Rating Scale), and teacher's or other professional's (Teacher Rating Scale). Information from the BERS-2 is useful for prereferral, placement, and measuring outcomes.

Format: Rating scale; untimed: 10 minutes

Scoring: Examiner evaluated

Cost: Complete Kit (manual; 25 each of teacher, parent, and youth rating scales; 50 summary forms; storage box) $165.00

Burks' Behavior Rating Scales–Second Edition (BBRS-2)

2006	Western Psychological Services

Harold F. Burks

Population: Ages 4 to 18 years

Purpose: Identifies patterns of behavior problems in children; used as an aid to differential diagnosis

Description: Paper–pencil 100-item inventory used by parents and teachers to rate a child on the basis of descriptive statements of observed behavior. Seven subscales measure Disruptive Behavior, Attention and Impulse Control Problems, Emotional Problems, Social Withdrawal, Ability Deficits, Physical Deficits, and Weak Self-Confidence. Two new scales test response validity. The Parents' Guide and the Teacher's Guide define each of the scales, present possible causes for the problem behavior, and offer suggestions on how to deal with the undesirable behavior from the point of view of the parent or teacher. The manual discusses causes and manifestations and possible intervention approaches for each of the subscales, as well as use with special groups, such as individuals with educable mental retardation, educational and orthopedic disabilities, and speech and hearing impairments.

Format: Rating scale by teacher and/or parent; untimed 15 to 20 minutes

Scoring: Examiner evaluated; auto scored

Cost: Kit (manual, 25 each of parent and teacher forms) $105.00

Child Behavior Checklist for Ages 1½ to 5 (CBCL-1½ to 5)

2000	ASEBA® Research Center for Children, Youth, and Families

Thomas M. Achenbach

Population: Ages 1½ to 5 years

Purpose: Used in mental health and special education applications to assess behavioral and emotional problems

Description. Paper–pencil 100-item short-answer rating scales with the following profiles: Emotionally Reactive, Anxious/Depressed, Somatic Complaints, Withdrawn, Sleep Problems, Attention Problems, and Aggressive Behavior. A fifth-grade reading level is required. A Windows-based scoring module is available.

Format: Rating scale; untimed: 10 minutes

Scoring: Hand key; computer scored

Cost: Package of 50 Forms $25.00

Child Behavior Checklist for Ages 6 to 18 (CBCL 6 to 18)

2001	ASEBA® Research Center for Children, Youth, and Families

Thomas M. Achenbach

Population: Ages 6 to 18 years

Purpose: Used in mental health and special education applications to assess behavioral and emotional problems

Description: Paper–pencil short-answer rating scales with 120 problem items and 20 competence items. The following scales are yielded: Anxious/Depressed, Withdrawn/Depressed, Somatic Complaints, Rule Breaking Behavior, Aggressive Behavior, Social Problems, Thought Problems, and Attention Problems. DSM-oriented scales are Affective, Anxiety, ADHD, Oppositional Defiant, and Conduct Disorders. Separate scor-

ing profiles for males and females ages 6 to 11 and 12 to 18 are available. A form completed by the parent is used. A fifth-grade reading level is required. A computer-administered program and scoring program are available. Additional scales to be available in 2007 are Obsessive–Compulsive Problems, Post Traumatic Stress Problems, and Sluggish Cognitive Tempo.

Format: Rating scale; untimed: 10 minutes

Scoring: Hand key; machine scored; computer scored

Cost: Package of 50 Forms $25.00

Conduct Disorder Scale (CDS)

2002	PRO-ED, Inc.

James E. Gilliam

Population: Ages 5 to 22 years

Purpose: Helps to diagnose conduct disorder

Description: An efficient and effective instrument for evaluating students exhibiting severe behavior problems who may have conduct disorder. The 40 items describe the specific diagnostic behaviors characteristic of the disorder. These items comprise four subscales necessary for the diagnosis: Aggressive Conduct, Non-Aggressive Conduct, Deceitfulness and Theft, and Rule Violations. The test is useful for screening and clinical assessment in schools, clinics, and correctional facilities. Normed on a representative sample of over 600 persons who were diagnosed with conduct disorder. A detailed interview form (derived from DSM-IV-TR) is provided to document infrequent but serious behavior problems.

Format: Rating scale; untimed: 5 to 10 minutes

Scoring: Examiner evaluated

Cost: Complete Kit (manual, 50 forms, storage box) $89.00

Coping Inventory: A Measure of Adaptive Behavior (Observation Form)

1985	Scholastic Testing Service, Inc.

Shirley Zeitlin

Population: Ages 3 to 16 years

Purpose: Assesses personality

Description: Paper–pencil criterion-referenced test assesses two categories: coping with self (productive, active, flexible), and coping with environment (productive, active, and flexible). Scores yielded are 1 (*Not Effective*), 2 (*Minimally Effective*), 3 (*Effective in Some but Not Others*),

4 (*Effective More Often Than Not*), and 5 (*Effective Most of the Time*). A booklet and manual are used. Examiner must be certified for assessment. Also available in large print.

Format: Rating scale; untimed

Scoring: Examiner evaluated

Cost: Starter Set (manual, 20 forms) $56.50

Coping Inventory: A Measure of Adaptive Behavior (Self-Rated Form)

1985	Scholastic Testing Service, Inc.

Shirley Zeitlin

Population: Ages 15 years and older

Purpose: Assesses personality

Description: Paper–pencil criterion-referenced test assesses two categories: coping with self (productive, active, and flexible), and coping with environment (productive, active, and flexible). Scores yielded are 1 (*Not Effective*), 2 (*Minimally Effective*), 3 (*Effective in Some but Not Others*), 4 (*Effective More Often Than Not*), and 5 (*Effective Most of the Time*). A booklet and manual are used. Examiner must be certified for assessment. Also available in large print.

Format: Rating scale; untimed

Scoring: Examiner evaluated

Cost: Starter Set (manual, 10 forms) $36.80

Developmental Teaching Objectives and Rating Forms–Revised (DTORF-R)

1999 (paper-pencil); 2005 (online)	Developmental Therapy Institute, Inc.

Mary M. Wood

Population: Ages birth to 16 years

Purpose: Assesses social, emotional, cognitive, and behavioral development; used for FBA and BIP assessments, IEP planning, and AYI

Description: Four subscales for a total of 171 items: Behavior (33 items), Socialization (41 items), Communication (35 items), and Cognition/Academics (62 items). Yields individual and group developmental profiles; ratings of items mastered; shows mastered progression sequentially through each category. Three forms are available: Early Childhood, Elementary School, and Middle/High School. Also available in German, Spanish, and Norwegian. An online version is available through the publisher's Web site.

Format: Rating scale; untimed

Scoring: Examiner evaluated; training and scoring service available; online

Cost: Complete Kit (manuals, forms, test booklets) $75.00; Online $169.00 per teacher for annual membership

Devereux Behavior Rating Scale– School Form

1993	Harcourt Assessment, Inc.

Jack A. Naglieri, Paul A. LeBuffe, Steven I. Pfeiffer

Population: Ages 5 to 18 years

Purpose: Detects severe emotional disturbances in students

Description: Evaluates the existence of behaviors indicating severe emotional disturbance. The results can be compared across informants and in a variety of settings. The 40-item scale is especially effective used in conjunction with other findings to monitor and evaluate progress during educational interventions, or to determine whether a child or adolescent with severe emotional disturbance should be placed in a special education program. The four subscales address the individual areas identified in IDEA. Two forms are available: a child form for ages 5 to 12 and an adolescent form for ages 13 to 18. Problem Item Scores help to identify specific problem behaviors for treatment.

Format: Rating scale; untimed: 5 minutes

Scoring: Examiner evaluated

Cost: Complete Kit (manual, 25 each of child and adolescent answer documents) $185.00

Differential Test of Conduct and Emotional Problems (DT/CEP)

1990	Slosson Educational Publications, Inc.

Edward J. Kelly

Population: Grades K to 12

Purpose: Differentiates between three critical populations: conduct disorder, emotional disturbance, and noninvolved

Description: The DT/CEP facilitates educational decisions for special education and regular education. Emphasizes simple but effective screening identification, verification, and diagnostic steps to facilitate more accountable placement and programming. Includes nine case studies that illustrate test use and related procedural uses.

Format: Examiner required; group administration; untimed: 15 to 20 minutes

Scoring: Hand key

Cost: Complete Kit $99.75

Direct Observation Form (DOF)

| 1986 | ASEBA® Research Center for Children, Youth, and Families |

Thomas M. Achenbach

Population: Ages 5 to 14 years

Purpose: Used in mental health and special education to assess behavioral and emotional problems for individuals with behavioral and emotional disorders and learning disabilities

Description: Paper–pencil short-answer rating scales with 97 problem items; on-task behavior at 1-minute intervals. The following scales are yielded: Withdrawn–Inattentive, Nervous–Obsessive, Depressed, Hyperactive, Attention Demanding, and Aggressive. An observation form is used and scored by an observer. Examiner must be an experienced observer. DOS format scoring is available.

Format: Completed by observer; timed: 10 minutes

Scoring: Hand key; computer scored

Cost: Package of 50 Forms $25.00

Disruptive Behavior Rating Scale (DBRS)

| 1993 | Slosson Educational Publications, Inc. |

Bradley T. Erford

Population: Ages 5 to 10 years

Purpose: Identifies attention-deficit disorder, attention-deficit/hyperactivity disorder, oppositional disorders, and antisocial conduct problems

Description: Administration of the 50-item inventory can be performed by both professionals and paraprofessionals. The DBRS is ideal for individual and mass screenings. The wording of the teacher and parent versions is nearly identical, allowing legitimate comparisons between their responses. Scale items were specifically written to allow direct teacher transfer to behavior-modification plans, IEPs, or 504 plans. The DBRS provides separate norms for teacher, mother, and father responses. Normative data were obtained from 1,766 children, mothers of 1,399 children, and fathers of 1,252 children. Normative data are also provided to convert raw scores into t-scores

and percentile ranks, as well as standard error of measurement and critical item determination. The computer-generated report calculates a summary statistics table, t-scores, percentile ranks, interpretation ranges, and also identifies critical items of importance.

Format: Examiner required; individual or group administration; untimed: 7 minutes

Scoring: Hand key; computer scored

Cost: Complete $169.25

Draw A Person: Screening Procedure for Emotional Disturbance (DAP:SPED)

| 1991 | PRO-ED, Inc. |

Jack A. Naglieri, Timothy J. McNeish, Achilles N. Bardos

Population: Ages 6 to 17 years

Purpose: Helps to identify children and adolescents who have emotional problems and require further evaluation

Description: The DAP:SPED has items that are used to rate the drawings of a man, a woman, and the self. The items were based on an exhaustive review of the literature on human figure drawings, and the test was written to be objective and fast to score. The test blends the clinical skills and knowledge reported in the literature over the past 75 years with a modern psychometric approach to test construction. The DAP:SPED was normed on a nationwide sample of 2,260 students representative of the nation as a whole with regard to gender, race, ethnicity, geographic region, and socioeconomic status. Evidence of various types of reliability and validity is well documented in the test manual. The DAP:SPED yields a standard score (t-score) that is used to determine if further assessment is (a) not indicated, (b) indicated, or (c) strongly indicated.

Format: Examiner required; individual or group administration; untimed

Scoring: Examiner evaluated

Cost: Complete Kit (manual, 10 scoring templates, 25 record forms, storage box) $140.00

Emotional and Behavior Problem Scale–Second Edition (EBPS-2)

| 2001 | Hawthorne Educational Services, Inc. |

Stephen B. McCarney, Tamara J. Arthaud

Population: Ages 5 to 18 years

Purpose: Provides results for both a theoretical

and empirical construct of emotional disturbance/behavioral disorders, providing both an educational and more clinical perspective of emotional disturbance/behavioral disorders

Description: The empirical interpretation provides five "conditions" of behavior, while the theoretical interpretation is composed of five subscales representing the five characteristics of Emotional Disturbance/Behavior Disorders contained in IDEA. The School Form is completed by an educator; the Home Form is completed by the parent or guardian. Each has 58 items. A Windows Quick Score is available.

Format: Rating scale; untimed

Scoring: Examiner evaluated; computer scoring available

Cost: Complete Kit (2 technical manuals, IEP and intervention manual, 50 each of 2 forms) $125.00

Emotional/Behavioral Screening Program (ESP)

1988   McCarron-Dial Systems

Jack G. Dial, Garry Amann

Population: Ages 9 years and older

Purpose: Analyzes emotional and behavioral functioning; used with special needs students

Description: Paper–pencil 35-item checklist for rating an individual on the basis of observed behavior, reliable case history reports, or information provided by a reliable informant. The checklist, called the Behavioral Checklist for Students (BCS), contains seven categories of items: Impulsivity–Frustration, Anxiety, Depression–Withdrawal, Socialization, Self-Concept, Aggression, and Reality Discrimination. Raw subtest scores are entered into the computer. Users may choose from three types of reports. The Analysis Report is an analysis of emotional/behavioral functions with possible diagnostic categories. The Classroom Report describes emotional/behavioral characteristics the teacher may anticipate and lists specific recommendations for educational management. The Comprehensive Report integrates features of both the Analysis Report and the Classroom Report. The software operates on Macintosh and PC systems.

Format: Self-administered; untimed

Scoring: Computer scored; test scoring software included

Cost: Complete Kit (comprehensive manual, 25 copies of BCS, computer program with operating manual) $250.00

Emotional or Behavior Disorder Scale–Revised (EBDS-R)

2003   Hawthorne Educational Services, Inc.

Stephen B. McCarney, Tamara J. Arthaud

Population: Ages 5 to 18 years

Purpose: Contributes to the early identification and service delivery for students with emotional or behavioral disorders

Description: The EBDS is based on the National Mental Health and Special Education Coalition definition of emotional or behavioral disorder and the theoretical construct of IDEA. This is a multiple-item rating scale in the areas of academic performance, social relationships, and personal adjustment. The rating form contains two sections: the Behavioral Component with 64 items and the Vocational Component with 54 items. A Quick Score for Windows is available.

Format: Rating scale; untimed: 20 minutes

Scoring: Examiner evaluated

Cost: Complete Kit (technical manual, 50 forms, intervention manual) $80.00

Eyberg Child Behavior Inventory (ECBI)/Sutter-Eyberg Student Behavior Inventory–Revised (SESBI-R)

1999   Psychological Assessment Resources, Inc.

Sheila Eyberg

Population: Ages 2 to 16 years

Purpose: Measures conduct problems reported by parent or teacher

Description: The ECBI consists of 36 items and assesses problem behavior reported by parents. The SESBI-R consists of 38 items and assesses problem behavior reported by teachers.

Format: Self-administered; untimed: 5 to 10 minutes

Scoring: Examiner evaluated

Cost: Introductory Kit (manual, 50 test sheets for each) $170.00

Functional Assessment and Intervention System: Improving School Behavior

2000   Harcourt Assessment, Inc.

Karen Callan Stoiber, Thomas R. Kratochwill

Population: Children, adolescents

Purpose: Helps to design interventions based

on both socially competent and challenging behaviors

Description: Teachers, parents, and the student complete checklists informed by direct observation or knowledge of the student. The data is used to create an assessment record and design interventions. A detailed list of resources and materials related to promoting social competence in applied settings is included.

Format: Rating scale; untimed

Scoring: Examiner evaluated

Cost: Complete Kit (manual, 25 record forms) $95.00

Home & Community Social Behavior Scales (HCSBS)

2002   **Assessment-Intervention Resources**

Kenneth W. Merrell, Paul Caldarella

Population: Ages 5 to 18 years

Purpose: Screening, assessment, identification, and intervention planning

Description: The scale is designed to be completed by home- and community-based raters. It provides integrated comprehensive ratings of both social skills and antisocial problem behaviors and includes two co-normed scales. The Social Competence scale includes 32 items that measure adaptive, prosocial skills on two subscales: Peer Relations and Self-Management/Compliance. The Antisocial Behavior scale includes 32 items that measure socially linked problem behaviors on two subscales: Defiant/Disruptive and Antisocial-Aggressive. The HCSBS was standardized with a national sample of ratings of 1,562 children and adolescents. The norm sample closely approximates the 2000 U.S. Census. Raw scores are converted to t-scores, percentile ranks, and descriptive Social Functioning Levels. Internal consistency reliability of the scale is .96 to .97 for the two total scale scores, and .94 for the four subscales. Extensive validity evidence is documented in the user's guide.

Format: Rating scale; untimed: 5 to 10 minutes

Scoring: Examiner evaluated

Cost: User's Guide $50.00; 25 Rating Forms $37.00

Manifestation of Symptomatology Scale (MOSS)

2000   **Western Psychological Services**

Neil L. Mogge

Population: Ages 11 to 18 years

Purpose: Assesses youngsters who are in trouble at school or with the law to identify personality dynamics, environmental concerns, treatment issues, and placement needs

Description: The MOSS has 124 brief sentences that describe a range of behaviors and emotional states with a true-false format. The MOSS yields 13 content scores, three summary indexes, and four validity scores. Normed on an ethnically diverse sample of more than 700, the MOSS is specifically designed to evaluate young people who may not have the reading skills and concentration needed for valid administration of other broadband personality instruments. It can be used as a screener, an assessment instrument, or a program evaluation tool.

Format: Examiner required; individual or group administration; untimed: 15 to 20 minutes

Scoring: Auto scored; computer scored; test scoring service available

Cost: Complete Kit (manual, 25 forms) $99.00

McGhee-Mangrum Inventory of School Adjustment (MISA)

2007   **PRO-ED, Inc.**

Ronnie L. McGhee, Laurel Mangrum

Population: Ages 5 through 18 years

Purpose: Measures student's behavior in the classroom

Description: The MISA contains five 10-item scales, reflecting different aspects of social adjustment that affect academic progress in school settings: Aggressive Behavior Scale, Anxiety Scale, Attention and Academic Problems Scale, Hyperactivity and Impulsivity Scale, and Oppositional Behavior Scale. Results can be used as part of a comprehensive evaluation to assist with educational programming decisions.

Format: Examiner required; individual administration; untimed: 5 to 10 minutes

Scoring: Examiner evaluated

Cost: Complete Kit (manual, 25 record forms, storage box) $108.00

Preschool and Kindergarten Behavior Scale–Second Edition (PKBS-2)

2002   **PRO-ED, Inc.**

Kenneth W. Merrell

Population: Ages 3 to 6 years

Purpose: Assesses social skills and problem behaviors

Description: A rating scale with 76 items on two separate scales, the PKBS-2 provides an integrated and functional appraisal. The scales can be completed by a variety of behavioral informants, such as parents, teachers, and other caregivers. The PKBS-2 was standardized with a nationwide sample of ratings of 3,317 children. A wide variety of reliability and validity evidence in support of the test is included in the manual. A Spanish version is available.

Format: Rating scale; untimed: 8 to 12 minutes

Scoring: Examiner evaluated

Cost: Complete Kit (manual, 50 forms, storage box) $110.00

Psychosocial Evaluation & Threat Risk Assessment™ (PETRA)

2005	Psychological Assessment Resources, Inc.

Jay Schneller

Population: Ages 11 to 18 years

Purpose: Following a threat of violence, analyzes the context of psychosocial, social, and ecological factors to assist in the identification, assessment, and management of adolescents who pose a risk for targeted violence through intervention before the violent act occurs

Description: The PETRA provides four domain scores: Psychosocial Resiliency Problems, Ecological, Total, Domain; eight cluster scores: Depressed Mood, Alienation, Egocentricism, Aggression, Family/Home, School, Stress, Coping Problems; two Response Style Indicators: Inconsistency and Social Desirability; and eight Critical Items. Also included is the Threat Assessment Matrix, which is used to classify the content of a threat as low, medium, or high risk based on the information gleaned from the threat itself.

Format: Examiner required; individual administration; untimed: 10 to 15 minutes

Scoring: Examiner evaluated

Cost: Introductory Kit (manual, 25 rating forms, 25 summary forms) $115.00

Revised Behavior Problem Checklist (RBPC)–PAR Edition

1996	Psychological Assessment Resources, Inc.

Herbert C. Quay, Donald R. Peterson

Population: Grades K to 12

Purpose: Measures behavior problems in children and adolescents

Description: Paper–pencil 89-item 3-point rating scale with the following categories: Conduct Disorder, Socialized Aggression, Attention Problems/Immaturity, Anxiety/Withdrawal, Psychotic Behavior, and Motor Excess.

Format: Rating scale; untimed: 10 minutes

Scoring: Hand key

Cost: Introductory Kit (manual, 50 checklists, 50 scoring profiles) $192.00

School Social Behavior Scale– Second Edition (SSBS-2)

2002	Assessment-Intervention Resources

Kenneth W. Merrell

Population: Grades K to 12

Purpose: Provides an integrated rating of both social skills and antisocial problem behaviors

Description: The rating scale is completed by the teacher or other school personnel. It provides comprehensive ratings of both social skills and antisocial problem behaviors of children and adolescents in school settings. The SSBS-2 includes two co-normed scales. The Social Competence scale includes 32 items that measure adaptive, prosocial skills and includes three subscales: Peer Relations, Self Management/Compliance, and Academic Behavior. The Antisocial Behavior scale includes 32 items that measure socially relevant problem behaviors and also includes three subscales: Hostile/Irritable, Antisocial–Aggressive, and Defiant/Disruptive. The scale was standardized with a national sample of 2,280 students. The norming sample closely approximates the 2000 U.S. Census. Raw scores are converted to *t*-scores, percentile ranks, and descriptive Social Functioning Levels. Internal consistency reliability of the SSBS-2 is .96 to .98 for the two total scale scores, and .94 to .96 for the six subscales. Extensive validity evidence for the scale is documented in the user's guide.

Format: Rating scale; untimed: 5 to 10 minutes

Scoring: Examiner evaluated

Cost: User's Guide $50.00; 25 Rating Forms $37.00

School Social Skills (S3)

1984	Slosson Educational Publications, Inc.

Laura Brown, Donald Black, John Downs

Population: Grades 1 to 8

Purpose: Assists school personnel in identifying student deficits in school-related social behaviors

Description: The 40-item scale of observable prosocial skills has been socially validated and determined to be important for student school success in the areas of Adult Relations, Peer Relations, School Rules, and Classroom Behaviors. The S3 Rating Scale is quick and easy to administer, taking approximately 10 minutes per student. Ratings are done on a six-point Likert scale and are based on observation of student behavior over the previous month. The S3 Manual accompanies the S3 Rating Scale and provides complete behavioral descriptions of each of the 40 skills and the conditions under which they should be used. The S3 Rating Scale is a criterion-referenced instrument that yields knowledge of a student's strengths and deficiencies. Both the test-retest and the interrater reliability data indicate the S3 Rating Scale has comparable reliability with residential, special education, and regular education students.

Format: Rating scale; untimed; 10 minutes

Scoring: Hand key

Cost: Complete Kit $77.25

Semistructured Clinical Interview for Children and Adolescents (SCICA)

2001	ASEBA® Research Center for Children, Youth, and Families

Stephanie H. McConaughy, Thomas M. Achenbach

Population: Ages 6 to 18 years

Purpose: Used in mental health and special education applications to assess behavioral and emotional problems

Description: Paper-pencil short-answer rating scales with 247 problem items. The following profiles are yielded: Anxious; Anxious/Depressed; Withdrawn Depressed; Language/Motor Problems; Aggressive/Rule Breaking Behavior; Attention Problems; Self-Control Problems; and Somatic Complaints (ages 12 to 18 only). Protocol and rating forms are used by an interviewer. Examiner must be an experienced interviewer. A Windows-based scoring program is available.

Format: Completed by interviewer; untimed: 60 to 90 minutes

Scoring: Hand key; computer scored

Cost: Package of 50 Forms $50.00

Social Behavior Assessment Inventory (SBAI)

1992	Psychological Assessment Resources, Inc.

Thomas H. Stephens, Kevin D. Arnold

Population: Grades K to 9

Purpose: Used by teachers, counselors, and parents to measure social behaviors

Description: Paper-pencil 136-item rating scale with the following content areas and subscales: Environmental Behaviors (care for the environment, dealing with emergency, lunchroom behavior, and movement around environment), Interpersonal Behaviors (accepting authority, coping with conflict, gaining attention, greeting others, helping others, making conversation, organized play, positive attitude toward others, playing informally, and property: own and others), Self-Related Behaviors (accepting consequences, ethical behavior, expressing feelings, positive attitude toward self, responsible behavior, and self-care), and Task-Related Behaviors (asking and answering questions, attending behavior, classroom discussion, completing tasks, following directions, group activities, independent work, on-task behavior, performing before others, and quality of work). Four behavior scales and 30 subscales can be used to develop instructional strategies.

Format: Rating scale completed by teacher or parent; untimed: 30 to 45 minutes

Scoring: Examiner evaluated

Cost: Introductory Kit (Social Skills in the Classroom, 2nd Ed.; manual; 25 rating booklets) $144.00

Social-Emotional Dimension Scale–Second Edition (SEDS-2)

2004	PRO-ED, Inc.

Jerry B. Hutton, Timothy G. Roberts

Population: Ages 6 to 18 years

Purpose: Provides a means for rating student behavior problems that may interfere with academic functioning

Description: The 74-item scale rates behaviors to provide a total score that estimates the degree of problems exhibited. Norms are reported separately for males and females. A 15-item screener is provided, as well as a structured interview. Behavioral descriptors have been added to assist the examiner in rating behaviors on each item.

Format: Rating scale; untimed: 20 to 30 minutes

Scoring: Examiner evaluated

Cost: Complete Kit (manual, 25 comprehensive forms, 50 screener forms, 50 screener summary forms, storage box) $149.00

Social Skills Rating System (SSRS)

1990	AGS Publishing/Pearson Assessments

Frank M. Gresham, Stephen N. Elliott

Population: Ages 3 to 18 years

Purpose: Questionnaires that obtain information on social behaviors

Description: The SSRS allows the examiner to obtain a more complete picture of social behaviors from teachers, parents, and students. A broad range of socially validated behaviors are evaluated. The instrument is used to assess and select for treatment problem behaviors. There are three scales: Social Skills Scale, Problem Behavior Scale, and Academic Competence Scale. The Assessment–Intervention Record can be used to combine the perspective of each rater on a single form.

Format: Rating scale; untimed: 15 to 25 minutes for each questionnaire

Scoring: Examiner interpretation; computer scoring available for Windows

Cost: Starter Set: Preschool/Elementary (10 copies each of teacher, parent, and student questionnaires; 10 assessment–intervention records, manual) $129.99 Secondary Level $110.99

Special Needs Assessment Profile–Behaviour (SNAP-B)

2006	Hodder Murray

Rob Long, Charles Weedon

Population: Ages 5 to 16 years

Purpose: Measures behavioral, emotional, and social difficulties

Description: The core problem area(s) for each child are identified in an intuitive and user-friendly assessment. The SNAP-B computer-aided package "maps" a pupil's own mix of problems onto an overall matrix of difficulties. It provides a structured assessment that pulls together information from home and school. From this, clusters and patterns of behaviors help to pinpoint core problem areas. Uses a bank of carefully targeted questions that profile 12 problem areas under three broad headings: Conflict With Self, Conflict With Peers, and Conflict With Adults. The focus is on identifying specific skills a learner needs to

be successful, rather than speculating about possible causes of any behavior.

Format: Examiner required; individual administration; untimed

Scoring: Computer scored

Cost: CD with 2-Year License £145.00; User Kit £29.99; Pupil Assessment Pack £17.99

Systematic Screening for Behavior Disorders (SSBD)

1992	Sopris West Educational Services

Hill M. Walker, Herbert H. Severson

Population: Grades K to 6

Purpose: Used in public schools to screen for behavior disorders

Description: The SSBD screening process is proactive and incorporates a three-stage, multi-gated process. The SSBD relies on teacher judgments and direct observation. The SSBD was extensively field tested. In Stage I, the teacher identifies two groups of 10 students each that most closely resemble behavioral profiles of externalizing and internalizing behavior problems. The teacher then ranks the students, and the three highest ranked students on each list move to Stage II. In Stage II, the teacher completes three brief rating instruments for each of the six students. Only those students who exceed the SSBD Stage II screening criteria move to Stage III. Stage III involves assessing each student in two separate 15-minute classroom and 15-minute playground observations.

Format: Examiner required; judgment and observation; untimed

Scoring: Examiner evaluated

Cost: Kit (user's guide and administration manual, technical manual, observer training manual, videotape, reproducible forms) $107.49

Teacher's Report Form (TRF)

2001	ASEBA® Research Center for Children, Youth, and Families

Thomas M. Achenbach

Population: Ages 6 to 18 years

Purpose: Used in mental health and special education applications to assess behavioral and emotional problems for individuals with behavioral and emotional disorders and learning disabilities

Description: Paper–pencil short-answer rating scales with 120 problem items and five adaptive items. The following profiles are yielded: Anxious/Depressed; Withdrawn/Depressed; Somatic Complaints; Rule Breaking Behavior; Aggressive Behavior; Social Problems; Thought Problems; and Attention Problems. Separate scoring profiles for males and females ages 6 to 11 and 12 to 18 are available. A computer-administered program and scoring program are available. In 2007, DSM-oriented scales will be available that are similar to the CBCL 6 to 18.

Format: Rating scale; untimed: 15 to 20 minutes

Scoring: Hand key; machine scored; computer scored

Cost: Package of 50 Forms $50.00

Youth Self-Report (YSR)

2001	ASEBA® Research Center for Children, Youth, and Families

Thomas M. Achenbach

Population: Ages 11 to 18 years

Purpose: Used in mental health and special education applications to assess behavioral and emotional problems

Description: Paper–pencil short-answer rating scales with 102 problem items and 17 competence items. The following profiles are yielded: Anxious/Depressed, Withdrawn/Depressed, Somatic Complaints, Rule Breaking Behavior, Aggressive Behavior, Social Problems, Thought Problems, and Attention Problems. In 2007, DSM-oriented and additional scales will be available. A fifth-grade reading level is required. A computer-administered and scoring program are available.

Format: Rating scale; untimed

Scoring: Hand key; machine scored; computer scored

Cost: Package of 50 Forms $25.00

Self-Concept

ASK-KIDS Inventory for Children

2005	Australian Council for Educational Research Limited

Laurel Bornholt

Population: Ages 4 to 12 years

Purpose: Measures children's understanding of themselves

Description: The inventory provides a profile of self-concepts in relation to a diverse set of physical, cognitive, and social activities. Can be administered by a wide range of professionals, including counselors, clinicians, social workers, psychologists, and health professionals. This is a unique and engaging inventory that includes self-concepts in 10 areas: Reading, Numbers, Drawing, Friends, Communication, Individuality, Belonging, Movement, Body, and Appearance. Simple diagrams of the activities provide a frame of reference for each of the self-concepts that are indicated by responses to five direct questions. Responses are recorded using a simple one-to-five dot-point scale.

Format: Examiner required; can be group administered; untimed: 15 minutes

Scoring: Examiner evaluated

Cost: Manual $69.95; 10 Test Booklets $29.95

Joseph Picture Self-Concept Scale

2004	Western Psychological Services

Jack Joseph

Population: Ages 3 to 13 years

Purpose: Assesses self-concept

Description: The Joseph Scale employs a unique administration format that lets youngsters respond using pictures rather than words. Children are shown pairs of illustrations representing common self-appraisal situations and are asked to choose between a picture representing positive self-concept and another representing negative self-concept. For example, one picture might show a youngster being disciplined, and the other a youngster being praised. The examiner asks the child to indicate which of the two illustrated situations happens to him or her most frequently. The child may answer orally or may simply point to his or her choice. This interview-and-picture response format is particularly useful with preschoolers and older children who may have developmental problems or language difficulties. The scale consists of two forms: the Young Child Interview (Form Y), used to assess children ages 3-0 to 7-11, and the Older Child Interview (Form O), designed for children ages 7-0 to 13-11. Each form includes its own Stimulus Booklets—Light-Skin and Dark-Skin versions, which contain picture pairs for both boys and girls. Form Y includes 21 items; Form O includes 30 items. The Older Child Interview includes a Response Distortion Index and items geared specifically to older children. It also uses an interactive interview format, though, like the Young Child Interview, it requires no reading and can be essentially nonverbal. Both forms yield a Total Self-Concept Score.

Format: Examiner required; individual administration; untimed: 5 to 10 minutes

Scoring: Examiner evaluated

Cost: Complete Kit (manual, cards, identity drawings, 50 record forms) $150.00

Joseph Preschool and Primary Self-Concept Screening Test (JPPSST)

1979	Stoelting Company

Jack Joseph

Population: Ages 3 years 5 months to 9 years

Purpose: Measures social-emotional development of children; used to identify children who may have learning difficulties due to negative self-appraisals and to monitor progress in early childhood programs and special education classes

Description: Paper–pencil 16-item oral-response test in two parts. First, the child draws his or her own face on a blank figure of the corresponding gender. Next, the child answers two simple oral-response questions and 13 questions asking the child to select from pairs of pictures the one with which he or she identifies more closely. The face drawing is evaluated qualitatively, and the 15 questions are scored objectively. The test generates a Global Self-Concept Score based on five dimensions and provides objective high-risk cutoff points. The effects of socially desirable responses are corrected for upper ranges (ages 5 to 9). Both quantitative and qualitative indices regarding possible cognitive deficits and experiential or receptive language lags are developed. The manual provides normative data, measures of validity and reliability, item analysis, specific case illustrations, and research considerations.

Format: Examiner required; individual administration; untimed: 5 to 7 minutes

Scoring: Examiner evaluated

Cost: Complete Kit (manual, cards, identity drawings, 50 record forms) $150.00

Multidimensional Self-Concept Scale (MSCS)

1992	PRO-ED, Inc.

Bruce A. Bracken

Population: Grades 5 to 12

Purpose: Assesses global self-concept and six context-dependent self-concept domains that

are functionally and theoretically important in the social-emotional adjustment of youth and adolescents

Description: The six self-concept domains are Social, Competence, Affect, Academic, Family, and Physical, with 25 items per domain. The questions are asked in a self-report with a 4-point Likert scale.

Format: Rating scale; untimed: 20 minutes

Scoring: Examiner evaluated

Cost: Complete Kit (manual, 50 record booklets, storage box) $110.00

Piers-Harris Children's Self-Concept Scale–Second Edition (Piers-Harris 2)

2002	Western Psychological Services

Ellen V. Piers, Dale B. Harris

Population: Grades 4 to 12

Purpose: Measures a child's self-concept and identifies problem areas

Description: Paper–pencil 80-item test assessing six aspects of a child's self-esteem: behavior, intellectual and school status, physical appearance and attributes, anxiety, popularity, and happiness and satisfaction. Items are written at a third-grade reading level and require a simple yes–no answer. Percentile and standard scores are provided for the total score and for each of the six subscales. Scores can be used for research purposes or to identify extreme problem areas. The manual provides the information necessary for administering and interpreting the scale, as well as the information included in Research Monograph #1 concerning use of the scale with minority and special education groups.

Format: Examiner or self-administered; suitable for group use; untimed: 15 to 20 minutes

Scoring: Hand key; may be computer scored

Cost: Kit (manual, 40 AutoScore™ forms) $119.00

Student Self-Concept Scale (SSCS)

1993	AGS Publishing/Pearson Assessments

Frank M. Gresham, Stephen N. Elliott, Sally E. Evans-Fernandez

Population: Grades 3 to 12

Purpose: Measures self-concept

Description: This flexible 72-item self-report measure of self-concept gives the examiner detailed information from three content areas in each of three dimensions. Based on Bandura's theory of self-efficacy, the SSCS documents the child's confidence level and importance rating of specific behaviors influencing the development of students' self-concepts. The three dimensions are Self-Confidence, Importance, and Outcome Confidence. The areas in each dimension are Academic, Social, and Self-Image.

Format: Self-administration; untimed: 15 to 25 minutes

Scoring: Examiner evaluated

Cost: Manual $49.95; Level I and Level 2 Student Questionnaires (25) $46.99

Tennessee Self Concept Scale–Second Edition (TSCS-2)

1996	Western Psychological Services

William H. Fitts, W. L. Warren

Population: Ages 12 years to adult

Purpose: Measures an individual's self-concept in terms of identity, feelings, and behavior; used for a wide range of clinical applications

Description: Paper–pencil 100-item test con-

sisting of self-descriptive statements that subjects rate on a scale ranging from 1 (*completely false*) to 5 (*completely true*). The test is available in two forms: Counseling (Form C) and Clinical and Research (Form C & R). Form C is appropriate if the results are to be used directly with the subject. It provides a number of measures, including response defensiveness, a total score, and self-concept scales that reflect "What I Am," "How I Feel," and "What I Do." The scales include Identify, Self Satisfaction, Behavior, Physical Self, Moral-Ethical Self, Personal Self, Family Self, and Social Self. It does not require scoring keys. Form C & R yields the same scores as Form C, as well as the following six empirical scales, which require special scoring keys: Defensive Positive, General Maladjustment, Psychosis, Personality Disorder, Neurosis, and Personality Integration. Both forms use the same test booklet, but require different answer-profile sheets.

Format: Self-administered; untimed: 10 to 20 minutes

Scoring: Computer scored; hand key

Cost: Kit (12 of each AutoScore™ answer forms, manual) $110.00

Development and Readiness

Ages & Stages Questionnaire (ASQ)–Second Edition

1999	Brookes Publishing, Co.

Diane Bricker, Jane Squires, Linda Mounts, LaWanda Potter, Robert Nickel, Elizabeth Trimbly, Jane Farrell

Population: Ages 4 months to 5 years

Purpose: Screening and developmental monitoring of at-risk and general preschool populations

Description: The ASQ has 19 age-specific intervals with 30 questions at each interval. Domains: Fine Motor, Gross Motor, Communication, Problem Solving, and Personal-Social. Cutoff scores indicate whether further evaluation is warranted. Common materials such as toys and blocks are used. Also available in Spanish, French, and Korean. Computer-based scoring is available.

Format: Parent rating; untimed: 5 to 10 minutes

Scoring: Examiner evaluated; computer scoring

Cost: Questionnaire and Guide $199.00

Ages & Stages Questionnaires: Social Emotional (ASQ:SE)

2001	Brookes Publishing, Co.

Jane Squires, Diane Bricker, Elizabeth Trimbly, Suzanne Yockelson, Maura Schoen Davis, Yoon Ghee Kim

Population: Ages 3 months to 5 years

Purpose: Used for child-find screening and developmental monitoring for children who are at risk

Description: The ASQ:SE has 19 to 34 items with eight age-specific intervals (6, 12, 18, 24, 30, 36, 48, and 60 months). Deals with social and emotional competence and problem areas.

Cutoff scores indicate whether further evaluation is warranted.

Format: Parent rating; untimed: 5 to 10 minutes

Scoring: Examiner evaluated

Cost: Questionnaire and Guide $149.00

AGS Early Screening Profiles (ESP)

1990	AGS Publishing/Pearson Assessments

Patti Harrison, Alan Kaufman,
Nadeen Kaufman, Robert Bruininks,
John Rynders, Steven Ilmer,
Sara Sparrow, Domenic Cicchetti

Population: Ages 2 through 6 years

Purpose: Screens the five major developmental areas

Description: The ESP is an ecological assessment battery that uses multiple domains, settings, and sources to measure the cognitive, motor, self-help/social, articulation, and health development and the home environment of young children. The ESP screens the five major developmental areas specified by P.L. 99-457: cognitive, language, motor, self-help, and social development. Can be administered by paraprofessionals.

Format: Examiner required; individually administered; 15 to 30 minutes

Scoring: Two-level scoring system: Level I scores available for two subscales of Cognitive/Language Profile; subscales and subtests of the Cognitive/Language Profile can be scored using Level II scores

Cost: Test Kit (manuals, easel, 25 test records, 25 self-help/social profile questionnaires, 25 score summaries, sample home/health history survey, tape measure, beads) $313.99

Assessment of Behavioral Problems and Intervention Strategies in Early Childhood, Volume II

1995	Hawthorne Educational Services, Inc.

Louise Ferre

Population: Ages birth through 6 years

Purpose: Identifies behavioral problems and provides intervention strategies to modify behavior

Description: Pediatric Behavior checklist is included in the book and is reproducible; checklist has 107 items.

Format: Rating scale; untimed

Scoring: Examiner evaluated

Cost: $12.00

Assessment of Developmental Delays and Intervention Strategies in Early Childhood, Volume I

1993	Hawthorne Educational Services, Inc.

Louise Ferre

Population: Ages birth through 6 years

Purpose: Identifies children who are at risk in the areas of cognitive, socialization, receptive language, expressive language, self-help, fine motor, and gross motor

Description: Ten items in each of the seven areas: Cognitive, Socialization, Receptive Language, Expressive Language, Self-Help, Fine Motor, and Gross Motor. Checklists are included and are reproducible.

Format: Rating scale; untimed

Scoring: Examiner evaluated

Cost: $12.00

Basic School Skills Inventory–Third Edition (BSSI-3)

1998	PRO-ED, Inc.

Donald D. Hammill, James E. Leigh,
Nils A. Pearson, Taddy Maddox

Population: Ages 4 through 6 years

Purpose: Determines the special learning needs of children by pinpointing both the general areas and the specific readiness skills that need remedial attention

Description: The inventory of 137 items is based on teachers' judgments of desirable school performance in the areas of Daily Living Skills, Spoken Language, Reading, Writing, Mathematics, and Classroom Behavior.

Format: Checklist format completed by teacher; untimed: 5 to 8 minutes

Scoring: Examiner evaluated

Cost: Complete Kit (manual, 25 summary/response booklets, storage box) $105.00

Battelle Developmental Inventory–Second Edition (BDI-2)

2004	Riverside Publishing Company

Jean Newborg,

Population: Ages birth through 7 years 11 months

Purpose: Evaluates the development of children from infant to primary levels; screens and diagnoses developmental strengths and weaknesses

Description: Multiple-item test assessing key developmental skills in five domains: Personal–Social, Adaptive, Motor, Communication, and Cognitive. Information is obtained through structured interactions with the child in a controlled setting; observation of the child; and interviews with the child's parents, caregivers, and teachers. Test items contain content and sequence directly compatible with infant and preschool curricula. The test may be administered by a team of professionals or by an individual service provider. Directions for modifications are included for children with various disabilities. A screening test containing 96 items is included in the complete BDI kit. Also available in Spanish.

Format: Examiner required; individual administration; untimed: 1 to 2 hours for complete, 10 to 30 minutes for screening

Scoring: Examiner evaluated; computer software available

Cost: Complete Kit (test books, examiner's manual, scoring booklets, visuals, materials, and carrying case) $867.50

Bayley Scales of Infant Development®– Third Edition (BSID-III)

2005	Harcourt Assessment, Inc.

Nancy Bayley

Population: Ages 1 month to 42 months

Purpose: Measures development in five areas

Description: The third edition is a major revision and involves the family. All five areas (cognitive, motor, language, social-emotional, and adaptive behavior) in IDEA are addressed. Information obtained may be used in developing the IFSP for infants and toddlers. A caregiver report is now included. An extended floor and ceiling more easily identify lower and higher functioning individuals.

Format: Examiner required; individual administration; untimed: 30 to 90 minutes

Scoring: Examiner evaluated; scoring assistant available

Cost: Complete Kit (manuals, 25 of each of form, administration video, manipulatives, rolling case) $895.00

Bayley-III™ Screening Test

2005	Harcourt Assessment, Inc.

Nancy Bayley

Population: Ages 1 month to 42 months

Purpose: Screens for cognitive, language, and motor developmental delays

Description: Selected items from the full Bayley-III battery.

Format: Examiner required; individual administration; untimed: 15 to 25 minutes

Scoring: Examiner evaluated

Cost: Complete Kit (manual, stimulus book, 25 record forms, picture book, manipulatives, bag) $225.00

BCP–Behavioral Characteristics Progression

2001 VORT Corporation

Population: Ages 1 through 14 years

Purpose: Comprehensive curriculum-based assessment used by special education professionals to assess, set objectives, track progress, and prepare instruction for those with special needs

Description: The BCP Assessment Record booklet helps to quickly screen needs, record skill mastery and dates, and identify target objectives. This continuum of skills and behaviors, without labels or age ranges, focuses on the developmental needs of each individual. It groups the 2,300 skills/behaviors into 56 strands. The BCP Instructional Activities book provides thousands of teacher-developed instructional activities for 1,900 of the BCP skills. For most skills, prerequisite abilities and interest levels are listed to help adapt instruction for older individuals.

Format: Examiner required; individual administration; untimed

Scoring: Hand scored

Cost: Assessment Record $5.00; Instructional Activities Book $59.95

Birth to Three Assessment and Intervention System– Second Edition (BTAIS-2)

2000	PRO-ED, Inc.

Jerome J. Ammer, Tina E. Bangs

Population: Ages birth to 3 years

Purpose: Comprehensive program that allows examiners to identify, measure, and address developmental delays

Description: Instrument is updated to provide examiners with an integrated, three-component system for screening and assessing. The Screening Test will help the examiner to know within

15 minutes whether a child has developmental delays, and be able to identify each child's strengths and weaknesses using the Comprehensive Test. Also included is a manual for teaching.

Format: Examiner required; individual administration; untimed

Scoring: Examiner evaluated

Cost: Complete Kit (teaching manual, screening kit, comprehensive kit) $246.00; Screening Kit (manual, 25 record forms, storage box) $81.00; Comprehensive Kit (manual, 25 record forms, storage box) $101.00; Teaching Manual $71.00

Boehm Test of Basic Concepts–Preschool Version

2001	Harcourt Assessment, Inc.

Ann E. Boehm

Population: Ages 3 through 5 years

Purpose: Identifies children who lack understanding of basic relational concepts

Description: Measures concepts relevant to today's early childhood curriculum with efficient tests that are quick and easy to administer and score. In addition, children respond favorably to the colorful stimulus materials. Each concept is tested twice to determine the child's understanding of it across contexts.

Format: Examiner required; individual administration; untimed: 20 to 30 minutes

Scoring: Hand key

Cost: Complete Kit (picture book, manual, 20 individual record forms) $159.00

Boehm Test of Basic Concepts–Third Edition (Boehm-3)

2000	Harcourt Assessment, Inc.

Ann E. Boehm

Population: Grades K to 2

Purpose: Measures children's mastery of basic concepts used in classroom instruction. Identifies individual children with low level of concept development; targets specific areas for basic concept remediation

Description: Measures 50 basic concepts relevant to today's early childhood curriculum. Has two parallel forms to allow for pre- and posttesting. Directions available in Spanish.

Format: Examiner required; suitable for group use; untimed: 30 minutes

Scoring: Hand key

Cost: Examination Kit (manual, 1 of each form, directions) $68.00

Bracken Basic Concept Scale–Third Edition: Receptive (BBCS-3R)

2006	Harcourt Assessment, Inc.

Bruce A. Bracken

Population: Ages 3 through 6 years

Purpose: Measures a child's acquisition of basic concepts and receptive language skills

Description: This latest version contains colorful artwork, new norms, and new items. Leading directly to IEP development and remediation, the test assesses a child's receptive knowledge of 301 basic concepts in 11 distinct conceptual categories. The BBCS-3R is based on current norms and contains a school readiness composite. Also available in Spanish.

Format: Examiner required; individual administration; untimed: 30 to 45 minutes

Scoring: Examiner evaluated; computer scoring available

Cost: Complete Kit (manual, stimulus manual, 25 forms) $299.00

BRIGANCE® Early Preschool Screen II

2005	Curriculum Associates®, Inc.

Albert H. Brigance

Population: Ages 2 years to 2 years 6 months

Purpose: Evaluates basic developmental and readiness skills of children; used for program planning, placement, and special service referrals

Description: Multiple-item oral-response and task-performance test evaluating basic developmental and readiness skills. Children identify body parts, objects, and colors; demonstrate gross and visual motor skills; match colors; explain the use of objects; repeat sentences; build with blocks; and provide personal data. Number concepts; picture vocabulary; use of plural -s, -ing, prepositions, and irregular plural nouns are tested also. Rating forms and supplementary skill assessments allow for additional observations and extended screening options. Validation study completed in 1995.

Format: Examiner required; suitable for group use; untimed: 12 minutes

Scoring: Examiner evaluated

Cost: Assessment Manual $110.00; 30 Pupil Data Sheets $38.00

BRIGANCE® Infant & Toddler Screen

2002	Curriculum Associates®, Inc.

Albert H. Brigance

Population: Ages birth through 23 months

Purpose: Evaluates basic developmental and readiness skills of children; used for program planning, placement, and special service referrals

Description: Multiple-item oral-response and task-performance test evaluating basic developmental and readiness skills. Children identify body parts, objects, and colors; demonstrate gross and visual motor skills; match colors; explain the use of objects; repeat sentences; build with blocks; and provide personal data. Number concepts; picture vocabulary; use of plural -*s*, -*ing*, prepositions, and irregular plural nouns are tested also. Rating forms and supplementary skill assessments allow for additional observations and extended screening options. Validation study completed in 1995.

Format: Examiner required; suitable for group use; untimed: 12 minutes

Scoring: Examiner evaluated

Cost: Assessment Manual $110.00; 30 Pupil Data Sheets $38.00

BRIGANCE® Inventory of Early Development-II

2004	Curriculum Associates®, Inc.

Albert H. Brigance

Population: Ages birth to 7 years

Purpose: Measures the development of children functioning below the developmental age of 7 years; diagnoses developmental delays and monitors progress over a period of time; used to develop IEPs

Description: Paper–pencil 200 oral-response and direct-observation skill assessments measuring psychomotor, self-help, communication, general knowledge and comprehension, and academic skill levels. Test items are arranged in developmental sequential order in the following major skill areas: Preambulatory, Gross Motor, Fine Motor, Prespeech, Speech and Language, General Knowledge and Comprehension, Readiness, Basic Reading, Manuscript Writing, and Basic Math Skills. An introductory section outlines how to ad-

minister the tests, assess skill levels, record the results, identify specific instructional objectives, and develop IEPs. Results, expressed in terms of developmental ages, are entered into the individual record book, which indicates graphically at each testing the level of competency the individual has achieved. An optional group record book monitors the progress of 15 individuals.

Format: Examiner required; individual administration; untimed: varies

Scoring: Examiner evaluated

Cost: Inventory with Standardization and Validation Manual $185.00; 10 Developmental Record Booklets $35.00; 10 Standardized Assessment Record Booklets $35.00

BRIGANCE® K & 1 Screen II

2005	Curriculum Associates®, Inc.

Albert H. Brigance

Population: Grades K and 1

Purpose: Screens the basic skills necessary for success; identifies students needing special service referral, determines appropriate pupil placement, and assists in planning instructional programs and developing IEPs

Description: Multiple-item paper–pencil oral-response and direct-observation assessments measuring the following basic skills: personal data response, color recognition, picture vocabulary, visual discrimination, visual-motor skills, standing gross-motor skills, draw-a-person, rote counting, identification of body parts, reciting the alphabet, following verbal directions, numeral comprehension, recognizing lowercase letters, auditory discrimination, printing personal data, syntax and fluency, and numerals in sequence. Five optional advanced assessments are included for students scoring 95% or above on the basic first-grade assessment. Optional forms for teacher–parent rating and examiner observations are reproducible. Separate pupil data sheets are required, and class summary record folders are available. Criterion-referenced results are translated directly into curriculum or program objectives to meet the needs of individual pupils. Test items are cross-referenced to the *BRIGANCE Inventory of Basic Skills* and the *Inventory of Early Development-II* to facilitate further evaluation of skill deficiencies. Validation study completed in 1995.

Format: Examiner required; individual administration; untimed: 12 minutes

Scoring: Examiner evaluated

Cost: Assessment Manual $110.00; 30 Pupil Data Sheets $38.00

BRIGANCE® Preschool Screen II

| 2005 | Curriculum Associates®, Inc. |

Albert H. Brigance

Population: Ages 3 to 4 years

Purpose: Evaluates basic developmental and readiness skills of children; used for program planning, placement, and special service referrals

Description: Multiple-item oral-response and task-performance test evaluating basic developmental and readiness skills. Children identify body parts, objects, and colors; demonstrate gross and visual motor skills; match colors; explain the use of objects; repeat sentences; build with blocks; and provide personal data. Number concepts; picture vocabulary; use of plural -s, -ing, prepositions, and irregular plural nouns are tested also. Rating forms and supplementary skill assessments allow for additional observations and extended screening options. Validation study completed in 1995.

Format: Examiner required; suitable for group use; untimed: 12 minutes

Scoring: Examiner evaluated

Cost: Assessment Manual $110.00; 30 Pupil Data Sheets $38.00

Child Development Chart (CDC)

| 2005 | Behavior Science Systems, Inc. |

Harold R. Ireton

Population: Ages birth to 5 years

Purpose: Screens for development in five areas: social, self-help, fine motor, gross motor, and language; used for well-child visit, preschool screening

Description: The standardized chart has one side for infants (birth to 21 months) and the other for the first five years. The chart is used to ask the parent what the child has been doing, to observe the child directly, and to record the child's skills. Also available in Spanish.

Format: Examiner required; individual administration; untimed: 3 to 5 minutes

Scoring: Examiner evaluated

Cost: $12.50 per pad of 25

Child Development Inventory (CDI)

| 1992 | Behavior Science Systems, Inc. |

Harold R. Ireton

Population: Ages 18 months to 5 years

Purpose: Assesses children whose development is a concern

Description: The yes–no statement inventory gives detailed information about the child's development, including strengths, delays, and needs. There are 270 items in the developmental scales: Social, Self-Help, Fine Motor, Gross Motor, Expressive Language, Language Comprehension, Letters, and Numbers. Also included is a 30-item Problems List that records the parent's concerns about health, vision and hearing, development, and behavior. A sixth-grade reading level is required. Also available in Spanish.

Format: Parents complete; untimed: 20 to 30 minutes

Scoring: Examiner evaluated

Cost: Starter Kit $72.00 (manual, scoring template, 10 booklets, 25 answer sheets, 25 profiles)

Child Development Review Parent Questionnaire (CDR-PQ)

| 2005 | Behavior Science Systems, Inc. |

Harold R. Ireton

Population: Ages 18 months to 5 years

Purpose: Screens for development in five areas: social, self-help, fine motor, and language; used for well-child visits and for preschool screening

Description: Parents report on child's present health, development, and behavior using two sections: six questions and a 26-item possible problems checklist. The responses are classified as indicating a problem or not. The reverse contains a Child Development Chart that helps determine the child's developmental skills. Also available in Spanish.

Format: Examiner required; individual administration; untimed: 5 to 10 minutes

Scoring: Examiner evaluated

Cost: Manual $33.00; 25 Questionnaires $12.50

Child Observation Record– Second Edition (COR)

| Date not provided | High/Scope Educational Research Foundation |

Population: 6 weeks to 3 years (Infant–Toddler version); Ages 2 years 6 months to 6 years (Preschool version)

Purpose: Measures a child's behavior and activities

Description: The trained teacher or observer assesses in six categories of development: Initiative, Social Relations, Creative Representation, Music and Movement, Language and Literacy, and Logic and Mathematics. Over several months, the teacher writes brief notes describing examples of children's behavior. The teacher then uses these notes to rate the child's behavior on 30 five-level COR items. The COR is an observational assessment tool that charts children's development and progress over time.

Format: Examiner required; observation; untimed: several months

Scoring: Examiner evaluated; computer program available

Cost: Kit (manual, 25 assessment booklets, 4 sets of note cards, 50 parent report forms, poster, box) $174.95

Cognitive Abilities Scale–Second Edition (CAS-2)

2001	PRO-ED, Inc.

Sharon Bradley-Johnson, Carl Johnson

Population: Ages 3 months to 3 years 11 months

Purpose: Identifies children who have delays in cognitive development

Description: A General Cognitive Quotient describes overall performance across all test items. A Nonvocal Cognitive Quotient describes children's ability excluding performance on vocal items. Results from the CAS-2 provide detailed information for planning instructional programs. The CAS-2 is playful in nature, and the toys enhance children's interest, as well as the validity of the results. Two forms are available in this revision: the Infant Form and the Preschool Form. The Infant Form allows testing of children as young as 3 months. It consists of 79 items divided into three sections: Exploration of Objects, Communication with Others, and Initiation and Imitation. The Preschool Form contains 88 items divided into five sections: Oral Language, Reading, Math, Writing, and Enabling Behaviors. The CAS-2 was normed on 1,106 children from 27 states. Reliability and validity are addressed in the manual.

Format: Examiner required; individual administration; untimed: 20 to 30 minutes

Scoring: Examiner evaluated

Cost: Complete Kit (manual, 25 each profile/ex-

aminer record booklets for Infant and Preschool, 25 symbol reproduction forms, 25 copies of "Mikey's Favorite Things," picture cards, ramp, manipulatives, attaché case) $437.00

Cognitive, Linguistic, and Social-Communicative Scales (CLASS)

1997	Academic Communication Associates

Dennis C. Tanner, Wendy M. Lamb, Wayne Secord

Population: Ages Preschool through 6 years

Purpose: Assesses development

Description: Using a parent interview, the examiner assesses basic concepts, comprehension and production of grammar, and communicative effectiveness. Examples of developmental milestones are presented to the parent, and the parent indicates whether the child displays each behavior. The developmental norms in the manual can be used to identify areas in which delays are demonstrated. An interview questionnaire for the classroom teacher is available.

Format: Examiner required; individual administration; untimed

Scoring: Hand key

Cost: Complete Kit $59.00

Communication and Symbolic Behavior Scales (CSBS)

1993	Brookes Publishing, Co.

Amy M. Wetherby, Barry M. Prizant

Population: Ages 8 to 24 months or up to 72 months if developmental delays present

Purpose: Assesses communicative, social–affective, and symbolic abilities; used for intervention planning

Description: Instrument consists of a caregiver questionnaire and behavior sample. Results are converted into seven clusters and one composite score to measure Communication Functions, Gestural Communicative Means, Vocal Communicative Means, Verbal Communicative Means, Social–Affective Signaling, and Symbolic Behavior. Scores are reported as percentile ranks and standard scores by chronological age or language stage. May be used for persons with visual, physical, hearing, or mental impairments.

Format: Examiner required; individually administered; untimed: 45 to 60 minutes

Scoring: Examiner evaluated

Cost: Complete Kit (manual, toy kit, 2 outline cards, 25 caregiver questionnaire forms, 25 record forms, sampling VHS videotape, scoring VHS videotape, bag) $599.00

Comprehensive Identification Process (CIP)–Second Edition

1997	Scholastic Testing Service, Inc.

R. Reid Zehrbach, Joan Good Erickson

Population: Ages 2 years to 6 years 6 months

Purpose: Evaluates the mental and physical development of young children; used to identify those in need of special medical, psychological, or educational help before entering kindergarten or first grade

Description: Criterion-referenced multiple-item verbal response and task-assessment test of eight areas of child development: Cognitive–Verbal, Fine Motor, Gross Motor, Speech and Expressive Language, Hearing, Vision, Social/Affective Behavior, and Medical History. The test can be administered by trained paraprofessionals supervised by professionals in the preschool area. The test helps meet the child-find requirements of P.L. 99-457. Also available in Spanish.

Format: Examiner required; individual administration; untimed

Scoring: Examiner evaluated

Cost: Screening Kit (administrator's and interviewer's manuals, screening booklet, 35 parent interview forms, 35 observation of behavior forms, 35 speech and expressive language forms, symbol booklet, 35 record folders, manipulatives) $310.00

DABERON Screening for School Readiness– Second Edition (DABERON-2)

1991	PRO-ED, Inc.

Virginia A. Danzer, Mary Frances Gerber, Theresa M. Lyons, Judith K. Voress

Population: Ages 4 to 6 years

Purpose: Provides a standardized assessment of school readiness in children, including those with learning or behavior problems who are functioning at the early elementary level

Description: Measurement of development, categorization, and other developmental abilities that relate to early academic success. The Learning Readiness Equivalency Age score may be used to identify children at risk for school failure. The test can help identify instructional objectives and

develop IEPs. It includes the Classroom Summary Form and the Report on Readiness, a summary of performance, and practical suggestions for parents. The test samples knowledge of body parts, color and number concepts, gross motor skills, and fine motor skills.

Format: Examiner required; individual administration; untimed: 20 to 40 minutes

Scoring: Examiner interpreted

Cost: Complete Kit (manual, 25 screen forms, 25 reports on readiness, 5 classroom summary forms, cards, object kit of manipulatives, storage box) $170.00

Denver Prescreening Questionnaire II (PDQ-II)

1998	Denver Developmental Materials, Inc.

Population: Ages birth to 6 years

Purpose: Determines whether a child possesses developmental skills acquired by most other same-age children; used to indicate further testing

Description: Paper–pencil 105-item prescreening test administered by the child's parents. This updated version is designed to include more age-appropriate items, simplified parent scoring, and easier norm comparisons. Forms are available for the following age ranges: 0 to 9 months, 9 to 24 months, 2 to 4 years, and 4 to 6 years. Examiners must have at least a high school education. Also available in Spanish.

Format: Examiner required; suitable for group use; untimed: office assistant, 2 minutes; parents, 10 minutes

Scoring: Hand key

Cost: 100 Forms $22.00 to $25.00

Denver II

1989	Denver Developmental Materials, Inc.

William K. Frakenburg, Josiah Dodds, Philip Archer, Howard Shapiro, Beverly Bresnick

Population: Ages birth to 6 years

Purpose: Assesses developmental skills

Description: A series of developmental tasks are used to determine if a child's development is within the normal range. Identifies children likely to have significant motor, social, or language delays. Also available in Spanish.

Format: Examiner required; individual administration; untimed: 10 to 20 minutes

Scoring: Examiner evaluated

Cost: Complete Package (manuals, test forms, manipulatives) $90.00

Developmental Activities Screening Inventory–Second Edition (DASI-II)

| 1984 | PRO-ED, Inc. |

Rebecca R. Fewell, Mary Beth Langley

Population: Ages birth to 5 years

Purpose: Detects early developmental disabilities in children

Description: Total-response and task-performance test assessing 67 items in 15 developmental skill categories ranging from sensory intactness, means-end relationships, and causality to memory, seriation, and reasoning. Test items may be administered in different sequences in one or two sittings. Instructions are given either verbally or visually. Each test item includes adaptations for use with children with visual impairments.

Format: Examiner required; individual administration, timed and untimed: 20 to 40 minutes

Scoring: Examiner evaluated

Cost: Complete Kit (manual, 50 protocols, picture cards, configuration cards, numeral cards, word cards, shape cards, storage box) $92.00

Developmental Assessment of Young Children (DAYC)

| 1998 | PRO-ED, Inc. |

Judith K. Voress, Taddy Maddox

Population: Ages birth through 5 years

Purpose: Assesses development in five areas: cognition, communication, adaptive behavior, social-emotional, and physical

Description: The instrument has five subtests for each of the five areas mandated by federal law to identify infants and young children who may benefit from early intervention. Assessment is tailored to each client's needs by assessing any combination of these domains. Parents and caregivers are interviewed as part of the assessment process. Standard scores (mean of 100 and standard deviation of 15) and percentiles, as well as age equivalents, are provided. The DAYC may also be used in arena assessment so that each discipline may use the evaluation tool independently. Specific manipulatives are not required; the examiner uses what is available in the child's environment.

Format: Examiner required; parental interview;

observation; untimed: 10 to 15 minutes per domain

Scoring: Examiner evaluated

Cost: Complete Kit (manual, 25 each of Adaptive, Cognitive, Communication, Physical, Social-Emotional forms; 25 profile/summary forms; 25 miniposters of Early Childhood Development Chart, storage box) $235.00

Developmental History Checklist™ (DHC™)

| 1989 | Psychological Assessment Resources, Inc. |

Edward H. Dougherty, John A. Schinka

Population: Ages 5 to 12 years

Purpose: Assesses children's development

Description: Designed to be completed by a parent, guardian, or clinician, with 136 items that cover family history, developmental history, educational history, family background, medical history, and current behavior. Computer version using PCs available.

Format: Rating scale; untimed

Scoring: Examiner evaluated

Cost: Package of 25 $52.00

Developmental Indicators for the Assessment of Learning–Third Edition (DIAL-3)

| 1998 | AGS Publishing/Pearson Assessments |

Carol Mardell-Czudnowski, Dorothea S. Goldenberg

Population: Ages 3 through 6 years

Purpose: A global screener for assessing large groups of children quickly and efficiently

Description: The DIAL-3 is an individually administered screening test designed to identify young children in need of further diagnostic assessment of curricular modification. Subtests assess behaviors in the motor, concepts, and language areas. Test includes a checklist of social development and self-help development. English and Spanish materials are included. A new feature of the revision is the Speed DIAL, a brief screener that can be given in 5 minutes per area.

Format: Examiner required; individual administration; untimed: 20 to 30 minutes

Scoring: Examiner evaluated

Cost: Complete Kit (manual, 50 English record forms, 1 Spanish record form, 50 cutting cards,

50 parent questionnaires, manipulatives, dials, Spanish and English Operator's Handbooks for subtests, speed DIAL, training packet) $469.99

Developmental Observation Checklist System (DOCS)

| 1994 | PRO-ED, Inc. |

Wayne P. Hresko, Shirley A. Miguel, Rita J. Sherbenou, Steve D. Burton

Population: Ages birth through 6 years

Purpose: Measures the areas of language, motor, social, and cognitive development to identify possible developmental delays

Description: This multiple-item screening questionnaire meets the mandates of P.L. 99-457 and is based on current theory. The test can be completed by parents or caregivers. It has a sufficient number of items, interactive play items at the earlier developmental levels, and environmental input on family stress and support, as well as problematic child behaviors. Responses are based on careful observation of the child's daily behaviors. The three-part system provides standard scores, percentiles, and NCE equivalents in Overall Development, Developmental Cognition, Developmental Language, Developmental Social Skills, and Developmental Motor Skills.

Format: Examiner required; parental interview; observation; untimed: 30 minutes

Scoring: Examiner evaluated

Cost: Complete Kit (manual, protocols, storage box) $165.00

Developmental Profile II (DP-II)

| 1986 | Western Psychological Services |

Gerald D. Alpern, Thomas Boll, Marsha Shearer

Population: Ages birth to 9 years 6 months

Purpose: Evaluates the age-equivalent physical, social, and mental development of children with or without disabilities

Description: Paper–pencil or computer-administered 186-item interview covering five areas: Physical, Self-Help, Social, Academic, and Communication. Developmental age scores are derived by interviewing a parent or through teacher observation. From birth to age 4, the scales are graded by half-year increments. From ages 5 to 9, they are graded in yearly increments. The test also provides an IQ equivalency score. Materials

include step-by-step procedures for test administration and interpretation. The computer version is suitable for use with PC-compatible systems. The manual must be purchased separately for the computer version. A computer report is available through mail-in service or on-site (if the computer version is used).

Format: Examiner required; individual administration; untimed: 20 to 40 minutes

Scoring: Examiner evaluated; may be computer scored; scoring service available

Cost: Complete Kit (25 scoring/profile forms, manual, 2-use PC disk, 2 PC answer sheets) $126.50

Developmental Tasks for Kindergarten Readiness–II (DTKR-II)

| 1994 | PRO-ED, Inc. |

Walter J. Lesiak, Judi Lucas Lesiak

Population: Ages 4 years 6 months to 6 years 2 months

Purpose: Assesses performance of skills and abilities necessary for success in kindergarten

Description: The DTKR-II has 15 subtests (Social Interaction, Name Printing, Body Concepts–Awareness, Body Concepts–Use, Auditory Sequencing, Auditory Association, Visual Discrimination, Visual Memory, Visual Motor, Color Naming, Relational Concepts, Number Counting, Number Use, Number Naming, and Alphabet Knowledge) that provide standard scores with a mean of 10 and standard deviation of 3. The composite score has a mean of 100 with a standard deviation of 15.

Format: Examiner required; individual administration; untimed: 20 to 30 minutes

Scoring: Examiner evaluated

Cost: Complete Kit (manual, materials book, 25 protocols) $134.00

Devereux Early Childhood Assessment

| 1999 | Kaplan Early Learning Company |

Population: Ages 2 to 5 years

Purpose: Screens for emotional and behavioral concerns

Description: The scale is completed by parents, family caregivers, or early childhood professionals to evaluate the frequency of 27 positive behaviors exhibited by preschoolers. The DECA also contains a 10-item behavioral concerns screener. The three scales measure attachment, self-control, and initiative. It was normed on a representative, nationwide sample of 2,000 children. Available online in English or Spanish. The Clinical version supports early intervention efforts to reduce or eliminate significant emotional and behavioral concerns.

Format: Examiner required; individual administration; untimed: 10 minutes

Scoring: Scoring service

Cost: Complete Kit (2 manuals, user's guide, 40 record forms, observation journal, 20 parent strategies) $199.95; Online Annual License Fee $249.95; Clinical Kit (manual, 30 record forms, 1 norms reference card) $125.95

Early Childhood Behavior Scale (ECBS)
1994   Hawthorne Educational Services, Inc.

Stephen B. McCarney

Population: Ages 36 to 72 months

Purpose: Provides the standardized profile information and specific indicators necessary to determine which students are in need of intervention, behavioral support, and the opportunity to learn more appropriate behavior

Description: The subscales of Social Relationships, Personal Adjustment, and Academic Progress were carefully developed with the use of behaviors appropriate for children ages 36 to 72 months, in preschool and kindergarten situations. Results provided by primary observers such as teachers, mental health workers, or parents are used to document the behaviors that indicate areas of most concern. Children in the standardization sample represented all geographic regions of the United States, with attention given to racial and ethnic minorities in the creation of the national norms. Internal consistency, test–retest, and interrater reliability; item and factor analysis; and content, criterion-related, diagnostic, and construct validity are well documented and reported for the scale. A Quick Score for Windows is available.

Format: Rating scale; untimed: 15 minutes

Scoring: Examiner evaluated; computer scoring available

Cost: Complete Kit (technical manual, 50 each of 2 forms, intervention manual) $105.00

Early Coping Inventory: A Measure of Adaptive Behavior
1988   Scholastic Testing Service, Inc.

Shirley Zeitlin, G. Gordon Williamson, Margery Szczepanski

Population: Ages 4 to 36 months

Purpose: Assesses the coping-related behaviors of infants and toddlers

Description: Behavioral observation inventory designed to assess the coping-related behaviors of infants and toddlers. The 48 items are divided into three subtests: Sensorimotor Organization, Reactive Behavior, and Self-Initiated Behaviors. The manual contains instructions for rating, scoring, and implementing results. Also available in large print.

Format: Examiner required; suitable for group use; untimed

Scoring: Hand key

Cost: Starter Set (manual, 20 forms) $56.50

Early Language Proficiency Test Series (ELPTS)
2004   MetriTech, Inc.

Population: Ages 3 to 5 years

Purpose: Measures language proficiency and early academic skills

Description: The ELPTS is a standardized assessment that can be used to document growth in the preacademic skills of students. Scores are provided for Listening, Speaking, Vocabulary, Sound Repetition, Following Directions and Explaining, School Concepts, and Alphabet. Two alternate forms are available. Answers are marked by the administrator on a scannable answer sheet.

Format: Examiner required; individually administered; untimed: 10 to 15 minutes

Scoring: Scoring service

Cost: Complete Administration Set $120.00

Early Literacy Skills Assessment (ELSA)
2004   High/Scope Educational Research Foundation

Andrea DeBruin-Parecki

Population: Ages 3 to 6 years

Purpose: Measures literacy skills

Description: An authentic assessment that measures comprehension, phonological awareness, alphabetic principle, and concepts about print. A child's storybook is used to conduct the assessment. A teacher reads the story with the child, stopping where indicated in the book to ask questions or elicit ideas. Can be used to measure progress in early childhood programs. The assessment meets the psychometric standards of reliability and validity. Also available in Spanish.

Format: Examiner required; individual administration; untimed: 15 minutes

Scoring: Examiner evaluated

Cost: Year One Kit (2 storybooks, user's guide, 60 each of score sheet and summary forms, class summary forms, family report forms) $149.95

Early Literacy Test

2000	Hodder Murray

Bill Gillham

Population: Ages 4 years 6 months to 7 years 5 months

Purpose: Provides diagnosis of strengths and weaknesses in early literacy

Description: The test profiles three key predictors of later reading attainment: book and story concepts, word recognition skills, and knowledge of sounds and letters. Each pupil's literacy needs are targeted with individualized teaching strategies. Norms provided as literacy/reading ages, percentiles, and standardized scores.

Format: Examiner required; individual administration; untimed: 15 minutes

Scoring: Examiner evaluated

Cost: Test £8.50 for 10; User's Handbook £18.99

Early Screening Inventory– Revised (ESI-R)

1998	Pearson Early Learning

Samuel J. Meisels, Dorothea B. Marsden, Martha Stone Wiske, Laura W. Henderson

Population: Ages 3 to 6 years

Purpose: Identifies children who may need special education services in order to perform successfully in school

Description: The revised version is available for two age groups. The ESI-P is for children ages 3 years to 4½ years and the ESI-K is for children ages 4½ to 6 years. They are brief developmental screening instruments. The following areas are measured: Visual Motor/Adaptive, Language and Cognition, and Gross Motor. The instrument was standardized and validated with 6,000 children,

many in Head Start. A Spanish language version is available.

Format: Examiner required, individual administration, untimed: 15 to 20 minutes

Scoring: Examiner evaluated

Cost: Kit (manual, 30 score sheets, 30 parent questionnaires, screening materials, tote) $120.95 per level

Egan Bus Puzzle Test

Date not provided	Hogrefe Limited

Dorothy F. Egan

Population: Ages 2 to 4 years

Purpose: Assesses developmental delay and disability

Description: Multiple-item response screening test consisting of display board with a printed street scene and nine lift-out pieces for assessing verbal labels, comprehension of illustrated situations related to experience, expressive language response, and the beginnings of intuitive verbal thinking.

Format: Requires examiner; individually administered; untimed

Scoring: Examiner evaluated

Cost: Contact publisher

FirstSTEP Screening Test for Evaluating Preschoolers™

1993	Harcourt Assessment, Inc.

Lucy J. Miller

Population: Ages 2 years 9 months to 6 years 2 months

Purpose: Identifies developmental delays

Description: A screening instrument that is sensitive enough to detect even mild developmental delays and identify children who need in-depth diagnostic testing. Addresses the IDEA domains of Cognition, Communication, Motor, Social-Emotional, and Adaptive. Results are classified as Within Acceptable Limits, Caution, or At-Risk. Available for three levels depending on age of child.

Format: Examiner required; individual administration; untimed: 15 minutes

Scoring: Examiner evaluated

Cost: Complete Kit (manual, stimulus booklet, 5 record forms for each level, 25 Social-

Emotional/Adaptive Behavior booklets, 25 parent booklets, manipulatives, case) $240.00

Five P's: Parent/Professional Preschool Performance Profile

| 1987 | Variety Child Learning Center |

Judith Simon Bloch, John S. Hicks, Janice L. Friedman

Population: Ages 2 to 6 years functioning between 6 and 60 months

Purpose: Assesses the development of young children with disabilities in the home and at school

Description: Observational assessment instrument consisting of 458 items on 13 scales grouped in six developmental areas: Classroom Adjustment, Self-Help Skills, Language Development, Social Development, Motor Development, and Cognitive Development. Scale items describe developmental skills and interfering behaviors. Items are observed and rated by teacher and parent on a 3-point Likert scale. The assessment is completed periodically to monitor change and to provide a means of ongoing assessment linked to remediation. Also available in Spanish.

Format: Examiner required; individual administration, untimed

Scoring: Examiner evaluated

Cost: Sample Packet $85.00; Educational Assessment for Class of 10 Children $135.00; Video $45.00; Manual $25.00

Fox Adds Up™

| 2005 | CTB/McGraw-Hill |

Population: Grades K to 3

Purpose: Provides observational insights into how young children are progressing on conceptual understanding of early mathematics

Description: *Fox Adds Up* is an observational assessment that measures Kindergarten through Grade 3 mathematics skills. The assessment contains performance-based activities. Children are actively involved in the assessment through the use of math manipulatives, including pattern blocks, attribute blocks, connecting cubes, and base-ten models. Teachers observe each child's performance, determine individual strengths and needs, and identify children who need additional help in acquiring mathematics skills.

Format: Examiner required; individual assessment; untimed: 90 minutes

Scoring: Examiner evaluated

Cost: Complete Kit (guide, observation and scoring records, activity cards, manipulatives, DVD) $245.00

Fox in a Box®–Second Edition

| 2005 | CTB/McGraw-Hill |

Population: Ages 5 to 8 years

Purpose: Provides diagnostic information about a child's literacy growth along a continuum of learning benchmarks

Description: *Fox in a Box* is an observational assessment that measures Kindergarten to Grade 3 literacy skills. The assessment contains performance-based activities. Children are actively involved in the assessment through the use of readers, a storybook, and an engaging fox puppet. Teachers observe each child's performance, determine individual strengths and needs, and identify children who need additional help in acquiring literacy skills.

Format: Examiner required; individual assessment; untimed: 90 minutes

Scoring: Examiner evaluated

Cost: Complete Kit (guide, observation and scoring records, activity cards, window card, reader, puppet, book, DVD) $245.00

Fox Letters and Numbers™

| 2003 | CTB/McGraw Hill |

Population: Age 4 years

Purpose: Identifies struggling learners in early literacy and math, provides focused instruction, and monitors progress

Description: *Fox Letters and Numbers* is an observational assessment that measures Pre-Kindergarten literacy skills. The assessment contains performance-based activities. Children are actively involved in the assessment through the use of hands-on manipulatives, readers, and other materials. Teachers observe each child's performance, determine individual strengths and needs, and identify children who need additional help in acquiring literacy and mathematics skills.

Format: Examiner required; individual assessment; untimed: 90 minutes

Scoring: Examiner evaluated

Cost: Complete Kit (guide, observation and scoring records, activity cards, manipulatives, DVD) $245.00

Gardner Social (Maturity) Developmental Scale (GSDS)

| 1994 | Academic Therapy Publications |

Morrison F. Gardner

Population: Ages 6 months to 8 years

Purpose: Measures developmental skills in reflexes, motor, social, and cognition

Description: A 61-item survey of behavioral observations that is completed by parents. The observations are related to familiar developmental milestones and behaviors. Each statement is clearly presented in a forced choice (yes–no) format. The manual contains a sample completed and scored survey. Also included is an appendix showing the usual age ranges for success with each behavior.

Format: Rating scale; untimed: 15 to 30 minutes

Scoring: Examiner evaluated

Cost: Test Kit (manual, 35 forms) $55.00

Griffiths Mental Development Scales

| 1996 | Hogrefe Limited |

Ruth Griffiths

Population: Ages birth to 8 years

Purpose: Measures developmental skills

Description: Multiple-item test of development measuring social development, fine and gross motor skills, hearing, eye–hand coordination, and speech. The test is available on two levels. Scale 1 (35 items) is for children from birth to age 2. Scale 2 (22 items) is for children from ages 2 to 8. Some items appear on both scales. Materials include toys, form boards, pictures, and models packed in a carrying case. There are different materials for each age group.

Format: Examiner required; individually administered; untimed

Scoring: Examiner evaluated

Cost: Contact publisher

HELP for Preschoolers (3–6)

| 2001 | VORT Corporation |

Population: Ages 3 to 6 years

Purpose: Designed as a curriculum-based assessment

Description: Provides a comprehensive coverage of 622 skills in six developmental domains: Cognitive, Language, Gross Motor, Fine Motor, Social, and Self-Help. The Assessment and Curriculum Guide is necessary for proper use of all HELP 3–6 materials. Includes sections on Structure and Link to HELP 0–3, Preparing for the Assessment—Overview, Conducting the Assessment, Characteristics of Children: 3–6, Information on Language Skills, Techniques for Children with Special Needs, and Tips for Effective Instruction.

Format: Examiner required; individual administration; untimed

Scoring: Examiner evaluated

Cost: $64.95

HELP–Hawaii Early Learning Profile (Inside HELP)

| 2001 | VORT Corporation |

Population: Ages birth to 3 years

Purpose: Developmental assessment, intervention, planning, and instruction with infants and toddlers and their families

Description: Provides comprehensive coverage of 685 skills in six developmental domains: Cognitive, Language, Gross Motor, Fine Motor, Social, and Self-Help. Easy-to-follow developmental sequence, starting at birth to 3 years in month-by-month increments. Used by professionals, the profile provides guidelines for individuals involved in assessment and planning. Designed for use with all young children, including those who have disabilities or are at risk. Focuses on the whole child.

Format: Examiner required; individual administration; untimed

Scoring: Examiner evaluated

Cost: $59.95

Infant Development Inventory (IDI)

| 2005 | Behavior Science Systems, Inc. |

Harold R. Ireton

Population: Ages birth to 18 months

Purpose: Screens for development

Description: There are five developmental scales: Social, Self-Help, Gross Motor, Fine Motor, and Language. Results are classified as around age level, borderline, and delayed. The parent questionnaire is one page; an infant development chart is on the opposite side. Monthly developmental milestones on the chart help parents to understand development. Also available in Spanish.

Format: Parent completed; untimed: 3 to 5 minutes

Scoring: Examiner evaluated

Cost: Manual $10.00; 25 Questionnaires $10.00

Infant/Toddler Symptom Checklist

1995   Harcourt Assessment, Inc.

Georgia De Gangi, Susan Poisson, Ruth Sickel, Andrea Santman Wiener

Population: Ages 7 months to 30 months

Purpose: Screens for sensory and regulatory diseases

Description: A symptom checklist to determine whether a child may have a predisposition toward developing sensory integrative difficulties. Scores are criterion-referenced.

Format: Parent interview; untimed: 10 minutes

Scoring: Hand key

Cost: Test Kit (manual, score sheet sets) $77.00

Kaufman Developmental Scale (KDS)

1974   Stoelting Company

Harvey Kaufman

Population: Infants through 9 years

Purpose: Evaluates school readiness, developmental deficits, and all levels of retardation for normal children through age 9 and persons with mental retardation of all ages; used in programming accountability

Description: Task-assessment test consisting of 270 behavioral evaluation items that are expandable teaching objectives. The KDS yields a Developmental Age and Developmental Quotient, as well as individual age scores and quotients for the following areas of behavioral development: Gross Motor, Fine Motor, Receptive, Expressive, Personal Behavior, and Interpersonal Behavior.

Format: Examiner required; individual administration; untimed: 30 minutes

Scoring: Examiner evaluated

Cost: Complete Kit (testing materials, manual, 25 record forms, carrying case) $425.00

Kaufman Infant and Preschool Scale (KIPS)

1981   Stoelting Company

Harvey Kaufman

Population: Ages 1 month to 4 years

Purpose: Measures early high-level cognitive process and indicates possible need for intervention in normal children ages 1 month to 4 years and in children and adults with mental ages of 4 years or less

Description: Multiple-item task-assessment and observation measure of high-level cognitive thinking. The child is observed and asked to perform a number of tasks indicative of his or her level. All test items are "maturational prototypes" that can be taught to enhance maturation. The test covers general reasoning, storage, and verbal communication. The test yields the following scores: Overall Functioning Age (Mental Age) and Overall Functioning Quotient. Based on a child's performance on the scale, the manual suggests types of activities and general experience the child needs for effective general adaptive behavior.

Format: Examiner required; individual administration; untimed: 30 minutes

Scoring: Examiner evaluated

Cost: Complete Kit (manual, manipulatives, stimulus cards, 10 evaluation booklets) $300.00

Kaufman Survey of Early Academic and Language Skills (K-SEALS)

1993   AGS Publishing/Pearson Assessments

Alan S. Kaufman, Nadeen L. Kaufman

Population: Ages 3 through 6 years

Purpose: Measures language skills, preacademic skills, and articulation

Description: Three subtests (Vocabulary; Numbers, Letters, and Words; and Articulation) provide an expanded and enhanced version of the Cognitive/Language Profile in the *AGS Early Screening Profiles*. The scores reflect many aspects of the child's language and early academic development.

Format: Examiner required; individual administration; untimed: 15 to 25 minutes

Scoring: Examiner interpreted

Cost: Complete Kit (manual, easel, test protocols, carrying bag) $244.99

Kent Inventory of Developmental Skills (KIDS)

1978 to 1995	Western Psychological Services

Jeanette M. Reuter, Lewis Katoff

Population: Developmental ages birth to 14 months

Purpose: Uses caregiver reports to screen and assess the developmental strengths and needs of infants and young children with disabilities

Description: Paper–pencil or computer-administered 252-item inventory that has caregivers describe behaviors characteristic of infants in the first year of life. Test items cover five behavioral domains: Cognitive, Motor, Language, Self-Help, and Social. Developmental ages for each domain and for the full scale are based on a normative sample of healthy infants. Specifically, the test can be used to assess the developmental status of healthy infants (0 to 14 months), infants at risk (0 to 20 months), and children with severe handicaps (2 to 8 years). The scale has been used for evaluating early intervention projects; monitoring the developmental progress of neonatal intensive care unit graduates; teaching teenage mothers about their child's development; and evaluating at-risk infants. Also available in Spanish, Dutch, German, Russian, and Hungarian.

Format: Examiner required; individual administration; untimed: 30 to 40 minutes

Scoring: Hand key; computer scored

Cost: Kit (administration booklet, 25 answer sheets, 25 profile forms, manual, scoring templates, developmental timetables) $120.00

Kindergarten Diagnostic Instrument–Second Edition (KDI-2)

2000	Kindergarten Interventions and Diagnostic Services, Inc.

Daniel C. Miller

Population: Ages 4 through 6 years

Purpose: Designed to assess developmental readiness skills

Description: A comprehensive and time-efficient screening instrument measuring 13 areas: Body Awareness, Concept Mastery, Form/Letter Identification, General Information, Gross Motor, Memory for Sentences, Number Skills, Phonemic Awareness, Verbal Associations, Visual Discrimination, Visual Memory, Visual-Motor Integration, and Vocabulary. *My Kindergarten Fun Book* contains over 90 learning activities related to the KDI-2 areas.

Format: Examiner required; individual administration; untimed: 35 minutes

Scoring: Examiner evaluated; computer scoring available

Cost: Starter Kit (manual, 3 stimulus booklets, blocks, 50 forms, 50 student fun books, computer scoring for 300, carrying case) $500.00

Kindergarten Inventory of Social-Emotional Tendencies (KIST)

1997	Kindergarten Interventions and Diagnostic Services, Inc.

Daniel C. Miller

Population: Ages 4 to 6 years

Purpose: Designed to provide information about social-emotional status

Description: The KIST has seven domains that measure the following areas: Communication, Daily Living, Hyperactivity/Inattentive Behaviors, Maladaptive Behaviors, Separation Anxiety Symptoms, Sleeping and Eating Behaviors, and Socialization.

Format: Examiner required; individual administration; untimed: 35 minutes

Scoring: Examiner evaluated; computer scoring available

Cost: Starter Set (manual, 50 rating forms, 50 interpretation forms) $80.00

Kindergarten Readiness Test (KRT)

1988	Slosson Educational Publications, Inc.

Sue Larson, Gary J. Vitali

Population: Ages 4 to 6 years

Purpose: Identifies school readiness

Description: Consolidates critical areas of various developmental tests into one single form, making identification of school readiness more efficient and valid. The KRT targets and screens key developmental traits across a broad range of skills necessary to begin school: Reasoning, Language, Auditory and Visual Attention, Numbers, Fine Motor Skills, and several other cognitive and sensory–perception areas. Test booklet and additional forms are designed for use in parent conferences or interprofessional presentations. The KRT may be used to identify possible handicapping conditions at an early age and facilitate writing developmental objective programs for teachers or parents. Tasks are presented in a sequential developmental–maturational format.

Format: Examiner required; individual administration; 15 minutes

Scoring: Hand key

Cost: Complete Kit $145.75

Kindergarten Readiness Test (KRT)

2006	Scholastic Testing Service, Inc.

O. F. Anderhalter, Jan Perney

Population: Ages 4 to 6 years

Purpose: Measures kindergarten preparedness

Description: The KRT tests vocabulary, letter identification, visual discrimination, phonemic awareness, comprehension and interpretation, and mathematical knowledge to establish readiness for kindergarten instruction. Four levels of readiness scores are provided. The test is designed to be administered either at the end of preschool or before the third full week of kindergarten.

Format: Examiner required; appropriate for small group use; timed: 25 to 30 minutes

Scoring: Examiner evaluated

Cost: Starter Set (manual, answer key, 20 test booklets, class record sheet, class summary report) $46.60

Learning Assessment Profile System

Date not provided	Kaplan Early Learning Company

Population: Ages birth to 72 months

Purpose: Assesses individual skill development in language, cognition, social-emotional, and fine and gross motor

Description: A set of three instruments: Early LAP, criterion referenced, for birth to 36 months; LAP-3, criterion referenced, for ages 36 to 72 months; and LAP-Diagnostic, norm referenced, for ages 30 to 72 months. All are available in Spanish. Computer scoring is available in either Web-based or CD format. The materials can be used to address requirements for any early childhood program. Assessment results help prepare and facilitate the design of learning activities. The LAP System includes curriculum guides and activity cards. All LAP System materials are designed to support the inclusion of children with disabilities and developmental delays in early childhood settings.

Format: Examiner required; individual administration; untimed

Scoring: Examiner evaluated; computer and online available

Cost: E-LAP Kit $334.95; LAP-3 $474.95; LAP-D $799.95

McCarthy Screening Test (MST)

1978	Harcourt Assessment, Inc.

Dorothea McCarthy

Population: Ages 4 years through 6 months 6 years

Purpose: Screens for potential learning problems.

Description: Includes six component scales, all drawn from the *McCarthy Scales of Children's Abilities,* that are predictive of a child's ability to cope with schoolwork in the early grades. The MST helps educators to identify children who may be at risk for learning problems. The subtests measure cognitive and sensorimotor functions central to the successful performance of school tasks, including Verbal Memory, Right–Left Orientation, Leg Coordination, Draw-A-Design, Numeric Memory, and Conceptual Grouping. Although interpretation of the MST requires training in psychology, it can be easily administered and scored by the classroom teacher or trained paraprofessional.

Format: Examiner required; individual administration; untimed: 20 minutes

Scoring: Examiner evaluated

Cost: Complete Set (manual, 25 record forms, 25 drawing booklets, carrying case) $250.00

Merrill-Palmer Scale–Revised

2004	Stoelting Company

Gale H. Roid, Jacqueline Sampers

Population: Ages birth through 6 years

Purpose: Measures early development in cognition, communication, physical, social-emotional, and adaptive areas

Description: Developed to examine prematurity and children with talents or disabilities. The scales for younger children are based on play with enticing toys and, with removal of the language scale and a few others, the test can be used with limited verbal interaction. Cognitive items fall into small, highly unified subtests showing progression and high relationship to total scale scores. Rasch Scaling allows the cognitive scale to be used as a criterion measure with precise intervals between items. Also available in Spanish.

Format: Examiner required; individual administration; timed and untimed

Scoring: Examiner evaluated

Cost: Complete Kit (manual, picture stimuli, manipulatives, record forms, easel, rolling case) $925.00

Metropolitan Performance Assessment (MPA)

1994	Harcourt Assessment, Inc.

Joanne R. Nurss

Population: Ages 4 to 7 years

Purpose: Measures skills in playlike activities

Description: Tasks in Level 1 for Pre-K and beginning Kindergarten children involve playlike interactions to hold the child's interest and to maximize performance. Level 2 has more complex language/literacy and quantitative/mathematics tasks for children in Kindergarten and beginning Grade 1. Included are a Developmental Inventory, Classroom Literacy Environment Inventory, Home Literacy Environment Inventory, Portfolio Assessment Guideline, and Preliteracy Inventory.

Format: Examiner required; group administration; untimed

Scoring: Hand key

Cost: Exam Kit per Activity $42.00

Metropolitan Readiness Tests: Sixth Edition (MRT6)

1995	Harcourt Assessment, Inc.

Joanne R. Nurss

Population: Ages 4 to 7 years

Purpose: Assesses underlying skills important for early school learning; for use in identifying each child's needs

Description: Multiple-item paper–pencil test of skills important for learning reading and mathematics and for developing language. The test is divided into two levels. Level 1 assesses literacy development in Pre-K and beginning Kindergarten children. Level 2 assesses beginning reading and mathematics development in the middle and end of Kindergarten and at the beginning of Grade 1.

Format: Examiner required; Level 1—individual administration, Level 2—suitable for group use; timed: Level 1, 85 minutes; Level 2, 100 minutes

Scoring: Hand scorable; scoring service available

Cost: Examination Kit $42.00 per level

Miller Assessment for Preschoolers™ (MAP™)

1982	Harcourt Assessment, Inc.

Lucy J. Miller

Population: Ages 2 years 9 months through 5 years 8 months

Purpose: Identifies preschoolers with moderate to severe developmental delays

Description: The MAP can be used for screening or for the in-depth assessment needed for formulating IEPs. There are five indices (Neural Foundations, Coordination, Verbal, Nonverbal, and Complex Tasks) that help identify developmental delays in sensorimotor and cognitive abilities. The scoring is divided by age into six levels.

Format: Examiner required; individual administration; untimed: 30 to 40 minutes

Scoring: Examiner evaluated

Cost: Complete Kit (manual, 6 levels of 25 score sheets, manipulatives, briefcase) $699.00

Missouri Kindergarten Inventory of Developmental Skills (KIDS)

1982	Assessment Resource Center

Population: Ages 4 to 6 years

Purpose: Assesses the development of academic skills

Description: The KIDS is a screening battery developed by a Missouri State Task Force on Early Childhood Screening. A parent questionnaire is included to obtain additional relevant information about each child's development. The following areas of development are surveyed: Number Concepts, Language Concepts, Auditory Skills, Visual Skills, Paper and Pencil Skills, and Gross Motor Skills.

Format: Examiner required; individual administration; untimed: 35 minutes

Scoring: Examiner evaluated

Cost: Contact publisher

Parents' Evaluations of Developmental Status (PEDS)

1998 Ellsworth & Vandemeer Press, Ltd.

Frances Page Glascoe

Population: Ages birth through 8 years

Purpose: Detects developmental and behavioral problems

Description: A screening test and a tool for managing a wide range of developmental, behavioral, and family issues. With 10 short questions to parents, PEDS helps professionals to identify children at risk for school problems and those with undetected developmental and behavioral disabilities. The questions are written at the fifth-grade level, which ensures that almost all parents can read and respond independently to the items. There is a Spanish version. An online version is completed and scored online. Results may be printed.

Format: Completed independently; untimed: 2 minutes

Scoring: Examiner evaluated

Cost: Complete Set (guide, 50 response forms, 50 scoring forms) $30.00; Manual $69.95; Online $9.95

Pre-Kindergarten Screen (PKS)

2000	Academic Therapy Publications

Raymond E. Webster, Angela Matthews

Population: Ages 4 through 5 years

Purpose: Measures kindergarten readiness and detects at-risk difficulties due to experiential or neurological immaturity

Description: The PKS identifies deficiencies in skills shown by research to be indicators of a child's later academic success: fine and gross motor skills, following directions, visual-spatial ability, elementary number and color concepts, letter identification, and impulse control. Administered prior to kindergarten entry, it allows teachers to provide extra help in areas that are problematic for the child. The PKS reliably identified children who later had academic problems in first grade. Thirty-nine items are clustered within five subtests. Cutoff scores are provided; standard scores and percentiles define the child's risk category.

Format: Examiner required; individually administered; timed and untimed: 10 to 15 minutes

Scoring: Examiner evaluated

Cost: Complete Kit (manual, test plates, 50 forms, in vinyl folder) $65.00

Pre-School Behavior Checklist (PBCL)

1988	Academic Therapy Publications

Jacqueline McGuire, Naomi Richman

Population: Ages 2 through 5 years

Purpose: Measures behavior and emotional factors; used to help determine if intervention is necessary

Description: A 22-item screen tool. The checklist consists of a series of items within specific areas (Soiling, Temper, Fears, Worries, and Moods). The examiner describes the degrees of usually observed behaviors. The total score can be compared to criterion cutoff scores that indicate the possibility of behavioral or emotional problems.

Format: Examiner required; untimed

Scoring: Examiner evaluated

Cost: Test Kit (manual, 25 forms, scoring acetate, 50 developmental activities checklist forms, in vinyl folder) $67.00

Preschool Evaluation Scale (PES)

1992	Hawthorne Educational Services, Inc.

Stephen B. McCarney

Population: Ages birth to 72 months

Purpose: Used in child development to screen for developmental delays and behavior problems

Description: Subscales are Large Muscle Skills, Small Muscle Skills, Cognitive Thinking, Expressive Language, Social/Emotional Behavior, and Self-Help Skills. Irregularities in normal development are determined in order to provide an appropriate intervention plan to remediate. Two forms are available: Birth to 35 months (94 items) and 36 to 72 months (85 items). A Windows Quick Score is available. Spanish forms are also available.

Format: Rating scale; untimed

Scoring: Examiner evaluated; computer scoring available

Cost: Complete Kit (2 technical manuals, 50 each of 4 forms) $180.00

Preschool Screening Instrument (PSI)

1994	Stoelting Company

Stephen Paul Cohen

Population: Ages 4 years to 5 years 3 months

Purpose: Identifies prekindergarten children with learning disabilities

Description: Multiple-item task-assessment test in which the child is told he or she will be "playing some games" with the examiner, who administers the following subtests: Figure Drawing, Circle Drawing, Tower Building, Cross Drawing, Block Design, Square Drawing, Broad Jumping,

Balancing, Ball Throwing, Hopping, Whole Name, Picture Responses, Comprehension, and Oral Vocabulary. The child's responses are evaluated in seven developmental areas: Visual-Motor Perception, Fine-Motor Development, Gross-Motor Development, Language Development, Verbal Fluency, Conceptual Skills, and Speech and Behavioral Problems.

Format: Examiner required; individual administration; untimed: 5 to 8 minutes

Scoring: Examiner evaluated

Cost: Complete Kit (25 each of student record books and parent questionnaires, manual, manipulatives, story card) $90.00

Primary Test of Cognitive Skills (PTCS)

1990	CTB/McGraw-Hill

Population: Grades K and 1

Purpose: Assesses intellectual functioning of young children, including verbal, spatial, memory, and concepts; used by teachers to identify students who may be gifted, have learning disabilities, or have unique developmental delays

Description: Multiple-item paper–pencil multiple-choice test divided into four subtests: Verbal, Spatial, Memory, and Concepts. It yields four subscales that combine with the child's age to produce a single Cognitive Skills Index (CSI). May be used with the *California Achievement Test–Fifth Edition* or *California Test of Basic Skills–Fourth Edition* to produce an Anticipated Achievement score to screen children for potential learning disabilities.

Format: Examiner required; suitable for group use; untimed: 30 minutes per subtest

Scoring: Machine scored; examiner evaluated

Cost: Review Kit $18.20

Reading Readiness Test: Reversal Tests (Bilingual)

Date not provided	Institute of Psychological Research, Inc.

Ake W. Edfeldt

Population: Grade 1

Purpose: Measures degree of speech reversal tendencies in young children before they learn to read; used by educators and speech therapists to predict reading problems in first grade

Description: Oral-response test based on re-search into the cause and effect of word transposition tendencies of children. The test was developed to diagnose and prevent these difficulties. A child who is scored either as "control case" or as "not yet ready to read" is not considered ready to master reading and, therefore, should postpone instruction.

Format: Examiner required; individual administration; untimed

Scoring: Hand key; examiner evaluated

Cost: Contact publisher

Revised Pre-Reading Screening Procedures to Identify First Grade Academic Needs

1997	Educators Publishing Service, Inc.

Beth H. Slingerland

Population: Grades K and 1

Purpose: Evaluates auditory, visual, and kinesthetic strengths in order to identify children who may have some form of dyslexia or specific language disability; should be used with students who have had no introduction to reading

Description: Series of 12 verbal–visual subtests measuring visual perception; visual discrimination; visual recall; visual-motor skills; auditory recall; auditory discrimination; auditory perception; letter knowledge; and language skills, such as vocabulary, enunciation, comprehension of oral directions, oral expression, and recall of new words. The test also evaluates motor coordination, hobbies and interests, attention span, and mental growth. The test identifies children who are ready for formal instruction in reading, writing, and spelling and are able to learn through conventional methods; children who, while appearing to be ready, reveal indications of a language disability and need immediate multisensory instruction; children who show language confusion but whose maturity indicates a need to begin strengthening their language background; and children of any age who are unready to begin reading instruction and who would benefit from more readiness and social development training. The examiner first explains the directions to the students and then they proceed with the task.

Format: Examiner required; suitable for group use; untimed: 2 to 3 hours

Scoring: Examiner evaluated

Cost: Specimen Set $23.55

Rockford Infant Developmental Evaluation Scales (RIDES)

| 1979 | Scholastic Testing Service, Inc. |

Population: Ages birth to 4 years

Purpose: Evaluates the level of a child's skill and behavioral development

Description: Multiple-item criterion-referenced evaluation of 308 developmental behaviors in five skill areas: Personal-Social, Self-Help, Fine Motor, Adaptive, Receptive Language, Expressive Language, and Gross Motor. Children respond verbally or by pointing. Each behavioral item is determined to be present, emerging, or absent in the child. Test results relate these single items to major developmental patterns and competencies and provide an informal indication of a child's development. The format calls for one eight-page booklet per child. An Individual Child Progress Graph on the back page shows progress and allows comparison of levels across developmental areas. The manual contains a section detailing development, use, and interpretation of the test. The entries for all 308 behaviors provide scoring criteria, developmental significance, equipment specifications, and references to further information. An appendix containing master equipment list, skill group listing, notes, and bibliography are included. Examiner must be certified for assessment.

Format: Examiner required; individual administration; untimed: one week

Scoring: Examiner evaluated

Cost: Starter Set (manual, 20 checklists) $50.50

Rossetti Infant-Toddler Language Scale

| 2006 | LinguiSystems, Inc. |

Louis Rossetti

Population: Ages birth to 3 years

Purpose: Assesses language skills

Description: Oral response 291-item criterion-referenced projective, verbal, point-to, gesture, vocalization test comprised of six domains: Interaction Attachment, Pragmatics, Gesture, Play, Language Comprehension, and Language Expression. An examiner's manual with scoring standards and interpretation is available. A Parent Questionnaire is also included. The Rossetti has a new look and is now available in English and Spanish (Mexican-American dialect). Both translations are included in the manual.

Format: Examiner required; individual administration; untimed

Scoring: Examiner evaluated

Cost: Kit (manual, 15 test forms, CD w/parent questionnaires in English and Spanish on CD) $89.95

School Readiness Test (SRT)

| 2004 | Scholastic Testing Service, Inc. |

O. F. Anderhalter, Jan Perney

Population: End of Kindergarten or before the third full week of Grade 1

Purpose: Determines individual and group readiness for first grade

Description: Multiple-choice criterion-referenced test designed for children entering first grade. The test reveals readiness for formal instruction by assessing eight skill areas: Number Knowledge, Handwriting Ability, Vocabulary, Identifying Letters, Visual Discrimination, Auditory Discrimination, Comprehension and Interpretation, and Spelling Ability. Raw scores, national percentiles, stanines, and norm curve equivalents are yielded. The test results, which can be used as the basis for placement, show a child at one of six readiness levels. Examiner must be certified for assessment.

Format: Examiner required; individual administration; untimed and timed portions: 90 minutes

Scoring: Hand key

Cost: Starter Set (manual, answer key, 35 test booklets, class record sheet, class summary report) $71.25

Screening of Reading Readiness (SORR)

| 2003 | Kindergarten Interventions and Diagnostic Services, Inc. |

Population: Ages 4 to 6 years

Purpose: Assesses reading readiness skills

Description: The SORR assesses reading readiness across seven subtests and includes one supplemental subtest: Rhyming Words in Context, Rhyming Words in Isolation, Identifying Sounds, Blending of Sounds, Verbal List Learning, Memory for Sentences, Rapid Picture Naming, and Print and Book Awareness.

Format: Examiner required; individual assessment; untimed: 25 minutes

Scoring: Examiner evaluated; Web-based scoring available

Cost: Complete Kit (manual, stimulus booklet, Verbal List Learning Color Interference Card, Audio CD pronunciation guide, minibook for the Print and Book Awareness subtest, 25 Student Test Booklets, 30 free credits for the Web-based Scoring Program) $195.00

Screening Test for Educational Prerequisite Skills (STEPS)

1990	Western Psychological Services

Frances Smith

Population: Ages 4 to 5 years

Purpose: Provides a clear picture of needs and skills of beginning kindergartners

Description: The STEPS screens five areas: Intellectual Skills, Verbal Information Skills, Cognitive Strategies, Motor Skills, and Attitudes in Learning Styles. The child performs several tasks: copying shapes and words, identifying colors, classifying objects, following directions, and remembering digits. The test is scored as it is given.

Format: Examiner required; individual administration; untimed: 8 to 10 minutes

Scoring: Hand key; computer scored

Cost: Kit (set of test materials, 25 AutoScore™ forms, 25 AutoScore™ home questionnaires, manual) $165.00

Slosson Test of Reading Readiness (STRR)

1991	Slosson Educational Publications, Inc.

Leslie Anne Perry, Gary J. Vitali

Population: Late Kindergarten to Grade 1

Purpose: Assesses reading readiness in young children

Description: The test was designed to identify children who are at risk of failure in programs of formal reading instruction. STRR subtests include recognition of capital letters, recognition of lowercase letters, matching capital and lowercase letters, visual discrimination, auditory discrimination, sequencing, and opposites. Test items focus on cognitive, auditory, and visual abilities.

Format: Examiner required; individual administration; untimed: 15 minutes

Scoring: Examiner evaluated

Cost: Complete Kit $91.50

Teacher's Observation Guide (TOG)

1995	Behavior Science Systems, Inc.

Harold R. Ireton

Population: Ages 18 months to 5 years

Purpose: Used to observe and record behavior and development and to plan educational activities

Description: There are 340 items in these categories: Social Development, Self-Help, Gross Motor, Fine Motor, Language, and School Readiness Skills. Development is classified in each area as around age level, borderline, and delayed. Twenty-three items record the teacher's concerns about the child's social adjustment/behavior problems, maturity, motor, and language development. Also available in Spanish.

Format: Teacher observation; untimed

Scoring: Examiner evaluated

Cost: Starter Set (manual, 20 booklets) $45.00

Test of Kindergarten/First Grade Readiness Skills (TKFGRS)

1987	Academic Therapy Publications

Karen Gardner Codding

Population: Ages 3 years 6 months through 6 years

Purpose: Evaluates the basic skills in reading, spelling, and arithmetic

Description: The skills measured in the three areas are Letter, Phonetic, and Word Identification; Story Comprehension; Letter and Word Identification; Number Identification; Written Computation; Time Identification; and Verbal Word Problems. Results are given in standard scores for the three areas.

Format: Examiner required; individual administration; untimed: 10 minutes

Scoring: Examiner evaluated

Cost: Complete Kit (manual, 25 record booklets, 8 cards) $60.00

Test of Preschool Early Literacy (TOPEL)

2007	PRO-ED, Inc.

Christopher J. Lonigan, Richard K. Wagner, Joseph K. Torgesen, Carol A. Rashotte

Population: Ages 3 to 5 years

Purpose: Identifies preschoolers who are at risk for literacy problems

Description: The TOPEL has three subtests: Print Knowledge (36 Items), Definitional Vocabulary (35 items), and Phonological Awareness (27 items). The three are combined into an overall composite score. Scores are reported as standard scores and percentile ranks.

Format: Examiner required; individual administration; untimed: 25 to 30 minutes

Scoring: Examiner evaluated

Cost: Complete Kit (manual picture book, 25 record booklets, box) $225.00

Test of Sensory Functions in Infants (TSFI)

1989	Western Psychological Services

Georgia A. DeGangi, Stanley I. Greenspan

Population: Ages 4 to 18 months

Purpose: Identifies infants with sensory integrative dysfunction

Description: Composed of 24 items, the test provides objective criteria for determining presence and extent of deficits in sensory functioning in infants. The TSFI provides an overall measure of sensory processing and reactivity and assesses these subdomains: reactivity to tactile deep pressure, visual tactile integration, adaptive motor function, ocular motor control, and reactivity to vestibular stimulation.

Format: Examiner required; individually administered; untimed: 20 minutes

Scoring: Examiner evaluated

Cost: Kit (set of test materials, 100 administration and scoring forms, manual, plastic carrying case) $192.50

Tests of Basic Experiences– Second Edition (TOBE 2)

1978	CTB/McGraw-Hill

Margaret H. Moss

Population: Grades K and 1

Purpose: Measures the degree to which young children have acquired concepts and experiences related to effective school participation; used for evaluation of school readiness

Description: Multiple-item battery of paper–pencil tests measuring quantity and quality of children's early learning experiences. The test is divided into two overlapping levels, covering programs from preschool through first grade. Each level contains a language, mathematics, science, and social studies test. Each test item consists of a verbal stimulus and four pictured responses. An instructional activities kit contains materials for teaching concepts and skills.

Format: Examiner required; suitable for group use; untimed: 45 minutes per test

Scoring: Hand key

Cost: 30 Test Books $58.90

Ullmann Scales of Early Learning: AGS Edition

1995	AGS Publishing/Pearson Assessments

Eileen M. Ullmann

Population: Ages birth to 68 months

Purpose: A comprehensive scale of cognitive functioning in multiple developmental domains; used to assess learning styles, strengths, and weaknesses

Description: Consists of a Gross Motor Scale (birth to 33 months), together with four cognitive scales: Visual Reception, Fine Motor, Receptive Language, and Expressive Language (birth to 68 months each). An Early Learning Composite score is derived from the scores on the cognitive scales. Results provide a profile of cognitive strengths and weaknesses that can be used to develop individualized program plans. Items are performance based, involving the child in a variety of activities.

Format: Examiner required; individual administration; untimed: birth to 2 years, 15 to 30 minutes; 3 to 5 years, 40 to 60 minutes

Scoring: Examiner interpretation; computer scoring is available for Macintosh and Windows formats

Cost: Complete Kit (manuals, picture books, 25 record forms, all manipulatives, briefcase) $679.99

Vineland Social-Emotional Early Childhood Scales (Vineland SEEC)

1998	AGS Publishing/Pearson Assessments

Sara Sparrow, David Balla, Domenic Cicchetti

Population: Ages birth through 5 years

Purpose: Measures social-emotional skills

Description: Information is collected by interview with parents or caregivers. The SEEC Scales identify strengths and weaknesses in specific areas of social-emotional behavior. The results can be used to plan a program and to select activities best suited to a child's needs.

Format: Examiner required; untimed: 15 to 25 minutes

Scoring: Examiner evaluated; computer scoring available

Cost: Complete Kit (manual, 25 record forms) $71.99

Vulpe Assessment Battery–Revised (VAB-R)

1994	Slosson Educational Publications, Inc.

Shirley German Vulpe

Population: Ages birth to 6 years

Purpose: Evaluates the developmental status of children developing atypically

Description: Performance analysis/developmental assessment of functioning with 1,127 items in multiple developmental skill areas (basic senses and functions, gross motor behaviors, fine motor behaviors, language behaviors, cognitive processes and specific concepts, the organization of behavior, activities of daily living) and an environmental domain. Information about an individual child is obtained through direct observation or from a knowledgeable informant.

Format: Examiner required; individual administration; untimed

Scoring: Examiner evaluated

Cost: Complete Battery $136.50

English Language Learners and Bilingual Education

Adult Language Assessment Scales (Adult LAS®)

1991	CTB/McGraw-Hill

Sharon E. Duncan, Edward A. DeAvila

Population: Adults

Purpose: Assesses English language proficiency in adults whose primary language is not English

Description: Multiple-item paper–pencil multiple-choice, oral response, and short-answer test available in two levels. The test consists of Oral Language, Writing, Reading, and Mathematics components. There are four subtests, divided into subsections that allow for identification of problem areas. Results of all test components are combined to give one measure of language proficiency.

Format: Examiner required; suitable for group use; untimed 5 to 30 minutes per subsection

Scoring: Examiner evaluated; hand key

Cost: Oral Examiner's Kit (Form A) $201.95; 50 Oral Answer Books $51.95; 25 Reading/Math Test Books $110.15; 50 Reading/Math Answer Sheets $43.50; 50 Writing Combination Test Books and Answer Sheets $76.50

Adult Rating of Oral English (AROE)

1995	Development Associates, Inc.

Population: Adults

Purpose: Informally assesses oral proficiency

Description: Eleven categories are rated to guide instruction, track progress, and guide placement. The instructor rates the individual based on interaction over time. Subtotals for each of two matrices are available: Building Blocks and Discourse Matrices.

Format: Rating scale; untimed

Scoring: Examiner evaluated

Cost: Introductory Kit (5 user handbooks, 25 matrices) $75.00

Basic English Skills Test (BEST)

Date not provided	Center for Applied Linguistics

Population: Adults

Purpose: Measures basic oral and literacy skills

Description: The BEST is a competency-based survival-level ESL performance test; widely used in adult ESL literacy programs; includes a structured oral interview component. The Oral Interview Section measures communication, fluency, pronunciation, and listening comprehension. The Literacy Skills Section provides scores for reading and writing. The BEST is available in two parallel forms.

Format: Examiner required; individual or group administered; timed: 45 minutes

Scoring: Examiner evaluated; test scoring service available

Cost: Complete Kit $150.00

Batería III Woodcock-Muñoz™

| 2005 | Riverside Publishing Company |

Ana F. Muñoz Sandoval,
Richard W. Woodcock, Kevin S. McGrew,
Nancy Mather

Population: Ages 2 to 90+ years

Purpose: Assesses cognitive abilities and achievement levels in Spanish-speaking individuals

Description: Completely revised and updated, the Batería III is a comprehensive set of tests that assess both cognitive abilities and achievement levels of Spanish-speaking individuals. This battery is used for measurement of general intellectual ability, specific cognitive abilities, oral language, and academic achievement. In addition, the battery also provides a language-reduced general intellectual ability score to measure the intellectual ability of bilingual or multilingual individuals, a Broad Cognitive Ability–Low Verbal Score, and a Comparative Language Index to determine language dominance. Using both the cognitive and achievement batteries of the Batería III will allow practitioners to make accurate comparisons among a person's general intellectual, oral language, and achievement scores and to obtain several types of discrepancies.

Format: Examiner required; individually administered; untimed: 5 to 10 minutes per subtest

Scoring: Computer scored

Cost: Complete Battery (cognitive test books, extended test books, achievement test books, cassettes, manuals, 25 each of both test records and response booklets, norm tables, scoring guide) $1,098.00

Bilingual Verbal Ability Tests (BVAT-NU) Normative Update

| 2005 | Riverside Publishing Company |

Ana F. Muñoz-Sandoval, Jim Cummins,
Criselda G. Alvarado, Mary L. Ruef,
Fredrick A. Schrank

Population: Ages 5 years to adult

Purpose: Provides a measure of overall verbal ability for bilingual individuals

Description: A test of the unique combination of cognitive–academic language abilities possessed by bilingual individuals in English and another language. The need for this test is based on the reality that bilingual persons know some things in one language, some things in the other language, and some things in both languages. Traditional procedures only measure a person's ability in one language, usually the one considered dominant. The BVAT may be administered either by one examiner who is fluent in the individual's two languages or by a primary and ancillary examiner team. The test can be used to determine entry and exit criteria for bilingual programs or to assess the academic potential of a bilingual student. The BVAT is comprised of three subtests from the *WJ-R Tests of Cognitive Ability*—Picture Vocabulary, Oral Vocabulary, and Verbal Analogies. The subtests have been translated from English into 18 languages. The subtests are administered in English first. Items that were missed are then administered in the individual's native language and added to the score.

Format: Examiner required; individual administration; untimed: 30 minutes

Scoring: Computer scored; examiner evaluated

Cost: Complete Test Kit (easel, manual, test records, normative update package, box) $778.00

Bilingual Vocabulary Assessment Measure

| 1995 | Academic Communication Associates |

Larry J. Mattes

Population: Ages 3 to 11 years

Purpose: Determines if basic picture-naming vocabulary for common nouns has been acquired

Description: Measures basic expressive vocabulary in a variety of languages. The instrument is criterion referenced and designed for use as an initial screening. Helpful in determining whether or not the child is able to label articles of clothing; tools; motor vehicles; and other nouns commonly encountered in school, in the supermarket, and at home. The standard record forms are designed so that responses can be recorded in any language spoken by the child.

Format: Examiner required; individual administration; untimed

Scoring: Hand key

Cost: Complete Kit $52.00

BRIGANCE® Assessment of Basic Skills–Spanish Edition

| 2007 | Curriculum Associates®, Inc. |

Albert H. Brigance

Population: Grades Pre-K to 9

Purpose: Measures the academic skills of Spanish-speaking students; distinguishes language barriers from learning disabilities; used by bilingual, ELL, migrant, and bilingual special educators to identify, develop, and implement academic programs

Description: A total of 102 skill sequences assessing Spanish-speaking students' abilities in readiness, speech, functional word recognition, oral reading, reading comprehension, word analysis, listening, writing and alphabetizing, numbers and computation, and measurement. Directions to the examiner are written in English; directions to the student are written in Spanish. Assessments used for dominant language screening present directions to the student in English and Spanish. The diagnostic tests identify skills the student has and has not mastered and students who might have learning disabilities. The diagnostic tests help to determine individual instructional objectives. The dominant language screening form provides a means of comparing a student's performance in English and Spanish on all of the oral language and literacy diagnostic assessments. Results of the screening are used to place students in appropriate ESL and bilingual programs. The seven grade-level screens assess skills that indicate grade-level competency in Grades K to 6. The results are used to place students at their appropriate instructional levels and to identify students who need further evaluation. Individual student record books record the level of competency the student has achieved.

Format: Examiner required; many sections are suitable for group use; untimed

Scoring: Examiner evaluated

Cost: Assessment Book $185.00; Class Record Book $14.00; 10 Student Record Books $35.00

Computerized Adaptive Placement Assessment and Support System and English as a Second Language (COMPASS/ESL)

2000	ACT, Inc.

Population: Ages 18 years and older

Purpose: Used for placement and diagnosis to assess writing, reading, and math skills

Description: Multiple-choice computer-administered test with placement tests and diagnostic tests. The categories are (a) Writing Skills Placement (465 items); (b) Reading Placement (205 items); (c) Math Placement: Prealgebra (234 items), Algebra (235 items), College Algebra (165 items), Geometry (187 items), and Trigonometry (200 items); (d) Math Diagnostic Tests (20 items per category): Operations with Integers, Operations with Fractions, Operations with Decimals, Exponents, Ratios and Proportions, Percentages, and Averages; (e) Reading Diagnostic Tests: Main Idea (30 items), Implicit Information (90 items), Explicit Information (60 items), and Vocabulary (100 items); and (f) Writing Skills Diagnostic Tests: Punctuation (40 items), Verbs (40 items), Usage (40 items), Relationships of Clause (40 items), Shifts in Construction (40 items), Organization (40 items), Spelling (40 items), and Capitalization (40 items). Contact publisher about computer requirements.

Format: Computer administered; examiner required; untimed

Scoring: Computer scored

Cost: Site License $450.00; Administration Unit $1.30 each

Dos Amigos Verbal Language Scales (DAVLS)

1996	Academic Therapy Publications

Donald E. Critchlow

Population: Ages 5 to 13 years

Purpose: Measures functional language levels of English and Spanish

Description: A screening tool that uses 85 pairs of opposites in both English and Spanish. By comparing scores for both sets of words, mixed language proficiency or language dominance can be seen so that, if needed, appropriate remediation can take place. Since verbal administration and responses are utilized, the child's reading proficiency is not a factor. Cutoff scores are provided to determine the child's quartile performance.

Format: Examiner required; individual administration; untimed: 20 minutes

Scoring: Examiner evaluated

Cost: Test Kit (manual, 25 forms, in vinyl folder) $45.00

English Placement Test (EPT)

1993	English Language Institute, University of Michigan

Mary Spann, Laura Strowe, A. Corrigan, B. Dobson E. Kellman, S. Tyma

Population: Adults

Purpose: Assesses facility with the English language; used to group low to advanced intermediate proficiency adult nonnative speakers of English into homogenous ability levels as they enter an intensive English course

Description: Paper-pencil 100-item multiple-choice test of listening comprehension, grammar in conversational contexts, vocabulary recognition, and reading comprehension of sentences. A tape is available for use with the listening comprehension items. Three forms (A, B, C) are available.

Format: Examiner required; suitable for group use; timed: 1 hour 15 minutes

Scoring: Hand key

Cost: Testing Package (examiner's manual, scoring stencil, 20 test booklets, 100 answer sheets, cassette) $85.00

ESL/Literacy Scale (ELS)

1989	Academic Therapy Publications

Michael Roddy

Population: Ages 16 years to adult

Purpose: Measures starting level for ESL and literacy instruction

Description: After a brief oral screening, the remainder includes Listening Comprehension, Grammar, Life Skills, Reading Comprehension, and Composition. The assessment was developed and field-tested over a five-year period with adult school students of many different backgrounds, including Hispanic, Asian, Middle Eastern, and European. Test results are charted on a profile showing whether beginning, intermediate, or advanced ESL classes are appropriate.

Format: Examiner required; individual and group administration; untimed: 15 to 20 minutes

Scoring: Examiner evaluated

Cost: 25 Test Booklets $25.00; Instructions Card $5.00; Scoring Template $5.00

Expressive One Word Picture Vocabulary Test–Spanish Bilingual Edition

2001	Academic Therapy Publications

Rick Brownell

Population: Ages 4 to 12 years

Purpose: Measures speaking vocabulary in Spanish and English

Description: Provides a measure of total acquired expressive vocabulary. Examinees may respond in both languages. The test was co-normed with the *Receptive One Word Picture Vocabulary Test-Spanish Bilingual Edition* on a national sample of Spanish-bilingual individuals. Administration procedures permit examiners to cue examinees so that they will attend to the relevant aspects of each illustration. Record forms provide cues and acceptable responses in both languages and common Spanish dialects. Raw scores are converted to standard scores, percentiles, and age equivalents. Utilizes the same plates as the English version, so users of the English version should order only the Spanish-Bilingual Manual and Record Forms.

Format: Examiner required; individual administration; untimed: 20 minutes

Scoring: Examiner evaluated

Cost: Test Kit (manual, test plates, 25 forms, in portfolio) $140.00

Institutional Testing Program (ITP)

Date not provided	Educational Testing Service

Population: Adolescents, adults

Purpose: Measures English proficiency of nonnative speakers of English

Description: Multiple-choice test composed of Listening Comprehension (50 items), Structure and Written Expression (40 items), and Vocabulary and Reading Comprehension (60 items). This test uses retired forms of the *Test of English as a Foreign Language* (TOEFL). The test yields three section scores and one total score. Suitable for individuals with visual, physical, or hearing impairments.

Format: Examiner required; suitable for group use; timed: 150 minutes

Scoring: Hand key; test scoring service available

Cost: 200 or Fewer Tests $14.00 each; More Than 200 Tests $12.00 each (minimum order of 10 tests)

IPT® 2004 Oral Language Proficiency Tests

2004	Ballard & Tighe Publishers

Population: Grades Pre-K to 12

Purpose: Assesses listening and speaking skills in English and Spanish

Description: The instruments measure BICS

and CALP in second language learners. Can be used for initial identification and redesignation and are effective for tracking and reporting student growth. Scores are reported as non-, limited, and fluent speaking. Three forms are available to make the instrument age appropriate. A training kit is available.

Format: Examiner required; group administration; untimed

Scoring: Examiner evaluated; computer scoring available

Cost: Pre-IPT Oral Test Set $172.00; Oral Test Set $162.00

IPT® 2004 Reading & Writing Tests

2004	Ballard & Tighe Publishers

Population: Grades K to 12

Purpose: Measures reading and writing ability

Description: Early Literacy Kit includes eight reading subtests and four writing subtests for younger, less experienced test takers. There are four forms for English and three forms for Spanish. Scores are reported as Pre-, Beginning, and Early Reading and Writing stages. Includes clear rubrics to make rating students' writing easy. Training kit available. The kits for older students provide comprehensive assessment. Scores are reported as Non-, Limited, or Competent.

Format: Examiner required; group administration; untimed

Scoring: Examiner evaluated; computer scoring available

Cost: Early Literacy Kit $229.00; IPT I $229.00; IPT 3 & 4 $239.00

Language Assessment Scales–Oral (LAS®-O)

2004	CTB/McGraw-Hill

Sharon E. Duncan, Edward A. DeAvila

Population: Grades 1 to 12

Purpose: Assesses the oral language abilities of students whose primary language is not English

Description: Multiple-item paper–pencil multiple-choice/oral response test available in two levels and two forms in English, two levels and one form in Spanish. The test is based on an analysis of four primary language subsystems: phonemic, lexical, syntactical, and pragmatic. Its five sections are divided into two components: the Oral Language Component and the Pronunciation Component. Can be used with *LAS Reading/Writing*.

Format: Examiner required; individually administered; untimed 10 to 20 minutes

Scoring: Examiner evaluated

Cost: Examiner's Kit $192.00

Language Assessment Scales Reading/Writing (LAS® R/W)

2004	CTB/McGraw-Hill

Sharon E. Duncan, Edward A. DeAvila

Population: Grades 2 to 12

Purpose: Assesses written language skills in Spanish or English

Description: Multiple-item paper–pencil multiple-choice and essay test available in two forms and three levels in English, and one form and three levels in Spanish. Vocabulary, fluency, reading comprehension, and mechanics are assessed objectively with multiple-choice items, while writing is evaluated directly using performance assessment.

Format: Examiner required; suitable for group use; timed 90 minutes

Scoring: Examiner evaluated

Cost: Contact publisher

Language Proficiency Test Series (LPTS)

1999	MetriTech, Inc.

Population: Grades K to 12

Purpose: Measures English proficiency; identifies students requiring services, monitors student progress over time, and provides information for mainstreaming

Description: Categories are Reading, Writing, and Listening/Speaking, each available for Grades K to 2, 3 to 5, 6 to 8, and 9 to 12. There are four proficiency levels for Reading and Writing. Proficiency cut scores for Listening/Speaking. Forms A and B available for each genre at each of four grade clusters, for a total of 24 total test booklets.

Format: Examiner required; group administered; untimed: 15 to 60 minutes

Scoring: Hand key; examiner evaluated; test scoring service is available

Cost: Administrator's Sample Set (administration and scoring guide, 1 of each test booklet at grade level of choice) $32.00

LAS™ Benchmark Assessments

| 2005 | CTB/McGraw-Hill |

Population: Grades K to 12

Purpose: Measures language proficiency growth

Description: A series of three, low-stakes benchmark tests provides information about students' language proficiency and growth at any time during the year. Three forms per grade span (K-1, 2-3, 4-5, 6-8, 9-12). The Benchmark Assessments work with any English language proficiency test.

Format: Examiner required; group administration; untimed: 30 minutes

Scoring: Examiner evaluated; scoring service available

Cost: Contact publisher

Listening Comprehension Test (LCT)

| 1986 | English Language Institute, University of Michigan |

John Upshur, H. Koba, Mary Spaan, Laura Strowe

Population: Adults

Purpose: Measures understanding of spoken English for a nonnative speaker; used to predict readiness to pursue studies in an English-speaking institution

Description: Paper-pencil 45-item multiple-choice test of aural comprehension of English. The student is read a short question or statement and responds by marking the appropriate written answer. A tape recording of the verbal questions and statements is available. The test is available in three forms: 4, 5, and 6. This test is a retired, nonsecure component of the *Michigan Test Battery*. It is sold only to educational institutions for internal use (e.g., to measure the learning progress of ESL/EFL students who have already been admitted to a program or to confirm the level of proficiency of matriculated students). The tests are not to be used for initial university admission purposes or to report scores to other institutions.

Format: Examiner required; suitable for group use; timed: 15 minutes

Scoring: Hand key

Cost: Testing Package (manual, 20 test book-

lets, 100 answer sheets, 3 scoring stencils) $125.00

MAC II Test of English Language Proficiency

| 2001 | Touchstone Applied Science Associates, Inc. |

Population: Ages 5 years and older

Purpose: Measures English language proficiency

Description: Applications include placement, measuring progress, determining readiness for ESL program exit, and evaluating ESL programs. Four subtests measure English proficiency: Speaking, Listening, Reading, and Writing. Results are reported as standard scores for each, Degrees of Reading Power scores (Grades 4 and up), and percentiles. Forms available: A1, A2, A3, A4, and A5 for Grades K to 12.

Format: Requires examiner; suitable for group use; both timed and untimed

Scoring: Hand key; machine scored; scoring service available

Cost: A1 and A2 Classroom Sets (manual picture booklet, 25 test booklets, 25 record forms) $162.00; A3-A5 Classroom Sets (manual, 25 each of test booklets, writing forms, answer sheets, record forms) $215.00; Handbook with Norms Tables $40.00

Michigan Test of English Language Proficiency (MTELP)

| 1977 | English Language Institute, University of Michigan |

John Upshur

Population: Adults

Purpose: Assesses the English language proficiency of nonnative speakers of English; used to predict the readiness to study at the college level or in a professional training program in an English-speaking institution.

Description: Paper-pencil 100-item multiple-choice test of grammar, reading comprehension, and vocabulary. Available in three alternate forms (P, Q, R). These materials are retired, nonsecure components of the *Michigan Test Battery* and should not be used as an admission test; however, the test is suitable for placement of students who have already been admitted.

Format: Examiner required; suitable for group use; timed: 1 hour 15 minutes

Scoring: Hand key

Cost: Testing Package (includes manual, scoring stencil, 20 test booklets, 100 answer sheets) $60.00

Oral English or Spanish Proficiency Placement Test

| 1995 | Moreno Education Company |

Population: Grades 1 to 6 and Grades 7 to 12

Purpose: Measures oral English-speaking ability of limited English-speaking students

Description: Oral test administered in English that measures language speaking ability. Initial directions given in the student's native language. Spanish placement test measures the oral Spanish speaking ability of the student.

Format: Examiner required; individual administration; untimed

Scoring: Examiner evaluated

Cost: $20.00

Pre-LAS®

| 2004 | CTB/McGraw-Hill |

Sharon E. Duncan, Edward A. DeAvila

Population: Ages 4 to 6 years

Purpose: Assesses oral language abilities of nonnative English-speaking children

Description: Multiple-item paper–pencil verbal-oral response test available in two forms in English and one form in Spanish. The test assesses expressive and receptive abilities in three linguistic components of oral language: morphology, syntax, and semantics.

Format: Examiner required; individually administered; untimed 15 to 20 minutes

Scoring: Examiner evaluated

Cost: Examiner's Kit (specify form) $216.00

Quick Informal Assessment–Second Edition (QIA)

| Date not provided | Ballard & Tighe Publishers |

Population: Grades 1 to 12

Purpose: Evaluates proficiency in English and Spanish

Description: An informal assessment that complements standardized tests. It is easy to administer and score. Includes oral and literacy tests in English and Spanish. This edition provides revised test questions and a new format to make students' proficiency levels more easily identifiable.

Format: Examiner required; group administration; untimed: 5 minutes

Scoring: Examiner evaluated

Cost: Set $130.00

Receptive One Word Picture Vocabulary Test–Spanish Bilingual Edition

| 2001 | Academic Therapy Publications |

Rick Brownell

Population: Ages 4 to 12 years

Purpose: Measures receptive vocabulary in Spanish and English

Description: Provides a measure of total acquired receptive vocabulary. Examinees may respond to stimulus words in both languages. The test was co-normed with the *Expressive One Word Picture Vocabulary Test–Spanish Bilingual Edition* on a national sample of Spanish-bilingual individuals. Administration procedures permit examiners to cue examinees so that they will attend to the relevant aspects of each illustration. Record forms include acceptable responses and stimulus words in both languages and common Spanish dialects. Raw scores are converted to standard scores, percentiles, and age equivalents. Utilizes the same plates as the English version, so users of the English version should order only the Spanish-Bilingual Manual and Record Forms.

Format: Examiner required; individual administration; untimed: 20 minutes

Scoring: Examiner evaluated

Cost: Test Kit (manual, test plates, 25 forms, in portfolio) $140.00

Secondary Level English Proficiency Test (SLEP)

| Date not provided | Educational Testing Service |

Population: Ages 12 to 17 years

Purpose: Assesses English language proficiency of nonnative speakers; used as an admissions test by private secondary schools and as a placement test by both public and private secondary schools

Description: Paper–pencil 150-item multiple-choice test measuring two components (75 items each) of English proficiency: listening comprehension and reading comprehension (structure and vocabulary). The test does not measure productive language skills. A tape recorder is required to administer the listening comprehension sections. A cassette tape is included. Raw and converted scores are provided for both the listening comprehension and reading comprehension sections. The test is available in three equivalent forms.

Format: Examiner required; suitable for group use; timed: 1 hour 20 minutes

Scoring: Hand key

Cost: Complete Kit (reusable materials, 25 test booklets, 100 answer sheets, cassette, 2 keys, manual) $100.00

Spanish and English Reading Comprehension Test

1993	Moreno Education Company

Population: Grades 1 to 6 and Grades 7 to 12

Purpose: Measures Spanish reading achievement based on Mexican norms to determine learning ability and learning potential; used as a tool to evaluate bilingual education programs, and for research

Description: Compares Spanish reading ability with that of Mexican neighbors. Based on Mexican curriculum materials; standardized and normed in Mexico. Measures both Spanish and English reading comprehension. Developed and designed for use in the United States. Can be used by psychologists and evaluators for the identification of students who are mentally gifted or who have learning disorders

Format: Individual administration; suitable for group use; untimed: 25 minutes

Scoring: Examiner evaluated

Cost: Elementary $20.00; Secondary $20.00 (Answer sheets may be duplicated as needed)

Spanish Articulation Measures (SAM)

1995	Academic Communication Associates

Larry J. Mattes

Population: Ages 3 years to adult

Purpose: Measures articulation and phonological processes in Spanish

Description: Vocabulary words that are familiar to young children are emphasized in the tasks. The Spontaneous Word Production Task is used to assess production of individual phonemes and use of phonological processes such as cluster reduction, stridency deletion, velar fronting, stopping, and syllable reduction. Tasks for assessing

individual phonemes in a variety of words are also included. The instrument is criterion referenced.

Format: Examiner required; individual administration; untimed

Scoring: Examiner evaluated

Cost: Complete Kit $75.00

Spanish Language Assessment Procedures (SLAP)

1995	Academic Communication Associates

Larry J. Mattes

Population: Ages 3 to 9 years

Purpose: Assesses pragmatic and structural aspects of the Spanish language

Description: A criterion-referenced measure of the ability to understand basic concepts, communicate basic needs, follow oral directions, retell short stories, request information, describe events in sequence, make inferences, express opinions, ask questions, and so on. An articulation screening instrument is included. The manual includes guidelines for using the assessment results in the identification of children with communication disorders.

Format: Examiner required; individual administration; untimed

Scoring: Examiner evaluated

Cost: Complete Kit $79.00

Spanish Reading Comprehension Test (Evaluación de Comprensión de la Lectura)

1994	CASAS

Population: Spanish-speaking adults and adolescents

Purpose: Assesses basic reading comprehension in Spanish

Description: Multiple-choice competency-based test of reading comprehension in Spanish. Contains reading selections drawn from authentic Spanish language material in functional life skill contexts. Difficulty levels range from 3 to 9 years of schooling. May be used as an entrance appraisal, a progress test, or an exit measure in Spanish language instructional programs. Two forms are available.

Format: Examiner required; group administered; untimed

Scoring: Self-scoring answer sheets

Cost: Set of 25 Reusable Booklets $70.00; Set

of 25 Answer Sheets $30.00; Administration Manual $45.00

Spanish Test for Assessing Morphologic Production (STAMP)

1991   Academic Communication Associates

Therese M. Nugent, Kenneth G. Shipley, Dora O. Provencio

Population: Ages 5 to 11 years

Purpose: Assesses production of Spanish morphemes

Description: An incomplete sentence is presented to the child, and the child is asked to complete that sentence using a pictorial prompt. Plurals, verb endings, and various other structures are examined. The instrument was developed based on an analysis of structure of the Spanish language. Means and standard deviations are reported for Spanish-speaking students. The test is designed so that it can be adapted for use with speakers of different Spanish dialects. When used in conjunction with conversational speech samples, the results will be helpful in identifying children with communication disorders.

Format: Examiner required; individual administration; untimed

Scoring: Hand key

Cost: Complete Kit $70.00

Speaking Proficiency English Assessment Kit (SPEAK)

Yearly   Educational Testing Service

Population: Adults, international teaching assistants

Purpose: Assesses spoken English for international teaching assistants

Description: Oral-response 12-item test available for purchase by institutions. Under this program, test forms are administered and scored by institutions, at their convenience, using their own facilities and staff. Scores are reported on a scale from 20 to 60 in 5-point increments. Materials used include a test book, test audiocassette, and an answer audiocassette/response tape.

Format: Examiner required; suitable for group use; timed: 30 minutes total

Scoring: Examiner evaluated

Cost: Contact publisher

Student Oral Proficiency Rating (SOPR)

1986   Development Associates, Inc.

Population: Grades K to 12

Purpose: Informally assesses oral proficiency

Description: Five categories are rated to guide instruction, track progress, and guide placement. The instructor rates the individual based on interaction over time.

Format: Rating scale; untimed

Scoring: Examiner evaluated

Cost: $5.00 for introductory information and matrix; $10.00 for teacher's training packet

TerraNova Supera®

2000   CTB/McGraw-Hill

Population: Grades K to 10

Purpose: Measures academic achievement in Spanish

Description: Supera is the Spanish-language version of the TerraNova assessments. Three test components are offered to measure Reading/Language Arts and Mathematics. Supera allows educators to observe student progress and achievement in their primary language.

Format: Examiner required; suitable for group administration; timed: 88 to 368 minutes depending on grade

Scoring: Examiner evaluated; scoring service available

Cost: Contact publisher

Test de Vocabulario en Imagenes Peabody (TVIP)

1986   AGS Publishing/Pearson Assessments

Lloyd M. Dunn, Delia E. Lugo, Eligio R. Padilla, Leota M. Dunn

Population: Ages 2 years 6 months to 17 years

Purpose: Measures receptive vocabulary for Spanish-speaking individuals

Description: Based on the *Peabody Picture Vocabulary Test–Revised,* the TVIP contains 125 translated items to assess the vocabulary of Spanish-speaking and bilingual students. Items were carefully selected through rigorous item analysis for their universality and appropriateness to Spanish-speaking communities.

Format: Examiner required; individual administration; untimed: 10 to15 minutes

Scoring: Examiner evaluated

Cost: Test Kit (test easel, Spanish manual, 25 record forms, shelf box) $149.99

Test of English as a Foreign Language (TOEFL)

| 1986 | Educational Testing Service |

Date not provided   Educational Testing Service

Population: Adults

Purpose: Assesses proficiency in English for non-native speakers; used as a college admission and placement test

Description: Paper–pencil 150-item multiple-choice test measuring three aspects of English ability: listening comprehension, structure and written expression, and reading comprehension. Items involve comprehension of spoken and written language. The test is administered monthly on either Friday or Saturday.

Format: Examiner required; suitable for group use; timed: 3 hours

Scoring: Computer scored

Cost: Contact publisher

Test of Spoken English (TSE)

Date not provided   Educational Testing Service

Population: Adults

Purpose: Assesses nonnative speakers' proficiency in spoken English; used to evaluate applicants for graduate-level teaching assistantships and for certification in health-related professions whose native language is not English

Description: Oral-response 12-item test assessing nonnative speakers' proficiency in spoken English. A test audiotape leads the examinee through questions requiring controlled responses or less structured free answers that demand more active use of English. The subject's answers are taped and evaluated by two raters at Educational Testing Service (ETS). The test yields scores in three areas: grammar, fluency, and pronunciation. The TSE is part of the *Test of English as a Foreign Language* (TOEFL) program and is designed to compliment the TOEFL, which does not measure oral English proficiency. The institutional version, the *Speaking Proficiency English Assessment Kit* (SPEAK), is available for local testing.

Format: Examiner required; individual administration; untimed: 20 minutes

Scoring: Computer scored; examiner evaluated

Cost: Contact publisher

Test of Written English (TWE)

1986   Educational Testing Service

Velma R. Andersen, Sheryl K. Thompson

Population: Students entering college

Purpose: Measures written English ability of nonnative speakers of English who wish to study at the college level; used for admissions and placement

Description: Paper–pencil criterion-referenced essay test on a specific topic. The TWE uses a 6-point holistic score scale. This is a secure test; the publisher arranges all administrations, scoring, and so on. Suitable for individuals with visual, physical, or hearing impairments.

Format: Examiner evaluated; group administration; timed: 30 minutes

Scoring: Examiner evaluated; test scoring service required

Cost: The TWE is given with the TOEFL test; no additional fee

Woodcock Language Proficiency Battery–Revised (WLPB-R) Spanish Form

1995   Riverside Publishing Company

Richard W. Woodcock, Ana F. Muñoz-Sandoval

Population: Ages 2 to 90+ years

Purpose: Assesses language skills in Spanish; used for purposes of eligibility and determination of level of language proficiency

Description: Provides an overall measure of language proficiency in measures of oral language, reading, and written language. The subtests are Memory for Sentences, Picture Vocabulary, Oral Vocabulary, Listening Comprehension, Verbal Analogies, Letter-Word Identification, Passage Comprehension, Word Attack, Reading Vocabulary, Dictation, Writing Samples, Proofing, Writing Fluency, Punctuation and Capitalization, Spelling and Usage, and Handwriting. There are cluster scores for Oral Language, Reading, and Written Language. The tests are primarily measures of language skills predictive of success in situations characterized by cognitive-academic language proficiency (CALP) requirements. When both versions of the WLPB-R have been administered, a comparative language index that allows direct comparison between English and Spanish scores can be obtained. CALP levels from advanced to negligible are provided.

Format: Examiner required; individual administration; untimed: 20 to 60 minutes depending on number of subtests

Scoring: Examiner evaluated; computer software available

Cost: Complete Program (test book, audiocassette, 25 each of test records and response booklets, English manual, English norm tables, supplemental manual) $381.50

Woodcock-Muñoz Language Survey (WMLS) Normative Update

2001	Riverside Publishing Company

Richard W. Woodcock, Ana F. Muñoz-Sandoval

Population: Ages 4 to adult

Purpose: Establishes language proficiency level in English or Spanish

Description: Provides a broad overview of language ability in oral language, reading, and writing. Use of the English Form in conjunction with the Spanish Form enables examiners to obtain information about the individual's dominant language and information regarding the subject's proficiency in each language compared to others at the same age or grade level. The Language Survey provides five cognitive–academic language proficiency (CALP) levels. This gives examiners a sound procedure for classification of a subject's English or Spanish language proficiency, for determining eligibility for bilingual services, and to assess a subject's progress or readiness for English-only instruction. Age and grade equivalents can be obtained directly from the test record. Percentile ranks, standard scores, relative proficiency indexes, and CALP levels can be obtained through use of the Scoring and Reporting Program, which comes with the test.

Format: Examiner required; individual administration; untimed: 5 minutes per subtest

Scoring: Computer scored; examiner evaluated

Cost: Complete Kit English or Spanish (comprehensive manual, 25 test records, test book, software) $281.00

Fine Arts

Harmonic Improvisation Readiness Record and Rhythm Improvisation Readiness Record

1998	GIA Publications, Inc.

Edwin E. Gordon

Population: Grades 3 to music graduate school

Purpose: Help determine objectively whether individual students have the necessary harmonic and rhythmic readiness to learn to improvise

Description: The tests will indicate what types of general instruction in improvisation are most beneficial for individual students and assist teachers in adapting instruction to each student's individual needs.

Format: Examiner required; individual administration; untimed: 20 minutes

Scoring: Hand key; machine scoring available

Cost: Complete Kit (harmonic answer sheets, rhythm answer sheets, scoring masks, CD, manual—enough to test 100 students) $110.00

Instrument Timbre Preference Test

1984	GIA Publications, Inc.

Edwin E. Gordon

Population: Ages 9 years and older

Purpose: Assesses the timbre preference; used to help students select appropriate brass or woodwind instruments

Description: Multiple-item paper–pencil test identifying the timbre preferences of students. Students listen to different melodic synthesized sounds on a cassette recording and indicate their preferences on an answer sheet. Results help students choose instruments that match their timbre preferences, which improves the performance of beginning band students and reduces dropout rates.

Format: Examiner required; group administration; untimed: 30 minutes

Scoring: Hand key

Cost: Complete Kit (CD, 100 test sheets, scoring masks, manual, research monographs) $59.00

Intermediate Measures of Music Audiation (IMMA)

| 1986 | GIA Publications, Inc. |

Edwin E. Gordon

Population: Grades 1 to 6

Purpose: Measures the music aptitude of children

Description: Multiple-item paper-pencil test measuring and discriminating among the music aptitudes of children who obtained exceptionally high scores on the *Primary Measures of Music Audiation* or who are slightly older than the students targeted for the primary test. The test requires no language or music skills. Children listen to tonal and rhythm tape recordings, decide if pairs of patterns are the same or different, and circle an appropriate picture on the answer sheet. The manual contains information on converting raw scores to percentile ranks, interpreting results, and formal and informal music instruction suggestions. Also available in Portuguese and Polish.

Format: Examiner required; suitable for group use; untimed: 24 minutes

Scoring: Hand key

Cost: Complete Kit (100 rhythm answer sheets, 100 tonal answer sheets, 100 student profile cards, 4 class records sheets, manual, scoring masks, research monographs, CD) $100.00

Iowa Tests of Music Literacy (ITML)

| 1991 | GIA Publications, Inc. |

Edwin E. Gordon

Population: Grades 4 to 12

Purpose: Assesses strengths and weaknesses in music achievement

Description: Six-level multiple-choice paper-pencil test with two categories: Tonal Concepts (45 minutes) and Rhythm Concepts (45 minutes). Listening, reading, and writing reports are available. There are six levels divided by grade.

Format: Examiner required; suitable for group use; timed: 90 minutes

Scoring: Hand key

Cost: Complete Kit (manual, 50 rhythm answer sheets for each level, 50 tonal answer sheets for each level, 50 record folders, CD for Level 1, cassettes for other levels, scoring masks for each level, class record sheets, research monographs) $350.00

Keynotes-Music Evaluation Software Kit

| 2001 | Australian Council for Educational Research Limited |

Jenny Bryce, Margaret Wu

Population: Upper primary, junior secondary

Purpose: Provides information about a student's existing strengths and weaknesses in pitch, rhythm, and music notation

Description: A computer interactive measure in two parts. Part I is multiple choice with three domains: Pitch and Intervals Discrimination, Recognition of Rhythmic and Melodic Patterns, and Music Reading (traditional Western notation). Part II provides video clips of students demonstrating their musical instruments and discussing why they decided to learn particular instruments. The clips cover instruments commonly available in school instrumental programs.

Format: Examiner required; computer administered; individual administration; untimed: varies

Scoring: Computer scored

Cost: Contact publisher

Modern Photography Comprehension

| 1969 | Martin M. Bruce, PhD |

Martin M. Bruce

Population: Adolescents, adults

Purpose: Assesses knowledge of photography; used for vocational guidance and as a measure of classroom progress

Description: Paper-pencil 40-item multiple-choice test measuring photographic understanding. Individuals are rated on a scale of superior, high average, average, and low average. Materials include a manual and grading keys. Suitable for individuals with physical, hearing, or visual impairments.

Format: Self-administered; untimed: 20 to 25 minutes

Scoring: Hand key

Cost: Specimen Test $10.50

Music Aptitude Profile (MAP)

1995	GIA Publications, Inc.

Edwin E. Gordon

Population: Grades 5 to 12

Purpose: Measures a student's aptitude for music

Description: The MAP is a complete test with seven components: Tonal Imagery (melody and harmony), Rhythm Imagery (tempo and meter), and Musical Sensitivity (phrasing, balance, and style). Features remastered recordings and an updated manual.

Format: Examiner required; individual administration; untimed: 3 hours 30 minutes

Scoring: Hand key

Cost: Complete Kit (manual, 2 CDs, class record sheets, 50 answer sheets and profile cards, scoring masks, research monographs) $140.00

Primary Measures of Music Audiation (PMMA)

1986	GIA Publications, Inc.

Edwin E. Gordon

Population: Grades K to 3

Purpose: Measures the music potential of students

Description: Multiple-item paper–pencil test diagnosing the musical potential of students with average to low musical aptitudes. The test requires no language or music skills. Children listen to tonal and rhythm recordings, decide whether patterns sound the same or different, and circle an appropriate picture on the answer sheet. The manual contains information on converting raw scores to percentile ranks, interpreting results, and formal and informal music instruction. Also available in Greek and Korean.

Format: Examiner required; suitable for group use; untimed: 30 minutes

Scoring: Hand key

Cost: Complete Kit (manual, 100 each answer sheets and profile cards, CD, scoring masks, class record sheets, research monographs) $100.00

Foreign Language

AATG National German Examination for High School Students

Yearly	American Association of Teachers of German

Population: Grades 9 to 12

Purpose: Measures German language achievement of students, assesses the progress of students in their second, third, and fourth years of study; assesses the progress of individual students and entire classes

Description: Multiple-item paper–pencil test assessing German language competency. Test sections include listening comprehension, grammar, situational questions, and comprehension of connected passages. Questions are of graded difficulty. Tests are administered annually in school under the supervision of the school's testing personnel. The test company returns scores to test administrators. A total score, as well as scores for each section of the test, are provided. Practice tests are available. Knowledge of German is not necessary for the examiner.

Format: Examiner required; individual or group administration; timed: 1 hour

Scoring: All tests scored by Software Design, Inc.

Cost: $5.00 per student

Advanced Russian Listening Comprehension/Reading Proficiency Test (ARPT)

Date not provided	Educational Testing Service

Population: Adults, college students

Purpose: Measures the listening comprehension and reading proficiency of native English-speaking students' Russian; appropriate for use with students who have completed the equivalent of 3 to 5 years or more of college-level study

Description: Multiple-item orally administered paper–pencil test in two major sections: Listening Comprehension and Reading Proficiency. The Listening Comprehension section is administered via a tape recording that presents the student with a variety of material spoken in Russian. Questions about this material are printed in a test booklet, and students respond on machine-scorable answer sheets. In the Reading Proficiency section, students read passages printed in Russian and select responses that complete or answer the questions.

Format: Examiner required; suitable for group use; timed: 2 hours

Scoring: Computer scored

Cost: Test Booklet $15.00 each

Arabic Proficiency Test (APT)

1992	Center for Applied Linguistics

Raji M. Rammuny

Population: Adolescents, adults; college and above

Purpose: Measures reading and listening proficiency for placement, selection, and evaluation

Description: Paper–pencil 100-question multiple choice test comprised of Listening and Reading Comprehension. Forms A and B available. Materials used include an audiocassette player, test booklet, and test answer sheet. Suitable for individuals with physical impairments.

Format: Examiner required; individual or group administered; timed: 110 minutes

Scoring: Hand key; machine scored; test scoring service available

Cost: $14.00 to $25.00 per examinee depending on the number of examinees

Arabic Speaking Test (AST)

1992	Center for Applied Linguistics

Raji M. Rammuny

Population: Adolescents, adults; college and above

Purpose: Measures oral proficiency in Arabic

Description: Oral-response 15-item test measuring oral language proficiency in Arabic. Ratings are based on the speaking proficiency scale of the American Council on the Teaching of Foreign Languages (ACTFL). Available in Forms A and B. Playback and tape-recording equipment used. Test available on audiocassette. May be used with individuals with physical impairments.

Format: Examiner required; individually administered; timed: 55 minutes

Scoring: Examiner evaluated; test scoring service available

Cost: $115.00 per examinee for operational costs and certified rating service

Chinese Proficiency Test (CPT)

1983	Center for Applied Linguistics

Population: Adolescents, adults; high school and above

Purpose: Measures listening and reading proficiency used for placement, evaluation, and selection

Description: Multiple-choice 150-question paper–pencil test comprised of Listening Comprehension, Reading Comprehension, and Structure. Materials used include an audiocassette player, test booklet, and test answer sheet. Suitable for those with physical impairments.

Format: Examiner required; individual or group administered; timed: 120 minutes

Scoring: Machine scored

Cost: $14.00 to $25.00 per examinee depending on the number of examinees

Chinese Speaking Test (CST)

1994	Center for Applied Linguistics

Population: Adolescents, adults; college and above

Purpose: Assesses the ability to speak Chinese in contemporary, real-life language use contexts

Description: Oral-response 15-item test measuring oral language proficiency in Chinese. Via a question tape and test booklet, the examinees are asked six types of questions: Personal Conversation, Giving Directions, Detailed Descriptions, Picture Sequences, Topical Discourse, and Situations. The examinee's oral responses to the six item types are recorded and then sent to the publisher for scoring. Ratings are based on the speaking proficiency scale of the American Council on the Teaching of Foreign Language (ACTFL). Three forms (A, B, and C) are available. May be used with individuals with physical impairments.

Format: Examiner required; suitable for group use; timed: 45 minutes

Scoring: Publisher scored

Cost: $115.00 per examinee for operational costs and certified rating service

ESL Computerized Adaptive Placement Exam (ESL-CAPE)

2005   Brigham Young University

Jerry W. Larson, Kim L. Smith, Diane Strong-Krause

Population: Adults

Purpose: Measures achievement in English as a second language; used for placement into English language courses

Description: The ESL-CAPE is a computerized adaptive test of English grammar, reading, and listening comprehension. The items are multiple-choice response. The scores indicate in which ESL course the examinee should enroll. Requires a basic level of English reading ability.

Format: Self-administered; online administration; timed and untimed

Scoring: Online scoring

Cost: $995.00 for site license

French Computerized Adaptive Placement Exam (F-CAPE)

1996   Brigham Young University

Jerry W. Larson, Kim L. Smith, Don C. Jensen

Population: Adults

Purpose: Measures the student's achievement level in French; used for placement into first-, second-, and third-semester university or college classes

Description: Total number of items varies according to the ability of the examinee. Categories include Grammar, Vocabulary, and Reading. Full performance or simplified compiled reports are available. A PC computer test disk is used. Available on the Web.

Format: Self-administered; untimed

Scoring: Computer scored

Cost: $995.00 for site license

French Speaking Test (FST)

1995   Center for Applied Linguistics

Population: Adolescents, adults; high school and above

Purpose: Measures oral proficiency in French

Description: Oral-response 16-item test measuring oral language proficiency in French. Via playback and tape-recording equipment, the oral response is recorded. Forms A, B, and C are available. Ratings are based on the speaking

proficiency scale of the American Council on the Teaching of Foreign Languages (ACTFL). Available on audiocassette. Suitable for individuals with physical impairments.

Format: Examiner required; individual or group administered; timed: 45 minutes

Scoring: Examiner evaluated; test scoring service available

Cost: $115.00 per examinee for operational costs and certified rating service

German Computerized Adaptive Placement Exam (G-CAPE)

1996   Brigham Young University

Jerry W. Larson, Kim L. Smith, Randall L. Jones

Population: Adults

Purpose: Measures the student's achievement level in German; used for placement into first-, second-, and third-semester university or college classes

Description: Total number of items varies according to the ability of the examinee. Categories include grammar, vocabulary, and reading. Full performance or simplified compiled reports are available. A PC computer test disk is used. Available on the Web.

Format: Self-administered; untimed

Scoring: Computer scored

Cost: $995.00 for site license

German Speaking Test (GST)

1995   Center for Applied Linguistics

Population: Adolescents, adults; high school and above

Purpose: Measures oral proficiency in German

Description: Oral-response 16-item test measuring oral language proficiency in German. Via playback and tape-recording equipment, the examinee's oral response is recorded. The test is available on audiocassette. Forms A, B, and C are available. Suitable for individuals with physical impairments.

Format: Examiner required; individual or group administration; timed: 45 minutes

Scoring: Examiner evaluated; test scoring service available

Cost: $115.00 per examinee for operational costs and certified rating service

Hausa Speaking Test (HAST)

1989	Center for Applied Linguistics

Population: Adolescents, adults; high school and above

Purpose: Assesses the ability to speak Hausa in contemporary, real-life language-use contexts

Description: Oral-response 16-item test measuring oral language proficiency in Hausa. Via a question tape and test booklet, the examinee's oral responses of five item types are recorded and then sent to the publisher for scoring. Ratings are based on the speaking proficiency scale of the American Council on the Teaching of Foreign Languages (ACTFL). Forms A and B, and male and female forms are available. May be used with individuals with physical impairments.

Format: Examiner required; suitable for group use; timed: 45 minutes

Scoring: Publisher scored

Cost: $115.00 per examinee for operational costs and certified rating service

Hebrew Speaking Test (HEST)

1989	Center for Applied Linguistics

Population: Adolescents, adults; college and above

Purpose: Assesses the ability to speak Hebrew in contemporary, real-life language-use contexts

Description: Oral-response 16-item test measuring oral language proficiency in Hebrew. Via a question tape and test booklet, the examinees are asked six types of questions. Personal Conversation, Giving Directions, Detailed Descriptions, Picture Sequences, Topical Discourse, and Situations. The examinee's oral responses to the six item types are recorded and then sent to the publisher for scoring. Ratings are based on the speaking proficiency scale of the American Council on the Teaching of Foreign Language (ACTFL). U.S. and Israeli versions are available for males and females, Forms A and B. May be used with individuals with physical impairments.

Format: Examiner required; suitable for group use; timed: 45 minutes

Scoring: Publisher scored

Cost: $115.00 per examinee for operational costs and certified rating service

Indonesian Speaking Test (IST)

1989	Center for Applied Linguistics

Population: Adolescents, adults; college and above

Purpose: Assesses the ability to speak Indonesian in contemporary, real-life language-use contexts

Description: Oral-response 27-item test measuring oral language proficiency in Indonesian. Via a question tape and test booklet, the examinees are asked five types of questions: Personal Conversation, Giving Directions, Picture Sequences, Topical Discourse, and Situations. The examinee's oral responses to the five item types are recorded and then sent to the publisher for scoring. Ratings are based on the proficiency scale on the American Council on the Teaching of Foreign Language (ACTFL). Two forms (A, B) are available. May be used with individuals with physical impairments.

Format: Examiner required; suitable for group use; timed: 45 minutes

Scoring: Publisher scored

Cost: $60

Japanese Speaking Test (JST)

1992	Center for Applied Linguistics

Population: Adolescents, adults; college and above

Purpose: Measures oral proficiency in Japanese for evaluation, placement, and selection

Description: Oral response 15 item test using playback and tape-recording equipment to record examinee's oral response. Ratings are based on the speaking proficiency scale of the American Council on the Teaching of Foreign Languages (ACTFL). Suitable for individuals with physical impairments.

Format: Examiner required; suitable for group use; timed: 45 minutes

Scoring: Examiner evaluated; test scoring service available

Cost: $115.00 per examinee for operational costs and certified rating service

LOTE Tests

1998	Australian Council for Educational Research Limited

Population: Primary to Year 10

Purpose: Analyze competency in listening and reading comprehension after a minimum of 80 hours teaching

Description: These tests are based on Australian Language Level Guidelines. Languages available are Italian, German, French, Modern Greek, and Japanese. Responses are given using paper-pencil and orally. An audiocassette is used.

Format: Examiner required; individual or group administration; untimed: 60 minutes

Scoring: Examiner evaluated

Cost: Contact publisher

National Spanish Examinations (NSE)

New exam created each year	National Spanish Exam

Population: Grades 6 to 12

Purpose: Motivational competition to assess reading and listening comprehension skills in Spanish

Description: Spanish exams covering six levels developed each year by teachers who are members of the American Association of Teachers of Spanish and Portuguese (AATSP). A multiple-choice test that has both aural and written sections that measure the knowledge of Spanish after each year of study at the secondary school level. There are 30 listening comprehension questions, 30 reading comprehension questions, and an additional 10 reading comprehension questions for bilingual-native students. As of 1997, NSE became proficiency based. As of 2006, the exam is administered online only.

Format: Online administration; timed: 1 hour

Scoring: Online scoring

Cost: Contact publisher

Polish Proficiency Test (PPT)

1992	Center for Applied Linguistics

Population: Adolescents, adults; college and above

Purpose: Measures listening and reading proficiency; used for placement, evaluation, and selection

Description: Paper–pencil 135-question multiple-choice test comprised of listening comprehension, reading comprehension, structure, and total. Test available on audiocassette. Suitable for individuals with physical impairments.

Format: Examiner required; individual or group administration; timed: 150 minutes

Scoring: Machine scored; test scoring service available

Cost: $14.00 to $25.00 per examinee depending on the number of examinees

Portuguese Speaking Test (PST)

1988	Center for Applied Linguistics

Population: Adolescents, adults; college and above

Purpose: Assesses the ability to speak Portuguese in contemporary, real-life language-use contexts

Description: Oral-response 16-item test measuring oral language proficiency in Portuguese. Via a question tape and test booklet, the examinees are asked six types of questions: Personal Conversation, Giving Directions, Detailed Descriptions, Picture Sequences, Topical Discourse, and Situations. Their oral responses are recorded and then sent to the publisher for scoring. Ratings are based on the speaking proficiency scale of the American Council on the Teaching of Foreign Languages (ACTFL). Forms A, B, and C are available. Available also in Brazilian and Lusitanian.

Format: Examiner required; suitable for group use; timed: 45 minutes

Scoring: Scored by publisher

Cost: $115.00 per examinee for operational costs and certified rating service

Preliminary Chinese Proficiency Test (Pre-CPT)

1991	Center for Applied Linguistics

Population: Adolescents, adults; high school and above

Purpose: Measures reading and listening proficiency for placement, evaluation, and selection

Description: Paper–pencil 125-question multiple-choice test comprised of Listening Comprehension, Reading Comprehension, and Structure. Materials used include audiocassette player, test booklet, and test answer sheet. Suitable for individuals with physical impairments.

Format: Examiner required; suitable for group use; timed: 90 minutes

Scoring: Machine scored; test scoring service available

Cost: $14.00 to $25.00 per examinee depending on the number of examinees

Preliminary Japanese Speaking Test (Pre-JST)

1991	Center for Applied Linguistics

Population: Adolescents, adults; high school and above

Purpose: Measures oral proficiency in Japanese for placement, evaluation, and selection

Description: Oral-response 8-item test using playback tape and recording equipment to record oral response. Forms A and B available. Ratings are based on the speaking proficiency scale of the American Council on the Teaching of Foreign Languages (ACTFL). Suitable for individuals with physical impairments.

Format: Examiner required; suitable for group use; timed: 25 minutes

Scoring: Examiner evaluated; test scoring service available

Cost: $90.00 per examinee for operational costs and certified rating service

Russian Computerized Adaptive Placement Exam (R-CAPE)

1996	Brigham Young University

Jerry W. Larson, Kim L. Smith, Marshall R. Murray

Population: Adults

Purpose: Measures the student's achievement level in Russian; used for placement into first-, second-, and third-semester university or college classes

Description: Total number of items varies according to the ability of the examinee. Categories include grammar, vocabulary, and reading. Full performance or simplified compiled reports are available. A PC computer test disk is used.

Format: Self-administered; untimed

Scoring: Computer scored

Cost: $995.00 for site license

Spanish Assessment of Basic Education, Second Edition (SABE®/2)

1991	CTB/McGraw-Hill

Population: Grades 1 to 8

Purpose: Assesses the basic reading and mathematics skills of Spanish-speaking students with limited English proficiency

Description: Multiple-item paper–pencil multiple-choice test covering Word Attack, Vocabulary, Reading Comprehension, Mathematics Computation, Mathematics Concepts and Applications, Spelling, Language Mechanics, Language Expression, and Study Skills. The examiner must speak fluent Spanish.

Format: Examiner required; suitable for group use; timed: 180 to 255 minutes

Scoring: Hand key; machine scored; test scoring service available

Cost: Package of 35 Tests $87.00

Spanish Computerized Adaptive Placement Exam (S-CAPE)

1995	Brigham Young University

Jerry W. Larson, Kim L. Smith

Population: Adults

Purpose: Measures the student's achievement level in Spanish; used for placement into first-, second-, and third-semester university or college classes

Description: Total number of items varies according to the ability of the examinee. Categories include grammar, vocabulary, and reading. Full performance or simplified compiled reports are available. A PC computer test disk is used. Available on the Web.

Format: Self-administered, untimed

Scoring: Computer scored

Cost: $995.00 for site license

Spanish Proficiency Test (SPT)

1994	Educational Testing Service

Population: Adolescents, adults

Purpose: Assesses Spanish language proficiency of nonnative speakers of Spanish; used for assessment, placement, evaluation of programs, and selection of students for immersion programs

Description: Multiple-choice paper pencil oral response, essay, verbal test composed of four categories: Listening (25 multiple-choice questions), Reading (40 multiple-choice questions), Writing (3 essay or constructed response prompts), and Speaking (simulated dialog with 15 inquiries). Raw scores and American Council on the Teaching of Foreign Languages (ACTFL) proficiency ratings for Listening and Reading (scored by the Educational Testing Service); ACTFL proficiency ratings for Writing and Speaking (scored at institutions).

Format: Examiner required; suitable for group use; timed: 90 minutes total

Scoring: Scoring service available

Cost: 4 Skills $25.00; Listening and Reading $17.00; Writing and Speaking $15.00

Spanish Speaking Test (SST)

| 1995 | Center for Applied Linguistics |

Population: Adolescents, adults

Purpose: Measures oral proficiency in Spanish for placement, evaluation, and selection

Description: Oral-response 16-item test. Oral response of examinee is recorded using playback and tape-recording equipment. Forms A, B, and C available. Ratings are based on the speaking proficiency scale of the American Council on the Teaching of Foreign Languages (ACTFL).

Format: Examiner required; individual or group administered; timed: 45 minutes

Scoring: Examiner evaluated; test scoring service available

Cost: $115.00 per examinee for operational costs and certified rating service

Guidance

General

Armed Services Vocational Aptitude Battery (ASVAB)

| Updated annually | ASVAB Career Exploration |

Department of Defense

Population: Grades 10 and above

Purpose: Evaluates high school students' vocational interests and aptitudes; used for counseling and by the military services to identify eligible graduates for possible recruitment

Description: Paper–pencil 334-item test of aptitudes in various vocational and technical fields. Factors measured include electronics, mechanical comprehension, general science, automotive and shop information, numerical operations, coding speed, word knowledge, arithmetic, reasoning, paragraph comprehension, and mathematics knowledge. Indicates ability in the following areas: Verbal; Math; Academic; Mechanical and Crafts; Business and Clerical; Electronics and Electrical; and Health, Social, and Technologies. A military service recruiter will assist each school in administering the test, and the Defense Manpower Data Center provides the examiner. Individual test results are delivered to school counselors, and copies of the scores are given to the recruiting services.

Format: Examiner required; suitable for group use; timed: 3 hours

Scoring: Computer scored

Cost: No charge to schools for administration, materials, and scoring

Aviator 3

| 2002 | Valpar International Corporation |

Population: Ages 15 years and older

Purpose: Assesses aptitudes and vocational interests

Description: Computerized battery of screening tests. Matches skills/interests with two occupational databases of about 1,000 occupations each. Criterion-referenced to scholastic curricula and Department of Labor's job analysis system. Requires a fifth-grade reading level. Also available in Spanish. Requires a Windows-based computer. Software may be automatically updated.

Format: Examiner required; may be group administered; timed and untimed

Scoring: Computer scored

Cost: $2,500.00

Barriers to Employment Success Inventory–Second Edition (BESI)

| 2002 | JIST Publishing |

John J. Liptak

Population: Adolescents, adults

Purpose: Identifies key barriers that keep people from getting and keeping a job

Description: Examinees rate 50 simple statements in five categories: Personal/Financial, Emotional/Physical, Career Decision Making/ Planning, Job Seeking Knowledge, and Education and Training. Identifies major barriers to employment based on results and then suggests ways to overcome those barriers. Includes an action plan. Ideal for job retention programs.

Format: Self-administered; untimed: 20 minutes

Scoring: Self-scored

Cost: 25 Forms and User's Guide $39.95

Becker Work Adjustment Profile– Second Edition (BWAP-2)

2005	Elbern Publications

Ralph L. Becker

Population: Ages 12 to years to adult

Purpose: Matches work competency with a vocational program level and level of supports

Description: Likert-type questionnaire with 63 items completed by someone familiar with the individual's work. A single edition is available for males and females. Vocational adjustment/competency and work supports are evaluated in four domains: Work Habits/Attitudes (10 items), Interpersonal Relations (12 items), Cognitive Skills (19 items), and Work Performance Skills (22 items). A global score is also obtained across the domains. The raw scores are converted to percentiles and *t*-scores using an appropriate norm for individuals with mental retardation, physical disabilities, economic deprivation, emotional disturbance, or learning disability. The Vocational Competency Profile provides a graphic picture of the person's vocational competency for placement in one of five program tracks: Day Care, Work Activity, Sheltered (High, Low), Transitional, and Community Competitive. Individuals are evaluated in each program tract for the amount of Work Supports Needed as Limited, Low, Moderate, High, and Extensive. A complete report-analysis is given on different individuals with disabilities.

Format: Examiner required; individual administration; untimed: 10 to 20 minutes

Scoring: Examiner evaluated

Cost: Value Kit (manual, 25 booklets) $70.75

Becker Work Assessment System (BWAS)

2005	Elbern Publications

Ralph Leonard Becker

Population: Ages 12 to 69 years

Purpose: Identifies vocational strengths and needs of people with diverse disabilities

Description: *Combines the Reading-Free Vocational Interest Inventory–Second Edition and the Becker Work Adjustment Profile–Second Edition to*

evaluate the vocational interest and work competence of individuals with disabilities. Allows the examiner to assess the amount of work supports an individual needs to succeed at a job and suggests the support activities needed to lessen the gap between an individual's level of competence and the demands of the job.

Format: Examiner required; suitable for group use; untimed: 20 minutes or less

Scoring: Hand key

Cost: Assessment System (R-FVII:2 and BWAP-2, Occupational Title Lists) $179.75

BRIGANCE® Diagnostic Employability Skills Inventory

1995	Curriculum Associates®, Inc.

Albert H. Brigance

Population: High school students, adults

Purpose: Assesses the basic skills and employability skills in job-seeking and employment contexts

Description: The inventory provides specific feedback on curriculum needs, allowing instructors to plan, monitor, and asses learning growth. A total of 124 in-depth skill sequences are covered in eight life-skill sections: Reading Grade Placement, Rating Scales, Career Awareness and Self-Understanding, Job-Seeking Skills and Knowledge, Reading Skills, Speaking and Listening, Preemployment Writing, and Math Skills and Concepts. The inventory correlates with the *Comprehensive Adult Student Assessment System* (CASAS) and SCANS Foundation Skills and meets the requirements of the Perkins Act.

Format: Examiner required; suitable for group use, untimed: 12 minutes

Scoring: Examiner evaluated

Cost: Inventory $89.95; 10 Record Books $24.95

California Critical Thinking Disposition Inventory (CCTDI)

1992	Insight Assessments

Peter A. Facione, Noreen C. Facione

Population: Grades 7 to 12, adults

Purpose: Measures disposition toward critical thinking; used for evaluation of groups and programs, personnel development, and management training

Description: Electronic or paper–pencil 75-item Likert-style inventory/survey. Five-page test booklet includes specialized answer sheet. Categories include Truth-Seeking, Inquisitiveness, Analyticity, Systematically, Open-Mindedness, Cognitive Maturity, and Reasoning Confidence. Available also in Spanish, French, Hebrew, Chinese, Thai, Korean, Finnish, Arabic, Portuguese, and Japanese.

Format: Self-administered; untimed: 20 minutes

Scoring: Machine or electronic scored; scoring service available

Cost: Specimen Kit (manual, 1 protocol, 1 CapScore™ answer form) $45.00

Career Assessment Inventory™– Enhanced Version (CAI-E)

1986	Pearson Assessments

Charles B. Johansson

Population: Grades 9 and above

Purpose: Assesses the career interests of students and individuals reentering the job market or considering a career change; used for making decisions about career interests, screening job applicants, and providing career and vocational assistance

Description: Paper–pencil 370-item test in which items are answered on a 5-point Likert-type scale ranging from *like very much* to *dislike very much*. Items are divided into three major categories: Activities, School Subjects, and Occupations. The test, which focuses on careers requiring up to and including 4 years of college, covers 111 occupations. Six General Occupational Theme scores (Holland's RIASEC model: Realistic, Investigative, Artistic, Social, Enterprising, and Conventional) and 25 Basic Interest scale scores that divide the six general scores into specific areas are provided. A narrative report, profile report, and optional group reports are available. Items are written at an eighth-grade reading level. This is a revision of the *Career Assessment Inventory–The Vocational Version,* which focuses on skilled trade occupations and careers requiring little or no postsecondary education. The inventory may be computer scored in one of three ways: via mail-in services, Arion II teleprocessing, or MICROTESTQ Assessment system.

Format: Self-administered; untimed: 40 minutes

Scoring: Scoring service

Cost: Preview Package with Interpretive Report $55.00

Career Beliefs Inventory (CBI)

1991	CPP, Inc.

John D. Krumboltz

Population: Ages 13 years and older

Purpose: Assesses individuals' beliefs and assumptions about themselves and the world of work

Description: Paper–pencil 96-item multiple-choice test intended for career counseling for use in high school, college, or during midlife career transitions. The profile yields 25 scales organized into five categories: My Current Career Situation, What Seems Necessary for My Happiness, Factors That Influence My Decisions, Changes I Am Willing to Make, and Effort I Am Willing to Initiate. Response choices range from *strongly agree* to *strongly disagree.* An eighth-grade reading level is required. Also available in French-Canadian. A client workbook is also available.

Format: Self-administered; untimed: 20 to 30 minutes

Scoring: Self-scored; scoring service

Cost: Preview Kit (item booklet, prepaid answer sheet, guide, manual) $81.50

Career Decision Scale™ (CDS™)

1987	Psychological Assessment Resources, Inc.

Samuel H. Osipow

Population: Grades 9 to college

Purpose: Identifies barriers preventing an individual from making career decisions; used as a basis for career counseling, to monitor the effectiveness of career counseling programs, and for research on career indecisiveness

Description: Paper–pencil 19-item inventory assessing a limited number of circumstances that cause problems in reaching and implementing educational and career decisions. Items 1 and 2 measure degree of certainty (Certainty scale). Items 3 to 18 measure career indecision (Indecision scale). Item 19 is open-ended. Individuals rate each item on a 4-point scale from 1 (*not like me*) to 4 (*like me*) to indicate the extent to which each item describes their personal situations. Scores are reported as percentiles. The manual includes data regarding validity and reliability and norms for various age and grade levels.

Format: Self-administered; untimed: 10 to 15 minutes

Scoring: Examiner evaluated

Cost: Introductory Kit (manual, 50 test booklets) $70.00

Career Planning Survey

1997	ACT, Inc.

Population: Grades 8 to 10

Purpose: Measures and profiles students' work-relevant interests and abilities; used in guidance and vocational counseling

Description: A comprehensive guidance-oriented career (educational and vocational) assessment system designed to help students in Grades 8 to 10 identify and explore personally relevant occupations and high school courses. The formal assessment components consist of an interest inventory (90 items), an inventory of ability self-estimates (15 items), and two optional academic ability tests: Reading Skills (32 items) and Numerical Skills (24 items). In addition, the Career Planning Guide workbook provides students with the opportunity to complete checklists examining their work-relevant experiences and the job characteristics they want in a work setting. Testing can be scheduled as one, two, or more sessions. The interest and ability scales were built around a two-dimensional model: people–things and data–ideas.

Format: Self-administered; timed: 45 minutes for each

Scoring: Scoring service

Cost: $3.80 per Assessment Set Option A (with Ability Measures); $3.25 per Assessment Set Option B (without Ability Measures) (answer sheet, student guidebook, prepaid scoring, 2 copies of the student report)

Career Scope–Version 7.2

2006	Vocational Research Institute

Population: Adolescents, adults (middle school and above)

Purpose: Measures career interest and aptitudes

Description: Computer administered with Interest Inventory having 145 items that measure 12 interest areas used by the U.S. Department of Labor. The Aptitude section has seven subtests with 203 items: Object Identification (30 items), Abstract Shape Matching (30 items), Clerical Matching (30 items), Pattern Visualization (30 items), Computation (30 items), Numerical Reasoning (23 items), and Word Meanings (30 items). Score reports include Assessment Profile, Counselor Report, and Summary Report.

Format: Self-administered; Interest: untimed, Aptitude: timed

Scoring: Computer scored

Cost: Contact publisher

Child Occupational Self Assessment, Version 2.1 (COSA)

2003	Model of Human Occupation Clearinghouse

Jessica Keller, Ana Kafkes, Semonti Basu, Jeanne Federico, Gary Kielhofner

Population: Ages 8 to 13 years

Purpose: Measures occupational competence in everyday activities and value for everyday activities

Description: A client-directed assessment tool and an outcome measure designed to capture individuals' perception of the importance of everyday activities. The COSA consists of a series of statements pertaining to everyday occupational participation and includes tasks related to school, home, and the community. Its self-rating design allows the client to document his or her understanding of occupational competence and values using familiar visual symbols and simple language. There are two versions: a card sort version and a checklist form version. The manual provides instructions on administration, interpretation, and modifications to ensure access for clients of all abilities. The manual also includes three case illustrations.

Format: Self-report; untimed: 35 to 45 minutes

Scoring: Examiner evaluated

Cost: Manual $35.00

Computerized Assessment (COMPASS)

1994	Valpar International Corporation

Population: Ages 15 years and older

Purpose: Used in occupational exploration and career counseling to screen for work-related factors from the Department of Labor's *Dictionary of Occupational Titles*

Description: Multiple-choice computer-administered test with 12 computer-based subtests plus three short work samples, and a paper–pencil survey. The three work samples are Alignment and Driving, Machine Tending, and Wiring. The 12 subtests are Placing, Color Discrimination, Reading, Size Discrimination, Shape Discrimination, Short-Term Visual Memory, Spelling, Vocabulary, Mathematics, Language Development (Editing), Problem Solving, and Eye–Hand–Foot Coordination. The paper–pencil survey is Guide to Occupational Exploration (GOE). Subtest level scores and DOT-type factors are yielded. A computer, control panel, foot pedal, and three out-of-computer work samples are used. A fifth-grade reading level is required. Designed to quickly establish that evaluees have various degrees of work-related and academic skills.

Format: Examiner required; individual administration; timed and untimed

Scoring: Computer scored

Cost: Contact publisher

Differential Aptitude Tests™– Fifth Edition (DAT™)

| 1990 | Harcourt Assessment, Inc. |

G. K. Bennett, H. G. Seashore, A. G. Wesman

Population: Grades 7 to 12, adults

Purpose: Assesses aptitude and interest; used for educational and vocational guidance in junior and senior high schools

Description: Multiple-item paper–pencil test of eight abilities: Verbal Reasoning, Numerical Ability, Abstract Reasoning, Clerical Speed and Accuracy, Mechanical Reasoning, Space Relations, Spelling, and Language Usage. A ninth score is obtained by summing the Verbal Reasoning and the Numerical Ability scores. The Career Planning Questionnaire is optional. Two levels: Level 1 for Grades 8 and 9; Level 2 for Grades 10 to 12.

Format: Examiner required; suitable for group use; timed: complete battery, 2.5 hours; partial battery, 1.5 hours

Scoring: Hand key; may be machine scored; scoring service available

Cost: Examination Kit with Career Interest Inventory $42.00

Educational Development Series

| 1999 | Scholastic Testing Service, Inc. |

O. F. Anderhalter, Jan Perney, Sandra Carlson, Peter Fisher, Sharon Weiner, Stephen Bloom, Charles Hamburg, Carol F. Larson

Population: Grades K to 12

Purpose: Assesses academic achievement, aptitude, and career interests

Description: The multiple-choice battery is comprised of the following subtests: Reading (R), Language Arts (LA), Mathematics (M), Science (S), Social Studies (SS), Reference Skills (RS), as well as Quantitative (Q) and Verbal Cognitive (VC) skills subtests. Future Plans (FP) and School Interests (SI) sections are also included in the battery. These 10 areas can be administered in one of four ways: Complete Battery (all subtests), Core Achievement Battery (R, LA, M, S, SS, RS), Cognitive and Basic Skills Battery (R, LA, M, S, SS, Q, VC), and Basic Skills Battery (FP, SI, R, LA, M). Various reports are provided.

Format: Examiner required; suitable for group use; timed: 2½ to 5½ hours

Scoring: Machine scored; hand key; computer scored; test scoring service available

Cost: Starter Set (Levels 13G to 16G/H) $61.50; Levels 17G/H to 18G/H $70.65

Employability Competency System (ECS)

| 1994 | CASAS |

Population: Adults, adolescents; native and nonnative speakers of English

Purpose: Helps programs to identify the skills needed by adults and youth in today's workforce and to place them into appropriate education and employment training programs and jobs; helps agencies to place learners into appropriate instructional levels

Description: Multiple-choice survey achievement tests assess reading comprehension and basic math skills at four levels, and listening comprehension tests assess English as a second language (ESL) at three levels. Each test has two forms, for pre-/posttesting. Includes an appraisal for placement purposes, certification tests, pre-employment and work maturity checklists, critical-thinking assessment, and occupation specific tests. Tests are competency based. Content covers a range of employment-related contexts. CASAS scaled scores identify general skill level and enable comparison of performance across CASAS tests. Scannable answer sheets are available.

Format: Examiner required; group administered; untimed

Scoring: Self- or computer scored

Cost: 25 Reusable Tests $70.00; 25 Listening Tests with Audiocassette $50.00; Manual $15.00

Harrington-O'Shea Career Decision-Making System–Revised (CDM-R)

| 1993 | AGS Publishing/Pearson Assessments |

Thomas F. Harrington, Arthur J. O'Shea

Population: Grade 7 to adult

Purpose: Involves the client with self-understanding of values and abilities needed for successful career choices and development

Description: The CDM-R is an interest inventory with a sound theoretical basis that provides valid and reliable assessment of career interests. It also surveys values, training plans, and abilities. It incorporates career information and presents a model for career decision making. The CDM-R is based on the Holland theory of vocational development—that is, that most people can be categorized by a single type or a combination of personality types. The CDM-R uses these six types: Crafts, Scientific, The Arts, Social, Business, and Office Operations. These six areas provide raw scores that are used to define a client's preferred work environment. Spanish and English versions are available.

Format: Examiner required; individual or group administration; untimed: Level 1, 20 minutes; Level 2, 30 to 40 minutes

Scoring: Level 1 is hand scored; Level 2 is hand or machine scored

Cost: Classroom Set (25 workbooks, teacher's guide, video) $349.95

Hilson Personnel Profile Success Quotient–Adolescent Version (HPPA)

1991	Hilson Research, Inc.

Robin E. Inwald

Population: Ages 9 to 19 years

Purpose: Measures adjustment

Description: A total of 50 true-false items measure Social Ability, Achievement History, and Goal Orientation. An adaptation of the *Hilson Personnel Profile/Success Quotient* (HPP/SQ) for students. This is the adolescent version of the HPP/SQ for measuring emotional IQ and social skills.

Format: Self-administered; untimed: 10 minutes

Scoring: Computer scored; scoring service available

Cost: $16.00 to $20.00 depending on scoring method

Interpersonal Intelligence Inventory (III)

2005	Scholastic Testing Service, Inc.

Paris S. Strom, Robert D. Strom

Population: Grade 6 to adult

Purpose: Measures teamwork skills

Description: The III focuses on 25 clustered items into five categories: Attends to Teamwork, Seeks and Shares Information, Communicates with Teammates, Thinks Critically and Creatively, and Gets Along with Others. The inventory presents formative and summative feedback, monitors progress, and recognizes achievement of an individual in a team setting.

Format: Rating scale; untimed

Scoring: Examiner evaluated

Cost: Starter Set (manual, 10 definitions booklets, 10 profile forms, 20 scoring forms, 20 skills forms) $38.00

Job Readiness Skills Pre/Post Assessment

2000	Education Associates, Inc.

Shelley M. Mauer

Population: Ages 14 years and older

Purpose: Measures job readiness and employ ability skills for workforce counseling, school-to-work, and career counseling

Description: Ten multiple-choice questions in each of the following sections: Career Goals, Finding Job Opportunities, Job Applications, Interviewing, Positive Attitudes, Good Appearance, Written Communication, Communication, and Resumes. A self-prescribed plan of study based on the score is provided.

Format: Examiner required; individually administered; untimed

Scoring: Hand key

Cost: 25 Pretests or Posttests $52.00

Job Search Attitude Inventory– Third Edition (JSAI)

2006	JIST Publishing

John J. Liptak

Population: High school students to adults

Purpose: Measures self-motivation of job seekers and fosters self-directed attitudes

Description: Test takers agree or disagree with 32 statements on a 4-point scale. They then self-score the instrument and place their scores on a graphic profile that shows four measures: Luck vs. Planning, Involved vs. Uninvolved, Self-Directed vs. Other-Directed, Active vs. Passive. Higher scores indicate the belief that persons can find their own jobs. A worksheet at the end offers suggestions and space to plan how best to improve one's job search attitude. Can be used as a pre- and posttest.

Format: Self-administered; untimed: 15 minutes

Scoring: Self-scoring

Cost: Administrator's Guide and 25 Forms $42.95

Job Search Knowledge Scale (JSKS)

2005	JIST Publishing

John J. Liptak

Population: High school students to adults

Purpose: Measures job search knowledge

Description: Provides an easy-to-use-and-interpret way to measure knowledge in five areas: Identifying Job Leads, Direct Application to Employers, Resumes and Cover Letters, Employment Interviews, and Follow Up. Includes 60 true–false statements. Scores lead to discovering topics on which they need more information or instruction in order to be more effective in a job search. Test takers also get some guidance on the job search methods that work best so they can find jobs more quickly. Space is included for a Job Search Journal and for Job Search Goals. Can be used for pretest and posttest for educators, workforce development professionals, and counselors. Online version available.

Format: Self-administered; untimed: 20 minutes

Scoring: Self-scored

Cost: 25 Forms and Administration Manual $34.95

Job Survival and Success Scale (JSSS)

2005	JIST Publishing

John J. Liptak

Population: High school students to adults

Purpose: Measures "softskills" necessary for surviving at work; used for career counseling, job retention, and job searching

Description: Helps trainers and programs to identify an individual's strong and weak skills. Composed of 60 statements, the JSSS provides a profile of the user in five categories: Dependability, Responsibility, Human Relations, Ethical Behavior, and Getting Ahead. Also includes space for developing a success plan. Can be used as a pre- and posttest.

Format: Self-administered; appropriate for groups; untimed: 15 to 20 minutes

Scoring: Self-scored

Cost: 25 Forms and Administration Manual $37.95

Jobs Observation and Behavior Scales (JOBS)

2000	Stoelting Company

Howard Rosenberg, Michael P. Brady

Population: Ages 15 years to adult

Purpose: Measures job performance for entry-level workers and high school students' transition to work

Description: This employee performance evaluation is for use by educators, job coaches, rehabilitation professionals, and employers involved in the evaluation, training, and placement of secondary students or adults, with and without disabilities, into the competitive workforce. The 30 items that make up the three subscales are designed to represent critical patterns of performance in work-required daily living skills, work-required behavior, and work-required job duties.

Format: Examiner required; individual administration; untimed: 5 to 8 minutes

Scoring: Examiner evaluated

Cost: Complete Kit (manual, 25 record forms) $75.00

Life Style Questionnaire (LSQ)

Date not provided	Hogrefe Limited

Jim Barrett

Population: Adolescents

Purpose: Provides insight regarding interest, attitudes, and behaviors of people about to begin work or already working

Description: The LSQ is a 132-item paper–pencil test for self-assessment of vocational interests and attitudes. Items are statements about work activities. Scores are provided on 13 scales: 6 dealing with general motivation, 5 examining consistency of outlook with interest, and 2 estimating the degree of certainty about questionnaire responses. The test booklet contains instructions on how to respond to test items.

Format: Examiner required; suitable for group use; untimed

Scoring: Test scoring service available

Cost: Contact publisher

Light's Retention Scale–2006 Edition (LRS)

| 2006 | Academic Therapy Publications |

H. Wayne Light

Population: Ages 6 to 18 years

Purpose: Provides opportunities for dialogue between parents and educators about grade retention

Description: Designed to be used in a parent conference, the LRS evaluates 20 areas of interest. Each factor is scored to reflect the impact on the question of retention or not. This revised edition includes a consideration of whether a student has preschool experience, up-to-date review of the current findings on both sides of the issue, a changed score structure, revised item descriptions, and new cutoff scores. The parent guides are available in Spanish. An optional school administrator's kit contains worksheets, parent consent forms, and appeal forms that may be useful in documenting the decision process.

Format: Rating scale; untimed

Scoring: Examiner evaluated

Cost: Test Kit (manual, 50 recording forms, 50 English parent guides, in vinyl folder) $95.00; 50 Spanish Parent Guides $25.00; School Administrator's Kit $20.00

Magellan 6

| 1997 | Valpar International Corporation |

Population: Ages 14 years and older

Purpose: Informally assesses aptitudes and vocational interests; used for occupational exploration and guidance

Description: Computerized battery of aptitude tests with vocational interest survey. Match students' scores to occupations in database of 1,000+ occupations. Suggests courses of study to achieve skills required by selected occupations. Designed for repeated use through high school years. Requires a fifth-grade reading level.

Format: Self-administered; untimed

Scoring: Computer scored

Cost: Stand-Alone $1,295.00

Missouri Comprehensive Student Needs Survey

| 1989 | Assessment Resource Center |

Population: Grades 4 to 12

Purpose: Identifies needs to develop guidance programs

Description: Students are asked to respond to needs grouped into areas of concern. Some of the categories are Exploring and Planning Careers, Understanding and Accepting Self, Making Decisions, Finding Jobs, and Planning for School. Three levels of the instrument are available: Elementary (Grades 4 to 6), Middle (Grades 6 to 9), and Senior (Grades 9 to 12). Adult/Teacher versions are available for the same groups.

Format: Rating scale; untimed

Scoring: Machine-scored; test scoring service available

Cost: Survey Materials $.61 (student), $.40 (adult/teacher); Scoring Services $.87 (student), $.61 (adult/teacher)

Missouri Guidance Competency Evaluation Surveys (MGCES)

| 1992 | Assessment Resource Center |

Population: Grades 6 to 12

Purpose: Assesses the impact of guidance curriculum units on student attainment of guidance competencies

Description: The areas targeted are career planning and exploration, knowledge of self and others, and educational and vocational development. The surveys have two forms for middle school (Grades 6 to 9) and high school (Grades 9 to 12) students. The MGCES provides school counselors and teachers with measures of students' self-reported confidence in their achievement of guidance curriculum competencies. The items are rated on a 7-point scale. This survey must be administered in a pre-/post situation to yield any useful data. Please order enough materials to have two per student.

Format: Rating scale; untimed

Scoring: Machine-scored; test scoring service available

Cost: Package (50 surveys, identification sheets, manual) $36.44; Scoring Service $.50 each

Mobile Vocational Evaluation (MVE)

| 1983 | Hester Evaluation Systems, Inc. |

Edward J. Hester

Population: Ages 14 and older

Purpose: Measures vocational ability factors and interests for vocational guidance

Description: Vocational guidance testing system measures 19 vocational ability factors and 12 interest areas resulting in a computer-generated report, which considers physical limitations, working condition restrictions, and people relationships, and lists feasible jobs ranked according to the individual's interests. A comprehensive system based on a normative group of 1,500 individuals, the MVE uses a combination of paper–pencil tests along with performance tests. Of the total testing time, 85% is group administered. The job database used in the system contains over 2,000 representative jobs from the current Department of Labor *Dictionary of Occupational Titles.*

Format: Examiner required; individual and group administration; timed and untimed

Scoring: Scoring software included

Cost: Complete System (manual, software, forms, performance tasks, carrying case) $5,300.00

Model of Human Occupation Screening Tool, Version 2.0 (MOHOST)

2005	Model of Human Occupation Clearinghouse

Sue Parkinson, Kirsty Forsyth, Gary Kielhofner

Population: Adolescents, adults, and older adults

Purpose: Measures how personal and environmental factors affect occupational participation

Description: Allows the therapist to gain an overview of the client's occupational functioning. Developed in Britain by practicing occupational therapists, the instrument seeks to objectify the information a therapist gathers while determining the need for occupational therapy services. A variety of data-collection methods (observation, chart review, or interviews) and a variety of intervention settings may be used. The MOHOST uses language that enables therapists to communicate findings clearly with clients, their families, and other professionals. Progress toward occupational therapy intervention goals may be documented.

Format: Rating scale, observation, interview; untimed: 10 to 40 minutes

Scoring: Examiner evaluated

Cost: Manual $38.50

My System of Career Influences (MSCI)

2005	Australian Council for Educational Research Limited

Mary McMahon, Wendy Patton, Mark Watson

Population: Ages 14 to 18 years

Purpose: Identifies students' systems of career influences to help decision making about subjects, further evaluation, training, and employment

Description: A reflection activity that provides qualitative information to facilitate more holistic career decisions. Derived from the Systems Theory Framework of career development, the MSCI provides an opportunity to visually represent the constellation of influences relevant to an individual's own career story at any given point in time. It is ideally suited as a resource for classroom-based education programs. It consists of an 11-page booklet that is completed by the student. The Facilitator's Guide contains decision case studies and suggested learning activities that are particularly useful for practitioners working in school contexts to introduce career concepts and terms. The booklet is designed so that it can be administered on two separate occasions.

Format: Examiner required; group administration; untimed: 30 to 40 minutes

Scoring: Examiner evaluated

Cost: Specimen Set $36.95

My Vocational Situation

1980	CPP, Inc.

John L. Holland

Population: Adults

Purpose: Assesses the problems that may be troubling an individual seeking help with career decisions; used in career counseling and guidance

Description: Two-page multiple-item paper–pencil questionnaire determining which of three difficulties may be troubling an individual in need of career counseling: lack of vocational identity, lack of information or training, or environmental or personal barriers. The questionnaire is completed by the individual just prior to the counseling interview and may be tabulated by the counselor at a glance. Responses may offer clues for the interview itself and treatments relevant to each individual's need. The manual discusses development of the diagnostic scheme and reports statistical properties of the three variables.

Format: Self-administered; untimed: 5 to 10 minutes

Scoring: Examiner evaluated

Cost: 25 Booklets $20.00; Manual $7.50

Occupational Circumstances Assessment Interview and Rating Scale, Version 4.0 (OCAIRS)

2005	Model of Human Occupation Clearinghouse

Kirsty Forsyth, Shilpa Deshpande,
Gary Kielhofner, Chris Henriksson,
Lena Haglund, Linda Olson,
Sarah Skinner, Supriya Kulkarni

Population: Adolescents, adults, and older adults

Purpose: Measures occupational participation

Description: The occupational therapist administers a semistructured interview and then uses a rating scale to determine how the client's role, sense of personal causation, skills, and ability to set goals impacts his or her occupational participation. This newest version has three interview formats for use in specific rehabilitation contexts: mental health, forensic mental health, and physical disabilities. The instrument can be used with a wide range of clients and would be appropriate for any adolescent or adult client who has the cognitive and emotional ability to participate in an interview. The manual includes a variety of reporting formats, semistructured interview, extensive rating criteria for each item, and three in-depth case illustrations.

Format: Interview; untimed: 40 to 60 minutes

Scoring: Examiner evaluated

Cost: Manual $38.50

Occupational Performance History Interview II, Version 2.1 (OPHI-II)

2004	Model of Human Occupation Clearinghouse

Gary Kielhofner, Trudy Mallinson,
Carrie Crawford, Meika Nowak, Matt Rigby,
Alexis Henry, Deborah Walens

Population: Adolescents, adults, and older adults

Purpose: Measures occupational adaptation via occupational competence, identity, and environment, and generates occupational history with a narrative slope

Description: A semistructured interview in the areas of work, leisure, and daily life activities. Enhances the therapeutic relationship by facilitating rapport with the client. Flexible interview formats are designed for both novice and experienced interviewers. Version 2.1 includes paper key forms that can be used to obtain numerical client scores from the scale ratings. The OPHI-II is designed for use with an occupational therapy client who is capable of responding to a life history interview. A series of recommended questions and flowcharts for guiding the interview are provided to help the therapist learn how to conduct the interview. The manual also includes a variety of reporting formats and extensive rating criteria for each item.

Format: Interview; untimed: 40 to 60 minutes

Scoring: Examiner evaluated

Cost: $38.50

O*NET Career Values Inventory

2002	JIST Publishing

Population: Grade 8 to adult

Purpose: Used in career exploration

Description: Relates work values to jobs described in the Department of Labor's O*NET database. Uses a card sort mechanism to discover the examinee's most important work values.

Format: Self-administered; untimed: 20 to 30 minutes

Scoring: Self-scored

Cost: Administrator's Guide and 25 Forms $29.95

Perceptions Expectation, Emotions, and Knowledge about College (PEEK)

1995	H & H Publishing Company, Inc.

Claire E. Weinstein, David R. Palmer

Population: High school seniors and college freshmen

Purpose: Assesses thoughts, beliefs, and expectations about personal, social, and academic changes that may occur in a college setting; used for counseling, course development, and college success courses

Description: Three-scale 30-item multiple-choice computer-administered test measuring Academic Experiences (10 items), Personal Experiences (10 items), and Social Experiences (10 items). A Distribution Report showing responses, percents, median, mode, mean, and standard deviation; a Student Profile; and a Summary Report are yielded.

Format: Self-administered; untimed: 20 to 30 minutes

Scoring: Machine scored; test scoring service available; computer version available

Cost: Up to 500 Forms $1.25 each; Computer Version Up to 99 Administrations $2.25 each

Program for Assessing Youth Employment Skills (PAYES)

Date not provided	Educational Testing Service

Population: Adolescents

Purpose: Measures the attitudes, knowledge, and interests of students preparing for entry-level employment; used by program directors, counselors, and teachers working with dropouts and disadvantaged youth in government training programs and skill centers

Description: Three orally administered paper–pencil tests assessing attitudes, knowledge, and interests related to entry-level employment. Test Booklet I measures attitudes toward job-holding skills (supervisor's requests, appropriate dress, and punctuality), attitudes toward supervision by authority figures, and self-confidence in social and employment situations. Measurements are made by assessing responses to multiple-choice questions based on statements, real-life situations, and scenes. Test Booklet II provides cognitive measures, including job knowledge, job seeking skills, and practical job-related reasoning in situations that require following directions. Test Booklet III measures seven vocational interest clusters. Respondents indicate their degree of interest in specific job tasks that are described verbally and pictured. Students mark answers directly in test booklets.

Format: Examiner required; suitable for group use; untimed

Scoring: Examiner evaluated

Cost: Complete Set (20 each of Test Booklets I, II, and III; score sheets) $90.00; User's Guide $4.50; Administrators' Manual $5.50

PSB Health Occupations Aptitude Examination

1995	Psychological Services Bureau, Inc.

Population: Adults; health occupations students

Purpose: Measures abilities, skills, knowledge,

and attitudes important to successful performance in various health-care occupations; used as an admission test for schools and programs in health occupations

Description: Multiple-item paper–pencil or electronic battery of five tests assessing areas important to performance in health-care occupations: academic aptitude, spelling, reading comprehension, the natural sciences, and vocational adjustment. The test predicts an individual's readiness for specialized instruction in numerous health-care positions, including medical record technician, dental assistant, psychiatric aide, histologic technician, nursing assistant, respiratory therapy technician, and radiologic technologist.

Format: Examiner required; suitable for group use; timed: 2 hours 15 minutes

Scoring: Machine and electronically scored

Cost: Contact publisher

Responsibility and Independence Scale for Adolescents (RISA)

1990	Riverside Publishing Company

John Salvia, John T. Neisworth, Mary W. Schmidt

Population: Ages 12 to 19 years

Purpose: Measures adolescents' adaptive behavior

Description: Nationally standardized instrument specifically designed to measure adolescents' behavior in terms of responsibility and independence. Whereas most measures of adaptive behavior target low-level skills, the RISA assesses higher level behaviors. Subscales include Domestic Skills, Money Management, Citizenship, Personal Planning, Transportation Skills, Career Development, Self-Management, Social Maturity, and Social Communication.

Format: Examiner required; individual administration; untimed: 30 to 45 minutes

Scoring: Examiner evaluated

Cost: Complete Program (test book, examiner's manual, 25 response forms) $210.50

Self-Directed Search (SDS) Australian Edition

2006	Australian Council for Educational Research Limited

Meredith Shears, Adrian Harvey-Beavis

Population: Ages 14 years to adult

Purpose: Explores career options by matching interests and abilities to occupations

Description: A career counseling tool that yields six scores based on Holland's theory of careers. The Australian edition has undergone a major revision to incorporate changes that have occurred in the workplace. New items reflect changes in technology and the world of work. Occupations in the Occupations Finder have been revised and linked to the revised *Australian Standard Classification of Occupations* (ASCO II). Instructions have been modified for easier completion.

Format: Self-administered; group administration; untimed: 30 to 45 minutes

Scoring: Self-scored

Cost: Specimen Set $70.40

Self Directed Search® Career Planner (SDS®) Form CP: Career Planning

| 1990 | Psychological Assessment Resources, Inc. |

John L. Holland

Population: Adults

Purpose: Used in career counseling as an assessment for long-term career planning; intended for individuals on the career development path

Description: Paper–pencil yes–no test. Materials used include a professional user's guide, technical manual, Form CP assessment booklets, career option finders, and exploring career options booklet. An eighth-grade reading level is required. A PC computer version is available.

Format: Self-administered; untimed: 20 to 30 minutes

Scoring: Self-scored; computer scored; scoring service available

Cost: Introductory Kit (user's guide, manual, 25 of each form) $188.00

SIGI3

| 2005 | Valpar International Corporation |

Population: Grades 11 to adult

Purpose: Assesses work values, interests, and skills; used for occupational planning and preparation

Description: Primarily designed for 11th and 12th grade, and freshman and sophomore college students. Administered online only. Assessment is informal and is designed for repeated use. Practical advice and occupation-specific links and video. Database of about 350 occupations. Requires a 10th-grade reading level.

Format: Self-administered online; untimed: unlimited

Scoring: Online scoring

Cost: Subscription per Year for Unlimited Use $975.00

Student Adaptation to College Questionnaire (SACQ)

| 1999 | Western Psychological Services |

Robert W. Baker, Bohad Siryk

Population: Adults

Purpose: Measures overall student adjustment to college; used for college counseling

Description: Multiple-choice 67-item questionnaire with four subscales that measure academic adjustment, social adjustment, personal-emotional adjustment, and attachment to the college. Yields *t*-scores. A PC computer version is available.

Format: Self-administered; untimed: 30 minutes

Scoring: Machine scored; computer scored; self-scored; test scoring service available

Cost: Kit (25 hand-scored questionnaires, 1 manual, 2-use PC disk, 2 PC answer sheets) $98.50

System for Assessment and Group Evaluation (SAGE)

| 1980 | PESCO International |

Population: Ages 14 years and older

Purpose: Measures educational development, vocational aptitudes, vocational interests, temperaments, and work attitudes

Description: Paper–pencil, multiple-choice, hands-on assessment battery measuring four categories. A fourth-grade reading level is required. Used for vocational planning and guidance with populations who have physical/mental disabilities, are disadvantaged, or are dislocated/injured workers. Computer scoring is available.

Format: Examiner required; suitable for groups; timed and untimed

Scoring: Machine scored; computer scored

Cost: Contact publisher

Transition Behavior Scale– Second Edition (TBS-2)

| 2000 | Hawthorne Educational Services, Inc. |

Stephen B. McCarney, Paul D. Anderson

Population: Ages 12 to 18 years

Purpose: Provides a measure of behaviors necessary for success in employment and independent living

Description: The subscales measure a student's behavior in the areas of Work Related Behavior, Interpersonal Relations, and Social/Community Expectations. The TBS-2 provides teachers with a convenient mechanism for measuring a student's skills and readiness for transition activities. Students in the standardization sample represented all geographic regions of the United States, with particular attention given to the inclusion of racial and ethnic minorities in the creation of the national norms. Internal consistency, test–retest, and interrater reliability; item and factor analysis; and content, criterion-related, diagnostic, and construct validity are well documented and reported for the scale. The School Form is completed by an educator; the Self-Report Form is completed by the student. A Quick Score for Windows is available.

Format: Rating scale; untimed

Scoring: Examiner evaluated

Cost: Complete Kit (2 technical manuals, IEP and intervention manual, 50 each of 2 forms) $125.00

Transition Planning Inventory–Updated Version (TPI-UV)

1997	PRO-ED, Inc.

Gary M. Clark, James R. Patton

Population: Ages 14 to 22 years

Purpose: Provides school personnel with a systematic way to address critical transition planning areas that are mandated by IDEA

Description: Information on transition needs is gathered from the student, parents or guardians, and school personnel through the use of three forms designed specifically for each of the target groups. The forms contain the same 46 items. The student form also contains 15 open-ended questions. The Administration and Resource Guide includes three extensive case studies, blackline master of the Planning Notes Form, and an extensive list of more than 600 transition goals that are correlated to each planning statement. Informal Assessments for Transition Planning consists of three major components. This is a criterion-referenced instrument. A new component, Case Studies in Transition Planning,

provides 15 comprehensive case studies. A set of Home Forms in Spanish are also available as an optional component.

Format: Rating scales; untimed

Scoring: Examiner evaluated; computer version available

Cost: Complete Kit (Administration and Resource Guide, 25 profile and further assessment recommendation forms, 25 school forms, 25 home forms, 25 student forms, Informal Assessments for Transition Planning Resource, case studies, storage box) $175.00

Valpar Computerized Ability Test (VCAT)

2004	Valpar International Corporation

Population: Ages 15 years and older

Purpose: Assesses aptitudes and vocational interests; used for occupational exploration

Description: Assesses seven aptitudes: General Learning Ability; Verbal, Numeral, and Spatial Perception; Form Perception; Clerical Skills; and Color Discrimination. The interest survey is presented in a pictorial format with audio. The test is administered online. Requires a fifth-grade reading level. Also available in Spanish.

Format: Examiner required; may be group administered; timed and untimed

Scoring: Online scoring

Cost: Access and 50 Uses $495.00

Vocational Decision-Making Interview

1999	JIST Publishing

Shirley Chandler, Thomas Czerlinsky

Population: Grades 7 to adult

Purpose: Designed to improve vocational decision making of people with learning and other disabilities

Description: This revised edition has high reliability, validity, and consistency measures that are important in vocational guidance instrument. A professional asks the 54 structured questions. Three scales provide immediate feedback: Decision-Making Readiness, Employment Readiness, and Self-Appraisal. Problems that need to be corrected are clarified.

Format: Examiner required; individual administration; untimed: 20 to 40 minutes

Scoring: Examiner evaluated

Cost: Manual $24.95; 10 Forms $29.95

Vocational Interest, Temperament, and Aptitude System (VITAS)

1981	Vocational Research Institute

Population: High school students, adults

Purpose: Assesses aptitudes, vocational interests, and work-related temperaments of individuals who are disadvantaged and have developmental delays; used for vocational guidance

Description: Performance test of vocational aptitudes consisting of work samples in 21 areas: Nuts, Bolts, and Washers Assembly; Packing Matchbooks; Tile Sorting and Weighing; Collating Material Samples; Verifying Numbers; Pressing Linens; Budget Book Assembly; Nail and Screw Sorting; Pipe Assembly; Filing by Letters; Lock Assembly; Circuit Board Inspection; Calculating; Message Taking; Bank Teller; Proofreading; Payroll Computation; Census Interviewing; Spot Welding; Laboratory Assistant; and Drafting. The assessment process includes orientation, assessment, a motivational group session, feedback, and an interest interview. The test hardware is provided for all work samples.

Format: Examiner required; suitable for group use (10 persons per week); untimed: 2½ days

Scoring: Examiner evaluated

Cost: Contact publisher

Work Adjustment Inventory (WAI)

1994	PRO-ED, Inc.

James E. Gilliam

Population: Ages 12 to 22 years

Purpose: Assesses work-related temperament

Description: A multidimensional, norm-referenced instrument designed for use in schools and clinics. The WAI provides vital information to counselors, psychologists, personnel directors, and others. It can be used in the development of individual transition plans for students with disabilities (required under IDEA) and has application for students at risk. Six scales measure six work-related temperament traits: Activity, Empathy, Sociability, Assertiveness, Adaptability, and Emotionality. Each scale provides a standard score for age and gender, and a combination of the standard scores generates an overall quotient of work temperament and adjustment. These scores can be displayed graphically. The WAI standardization (on more than 7,000 students, 10% with disabilities) is the largest and most representative of the 1990 U.S. population of any test of temperament. The WAI norms constitute the most current and representative temperament norms available. Studies of both internal consistency and test-retest reliability produced appropriately high coefficients. Evidence of reliability of the WAI is provided in the form of coefficients alpha.

Format: Rating scale; untimed: 20 minutes

Scoring: Examiner evaluated

Cost: Complete Kit (manual, 50 response record forms, storage box) $105.00

Work Orientation and Values Survey (WOVS)

2002	JIST Publishing

Robert P. Brady

Population: Grades 9 and above

Purpose: Measures work values in relation to career satisfaction; used for career counseling, job placement, and job searching

Description: This easy-to-use 32-item survey asks users to rate the importance of key work values and then suggests a hierarchy of those concerns for use in determining job satisfaction or a career path.

Format: Self-administered; untimed: 15 minutes

Scoring: Self-scored

Cost: 25 Forms and Administration Manual $24.95

Workforce Skills Certification System

2000	CASAS

Population: Grades 11 to adult

Purpose: Measures job readiness skills in reading, math, critical thinking, problem solving, and oral communication in specific job areas; provides job readiness certification

Description: Includes 13 subtests plus a portfolio assessment system. Each subtest is individually scored. Reading and Math test yields CASAS scaled score. Tests: Reading and Math; Critical Thinking/Problem Solving tests in Banking, Construction, Health, High-Tech, and Telecommunication; Applied Performance assessments in Banking, Construction, Health, and Telecommunications. Test is multiple-choice, paper–pencil, oral response, and short answer.

Format: Examiner required; individual and group administration; timed and untimed

Scoring: Examiner evaluated; machine scored

Cost: 25 Tests $70.00; 25 Listening Tests with Audiocassette $50.00; Manual $60.00

World of Work and You–Third Edition

| 2002 | JIST Publishing |

J. Michael Farr

Population: Grades 8 to 12

Purpose: Used in career exploration; teaches the importance of values and education in career planning

Description: Career exploration booklet (32 pages) identifies such factors as work satisfiers, values, and training in educational options. Job matching chart included. An eighth-grade reading level is required.

Format: Self-administered; untimed

Scoring: Self-scored

Cost: 10 Forms $24.95

Aptitude

Ability Explorer–Second Edition

| 2006 | JIST Publishing |

Joan C. Harrington, Thomas F. Harrington

Population: Middle school students to adults

Purpose: Measures work-related abilities with careers, courses, and activities for future planning

Description: *Ability Explorer* matches 14 abilities: Artistic, Clerical, Interpersonal, Language, Leadership, Manual, Musical/Dramatic, Numerical/Mathematical, Organizational, Scientific, Persuasive, Spatial, Social, and Technical/Mechanical. Assessment directly links to resources from the U.S. Department of Labor. Written at an eighth-grade reading level. Individuals are asked to read each statement and then indicate how good they are or would be at doing an activity. Excellent reliability and validity. Normed on over 8,000 people. Used in many states and settings.

Format: Self-administered; untimed: 30 to 45 minutes

Scoring: Self-scoring

Cost: 25 Forms and Administration Guide $39.95

Kuder® Skills Assessment (KSA)

| 2004 | National Career Assessment Services, Inc. |

Darrell A. Luzzo, Don Zytowski

Population: Grades 7 and above, adults

Purpose: Assesses skills confidence; used for career education, development, and counseling

Description: The KSA is a component of the *Kuder Career Planning System*. Respondents rate themselves on their confidence that they can successfully perform a wide variety of tasks (e.g., fix a faucet that is dripping). Assessment may be customized to other career cluster systems such as the States' 16 clusters. A joint profile is available with the Kuder Career Search. Results link to numerous occupational (e.g., O*Net) and educational resources through the system's online career portfolio. Administrator oversight is included in the system.

Format: Self-administered online; untimed: 15 minutes

Scoring: Online scoring

Cost: Individual Online $19.95

McCarron-Dial System (MDS)

| 1986 | McCarron-Dial Systems |

Lawrence T. McCarron, Jack G. Dial

Population: Ages 16 years and older

Purpose: Assesses verbal–spatial–cognitive, sensory, motor, emotional, and integration-coping factors; used primarily in educational and vocational programming, development, and placement of special education and rehabilitation populations

Description: Multiple-item paper–pencil oral-response point-to task-performance battery consisting of six instruments: *Peabody Picture Vocabulary Test–Third Edition* (PPVT-III), *Bender Visual Motor Gestalt Test* (BVMGT), *Behavior Rating Scale* (BRS), *Observational Emotional Inventory* (OEI), *Haptic Visual Discrimination Test* (HVDT), and *McCarron Assessment of Neuromuscular Development* (MAND). The standard format for comprehensive reporting includes specific scores, vocational and residential placement scores, behavioral observations, case history information, lists of strengths and weaknesses, programming priorities, and programming recommendations. The system is designed to predict the level of vocational and residential functioning the individual may achieve after training. This level can be used to establish vocational goals and/or appropriate vocational program placement. The system is targeted toward individuals with learning disabilities, emotional disturbance, mental retardation, cerebral palsy, closed head injuries, social disabilities, and cultural disadvantages. It also can be used with persons who are blind or deaf. The examiner must be trained.

Format: Examiner required; individual administration; untimed

Scoring: Hand key; examiner evaluated

Cost: Complete MDS $3,115.00; HVDT $1,125.00; MAND $1,350.00

Non-Verbal Reasoning
1994	Valpar International Corporation

Population: Ages 15 years and older

Purpose: Assesses nonverbal reasoning of the Department of Labor's GED R Levels 4, 5, and 6; used in career counseling and vocational exploration

Description: The examinee is presented with a series of 3 × 3 grids. Eight of the cells contain geometric pictures that bear some relationship to one another. The examinee must choose from a list the item that best completes the grid. A test booklet, answer sheet, and a manual are used.

Format: Examiner required; individual or group administration; timed: 20 minutes

Scoring: Machine scored; computer scored

Cost: Contact publisher

Occupational Aptitude Survey and Interest Schedule-Aptitude Survey: Third Edition (OASIS-AS:3)
2002	PRO-ED, Inc.

Randall M. Parker

Population: Grades 8 to adult

Purpose: Evaluates a student's aptitude for various occupations; used for occupational guidance and counseling

Description: Paper–pencil 245-item survey measuring general, verbal, numerical, spatial, perceptual, and manual abilities through five subtests: Vocabulary (40 items, 9 minutes), Computation (30 items, 12 minutes), Spatial Relations (20 items, 8 minutes), Word Comparison (95 items, 5 minutes), and Making Marks (60 items, 1 minute). Subtest raw scores, percentiles, stanines, and 5-point scores are yielded. A companion test to the Interest Schedule, scores for both surveys are keyed directly to the *Dictionary of Occupa-*

tional Titles, Guide for Occupational Exploration, and the *Worker Trait Group Guide.*

Format: Examiner required; suitable for group use; timed: 35 minutes

Scoring: Examiner evaluated; scoring service available

Cost: Complete Kit (manual, 10 student test booklets, 50 hand-scorable answer sheets, 50 profile sheets, interpretation workbook, storage box) $170.00

Skills Assessment Module (SAM)
2005	Piney Mountain Press, Inc.

Michelle Rosinek

Population: Ages 14 years and older

Purpose: Assesses basic skill level in 12 work-performance and basic skills locator test areas; used for career training placement

Description: Paper–pencil show–tell format with 12 hands-on modules: Digital Discrimination, Clerical Verbal Perception, Motor Coordination, Clerical Numerical Perception, Written Instructions, Aiming Finger Dexterity, Manual Dexterity, Form Perception, Spatial Perception, Color Discrimination, Diagrammed Instructions, Oral Instructions. A Career Training Performance matrix is generated. A computer version for Windows is available. Also available in Spanish.

Format: Examiner required; suitable for group or individual use; timed: 1 hour 45 minutes

Scoring: Examiner evaluated; computer scored

Cost: $2,195.00

Spatial Aptitude
1994	Valpar International Corporation

Population: Ages 15 years and older

Purpose: Used in career counseling and vocational exploration to assess the top three levels of the APT-S

Description: The examinee is presented with a series of two-dimensional drawings that could fold into a three-dimensional object. The examinee must select the proper object from a group of three-dimensional projections. Department of Labor Spatial Aptitude Levels 1 and 2 scores are yielded. A test booklet, answer sheet, and manual are used.

Format: Examiner required; individual or group administration; timed: 10 minutes

Scoring: Machine scored; computer scored

Cost: Contact publisher

Interest

Career Assessment Battery (CAB)

2004	Piney Mountain Press, Inc.

Population: Ages 13 years to adult

Purpose: Measures career interests for career counseling

Description: A live action video and multimedia CD provide participants access to 12 occupational situations to make informed choices. Each category takes 3 minutes and provides aptitude, career cluster, and job title matches. Computer scoring on Windows is included in the package.

Format: Examiner required; individual or group administration; untimed: 40 minutes

Scoring: Examiner interpretation; computer scored; machine scored; scoring service

Cost: Stand-Alone Version $195.00; Multistation Version $495.00; Network Version $995.00

Career Assessment Inventory™– Vocational Version (CAI-V)

1982	Pearson Assessments

Charles B. Johansson

Population: Adolescents, adults

Purpose: Measures occupational interests of high school students who want immediate, non–college-graduate business or technical training; used for employment decisions, vocational rehabilitation, and self-employment

Description: Compares an individual's vocational interests to those of individuals in 91 specific careers that reflect a range of positions in today's workforce requiring two years or less of post-secondary training. Helps to guide students to focus on the patterns of interest that are important in making educational and occupational choices. Has 305 items with a 5-point rating scale.

Format: Self-administered; online administration available; untimed: 25 to 30 minutes

Scoring: Computer scoring; scoring service available

Cost: Preview Package with Interpretive Reports $55.00

Career Directions Inventory

2001	Sigma Assessment Systems, Inc.

Douglas N. Jackson

Population: Adolescents, adults

Purpose: Helps evaluate career interests of high school and college students, and adults

Description: Paper–pencil or computer-administered 100-item inventory consisting of a triad of statements for each item, describing job-related activities. Computer scoring yields a gender-fair profile of 15 basic interest scales. The pattern of these interests is compared to the interest patterns shown by individuals in a wide variety of occupations. This new test evolved from the *Jackson Vocational Interest Survey;* the content and vocabulary are easier and more emphasis is placed on activities involved in sales, service, and technical occupations. Reports are available through the mail-in batch scoring service. The computer version operates on IBM PC and compatible systems.

Format: Examiner required; suitable for group use; untimed: 30 to 45 minutes

Scoring: Computer scored; scoring service available

Cost: Contact publisher

Career Exploration Inventory– Third Edition (CEI)

2006	JIST Publishing

John J. Liptak

Population: Grades 7 and above

Purpose: Career test that integrates work, leisure, and learning interests; used for career guidance

Description: The CEI asks individuals to consider their past, present, and future interests by reflecting on 128 brief activity statements. They then indicate whether they like, or would like, to engage in that activity. By assessing leisure interests, the CEI can be used successfully with people who have limited work or education experience. The responses are totaled on a grid and the Interest Profile provides an immediate graphic picture of interest levels in 16 categories. The guide then provides the areas of strongest interest and information is given on related occupation, typical leisure activities, and related education and training programs. Results are related to codes in the Guide for Occupational Exploration. Formal validity data are provided. Available in Spanish using 15 career clusters. Instructors Manual is available online.

Format: Self-administered; untimed: 20 to 30 minutes

Scoring: Self-scored

Cost: 25 Forms and Administrator's Guide $36.95

Educational Opportunities Finder (EOF)

| 1997 | Psychological Assessment Resources, Inc. |

Donald Rosen, Kay Holmberg, John L. Holland

Population: Adolescents

Purpose. Used in college counseling to aid in identifying fields of study that match one's interests; intended for college or college-bound individuals

Description: The EOF is used with the Self-Directed Search assessment.

Format: Self-administered; untimed: 20 to 30 minutes

Scoring: Hand key

Cost: Package of 25 $50.00

Geist Picture Interest Inventory

| 1975 | Western Psychological Services |

Harold Geist

Population: Grades 8 and above

Purpose: Identifies an individual's vocational and avocational interests

Description: Multiple-item paper–pencil multiple-choice test requiring minimal language skills. The subject circles one of three pictures depicting the vocational and avocational scenes he or she prefers. Occupational norms are provided. A Motivation Questionnaire can be administered separately to explore motivation behind occupational choices.

Format: Self-administered; untimed: 20 to 30 minutes

Scoring: Hand key

Cost: Kit (10 male and 10 female tests, manual) $87.95

Guide for Occupational Exploration Interest Inventory–Second Edition (GOE)

| 2002 | JIST Publishing |

J. Michael Farr

Population: High school students to adults

Purpose: Explores career, education, and lifestyle options; used in career counseling

Description: Multiple-choice, true–false test yielding a graphic interest profile on seven factors leading to career options: Leisure Activities, Home Activities, Education and School Subjects, Training, Work Settings, Work Experience, and Overall Interest. An eighth-grade reading level is required.

Format: Self-administered; untimed: 20 to 30 minutes

Scoring: Self-scored

Cost: $29.95 (administrator's guide, 25 forms)

Hall Occupational Orientation Inventory–Fifth Edition

| 2002 | Scholastic Testing Service, Inc. |

Lucy G. Hall

Population: Adults with reading deficiencies

Purpose: Used in career guidance and counseling to assess vocational interests for adults in basic education programs

Description: Paper pencil criterion-referenced test with 175 items focusing on 35 occupational and personality characteristics. A booklet, response sheet, and interpretive folder are used. Examiner must be certified for assessment. Reading level can be modified for the test. Also available in large print.

Format: Examiner required; individual and group administration; untimed: 45 minutes

Scoring: Self-scored; examiner evaluated

Cost: Sample Set (inventory booklet, manual, response sheet) $16.50

Hall Occupational Orientation Inventory (HALL)–Form II

| 1989 | Scholastic Testing Service, Inc. |

Lacy G. Hall

Population: Adolescents, adults

Purpose: Used in career guidance and counseling to assess vocational interests

Description: Paper–pencil criterion-referenced test with 150 items focusing on career opportunities and development. Items are referenced to six interest scales, eight worker trait scales, and nine value/needs scales. A booklet, response sheet, and interpretive folder are used. Examiner must be certified for assessment. Also available in large print.

Format: Examiner required; individual and group administration; untimed: 45 minutes

Scoring: Self-scored; examiner evaluated

Cost: Sample Set (inventory booklet, digest, response sheet) $19.50

Interest Determination, Exploration, and Assessment System (IDEAS™)

1990	Pearson Assessments

Charles B. Johansson

Population: Grades 6 to 12

Purpose: Measures career-related interests of junior high and high school students; used in career planning and occupational exploration

Description: Paper–pencil 128-item inventory assessing a range of career interests. The areas covered are Mechanical/Fixing, Nature/Outdoors, Science, Writing, Child Care, Protective Services, Mathematics, Medical, Creative Arts, Community Service, Educating, Public Speaking, Business, Sales, Office Practices, and Food Service. The test is scored on a 5-point Likert-type scale and is sold in a self-contained package that can be scored and interpreted by the student. A sixth-grade reading level is required.

Format: Self-administered; untimed: 30 to 40 minutes

Scoring: Self-scoring

Cost: Starter Package with Self-Scored Reports $25.00

InterSurvS (ISS)

1994	Hester Evaluation Systems, Inc.

Edward J. Hester

Population: Ages 14 years and older

Purpose: Measures vocational interests

Description: Vocational guidance testing system that measures 12 interest areas of the Guide to

Occupational Exploration, resulting in a computer report listing feasible jobs that consider the individual's physical limitations, working condition restrictions, and people relationships using a database of over 2,000 jobs from the *Dictionary of Occupational Titles*.

Format: Examiner required; group administration; untimed: 15 minutes

Scoring: Scoring software included

Cost: Complete System (manual, software, 25 forms) $495.00

Jackson Vocational Interest Survey (JVIS)

1999	Sigma Assessment Systems, Inc.

Douglas N. Jackson

Population: Ages 14 years and older

Purpose: Helps evaluate career interests of high school and college students, and adults in career transition; used for educational and vocational planning and counseling and for personnel placement

Description: Paper–pencil or computer-administered 289-item inventory consisting of paired statements covering 34 basic interest scales and 10 occupational themes: Expressive, Logical, Inquiring, Practical, Assertive, Socialized, Helping, Conventional, Enterprising, and Communicative. The subject marks one of two responses. Scoring yields a gender-fair profile of 34 basic interest scales. A seventh-grade reading level is required. The computer version operates on PC systems. Also available in French and Spanish.

Format: Examiner required; suitable for group use; untimed: 45 to 60 minutes

Scoring: Hand key; computer scored; scoring service available from publisher

Cost: Contact publisher

Kuder® Career Search (KCS)

2004	National Career Assessment Services, Inc.

Frederic Kuder, Don Zytowski

Population: Grades 7 and above, adults

Purpose: Assesses activity preferences or interests; used for career education, development, and counseling

Description: The KCS is a component of the *Kuder Career Planning System*. Respondents rank-order 60 triads consisting of ordinary activities (e.g., paint with watercolors). There are two levels of Scoring: (1) similarity with employed adults in the Big Six career clusters and (2) Person Matches, revealing the occupation and short "job sketch" of several employed persons the inventory taker most resembles. Assessment may be customized to other career cluster systems such as the States' 16 clusters. A joint profile is available with the *Kuder Skills Assessment.* Results link to numerous occupational (e.g., O*Net) and educational resources through the system's online career portfolio. Administrator oversight is included in the system.

Format: Self-administered; untimed. 15 minutes

Scoring: Examiner evaluated; online administration and scoring; scoring service available

Cost: Individual Online $19.95

Occupational Aptitude Survey and Interest Schedule-Interest Survey: Third Edition (OASIS-IS:3)

1991	PRO-ED, Inc.

Randall M. Parker

Population: Grades 8 to 12

Purpose: Evaluates a student's areas of interest, as related to various occupations, used for occupational guidance and counseling

Description: Paper-pencil 240-item self-rating scale measuring the following interest areas: Artistic, Scientific, Nature, Protective, Mechanical, Industrial, Business Detail, Selling, Accommodating, Humanitarian, Leading/Influencing, and Physical Performing. The test yields scale raw scores, percentiles, and stanines. A companion test is the Aptitude Survey. Scores for both surveys are keyed directly to the *Dictionary of Occupational Titles, Guide for Occupational Exploration* and the *Worker Trait Group Guide.* Questions may be read aloud to students who have visual impairments or reading disabilities.

Format: Examiner required; suitable for group use; untimed: 30 minutes

Scoring: Examiner evaluated; scoring service available

Cost: Complete Kit (manual, 25 student test booklets, 50 hand-scorable answer sheets, 50 profile sheets, 50 scoring forms, interpretation workbook, storage box) $184.00

O*NET Career Interests Inventory

2002	JIST Publishing

Population: Grades 8 to adult

Purpose: Used in career exploration

Description: Relates career interests to jobs described in the Department of Labor's O*NET database. Based on the RIASEC system, users rate their likes and dislikes of 180 activity statements. The resulting scores are matched directly to lists of job titles based on personality type.

Format: Self-administered; untimed: 20 to 30 minutes

Scoring: Self-scored

Cost: Administrator's Guide and 25 Forms $29.95

Picture Interest Career Survey (PICS)

2007	JIST Publishing

Robert P. Brady

Population: Middle school students to adults

Purpose: Language-free assessment helps users discover career Interests

Description: A picture based assessment that presents 36 sets of three pictures each. Examinees choose the picture most interesting to them. Based on the number and kind of pictures selected, a profile is created that is based on the RIASEC coding system. The PICS code can lead directly to career information and potential job matches. Highly valid and reliable, it is usable with all populations, but is particularly useful for individuals with limited reading ability or special needs.

Format: Self-administered; untimed: 10 to 20 minutes

Scoring: Self scored

Cost: 25 Forms and Administration Manual $39.95

Reading-Free Vocational Interest Inventory: 2 (R-FVII:2)

2000	Elbern Publications

Ralph Leonard Becker

Population: Ages 13 years to adult

Purpose: Measures vocational interests of individuals in job areas that may be within the individuals' capabilities

Description: Consists of a series of 55 sets of three drawings each, depicting different job tasks. The individual is asked to mark the one occupational activity most preferred in each set. Responses are keyed to yield scores in 11 interest areas and five clusters. The interest areas are Animal Care, Automotive, Building Trades, Clerical, Food Service, Horticulture, Housekeeping,

Laundry Service, Materials Handling, Patient Care, and Personal Service. The clusters are Mechanical, Outdoor, Mechanical/Outdoor, Clerical/Personal Care, and Food Service/Handling Operations. A Cluster Quotient is obtained for each examinee from a combination of related interest area scores. The manual contains the normative tables and a description of the Scales and Clusters and suggested jobs within each of the categories. A single booklet is used for both males and females. Each booklet has two detachable pages that provide a complete record of interest and cluster scores that is used as a permanent record. The *Occupational Title Lists–Second Edition* (2001) provides 954 occupations with their unique DOT and new O*NET codes distributed among the 11 interest categories. A seven-step guide allows the examiner to narrow the choice of jobs for each trainee.

Format: Examiner required; suitable for group use; untimed: 20 minutes or less

Scoring: Hand key; self-scored

Cost: Complete Kit (manual, 20 booklets, Occupational Title Lists) $109.00

Safran Students' Interest Inventory (Third Edition)

1985	Thomson Nelson

C. Safran

Population: Grades 5 to 12

Purpose: Assesses occupational interests of students

Description: Multiple-item three-part paper–pencil inventory determining the relationship of students' interests and occupational characteristics. Section 1 requires students to choose one alternative from 168 pairs of occupational alternatives categorized in the area of Economic, Technical, Outdoor, Service, Humane, Artistic, and Scientific preferences. Section II measures school subject interests, and Section III contains a self-rated Levels of Ability Chart (academic, mechanical, social, and clerical). Student interests are referenced to the *Canadian Classification and Dictionary of Occupations* (CCDO) and the *Student Guidance Information System* (SGIS). The inventory is available on two levels: Level 1 (Grades 5 to 9) and Level 2 (Grades 8 to 12). Reading levels are matched to the grades indicated for test levels. For remedial and special education students in Grades 8 and 9, the Level 1 instrument should be used. This new edition includes occupational selections relevant to a student's world.

Format: Self-administered; untimed: 40 minutes

Scoring: Hand key

Cost: Specimen Set (test booklets Levels 1 and 2, student manual, counselor's manual) $33.95; 35 Student Booklets $59.00

Self Directed Search® Career Explorer (SDS® CE)

1994	Psychological Assessment Resources, Inc.

John L. Holland, Amy B. Powell

Population: Grades 5 to 8

Purpose: Used to help students assess and explore interests for future education and career planning

Description: Paper–pencil yes–no test. Materials used include a technical information book, teacher's guide, self-assessment booklet, careers booklet, and guidance booklet. A sixth-grade reading level is required. A computer version using PCs is available.

Format: Self-administered; untimed: 30 minutes

Scoring: Self-scored; computer scored

Cost: Introductory Kit (user's guide, manual, teacher's guide, 35 of each booklet) $230.00

Self Directed Search® (SDS®) Form E–4th Edition

1990	Psychological Assessment Resources, Inc.

John L. Holland

Population: Adolescents, adults

Purpose: Assesses career interests; used in career counseling to assess career interests among individuals with lower educational levels

Description: Asks simple questions about individuals' likes and dislikes, their competencies, the jobs they find interesting, and their personal abilities. After answering the questions in the Assessment Booklet, they obtain a two-letter summary code using a simplified scoring system. Requires a fourth-grade reading level and focuses on training and jobs that require a high school diploma or less.

Format: Self-administered; untimed: 20 to 30 minutes

Scoring: Self-scored

Cost: Introductory Kit (user's guide, manual, 25 of each form) $150.00

Self Directed Search® Form R– 4th Edition (SDS® Form R)

| 1994 | Psychological Assessment Resources, Inc. |

John L. Holland

Population: Adolescents, adults

Purpose: Used to explore career interests

Description: A simulated career counseling experience. The SDS enables individuals to choose careers and fields of study that best match their self-reported skills and interests. Individuals answer questions about their aspirations, activities, competencies, occupations, and other self-estimates and discover occupations that best fit their interests and skills. Yields a three-letter summary code that designates the three personality types an individual most closely resembles.

Format: Self-administered; untimed: 35 to 45 minutes

Scoring: Self-scored; computer scored; scoring service available; online administration and scoring available

Cost: Comprehensive Kit (user's guide, manual, 25 of each form, 10 each of finder's booklet) $194.00

Strong Interest Inventory®

| 2004 | CPP, Inc. |

E. K. Strong, Jr., Jo-Ida C. Hansen, David P. Campbell

Population: Ages 14 years and older

Purpose: Measures occupational interests in a wide range of career areas; used to make long-range curricular and occupational choices and for employee placement, career guidance, development, and vocational rehabilitation placement

Description: Paper–pencil 291-item multiple-choice test requiring the examinee to respond in various ways to items covering a broad range of familiar occupational tasks and daily activities. Topics include occupations, school subjects, activities, leisure activities, types of people, preference between two activities, and your characteristics and preference in the world of work. The response is scored on six general occupational themes, 30 basic interest scales, occupational scales, and four Personal Style scales. The scoring services provide 11 additional nonoccupational

and administrative indexes as a further guide to interpreting the results. Also available in Spanish, French-Canadian, and Hebrew.

Format: Self administered; untimed: 30 minutes

Scoring: Scoring service; online

Cost: Preview Kit $14.65; College Preview Kit $9.60; Profiles $7.80 each for 1 to 99

Super's Work Values Inventory– Revised (SWV)

| 2004 | National Career Assessment Services, Inc. |

Donald E. Super, Don Zytowski

Population: Grades 7 and above, adults

Purpose: Assesses work values; used for career education, development, and counseling

Description: The SWV is a component of the *Kuder Career Planning System.* Respondents rate themselves on their value for 12 aspects of jobs and careers (e.g., prestige, independence, security). Results link to numerous occupational (e.g., O*Net) and educational resources through the system's online career portfolio. Administrator oversight is included in the system.

Format: Self-administered online; untimed: 10 minutes

Scoring: Online scoring

Cost: Individual Online $19.95

Transition-to-Work Inventory (TWI)

| 2004 | JIST Publishing |

John J. Liptak

Population: Ages 14 to 65

Purpose: Measures nonwork activity interest as it relates to potential occupations; used for career change, entry into the workforce, and career counseling

Description: Mates ratings on 84 activities to 14 major career interest areas based on the *Guide for Occupational Exploration.* Includes spaces for self-reflection and listings of specific jobs. Administrators Guide has information on construction, interpretation, validity, and reliability.

Format: Self-administered; untimed: 25 minutes

Scoring: Self-scored

Cost: 25 Forms and Administration Manual $34.95

Vocational Interest, Experience and Skill Assessment (VIESA)– Second Canadian Edition

1995	Thomson Nelson

Population: Grades 8 and above

Purpose: Measures vocational interests, experiences, and skills of individuals; used by educators and professionals in career counseling with individuals and for group programs

Description: Multiple-item two-part paper–pencil assessment providing career counseling information. Individuals link personal characteristics determined using the Career Guidebook to more than 500 occupations on a World of Work Map that shows how occupations relate to each other. The Job Family Charts list occupations according to typical preparation level, including high school courses, post–high school preparation, and college majors. Occupations are referenced to the *National Occupational Classification* (NOC) and the *Canadian Classification and Dictionary of Occupations* (CCDO). The test is available on two levels: Level 1 (Grades 8 to 10) and Level 2 (Grades 11 to adult). A seventh-grade reading level is required.

Format: Self-administered; untimed: 40 to 45 minutes

Scoring: Hand key

Cost: Examination Kit Level 1 and 2 $28.65; 25 Student Booklets $55.00

Vocational Interest Exploration (VIE) System

1991	McCarron-Dial Systems

Lawrence T. McCarron, Harriette P. Spires

Population: Ages 14 years and older

Purpose: Assesses preferences for work conditions and orientation to work. Used for vocational guidance, work adjustment, and occupational planning.

Description: Six to 10 entry-level jobs (computer-generated) are described with matching responses from a multiple-choice work preference questionnaire. Each job can then be reviewed in the VIE Job Manuals that contain color photographs and descriptive information about job duties, abilities required, training needed, suggestions on where to look for the job, occupational outlook, and estimated earnings. A fourth-grade reading level is required.

Format: Examiner required; individual or group administration; untimed

Scoring: Test scoring software included

Cost: $350.00

Vocational Training Inventory and Exploration Survey (VOC-TIES)

2006	Piney Mountain Press, Inc.

Nancy Scott

Population: Ages 13 years to adult

Purpose: Identifies technical training interests of junior high and high school students

Description: Presents 15 career/technical pathways available in most career/technical schools. Provides critical information about the training area to assist the student in making a more informed choice. A parent/student option gives a quick method of documenting students' interests and notifying parents about local training opportunities. Also included is a Career Development Plan with an ITEP generator consisting of over 2,000 career technical objectives. Spanish version available.

Format: Group administration; presented in video or CD format

Scoring: Examiner evaluated

Cost: Stand-Alone Version $195.00; Multistation Version $495.00; Network Version $995.00

Wide Range Interest-Opinion Test– Second Edition (WRIOT-2)

Date not provided	Harcourt Assessment, Inc.

Joseph J. Glutting, Gary Wilkinson

Population: Ages 9 to 90 years

Purpose: Provides information about vocational interests (without language requirements)

Description: The instrument contains 238 full-color pictures to help students and adults determine whether they like, dislike, or are undecided about the work situations depicted. The test can be administered with the picture book or with a computer by using the CD. Results are depicted graphically to help guide individuals toward career choices based on their strengths in 17 Occupational, 16 Interest, and 6 Holland Type Scales. The WRIOT-2 does not require reading or language understanding and is ideal for use with individuals with disabilities or those who are educationally or culturally disadvantaged. The test is appropriate for use with employees ranging from unskilled laborers to managers to highly trained professionals.

Format: Examiner required; suitable for group use, untimed. 40 minutes

Scoring: Examiner evaluated; computer scoring

Cost: Complete Kit (manual, 25 response forms, picture book, 25 computer administrations, box) $295.00

Work Preference Match (WPM)

2006	JIST Publishing

Lynn R. Dowd

Population: Grades 8 and above

Purpose: Measures work needs, interests, skills,

and desires; used for career counseling and job searching

Description: Test takers complete a grid of their most important work-related preferences, which they can then use to explore careers. Examines work-related factors in seven categories: Work Tasks, Environment, Schedule, Supervision, Compensation, Work Culture, and Social Issues. Uses "discrepancy analysis" to identify and resolve conflicts between work interests, values, and needs.

Format: Self-administered; untimed: 30 minutes average

Scoring: Self-scored

Cost: 25 Forms and Administration Manual $39.95

Health Education

Safe and Drug-Free Schools and Communities Survey

1993	Assessment Resource Center

Population: Grades 6 to 12

Purpose: Assesses use of alcohol, tobacco, drugs, violence, weapons, suicide, and AIDS awareness

Description: An anonymous 51-item questionnaire designed to determine high school students' attitudes toward, observations of, and experiences with tobacco, alcohol, driving under

the influence, drugs (legal and illegal), weapons, violence, vandalism, and suicide (on and off school property). The survey is an adaptation of the longer *Youth Risk Behaviors Survey* administered by the federal Centers for Disease Control.

Format: Examiner required; group administration; untimed: 50 minutes

Scoring: Machine scored; test scoring service available

Cost: Survey Materials $.99 each; Scoring $.99 each

Industrial Arts

VCWS 202—Mechanical Assembly/ Alignment and Hammering

1982	Valpar International Corporation

Population: Ages 15 years and older

Purpose: Assesses worker qualification profile factors for job, curricula placement, and career planning

Description: Criterion-referenced work sample consisting of demonstrated performance of block

assembly, alignment driving, block disassembly, and hammering. Spatial aptitude, motor coordination, finger dexterity, and manual dexterity are measured. The work sample yields methods–time measurement percentage scores. Materials include assembly block, assorted small tools and parts, and hammering cards. This work sample is suitable for individuals with hearing, physical, or mental impairments. Signing for individuals with hearing impairments is necessary. Learning curve allows for multiple administrations as needed.

Format: Examiner required; individual administration; untimed: 10 to 15 minutes

Scoring: Examiner evaluated

Cost: $1,295.00

VCWS 203—Mechanical Reasoning and Machine Tending

| 1982 | Valpar International Corporation |

Population: Ages 15 years and older

Purpose: Assesses worker qualification to profile factors for job, curricula placement, and career planning

Description: Criterion-referenced work sample consisting of demonstrated performance of plat-form assembly and disassembly using fingers and small tools. Measures vocational reasoning, motor coordination, manual dexterity, finger dexterity, and general learning ability. The work sample yields methods–time measurement percentage scores. Materials include four-legged platform, machine tending board, nut driver, and felt marker. This work sample is suitable for individuals with hearing, physical, or mental impairments. Signing for individuals with hearing impairments is necessary. Learning curve allows for multiple administrations as needed.

Format: Examiner required; individual administration; untimed: 10 to 15 minutes

Scoring: Examiner evaluated

Cost: $1,095.00

Library Skills

Essential Skills Assessments: Information Skills (ESA:IS)

| 2000 | New Zealand Council for Educational Research |

Cedric Croft, Karyn Dunn, Gavin Brown

Population: Ages 10 to 15 years

Purpose: Measures information-finding skills

Description: The ESA:IS are set within the Information Skills of the Essential Skills of the New Zealand Curriculum Framework and consist of six modules incorporating 14 tests: Finding Information in a Library, Finding Information in Books, Finding Information in Reference Sources, Finding Information in Graphs and Tables, Finding In-formation in Prose Text, and Evaluating Information in Text. The tests are designed for formative assessment and can be used for comparative purposes as each student's score can be converted into a stanine. They cover two years at each level, so the tests may be used to identify strengths and weaknesses and to monitor progress over time. The tests contain a range of item types.

Format: Examiner required; group administration; timed: 30 minutes

Scoring: Hand key

Cost: Full Specimen Set (1 each of Primary, Intermediate, and Secondary; manual) $36.00

Mathematics

Basic

Basic Number Diagnostic Test

| 2001 | Hodder Murray |

Bill Gillham

Population: Ages 5 to 9 years

Purpose: Determines which pupils are underperforming in numeracy and how to address individual needs

Description: This diagnostic test measures and profiles key aspects of developing numeracy, from reciting and writing numbers to simple addition and subtraction. Pinpoints the bottom 20% before problems become severe. Matches teaching activities and strategies to each pupil's needs. Designed for retesting at intervals.

Format: Examiner required; individual administration; untimed: 15 to 20 minutes

Scoring: Examiner evaluated

Cost: Set of 10 Copies £9.50; Manual £13.99

Basic Number Screening Test

| 2001 | Hodder Murray |

Bill Gillham, K. A. Hesse

Population: Ages 7 to 12 years

Purpose: Identifies pupils whose number attainments are low for their age

Description: The assessment in two parallel forms focuses on pupils' understanding of the number system and ability to carry out mental operations. Instructions are presented verbally; no reading involved. Provides a needs indicator for pupils in the bottom 20% of their age group. Scores are reported as number ages, percentiles, and standardized scores.

Format: Examiner required; group administration; untimed: 30 minutes

Scoring: Examiner evaluated

Cost: 10 Copies of Either Form A or Form B £6.50; Manual £12.99

Booker Profiles in Mathematics: Numeration and Computation

| 1994 | Australian Council for Educational Research Limited |

George Booker

Population: Early primary grades to adult

Purpose: Assesses and analyzes strengths and weaknesses in numeration and computation

Description: The test components contain a series of test questions to measure basic math knowledge. The criterion-referenced tests are intended to serve a wide range of examinees. Materials include an easel, blackline masters, and a manual that includes suggestions for interpretations and reteaching.

Format: Examiner required; individual administration; untimed: 35 to 40 minutes

Scoring: Examiner evaluated

Cost: Complete Kit $132.00

Collegiate Assessment of Academic Progress (CAAP) Mathematics Test

| 2001 | ACT, Inc. |

Population: Ages 17 years and older

Purpose: Assesses mathematics skills

Description: Paper–pencil 35-item multiple-choice test. May be used for persons with visual, physical, hearing, or mental impairments.

Format: Examiner required; suitable for group use; timed: 40 minutes

Scoring: Machine scored; test scoring service available

Cost: $10.75

Comprehensive Assessment of Math Strategies (CAMS®)

| 2006 | Curriculum Associates®, Inc. |

Population: Grades 1 to 8

Purpose: Diagnoses individual instructional needs

Description: The assessment identifies weaknesses in 12 standards-based reading strategies and encourages students to use higher-order thinking skills. Supports NCLB goals. Reinforces understanding of performance through self-assessment. Management software is available. Available in Spanish for Grades 1 to 5.

Format: Examiner required; group administration; untimed

Scoring: Examiner evaluated; computer scoring available

Cost: 10-Pack of Student Booklets $25.90; Teacher Guide $1.95 per grade; Software $25.95

Diagnostic Test of High School Math (DT-HSM)

| 2002, 2003 | APR Testing Services |

Joel Peter Wiesan

Population: Grades 8 to 10

Purpose: Measures competencies

Description: The test yields a score from 60 multiple-choice questions for 20 different areas including addition, subtraction, multiplication, and division of common fractions and mixed numbers; solving algebraic equations; setting up equations; word problems; and probability and statistics. Each student is provided with a diagnostic profile.

Format: Examiner required; suitable for group use; untimed: 90 minutes

Scoring: Online scoring; examiner evaluated

Cost: Specimen Set (test booklet, answer sheet, sample reports) $75.00; Manual $45.00; Price per Student $4.10 to $7.50 depending on number of students and option

I Can Do Maths...

2000	Australian Council for Educational Research Limited

Brian Doig, Marion de Lemos

Population: First 3 years of school

Purpose: Assesses early numeracy skills

Description: This test comes in two levels to enable continuous monitoring focusing on number, space, and measurement. Provides a basis for planning programs for individual needs. Appropriate for new English learners. Administration is oral.

Format: Examiner required; individual or group administration; untimed: 20 minutes

Scoring: Examiner evaluated

Cost: Contact publisher

Mathematics Competency Test

1996	Australian Council for Educational Research Limited

John F. Izard, Ken M. Miller

Population: Ages 11 to 18 years

Purpose: Used for general screening and identification of strengths and weaknesses to provide a profile of math competency

Description: Paper–pencil 46-item objective test. Scores: Full Test, Using and Applying Mathematics, Number and Algebra, Shape and Space, and Data.

Format: Examiner required; suitable for group use; timed

Scoring: Hand key; examiner evaluated

Cost: Contact publisher

Math Placement Test for Grade 6 (MPT-6)

2003, 2004	APR Testing Services

Joel Peter Wiesen

Population: Grade 6

Purpose: Measures competencies required for success in junior high mathematics

Description: Along with an overall score, the test yields a diagnostic score from 40 multiple-choice questions for 13 areas, including addition, subtraction, multiplication, and division of whole numbers; common fractions; percentages; tables; estimation; and word problems. Student and school score reports are provided.

Format: Examiner required; suitable for group use; untimed

Scoring: Online scoring; examiner evaluated

Cost: Specimen Set (test booklet, answer sheet, sample reports) $75.00; Manual $45.00; Price per Student $4.10 to $7.50 depending on number of students and option

Numeracy Progress Tests

2000	Hodder Murray

Denis Vincent, Mary Crumpler

Population: Ages 5 to 11 years

Purpose: Provides baseline assessment in math skills

Description: Standardized tests that allow progress monitoring throughout the primary school. Ideal for identifying pupils making slower or better progress than expected. Minimal reliance on reading ability. Each test gives a standardized score, numeracy age, and an NC level. Stage One is for ages 5 to 8; Stage Two is for ages 7 to 11.

Format: Examiner required; group administration; untimed: 40 to 45 minutes

Scoring: Examiner evaluated; computer scoring available

Cost: Stage One or Stage Two Specimen Set £15.99 each

Comprehensive

Booker Profiles in Mathematics: Thinking Mathematically

2001	Australian Council for Educational Research Limited

George Booker

Population: Children, adolescents

Purpose: Measures capacity to think, reason, and problem-solve in mathematics

Description: The assessment reflects contemporary approaches to the development of math problem solving. The instrument contains an easel of items organized in four levels of difficulty; blackline masters; and a manual containing directions for administering, recording, and interpreting the assessment items and ideas for a follow-up program.

Format: Examiner required; suitable for group use; untimed: 30 minutes

Scoring: Scored with key

Cost: Complete Kit $198.00

Collis-Romberg Mathematical Problem-Solving Profiles

1992	Australian Council for Educational Research Limited

Kevin Collis, Thomas Romberg

Population: Ages 9 to 17+ years

Purpose: Assesses math problem solving

Description: The test profiles assessment items in five aspects of math, which form a foundation for problem solving in Algebra, Chance and Data, Measurement, Number, and Space. Gives suggestions for further teaching based on the student's current level of functioning.

Format: Examiner required; suitable for group use; timed: 40 to 50 minutes

Scoring: Examiner evaluated

Cost: Contact publisher

Comprehensive Mathematical Abilities Test (CMAT)

2002	PRO-ED, Inc.

Wayne P. Hresko, Paul L. Schlieve, Shelley R. Herron, Colleen Swain, Rita J. Sherbenou

Population: Ages 7 to 18 years

Purpose: Measures all aspects of mathematics

Description: The CMAT has 12 subtests: Addition; Subtraction; Multiplication; Division; Problem Solving; Charts, Tables, and Graphs; Algebra; Geometry, Rational Numbers, Time, Money; and Measurement. They are combined into six composites: General Mathematics, Basic Calculations, Reasoning Core, Advanced Calculations, Practical Applications, and Overall Mathematics. The General Mathematics Composite provides a concise analysis of the two critical areas used in defining math learning disabilities: Basic Calculations and Reasoning.

Format: Examiner required; individual administration; untimed; 30 minutes to 2 hours

Scoring: Examiner evaluated

Cost: Complete Kit (manual, picture book, 25 record forms, 25 each of 2 response books, storage box) $285.00

DART (Developmental Assessment Resource for Teachers) Mathematics

1998	Australian Council for Educational Research Limited

E. Recht, M. Forster, G. Masters

Population: Children, adolescents

Purpose: Assesses students' level of performance in mathematics

Description: Contains five strands: Number, Space, Measurement, Chance and Data, and Data Sense in Form A and Form B. They are designed to be integrated into day-to-day teaching programs and are aligned with outcome statements. The questions are grouped around specific stimuli related to the workings and life of the zoo.

Format: Examiner required; suitable for group use; untimed: 60 minutes each strand

Scoring: Examiner evaluated

Cost: Contact publisher

Diagnostic Screening Test: Math, Third Edition (DSTM)

1980	Slosson Educational Publications, Inc.

Thomas D. Gnagey

Population: Grades 1 to 10

Purpose: Determines a student's conceptual and computational mathematical skills

Description: Multiple-item paper–pencil test in two sections: Basic Processes Section and Specialized Section. The Basic Processes Section consists of 36 items arranged developmentally within four major areas: addition skills, subtraction skills, multiplication, and division. Each area yields a separate Grade Equivalent Score and Consolidation Index Score and scores in nine supplemental categories: process, sequencing, simple computation, special manipulations, use of zero decimals, simple fractions, and manipulation in fractions. The Specialized Section consists of 37 to 45 items evaluating conceptual and computational skills in five areas: money, time, percent, U.S. measurement, and metric measurement. The examiner explains the procedure and student completes the problems. Contains forms A and B.

Format: Examiner required; suitable for group use; untimed: 5 to 20 minutes

Scoring: Hand key

Cost: Complete Kit (manual, 25 each of Form A and B) $72.25

Graded Arithmetic-Mathematics Test

2002	Hodder Murray

P. E. Vernon, K. M. Miller

Population: Ages 5 to 12 years

Purpose: Provides assessment of overall mathematical attainment

Description: The instrument samples a wide range of math skills and can be administered orally. Pupils begin at an age-appropriate level. Scores are provided for ages and as standardized scores.

Format: Examiner required; individual or group administration; untimed: 30 minutes

Scoring: Examiner evaluated

Cost: Set of 10 Copies £6.99; Manual £12.99

KeyMath-Revised/NU: A Diagnostic Inventory of Essential Mathematics–Revised–Normative Update

1998	AGS Publishing/Pearson Assessments

Austin J. Connolly

Population: Ages 5 to 22 years

Purpose: Measures understanding and application of important math concepts and skills

Description: Provides an accurate measurement of students' math skills with 516 items. Does not require reading ability. The age range has been extended in the update. NCTM standards are reflected. It includes estimating, interpreting data, and problem solving. It also tests knowledge of the metric system in 13 subtests.

Format: Examiner required; individual administration; untimed: 35 to 50 minutes depending on grade level

Scoring: Examiner interpreted; computer scoring available

Cost: Complete Form A and Form B Kit (2 easels, 25 each of Form A and Form B record forms, NU manual, sample report to parents, carrying bag) $532.99

Mathematics Assessment for Learning and Teaching (MaLT)

2005	Hodder Murray

Julian Williams

Population: Ages 5 to 14 years

Purpose: Measures comprehensive mathematical ability and provides diagnostic error analysis

Description: The MaLT samples all aspects of math from Reception to Year 9, generating comprehensive assessments and providing standardized scores, year-on-year progress assessment,

attainment target performance profiles, individualized formative and diagnostic feedback to pupils, and whole-class profiles identifying weaknesses. Tests are available in both paper–pencil and computer-adaptive formats. Tests for ages 5 to 7 are presented orally. Samples the full range of math skills appropriate to each year group.

Format: Examiner required; individual administration; untimed: 45 minutes

Scoring: Examiner evaluated; computer scoring available

Cost: Primary Evaluation Pack (manual, 1 copy of each 5 to 11) £15.00; Secondary Evaluation Pack (manual, 1 copy of each 12 to 14) £15.00

Mathematics Competency Test

2002	Hodder Murray

P. E. Vernon, K. M. Miller, J. F. Izard

Population: Ages 12 to 16 years

Purpose: Measures math skills and provides skills profile

Description: Skills measured mirror National Curriculum attainment targets. The test is suitable for schools, further education colleges, and preemployment. Scores are reported as a norm-referenced total score. Open-ended questions are presented in ascending order of difficulty.

Format: Examiner required; group administration; untimed: 30 to 40 minutes

Scoring: Examiner evaluated

Cost: Set of 10 Copies £7.99; Manual £15.99

Progressive Achievement Test (PAT): Mathematics (Revised)

2006	New Zealand Council for Educational Research

Neil Reid

Population: Ages 8 to 14 years

Purpose: Measures mathematical achievement

Description: 50-item multiple-choice revised test has an emphasis on power rather than speed. Measures math skills and understandings in each of the learning strands of the current curriculum. The questions are arranged roughly in order of difficulty in two cycles so that a student attempts blocks of Recall, Computation, Understanding, and Application items in each half of the test. Raw scores may be converted to percentile rank norms and stanines by age and/or class.

Format: Examiner required; group administration; timed: 55 minutes

Scoring: Examiner evaluated

Cost: Manual $9.00; Booklets $1.80; 10 Answer Sheets $1.80; Keys $.99

Progressive Achievement Tests in Mathematics–Third Edition

2005	Australian Council for Educational Research Limited

Population: Years 4 to 9

Purpose: Assesses levels of achievement in mathematics

Description: Provides information to teachers about the level of achievement in skills and understanding. All items have been assigned to an appropriate level from the National Profiles. Features: battery of six tests covering levels 1 to 5 of the National Profiles; tests arranged in three parallel pairs for test–retest options; reusable test booklets; multiple-choice format; and calculator and noncalculator use items provided.

Format: Examiner required; group administration; timed: 45 minutes

Scoring: Examiner evaluated; scoring service available

Cost: Contact publisher

Quant Q

2005	Insight Assessments

Stephen W. Blohm

Population: Ages 18 years and older

Purpose: Measures quantitative reasoning

Description: The instrument has 28 multiple-choice items. They are designed to measure one's ability to think outside of the box when solving quantitative problems. Available in paper–pencil or electronic format.

Format: Examiner required; group administration, timed and untimed

Scoring: Machine or electronic scored; scoring service available

Cost: Specimen Kit (manual, 1 protocol, 1 CapScore™ answer form) $40.00

Slosson-Diagnostic Math Screener (S-DMS)

2004	Slosson Educational Publications, Inc.

Bradley T. Erford, Rita R. Boykin

Population: Grades 1 to 8

Purpose: Measures mathematical abilities

Description: Three areas are assessed (Math Conceptual Development, Math Problem-Solving, and Math Computation Skills) in five grade ranges: 1 to 2, 3, 4 to 5.4, 5.5 to 6, and 7 to 8. The S-DMS yields standard scores for both grade and age norms.

Format: Examiner required; group administration; untimed: 30 to 50 minutes

Scoring: Examiner evaluated

Cost: Complete Multilevel $229.25

Stanford Diagnostic Mathematics Test, Fourth Edition (SDMT 4)

1995	Harcourt Assessment, Inc.

Population: Grades 1 to 13

Purpose: Measures competence in the basic concepts and skills that are prerequisite to success in mathematics

Description: The SDMT 4 identifies specific areas of difficulty for each student so that appropriate intervention may be planned. This revised version reflects current trends in mathematics instruction. Each test provides both a multiple-choice and free-response assessment format. Students select and apply problem-solving strategies and use their reasoning and communication skills. Norm-referenced and criterion-referenced information is provided. Calculators may be used by Grades 3.5 to 13.

Format: Examiner required; suitable for group use; timed: varies

Scoring: Hand key; scoring service available

Cost: Examination Kit $42.00

STAR Math

2006	Renaissance Learning, Inc.

Population: Grades 1 to 12

Purpose: Provides periodic progress monitoring of mathematic skills

Description: STAR Math provides teachers with quick, accurate estimates of students' math ability relative to national norms, provides criterion-referenced diagnostic assessment of math skills development, and provides a way to track student growth through the year. STAR Math uses computer-adaptive technology to tailor each student's assessment based on his or her responses to previous items. By administering test items that are closely matched to student achievement levels, reliability is enhanced.

Format: Computer administered; timed: 12 minutes

Scoring: Computer scored

Cost: One-Time Setup (per school) $1,499.00; Annual Student Fee: $.39 per student

Test of Early Mathematics Ability–Third Edition (TEMA-3)

2003	PRO-ED, Inc.

Herbert P. Ginsburg, Arthur J. Baroody

Population: Ages 3 to 8 years

Purpose: Measures math performance; identifies individual strengths and weaknesses

Description: Measures informal and formal (school-taught) concepts and skills in the following domains: Numbering Skills, Number-Comparison Facility, Numeral Literacy, Mastery of Number Facts, Calculation Skills, and Understanding of Concepts. It has two parallel forms, each containing 72 items. Results are reported as standard scores, percentile ranks, and age/grade equivalents. Includes a book of remedial techniques.

Format: Examiner required; individual administration; untimed: 20 to 45 minutes

Scoring: Examiner evaluated

Cost: Complete Kit (manual, 2 picture books [A and B], 25 each A and B examiner record forms, 25 each A & B worksheets, assessment probes and instructional activities, storage box) $265.00

Test of Mathematical Abilities–Second Edition (TOMA-2)

1994	PRO-ED, Inc.

Virginia L. Brown, Mary E. Cronin, Elizabeth McEntire

Population: Grades 3 to 12

Purpose: Assesses the mathematical attitudes and aptitudes of students

Description: Five paper-pencil subtests assessing knowledge, mastery, and attitudes in two

major skill areas: story problems and computation. In addition to measuring the student's abilities, the following broad diagnostic areas are assessed: expressed attitudes toward mathematics, understanding of vocabulary as applied to mathematics. Standard scores differentiate diagnostically between students who have problems in mathematics and those who do not.

Format: Examiner required; individual or group administration; untimed: 60 to 90 minutes

Scoring: Examiner evaluated

Cost: Complete Kit (manual, 25 profile/record forms, storage box) $92.00

Specific

Acuity™ Algebra

2005	CTB/McGraw-Hill

Population: Grades 7 to 12

Purpose: Measures readiness for Algebra 1 and identifies student needs throughout instruction

Description: Includes a readiness exam, formative (monitor student understanding) assessments, proficiency (assess mastery) exam, and item bank.

Format: Online assessment; timed: 45 minutes

Scoring: Online scoring

Cost: Contact publisher

Diagnostic Test of Pre-Algebra Math (DT-PAM)

2001	APR Testing Services

Joel Peter Wiesen

Population: Grades 6 to 8

Purpose: Measures competencies required for success in algebra

Description: The test yields a score from 50 forced-choice questions for 21 different competencies, including addition, subtraction, multiplication, and division of common fractions and mixed numbers; signed numbers, rounding, and estimating; word problems; and reading tables and graphs. Each student is provided with a diagnostic profile. Class and school summaries will be provided with group testing. Paper–pencil and online administration available.

Format: Examiner required; suitable for group use; untimed: 1 to 2 class periods

Scoring: Online scoring; examiner evaluated

Cost: Specimen Set (test booklet, answer sheet, sample reports) $75.00; Manual $45.00; Price per Student $4.10 to $7.50 depending on number of students and option

Iowa Algebra Aptitude Test™ (IAAT™)

| 1993 | Riverside Publishing Company |

Harold L. Schoen, Timothy N. Ansley,
H. D. Hoover, Beverly S. Rich,
Sheila I. Barron, Robert A. Bye

Population: Grades 7 and 8; suitable for high school or junior college testing

Purpose: Assesses readiness for Algebra 1

Description: The IAAT can promote student success in algebra classes by helping educators determine which students should be placed into Algebra 1 or into prealgebra courses. The content of the IAAT has been aligned with current NCTM recommendations, both for prealgebra and algebra curricula and for testing.

Format: Examiner required; group administered; untimed: 50 minutes

Scoring: Examiner evaluated; machine scoring available

Cost: Test Booklets (25, includes Directions for Administration) $78.00 per level; 25 Self-Scoring Answer Sheets $35.00

Orleans-Hanna Algebra Prognosis Tests–Third Edition

| 1998 | Harcourt Assessment, Inc. |

Gerald S. Hanna

Population: Grades 7 to 11

Purpose: Determines algebra readiness

Description: This new edition retains the reliability of the previous edition, but aligns with the NCTM standards. More problem-solving items are included. The items cover algebraic topics such as exponents, integers, and algebraic expressions. A new, open design makes it easy for students to proceed through the test.

Format: Examiner required; suitable for group use; timed: 40 minutes

Scoring: Hand key; may be machine scored

Cost: 25 Test Booklets and Directions $90.00; 25 Hand-Scorable Answer Sheets $36.00

Motor Skills

Bruininks-Oseretsky Test of Motor Proficiency–Second Edition (BOT-2)

| 2005 | AGS Publishing/Pearson Assessments |

Robert H. Bruininks, Brett D. Bruininks

Population: Ages 4 to 21 years

Purpose: Provides a comprehensive picture of a child's motor development

Description: The test provides a comprehensive index of motor proficiency, as well as differentiated measures of gross and fine motor skills. Eight subtests measure fine motor precision, fine motor integration, manual dexterity, bilateral coordination, balance, running speed and agility, upper limb coordination, and strength. Composite scores are provided in four motor areas and one comprehensive measure of overall motor proficiency.

Format: Examiner required; individually administered; Complete Battery, 45 to 60 minutes; Short Form, 15 to 20 minutes

Scoring: Examiner evaluated

Cost: Complete Kit (manual, easel, 25 protocols, scoring transparency, balance beam, manipulatives) $699.99

Movement Assessment Battery for Children (Movement ABC)

| 1992 | Harcourt Assessment-UK |

Shelia E. Henderson, David A. Sugden

Population: Ages 4 to 12 years

Purpose: Provides screening, assessment, and management of movement problems

Description: Evaluates the movement problems

that can determine a child's participation and social adjustment at school and helps plan programs for remediation and management. There are four age bands: 4 to 6 years, 7 to 8 years, 9 to 10 years, and 11 to 12 years.

Format: Examiner required; individual administration; untimed: 30 minutes

Scoring: Examiner evaluated

Cost: Complete Kit (manual, 50 checklists, 10 of each age band record forms, manipulatives, in briefcase) £575.50

Peabody Developmental Motor Scale–Second Edition (PDMS-2)

2000	PRO-ED, Inc.

M. Rhonda Folio, Rebecca R. Fewell

Population: Ages birth to 5 years

Purpose: Assesses gross and fine motor development

Description: An early childhood motor development program that provides both in-depth assessment and training or remediation of gross and fine motor skills in six subtests: Reflexes, Stationary, Locomotion, Object Manipulation, Grasping, and Visual-Motor Integration. The normative sample consisted of 2,003 persons residing in 46 states. The PDMS-2 can be used by occupational therapists, physical therapists, diagnosticians, early intervention specialists, adapted physical education teachers, and psychologists. There are three composite scores: Gross Motor Quotient, Fine Motor Quotient, and Total Motor Quotient. The new Illustrated Guide to Item Administration provides detailed descriptions of every item in the PDMS-2. The Examiner Record Booklets contain all of the items to be given to the child and allow the examiner to use the same form for four administrations. The Peabody Motor Activities Program is the instruction/treatment program. It contains units organized developmentally by skill area. The Peabody Motor Development Chart provides a convenient reference for the motor skills measured and the ages at which 50% of the normative sample performed the skill.

Format: Examiner required; individual administration; untimed: 20 to 30 minutes

Scoring: Examiner evaluated; computer scoring program available for Windows

Cost: Complete Kit (manual, guide to item administration, 25 profile/summary forms, 25 examiner record booklets, the Peabody Motor

Activities Program Manual, a black-and-white Peabody Motor Development chart, manipulatives, storage box) $445.00

Test of Gross Motor Development–Second Edition (TGMD-2)

2000	PRO-ED, Inc.

Dale A. Ulrich

Population: Ages 3 to 10 years

Purpose: Assess common motor skills of children; used for educational planning and research and to evaluate existing special education programs

Description: Multiple-item task-performance test consisting of two subtests. The Locomotor Skills subtest measures the run, gallop, hop, horizontal jump, and slide. The Object Control Skills subtest measures striking a stationary ball, stationary dribble, catch, kick, overhand throw, and underhand roll. Test findings are reported in terms of subtest standard scores, percentiles, and a composite quotient that represents total gross motor development performance.

Format: Examiner required; individual administration; untimed: 15 minutes

Scoring: Examiner evaluated

Cost: Complete Kit (manual, 50 protocols, storage box) $105.00

300 Series Valpar Dexterity Modules

1995	Valpar International Corporation

Population: Ages 15 years and older

Purpose: Used in cognitive assessment and psychomotor functioning to assess motor, manual, and finger coordination; intended for individuals with brain injuries and industrial rehabilitation

Description: Criterion-referenced performance work sample. The 300 Series Dexterity Modules include five six-inch square plates (numbered 301 to 305) that fasten, one at a time, onto a lightweight plastic box (the Basic Unit). Each plate has several unique short exercises that assess various aspects of hand function and upper extremity range of motion. The exercises may be administered to the client either horizontally or at a 45-degree angle of presentation. The exercises focus primarily on tasks that require fine finger and manual dexterity and eye–hand coordination. The exercises assess upper body range of motion, strength, flexibility, ability to follow instructions, memory, and many secondary work-related characteristics. All of the exercises have methods-time measurement industrial work rate standards to aid in the interpretation of scores. Learning curve allows for multiple administrations as needed.

Format: Examiner required; individual administration; untimed

Scoring: Examiner evaluated

Cost: Complete Set $1,810.00; modules may be purchased individually

VCWS 4—Upper Extremity Range of Motion

| 1993 | Valpar International Corporation |

Population: Ages 15 years and older

Purpose: Assesses an individual's upper extremity range of motion, including the shoulders, upper arms, forearms, elbows, wrists, and hands; provides insight into factors such as neck and back fatigue, finger dexterity, and finger tactile sense

Description: Work sample assessment of the range of motion and work tolerances of an individual in relation to the upper torso. The individual works through an opening in front of the work sample, the inside of which is half red and half blue. Using opposite hands for each color, the individual fastens two sizes of nuts to bolts on each of five panels. The design of the work sample allows the examiner to view muscle action in the individual's wrist and fingers. Performance indicates coordination, spatial, and perceptual skills; susceptibility to fatigue; and the ability to succeed in jobs requiring reaching, handling, fingering, feeling, and seeing. The test should not be used with individuals with severe impairment of the upper extremities. Learning curve allows for multiple administrations as needed.

Format: Examiner required; individual administration; timed

Scoring: Examiner evaluated

Cost: $1,660.00

VCWS 7—Multi-Level Sorting

| 1974 | Valpar International Corporation |

Population: Ages 15 years and older

Purpose: Assesses an individual's decision-making ability while performing tasks requiring physical manipulation and visual discrimination of colors, color-numbers, color-letters, and combinations of the three

Description: Work sample assessment of an individual's ability to make decisions while performing work tasks requiring physical manipulation and visual discrimination. The individual sorts 168 coded chips into 48 sorting slots showing on a board. Each chip is coded in one of the following ways: color; color and number; color and letter; or color, letter, and number. The work sample allows the examiner to observe the individual's orientation, approach, and organization with regard to the task, color, and letter; number discrimination skills; simple decision making; and physical manipulation. Methods-time measurement and error scores are used to determine performance level. Learning curve allows for multiple administrations as needed.

Format: Examiner required; individual administration; timed

Scoring: Examiner evaluated

Cost: $1,895.00

VCWS 9—Whole Body Range of Motion

| 1974 | Valpar International Corporation |

Population: Ages 15 years and older

Purpose: Assesses the ability to perform successfully gross and fine finger dexterity tasks while in kneeling, crouching, stooping, bending, and stretching positions

Description: Nonmedical assessment of gross body movements of the trunk, hands, arms, legs, and fingers as they relate to an individual's functional ability to perform job tasks. The individual stands in front of the work sample, with the frame adjusted to six inches above the head. The individual takes three colored shapes, one at a time, and transfers them from shoulder height to overhead. The individual then transfers the shapes to waist level, which requires bending forward at the waist; to knee level, which requires crouching or kneeling; and then back to shoulder height. In each transfer, the individual must remove a total of 22 nuts and then replace them, using one hand, onto each of the three colored shapes. May be used with individuals who are hearing or visually impaired. Methods-time measurement and error scores used to determine performance level. Learning curve allows for multiple administrations as needed.

Format: Examiner required; individual administration; timed

Scoring: Examiner evaluated

Cost: $2,395.00

VCWS 201—Physical Capacities/ Mobility Screening

1982 Valpar International Corporation

Population: Ages 15 years and older

Purpose: Screens physical demands required in work/training settings; used for placement and career planning

Description: Criterion-referenced work sample consisting of demonstrated performance of lifting, continuous lifting, two-handed grip, palm press, horizontal press, vertical press, balancing, walk forward, walk backward, walk heel-toe, and climbing. Examiner qualifications as required by testing site. Materials include weight scale, standing platform, lifting apparatus, hinged climbing board, and tape measure. This work sample is suitable for individuals with hearing, physical, or mental impairments. Signing for individuals with hearing impairments necessary.

Format: Examiner required; individual administration; untimed: 10 to 15 minutes

Scoring: Examiner evaluated

Cost: $795.00

VCWS 204—Fine Finger Dexterity

1992 Valpar International Corporation

Population: Ages 15 years and older

Purpose: Assesses worker qualification to profile factors for job, curricula placement, and career planning

Description: Criterion-referenced work sample consisting of demonstrated performance of dominant and nondominant fine finger dexterity. The work sample yields methods–time measurement percentage scores. Materials include wiring box and tweezers. This test is suitable for individuals with hearing, physical, or mental impairments. Signing for individuals with hearing impairments is necessary. Learning curve allows for multiple administrations as needed.

Format: Examiner required; individual administration; untimed: 10 to 15 minutes

Scoring: Examiner evaluated

Cost: $725.00

Reading, Language Arts, and English

Elementary

Assessing and Teaching Phonological Knowledge

1998 Australian Council for Educational Research Limited

John Munro

Population: First 3 years of school

Purpose: Identifies developmental level of phonological knowledge; assesses whether difficulties are due to delayed or immature development; used to recommend teaching procedures and follow-up tasks

Description: The materials include a manual, record book, checklist, task sheet, and starter sheet. The following skills are measured: awareness of sound patterns in words, segmenting words into sounds, sound blending, manipulating sounds in words, and phonemic recoding.

Format: Examiner required; individual administration; untimed

Scoring: Examiner evaluated

Cost: Starter Set $133.00

Burt Word Reading Test– New Zealand Revision

1981 New Zealand Council for Educational Research

Alison Gilmore, Cedric Croft, Neil Reid

Population: Ages 6 to 13 years

Purpose: Measures word recognition

Description: Provides a measure of an aspect of a child's word reading skills (i.e., word recognition). The Test Card consists of 110 words printed in decreasing size of type and graded in approximate order of difficulty. Used in conjunction with other information, the *Burt Word Reading Test* should allow teachers to form a broad estimate of a child's reading achievement to aid decisions about appropriate teaching and reading materials, instructional groupings, and so on. In addition, the *Burt Word Reading Test* should prove useful as an indicator of possible wider reading problems.

Format: Examiner required; individual administration; untimed: 5 minutes

Scoring: Examiner evaluated

Cost: Specimen Set $8.10

Comprehensive Assessment of Reading Strategies (CARS®)

| 2006 | Curriculum Associates®, Inc. |

Population: Grades 1 to 8

Purpose: Diagnoses individual instructional needs

Description: The assessment identifies weaknesses in 12 standards-based reading strategies and encourages students to use higher-order thinking skills. Supports No Child Left Behind goals. Reinforces understanding of performance through self-assessment. Management software is available. Available in Spanish for Grades 1 to 5.

Format: Examiner required; group administration; untimed

Scoring: Examiner evaluated; computer scoring available

Cost: 10-Pack of Student Booklets $25.90; Teacher Guide $4.95 per grade; Software $25.95

Diagnostic Reading Scales Revised Edition (DRS)

| 1982 | CTB/McGraw-Hill |

George D. Spache

Population: Children

Purpose: Identifies a student's reading strengths and weaknesses; used by educators to determine placement and to prescribe instruction

Description: Multiple-item reading skills test consisting of a series of graduated scales containing three word-recognition lists, 22 reading sections, and 12 phonics and word analysis tests.

Format: Examiner required; individual administration; timed: 1 hour

Scoring: Examiner evaluated

Cost: Contact publisher

Durrell Analysis of Reading Difficulty: Third Edition (DARD)

| 1980 | Harcourt Assessment, Inc. |

Donald D. Durrell, Jane H. Catterson

Population: Grades 1 to 6

Purpose: Assesses reading behavior; used for diagnosis, measurement of prereading skills, and planning remedial programs

Description: Multiple-item series of tests and situations measuring 10 reading abilities: oral reading, silent reading, listening comprehension, listening vocabulary, word recognition/word analysis, spelling, auditory analysis of words and word elements, pronunciation of word elements, visual memory of words, and prereading phonics abilities. Supplementary paragraphs for oral and silent reading are provided for supplementary testing or retesting. Materials include a spiral-bound booklet containing items to be read and a tachistoscope with accompanying test card.

Format: Examiner required; individual administration; untimed: 30 to 45 minutes

Scoring: Examiner evaluated

Cost: Examiner's Kit (5 record booklets, tachistoscope, reading booklet, manual) $163.00

Dynamic Indicators of Basic Early Literacy Skills (DIBELS)

| 2003 | Sopris West Educational Services |

Roland H. Good III, Ruth Kaminski

Population: Grades K to 6

Purpose: Measures reading to predict success

Description: Students from Kindergarten to Grade 3 are given Benchmark Assessments three times a year that measure the critical areas of early reading: phonemic awareness, phonics, fluency, comprehension, and vocabulary. Students in Grades 4 to 6 are assessed in the areas of fluency and comprehension. For those with reading difficulties, Progress Monitoring Assessments are given as often as necessary to determine the effectiveness of the intervention(s) being used. Also available in Spanish.

Format: Examiner required; group administration; untimed

Scoring: Examiner evaluated

Cost: K to 3 Classroom Set (specify grade) $69.00; 4 to 6 Classroom Set (specify grade) $55.00

Group Reading Test–Fourth Edition

| 1999 | Hodder Murray |

Dennis Young

Population: Ages 6 to 9 years

Purpose: Measures reading accuracy and understanding

Description: Looks at a pupil's use of picture, context, sight, and phonic cues in silent reading. Provides standardized scores and reading ages. Has parallel forms.

Format: Examiner required; group administration; untimed: 20 to 25 minutes

Scoring: Examiner evaluated

Cost: Specimen Set (manual, 1 each of Form A and Form B) £13.99

NewGAP

1990	Academic Therapy Publications

John McLeod, Rita McLeod

Population: Ages 7 to 10 years

Purpose: Measures reading comprehension

Description: A norm-referenced instrument that uses the cloze technique, which involves omitting simple, common words within sentences in several short passages and asking students to insert the best-fitting word. This method allows an assessment of expressive language since students must generate words that fit a specific context. Since there are two equivalent forms, the instrument is appropriate for pre- and posttesting. A template facilitates scoring. Correlates with the Reading Comprehension subtest of the *Comprehensive Tests of Basic Skills.*

Format: Examiner required; group administration; untimed: 20 minutes

Scoring: Examiner evaluated

Cost: Test Kit (manual, 25 of each form [I and II], scoring template, in vinyl folder) $55.00

Phonemic-Awareness Skills Screening (PASS)

2000	PRO-ED, Inc.

Linda Crumrine, Helen Lonegan

Population: Grades 1 and 2

Purpose: Identifies specific weaknesses in phonological processing ability

Description: The PASS includes eight sections: Rhyme, Sentence Segmentation, Blending, Syllable Segmentation, Deletion, Phoneme Isolation, Phoneme Segmentation, and Phoneme Substitution.

Format: Examiner required; individual administration; untimed: 15 minutes

Scoring: Examiner evaluated

Cost: Complete Kit (manual, 25 record forms) $30.00

Phonics-Based Reading Test (PRT)

2002	Academic Therapy Publications

Rick Brownell

Population: Grades 1 to 6

Purpose: Measures decoding, fluency, and comprehension

Description: The instrument determines what phonics skills a student uses in reading. There are word lists and words within passages that are coordinated to the typical sequences of phonics skill acquisition. Reading materials are progressively more complex. Scores can be interpreted using either criteria or notionally representative norms to assist with instructional planning.

Format: Examiner required; individual administration; untimed: 20 to 30 minutes

Scoring: Examiner evaluated

Cost: Test Kit (manual, stimulus book, 25 forms, portfolio) $82.00

Pre-Literacy Skills Screening (PLSS)

1999	PRO-ED, Inc.

Linda Crumrine, Helen Lonegan

Population: Pre-K to K

Purpose: Identifies incoming kindergarten children who may be at risk for literacy failure

Description: The PLSS includes nine subtests: Rhyme, Sentence Repetition, Naming, Blending, Sentence Segmentation, Letter Naming, Syllable Segmentation, Deletion, and Multisyllabic Word Repetition.

Format: Examiner required; individual administration; untimed: 15 minutes

Scoring: Examiner evaluated

Cost: Complete Kit (manual and picture book, 25 record forms) $51.00

Process Assessment of the Learner™ (PAL™): Test Battery for Reading and Writing

2000	Harcourt Assessment, Inc.

Virginia Wise Beringer

Population: Grades K to 6

Purpose: Examines processes underlying reading and writing skills

Description: The PAL screens by identifying students at risk, monitors by tracking progress, and diagnoses by evaluating the nature of reading- and writing-related processing problems. The subtests are developmentally appropriate, and the examiner may choose which subtests to administer; the test does not need to be given in its entirety. The PAL was standardized with the *Wechsler Individual Achievement Test–Second Edition,* providing an empirically based sequence of decision making. The battery includes measures of phonological processing; orthographic coding; rapid automatized naming; and integration of listening, note taking, and summary writing skills.

Format: Examiner required; individual administration; untimed: 30 to 60 minutes

Scoring: Examiner evaluated

Cost: Complete Kit (manual, stimulus booklets, 25 each of record forms and response forms, word card, audiotape, manipulatives, bag) $355.00

Reading Progress Tests

1997	Hodder Murray

Denis Vincent, Mary Crumpler, Mike de la Mare

Population: Ages 5 to 12 years

Purpose: Measures progress in reading

Description: The tests can be used separately, with selected year groups, but are most informative when used annually to provide an ongoing measure of attainment. The combination of text and illustration seeks to make the tests motivating and accessible to children across a wide ability range. Standardized scores and reading ages are provided for each year group. Additionally, "progress norms" make the tests particularly suitable for continuous year-on-year tracking of individual progress relative to a child's previous performance. Available for Stage One and Stage Two. Stage Two assesses literal and inferential comprehension and reading vocabulary on reusable full-color broadsheets.

Format: Examiner required; group administration; untimed: 45 to 50 minutes

Scoring: Examiner evaluated; computer scoring available

Cost: Stage One Specimen Set (manual; 1 each of Literacy Baseline, Test 1, Test 2) £18.99; Stage

Two Specimen Set (manual; 1 each of Test 3, Test 4, Test 5, Test 6; 1 each of broadsheets for all tests) £22.99

Signposts Early Literacy Battery

2000	Touchstone Applied Science Associates, Inc.

Population: Ages 5 to 8 years

Purpose: Measures language arts competency (reading and prereading), helps to design instruction, and evaluates progress

Description: A total of 68 to 88 items, depending on level, with four categories (Speaking, Listening, Reading, and Writing) that measure a number of elements of emerging literacy. Pre-DRP/DRP (Degrees of Reading Power) subscores, battery scale score, and percentile rank scores provided.

Format: Examiner required; suitable for group use; untimed: 110 to 165 minutes

Scoring: Examiner evaluated; software scoring available

Cost: Classroom Set (25 test booklets, administration procedures, class record sheet, handbook, norms) $99.00

Signposts Pre-DRP Test

2000	Touchstone Applied Science Associates, Inc.

Population: Ages 5 to 8 years

Purpose: Measures reading ability of emerging and beginning readers, monitors progress, and matches ability with appropriate reading materials

Description: A total of 28 to 32 items depending on level. Yields Pre-DRP (Degrees of Reading Power) scale score, and percentile rank.

Format: Examiner required; suitable for group use; untimed: 45 to 50 minutes

Scoring: Hand Key

Cost: Classroom Set (25 test booklets, administration procedures, handbook, norms) $79.00

Slosson Phonics and Structural Analysis Test (SP-SAT)

2004	Slosson Educational Publications, Inc.

Leslie Anne Perry, Bradley T. Erford

Population: Ages 6 to 9 years

Purpose: Measures ability to examine words for meaningful parts

Description: Phonics skills are measured by Phonics Clusters and Structural Analysis Clusters. Administration and scoring are quick and easy.

Format: Examiner required; group administration; untimed

Scoring: Examiner evaluated

Cost: Complete Kit $120.25

Spelling and Reading Tests– Third Edition (SPAR)

1998	Hodder Murray

Dennis Young

Population: Ages 7 to 9 years

Purpose: Measures reading and spelling skills

Description: Ideas for Year 3 pupils with a wide ability range and those with anticipated reading ages of up to 9 years. Spelling banks allow the selection of three 40-item spelling tests without overlap and more with partial overlap. Gives standardized scores (separately for reading and spelling).

Format: Examiner required; group administration; untimed: 20 to 25 minutes

Scoring: Examiner evaluated

Cost: Specimen Set (manual, 1 each of Form A, Form B) £14.99

Star Early Literacy

2006	Renaissance Learning, Inc.

Population: Grades Pre-K to 3

Purpose: Provides periodic progress monitoring of early literacy skills

Description: It tracks the development of 41 skills within the following seven literacy domains: General Readiness, Graphophonemic Knowledge, Phonemic Awareness, Phonics, Comprehension, Vocabulary, and Structural Analysis. The criterion-referenced scores enable educators to effectively plan instruction and monitor the progress of each student throughout the year. The *STAR Early Literacy* uses computer-adaptive technology to tailor each student's assessment based on his or her responses to previous items. The program is animated, auditory, and can be completed without teacher assistance.

Format: Computer administered; timed: 10 minutes

Scoring: Computer scored

Cost: One-Time Setup (per school) $1,499.00; Annual Student Fee: $.39 per student

STAR Supplementary Test of Achievement in Reading

2000, 2003	New Zealand Council for Educational Research

Warwick B. Elley

Population: Years 3 to 9

Purpose: Measures reading achievement

Description: The purpose of the STAR is to supplement the assessments teachers make about progress and achievement in reading. The STAR may be administered at any time in the school year. There are two parallel forms. Subtests are (1) Word Recognition: This subtest shows how well pupils can decode words that are familiar in their spoken vocabulary; in the absence of any verbal context, the pupils must decode, accurately, using letters and sounds; (2) Sentence Comprehension: The task is reading for meaning; this subtest assesses the skills of decoding and the ability to use a range of sources to gain meaning; (3) Paragraph Comprehension: The cloze procedure here assesses reading comprehension by requiring pupils to replace words that have been deleted from the text; pupils use the context of the surrounding text as cues to meaning; (4) Vocabulary Range: This subtest assesses pupils' knowledge of word meanings in context; Years 7 to 9 only; (5) The Language of Advertising: This subtest requires pupils to identify emotive words, which are typically said by advertisers when trying to attract consumers to buy; pupils read a series of sentences and circle the one that sounds appealing but provides no information, (e.g., "fabulous," "cosy," "gotta-go"); this skill is part of learning to be a critical reader and is stressed in "English in the New Zealand Curriculum" for Years 7 and 8 (or Curriculum Levels 4 and 5); (6) Reading Different Genres or Styles of Writing: Pupils in the senior levels of primary school are expected to read with understanding various styles or genres of writing, both formal and informal.

Format: Examiner required; group administration; timed: 20 to 30 minutes

Scoring: Examiner evaluated

Cost: Specimen Set Year 3 $36.90; Specimen Set Years 4 to 9 $61.65

Test of Early Reading Ability– Third Edition (TERA-3)

2001	PRO-ED, Inc.

D. Kim Reid, Wayne P. Hresko, Donald D. Hammill

Population: Ages 3 years 6 months to 8 years 6 months

Purpose: Measures mastery of early developing reading skills

Description: This edition has been redesigned to provide the examiner with three subtests: Alphabet (measuring knowledge of the alphabet and its uses), Conventions (measuring knowledge of the conventions of print), and Meaning (measuring knowledge of the construction of meaning from print). Standard scores are provided for each subtest. An overall Reading Quotient is computed using all three subtest scores. New items have been added to make the test more reliable and valid for the upper and lower ages covered by the test. All pictures have been drawn in color to present a more appealing look to children. All logos and labels are included.

Format: Examiner required; individual administration; untimed: 30 minutes

Scoring: Examiner evaluated

Cost: Complete Kit (manual, picture books, 25 each of Form A and Form B profile/examiner record forms, storage box) $265.00

Test of Early Written Language–Second Edition (TEWL-2)

1996	PRO-ED, Inc.

Wayne P. Hresko, Shelley R. Herron, Pamela K. Peak

Population: Ages 3 to 10 years

Purpose: Measures the emerging written language skills of young children; used to identify students with mild disabilities and to document student growth and program effectiveness

Description: Multiple-item paper–pencil test covering areas with a direct relationship to a young child's school-related activities, including transcription, conventions of print, communication, creative expression, and record keeping. Picture cards are used to prompt writing samples. The test yields standard scores and percentiles, which can be used with other cognitive and academic measures to identify intraindividual abilities. The scores obtained are Global Writing Quotient, Basic Writing Quotient, and Contextual Writing Quotient.

Format: Examiner required; individual administration; untimed: 30 to 45 minutes

Scoring: Examiner evaluated

Cost: Complete Kit (manual, 10 each of Forms A and B, 10 each of student workbooks Forms A and B, storage box) $190.00

Test of Oral Reading and Comprehension Skills (TCS)

2000	Academic Therapy Publications

Morrison F. Gardner

Population: Ages 5 to 14 years

Purpose: Measures reading skills

Description: Measures what the child reads or what is read to the child to determine how well a child will perform other academic subjects. Was constructed to include words, phrases, and sentences arranged developmentally. Information on reliability and validity is well documented in the manual.

Format: Examiner required; individual administration; untimed: 20 minutes

Scoring: Examiner evaluated

Cost: Complete Kit (manual, 15 test booklets, oral reading stories booklet) $52.00

Test of Phonological Awareness in Spanish (TPAS)

2004	PRO-ED, Inc.

Cynthia A. Riccio, Brian Imhoff, Jan E. Hasbrouck, G. Nicole Davis

Population: Ages 4 to 10 years

Purpose: Measures phonological awareness ability in Spanish-speaking children; identifies children who may benefit from instructional activities that enhance their phonological abilities

Description: Using four subtests (Initial Sounds, Final Sounds, Rhyming Words, and Deletions), the TPAS provides standard scores and percentiles.

Format: Examiner required; individual administration; untimed: 15 to 30 minutes

Scoring: Examiner evaluated

Cost: Complete Kit (manual, 25 record booklets, storage box) $84.00

Test of Phonological Awareness Skills (TOPAS)

2003	PRO-ED, Inc.

Phyllis L. Newcomer, Edna Barenbaum

Population: Ages 5 to 10 years

Purpose: Identifies children who have problems in phonological awareness

Description: The TOPAS has four subtests (Rhyming, Incomplete Words, Sound Sequencing, and Sound Deletion) that measure three areas of phonological awareness: Sound Comparison, Phoneme Blending, and Phoneme Segmentation. Raw scores are converted into percentiles, standard scores, and age equivalents.

Format: Examiner required; individual administration; untimed: 15 to 30 minutes

Scoring: Examiner evaluated

Cost: Complete Kit (manual, 25 record booklets, block kit, audiocassette, storage box) $110.00

Test of Silent Reading Skills (TSRS)

2001	Academic Therapy Publications

Morrison F. Gardner

Population: Ages 7 to 13 years

Purpose: Measures ability to gain information from silent reading

Description: Measures not only story comprehension and paragraph comprehension, but also word meaning, word identification, and speed of reading. All six stories and all six paragraphs are followed by multiple-choice questions. A Spanish version is available.

Format: Examiner required; individual or group administration; untimed: 25 to 35 minutes

Scoring: Examiner evaluated

Cost: Complete Kit (manual, 25 test booklets, template, reading card) $96.00

Word Recognition and Phonic Scale–Second Edition (WRaPS-2)

2003	Hodder Murray

David Moseley

Population: Ages 5 to 9 years

Purpose: Assesses developing word recognition and phonics skills

Description: The WRaPS-2 has been extensively refined in light of ongoing research and is now available in parallel Forms A and B. Fully restandardized, the coverage of the test has been extended to map fully to the Literacy Strategy Progression in Phonics "steps," making it suitable for use with pupils aged 4-6 to 9-0 years. The practical suggestions for teaching follow-up have also been expanded. The WRaPS-2 is easily administered to a full class in a single period and is quickly scored using the scoring keys, which also now provide a sharper diagnostic analysis. The test format ensures that almost all children can identify some features of spoken words in printed form and can complete the test without experiencing failure. The WRaPS-2 can be repeated using the parallel forms at intervals to assess progress from Reception to Year 4, and in working with older pupils with reading difficulties.

Format: Examiner required; group administration; untimed: 20 to 30 minutes

Scoring: Examiner evaluated

Cost: Specimen Set (manual, diagnostic keys, 1 each of Form A and Form B) £29.99

High School and College

Collegiate Assessment of Academic Progress (CAAP) Reading Test

2001	ACT, Inc.

Population: Ages 17 years and older

Purpose: Assesses reading skills

Description: Paper–pencil 36-item multiple-choice test with two categories: Referring and Reasoning. A test booklet, answer sheet, and pencil are used. May be used with persons with visual, physical, hearing, or mental impairments.

Format: Examiner required; suitable for group use; timed: 40 minutes

Scoring: Machine scored; test scoring service available from publisher

Cost: $10.75

Collegiate Assessment of Academic Progress (CAAP) Writing Essay Test

2001	ACT, Inc.

Population: Ages 17 years and older

Purpose: Assesses writing skills

Description: Paper–pencil essay test. A test booklet, answer sheet, and pencil are used. May be used for persons with visual, physical, hearing, or mental impairments.

Format: Examiner required; suitable for group use; timed: 40 minutes

Scoring: Examiner evaluated; test scoring service available

Cost: $10.75

Collegiate Assessment of Academic Progress (CAAP) Writing Skills Test

| 2001 | ACT, Inc. |

Population: Ages 17 years and older

Purpose: Assesses English usage/mechanics and rhetorical skills

Description: Paper-pencil 72-item multiple-choice test with the following categories: Usage/Mechanical and Rhetorical Skills. Two subscores are yielded. May be used for persons with visual, physical, hearing, or mental impairments.

Format: Examiner required; suitable for group use; timed: 40 minutes

Scoring: Machine scored; test scoring service available

Cost: $10.75

English Language Understanding Test (ELT)

| 2000 | Hogrefe Limited |

Geoff Williams

Population: Ages 16 years and older

Purpose: Measures an individual's level of competence in, understanding of, and ability to work effectively with the English language

Description: The test consists of two short sections. In Part One, the candidate chooses from a selection of four words the one word that best fits the meaning of the text. This part is primarily word knowledge, but also requires a basic understanding of grammar in looking at contextual cues. Part Two is more concerned with accuracy and understanding. The candidate is required to find the errors in a passage of text that can be spelling, punctuation, grammar, or the use of inappropriate words. In addition, the subject of the text is unlikely to be familiar to the candidates, and therefore the ability to grasp new topics can also be assessed.

Format: Examiner required; individually administered; timed: 10 minutes

Scoring: Hand key; test scoring service available from publisher

Cost: Contact publisher

Functional Writing Assessment

| 2006 | CASAS |

Population: Adolescents, adults; native and nonnative speakers of English

Purpose: Assesses learners' general writing level and provides diagnostic information about which writing skills the learner needs to target; appropriate for low literacy levels

Description: Three writing tasks: Letter Task, Picture Task, and Form Task. Students write a letter, describe the process or picture, or fill out the form. In addition, two beginning-level writing tasks are available. Training is required for examiners. Writing samples are scored analytically or holistically using standardized detailed rubrics and annotated scoring anchors.

Format: Examiner required; individual or group administration; untimed

Scoring: Examiner evaluated

Cost: Contact publisher

Life and Work Reading

| 2006 | CASAS |

Population: Adolescents, adults; native and nonnative speakers of English

Purpose: Used by programs to identify basic skills in reading needed by individuals to function successfully in today's workplace, community, and society; learners can be placed into educational programs to assess learning gains

Description: Contains progress tests at Levels A, B, C, and D. The reading tests are appropriate for both adult basic education and English as a second language individuals. The tests for Levels A and B follow a storyline to enhance interest and increase the accessibility and relevance of the items. The tests can be used for progress testing. The student takes a pretest, and after approximately 70 to 100 hours of instruction, a posttest is administered.

Format: Self-administered; untimed

Scoring: Self- and computer scored

Cost: 25 Reusable Tests $70.00; 25 Listening Tests with Audiotape $75.00; Manual $15.00

Nelson-Denny Reading Test: Forms G and H

| 1993, 2000 | Riverside Publishing Company |

James I. Brown, Vivian Vick Fishco, Gerald S. Hanna

Population: Grades 9 to adult

Purpose: Assesses student achievement and progress in vocabulary, comprehension, and reading rate

Description: A two-part test. Part I (Vocabulary) is a 15-minute timed test; Part II (Comprehension and Rate) is a 20-minute test. The Vocabulary section focuses on words students need for success in today's classroom, and the Comprehension passages are drawn from widely used current high school and college texts.

Format: Examiner required; suitable for group use; untimed: 35 minutes

Scoring: Hand key; may be machine scored; computer scoring

Cost: 25 Test Booklets $59.35; 50 Self-Scorable Answer Sheets $96.50; CD $6.95 per administration

PSB Reading Comprehension Examination

1993	Psychological Services Bureau, Inc.

Population: Health occupations students

Purpose: Measures an individual's ability to understand material read; used to identify students in the health professions who need counseling or remedial assistance

Description: Multiple-item paper–pencil or electronic test sampling essential functional elements of reading comprehension. It is specifically designed for secondary, postsecondary, and professional programs and may be used as an adjunct to PSB tests in practical nursing, health occupations, and nursing.

Format: Examiner required; suitable for group use; timed: 60 minutes

Scoring: Machine and electronically scored

Cost: Contact publisher

Multiage

Cloze Reading Tests

1992	Hodder Murray

Dennis Young

Population: Ages 7 years 6 months to 12 years 7 months

Purpose: Measures ability to read

Description: Adapts the well-researched cloze technique to the practical purpose of assessing pupils' reading. Three test levels provide standardized scores and reading ages.

Format: Examiner required; group administration; untimed: 35 to 40 minutes

Scoring: Examiner evaluated

Cost: Each Level (10) £6.50; Manual £13.99

CTB Writing Assessment System®

1993	CTB/McGraw-Hill

Population: Grades 2 to 12

Purpose: Assesses independent and reading-related writing skills

Description: Multiple-item paper–pencil essay test used independently or combined with results from the *California Achievement Test, Fifth Edition.* The test offers two kinds of writing assignments or prompts: independent and reading-related. Independent prompts test writing ability independent of the ability to comprehend a reading passage. Reading-related prompts combine reading comprehension with writing tasks to reflect the whole-language instructional approach. Writing tasks elicit one of the following types of writing: personal expression (narrative or descriptive), informative, or persuasive. The assessment has four levels, ranging from Grades 2 to 12.

Format: Examiner required; suitable for group use; timed

Scoring: Examiner evaluated; scoring service available

Cost: Contact publisher

DART (Developmental Assessment Resource for Teachers) English

1997	Australian Council for Educational Research Limited

W. Bodey, L. Darkin, M. Forster, G. Masters

Population: Levels 1 to 5

Purpose: Assesses students' level of performance in terms of skills and understanding

Description: The tests contain five strands: viewing, reading, listening, speaking, and writing. DART activities can be used as the basis for a classroom language unit. Descriptive and Diagnostic reports are provided.

Format: Examiner required; suitable for group use; untimed

Scoring: Examiner evaluated

Cost: Contact publisher

Degrees of Reading Power® (DRP)

2000	Touchstone Applied Science Associates, Inc.

Population: Grades 1 to 12+, college

Purpose: Assesses reading comprehension of students; used to identify and place students in reading programs, assess reading goals and standards, relate reading ability to appropriate reading materials, and make admission decisions

Description: Multiple-item multiple-choice text-referenced paper–pencil test in which students read a series of nonfiction prose passages, each with seven deleted words. Students supply the missing words from among five choices provided for each deletion. The passages progress from easy to difficult. The test yields six scores: raw score, independent level score (indicates the difficulty of books the student can read with a 90% chance of understanding the material), three instructional level scores (70%, 75%, and 80% chance of student comprehending materials), and frustration level score (indicates probability of comprehension of 50% or less). Percentile ranks and NCEs are available for Grades 1 to 12. The test is available in two alternate series, J and K, for Grades 1 to 12: Primary Forms (machine scorable) and Standard (reusable) for the various grades.

Format: Examiner required; suitable for group use; untimed: about one class period

Scoring: Hand key; computer scoring available

Cost: Examination Set $45.00

Diagnostic Assessments of Reading (DAR)

| 2006 | Riverside Publishing Company |

Florence G. Roswell, Jeanne S. Chall, Mary E. Curtis, Gail Kearns

Population: Ages 5 years to adult

Purpose: Assesses achievement in print awareness, letters and sounds, word recognition, word analysis, oral reading accuracy and fluency, silent reading comprehension, spelling, and word meaning

Description: Revision includes new tests and enhanced subtests. Comprehension assessment has been added to the lower levels. All data have been updated and have a four-color format. Computer scoring allows aggregation and desegregation of student scores. Trial Teaching Strategies available.

Format: Examiner required; suitable for group use; untimed: 40 minutes

Scoring: Examiner evaluated; computer scoring

Cost: Classroom Kit (manual, student book, 30 response record forms) $219.25

Diagnostic Reading Analysis

| 2004 | Hodder Murray |

Mary Crumpler, Colin McCarty

Population: Ages 7 to 16 years

Purpose: Provides reading analysis for less able readers

Description: The test provides an initial listening comprehension passage that helps to determine each pupil's starting point. Pupils read and answer questions on three graded passages (two fiction and one nonfiction) pitched at appropriate levels of difficulty. The student does not have to take the whole test, but is directed to the next appropriate reading passage. The test uses NLS sight words and includes full-color illustrations. Assesses reading accuracy, reading comprehension, and fluency/reading rate. Scores are fully standardized. Detailed advice on interpretation and diagnostic follow-up are provided. Parallel forms allow for retesting. An optional computer scoring provides a detailed report.

Format: Examiner required; individual administration; untimed: 15 minutes

Scoring: Examiner evaluated; computer scoring available

Cost: Specimen Set (manual, 1 each of Form A and Form B record forms, reading booklet) £50.00; CD scoring £75.00+VAT

Diagnostic Screening Test: Language—Second Edition (DSTL)

| 1980 | Slosson Educational Publications, Inc. |

Thomas D. Gnagey, Patricia A. Gnagey

Population: Grades 1 to 13

Purpose: Determines a student's ability to write English and diagnoses common problems in the use of the language

Description: Paper–pencil 110-item multiple-choice test yielding six scores: Total, Sentence Structure, Grammar, Punctuation, Capitalization, and Formal Spelling Rules. All subtests yield applied versus formal knowledge for a total of 12 scores in all. The examiner explains the procedure to individuals or groups and reads the test if the students have poor reading skills.

Format: Examiner required; suitable for group use; untimed: 5 to 10 minutes

Scoring: Hand key

Cost: Manual and 50 Test Forms $72.25

Diagnostic Screening Test: Reading-Third Edition (DSTR)

1982	Slosson Educational Publications, Inc.

Thomas D. Gnagey, Patricia A. Gnagey

Population: Grades 1 to junior college

Purpose: Determines reading achievement levels and diagnoses common reading problems by testing word recognition, reading, and listening comprehension

Description: Paper-pencil 84-word test yielding two major scores (Word Recognition and Reading Comprehension Grade Equivalents) and eight diagnostic scores that reflect skills in using seven basic word attack skills, as well as sight vocabulary. The student reads a word list and comprehension passages aloud and answers prescribed questions. The examiner then reads a passage aloud and the student answers questions. The test yields a consolidation index that reflects how solid or spotty each skill is. The test is available in two equivalent forms, A and B.

Format: Examiner required; individual administration; untimed: 5 to 10 minutes

Scoring: Hand key

Cost: Complete Kit (manual, 25 each of Form A and B) $72.25

Diagnostic Screening Test: Spelling-Third Edition (DSTS)

1982	Slosson Educational Publications, Inc.

Thomas D. Gnagey

Population: Grades 1 to 12

Purpose: Measures a student's ability to spell words and diagnoses common spelling problems

Description: Paper-pencil 78-item test measuring sight or phonics orientation for spelling instruction; relative efficiency of verbal and written testing procedures; analysis of sequential and gross auditory memory; and spelling potential. A pretest is available to determine the appropriate level of entry. The examiner, using the test form, pronounces 78 developmentally arranged words and the student spells them orally; the examiner then repronounces difficult words and the student writes them. When administered to groups, the test yields a grade equivalent score. The test is available in Forms A and B.

Format: Examiner required; suitable for group use; untimed: 5 to 10 minutes

Scoring: Hand key

Cost: Complete Kit (manual, 25 each of Form A and B) $72.25

Edinburgh Reading Tests-Third Edition

2002	Hodder Murray

Population: Ages 7 to 16+ years

Purpose: Assesses a range of literacy skills and provides a diagnostic profile of strengths and weaknesses

Description: Four overlapping tests provide reliable standardized scores, reading ages, and individual diagnostic profiles for vocabulary, sequencing, and comprehension. Provides effective progress monitoring in reading. A computerized interactive version is available for ages 11 to 16+. A shortened test covers a wide ability range at ages 10 years to 11 years 6 months. Gives standardized scores and reading ages.

Format: Examiner required; group administration; untimed: varies by age

Scoring: Examiner evaluated; computer scoring available

Cost: Varies by Level (1 to 4)

Gates-MacGinitie Reading Test-Second Canadian Edition (GMRT)

1992	Thomson Nelson

Walter MacGinitie

Population: Grades K to 12

Purpose: Measures students' reading and vocabulary achievement levels; used for placement and class planning

Description: Multiple-item paper-pencil test of vocabulary and reading comprehension. The basic Level R contains 54 items. Levels A to F contain 85 to 89 items.

Format: Examiner required; suitable for group use; timed: 55 minutes; untimed: Level R, 65 minutes

Scoring: Hand key; may be computer scored

Cost: Contact publisher

Gates-MacGinitie Reading Tests™-Fourth Edition (GMRT™)

2000	Riverside Publishing Company

Walter H. MacGinitie, Ruth K. MacGinitie, Katherine Maria, Lois G. Dreyer

Population: Grades K to 12, adults

Purpose: Measures the general level of reading achievement

Description: The test places emphasis on comprehension at all levels. Each level is developmentally appropriate and alternate forms provide for pre- and posttesting. Level AR is designed for adult education programs. The tests were standardized nationally in the 1998–1999 school year. The empirical norms dates for most levels are November 9 and April 22, except for Level 1, which are February 24 and April 22. National norms are available for all times of the year. A broad range of out-of-level norms is also available.

Format: Examiner required; suitable for group use; timed: varies per level

Scoring: Hand key; may be machine scored; scoring service available

Cost: Contact publisher

Graded Word Spelling Test

1998	Hodder Murray

P. E. Vernon

Population: Ages 6 years to adult

Purpose: Measures spelling ability

Description: An 80-word list, graded in order of difficulty, is presented. Each is placed in the context of a short sentence. Pupils use only those test items appropriate to their age and ability. Norms given as both spelling ages and standardized scores. Recognized by the Joint Council for Qualifications to support examination concessions at 16+.

Format: Examiner required; group administration; untimed: 20 to 30 minutes

Scoring: Examiner evaluated

Cost: Test Booklet £9.99

Gray Diagnostic Reading Test–Second Edition (GDRT-2)

2004	PRO-ED, Inc.

Brian R. Bryant, J. Lee Wiederholt, Diane P. Bryant

Population: Ages 6 to 13 years

Purpose: Assesses students who have difficulty in reading continuous print and require an evaluation of specific abilities and weaknesses

Description: The GDRT-2 uses two parallel forms

with four core subtests (Letter/Word Identification, Phonetic Analysis, Reading Vocabulary, and Meaningful Reading) to measure reading skill. Three supplemental subtests (Listening Vocabulary, Rapid Naming, and Phonological Awareness) measure skills important in the diagnosis of reading difficulty. Standard scores and percentiles, as well as age/grade equivalents, are available.

Format: Examiner required; individual administration; untimed: 45 to 60 minutes

Scoring: Examiner evaluated

Cost: Complete Kit (manual, storybook, A and B student book, 25 each A and B record forms, storage box) $169.00

Gray Oral Reading Test–Fourth Edition (GORT-4)

2001	PRO-ED, Inc.

J. Lee Wiederholt, Brian R. Bryant

Population: Ages 6 to 18 years

Purpose: Measures growth in oral reading and diagnoses reading difficulties in students

Description: Multiple-item oral-response test in two alternate, equivalent forms. The student reads 14 developmentally sequenced passages aloud and responds to five comprehension questions. The Fluency Score, derived from reading rate and errors, and Oral Reading Comprehension are reported as standard scores, percentiles, and grade equivalents. A system of miscue analysis provides criterion information in Meaning Similarity, Function Similarity, Graphic/Phonemic Similarity, and Self-Correction. A total standard score for Oral Reading is also provided.

Format: Examiner required; individual administration; portions timed: 15 to 30 minutes

Scoring: Examiner evaluated

Cost: Complete Kit (manual, student book, 25 each of forms A and B, storage box) $225.00

Gray Silent Reading Tests (GSRT)

2000	PRO-ED, Inc.

J. Lee Wiederholt, Ginger Blalock

Population: Ages 7 to 25 years

Purpose: Measures an individual's silent reading comprehension ability

Description: The test consists of two parallel forms each containing 13 developmentally sequenced reading passages with five multiple-choice questions. Each form of the test yields raw scores, grade equivalents, age equivalent percentiles, and a Silent Reading Quotient. Unlike many other tests of reading, internal consistency is reported for each 1-year interval. Sources of cultural, racial and gender bias are eliminated. Validity data also show that the GSRT can be used with the *Gray Oral Reading Tests–Fourth Edition* (GORT-4).

Format: Examiner required; individual or group administration; untimed: 15 to 30 minutes

Scoring: Examiner evaluated

Cost: Complete Kit (manual, 25 each forms A and B, 10 reading booklets A and B, storage box) $160.00

Group Literacy Assessment–Second Edition

1999	Hodder Murray

Frank Spooncer

Population: Ages 7 to 14 years

Purpose: Measures reading ability

Description: This test reflects current concerns in focusing on literacy at the critical stage of primary/secondary transfer. Provides a quick and convenient assessment of pupils' abilities. Measures ability to combine pictorial, contextual, and grammatical cues; to note significant details; to carry information in short-term memory; and to make inferential judgments. Ideal for screening pupils at the beginning of Year 7 or assessing older, special needs groups. Gives standardized scores for ages 10 years 6 months to 12 years 6 months, plus reading ages for 7 to 14 years.

Format: Examiner required; group administration; untimed: 30 minutes

Scoring: Examiner evaluated

Cost: 20 Test Forms £9.50; Manual £14.99

Hodder Group Reading Tests

2000	Hodder Murray

Denis Vincent, Mary Crumpler

Population: Ages 5 to 16 years

Purpose: Assesses reading comprehension at the word, sentence, and continuous text level

Description: The tests are useful in assessing mixed-ability groups and are easy to administer and score. Standardized on over 13,000 pupils. The tests provide reading ages, standardized scores, and National Curriculum levels. Parallel forms are available for three age levels.

Format: Examiner required; group administration; untimed: 40 to 45 minutes

Scoring: Examiner evaluated; computer scoring available

Cost: Each Level: Form A or Form B (10) £6.50; Manual £12.99

Iowa Writing Assessment

1994	Riverside Publishing Company

H. D. Hoover, A. N. Hieronymus, D. A. Frisbie, S. B. Dunbar, L. S. Feldt, R. A. Forsyth, T. N. Ansley, S. D. Alnot

Population: Grades 3 to 12

Purpose: Assesses students' ability to generate, organize, and express ideas in a variety of written forms

Description: Measures students' ability to generate, organize, and express ideas in four modes of discourse: Narrative, Descriptive, Persuasive, and Expository. Used in conjunction with the *Iowa Tests of Basic Skills, Tests of Achievement and Proficiency*, and *Iowa Tests of Educational Development*, the *Iowa Writing Assessment* provides a measure of students' productive writing skills in response to specific writing tasks.

Format: Examiner required; suitable for group use; untimed: 50 minutes

Scoring: Examiner evaluated

Cost: Classroom Test Packages (directions and testing materials for 25 students) $46.75 per level/writing mode; Manual for Scoring and Interpretation $28.90 per level/writing mode

Neale Analysis of Reading Ability–3rd Edition

1999	Australian Council for Educational Research Limited

Marie D. Neale

Population: Ages 6 to 12+ years

Purpose: Assesses reading progress objectively

Description: A series of reading passages that the student reads aloud. The test is available in two parallel forms, Form 1 and Form 2, and a Diagnostic Tutor Form that extends test options. The test yields stanine and percentile rank and range scores, Neale (Rasch) scale scores, and reading ages. This test is a revised version of the *Neale Analysis of Reading Ability,* published by Macmillan Education.

Format: Examiner required; individual administration; timed and untimed

Scoring: Hand key; examiner evaluated

Cost: Contact publisher

Nonword Reading Test

2004   **Hodder Murray**

Mary Crumpler, Colin McCarty

Population: Ages 6 to 16 years

Purpose: Provides diagnostic information for pupils struggling with basic phonics

Description: Using nonwords (words that do not exist, but do use common and acceptable letter–sound correspondences), the test helps to identify pupils who are slow to establish phonological decoding skills when first beginning to read. With dyslexic and older pupils reading below the level for their age, the test helps to diagnose phonological problems and to pinpoint the special provision that the pupils are likely to require. Two equivalent forms allow assessment of progress over time.

Format: Examiner required; individual administration; untimed: 5 to 10 minutes

Scoring: Examiner evaluated

Cost: Test Booklet £25.00; Manual £19.99; 10 Record Sheets £9.99

Parallel Spelling Test-Second Edition

1998   **Hodder Murray**

Dennis Young

Population: Ages 8 to 12

Purpose: Charts pupil's progress in spelling

Description: Banks of sentences allow selection of 12 matched tests with no overlap, or more with partial overlap. Gives standardized scores and spelling ages. Minimal preparation required.

Format: Examiner required; group administration; untimed: 20 to 30 minutes

Scoring: Examiner evaluated

Cost: Test Booklet £16.99

Phonological Awareness & Reading Profile-Intermediate

2001   **LinguiSystems, Inc.**

Wanda Salter, Carolyn Robertson

Population: Ages 8 to 14 years

Purpose: Assesses phonological awareness, decoding, spelling, and fluency skills of students who continue to have difficulty with reading and spelling skills past Grade 2.

Description: Oral response criterion-referenced test with four subtests: Phonological Awareness (65 items measuring blending, isolation, segmentation, deletion, and manipulation skills),

Decoding (41 items assessing phonetic patterns), Spelling (20 items to assess phonetic patterns), and Fluency (rapid letter naming and paragraph reading tasks).

Format: Examiner required; individual administration; untimed: 25 to 35 minutes

Scoring: Examiner evaluated

Cost: Test Kit (manual, 15 forms, cubes) $41.95

Progressive Achievement Test (PAT) Reading: Comprehension and Vocabulary

1990   **New Zealand Council for Educational Research**

Neil Reid, Warwick B. Elley

Population: Ages 8 to 14 years

Purpose: Assesses comprehension and vocabulary skills

Description: Short, graded prose passages are presented to assess both factual and inferential reading comprehension. All passages have brief lead-in statements and are illustrated. The tests present level scores that provide a guide to appropriate instructional levels in reading. Also provided are age and class percentile ranks. The vocabulary test is a test of words systematically chosen from the 10,000 most commonly used English words. The words are presented in the context of short sentences, with all questions in a multiple-choice format. The child's task is to select the best synonym from five alternatives.

Format: Examiner required; group administration; timed: 75 minutes

Scoring: Examiner evaluated

Cost: Manual $9.00; 10 Answer Sheets $1.98; Booklets $1.80; Keys $.99

Progressive Achievement Tests: Reading, Third Edition

2001   **Australian Council for Educational Research Limited**

Population: Years 3 to 9

Purpose: Assesses reading abilities in vocabulary and comprehension

Description: Vocabulary questions are presented with each test word in context in a short sentence. The task is to select the best synonym from a choice of five. Comprehension questions are designed measure factual and inferential comprehension. Multiple-choice items follow each reading passage. Available in parallel forms.

Format: Examiner required; individual and group administration; untimed: Vocabulary, 30 minutes; Comprehension, 40 minutes

Scoring: Examiner evaluated; scoring service available

Cost: Contact publisher

Proof Reading Tests of Spelling (PRETOS)

1981	New Zealand Council for Educational Research

Cedric Croft, Alison Gilmore, Neil Reid, Peter Jackson

Population: Ages 8 to 13 years

Purpose: Measures discrimination between misspelled and correctly spelled words in meaningful text

Description: The *Proof Reading Tests of Spelling* are broad measures of a child's ability to discriminate between misspelled words and correctly spelled words, presented in the context of meaningful paragraphs. The tests provide a measure of spelling achievement within the context of a proofreading task and present diagnostic information about an individual pupil's spelling accomplishments.

Format: Examiner required; group administration; timed: 30 minutes

Scoring: Hand key

Cost: Specimen Set $17.10

Rapid Automatized Naming and Rapid Alternating Stimulus Tests (RAN/RAS)

2005	PRO-ED, Inc.

Maryanne Wolf, Martha Bridge Denckla

Population: Ages 5 to 18 years

Purpose: Measures an individual's ability to recognize a visual symbol and to name it accurately and rapidly; identifies students who may be at risk for reading failure

Description: The tests consist of rapid automatized naming (RAN) tests (Letters, Numbers, Colors, Objects) and rapid alternating stimulus (RAS) tests (2-Set Letters and Numbers and 3-Set Letters, Numbers, and Colors). The RAN tests comprise five high-frequency stimuli that are randomly repeated 10 times in an array of five rows. The RAS tests are high-frequency stimuli that are randomly repeated in an array of five rows. On all tests, the examinee is asked to name each stimulus item as quickly as possible without making any mistakes. Scores are based on the amount of time required to name all of the stimulus items on each test. Raw scores are converted to percentiles, standard scores, and age/grade equivalents.

Format: Examiner required; individual administration; timed: 5 to 10 minutes

Scoring: Examiner evaluated

Cost: Complete Kit (manual 50 record forms, card packs, storage box) $130.00

Reading Style Inventory® (RSI)

2000	National Reading Styles Institute, Inc.

Marie L. Carbo

Population: Ages 6 years to adult

Purpose: Assesses learning style for reading; used to implement reading instruction

Description: The RSI reports help the teacher to target and tailor reading instruction so that students enjoy learning to read and learn to read well in the shortest possible time. At a glance, the reports list the child's strengths and weaknesses and the best reading strategies to use for fast progress. There are seven different reports for individuals and groups. Provides descriptions of 14 reading methods and dozens of teaching strategies. Produces personalized letters to parents, plus a special RSI profile lists extensive recommendations for working with the child at home.

Format: Online administration; untimed

Scoring: Examiner evaluated; computer scored

Cost: Order Online Access to a Specific Number of Administrations (e.g., 5 to 24 $3.00 each)

Slosson Oral Reading Test–Revised (SORT-R3)

2004	Slosson Educational Publications, Inc.

Richard L. Slosson, Charles L. Nicholson

Population: Grades Preschool to adult

Purpose: Measures reading ability

Description: Oral screening test of 200 words providing an estimate of a person's word recognition level. The SORT-R3 is based on the ability to pronounce words at different levels of difficulty, primer through high school. Scores provided are standard scores and grade equivalents.

Format: Examiner required; individual administration; untimed: 3 to 5 minutes

Scoring: Examiner evaluated

Cost: Complete Kit $81.25

Slosson Written Expression Test (SWET)

| 2002 | Slosson Educational Publications, Inc. |

Donald B. Hofler, Bradley T. Erford, William J. Amoreill

Population: Ages 8 to 17 years

Purpose: Measures spontaneous written expression skills

Description: The test allows for description of the individual child's authentic written expressive skills and a comparison of the child's performance to his or her age peers. Student responses are analyzed in the context of an authentic composition. The SWET's dinosaur, space, and shipwreck themes are highly stimulating picture prompts that help to tap creative-writing skills and are ideal for portfolio/performance-based assessment approaches. The standardized scoring system—featuring specially designed, user-friendly scoring and profile forms—yield subscale scores for Spelling, Capitalization, and Punctuation, as well as two writing maturity measures: Sentence Length and Type–Token Ratio.

Format: Examiner required; individual and group administration; untimed. 15 minutes

Scoring: Examiner evaluated

Cost: Complete Kit $115.50

Spadafore Diagnostic Reading Test (SDRT)

| 1983 | Academic Therapy Publications |

Gerald J. Spadafore

Population: Ages 6 years to adult

Purpose: Assesses reading skills; used as a screening and diagnostic instrument for academic placement and career guidance counseling

Description: Four subtests assess Word Recognition, Oral Reading and Comprehension, Silent Reading Comprehension, and Listening Comprehension. Criterion-referenced test items are graded for difficulty. Independent, Instructional, and Frustration reading and comprehension levels are designated for performance at each grade level. Test results may be used for screening to determine whether reading problems exist at a student's current grade placement. Administration for diagnostic purposes requires 30 minutes for all four subtests and yields a comparison of decoding reading skills. Guidelines are provided for interpreting performance in terms of vocational literacy. Provisions for conducting a detailed error analysis of oral reading are included.

Format: Examiner required; individual administration; screening, 30 minutes; diagnostic, 1 hour

Scoring: Examiner evaluated

Cost: Test Kit (manual, test plates, 10 test booklets) $65.00

Standardized Reading Inventory–Second Edition (SRI-2)

| 1999 | PRO-ED, Inc. |

Phyllis L. Newcomer

Population: Ages 6 to 14 years

Purpose: Evaluates a student's idiosyncratic reading skills

Description: In addition to being criterion-referenced, the instrument is now norm-referenced. The subtests include a measure of vocabulary proficiency and a supplemental measure of predictive comprehension. Designed like an informal reading inventory, each of the two forms consists of 10 graded passages, ranging from the lowest reading level (preprimer) to the highest level (eighth grade). Each passage incorporates key words extracted from five popular basal reading series. Evidence of construct validity is presented showing that the SRI-2 discriminates between good and poor readers. The comprehension questions are open ended.

Format: Examiner required; individual administration; untimed: 30 to 90 minutes

Scoring: Examiner evaluated

Cost: Complete Kit (manual, storybook, 25 each of Forms A and B vocabulary sheets, 25 each of Forms A and B Examiner record booklets, 50 profile scoring forms, storage box) $268.00

Stanford Diagnostic Reading Test, Fourth Edition (SDRT 4)

| 1995 | Harcourt Assessment, Inc. |

Bjorn Karlsen, Eric F. Gardner

Population: Grades 1.5 to 13

Purpose: Measures major components of the reading process

Description: Provides formal and informal diagnostic measures for determining students' strengths and needs in reading. Use the information to evaluate students for program placement or to design an appropriate instructional program. High-quality selections provide relevant information. There are six test levels with a single form at each of the first three levels and two alternate and equivalent forms at each of the upper three levels. The SDRT 4 enables teachers to determine how students' comprehension can vary according to the reading selection: recreational, textual, and functional.

Format: Examiner required; suitable for group use; timed: varies by level

Scoring: Hand key; scoring service available; online testing and scoring available

Cost: Examination Kit $42.00

STAR Reading

2006	Renaissance Learning, Inc.

Population: Grades 1 to 12

Purpose: Provides periodic progress monitoring of reading skills

Description: *STAR Reading* provides accurate, norm-referenced scores, criterion-referenced measures of students' instructional reading levels, and a way for teachers to track student growth throughout the year. *STAR Reading* uses computer-adaptive technology to tailor each student's test based on responses to his or her previous items. By administering test items that are closely matched to student achievement levels, *STAR Reading*'s reliability is enhanced and testing time is minimized.

Format: Computer administered; timed: 10 minutes

Scoring: Computer scored

Cost: One-Time Setup (per school) $1,499.00; Annual Student Fee $.39 per student

Test for Reception of Grammar Version 2 (TROG-2)

2003	Harcourt Assessment–UK

Dorothy Bishop

Population: Ages 4 years to adult

Purpose: Measures understanding of grammatical contrasts

Description: The TROG-2 is a fully revised and nationally restandardized version. The instrument tests understanding of 20 constructs four times each using different test stimuli. Each stimulus is presented in a four-picture multiple-choice format with lexical and grammatical foils. The difficulty range has been increased to effectively tap into receptive grammar.

Format: Examiner required; individual administration; untimed: 10 to 20 minutes

Scoring: Examiner evaluated

Cost: Complete Kit (manual, stimulus book, 25 record forms, in a bag) £151.50

Test of Reading Comprehension– Third Edition (TORC-3)

1995	PRO-ED, Inc.

Virginia L. Brown, Donald D. Hammill, J. Lee Wiederholt

Population: Ages 7 to 17 years

Purpose: Assesses students' reading comprehension; used to diagnose reading problems in terms of current psycholinguistic theories of reading comprehension as a constructive process involving both language and cognition

Description: Eight multiple-item paper–pencil subtests measuring aspects of reading comprehension. Three of the subtests (General Vocabulary, Syntactic Similarities, and Paragraph Reading) are combined to determine a basic Comprehension Core, which is expressed as a Reading Comprehension Quotient (RCQ). Three subtests measure students' abilities to read the vocabularies of math, science, and social studies. Subtest 7, Reading the Directions of Schoolwork, is a diagnostic tool for younger or remedial students. The eighth subtest is Sentence Sequences. Scaled scores are provided for each subtest.

Format: Examiner required; individual or group administration; untimed: 30 to 90 minutes

Scoring: Examiner evaluated

Cost: Complete Kit (manual, 50 answer sheets, 50 Subtest 8 forms, 50 profile/examiner record forms, 10 student booklets, storage box) $189.00

Test of Silent Contextual Reading Fluency (TOSCRF)

2006	PRO-ED, Inc.

Donald D. Hammill, J. Lee Wiederholt, Elizabeth A. Allen

Population: Ages 7 to 18 years

Purpose: Assesses silent general reading ability

Description: The test measures a student's essential contextual reading abilities (i.e., word identification, word meaning, word building, sentence structure, comprehension, and fluency). Using a series of printed passages adapted from the *Gray Oral Reading Test–Fourth Edition,* the TOSCRF can be used to identify both poor and good readers. Students are presented with short passages comprised of rows of contextually related words, ordered by reading difficulty. All words are printed in uppercase without any spaces or punctuation. Students are asked to draw a line between the boundaries of as many recognizable words as possible within 3 minutes. To do well, the student has to read the meaning of the text. The TOSCRF scores are reported as percentiles, standard scores, and age/grade equivalents. There are four alternate forms.

Format: Examiner required; group administration; timed: 3 minutes

Scoring: Examiner evaluated

Cost: Complete Kit (manual; 25 each of Forms A, B, C, D; storage box) $200.00

Test of Silent Word Reading Fluency (TOSWRF)

2004	PRO-ED, Inc.

Nancy Mather, Donald D. Hammill, Elizabeth A. Allen, Rhia Roberts

Population: Ages 6 years 6 months to 17 years

Purpose: Measures ability to recognize printed words accurately and efficiently

Description: The TOSWRF has two equivalent forms that use a testing format originally pioneered by Guilford in his Structure of Intellect studies to assess current reading skill by counting the number of printed words that the student can identify within 3 minutes. Students are presented with rows of words, ordered by reading difficulty, with no spaces between the words and instructed to draw a line between the boundaries of as many words as possible. The instrument accurately identifies students who are struggling with reading. Raw scores are converted to percentiles, standard scores, and age/grade equivalents.

Format: Examiner required; group administration; timed: 3 minutes

Scoring: Examiner evaluated

Cost: Complete Kit (manual, 25 each of Forms A and B, storage box) $135.00

Test of Word Reading Efficiency (TOWRE)

1999	PRO-ED, Inc.

Joseph K. Torgesen, Richard Wagner, Carol Rashotte

Population: Ages 6 to 24 years

Purpose: Measures word-reading accuracy and fluency

Description: Because it can be administered very quickly, the test provides an efficient means of monitoring the growth of two kinds of word reading skills that are critical in the development of overall reading ability: the ability to accurately recognize familiar words as whole units and the ability to "sound out" words quickly. The TOWRE contains two subtests: Sight Word Efficiency and Phonetic Decoding Efficiency. Each subtest has two forms that are of equivalent difficulty. Percentiles, standard scores, and age/grade equivalents are provided.

Format: Examiner required; individual administration; timed: 5 to 10 minutes

Scoring: Examiner evaluated

Cost: Complete Kit (manual, 25 each of Form A and Form B record booklets, word cards, storage box) $178.00

Test of Written Expression (TOWE)

1995	PRO-ED, Inc.

Ron McGhee, Brian R. Bryant, Stephen C. Larsen, Diane M. Rivera

Population: Age 6 years 6 months to 14 years 11 months

Purpose: Provides a comprehensive assessment of writing achievement

Description: The TOWE uses two assessment methods to evaluate a student's writing skills. The first method involves administering a series of 76 items that tap different skills associated with writing. The second method requires students to read or hear a prepared story starter and use it as a stimulus for writing an essay (i.e., the beginning of the story is provided, and the writer continues the story to its conclusion). The TOWE provides an excellent source of writing samples that can be used independently in a norm-referenced assessment of writing or as a component of a student's portfolio of written products. The 76 items assess a broad array of writing skills (i.e., ideation, vocabulary, grammar, capitalization, punctuation, and spelling) to determine the students' general writing proficiency. The overall writing score derived can be converted to normative data. Examiners also can conduct an item analysis to examine strengths and weaknesses across the content assessed by the items.

Format: Examiner required; individual administration; untimed: 60 minutes

Scoring: Examiner evaluated

Cost: Complete Kit (manual, 25 profile/

examiner record forms, 25 student booklets, storage box) $145.00

Test of Written Language– Third Edition (TOWL-3)

| 1988 | PRO-ED, Inc. |

Donald D. Hammill, Stephen C. Larsen

Population: Ages 7 years 6 months to 17 years

Purpose: Identifies students who have problems in written expression and pinpoints specific areas of deficit

Description: Paper–pencil test in which students write a story about a given theme. The test yields information in eight areas of writing competence, in contrived and spontaneous formats: Vocabulary, Spelling, Style, Logical Sentences, Sentence Combining, Contextual Conventions, Contextual Language, and Story Construction. The information is derived from an analysis of a sample of continuous writing, as well as from an analysis of subtest performance. Subtest raw scores, standard scores, percentiles, a Contrived Writing Quotient, Spontaneous Writing Quotient, and Overall Written Language Quotient are generated. The test is available in Forms A and B.

Format: Examiner required; suitable for group use; untimed: 90 minutes

Scoring: Examiner evaluated; computer scoring available

Cost: Complete Kit (manual, 25 each of student response booklets A and B, 50 profile/story scoring forms, storage box) $210.00

Test of Written Spelling– Fourth Edition (TWS-4)

| 1999 | PRO-ED, Inc. |

Stephen C. Larsen, Donald D. Hammill, Louisa Moats

Population: Grades 1 to 12

Purpose: Identifies those individuals whose scores are below those of their peers and who might need interventions designed to improve spelling

Description: The revised TWS-4 is a norm-referenced test of spelling. The test is administered using a dictated word format. The TWS-4 has two alternate or equivalent forms (A and B) that make it more useful in test-teach-test situations. This test was developed after a review of 2,000 spelling rules. The words to be spelled

are drawn from 10 basal spelling programs and popular graded word lists.

Format: Examiner required; individual or group administration; untimed: 20 minutes

Scoring: Examiner evaluated

Cost: Complete Kit (manual, 50 summary/ response forms, storage box) $85.00

Tests of Reading Comprehension– Second Edition (TORCH)

| 2003 | Australian Council for Educational Research Limited |

L. Mossenson, P. Hill, G. Masters

Population: Grades 3 to 10

Purpose: Assesses the extent to which a student is able to obtain meaning from the text

Description: Multiple-item paper–pencil modified-cloze-response reading comprehension test yielding both diagnostic and achievement information. The test consists of 14 passages of graded difficulty. Each passage contains approximately 24 items. The test yields both stanine and percentile rank scores and TORCH (Rasch) scale scores.

Format: Examiner required; suitable for group use; untimed: 30 minutes

Scoring: Hand key; examiner evaluated

Cost: Contact publisher

Woodcock Reading Mastery Tests– Revised–Normative Update (WRMT-R/NU)

| 1998 | AGS Publishing/Pearson Assessments |

Richard W. Woodcock

Population: Ages 5 to 75+ years

Purpose: Assesses reading skills

Description: The WRMT-R/NU is a comprehensive individual assessment of reading ability and is available in two parallel forms: Form G and H. Six tests: (1) Visual-Auditory Learning (Form G) measures ability to form associations between visual stimuli oral responses; (2) Letter Identification (Form G) measures ability to identify letters presented in uppercase or lowercase forms; Supplementary Letter Checklist (Form G) is used to determine which letters the subject can name or identify by sound; (3) Word Identification requires the subject to identify isolated words that appear in large type on the subject pages in the test easel; (4) Word Attack requires the subject to read either nonsense words or words with a very low frequency of occurrence in English, thus measuring ability to apply phonic and structural analysis skills to pronounce unfamiliar words; (5) Word Comprehension measures reading vocabulary at several different levels of cognitive processing and consists of three subtests: Antonyms, Synonyms, and Analogies; and (6) Passage Comprehension measures ability to identify a key word.

Format: Examiner required; individual administration; 10 to 30 minutes for each cluster of tests

Scoring: Examiner evaluated; computer scoring available for Macintosh and Windows

Cost: Combined Kit (Form G and H test books, 25 each Form G and H test records, sample Form G and H summary record form, pronunciation guide audiocassette, sample report to parents, manual) $443.99

Woodcock-Johnson Diagnostic Reading Battery (WJ III ® DRB)

2004	Riverside Publishing Company

Richard W. Woodcock, Nancy Mather, Fredrick A. Schrank

Population: Ages 2 to 80+ years

Purpose: Provides a diagnostic test that assesses reading achievement and important related abilities

Description: Comprised of 10 tests from the *WJ III Tests of Achievement*, Form B, and *WJ III Tests of Cognitive Abilities*. There are eight clusters available for interpretation: Basic Reading Skills, Reading Comprehension, Phonics Knowledge, Phonemic Awareness, Oral Language Comprehension, Brief Reading, Broad Reading, and Total Reading. Any of the tests or clusters can be used for progress monitoring or outcome research.

Format: Examiner required; individual administration; untimed: 50 to 60 minutes

Scoring: Examiner evaluated; computer scoring available

Cost: Complete Kit (test book, cassette, manual, norms tables, 25 test records) $382.00

Word Identification and Spelling Test (WIST)

2004	PRO-ED, Inc.

Barbara A. Wilson, Rebecca H. Felton

Population: Ages 7 to 18 years

Purpose: Measures word identification, spelling, and sound–symbol knowledge; identifies students who are struggling with reading and spelling

Description: The WIST provides detailed information that can be used to identify areas of difficulty to develop appropriate instructional interventions. Elementary and secondary versions are easy to administer and score. The three subtests can be used in either norm-referenced scoring or informal assessment. Information from the informal analyses helps to formulate a literacy intervention plan.

Format: Examiner required; individual administration; untimed: 40 minutes

Scoring: Examiner evaluated

Cost: Complete Kit (manual, 25 each elementary and secondary record forms, 50 spelling response forms, word cards, spelling cards, storage box) $235.00

Writing Assessment Program (WrAP)

2005	Educational Records Bureau

Population: Grades 3 to 12

Purpose: Assesses six elements of writing proficiency

Description: A direct measure of writing that lends itself to incorporation into writing portfolios. Students provide a writing sample on a prompt or topic. The papers are scored (scale of 1 to 6) on Overall Development, Organization, Support, Sentence Structure, Word Choice, and Mechanics. Five levels based on grade use the following modes: Narrative (3 to 4), Informative/Descriptive (5 to 6), Expository (7 to 8), Persuasive (9 to 10), and College Preparatory (11 to 12). Scores are norm referenced. A Writing Practice Program is also available online.

Format: Examiner required; group administration; timed: 50 to 60 minutes

Scoring: Scoring service

Cost: $7.75 per student (quantity discounts available)

Writing Process Test (WPT)

1992	PRO-ED, Inc.

M. Robin Warden, Thomas A. Hutchinson

Population: Ages 8 to 19 years

Purpose: Assesses both written product and writing process

Description: The norm-referenced WPT is a direct measure of writing that requires the student to plan, write, and revise an original composition. The Written Product is measured by scoring the first draft (or the revision if a student is given time to revise the composition). The same set of scales is used to analyze all students' writing, regardless of their age or grade. The scales rate the writer's effort on two scales: Development and Fluency. The six Development Scales assess Purpose and Focus, Audience, Vocabulary, Style and Tone, Support and Development, and Organization and Coherence. The four Fluency Scales assess Sentence Structure and Variety, Grammar and Usage, Capitalization and Punctuation, and Spelling.

Format: Examiner required; suitable for group use; untimed: 45 minutes, then 30 minutes for revision

Scoring: Examiner evaluated

Cost: Complete Kit (2 manuals, 25 analytical record forms, 25 each of Form A and B first draft booklets, 25 training and calibration record forms, 25 revision booklets, scorer folder) $179.00

Writing Roadmap™ 2.0

2005	CTB/McGraw-Hill

Population: Grades 3 to 12, college students, adults

Purpose: Helps students to improve their writing skills and helps teachers to monitor student progress

Description: This writing program is administered online and assesses student strengths and weaknesses in six writing dimensions: Ideas and Content, Organization, Voice, Word Choice, Conventions, and Fluency. Holistic and analytic scores are generated immediately. Instructional Tools keep students engaged in the writing process and help improve student writing over time. Graphic reports help instructors evaluate student performance and inform teaching strategies.

Format: Requires examiner; self-administered; untimed

Scoring: Online scoring

Cost: Contact publisher

Written Language Assessment (WLA)

1989	Academic Therapy Publications

J. Jeffrey Grill, Margaret M. Kirwin

Population: Ages 8 to 18+ years

Purpose: Assesses written language

Description: Essay test offering direct assessment of written language through an evaluation of writing samples that reflect three modes of discourse: expressive, instructive, and creative writing. Analytic scoring techniques are used to yield scores in General Writing Ability, Productivity, Word Complexity, and Readability. A Written Language Quotient that is a composite of the four subscores is also reported. Raw scores for the four subskill areas and the Written Language Quotient can be converted to scaled scores and percentile ranks and plotted on the scoring/profile form.

Format: Examiner required; individual or group administration; untimed: 1 hour

Scoring: Examiner evaluated

Cost: Test Kit (manual, 25 each of three writing record forms, 25 scoring/profile forms, hand counter, in vinyl folder) $80.00

Religion

Partial Index of Modernization: Measurement of Attitudes toward Morality

1972	Donna Bardis

Panos D. Bardis

Population: Adolescents, adults

Purpose: Measure attitudes toward traditional concepts of sin; used for clinical assessment, counseling, research on religion and morals, and discussions in religion and social science classes

Description: Paper–pencil 10-item test in which the subject rates 10 statements about sin and morality from 0 (least amount of agreement) to 10 (highest amount of agreement). The score equals the sum of the 10 numerical responses. The theoretical range of scores extends from 0 (least modern) to 100 (most modern).

Format: Rating scale; untimed: 5 minutes

Scoring: Examiner evaluated and interpreted

Cost: $1.00

Thanatometer

1986   Donna Bardis

Panos D. Bardis

Population: Adolescents, adults

Purpose: Measures awareness and acceptance of death

Description: Paper–pencil 20-item Likert scale assessing attitudes toward death and dying. Examinee responds by indicating degree of agreement with each item. Suitable for use with individuals with physical or hearing impairments.

Format: Self-administered; untimed: 12 minutes

Scoring: Hand key

Cost: $1.00

School and Institutional Environments

Breakthrough School Improvement Survey: Survey of Implementation

2006   National Study of School Evaluation

Population: Adults

Purpose: Monitors the extent of implementation of improvement efforts

Description: Responses provide valuable feedback on the status of actions, timelines, responsibilities, and impact of interventions. The survey is available in Resources and Tools and in a Web-based format. Statistical report with individual statements, as well as subgroup breakdown on a five-point scale.

Format: Self-administered; untimed

Scoring: Scoring service; online available

Cost: Web Setup Fee per School $150.00; $1.00 for each access code

Classroom Environment Scale

2002   Mind Garden, Inc.

Rudolf H. Moos

Population: Students in classrooms of junior and senior high schools

Purpose: Evaluates the effects of course content, teaching methods, teacher personality, class composition, and characteristics of the overall classroom environment

Description: This rating scale reveals an individual's perceptions of the classroom and his or her place in it. The results may contrast the teacher and student view by evaluating the impact of intervention programs for individual and classroom research and program evaluation. The 90

items are grouped into nine subscales with three dimensions.

Format: Rating scale; untimed

Scoring: Examiner evaluated

Cost: Manual/Sampler Set $40.00; 200 Permissions $150.00

Community College Student Experiences Questionnaire (CCSEQ)

1999   Center for the Study of Higher Education

Jack Friedlander, C. Robert Pace,
Patricia H. Murrell, Penny Lehman

Population: Ages 18 and older

Purpose: Intended for community and technical college students, to measure student progress, involvement, and experiences, as well as institutional effectiveness

Description: Multiple-choice, self-report (Likert scale) instrument with 170 items, plus 20 optional locally developed questions on six subtests: Student Background, College Program, Courses, College Activities, Estimate of Gains, and Campus Environment. Results include frequency reports of all data and Quality of Effort scores. The CCSEQ can be used for those with visual, hearing, and physical impairments.

Format: Self-administered; untimed: 20 to 30 minutes

Scoring: Computer scored; test scoring service available

Cost: Print Report and Data on Disk $125.00; $2.25 per instrument

Community Oriented Programs Environment Scale (COPES)

1996	Mind Garden, Inc.

Rudolf H. Moos

Population: Adults

Purpose: Assesses the social environments of community-based psychiatric treatment programs

Description: Paper–pencil 100-item true–false test of 10 aspects of social environment: Involvement, Support, Spontaneity, Autonomy, Practical Orientation, Personal Problem Orientation, Anger and Aggression, Order and Organization, Program Clarity, and Staff Control. Materials include the Real Form (Form R), which measures perceptions of a current program; the 40-item Short Form (Form S); and the Ideal Form (Form I), which measures conceptions of a new program. Forms I and E are reproducible, and instructions are printed in the appendix of the COPES manual. Items are modified from the *Ward Atmosphere Scale*. One in a series of nine Social Climate Scales.

Format: Examiner required; suitable for group use; untimed: 20 minutes

Scoring: Examiner evaluated

Cost: Sampler Set $30.00; Permission for Up to 200 Uses $200.00

Correctional Institutions Environment Scale (CIES)

1974, 1987	Mind Garden, Inc.

Rudolf H. Moos

Population: Adults

Purpose: Assesses the social environment of juvenile and adult correctional programs

Description: Paper–pencil 90-item true–false test of nine aspects of social environment: Involvement, Support, Expressiveness, Autonomy, Practical Orientation, Personal Problem Orientation, Order and Organization, Clarity, and Staff Control. Materials include four forms: the Real Form (Form R), which measures perceptions of the current correctional program; the 36-item Short Form (Form S); the Ideal Form (Form I), which measures conceptions of an ideal program; and the Expectations Form (Form E), which measures expectations of a new program. Forms I and E are reproducible, and items and instructions appear in the appendix of the CIES manual. Items and subscales are similar to those used in

the *Ward Atmosphere Scale*. One of a series of nine Social Climate Scales.

Format: Examiner administered; suitable for group use; untimed

Scoring: Examiner evaluated

Cost: Sampler Set $30.00, Permission for Up to 200 Uses $150.00

Early Childhood Environment Rating Scale–Revised (ECERS)

2005	Teachers College Press

Thelma Harms, Richard M. Clifford, Debby Cryer

Population: Adults who work in classrooms serving children ages 2 years 6 months to 5 years

Purpose: Designed to measure the quality of educational programs

Description: The new revision has been expanded to 43 items and includes many improvements. Examples of new items include Interaction items, such as staff–child interactions, interactions among children, and discipline; Curriculum items, such as nature/science and math/number; Health and Safety items; more inclusive and culturally sensitive indicators for many items; and more items focusing on staff needs. Training video available. Also available in Spanish.

Format: Rating scale; untimed

Scoring: Examiner evaluated

Cost: $16.95

Family Day Care Rating Scale (FDCRS)

1989	Teachers College Press

Thelma Harms, Richard M. Clifford

Population: Adults

Purpose: Designed to measure the quality of educational programs

Description: Consists of 32 items, organized under six major headings: Space and Furnishings for Care and Learning, Basic Care, Language and Reasoning, Learning Activities, Social Development, and Adult Needs. Eight additional items are included for rating a day care home's provisions for children with special needs. Video training program available.

Format: Rating scale; untimed

Scoring: Examiner evaluated

Cost: $15.95

Functional Assessment of Academic Behavior (FAAB)

2002	Sopris West Educational Services

James Ysseldyke, Sandra Christenson

Population: Grades 1 to 12

Purpose: Assesses the instructional needs of students in relation to the learning environment

Description: Based on the belief that student performance in school is a function of an interaction between the student and the learning (instructional) environment, the FAAB provides a set of observational and interview forms, administration procedures, and an organizational structure that allows educators to both identify and address the instructional needs of individual students. While the FAAB can be used to assess the learning needs of all students, it is especially useful when applied to the needs of those who are tough to teach. The FAAB enables education professionals to identify ways to change instruction—or the learning environment—so that the student will respond to instruction more positively and thus more successfully. The FAAB provides education professionals with essential information for prereferral intervention, instructional consultation, student/staff support teams (SSTs, TATs, etc.), intervention assistance, and collaborative intervention planning. This edition contains a section on interventions associated with the student's specific areas of need.

Format: Examiner required, individual administration; untimed

Scoring: Examiner evaluated

Cost: $61.95

Infant/Toddler Environment Rating Scale–Revised (ITERS)

2006	Teachers College Press

Thelma Harms, Debby Cryer, Richard M. Clifford

Population: Adults who work in child care settings with children ages birth to 30 months

Purpose: Measures the quality of educational programs

Description: The 39 items in the ITERS are divided into seven categories: Furnishings and Display for Children, Personal Care Routines, Listening and Talking, Learning Activities, Interactions, Program Structure, and Adult Needs. A video training program is available.

Format: Rating scale; untimed

Scoring: Examiner evaluated

Cost: $16.95

Institutional Functioning Inventory

Date not provided	Educational Testing Service

Earl J. McGrath

Population: Adults

Purpose: Evaluates functioning of educational institutions; used in self-studies for accreditation, planning, and research

Description: Paper–pencil 132-item test assessing 11 dimensions of institutional functioning: Intellectual–Aesthetic, Extracurricular, Freedom, Human Diversity, Concern for Undergraduate Learning, Democratic Governance, Meeting Local Needs, Self-Study and Planning, Concern for Advanced Knowledge, Concern for Innovation, and Institutional Esprit. The inventory is distributed to a random sample of college community members, including the faculty, administration, and students. Available in French for Canadian institutions.

Format: Self-administered; untimed: 45 minutes

Scoring: Computer scored

Cost: Reusable Faculty Booklet $0.50; Reusable Student Booklets $0.35; Answer Sheet $0.10 each

Inventory of School Effectiveness

2004	National Study of School Evaluation

Population: Adults

Purpose: Measures school effectiveness using an evidence-based scale

Description: This inventory is designed for schools that want to assess their use of 34 research-based factors that affect student performance. The inventory is available in Web-based and scannable paper formats. Statistical report with individual statements, as well as subgroup breakdown on a 5-point scale, provided.

Format: Self-administered; untimed

Scoring: Scoring service; online available

Cost: Paper Package of 25 $37.50; Web Setup Fee per School $150.00; $1.00 for each access code

Military Environment Inventory (MEI)

1986	Mind Garden, Inc.

Rudolph H. Moos

Population: Adults

Purpose: Assesses the social environment of various military contexts; used to detect individuals and units at risk of morale and performance problems

Description: Multiple-item paper–pencil inventory assessing individuals' and units' perceptions of the military environment. The test yields seven scores: Involvement, Peer Cohesion, Officer Support, Personal Status, Order and Organization, Clarity, and Officer Control. Additional subscales are related to military performance and sick-call rates.

Format: Self-administered; untimed

Scoring: Examiner evaluated

Cost: Sampler Set $30.00; Permission Set $150.00

Opinion Inventories for Students, Teachers, Parents, Support Staff, and Community Members

2002	National Study of School Evaluation

Population: All ages

Purpose: Measures the opinions of the school's stakeholders

Description: The NSSE's Opinion Inventories address a series of school climate issues of particular concern to teachers, students, parents, and community members. In addition, each of the inventories contains a section for up to 20 additional questions that can be developed by the school to address specific issues of concern or interest to the school. The inventories also include a section in which the respondents can write additional comments. Each of the NSSE's Opinion Inventories has been designed to incorporate the survey questions directly on optical scan answer sheets to provide for ease of administration. Consequently, survey participants do not need to transfer their responses to a separate answer sheet.

Format: Self-administered; untimed

Scoring: Scoring service; online available

Cost: Paper Package of 25 $25.00; Web Setup Fee per School $150.00; $1.00 for each access code

Preschool Program Quality Assessment, Second Edition (PQA)

Date not provided	High/Scope Educational Research Foundation

Population: Adults

Purpose: Rate a program

Description: A comprehensive rating instrument for evaluation of program quality and identifying staff training needs. It contains sections on the learning environment, daily routine, parent involvement and family services, staff qualifications and development, curriculum planning and assessment, adult–child interaction, and program management. A separate guide is available for using the PQA in Head Start program evaluation.

Format: Self-administered; untimed

Scoring: Self-scored

Cost: Starter Pak (manual, Head Start user's guide, form) $25.85

School-Age Care Environment Rating Scale (SACERS)

1996	Teachers College Press

Thelma Harms, Ellen Vineberg Jacobs, Donna Romano White

Population: Adults who work in child care settings

Purpose: Designed to measure the quality of educational programs

Description: Provides an easy-to-use resource for defining high-quality care and assessing levels of quality in child care programs offered by schools and other organizations. It consists of 49 items, organized under seven categories: Space and Furnishings, Health and Safety, Activities, Interactions, Program Structure, Staff Development, and Supplementary Items (for children with special needs).

Format: Rating scale; untimed

Scoring: Examiner evaluated

Cost: $15.95

School Improvement Follow-Up Survey

1994	Assessment Resource Center

Population: Adults; postsecondary, graduates

Purpose: Collects and reports follow-up data on students after graduation

Description: Multiple-choice response format with comments section. For students in their first and fifth years following graduation. Survey data can provide information about the success of academic programs, support services, teaching methods, extracurricular activities climate for learning, and other factors. Meets reporting requirements of the Missouri School Improvement Program.

Format: Survey mailed

Scoring: Machine-scored; test scoring service available

Cost: $50.00 (50 surveys and supportive materials); Scoring $.75 each

Small College Goals Inventory (SCGI)

| Date not provided | Educational Testing Service |

Population: College students

Purpose: Assesses the educational goals of small colleges; used to establish priorities and to provide direction for present and future planning

Description: Paper–pencil 90-item test assessing the educational goals of small colleges. The 20 goal areas are divided into two types: Outcome Goals and Process Goals. The Outcome Goals are Academic Development, Intellectual Orientation, Individual Personal Development, Humanism/Altruism, Cultural/Aesthetic Awareness, Traditional Religiousness, Vocational Preparation, Advanced Training, Research, Meeting Local Needs, Public Service, Social Egalitarianism, and Social Criticism/Activism. The Process Goals are Freedom, Democratic Governance, Community, Intellectual/Aesthetic Environment, Innovation, Off-Campus Learning, and Accountability/Efficiency. The inventory is distributed to a random sample of students, faculty, and administrators. Materials include space for 20 additional locally written goals.

Format: Self-administered; untimed: 45 minutes

Scoring: Computer scored

Cost: Booklets $0.65; Processing $1.75

Survey of Goals for Student Learning

| 1997 | National Study of School Evaluation |

Population: School professional staff

Purpose: Assesses the quality of the work of students across the curriculum

Description: The NSSE, working together with the Alliance for Curriculum Reform, conducted a comprehensive review of the subject area expectations for student learning defined by each of the national curriculum associations. Based on the results of this interdisciplinary analysis of the national standards, the following schoolwide goals for student learning were identified: Learning-to-Learn Skills, Expanding and Integrating Knowledge, Communications Skills, Thinking and Reasoning Skills, Interpersonal Skills, and Personal and Social Responsibility. Part 1 of the survey helps schools assess the extent to which students are achieving these goals for their learning. In Part 2 of the survey, the respondents are asked to determine the level of priority for improvement that should be assigned to each goal. Schools can further customize the survey by including additional goals on the survey. Included with the survey are a comprehensive set of rubrics for the six schoolwide goals.

Format: Self-administered; untimed

Scoring: Scoring service; online available

Cost: Paper Package of 25 $25.00; Web Setup Fee per School $150.00; $1.00 for each access code

Survey of Instructional and Organizational Effectiveness

| 1997 | National Study of School Evaluation |

Population: School professional staff

Purpose: Helps schools to identify the strengths and limitations focusing on the quality of the work of the school

Description: This survey is not designed for staff evaluation. Instead, the focus is placed on assessing the overall effectiveness of the school for the purpose of school improvement. This survey is based on the NSSE's Indicators of Schools of Quality, which include a comprehensive set of research-based principles and indicators that consistently distinguish the work of top-performing schools. The principles are defined within seven categories of instructional and organizational effectiveness: Curriculum Development, Instructional Strategies, Assessment of Student Learning, Educational Agenda, Leadership for School Improvement, Community-Building, and Culture of Continuous Improvement and Learning.

Format: Self-administered; untimed

Scoring: Scoring service; online available

Cost: Paper Package of 25 $25.00; Web Setup Fee per School $150.00; $1.00 for each access code

Transition Surveys: Eighth Grade Exit

| 2004 | National Study of School Evaluation |

Population: Students exiting Grade 8

Purpose: Questions students' experience in the school and their future plans

Description: These surveys are designed for schools that want to obtain information about the quality of programs, services, and activities. Statistical report with individual statements, as well as subgroup breakdown on a 5-point scale. May be administered online.

Format: Self-administered; untimed

Scoring: Scoring service; online available

Cost: Paper Package of 25 $37.50; Web Setup Fee per School $150.00; $1.00 for each access code

Transition Surveys: High School Exit

2005	National Study of School Evaluation

Population: Students exiting Grade 12

Purpose: Questions students' experience in the school and their future plans

Description: These surveys are designed for schools that want to obtain information about the quality of programs, services, and activities. Statistical report with individual statements, as well as subgroup breakdown on a 5-point scale. May be administered online.

Format: Self-administered; untimed

Scoring: Scoring service; online available

Cost: Paper Package of 25 $37.50; Web Setup Fee per School $150.00; $1.00 for each access code

Transition Surveys: High School Follow-up

2005	National Study of School Evaluation

Population: High school alumni

Purpose: Questions students' experience in the school and their future plans

Description: These surveys are designed for schools that want to obtain information about the quality of programs, services, and activities. Statistical report with individual statements, as well as subgroup breakdown on a 5-point scale. May be administered online.

Format: Self-administered; untimed

Scoring: Scoring service; online available

Cost: Paper Package of 25 $37.50; Web Setup Fee per School $150.00; $1.00 for each access code

University Residence Environment Scale (URES)

1988	Mind Garden, Inc.

Rudolf H. Moos

Population: College students, adults

Purpose: Assesses the social environment of university residence halls and dormitories

Description: Paper–pencil 100-item true–false test of 10 dimensions of the social climate of college dormitories: Involvement, Emotional Support, Independence, Traditional Social Orientation, Competition, Academic Achievement, Intellectuality, Order and Organization, Student Influence, and Innovation. Materials include the Real Form (Form R), which measures current perceptions of a residence; the 40-item Short Form (Form S); the Expectations Form (Form E), which measures expectations of a new residence; and the Ideal Form (Form I), which measures conceptions of an ideal residence hall environment. Forms I an E are reproducible, and items and instructions appear in the appendix of the URES manual. One in a series of nine Social Climate Scales.

Format: Examiner required; suitable for group use; untimed

Scoring: Examiner evaluated

Cost: Sample Set $30.00; Permission for Up to 200 Uses $150.00

Ward Atmosphere Scale (WAS)

1996	Mind Garden, Inc.

Rudolf H. Moos

Population: Adolescents, adults

Purpose: Assesses the social environments of hospital-based psychiatric treatment programs; used to evaluate organizational effectiveness

Description: Paper–pencil 100-item true–false test covering 10 aspects of social environment. Yields 10 scores: Involvement, Support, Spontaneity, Autonomy, Practical Orientation, Personal Problem Orientation, Anger and Aggression, Order and Organization, Program Clarity, and Staff Control. Three treatment outcome scales may be used: Dropout, Release Rate, and Community Tenure. Materials include the Real Form (Form R), which measures perceptions of a current program; the 40-item Short Form (Form S); the Ideal Form (Form I), which measures conceptions of an ideal program; and the Expectations Form (Form E), which measures expectations of a new program. Forms I and E are reproducible, and items and instructions appear in the appendix of the WAS. One in a series of nine Social Climate Scales.

Format: Examiner required; suitable for group use; untimed: 20 minutes

Scoring: Examiner evaluated

Cost: Sample Set $30.00; Permission for Up to 200 Uses $150.00

Science

General

Collegiate Assessment of Academic Progress (CAAP) Science Reasoning Test

2001	ACT, Inc.

Population: Ages 17 years and older

Purpose: Assesses science reasoning

Description: Paper-pencil 36-item multiple-choice test with two categories: Referring and Reasoning. May be used for persons with visual, physical, hearing, or mental impairments.

Format: Examiner required; suitable for group use; timed: 40 minutes

Scoring: Machine scored; test scoring service available

Cost: $10.75

Health Sciences Reasoning Test

2006	Insight Assessments

Noreen C. Facione, Peter A. Facione

Population: Adults

Purpose: Assesses reasoning skills in health professionals and health sciences contexts for college and graduate levels

Description: Targets those reasoning and core critical thinking skills regarded as essential for success in scientific study and professional practices, including analysis, interpretation, inferences, exploration, and explanation. Returns five scale scores: Inductive Reasoning, Deductive Reasoning, Analysis, Inference, and Evaluation.

Format: Individual online; examiner required; group administration; timed or untimed

Scoring: Machine or electronic scored; scoring service available

Cost: Specimen Kit (manual, 1 protocol, 1 CapScore™ answer form) $40.00

Optometry Admission Test (OAT)

Updated yearly	Association of Schools and Colleges of Optometry

Population: Adults

Purpose: Measures general academic ability and comprehension of scientific information

Description: Required by all optometry schools for admission. Participation in at least 1 year of collegiate education, including courses in biology, general and organic chemistry, and physics is recommended. The tests include Survey of the Natural Sciences (90 minutes), Reading Comprehension (60 minutes), Physics (50 minutes), and Quantitative Reasoning (45 minutes). All sections must be completed; partial credit is not granted.

Format: Examiner required; group administration; timed: 300 minutes

Scoring: Computer scoring

Cost: Test Fee $189.00

Specific

Dental Admission Test (DAT)

Updated annually	American Dental Association

Population: Ages 21 to 22; college students applying to dental schools; 63% have completed 60 to 120 semester hours

Purpose: Used for admission to dental school

Description: The testing program is designed to measure general academic ability, comprehension of scientific information, and perceptual ability. Completion of at least 1 year of collegiate education, which should include courses in biology, general chemistry, and organic chemistry, is required. The examinations are comprised exclusively of multiple-choice test items. There are four examinations included: Survey of the Natural Sciences (Biology, General Chemistry, and Organic Chemistry), Perceptual Ability, Reading Comprehension, and Quantitative Reasoning. The test is administered on computer almost any day of the year at Sylvan Technology Test Centers in the United States only.

Format: Computer administered; timed: 4 hours 15 minutes

Scoring: Computer scored; candidate receives official DAT scores immediately

Cost: Candidate Fee $160.00

PSB Aptitude for Practical Nursing Examination

1997   Psychological Services Bureau, Inc.

Population: Adults; practical nursing students

Purpose: Measures abilities, skills, knowledge, and attitudes important to successful performance as a practical nurse; used as an admission test for schools and programs of practical nursing

Description: Multiple-item paper–pencil or electronic battery of five tests assessing areas important for performance as a practical nurse: general mental ability, spelling, the natural sciences, judgment in practical nursing, and readiness for specialized instruction in practical nursing.

Format: Examiner required; suitable for group use; timed: 2 hours 15 minutes

Scoring: Machine and electronically scored

Cost: Contact publisher

PSB Nursing School Aptitude Examination (RN)

1996   Psychological Services Bureau, Inc.

Population: Adult; nursing school candidates

Purpose: Measures abilities, skills, knowledge, and attitudes important to successful performance as a professional nurse; used as an admission test for schools and departments of nursing

Description: Multiple-item paper–pencil or electronic battery of five tests assessing areas important for performance as a nurse: academic aptitude, spelling, reading comprehension, information in the natural sciences, and vocational adjustment. The battery predicts readiness for instruction in nursing at the diploma or associate degree levels.

Format: Examiner required; suitable for group use; timed: 1 hour 45 minutes

Scoring: Machine and electronically scored

Cost: Contact publisher

Social Studies

Informeter: An International Technique for the Measurement of Political Information

1972   Donna Bardis

Panos D. Bardis

Population: Grades 10 and above

Purpose: Measures political knowledge and awareness of local, national, and international affairs; used for research on political information in the general population and discussion in social sciences classes

Description: Paper–pencil 100-item test in which the subject is asked to list important names, dates, events, and issues in response to specific questions about politics, government, and current events. Suitable for use with individuals with physical or hearing impairments.

Format: Self-administered; untimed: 15 minutes

Scoring: Examiner evaluated

Cost: $1.00

Irenometer

1985   Donna Bardis

Panos D. Bardis

Population: Adolescents, adults

Purpose: Measures attitudes and beliefs concerning peace; used for discussion purposes

Description: Paper–pencil 10-item inventory in which an individual rates 10 statements about peace and its effects on individuals and society on a 5-point scale ranging from 0 (*strongly disagree*) to 4 (*strongly agree*). All statements express positive attitudes toward peace. The score equals the sum of the 10 numerical responses. Suitable for use with individuals with physical or hearing impairments.

Format: Self-administered; untimed: 15 minutes

Scoring: Self-Scored

Cost: $1.00

World Government Scale

1985   Donna Bardis

Panos D. Bardis

Population: Adolescents, adults

Purpose: Measures attitudes and beliefs concerning world government and the possible effects world government might have on society; used for discussion and educational purposes

Description: Paper–pencil 6-item inventory in which individuals rate six statements about world government and its effects on society on a 5-point scale from 0 (*strongly disagree*) to 4 (*strongly agree*). All statements express positive attitudes toward world government. The score equals the sum of the six numerical responses. The theoretical range extends from 0 (complete rejection of the concept of world government) to 24 (complete acceptance). Suitable for use with individuals with physical or hearing impairments.

Format: Self-administered; untimed: 15 minutes

Scoring: Self-scored

Cost: $1.00

Special Education

General

Adaptive Behavior Evaluation Scale Revised Second Edition: 4 12 years (ABES-R2:4-12 years)

2006	Hawthorne Educational Services, Inc.

Stephen B. McCarney, Tamara J. Arthaud

Population: Ages 4 to 12 years

Purpose: Provides a measure of adaptive skills necessary for success in educational and residential settings

Description: May be used as a general or specific measure of adaptive skills with any student experiencing academic or behavioral difficulties regardless of the severity or suspected disability. The ABES-R2 assesses 10 areas of adaptive skills grouped under three adaptive behavioral domains. The Conceptual domain assesses the adaptive skills areas of communication and functional academics. The Social domain assesses the social, leisure, and self-direction adaptive skills areas. Self-care, home living, community use, health and safety, and work are the adaptive skills areas assessed in the Practical domain. Each item is rated on a 6-point scale. Following administration, seven types of scores may be obtained: frequency rating, subscale raw score, subscale standard score, a domain quotient and percentile, and an adaptive skills quotient and percentile. Home and school versions are available, as is a Quick Score for Windows.

Format: Rating scale; untimed: 20 minutes

Scoring: Examiner evaluated; computer scoring available

Cost: Complete Kit (2 technical manuals, intervention manual, 50 each of 2 forms) $138.00

Adaptive Behavior Evaluation Scale–Revised Second Edition: 13–18 years (ABES-R2:13-18 years)

2006	Hawthorne Educational Services, Inc.

Stephen B. McCarney, Tamara J. Arthaud

Population: Ages 13 to 18 years

Purpose: Provides a measure of adaptive skills necessary for success in educational and residential settings

Description: May be used as a general or specific measure of adaptive skills with any student experiencing academic or behavioral difficulties regardless of the severity or suspected disability. The ABES-R2 assesses 10 areas of adaptive skills grouped under three adaptive behavioral domains. The Conceptual domain assesses the adaptive skills areas of communication and functional academics. The Social domain assesses the social, leisure, and self-direction adaptive skills areas. Self-care, home living, community use, health and safety, and work are the adaptive skills areas assessed in the Practical domain. Each item is rated on a six-point scale. Following administration, seven types of scores may be obtained: frequency rating, subscale raw score, subscale standard score, a domain quotient and percentile, and an adaptive skills quotient and percentile. Home and school versions are available, as is a Quick Score for Windows.

Format: Rating scale; untimed: 20 minutes

Scoring: Examiner evaluated; computer scoring available

Cost: Complete Kit (2 technical manuals, intervention manual, 50 each of 2 forms) $140.00

Analytic Learning Disability Assessment (ALDA)

| 1982 | Slosson Educational Publications, Inc. |

Thomas D. Gnagey, Patricia D. Gnagey

Population: Ages 8 to 14 years

Purpose: Measures the skills necessary to read, spell, write, and work with numbers; aids in the neuropsychological evaluation of individuals with learning disability, mental retardation, and behavior disorders

Description: Multiple-item test assessing a student's strengths and weaknesses in 77 skills underlying basic school subjects. The strengths and weaknesses are matched with the student's most appropriate learning method for each subject: 11 reading methods, 23 spelling methods, 6 math computation methods, and 8 handwriting methods. The results are transferred to the Recommendation Pamphlet to create an individualized teaching plan providing specific procedures and methods for teachers. Materials include a student learning plan; a teacher recommendation pamphlet, also with tear-out sections; four colored scoring pencils; tape; and a straightedge ruler—all in a leather carrying case. The test should not be used unless a learning dysfunction is suspected.

Format: Examiner required; individual administration; untimed: 75 minutes

Scoring: Hand key; computer scoring available

Cost: Complete Kit (test book, manual, scoring straightedge, four colored scoring pencils, tape, chalk, 20 complete testing forms, teaching plan, carrying case) $191.75

Anser System—Aggregate Neurobehavioral Student Health and Educational Review

| 1989 | Educators Publishing Service, Inc. |

Melvin D. Levine

Population: Ages 3 to 18 years

Purpose: Gathers information from parents and teachers for the educator or clinician who has questions about a child with learning or behavioral problems

Description: Three separate short-answer paper–pencil questionnaires for parents and school personnel to evaluate three age groups: Form 1 (ages 3 to 5), Form 2 (ages 6 to 11), and Form 3 (ages 12 and older). Form 4 is a self-administered student profile to be completed by students ages 9 and older. The parent questionnaire surveys family history, possible pregnancy problems, health problems, functional problems, early development, early educational experience, skills and interests, activity–attention problems, associated behaviors, and associated strengths. The school questionnaire covers the educational program and setting, special facilities available, and the results of previous testing. The self-administered Student Profile asks the student to rate himself or herself on a series of statements in the following categories: Fine Motor, Gross Motor, Memory, Attention, Language, General Efficiency, Visual-Spatial Processing, Sequencing, General Academic Performance, and Social Interaction. Follow-up questionnaires document frequency and changes of behaviors and environment, assisting in monitoring and evaluating progress and deficiency of intervention programs.

Format: Self-administered; untimed: 30 to 60 minutes

Scoring: Examiner evaluated

Cost: Specimen Set $18.60

Checklist of Adaptive Living Skills (CALS)

| 1991 | Riverside Publishing Company |

Lanny E. Morreau, Robert H. Bruininks

Population: All ages

Purpose: Comprehensive, criterion-referenced checklist that targets specific behaviors each individual needs to develop

Description: Organized into four broad domains: Personal Living Skills, Home Living Skills, Community Living Skills, and Employment Skills, CALS presents 24 specific skill modules spanning a wide range of behaviors. Evaluates 794 important life skills. It can be used to determine instructional needs, develop individual training objectives, and provide continuous record of progress. Linked to two norm-referenced tests: *Scales of Independent Behavior* and *Inventory for Client and Agency Planning.*

Format: Examiner required; individual administration; untimed

Scoring: Examiner evaluated

Cost: Complete Program (manual, 25 checklists) $117.50

Dynamic Assessment of Test Accommodations™ (DATA)

| 2003 | Harcourt Assessment, Inc. |

Lynn Fuchs, Douglas Fuchs, Susan Eaton, Carol Hamlett

Population: Grades 2 to 7

Purpose: Helps to determine appropriate test accommodations based on empirical evidence

Description: Practitioners administer brief tests, with and without testing accommodations. Student scores are compared to those of a nondisabled normative sample. When scores indicate that a student benefits from an accommodation more than would be expected, the accommodation is recommended. DATA includes tests that assess the following areas under various testing conditions: math computation, math concepts and applications, and reading comprehension. There are three grade-appropriate levels.

Format: Examiner required; suitable for group; untimed

Scoring: Examiner evaluated

Cost: Complete Kit (manual, 25 of 3 booklets) $175.00 per level

Functional Skills Screening Inventory (FSSI)

| 2003 | Functional Resources |

Heather Becker, Sally Schur, Michele Paoletti-Schelp, Ed Hammer

Population: Ages 7 to 80 years

Purpose: Assesses critical living and working skills

Description: The FSSI is an ipsilateral observation that uses the person with complex disabilities (deaf-blind, autistic, etc.) as both subject and control. This means that the results compare the person to self over time. For the most severely involved individuals with disabilities, baseline behavior and long-term progress can be measured. It is available in a Windows format and measures two variables: the degree of support a person needs to live in the community and the degree of support a person needs to occupy his or her time in a productive manner. Available in individual, employment, and environmental editions.

Format: Examiner required; individual administration; untimed

Scoring: Examiner evaluated

Cost: Computer Version $450.00; Print Version $125.00 or $190.00

Life Skills Assessment System

| 1998 | CASAS |

Population: Adult and adolescent native and nonnative speakers of English

Purpose: Used by programs to identify basic skills in math and listening needed by individuals to function successfully in today's workplace, community, and society; learners can be placed into educational programs to assess learning gains

Description: Multiple-choice survey achievement series includes math tests at four levels (A–D) and, for assessment in English as a second language (ESL), listening comprehension tests at three levels (A–C). Each test has two forms, for pre- and posttesting. Tests are competency-based; content covers general life skills in a variety of content areas. CASAS scaled scores identify general skill level and enable comparison of performance across CASAS tests. Scannable answer sheets are available.

Format: Self-administered; untimed: 20 to 25 minutes

Scoring: Self-/Computer scored

Cost: 25 Reusable Tests $70.00; 25 Listening Tests with Audiotape $75.00; Manual $60.00

Scales of Independent Behavior-Revised (SIB-R)

| 1996 | Riverside Publishing Company |

Robert H. Bruininks, Richard W. Woodcock, Richard F. Weatherman, Bradley K. Hill

Population: Infants to adults

Purpose: Measures adaptive and problem behavior; used to determine independence of individuals with varying degrees of mental, emotional, behavioral, or physical disability

Description: Multiple-item structured interview or checklist procedure with 14 subtests assessing motor skills, social interaction and communication skills, personal living skills, community living skills, and problem behaviors. In addition, four maladaptive behavior indexes measure the frequency and severity of problem behaviors: General Maladaptive Index, Internalized Maladaptive Index, Externalized Maladaptive Index, and Asocial Maladaptive Index. Age scores, percentile ranks, standard scores, relative mastery indexes, expected range of independence, and training implication range are obtained. The SIB-R offers five administration options: full battery, short form, early development scale, individual clusters, and a problem behavior scale. This test is related structurally and statistically to the WJ-R. Because common norms are provided for the two tests, an individual's adaptive behavior may be interpreted in relation to cognitive ability.

Format: Examiner required; individual administration; time varies to battery or scale

Scoring: Examiner evaluated; computer software available

Cost: Complete Program (interview book, manual, 15 full-scale response booklets, 5 short form response booklets, 5 early development response booklets) $204.50

School Function Assessment (SFA)

1998	Harcourt Assessment, Inc.

Wendy Coster, Theresa Deeney, Stephen Haley

Population: Grades K to 6

Purpose: Evaluates and monitors a student's performance of functional tasks and activities

Description: The instrument helps elementary school students with disabilities succeed by identifying their strengths and needs in important nonacademic functional tasks. Three scales are included for evaluating students: Participation, Task Supports, and Activity Performance. Criterion cutoff scores help to establish eligibility for special services.

Format: Examiner required; individual administration; untimed: 5 to 10 minutes

Scoring: Examiner evaluated

Cost: Complete Kit (manual, 25 record forms, 3 rating scales) $185.00

Special Needs Assessment Profile–Revised 2 (SNAP)

2005	Hodder Murray

Charles Weedon, Gavin Reid

Population: Ages 5 to 14 years

Purpose: Provides computer-aided diagnostic assessment and profiling

Description: This is an all-in-one package that profiles 18 specific learning difficulties and related factors (ADD; auditory processing; developmental coordination disorder; dyscalculia; dysgraphia; hyperactivity; hyperlexia; dyslexia; phonological difficulties; nonverbal learning difficulties; processing speed; social awareness and communicative difficulties; specific speech, language, and communication difficulties; visual processing difficulties; working memory difficul-

ties; essential fatty acid deficiency; educational self-esteem; and social self-esteem) and gives follow-up suggestions for both teachers and parents. Designed for use by SENCOs, learning support teachers, and specialist teachers. Maps each pupil's own mix of problems onto an overall matrix of learning, social, and personal difficulties. Helps to identify clusters of problems and the core features of a pupil's difficulties using focused assessments from a bank of diagnostic probes. Indicates the most appropriate teaching and/or specialist provision. Generates personalized information sheets that will help to strengthen home and teacher support.

Format: Examiner required; individual administration; untimed

Scoring: Computer scored

Cost: CD with 2-Year License £165.00; User Kit £39.99; Pupil Assessment Pack £17.99

Survey of Teenage Readiness and Neurodevelopmental Status (STRANDS)

2001	Educators Publishing Service, Inc.

Melvin D. Levine

Population: Ages 13 to 19 years

Purpose: Provides an overview of an individual's perceptions of functioning across a variety of neurocognitive and psychosocial domains

Description: Designed to be administered by any professionals who work with adolescents, STRANDS provides clues and guidance to the clinician, counselor, teacher, or researcher about how students process information and how they function in school and in their social lives. STRANDS can be used to suggest areas of adolescent functioning that require more detailed evaluation and follow-up and can provide additional guidance in selecting follow-up measures. Responses can indicate the need for specific teaching or counseling strategies based on students' perceived strengths and weaknesses. Based on a metacognitive theoretical model, STRANDS has been through 6 years of technical development, standardization, and test modification. Quantitative and qualitative scoring procedures have been incorporated. Assessment of Attention, Memory, Sequencing, Language, Visual Processing, Motor Functions, Organization and Strategies, Higher-Order Cognition, Metacognitive Awareness, Observations, School Skills, School Life, Social Life, School and Work Preferences, Reasons, and Academic Expectations.

Format: Examiner required and self-administered; individual administration; untimed: Rating, 20 minutes; Interview, 40 minutes

Scoring: Examiner evaluated

Cost: Complete Set (manual, 12 of each student form, 12 profile sheets) $86.95

Vineland Adaptive Behavior Scales–Second Edition (Vineland-II)

2004	AGS Publishing/Pearson Assessments

Sara S. Sparrow, Dominic V. Cicchetti, David A. Balla

Population: Ages birth to 90 years

Purpose: Measures personal and social skills

Description: Updated with new norms, expanded age range, and improved items. Maintains the semistructured interview format. There are five Domains and Indexes (Communication, Daily Living Skills, Socialization, Motor Skills, and optional Maladaptive Behavior Index). The examiner may use a survey interview form, parent/caregiver form, expanded interview form, and teacher rating form. Items have been added at the lower and upper age ranges to provide a reliable picture of the level of functioning. Some forms are available in Spanish.

Format: Interview and questionnaire; untimed 20 to 60 minutes

Scoring: Examiner evaluated; Computer scoring available for Macintosh and Windows

Cost: Survey Starter Set (manual, 10 of 3 forms) $124.99; Teacher Starter Set (manual, 10 of 3 forms) $89.99

Autism Spectrum

Asperger Syndrome Diagnostic Scale (ASDS)

2000	PRO-ED, Inc.

Brenda Myles, Stacy Jones-Bock, Richard Simpson

Population: Ages 5 to 18 years

Purpose: Helps to determine the presence of Asperger's syndrome

Description: Completed by anyone who knows the child, the rating scale has 50 yes–no items. The items were drawn from five specific areas

of behavior: cognitive, maladaptive, language, social, sensorimotor. The ASDS was normed on 227 persons with various disabilities. All items included represent behaviors that are symptomatic of Asperger's syndrome.

Format: Rating scale; untimed: 10 to 15 minutes

Scoring: Examiner evaluated

Cost: Complete Kit (manual, 50 record forms, storage box) $100.00

Autism Diagnostic Interview–Revised (ADI-R)

2003	Western Psychological Services

Michael Rutter, Ann LeCouteur, Catherine Lord

Population: Parents or caregivers of children whose developmental age is greater than 2 years

Purpose: Diagnoses autism, planning treatment, and distinguishing autism from other developmental disorders

Description: Composed of 93 items, the ADI-R focuses on three functional domains: Language and Communications; Reciprocal Social Interactions; and Restricted, Repetitive, and Stereotyped Behaviors and Interests. Interview questions cover eight content areas: Overview of the subject's behavior; the subject's background, including family, education, previous diagnoses, and medications; early development and developmental milestones; language acquisition and loss of language or other skills; current functioning in regard to language and communication; social development and play; interests and behaviors; and clinically relevant behaviors, such as aggression, self-injury, and possible epileptic features. The ADI-R provides categorical results, rather than scales or norms. Results can be used to support a diagnosis of autism or to determine the clinical needs of various groups.

Format: Examiner required; individual administration; untimed: 90 to 150 minutes

Scoring: Examiner evaluated; computer scoring available

Cost: Kit (manual, 10 interview booklets, 12 current behavior algorithms, 12 diagnostic algorithms) $192.50

Autism Diagnostic Observation Schedule (ADOS)

1999	Western Psychological Services

Catherine Lord, Michael Rutter,
Pamela C. DiLavore, Susan Risi

Population: All ages

Purpose: Evaluates anyone suspected of having autism

Description: The ADOS consists of various activities that allow the examiner to observe social and communication behaviors related to the diagnosis of pervasive developmental disorders (PDDs). These activities provide interesting, standard contexts in which interaction can occur. The ADOS consists of four modules. The individual being evaluated is given just one module, depending on his or her expressive language level and chronological age. Following guidance provided in the manual, the examiner selects the appropriate module for each person. Observations are recorded, then coded later to formulate a diagnosis. Cutoff scores are provided for both the broader diagnosis of PDD, atypical autism, or autism spectrum, as well as the traditional, narrower conceptualization of autism.

Format: Requires examiner; individually administered; untimed: 35 to 40 minutes

Scoring: Examiner evaluated

Cost: Complete Kit (manual, 4 of each module observation/coding booklets, manipulatives, container) $1,480.00

Autism Screening Instrument for Educational Planning– Second Edition (ASIEP-2)

1993	PRO-ED, Inc.

David A. Krug, Joel R. Arick,
Patricia J. Almond

Population: Ages 18 months to adult

Purpose: Assesses the behavioral, social, and educational development of students with autism, and other developmental disabilities; used to establish Individualized Education Programs, to evaluate program effectiveness, and to monitor student progress

Description: Multiple-item paper–pencil observational inventory consisting of five subtests: Autism Behavior Checklist (ABC), Sample of Vocal Behavior, Interaction Assessment, Educational Assessment, and Prognosis of Learning Rate. The observational methods involved in all five subtests allow all students to be "testable."

Format: Examiner required; individual administration; untimed

Scoring: Examiner evaluated

Cost: Complete Kit (manual, 25 each of all record forms, manipulatives, storage box) $230.00

Behavior Rating Instrument for Autistic and other Atypical Children–Second Edition (BRIAAC)

1991	Stoelting Company

Bertram Ruttenberg, Charles Wenar,
Enid G. Wolf

Population: Autistic children of all ages

Purpose: Evaluates the status of low functioning, atypical, and autistic children of all ages; used to evaluate children who will not or cannot cooperate with formal testing procedures.

Description: Paper–pencil inventory of observations taken over a two-day period assessing a child's present level of functioning and measuring behavioral change in eight areas: relationship to an adult, communication, drive for mastery, vocalization and expressive speech, sound and speech reception, social responsiveness, body movement (passive and active), and psychobiological development. Each of the eight scales begins with the most severe autistic behavior and progresses to behavior roughly comparable to that of a normally developing 3½- to 4½-year-old. The complete BRIAAC includes a manual, report forms, individual scale score sheet, total score sheet, intrascale and interscale profile forms, descriptive guides, and suggested individual plans.

Format: Examiner required; individual administration; untimed

Scoring: Examiner evaluated

Cost: Complete Kit (manual, all required forms) $130.00

Childhood Autism Rating Scale (CARS)

1988	Western Psychological Services

Eric Schopler, Robert J. Reichler,
Barbara Rochen Renner

Population: Children, adolescents

Purpose: Diagnoses children with autism syndrome and distinguishes them from children with developmental disabilities who are not autistic

Description: Items include relating to people; imitation; emotional response; body use; object use; adaptation to change; visual response; listening response; taste, smell, and touch response and use; fear or nervousness; verbal communication; nonverbal communication; activity level; level and consistency of intellectual response; and general impression. The child is rated on each of the 15 items using a 7-point scale that indicates the degree to which the child's behavior deviates from that of a normal child of the same age. A total score is then computed by summing the individual ratings. Children who score above a given point are categorized as autistic. Scores within the autistic range can then be divided into two categories: mild-to-moderate autism and severe autism.

Format: Rating scale; untimed

Scoring: Examiner evaluated

Cost: Kit (25 rating scales, manual) $77.00

Children's Communication Checklist–Second Edition (CCC-2)

| 2003 | Harcourt Assessment–UK |

Dorothy Bishop

Population: Ages 4 to 16 years

Purpose: Screens for communication problems

Description: A 70-item checklist that is completed by a caregiver. The instrument identifies pragmatic impairment and assists in determining who may merit from further assessment for an autistic spectrum disorder. There are 10 scales: Speech, Syntax, Semantics, Coherence, Inappropriate Initiation, Stereotyped Language, Use of Context, Nonverbal Communication, Social Relations, and Interests. Two composite scores are derived: General Communication Composite and Social Interaction Deviance Composite.

Format: Rating scale; untimed

Scoring: Examiner evaluated; computer scoring included

Cost: Complete Kit (manual, 25 checklists, 25 summary sheets, overlay keys, CD scorer, in a bag) £97.00

Evaluating Acquired Skills in Communication–Revised (EASIC-R)

| 1991 | PRO-ED, Inc. |

Anita Marcott Riley

Population: Ages 3 months to 8 years

Purpose: Measures receptive and expressive language; used also with individuals with developmental language delays

Description: Multiple-item oral-response test consisting of five inventories assessing a child's abilities in semantics, syntax, morphology, and pragmatics. The examiner uses picture stimuli to elicit spontaneous, cued, imitated, manipulated, noncompliant, or incorrect responses. The test helps to determine emerging communication skills, including before meaningful speech; understanding of simple noun labels, action verbs, and basic concepts; emerging modes of communication; understanding of more complex language functions; and use of more complex communication. The test includes goals for individual education prescriptions.

Format: Examiner required; individual administration; untimed: 15 to 30 minutes

Scoring: Examiner evaluated

Cost: Complete Kit (manual, picture book, cards, test booklets for all levels, skill profiles, storage box) $153.00

Gilliam Asperger Disorder Scale (GADS)

| 2001 | PRO-ED, Inc. |

James F. Gilliam

Population: Ages 3 to 22 years

Purpose: Evaluates unique behavioral problems of individuals who may have Asperger's disorder

Description: Based on the most current and relevant definitions and diagnostic criteria of Asperger's disorder, the rating scale is completed by a parent or a professional who knows the child. There are 32 clearly stated items divided into four subscales that describe specific, observable, and measurable behaviors. Eight additional items are included for parents to contribute data about their child's development during the first 3 years of life. Standard scores and percentiles are provided. A reference listing of resources for teachers and parents is included in the manual.

Format: Rating scale; untimed: 5 to 10 minutes

Scoring: Examiner evaluated

Cost: Complete Kit (manual, 25 protocols, storage box) $100.00

Gilliam Autism Rating Scale–Second Edition (GARS-2)

| 2006 | PRO-ED, Inc. |

James E. Gilliam

Population: Ages 3 to 22 years

Purpose: Helps to identify and diagnose autism and estimates the severity of the disorder

Description: Items on the GARS-2 are based on the definitions of autism adopted by the Autism Society of America and the *Diagnostic and Statistical Manual of Mental Disorders–Fourth Edition, Text Revision.* The items are grouped into three subtests: Stereotyped Behaviors, Communication, and Social Interaction. These core subtests describe specific and measurable behaviors. A structured interview form is included for gathering diagnostically important information from the individual's parents. The total score, with a mean of 100 and standard deviation of 15 is the Autism Index. A separate booklet, Instructional Objectives, is included.

Format: Rating scale; untimed: 5 to 10 minutes

Scoring: Examiner evaluated

Cost: Complete Kit (manual, 50 summary/response forms, objectives manual, storage box) $131.00

Krug Asperger's Disorder Index (KADI)

2003 PRO-ED, Inc.

Joel R. Arick, David A. Krug

Population: Ages 6 to 21 years

Purpose: Enables professionals to accurately distinguish individuals with Asperger's disorder from individuals with other forms of high-functioning autism

Description: The KADI can be a prescreening scale that immediately identifies individuals who do not have Asperger's disorder. Each item on the KADI has a weighted score, which was determined via statistical analysis of the item's predictive ability to differentiate.

Format: Rating scale; untimed: 10 to 15 minutes

Scoring: Examiner evaluated

Cost: Complete Kit (manual, 50 each ages 6 to 11 and ages 12 to 21 forms, storage box) $90.00

PDD Behavior Inventory™ (PDDBI)

2005 Psychological Assessment Resources, Inc.

Ira L. Cohen, Vicki Sudhalter

Population: Ages 1 year 6 months to 12 years 5 months

Purpose: Assesses responsiveness to intervention in children with pervasive developmental disorder

Description: An informant-based rating scale that is designed to measure both problem behavior and social communication skills. It was also designed to provide age-standardized scores for both parent and teacher ratings. It can be used for diagnosis and change over time. The standard forms for teacher and parent have six domains and are appropriate if the primary concerns are specifically related to autism. The extended form consists of 10 domains for both the parent and the teacher versions.

Format: Rating scale; untimed: standard, 20 to 30 minutes; extended form, 30 to 45 minutes

Scoring: Examiner evaluated

Cost: Introductory Kit (manual, 25 of each form, 25 of each summary form) $230.00

Psychoeducational Profile–Third Edition (PEP-3)

2005 PRO-ED, Inc.

Eric Schopler, Margaret D. Lansing, Robert J. Reichler, Lee M. Marcus

Population: Children with developmental disabilities functioning between the ages of 6 months and 7 years

Purpose: Measures the learning abilities and characteristics of autism and related developmental disabilities; used to establish individualized special education curricula or home programs

Description: The PEP-3 is a revision that provides a profile to graphically chart uneven and idiosyncratic development, emerging skills, and autistic behavioral characteristics. A Caregiver Report is now included that utilizes parent input. The test is also improved by offering normative data both from a group of children in the autism spectrum, as well as from a comparison group of children without autism. The scoring has been quantified as 0, 1, 2; and each score is clearly defined, making statistical comparisons more accurate. At the same time, the flexibility of the previous system—using pass, emerge, and fail—has been maintained.

Format: Examiner required; individual administration; untimed: 45 to 90 minutes

Scoring: Examiner evaluated

Cost: Complete Kit (manual, Guide to Item Administration, picture book, 10 scoring/summary booklets, 10 response booklets, 10 caregiver report forms, object kit, storage boxes) $450.00

Social Communication Questionnaire (SCQ)

2003	Western Psychological Services

Michael Rutter, Anthony Bailey, Catherine Lord

Population: Parents or caregivers of children with a developmental age greater than 2 years and chronological age of 4 years

Purpose: Screens for autism spectrum disorders

Description: Previously known as the *Autism Screening Questionnaire* (ASQ), this brief instrument helps to evaluate communication skills and social functioning in children who may have autism or autism spectrum disorders. It is available in two forms—Lifetime and Current—each composed of 40 yes–no questions. Both forms can be given directly to the parent, who can answer the questions without supervision. Forms are available in Spanish, Danish, Dutch, German, Hungarian, Italian, and Swedish. The Lifetime Form focuses on the child's entire developmental history, providing a Total Score that is interpreted in relation to specific cutoff points. This score identifies individuals who may have autism and should be referred for a more complete evaluation—with the *Autism Diagnostic Interview–Revised* (ADI-R) or the *Autism Diagnostic Observation Schedule* (ADOS), for example. SCQ content parallels that of the ADI-R, and the agreement between SCQ and ADI-R scores is high and substantially unaffected by age, gender, language level, and performance IQ. This indicates that the SCQ is a valid screener, providing a reasonable picture of symptom severity. Moving from developmental history to present status, the Current Form looks at the child's behavior over the most recent 3-month period. It produces results that can be helpful in treatment planning, educational intervention, and measurement of change over time. In addition to its screening and educational applications, the SCQ can also be used to compare symptom levels across various groups—children with developmental language disorders, for example, or youngsters with medical conditions typically associated with autism spectrum disorders.

Format: Rating scale; untimed: 10 minutes

Scoring: Examiner evaluated; computer scoring available

Cost: Kit (manual, 20 current AutoScore™ forms, 20 lifetime AutoScore™ forms) $104.50

Social Responsiveness Scale (SRS)

2005	Western Psychological Services

John N. Constantino, Christian P. Gruber

Population: Parents or teachers of children ages 4 to 18 years

Purpose: Distinguishes autism spectrum conditions from other child psychiatric conditions

Description: This 65-item rating scale measures the severity of autism spectrum symptoms as they occur in natural social settings. The SRS measures impairment on a quantitative scale across a wide range of severity—which is consistent with recent research indicating that autism is best conceptualized as a spectrum condition, rather than as an all-or-nothing diagnosis. This is important because even mild degrees of impairment can have significant adverse effects on social functioning. In addition to a Total Score reflecting severity of social deficits in the autism spectrum, the SRS generates scores for five Treatment Subscales: Receptive, Cognitive, Expressive, and Motivational aspects of social behavior, as well as Autistic Preoccupations.

Format: Rating scale; untimed: 15 to 20 minutes

Scoring: Examiner evaluated; computer scoring available

Cost: Kit (manual, 15 each of parent and teacher AutoScore™ forms) $91.00

TEACCH Transition Assessment Profile (TTAP)

2007	PRO-ED, Inc.

Gary B. Mesibov, John B. Thomas, S. Michael Chapman, Eric Schopler

Population: Adolescents and adults with developmental disability

Purpose: Measures the functional areas required to achieve positive outcomes in adulthood

Description: A major revision of the *Adolescent and Adult Psychoeducational Profile* (AAPEP) to measure transitional needs. The TTAP is structured to satisfy those provisions in IDEA 2004 that require evaluation for transition and provision of a transition plan.

Format: Examiner required; individual administration; untimed: 60 minutes

Scoring: Examiner evaluated

Cost: Complete Kit (manual, 10 forms) $72.00

Deaf and Hearing Impairment

Carolina Picture Vocabulary Test (CPVT)

| 1985 | PRO-ED, Inc. |

Thomas L. Layton, David W. Holmes

Population: Ages 4 to 11 years

Purpose: Measures receptive sign vocabulary in individuals who use manual signing as their primary mode of communication

Description: Norm-referenced, validated, receptive sign vocabulary test for children who are deaf or hearing impaired. The population (*N* = 767) used in the standardization research was based on a nationwide sample of children who use manual signs as their primary means of communication. Stratification of the sample was based on geographic region, educational facility, parental occupation, gender, race, age, grade, etiology, age of onset of hearing impairment, number of years of signing, IQ, and threshold of hearing loss in the better ear. The CPVT consists of 130 items with suggested basal and ceiling levels. Scale scores, percentile ranks, and age equivalency scores are provided.

Format: Examiner required; individual administration; untimed: 10 to 15 minutes

Scoring: Examiner evaluated

Cost: Complete Kit (manual, picture book, 50 record forms, storage box) $135.00

Central Institute for the Deaf Preschool Performance Scale (CID-PPS)

| 1984 | Stoelting Company |

Ann E. Geers, Helen S. Lane

Population: Ages 2 to 6 years

Purpose: Measures intellectual potential using completely nonverbal testing procedures; predicts school achievement in preschoolers with hearing impairment

Description: Multiple-item task-performance test assessing the intellectual abilities of preschoolers without requiring a single spoken word from either the examiner or the child (optional verbal clues are provided for hearing children). Six subtests assess intellectual abilities in the following areas: manual planning (block building, Montessori cylinders, and two-figure formboard); manual dexterity (buttons and Wallin pegs); form perception (Decroly pictures and Seguin formboard); perceptual/motor skills (Knox cube, drawing, and paper folding); preschool skills (color sorting and counting sticks); and part/whole relations (Manikin and Stutsman puzzles). Test materials were selected from existing mental tests for children ages 2 to 5 to obtain a broad, clinical picture of the child's ability and a numerical rating (Deviation IQ) that would correlate with a *Stanford-Binet IQ*. The test is an adaptation of the early *Randall's Island Performance Series*.

Format: Examiner required; individual administration; untimed: 40 minutes

Scoring: Examiner evaluated

Cost: Complete Kit (manual, 30 record forms, manipulatives) $850.00

CID Phonetic Inventory

| 1988 | Central Institute for the Deaf Publications |

Jean S. Moog

Population: Ages 3 years to adolescent with severe to profound hearing impairment

Purpose: Measures speech production in individuals with hearing impairment

Description: This is a rating form on which the teacher can record the child's ability to produce speech sounds. The Phonetic Skills Profile graphically illustrates the child's skills and progress. There are six subtests: Suprasegmental Aspects, Vowels/Diphthongs, Initial Consonants, Alternating Vowels, Final Consonants, and Alternating Consonants.

Format: Examiner required; individual administration; untimed: 30 minutes

Scoring: Examiner evaluated

Cost: Kit (manual, forms, cards) $50.00

CID Picture SPINE: The Speech Intelligibility Evaluation

| 1988 | Central Institute for the Deaf Publications |

Randall Monsen, Jean S. Moog, Ann E. Geers

Population: Ages 6 to 12 years

Purpose: Provides an estimation of speech intelligibility of children with severe to profound hearing impairment

Description: Uses colorful pictures in four sets

of 25 cards. Each set consists of phonemically confusable words.

Format: Examiner required; individual administration; untimed

Scoring: Examiner evaluated

Cost: Kit (manual, forms, full-color cards) $110.00

Early Speech Perception Test (ESP)

| 1990 | Central Institute for the Deaf Publications |

Jean S. Moog, Ann E. Geers

Population: Ages 3 years to adolescent with severe to profound hearing impairment

Purpose: Measures speech perception skills

Description: The ESP may be used to establish objectives and to measure effects of a hearing aid or a cochlear implant in terms of their impact on the child's speech perception ability. There are two versions: standard and low verbal.

Format: Examiner required; individual administration; untimed: 20 to 30 minutes

Scoring: Examiner evaluated

Cost: Kit (manual, forms, toys, full color picture cards, CD) $200.00

Rhode Island Test of Language Structure (RITLS)

| 1983 | PRO-ED, Inc. |

Elizabeth Engen, Trygg Engen

Population: Ages 3 to 20 years

Purpose: Measures English language development in hearing children ages 3 to 6 years or children with hearing impairments and adults ages 3 to 20 years

Description: Multiple-choice 100-item verification test assessing understanding of language structure (syntax). The test presents 20 sentence types, both simple and complex. The test is used for educational planning, such as determination of school readiness, bilingual programming, and language introduction procedures. It can also be used where language development is a concern, including students with mental retardation or learning disabilities, and in bilingual programs.

Format: Examiner required; individual administration; untimed: 30 minutes

Scoring: Examiner evaluated

Cost: Complete Kit (test booklet, 10 response sheets/10 analysis sheets, manual) $143.00

Scales of Early Communication Skills (SECS)

| 1975 | Central Institute for the Deaf Publications |

Jean S. Moog, Ann E. Geers

Population: Ages 2 to 8 years

Purpose: Evaluates speech and language development of individuals with hearing impairments

Description: Four scales measure receptive language, expressive language, nonverbal receptive skills, and nonverbal expressive skills. Ratings are based on observation of the child in structured lessons and in natural communication settings.

Format: Examiner required; individual administration; untimed

Scoring: Examiner evaluated

Cost: Manual $14.95; 25 Forms $12.00

Speech Perception Instructional Curriculum and Evaluation (SPICE)

| 1995 | Central Institute for the Deaf Publications |

Julia J. Biedenstein, Lisa S. Davidson, Jean S. Moog

Population: Ages 3 to adult

Purpose: Measures auditory speech perception and is an auditory training curriculum for individuals with hearing impairments

Description: There are four subtests. Detection of Speech, Suprasegmental Perception of Speech, Vowel and Consonant Perception of Speech, and Auditory Speech Perception in Connected Speech Activities. The evaluation and curriculum are used with children with cochlear implants or hearing aids.

Format: Examiner required; individual administration; untimed

Scoring: Examiner evaluated

Cost: Kit (manual, forms, toys, full-color illustrated word and sentence cards, auditory training screen, instructional video) $350.00

Teacher Assessment of Grammatical Structures (TAGS)

| 1983 | Central Institute for the Deaf Publications |

Jean S. Moog, Victoria J. Kozak

Population: Children

Purpose: Measures grammatical language use

Description: There are three levels of assessment of syntactic ability: Presentence, Simple Sentence, and Complex Sentence. The results assist teachers in planning goals and are used to rate progress.

Format: Examiner required; individual administration; untimed

Scoring: Examiner evaluated

Cost: Manual $19.95; 25 Forms $12.00

Test of Early Reading Ability–Deaf or Hard of Hearing (TERA-D/HH)

1991	PRO-ED, Inc.

D. Kim Reid, Wayne P. Hresko, Donald D. Hammill, Susan Wiltshire

Population: Ages 3 to 13 years

Purpose: Measures early literacy of children with moderate to profound sensory hearing loss (ranging from 41 to beyond 91 decibels, corrected)

Description: The instrument has equivalent forms and taps the child's ability to construct meaning, knowledge of the alphabet and its functions, and awareness of print conventions. Results are reported as standard scores, percentile rankings, and normal curve equivalents. TERA-D/HH was standardized on a national sample of more than 1,000 students from 20 states who are deaf or hard of hearing. Normative data are given for every 6-month interval. Internal consistency and test–retest reliability are reported in the manual. In all instances, coefficients approach or exceed .90. Validity coefficients for TERA-D/HH with other reading, language, intelligence, and achievement tests frequently used with students who are deaf or hard of hearing also are reported in the manual.

Format: Examiner required; individual administration; untimed: 20 to 30 minutes

Scoring: Examiner evaluated

Cost: Complete Kit (manual, picture book, 25 each of Form A and Form B profile/examiner record forms, storage box) $190.00

Developmental Disabilities

AAMR Adaptive Behavior Scale— Residential and Community: Second Edition (ABS-RC:2)

1993	PRO-ED, Inc.

Kazuo Nihira, Henry Leland, Nadine Lambert

Population: Ages 18 to 60+ years

Purpose: Identifies individuals who are significantly below their peers in important areas of adaptive behavior to determine strengths and weaknesses among adaptive domains and factors

Description: This instrument is a revision of the 1969 and 1974 *AAMD Adaptive Behavior Scales*. The items measure the following domains: Independent Functioning, Physical Development, Economic Activity, Language Development, Numbers and Time, Domestic Activity, Prevocational/Vocational Activity, Self-Direction, Responsibility, Socialization, Social Behavior, Conformity, Trustworthiness, Stereotyped/Hyperactive Behavior, Sexual Behavior, Self-Abuse Behavior, Social Engagement, and Disturbing Interpersonal Behavior. Factor scores of Personal Self-Sufficiency, Community Self-Sufficiency, Personal–Social Responsibility, Social Adjustment, and Personal Adjustment are available from the domain scores.

Format: Individual interview format; untimed: 15 to 30 minutes

Scoring: Examiner evaluated

Cost: Complete Kit (manual, 25 protocols, 25 scoring forms, storage box) $150.00

AAMR Adaptive Behavior Scale— School: Second Edition (ABS-S:2)

1993	PRO-ED, Inc.

Nadine Lambert, Kazuo Nihira, Henry Lambert

Population: Ages 3 to 18 years

Purpose: Identifies individuals who are significantly below their peers in important areas of adaptive behavior to determine strengths and weaknesses among adaptive domains and factors

Description: This instrument is a revision of the 1969 and 1974 *AAMD Adaptive Behavior Scales*. The items measure the following domains in Part One: Independent Functioning, Physical Development, Economic Activity, Language Development, Numbers and Time, Prevocational/Vocational Activity, Self-Direction, Responsibility, and Socialization. Behaviors in Part Two measured: Social Behavior, Conformity, Trustworthiness, Stereotyped/Hyperactive Behavior, Self-Abusive Behavior, Social Engagement, and Disturbing Interpersonal Behavior. Factor scores of Personal Self-Sufficiency, Community Self-Sufficiency, Personal–Social Responsibility, Social Adjustment, and Personal Adjustment are available from the domain scores.

Format: Individual interview format; untimed: 15 to 30 minutes

Scoring: Examiner evaluated

Cost: Complete Kit (manual, 25 protocols, 25 scoring forms, storage box) $150.00

Aberrant Behavior Checklist (ABC)

Residential 1986;	Slosson Educational
Community 1994	Publications, Inc.

Michael G. Aman, Nirbhay N. Singh

Population: Children to adults

Purpose: Assesses problem behaviors of children and adults with mental retardation at home, in residential facilities, ICFs/MR, and in work training centers

Description: Checklist with 58 items in five subscales: Irritability and Agitation, Lethargy and Social Withdrawal, Stereotypic Behavior, Hyperactivity and Noncompliance, and Inappropriate Speech. The ABC asks for degree of retardation, the person's medical status, and current medication condition; then 58 specific symptoms are rated and an extensive manual gives comprehensive descriptions for each assessed behavior. The checklist can be completed by parents, special educators, psychologists, direct caregivers, nurses, and others with knowledge of the person being assessed. Average subscale scores are available for both U.S. and overseas residential facilities and for children and adults living in the community.

Format: Rating scale; untimed: 25 minutes

Scoring: Examiner evaluated

Cost: Residential Complete $81.25; Community Complete $92.50

Adaptive Behavior Assessment System–Second Edition (ABAS-2)

2003	Harcourt Assessment, Inc.

Patti Harrison, Thomas Oakland

Population: Ages birth to 89 years

Purpose: Provides complete assessment of adaptive skills functioning

Description: The second edition adds a parent/primary caregiver form for infants through age 5. Assesses 10 areas of adaptive skills specified by AAMR and the DSM-IV: communication, community use, functional academics, home living, health and safety, leisure, self-care, self-direction, social, and work. Separate forms for teachers and parents are available for ages 5 to 21 years. The adult form can be completed by the individual's caregiver or by the individual. The ABAS-2 can also be used to determine if adults can live independently.

Format: Examiner required; suitable for group use; untimed: 15 minutes

Scoring: Examiner evaluated; computer scoring available

Cost: Examination Kit (manual, 5 each of 5 forms) $175.00

Adaptive Behavior Inventory (ABI)

1986	PRO-ED, Inc.

Linda Brown, James E. Leigh

Population: Ages 6 to 18 years

Purpose: Evaluates the functional, daily living skills of school-aged children; helps to identify children believed to have mental retardation or emotional disturbance

Description: Paper-pencil 150-item inventory assessing functional skills in five scale areas: Self-Care Skills, Communication Skills, Social Skills, Academic Skills, and Occupational Skills. The test yields an Adaptive Behavior Quotient, standard scores, and percentiles. The ABI-Short Form, which contains 50 items and yields the same scores as the complete form, is also available.

Format: Individual interview format; untimed: 15 to 30 minutes

Scoring: Examiner evaluated

Cost: Complete Kit (manual, short form and long form protocols, storage box) $92.00

Adult Life Skills

2000	CASAS

Population: Adolescents, adults

Purpose: Used with learners with developmental disabilities to assess competencies across a range of life skills and may be used to measure learning progress

Description: Multiple-choice tests. Highest test level provides transition into regular CASAS life skill series. Four levels of tests, AAAAA (most basic) through AA. Training is required to implement the program. CASAS-scaled scores identify general skill level and enable comparison of performance across CASAS tests.

Format: Examiner required; individual administration

Scoring: Hand-scored

Cost: Manual $15.00; $22.00 per reusable test

Assessment for Persons Profoundly or Severely Impaired (APPSI)

| 1998 | PRO-ED, Inc. |

Patricia Connrad, Sharon Bradley-Johnson

Population: Developmental ages birth to 8 months

Purpose: Assesses communication and motor performance of students and adults; diagnoses communication needs and evaluates prelinguistic behavior of preverbal individuals

Description: Discover clients' preferences for visual, auditory, and tactile stimuli on the receptive side, social interaction, and methods of communicative output. The APPSI is not normed, but it was piloted in three states with 32 individuals (ages 2 to 24) who have severe and profound impairments. Reliability coefficients for the test range from .76 to .92, indicating a very high level of reliability. The APPSI aids in defining individuals' preferred methods of communication.

Format: Examiner required; individual administration; untimed: 30 to 60 minutes

Scoring: Examiner evaluated

Cost: Complete Kit (manual, 25 record booklets, 25 profile/summary forms, set of cards and manipulatives, storage box) $185.00

Developmental Assessment for Students with Severe Disabilities–Second Edition (DASH-2)

| 1999 | PRO-ED, Inc. |

Mary K. Dykes, Jane N. Erin

Population: Developmental ages birth to 6 years

Purpose: Assesses the development of individuals with severe disabilities; used to establish goals and objectives

Description: Five Pinpoint Scales assess performance in Language, Sensory-Motor Skill, Activities of Daily Living, Basic Academic Skills, and Social-Emotional Skill. The skills assessed are identified as either present, emerging, task-resistive, nonrelevant, or unknown. This is a criterion-referenced instrument.

Format: Examiner required; individual administration; untimed

Scoring: Examiner evaluated

Cost: Complete Kit (manual, 5 each of 5 Pinpoint Scales, 25 daily plan sheets, 1 pad comprehensive program records, 25 individualized education plans) $210.00

Inventory for Client and Agency Planning (ICAP)

| 1986 | Riverside Publishing Company |

Robert H. Bruininks, Bradley K. Hill, Richard F. Weatherman, Richard W. Woodcock

Population: Infants to adults

Purpose: Measures adaptive and problem behaviors and service needs of individuals with moderate to severe disabilities or mental retardation in residential rehabilitation, education, and human service programs; also used by geriatric service agencies

Description: Multiple-item paper–pencil self-report inventory providing client information in the following areas: diagnostic and health status, adaptive behavior, problem behavior, service history, residential placement, projected service needs, functional limitations, and social/leisure history. The results can be used by administrators and supervisors to determine the client's current status and eligibility for services and to manage programs and facilities by assisting in their accreditation, coordinating and planning project costs and reimbursement, and obtaining funding. Age scores, adaptive behavior indexes, standard scores, and service level index scores are obtained. Response booklets are available in Spanish.

Format: Examiner required; individual administration; untimed: 20 to 30 minutes

Scoring: Examiner evaluated; software scoring available

Cost: Complete Program (manual, 25 response booklets) $167.50

Street Survival Skills Questionnaire (SSSQ)

| 1993 | McCarron-Dial Systems |

Dan Linkenhoker, Lawrence T. McCarron

Population: Ages 9 years and older

Purpose: Measures specific aspects of the adaptive behavior of special education students; used as a baseline behavioral measure of the effects of training and to predict one's potential for adapting to community living conditions and vocational placement

Description: Oral-response and point-to test consisting of 216 items on nine subtests, each containing 24 picture plates. The examiner orally presents the question, and the examinee responds by pointing to one of the four pictures presented. Fundamental reading skills are required. The large print and graphic format are designed for use with individuals with visual acuity of 20/200 or better in either eye. A booklet for administering the SSSQ in sign language is available. The SSSQ Report (sold separately) provides narrative interpretations of the examinee's performance in each area, as well as more specific area analyses.

Format: Examiner required; individual administration; untimed: 30 to 45 minutes

Scoring: Hand key; may be computer scored

Cost: Complete $400.00; SSSQ Computer Report $250.00

VCWS 14-Integrated Peer Performance

1974   **Valpar International Corporation**

Population: Ages 15 years and older with developmental disability

Purpose: Assesses an individual's instruction-following ability and color discrimination skills; stimulates interaction among workers

Description: Work sample assessing an individual's ability to follow instructions and discriminate between colors. The work sample emphasizes the ability to interact effectively with both peers and supervisors and the ability to work as a team member in order to complete a task. Three or four examinees are seated and given colored assembly pieces and an assembly pattern booklet. The examiner places assembly boards on the table and moves them from worker to worker every 20 seconds. Each examinee performs his or her portion of assembly and then waits for the next assembly board. As each assembly board is completed, the examiner inspects each board and informs the examinee of any errors made. Useful as a clinical assessment and training aid.

Format: Examiner required; suitable for group use; timed

Scoring: Examiner evaluated

Cost: $5,175.00

VCWS 17-Pre-Vocational Readiness Battery

1978   **Valpar International Corporation**

Population: Ages 15 years and older with developmental disability

Purpose: Assesses an individual's ability to function independently

Description: Assessment and training tool containing five subtests: Development Assessment, Workshop Evaluation, Vocational Interest Screening, Interpersonal/Social Skills, and Independent Living Skills. The developmental assessment subtest contains functional nonmedical measures of physical and mental abilities. The workshop evaluation is a simulated assembly process designed to determine if the examinee is appropriately placed in a work or training setting. The Vocational Interest screening subtest, presented in an audiovisual format, identifies job interests. The Interpersonal/Social Skills subtest identifies barriers to employment or independent living. The Independent Living Skills subtest measures skill and knowledge in transportation, money handling, grooming, and living environment. The tasks in each subtest vary in difficulty from very simple recognition of rooms to more complex processes relating to work. The work sample is designed in such a way that a lack of language or reading skills does not present a barrier to evaluation. The test should not be administered to individuals with severe impairment of the upper extremities.

Format: Examiner required; individual administration; timed

Scoring: Examiner evaluated

Cost: $4,735.00

Emotional Disturbance

Scale for Assessing Emotional Disturbance (SAED)

1998   **PRO-ED, Inc.**

Michael H. Epstein, Douglas Cullinan

Population: Ages 5 to 18 years

Purpose: Identifies children and adolescents who qualify for the federal special education category emotional disturbance (ED); the SAED is based on the federal terminology and definition as presented in the Individuals with Disabilities Education Act

Description: The SAED contains 52 items that measure the following seven areas of child functioning: inability to learn, relationship problems, inappropriate behavior, unhappiness or depression, physical symptoms or fears, social maladjustment, and overall competence. The scale is completed by teachers, counselors, parents, or other individuals familiar with the child. Information from the SAED is useful in understanding the emotional and behavioral disorder of children, identifying students who may meet the criteria for the ED educational disability category, selecting appropriate education goals for an IEP, and periodically evaluating student progress toward desired outcomes. The SAED was normed on a nationally representative sample of students without disabilities and students with ED.

Format: Rating scale; untimed

Scoring: Examiner evaluated

Cost: Complete Kit (manual, 50 record booklets, storage box) $100.00

Gifted and Talented

California Measure of Mental Motivation (CM3)

2004, 2005	Insight Assessments

Carol A. Giancarlo

Population: Ages 9 years and older

Purpose: Measures attitudes and inclinations about thinking

Description: Total of 72 Likert-style survey items that measure mental focus, learning orientation, creative problem solving, and cognitive integrity. Three versions of the CM3 are available: Level I targets students in Grade 6 and below; Level II targets students in Grade 6 to high school; and Level III targets college students, adults, and professionals. An electronic version is available for Level II and Level III; a paper–pencil version is available for all levels.

Format: Examiner required; group administration; timed and untimed

Scoring: Machine or electronic scored; scoring service available

Cost: Specimen Kit (manual, 1 protocol, 1 CapScore™ answer form) $40.00

Cornell Critical Thinking Test, Level X

1985	Critical Thinking Company

Robert H. Ennis, Jason Millman

Population: Grades 5 to 12+

Purpose: Assesses an individual's ability to think critically; used for research, teaching of critical thinking, or as one of several criteria for admission to positions/areas requiring ability to think critically

Description: Paper–pencil 71-item multiple-choice measure of critical thinking divided into four sections. In the first section, the examinee reads a conclusion and decides which of several premises supports the conclusion. The second section measures the examinee's ability to judge the reliability of information. The third section tests the examinee's ability to judge whether a statement follows from premises. The fourth section involves the identification of assumptions. Level X is easier than Level Z. Computer scoring and online versions are available.

Format: Examiner required for Grades 5 and 6; suitable for group use; timed: 50 minutes

Scoring: Computer or hand scored

Cost: Specimen Set (1 of each test, manual, answer sheets) $17.99

Cornell Critical Thinking Test, Level Z

1985	Critical Thinking Company

Robert H. Ennis, Jason Millman

Population: Grades 10+

Purpose: Assesses an individual's ability to think critically; used for research, teaching of critical thinking, or as one of several criteria for admission to positions or areas requiring ability for critical thinking

Description: Paper–pencil 52-item multiple-choice measure of critical thinking divided into seven sections directed at assessing the examinee's ability to decide whether a statement follows from a given premise, detect equivocal arguments, judge reliability of observation and authenticity of sources, judge direction of support for a hypothesis, judge possible predictions for their value in guiding experiments, and find assumptions of various types. Level Z is more difficult than Level X. Computer scoring and online versions are available.

Format: Self-administered; timed: 50 minutes

Scoring: Computer or hand scored

Cost: Specimen Set (1 of each test, manual) $17.99

Cornell Critical Thinking Test Software

2001	Critical Thinking Company

Robert Ennis, Jason Millman

Population: Grades 7 to adult

Purpose: Assesses an individual's ability to think critically; used for research, teaching of critical thinking, or as one of several criteria for admission to positions or areas requiring ability for critical thinking

Description: The examiner can set up a test and have students take it from the same computer or from many computers (either on standalone stations or over a network). Students can also take a test as a group or at different times. The administration program can be used to create student records, assign tests (individually or in batches), check testing status in progress, then grade and print.

Format: Computer administered to either groups or individuals; timed and untimed: 50 minutes

Scoring: Computer scored

Cost: CD with 50 Administrations $64.99 per Level X or Level Z; Both Levels $103.99

Creativity Assessment Packet (CAP)

1980	PRO-ED, Inc.

Frank E. Williams

Population: Ages 6 to 18 years

Purpose: Measures cognitive thought factors of fluency, flexibility, elaboration, originality, vocabulary, and comprehension that are related to the creative process; identifies gifted students

Description: Instrument consists of two group-administered instruments for children: the Test of Divergent Thinking (Forms A and B) and the Test of Divergent Feeling. A third instrument, The Williams Scale, is a rating instrument for teachers and parents of the same tested factors among children. All three instruments can be used to evaluate, screen, and identify the most important factors of creativity found in some degree among all children.

Format: Examiner required; group administration; untimed: 20 to 25 minutes

Scoring: Examiner evaluated

Cost: Complete Kit (manual, forms, storage box) $120.00

Gifted and Talented Evaluation Scales (GATES)

1996	PRO-ED, Inc.

James E. Gilliam, Betsy O. Carpenter, Janis R. Christensen

Population: Ages 5 to 18 years

Purpose: Identifies students who are gifted and talented

Description: Assesses the characteristics, skills, and talents of gifted students in a quick rating scale approach. Completed by someone who knows the child. Ratings are obtained in Intellectual Ability, Academic Skills, Creativity, Leadership, and Artistic Talent. The norms are based on a sample of gifted students. Scores are identified with the likelihood of giftedness from very unlikely to extremely probable.

Format: Rating scale; untimed: 5 to 10 minutes

Scoring: Examiner evaluated

Cost: Complete Kit (manual, 50 protocols, storage box) $110.00

Gifted Evaluation Scale– Second Edition (GES-2)

1998	Hawthorne Educational Services, Inc.

Stephen B. McCarney, Paul D. Anderson

Population: Ages 5 to 18 years

Purpose: Contributes to the identification of gifted and talented students based on the current federal definition of giftedness adopted by the U.S. Office of Education in 1978 and P.L. 95-561

Description: The scale has five subscales: Intelligence, Creativity, Specific Academic Aptitude, Leadership Ability, and Performing and Visual Arts Skills. An optional subscale, Motivation, is available. The completed rating form and student profile provides standard scores for the five subscales, a quotient score, and a percentile score based on the national standardization sample. The School Form is completed by an educator; the Home Form is completed by the parent or guardian. A Windows Quick Score is available.

Format: Rating scale; untimed

Scoring: Examiner evaluated; computer scoring available

Cost: Complete Kit (technical manual, intervention manual, 50 forms) $75.00

Group Inventory for Finding Creative Talent (GIFT)

| 1980 | Educational Assessment Service, Inc. |

Sylvia B. Rimm

Population: Grades K to 6

Purpose: Assesses creativity; used to identify gifted students

Description: Multiple-item paper–pencil test of interests and attitudes related to creativity. The test yields the following dimension scores: Imagination, Independence, and Many Interests. Validation groups include minorities, urban and suburban students, students who are learning disabled, and gifted students. Also available in Spanish.

Format: Examiner required; suitable for group use; untimed

Scoring: Scoring service

Cost: Specimen Set $15.00; Class Set of 30 $100.00 (indicate grade level) (scoring included in price)

Group Inventory for Finding Interests (GIFFI)

| 1979 | Educational Assessment Service, Inc. |

Gary A. Davis, Sylvia B. Rimm

Population: Grades 6 to 12

Purpose: Assesses creativity; used to identify gifted students

Description: Multiple-item paper–pencil test of interests and attitudes related to creativity. The test yields the following dimension scores: Creative Art and Writing, Confidence, Imagination, Challenge–Inventiveness, and Many Interests. Validation groups include minorities, urban and suburban students, students who are learning disabled, and gifted children. Also available in Spanish.

Format: Self-administered; untimed: 20 to 40 minutes

Scoring: Scoring service

Cost: Specimen Set $15.00; Class Set of 30 $120.00 (indicate grade level) scoring included in price

James Madison Test of Critical Thinking (JMTCT)

| 2004 | Critical Thinking Company |

Don Fawkes, Bill O'Meary, Dan Flage

Population: Ages 12 to adult

Purpose: Measures critical-thinking skills

Description: The JMTCT is a 55-item objective test that assesses approximately 47 critical-thinking skills. The assessment covers 24 skills not evaluated on other critical-thinking tests. These additional items include necessary and sufficient conditions and more emphasis on informal fallacies and unstated premises/conclusions. The instrument may be administered online, over a network, or on a standalone computer. There are two forms that may be used as pretest and posttest.

Format: Computer administered to either groups or individuals; timed: 50 minutes

Scoring: Computer scored

Cost: CD with 50 Administrations $64.99 per Level X or Level Z; Both Levels $103.99

Khatena-Morse Multitalent Perception Inventory (KMMPI)

| 1998 | Scholastic Testing Service, Inc. |

Joe Khatena, David T. Morse

Population: Ages 6 years to adult

Purpose: Assesses giftedness in art, music, and leadership

Description: Paper–pencil criterion-referenced test that measures five factors: art, music, creative imagination, initiative, and leadership. Form A has 19 items; Form B has 20 items. Raw scores, national percentile ranks, standard score, and stanines are yielded. Examiner must be certified for assessment. Also available in large print.

Format: Examiner required; individual and group administration; untimed: 20 to 40 minutes

Scoring: Examiner evaluated; self-scored

Cost: Starter Set (guide, manual, 35 questionnaires, 35 profile charts) specify which form $56.60

Khatena-Torrance Creative Perception Inventory (KTCPI)

| 1994 | Scholastic Testing Service, Inc. |

Joe Khatena, E. Paul Torrance

Population: Ages 12 years and older

Purpose: Identifies candidates for gifted programs

Description: Paper-pencil criterion-referenced test with two subtests: Something About Myself (SAM) and What Kind of Person Are You (WKOPAY). Both subtests have 50 items each. Raw scores and standard scores are yielded. Examiner must be certified for assessment. Also available in large print.

Format: Examiner required; individual and group administration; untimed: 20 to 40 minutes

Scoring: Examiner evaluated; self-scored

Cost: Starter Set (manual, 35 of each checklist, 35 scoring worksheets) $57.65

Preschool and Kindergarten Interest Descriptor (PRIDE)

1983	Educational Assessment Service, Inc.

Sylvia B. Rimm

Population: Parents of children ages 3 to 6 years

Purpose: Identifies creatively gifted preschool and kindergarten children; used for academic placement in gifted programs

Description: Paper-pencil 50-item inventory in which parents assess their child's attitudes and interests by responding "no," "to a small extent," "average," "more than average," or "definitely" to each item. Scores are provided on four dimensions: Many Interests, Independence-Perseverance, Imagination-Playfulness, and Originality.

Format: Self-administered; untimed: 20 to 35 minutes

Scoring: Scoring service

Cost: Specimen Set $15.00; Class Set of 30 $120.00 (indicate grade level) scoring included in price

Profile of Creative Abilities (PCA)

2007	PRO-ED, Inc.

Gail R. Ryser

Population: Ages 5 through 14 years

Purpose: Measures creative ability; used to identify and monitor progress

Description: The PCA is based on two models of creativity, J. P. Guildford's Structure of Intellect and T. M. Amabile's Component Model of Cre-

ativity. The instrument consists of two subtests, each measuring two aspects of divergent production (Drawing and Categories). A 36-item rating scale measures creative abilities, domain-relevant skills, creativity-relevant processes, and intrinsic task motivation. Each item is scored using a 4-point Likert scale. Separate rating scales are completed by an educator or a parent.

Format: Examiner required; small-group administration; timed and untimed: 30 to 40 minutes

Scoring: Examiner evaluated

Cost: Complete Kit (manual, 25 summary/scoring booklets, 25 picture booklets, 25 student booklets, 25 each of rating scales, storage box) $161.00

Scales for Identifying Students as Gifted (GIGS)

2004	Prufrock Press, Inc.

Gail R. Ryser, Kathleen McConnell

Population: Ages 5 to 18 years

Purpose: Assists in the identification of students as gifted and talented

Description: Measures seven areas: General Intellectual Ability, Language Arts, Mathematics, Science, Social Studies, Creativity, and Leadership. Twelve items per area are rated on a 5-point Likert scale. There are school and home rating forms. Standard scores and percentiles are provided, as well as qualitative information provided by the educator or caregiver if the student has six or more items rated with the highest rating. Home scale is available in Spanish.

Format: Rating scale; untimed

Scoring: Examiner evaluated

Cost: Complete Kit (manual, 25 school and home scales, 25 summary forms) $150.00

Screening Assessment for Gifted Elementary and Middle School Students (SAGES-2)

2001	PRO-ED, Inc.

Susan Johnsen, Anne Corn

Population: Ages 5 to 14 years

Purpose: Assesses aptitude and achievement; used to identify children who may be gifted

Description: Its three subtests sample aspects of two of the most commonly used areas for identifying gifted students: aptitude and achievement.

Aptitude is measured via the Reasoning subtest. The student is asked to solve analogical problems by identifying relationships among pictures and figures. The other two subtests assess achievement, one for language arts and social studies, the other for math and science. The SAGES-2 was normed on two large samples; a normal sample of 3,023 students who were in heterogeneous classrooms, the other a sample of 2,290 students who were identified as gifted by their local school districts. Reliability and validity are reported in the manual. There are separate forms for Grades K to 3 and 4 to 8.

Format: Examiner required; group administration; untimed: 20 minutes each subtest

Scoring: Examiner evaluated

Cost: Complete Kit (manual, 10 each of 3 forms for K to 3 and 4 to 8, storage box) $215.00

Special Abilities Scale

2000	Hodder Murray

Valsa Koshy, Ron Casey

Population: Ages 5 to 16 years

Purpose: Identifies high-ability pupils

Description: This is a fully validated observational assessment that provides a structured basis for accurate, consistent, and effective measurement. A five-scale profile of learning, social leadership, creative thinking, self-determination, and motivation is generated. These skills and abilities are shown to correlate highly with exceptional performance. Gives extensive guidance on how to support able pupils, plus practical strategies for appropriate follow-up.

Format: Rating scale; untimed: 10 minutes

Scoring: Examiner evaluated

Cost: Specimen Set (manual, 1 scale) £16.99

Teacher Observation Scales For Identifying Children with Special Abilities

1996	New Zealand Council for Educational Research

Don McAlpine, Neil Reid

Population: Ages 8 to 13 years

Purpose: Measures educational ability

Description: These scales are for use by classroom teachers at middle primary, intermediate, and junior secondary school levels. Essentially, children who are "borderline" gifted and talented, puzzling, unknown, new to the school, enigmatic,

and/or who display intermittent signs of unusual ability, should be rated by the scales. There are five scales, comprising between 8 and 13 statements. Each statement is to be considered separately and rated as being observed "Seldom or Never," "Occasionally," "Often," or "Almost Always or Always." The Learning Characteristics scale comprises such behaviors as easily grasps underlying principles. The Social Leadership Characteristics scale is made up of behaviors such as actively seeks leadership in social situations. The Creative Thinking Characteristics scale contains behaviors such as is not afraid to be different. The Self-Determination Characteristics scale is defined by behaviors such as pushes teachers and adults for explanations. The Motivational Characteristics scale includes behaviors such as is highly motivated; sets personal goals.

Format: Examiner required; individual administration; untimed

Scoring: Examiner evaluated

Cost: Manual $12.60; 20 Record Forms $12.60

Test of Mathematical Abilities for Gifted Students (TOMAGS)

1998	PRO-ED, Inc.

Gail R. Ryser, Susan K. Johnsen

Population: Grades K to 6

Purpose: Measures students' ability to use mathematical reasoning and mathematical problem solving

Description: There are two forms of the test: The Primary Level (Grades K to 3) or the Intermediate Level (Grades 4 to 6). The TOMAGS is a standardized, norm-referenced test. One composite score is provided that can be interpreted using two sets of national norms: for children who are identified as gifted in mathematics and normal children. The items were written to reflect the following National Council of Teachers of Mathematics curriculum and evaluation standards: Number Sense and Numeration, Concepts of Whole Number Operations, Whole Number Computation, Number and Number Relationships, Number Systems and Number Theory, Estimation, Geometry and Spatial Sense, Measurement, Statistics and Probability, Patterns and Relationships, and Algebra.

Format: Examiner required, group administration; untimed: 30 to 60 minutes

Scoring: Examiner evaluated

Cost: Complete Kit (manual, 25 each of Primary and Intermediate student booklets, 25 each of

Primary and Intermediate scoring forms, storage box) $175.00

Thinking Creatively in Action and Movement (TCAM)

| 1981 | Scholastic Testing Service, Inc. |

E. Paul Torrance

Population: Ages 3 to 6 years

Purpose: Assesses the creativity of young children; used as part of a program to develop promising creative talent among young children

Description: Show-and-tell test assessing the creativity of young children, especially preschoolers. The responses are appropriate to the developmental characteristics of the younger child and are physical in nature, although verbal responses are acceptable. A booklet, manual, and set of equipment are used. Raw scores and standard scores are yielded. Examiner must be certified for assessment.

Format: Examiner required; individual administration; untimed: 10 to 30 minutes

Scoring: Examiner evaluated

Cost: Starter Set (manual, 20 test booklets) $38.55

Thinking Creatively with Sounds and Words (TCSW)

| 1973 | Scholastic Testing Service, Inc. |

E. Paul Torrance, Joe Khatena, Bert F. Cunnington,

Population: Grades 3 and above

Purpose: Measures ability to create images for words and sounds; used to identify gifted and creative individuals and to teach imagery

Description: Two-test battery assessing creativity by measuring the originality of ideas stimulated by abstract sounds and spoken onomatopoeic words. The TCSW is a battery of two tests: Sounds and Images and Onomatopoeia and Images. It is available in equivalent forms (A and B) on two levels: Level I (Grades 3 to 12) and Level II (Adult). One cassette provides the stimuli for each level. Raw scores are yielded. Examiner must be certified for assessment.

Format: Examiner required; suitable for group use; untimed: 30 minutes per test

Scoring: Examiner evaluated

Cost: Starter Set (manual, 20 test booklets) specify level and form $37.65

Torrance Tests of Creative Thinking (TTCT)–Figural

| 1990 | Scholastic Testing Service, Inc. |

E. Paul Torrance

Population: Grades K to adult

Purpose: Assesses figural creativity

Description: The TTCT assess mental characteristics of fluency, originality, elaboration, abstractness of titles, and resistance to closure. The tests have three main activities or categories with 41 items: Picture Construction, Picture Completion, and Lines. The TTCT yields an individual student report. Materials used are a manual, test booklets, scoring worksheets, pencils, and crayons.

Format: Examiner required; suitable for group use; timed: 30 minutes

Scoring: Hand key; examiner evaluated; scoring service available

Cost: Starter Set (manual, 20 test booklets, 20 scoring worksheets, class record sheet) specify form $50.30

Torrance Tests of Creative Thinking (TTCT)–Verbal

| 1990 | Scholastic Testing Service, Inc. |

E. Paul Torrance

Population: Grades 1 to adult

Purpose: Assesses fluency, flexibility, and originality

Description: Paper-pencil and short-answer measure of verbal creativity with six categories: Asking, Guessing Causes, Guessing Consequences, Product Improvement, Unusual Uses, and Just Suppose.

Format: Examiner required; suitable for group use; timed: 40 minutes

Scoring: Hand key; examiner evaluated; scoring service available

Cost: Starter Set (manual, 20 test booklets, 20 scoring worksheets, class record sheet) specify form $50.30

Learning Disabilities

Boder Test of Reading–Spelling Patterns

| 1982 | Harcourt Assessment, Inc. |

Elena Boder, Sylvia Jarrico

Population: All ages

Purpose: Differentiates specific reading disability (developmental dyslexia) from nonspecific reading disability through reading and spelling performance; used to classify readers with dyslexia into one of three subtypes

Description: Paper–pencil 300-item tests of reading and spelling ability. The Reading Test uses 13 graded word lists of 20 words each, half of which are phonetic and half of which are non-phonetic. The words, which are presented in flash format and untimed, require sight vocabulary and phonic word analysis skills. The Spelling Test uses two individualized spelling lists (10 known words and 10 unknown) based on the student's reading performance. Both the reading and spelling tests tap the central visual and auditory processes required for reading and spelling, making it possible to diagnose developmental dyslexia by the joint analysis of reading and spelling as interdependent functions. The results should be supplemented with testing that uses instructional materials to which the child already has been and will be exposed.

Format: Examiner required; individual administration; untimed: 30 minutes

Scoring: Examiner evaluated

Cost: Complete Kit (manual, stimulus materials, 25 of each of 4 forms) $210.00

Decoding–Encoding Screener for Dyslexia (DESD)

2006	Western Psychological Services

John R. Griffen, Howard N. Walton, Garth N. Christenson

Population: Grades 1 to 8

Purpose: Assesses specific reading difficulties

Description: The DESD consists of three sections: Decoding, Encoding, and Letter Writing. The Decoding section provides a norm-referenced measure of sight-word recognition (Reading Standard Score). Additionally, qualitative indicators in the Encoding section allow you to distinguish deficits in sight-word recognition from deficits in phonetic analysis. The test identifies the specific skills that a child brings to bear on the task of reading words. This information makes it easier to detect and describe reading problems and to refer students for appropriate educational therapy.

Format: Examiner required; individual administration; untimed: 5 to 10 minutes

Scoring: Examiner evaluated

Cost: Kit (manual, stimulus booklet, 100 spelling response forms, 100 record sheets) $109.00

Dyslexia Diagnosis and Screening Kit

2003	Richmond Products, Inc.

Population: Grades K to adult

Purpose: Identifies if dyslexia is source of reading difficulty

Description: Consists of four age-related tests with decoding and encoding. The test sensitivity is 88% for dyseidesia and 84% for dysphonesia. Also available in French and Spanish. Available in four age groups: Kindergarten, Grade 1, Grades 2 to 9, and Adults.

Format: Examiner required; individual administration; untimed: 30 minutes

Scoring: Examiner evaluated

Cost: Test Kit (forms, interpretation forms) School-Age Group $64.00; Adults $84.00; Manual 34.50

Dyslexia Early Screening Test–Second Edition (DEST-2)

2004	Harcourt Assessment-UK

Rod Nicolson, Angela Fawcett

Population: Ages 4 years 6 months to 6 years 5 months

Purpose: Profiles strengths and weaknesses often associated with dyslexia

Description: The battery helps to determine whether a young child is experiencing difficulty in areas known to be affected by dyslexia. An "at risk" score for dyslexia determines whether further in-depth testing should be undertaken. A profile of skills provides information that can be used to guide in-school support. The 12 subtests are Rapid Naming, Bead Threading, Phonological Discrimination, Postural Stability, Rhyme/Alliteration, Forwards Digit Span, Digit Naming, Letter Naming, Sound Order, Shape Copying, Corsi Frog, and Vocabulary.

Format: Examiner required; individual administration; untimed: 30 minutes

Scoring: Examiner evaluated; scoring software available

Cost: Complete Kit (manual, stimulus materials, scoring software, 50 score sheets, in a bag) £125.00

Dyslexia Screening Instrument

| 1994 | Harcourt Assessment, Inc. |

Kathryn B. Coon, Mary Jo Polk, Melissa McCoy Waguespack

Population: Ages 6 to 21 years

Purpose: Screens for characteristics of dyslexia

Description: The test measures a cluster of characteristics associated with dyslexia and discriminates between those who have the cluster and those who do not. The classroom teacher rates 33 statements using a 5-point scale.

Format: Rating scale; untimed: under 20 minutes

Scoring: Computer scored

Cost: Complete Kit (manual, rating scale, scoring software) $99.00

Dyslexia Screening Test–Junior (DST-J)

| 2004 | Harcourt Assessment-UK |

Angela Fawcett, Rod Nicolson

Population: Ages 6 years 6 months to 11 years 5 months

Purpose: Identifies children who are at risk of dyslexia

Description: The DST is now two instruments for different age groups. New theoretical developments in dyslexia research suggest that early identification provides greater reading support. The DST-J consists of the following subtests: Rapid Naming, Bead Threading, One Minute Reading, Postural Stability, Phonemic Segmentation, Two Minute Spelling, Backwards Digit Span, Nonsense Passage Reading, One Minute Writing, Verbal Fluency, Rhyme, and Vocabulary.

Format: Examiner required; individual administration; untimed: 30 minutes

Scoring: Examiner evaluated; scoring software available

Cost: Complete Kit (manual, stimulus materials, scoring software, 50 score sheets, in a bag) £125.00

Dyslexia Screening Test–Secondary (DST-S)

| 2004 | Harcourt Assessment-UK |

Angela Fawcett, Rod Nicolson

Population: Ages 11 years 6 months to 16 years 5 months

Purpose: Identifies children who are at risk of dyslexia

Description: The DST is now two instruments for different age groups. New theoretical developments in dyslexia research suggest that early identification provides greater reading support. The DST-S consists of the following subtests: Rapid Naming, Bead Threading, One Minute Reading, Postural Stability, Phonemic Segmentation, Two Minute Spelling, Backwards Digit Span, Nonsense Passage Reading, One Minute Writing, Verbal Fluency, Semantic Fluency, Spoonerisms, and Non-Verbal Reasoning.

Format: Examiner required; individual administration; untimed: 30 minutes

Scoring: Examiner evaluated; scoring software available

Cost: Complete Kit (manual, stimulus materials, scoring software, 50 score sheets, in a bag) £125.00

Graded Nonword Reading Test

| 1996 | Harcourt Assessment-UK |

Margaret Snowling, Susan Stothard, Janet McLean

Population: Ages 5 to 11

Purpose: Assesses whether a child's nonword reading score is at the expected level for his or her age; useful in the diagnosis of developmental dyslexia

Description: This test has been developed on the basis of some 20 years of research with children who have reading difficulties. A recent review of more than 25 studies of nonword reading in children with dyslexia points to the importance of the assessment of these skills. It has high internal and test–retest reliability, and it correlates well with performance on other standardized reading tests. There are five practice and 20 nonwords that are graded in difficulty. Children who fail to reach criterion on the practice items are not tested further.

Format: Individually administered; untimed: 15 minutes

Scoring: Examiner evaluated

Cost: Complete kit (manual, 100 scoring sheets, stimulus book) £84.00

Learning Disabilities Diagnostic Inventory (LDDI)

| 1998 | PRO-ED, Inc. |

Donald D. Hammill, Brian R. Bryant

Population: Ages 8 to 17 years

Purpose: Helps in the diagnosis of learning disability

Description: The LDDI is a rating scale designed to help identify intrinsic processing disorders and learning disabilities. This is not an ability or achievement measure (i.e., it will not tell you how well or how poorly students read, write, or speak). Instead, the LDDI will tell you the extent to which students' skill patterns in a particular area are consistent with those of individuals known to have LD in that area. Thus, using the LDDI shifts the diagnostic emphasis away from interpreting norm-referenced ability test scores and toward studying an individual's skill patterns, especially those patterns that are indicative of people who are known to have specific learning disabilities. The test was normed on 2,152 students residing in 43 states and DC. The scores are reported in terms of stanines and percentiles.

Format: Rating scale; untimed: 10 minutes

Scoring: Examiner evaluated

Cost: Complete Kit (manual, 50 record booklets, storage box) $120.00

Learning Disabilities Evaluation Scale Renormed (LDES)

1996	Hawthorne Educational Services, Inc.

Stephen B. McCarney

Population: Ages 4 years 5 months to 18 years

Purpose: Aids in the diagnosis of learning disability

Description: The instrument utilizes performance observations of the classroom teacher or other instructional personnel. The instrument is designed to provide a profile based on the most commonly accepted IDEA definition of learning disabilities. This profile classifies whether the student's difficulties are in the areas of Listening, Thinking, Speaking, Reading, Writing, Spelling, or Mathematical Calculations. Appropriate for initial referral and screening procedures. Separate norms for males and females are provided. A Windows Quick Score is available. A revised edition will be available in 2007.

Format: Rating scale; untimed: 20 minutes

Scoring: Examiner evaluated; computer scoring available

Cost: Complete Kit (technical manual, interven-

tion manual, parent's guide, 50 each of 3 forms) $152.00

Listening and Literacy Index

2001	Hodder Murray

Charles Weedon, Gavin Reid

Population: Ages 6 to 9 years

Purpose: Screens and provides follow-up for dyslexia, dyspraxia, or dysgraphia

Description: Standardized group test for profiling literacy development and identifying specific learning difficulties. Linked assessments of listening comprehension, reading, and spelling give a clear profile of pupils' attainments and diagnose how their key skills are developing relative to each other. Two parallel forms are available.

Format: Examiner required; group administration; untimed: 50 minutes

Scoring: Examiner evaluated

Cost: Specimen Set (manual, 1 each of Form A, Form B) £16.99

Slingerland Screening Tests for Identifying Children with Specific Language Disability

1984	Educators Publishing Service, Inc.

Beth H. Slingerland

Population: Grades 1 to 6

Purpose: Screens elementary school children for indications of specific language disabilities in reading, spelling, handwriting, and speaking

Description: Four forms (A, B, C, and D) each contain eight subtests. Five of the subtests evaluate visual-motor coordination and visual memory linked with motor coordination. Three subtests evaluate auditory-visual discrimination or auditory-memory-to-motor ability. Form D contains a ninth subtest that evaluates personal orientation in time and space and the ability to express ideas in writing. All the forms contain separate Echolalia tests and include individual auditory tests. The Revised Pre-Reading Screening Procedures (1997 revision) are group tests for students who have had limited introduction to reading. These screenings evaluate auditory, visual, and kinesthetic strengths to identify dyslexia or specific language disability. Also available in Spanish.

Format: Examiner required; individual or group administration; untimed: 90 minutes

Scoring: Examiner evaluated

Cost: Specimen Set (manual, 1 of each form) $20.80

Test of Problem Solving 2-
Adolescent (TOPS 2-Adolescent)

2007	LinguiSystems, Inc.

Linda Bowers, Rosemary Huisingh, Carolyn LoGiudice

Population: Ages 12 to 17 years

Purpose: Evaluates critical-thinking abilities based on students' language abilities

Description: Test has 75 items in five subtests that measure making inferences, determining, solutions, expressing consequences, evaluating perspectives, and transferring insights to new contexts. Standard score, percentile rank, and age equivalency are provided for the total test.

Format: Examiner required; individual administration; untimed: 40 minutes

Scoring: Examiner evaluated

Cost: Manual and 20 Forms $129.95

Visual Impairment

Hill Performance Test of
Selected Positioned Concepts

1981	Stoelting Company

Everett Hill

Population: Ages 6 to 10 years

Purpose: Measures the development of spatial concepts in children with visual impairments

Description: Task-assessment of basic spatial concepts such as front, back, left, and right. The development of these positional concepts is tested through performance on 72 items in four types of tasks: identifying body relationships, demonstrating positional concepts of body parts to one another, demonstrating positional concepts of body parts to other objects, and forming object-to-object relationships. The test may be used as a criterion-referenced instrument to identify individual strengths and weaknesses in the area of spatial concepts or as a norm-referenced test.

Format: Examiner required; individual administration; untimed

Scoring: Examiner evaluated

Cost: Complete Kit (20 record forms, manual) $35.00

VCWS 18—Conceptual Understanding
Through Blind Evaluation (CUBE)

1980	Valpar International Corporation

Population: Adults who are blind or visually impaired

Purpose: Assesses the perceptive abilities that help a person compensate for visual handicaps, used with individuals who are congenitally and adventitiously blind

Description: Performance-based battery of six exercises assessing a person's perceptual skills in meeting the basic needs of judgment, mobility, orientation, discrimination, and balance. The subtests are Tactual Perception, Mobility/Discrimination Skills, Spatial Organization and Memory, Assembly and Packaging, and Audile Perception. Administration of the tests varies according to the factors being assessed: mobility or job skills. Useful as a clinical assessment and training aid.

Format: Examiner required; individual administration; timed

Scoring: Examiner evaluated

Cost: $4,795.00

Speech and Language

Aphasia, Apraxia, Dysarthria,
and Dysphagia

Aphasia Diagnostic Profiles (ADP)

1992	PRO-ED, Inc.

Nancy Helm-Estabrooks

Population: Adults

Purpose: Measures language and communication impairment associated with aphasia

Description: Designed to meet the demands of today's medical climate, the test contains nine brief subtests. Each subtest yields standard scores and percentile ranks. Subtest results are used to create composite scores and a series of five profiles addressing five critical areas of the patient's performance: Aphasia Classification Profile, Aphasia Severity Profile, Alternative Communication Profile, Error Profiles, and Behavioral Profile. The ADP was standardized on 290 adults with neurological impairments and 40 nonaphasic adults (median age 70).

Format: Examiner required; individual administration; untimed: 40 to 45 minutes

Scoring: Examiner evaluated

Cost: Complete Kit (manual, stimulus cards/letter board, 25 record forms) $169.00

Apraxia Battery for Adults–Second Edition (ABA-2)

2000	PRO-ED, Inc.

Barbara L. Dabul

Population: Adults

Purpose: Used in supporting or refuting a prior impression of apraxia to gain an estimate of severity

Description: Measures the presence and severity of apraxia in adolescents and adults. The instrument has six subtests: Diadochokinetic Rate, Increasing Word Length, Limb and Oral Apraxia, Latency Time and Utterance Time for Polysyllabic Words, Repeated Trials Test, and Inventory of Articulation Characteristics of Apraxia.

Format: Examiner required; individual administration; untimed: 20 minutes

Scoring: Examiner evaluated

Cost: Complete Kit (manual, picture book, 25 profile/examiner record forms, storage box) $130.00

Apraxia Profile

1997	Harcourt Assessment, Inc.

Lori A. Hickman

Population: Ages 3 to 13 years

Purpose: Identifies the presence of developmental verbal apraxia and documents a child's progress over time

Description: Used to assist in the differential diagnosis of developmental verbal apraxia, to identify the presence of oral apraxia, and to reveal the most problematic oral-motor sequences and movements. Documents a child's oral-motor se-

quencing deficits and establishes the level of oral movements and sequences produced successfully. There are preschool and school-age forms.

Format: Examiner required; individual administration; untimed: 25 to 35 minutes

Scoring: Examiner evaluated

Cost: Complete Kit (manual, 10 each of record forms for 2 age brackets) $73.00

Assessment of Intelligibility of Dysarthic Speech

1984	PRO-ED, Inc.

Kathryn Yorkston, David Beukelman, Charles Traynor

Population: Adolescents, adults

Purpose: Quantifies the single-word intelligibility, sentence intelligibility, and speaking rates of individuals with dysarthria

Description: Multiple-item verbal and listening test containing speaker tasks, recording techniques, and listener response formats to obtain a variety of intelligibility and communication efficiency measures. The instrument can be readministered repeatedly with reliable results.

Format: Speech–language pathologist required; individual administration

Scoring: Examiner evaluated

Cost: Complete Kit (manual w/ reproducible forms, picture book, storage box) $101.00

Bedside Evaluation of Dysphagia (BED)

1995	PRO-ED, Inc.

Edward Hardy

Population: Adults with neurological impairment

Purpose: Assesses adult patients with dysphagia at bedside

Description: Comprises a Screening of behavior, cognition, and communication abilities; Oral Motor assessment of structure and function of the lips, cheeks, tongue, soft palate, mandible, and larynx; and Oral–Pharyngeal Dysphagia Symptoms assessment of oral, and to some degree, pharyngeal abilities. The Summary Report is detachable.

Format: Examiner required; individual administration; untimed

Scoring: Examiner evaluated

Cost: Complete Kit (manual, 25 evaluation forms, 25 screening forms) $92.00

Bedside Evaluation Screening Test–Second Edition (BEST-2)

1998	PRO-ED, Inc.

Joyce Fitch-West, Elaine S. Sands, Deborah Ross-Swain

Population: Adults

Purpose: Assesses language deficits of patients to provide a profile of severity of aphasia

Description: Used to assess and quantify language disorders in adults resulting from aphasia. Highly efficient and effective tool for assessing communicative modalities. Pathologists, psychologists, neuropsychologists, and physicians using this test will obtain sufficient clinical information to set treatment goals and objectives.

Format: Examiner required; individual administration; untimed: 20 minutes

Scoring: Examiner evaluated

Cost: Complete Kit (manual, picture book, 25 record forms, 25 profile/summary sheets, storage box) $165.00

Boston Assessment of Severe Aphasia (BASA)

1989	PRO-ED, Inc.

Nancy Helm-Estabrooks, Gail Ramsberger, Alisa R. Morgan, Marjorie Nicholas

Population: Adults

Purpose: Provides diagnostic information needed for immediate treatment of stroke patients

Description: This test is designed to be given to poststroke cases soon after the onset of symptoms, preferably at bedside. It can be given long before most other assessments are appropriate. The BASA probes the spared language abilities of persons with severe aphasia and provides diagnostic information needed for immediate treatment. The 61 items measure a wide variety of tasks and modalities, including auditory comprehension, buccofacial or limb praxis, gesture recognition, oral and gestural expression, reading comprehension, writing, and visual-spatial tasks. Both gestural and verbal responses to the items are scored, and refusals, affective responses, and perseverative responses are recorded. Gestural and verbal responses may be scored in combination or separately, and both scores may be expressed as fully or partially communicative.

Format: Examiner required; individual administration; untimed: 30 to 40 minutes

Scoring: Examiner evaluated

Cost: Complete Kit (manual, custom clipboard, manipulatives, stimulus cards, 25 record forms, briefcase) $277.00

Boston Diagnostic Aphasia Examination–Third Edition (BDAE-3)

2000	PRO-ED, Inc.

Harold Goodglass, Edith Kaplan, Barbara Barresi

Population: Adults

Purpose: Measures the presence and type of aphasic syndrome, leading to inferences concerning cerebral localization for both initial determination and detection of change over time, as well as comprehensive assessment of the patient's assets and liabilities

Description: Multiple-item instrument that provides a severity rating in fluency, auditory comprehension, naming, oral reading, repetition, paraphasia, automatic speech, reading comprehension, writing, music, and spatial and computational areas. The patient responds to oral, pictorial, and written prompts. Also, includes the former *Boston Naming Test–Second Edition,* which is a 60-item test of line-drawn objects of graded difficulty from *bed* to *abacus.* The individual is provided with the initial sound, if he or she is unable to name it correctly. Norms for the Naming test are provided for children ages 5½ to 10½ and adults.

Format: Examiner required; individual administration; untimed: 35 to 45 minutes

Scoring: Examiner evaluated

Cost: Complete Kit (manual, standard form stimulus cards, 25 standard record booklets, short form stimulus cards, 25 short form record booklets, 25 Boston Naming Test record booklets, videotape, box) $400.00

Communication Activities of Daily Living–Second Edition (CADL-2)

1999	PRO-ED, Inc.

Audrey L. Holland, Carol M. Frattali, Davida Fromm

Population: Adults with aphasia

Purpose: Assesses functional communication skills; used for planning treatment programs

Description: Assessment of the functional communication skills of adults with neurogenic communication disorders. The test contains 50 items that assess communication activities in seven areas: Reading, Writing, and Using Numbers; Social Interaction; Divergent Communication; Contextual Communication; Nonverbal Communication; Sequential Relationships; and Humor/Metaphor Absurdity.

Format: Examiner required; individual administration; untimed: 30 minutes

Scoring: Examiner evaluated

Cost: Complete Kit (manual, picture book, 25 record booklets, 25 response forms, storage box) $195.00

Dysphagia Evaluation Protocol

1997	Harcourt Assessment, Inc.

Wendy Avery-Smith, Abbey Brod Rosen, Donna Dellarosa

Population: Adults

Purpose: Evaluates patients for swallowing problems

Description: Results help to determine whether a patient is appropriate for videofluoroscopy and assist in defining variables and factors that need to be evaluated further with videofluoroscopy. A pocket-sized version of the evaluation in a flipbook format is included for easy bedside administration.

Format: Examiner required; individual administration; untimed: 30 minutes

Scoring: Examiner evaluated

Cost: Complete Kit (manual, flipbook, 15 record forms) $79.00

Examining for Aphasia–Third Edition (EFA-3)

1994	PRO-ED, Inc.

Jon Eisenson

Population: Adolescents, adults

Purpose: Helps to determine areas of strength and weakness for receptive and expressive functions

Description: A revised version of a classic assessment of aphasia and aphasic impairments relative to receptive and evaluative (decoding) and expressive and productive (encoding) impairments. The EFA-3 acknowledges cognitive, personality, and linguistic modifications that are associated with acquired aphasia. The test reflects current positions and interpretations of aphasic impairments on subsymbolic and symbolic levels. The EFA-3's 33 subtests help to determine areas of strength and weakness for receptive and expressive functions. The EFA-3 tests for agnosia (visual, auditory, and tactile); linguistic reception (oral and written) of words, sentences, and paragraphs; and expressive impairments, including simple skills, automatic language, arithmetic computations, and language items that parallel those for receptive tasks. An optional Tell a Story test in response to a picture assesses self-organized language content. The Examiner's Manual has been rewritten and redesigned for ease of administration and interpretation. It includes the author's position on the nature and purposes of assessment for diagnosis, prognosis, and therapy.

Format: Examiner required; individual administration; untimed: 30 minutes to 2 hours

Scoring: Examiner evaluated

Cost: Complete Kit (manual, picture book, 25 profile/response forms, 25 examiner record booklets, object kit, storage box) $180.00

Frenchay Dysarthria Assessment–Second Edition

2008	PRO-ED, Inc.

Pamela M. Enderby, Rebecca Palmer

Population: Ages 12 years to adult

Purpose: Assesses and provides differential description and diagnosis of dysarthria

Description: Task-performance and behavioral-observation test with 29 items measuring speech impairment due to neuromuscular disorders. The test items cover reflex, respiration, lips, jaw, palate, larynx, tongue, intelligibility, influencing factors (sight, teeth, language, mood, posture), rate, and sensation. The results are recorded graphically on multicopy forms using a 9-point rating scale.

Format: Examiner required; individual administration; untimed: 20 minutes

Scoring: Examiner evaluated

Cost: Complete Kit (manual, 25 protocols) $100.00

Hines Functional Dysphagia Scale (HFDS)

2004	PRO-ED, Inc.

Barry M. Klor, Mary J. Bacon, Barbara Cook, Franklin J. Milianti

Population: Adults

Purpose: Distills the results of a videofloroscopic swallow study

Description: The clinician rates the patient's ability on five items: Food, Liquid, Aspiration, Efficiency, and Compensation. The sum of these five ratings provides the HFDS Total Score.

Format: Examiner required; untimed

Scoring: Examiner evaluated

Cost: Complete Kit (manual, 50 forms) $85.00

Reading Comprehension Battery for Aphasia–Second Edition (RCBA-2)

1998	PRO-ED, Inc.

Leonard L. LaPointe, Jennifer Horner

Population: Preadolescent to geriatric clients

Purpose: Evaluates the nature and degree of reading impairment in aphasic adults and provides a focus for therapy

Description: Multiple item stimulus–response test utilizing pictures to assess the reading comprehension of aphasic adults. The 10 subtests included are Single Word Comprehension (Visual Confusions, Auditory Confusions, and Semantic Confusions), Functional Reading, Synonyms, Sentence Comprehension (Picture), Short Paragraph Comprehension (Picture), Paragraphs (Factual and Inferential Comprehension–2 subtest), and Morpho-Syntactic Reading with Lexical Controls.

Format: Examiner required; individual administration; untimed: 30 minutes

Scoring: Examiner evaluated

Cost: Complete Kit (manual, picture book, supplementary picture book, 25 profile/summary record forms, storage box) $180.00

Revised Token Test (RTT)

1978	PRO-ED, Inc.

Malcolm M. McNeil, Thomas E. Prescott

Population: Ages 20 to 80 years

Purpose: Used for designing effective auditory rehabilitation programs and in quantifying small amounts of patient change for both clinical and research purposes

Description: A revision of the *Token Test* by DeRenzi and Vignolo, the RTT is a sensitive, quantitative, and descriptive test battery for auditory processing inefficiencies and disorders associated with brain damage, aphasia, and

certain language and learning disabilities. Percentile ranks are available for normal adults and for adults with right- and left-hemisphere brain damage for each of the 10 RTT subtests and for overall performance. Experimental evidence is reported for concurrent and construct validity, as well as for test–retest, intrascorer, and interscorer reliability.

Format: Examiner required; individual administration; untimed: 30 minutes

Scoring: Examiner evaluated

Cost: Complete Kit (examiner's manual, administration manual, scoring forms, profile forms, tokens, storage box) $153.00

Screening Test for Developmental Apraxia of Speech–Second Edition (STDAS-2)

2000	PRO-ED, Inc.

Robert W. Blakeley

Population: Ages 4 to 12 years

Purpose: Assists in the differential diagnosis of developmental apraxia of speech

Description: Multiple-item test diagnosing the developmental apraxia of speech through eight subtests. The subtests are Expressive Language Discrepancy, Vowels and Diphthongs, Oral Motor Movement, Verbal Sequencing, Motorically Complex Words, Articulation, Transpositions, and Prosody. The testing results of 169 children of normal intelligence with multiple articulation errors are reported.

Format: Examiner required; individual administration; untimed: 15 minutes

Scoring: Examiner evaluated

Cost: Complete Kit (examiner's manual, 50 response record forms, storage box) $95.00

Swallowing Ability and Function Evaluation (SAFE)

2002	PRO-ED, Inc.

Deborah Ross-Swain, Peggy Kipping, Patricia Yee

Population: Adolescents, adults

Purpose: Comprehensive evaluation of swallowing

Description: The test is based on the findings of the latest research in swallowing disorders and the practical needs of therapists conducting such assessments. It is designed to assist in providing a definitive diagnosis or label of dysphagia. Its results help generate treatment plans or suggest the need for referral to other professionals for further assessment. The SAFE's primary focus is on the oral and pharyngeal phases of the swallow. There are three stages of the SAFE: Evaluation of General Information Related to Swallowing Ability, Physical Examination of the Oropharyngeal Mechanism, and Functional Analysis of Swallowing. The results can be used to determine the effectiveness of various interventions on test performance.

Format: Examiner required; individual administration; untimed

Scoring: Examiner evaluated

Cost: Complete Kit (examiner's manual, treatment manual, 50 record forms, storage box) $130.00

Western Aphasia Battery–Enhanced (WAB-E)

| 2006 | Harcourt Assessment, Inc. |

Andrew Kertesz

Population: Ages 18 to 89 years

Purpose: Tests for aphasia syndromes and measures their severity

Description: The WAB-E is the updated version. It is an individually administered assessment for adults with acquired neurological disorders. The linguistic skills most frequently affected by aphasia are measured. There are eight subtests from 32 short tasks. Two new supplementary tasks (reading and writing of irregular and nonwords) aids the clinician in distinguishing between surface, deep (phonological), and visual dyslexia. A bedside instrument allows diagnosis of moderate to severe aphasia.

Format: Examiner required; individual administration; untimed: full battery, 30 to 45 minutes; enhanced subtests, additional 45 to 60 minutes

Scoring: Examiner evaluated

Cost: Complete Kit (manual, 25 each test booklets for full and bedside, stimulus book) $199.00

Articulation and Phonology

Arizona Articulation Proficiency Scale: Third Edition (Arizona-3)

| 2001 | Western Psychological Services |

Janet Barker Fudala

Population: Ages 1 year 6 months to 18 years

Purpose: Measures articulation skills

Description: The new edition retains the features from previous editions and adds a number of improvements: updated picture cards, gender-specific norms up to age 6 years, expanded age range, optional assessment tasks, and improved test booklet. It covers all major speech sounds in the English language, including initial and final consonants and blends, vowels, and diphthongs. Scores are provided in several formats: intelligibility descriptions, severity designations, percentile rankings, and standardized scores. Three optional tasks are included: Word Reading Administration, Language Screening Task, and Spontaneous Speech Task.

Format: Examiner required; individual administration; untimed: 3 minutes

Scoring: Examiner evaluated

Cost: Kit (picture cards, 25 protocols, manual) $147.50

Bankson-Bernthal Test of Phonology (BBTOP)

| 1990 | PRO-ED, Inc. |

Nicholas W. Bankson, John E. Bernthal

Population: Ages 3 to 9 years

Purpose: Assesses articulation and phonology

Description: Three points of view are represented: a whole word accuracy analysis, a traditional consonant articulation analysis, and a phonological process analysis. Practice exercises for scoring the Phonological Process Inventory are included.

Format: Examiner required; individual administration; untimed: 15 to 20 minutes

Scoring: Examiner evaluated

Cost: Complete Kit (manual, picture book, 25 record booklets, easel) $170.00

Children's Speech Intelligibility Measure (CSIM)

| 1999 | Harcourt Assessment, Inc. |

Kim Wilcox, Sherrill Morris

Population: Ages 3 to 10 years

Purpose: Measures the intelligibility of children's speech

Description: Can be used to establish baseline information and to monitor progress during the course of articulation/phonological treatment.

The manual provides over 100 versions of the stimulus list, so the examiner can test a child frequently using a different word list each time. To administer, the examiner models 50 words and the child repeats each one for tape-recording. Intelligibility is determined by a second individual (listening to the tape) who is not familiar with the child's speech errors or patterns. The CSIM meets new IDEA regulations for progress reports to parents on the same schedule as report cards for regular education.

Format: Examiner required; individual administration; untimed: 20 minutes

Scoring: Examiner evaluated

Cost: Complete Kit (manual, 15 record forms, microphone switch) $105.00

Comprehensive Test of Phonological Processing (CTOPP)

1999	PRO-ED, Inc.

Richard Wagner; Joseph K. Torgesen, Carol Rashotte

Population: Ages 5 to 24 years

Purpose: Assesses phonological awareness, phonological memory, and rapid naming

Description: The CTOPP was developed to aid in the identification of individuals from kindergarten through college who may profit from instructional activities to enhance their phonological skills. There are two versions of the instrument: a primary for ages 5 to 6 that contains seven core subtests and one supplemental test. The second version, for individuals ages 7 to 24, contains six core subtests and eight supplemental tests. The test contains the following subtests: Elision, Blending Words, Sound Matching, Memory for Digits, Nonword Repetition, Rapid Color Naming, Rapid Digit Naming, Rapid Letter Naming, Rapid Object Naming, Blending Nonwords, Phoneme Reversal, Segmenting Words, and Segmenting Nonwords. There are three composites: Phonological Awareness Quotient, Phonological Memory Quotient, and the Rapid Naming Quotient. Percentiles, standard scores, and age and grade equivalents are provided. The CTOPP was normed on more than 1,600 individuals.

Format: Examiner required; individual administration; untimed: 30 minutes

Scoring: Examiner evaluated

Cost: Complete Kit (manual, 25 each of ages 5 to 6 and ages 7 to 24 protocols, picture book, CD, storage box) $254.00

Compton Phonological Assessment of Children

1986	Carousel House

Arthur J. Compton

Population: Children

Purpose: Evaluates and analyzes patterns of speech errors in children

Description: Evaluation tool that uses a step-by-step approach that provides a visual display of error patterns, provides phonological rule analysis, and does a phonological process analysis. The first 15 items can function as a screening evaluation. Pictures are used as prompts. Response booklet provides results in a color-coded, easy-to-read format.

Format: Examiner required; individual administration; untimed: 45 to 60 minutes

Scoring: Examiner administration and interpretation

Cost: Set (manual, pictures, protocols) $48.00

Compton Phonological Assessment of Foreign Accent-Revised

2002	Carousel House

Arthur J. Compton

Population: All ages

Purpose: Identifies the accent patterns of non-native English speakers

Description: Evaluation kit gives a quick, detailed analysis of client's problem sounds and accent patterns. Assessment is based on research on over 1,500 people and 95 different languages. A tape-recorded speech analysis gives a phonetically balanced sampling of speech sounds in single words, sentences and phrases, oral reading, and conversational speech. The results are organized in a clear, color-coded display of problem sounds and accent patterns.

Format: Examiner required; individual administration; untimed: 90 minutes

Scoring: Examiner interpreted

Cost: Set (manual, stimulus words, reading passage, protocols) $46.00

Compton Screening Assessment of Foreign Accent

1998	Carousel House

Arthur J. Compton

Population: Adults

Purpose: Identifies the accent patterns of non-native English speakers

Description: Based on 15 stimulus words and a three-sentence reading passage that samples 70% of all consonants and 100% of the vowels and diphthongs, the instrument helps potential clients discover their degree of accent. The test is normed on 200 clients from 40 language backgrounds and objectively locates the person's accent into one of three categories: very mild, average, or severe. Speaking rate, volume, intonation, vocal quality, grammar, and perceived degree of accent are assessed from a conversation speech sample.

Format: Examiner required; individual administration; untimed: 6 to 10 minutes

Scoring: Examiner evaluated, Spanish version requires bilingual pathologist or aide

Cost: Set (stimulus items, instructions, response booklets) $10.50

Compton Speech and Language Screening Evaluation–Revised

1999	Carousel House

Arthur J. Compton

Population: Ages 3 to 6 years

Purpose: Estimates articulation and language development of young children

Description: Multiple-item oral-response test utilizing common objects to elicit verbal responses from the child. The test, which measures both production and comprehension, covers the following areas: articulation, vocabulary, colors, shapes, memory span, language (plurals, opposites, progressive and past tenses, prepositions, multiple commands, and possessive pronouns), spontaneous language, fluency, voice, and oral mechanism. The materials include revised response forms with age profiles, pass–fail guidelines, and an audiogram. Also available in Spanish.

Format: Examiner required; individual administration; untimed: 6 to 10 minutes

Scoring: Examiner evaluated; Spanish version requires bilingual pathologist or aide

Cost: Complete Kit (manual, carrying case, stimulus objects, pictures, 25 response forms) $55.00

Computerized Articulation and Phonology Evaluation System

2001	Harcourt Assessment, Inc.

Julie Masterson, Barbara Bernhardt

Population: Ages 2 years to adult

Purpose: Analyzes articulation and phonology

Description: This easy-to-use software provides a thorough, individualized evaluation and analysis in just a few minutes, and it includes treatment suggestions based on the respondent's error patterns, strengths, and weaknesses. The respondent states answers to onscreen stimuli and the administrator inputs the answers into the computer. The system consists of two separate evaluations: The Phonemic Profile, a quick screen of sound production and the Individualized Phonological Evaluation, a deeper analysis of 10 to 100 words that consists of multiple examples of target phonemes, phonological processes, or features that need remediating. A dialect filter is used to help determine which phonemes are produced in error.

Format: Examiner required; computer administered; untimed: 5 to 10 minutes

Scoring: Computer scored; examiner evaluated

Cost: $279.00

Denver Articulation Screening Exam (DASE)

1971	Denver Developmental Materials, Inc.

Amelia F. Drumwright

Population: Ages 2 years 6 months to 7 years

Purpose: Detects speech articulation problems in children

Description: The test measures a child's intelligibility. The examiner shows 22 pictures, displayed on 11 cards to the child, says a word, and the child repeats it.

Format: Examiner required; individual administration; untimed: 5 minutes

Scoring: Examiner evaluated

Cost: 25 Tests $8.00; Manual/Workbook $19.00; Picture Cards $8.00

Fisher-Logemann Test of Articulation Competence (F-LOTAC)

1971	PRO-ED, Inc.

Hilda B. Fisher, Jerilyn A. Logemann

Population: Children, adults

Purpose: Implements the examination of the phonological system, provides ease in recording and analyzing phonetic notations of articulation, and facilitates accurate analysis of articulation errors

Description: Two test forms (pictures and sentences) provide a method for eliciting spontaneous responses that are prestructured for required phonemic occurrence and analyzed and summarized according to distinctive features that are violated. The test consists of a Test Portfolio of 35 cards with 109 large, full-color illustrations and a Sentence Test with 15 sentences to be repeated.

Format: Examiner required; individual administration; untimed: 45 minutes

Scoring: Examiner evaluated

Cost: Complete Kit (manual, portfolio, 50 record forms) $195.00

Goldman Fristoe Test of Articulation–Second Edition

2000	AGS Publishing/Pearson Assessments

Ronald Goldman, Macalyne Fristoe

Population: Ages 2 to 21 years

Purpose: Provides descriptive information about an individual's articulation skills

Description: The test provides information about a child's articulation ability by sampling both spontaneous and imitative sound production. Examinees respond to picture plates and verbal cues from the examiner with single-word answers that demonstrate common speech sounds. Additional sections provide further measures of speech production. The revision contains new items, new artwork, and new norms.

Format: Examiner required; individual administration; untimed: 10 to 15 minutes

Scoring: Examiner evaluated; computer scoring available

Cost: Complete Kit (test easel, manual, 25 response forms, canvas bag) $229.99

Hodson Assessment of Phonological Patterns–Third Edition (HAPP-3)

2004	PRO-ED, Inc.

Barbara Williams Hodson

Population: Intelligibility: 2 years and older; Normative Score: 3 to 8 years

Purpose: Evaluates children with highly unintelligible speech

Description: Objects are used to elicit 50 stimulus words that are evaluated for phonological deviations, severity ratings, intervention goals, and

treatment effects over time. The Comprehensive Phonological Evaluation and two screening tools are included. Criterion-referenced and norm-referenced scores are included. The manual includes a chapter about phonological intervention principles and procedures. All materials are included.

Format: Speech-language pathologist required; individual administration; untimed: 15 to 20 minutes

Scoring: Examiner evaluated; computer software available

Cost: Complete Kit (manual, all protocols, objects, storage box) $189.00

Khan-Lewis Phonological Analysis–Second Edition (KLPA-2)

2002	AGS Publishing/Pearson Assessments

Linda Khan, Nancy Lewis

Population: Ages 2 to 5 years

Purpose: Measures phonological processes

Description: Used by transferring the scores of the Sounds-in-Words section of the *Goldman-Fristoe Test of Articulation* (GFTA) to the KLPA-2 Analysis Form. Easy to read and color-coded, the form gives you diagnostic information at a glance. A Goal Selection Worksheet is provided for developing treatment strategies.

Format: Uses administration of GFTA; 15 to 40 minutes

Scoring: Examiner evaluated; computer scoring available

Cost: Complete Kit (manual, 25 analysis forms, sound change booklet, progress report) $134.99

Phonological Abilities Test (PAT)

1997	Harcourt Assessment-UK

Valerie Muter, Charles Hulme, Margaret Snowling

Population: Ages 5 to 7 years

Purpose: Assesses the nature and extent of a child's phonological weakness

Description: The PAT consists of six subtests: Rhyme Detection, Letter-Knowledge, Rhyme Production, Speech Rate, Word Completion—Syllables and Phonemes, and Phoneme Deletion—Beginning Sounds and End Sounds. With colorful, child-friendly material, this easy to administer test provides scores that can be compared to normative data based on an extensive UK sample.

Format: Examiner required; individual administration; untimed: 25 to 30 minutes

Scoring: Examiner evaluated

Cost: Complete Kit (manual, stimulus manual, 25 record forms, in a case) £90.00

Phonological Awareness Profile

1995	LinguiSystems, Inc.

Carolyn Robertson, Wanda Salter

Population: Ages 5 to 8 years

Purpose: Used to diagnose deficits in phonological processing and phoneme–grapheme correspondence

Description: Oral response criterion-referenced test. Nine total tasks are assessed, divided into two areas. Suitable for individuals with visual, physical, hearing, or mental impairments.

Format: Examiner required; individual administration; untimed: 10 to 20 minutes

Scoring: Examiner evaluated

Cost: Manual and 20 Test Forms $34.95

Phonological Awareness Test

1997	LinguiSystems, Inc.

Carolyn Robertson, Wanda Salter

Population: Ages 5 to 9 years

Purpose: Measures phonological processing skills and phoneme–grapheme correspondence

Description: A total of 278 total items on eight subtests: Rhyming Discrimination and Production; Segmentation for Sentences, Syllables and Phonemes; Isolation for Initial, Medial, and Final Sounds; Deletion for Compound Words, Syllables, and Phonemes; Substitution with and without Manipulatives; Blending Syllables and Phonemes; Graphemes; and Decoding. Standard score, percentile rank, and age equivalency are given for each subtest and the total test. A revision is scheduled for 2007.

Format: Examiner required; individual administration; untimed: 40 minutes

Scoring: Examiner evaluated; computer scoring available

Cost: Complete Set (manual, cubes, flipbooks, 15 forms) $129.95

Photo Articulation Tests–Third Edition (PAT-3)

1997	PRO-ED, Inc.

Barbara A. Lippke, Stanley E. Dickey, John W. Selmar, Anton L. Soder

Population: Ages 3 to 8 years

Purpose: Measures articulation skills; used for screening and analysis in schools and clinics to plan therapy

Description: The PAT-3 meets the nationally recognized need for a standardized way to document the presence of articulation errors. Enables clinicians to rapidly and accurately assess and interpret articulation errors. Some of the new features of the PAT-3 include full-color photos used to elicit words, stimulus pictures that appeal to students, quick test administration, and easily scored and interpreted test results.

Format: Examiner required; individual administration; untimed: 5 minutes

Scoring: Examiner evaluated

Cost: Complete Kit (manual, photo album picture book, picture card deck, 50 summary/response forms, storage box) $180.00

Preschool and Primary Inventory of Phonological Awareness (PIPA)

2000	Harcourt Assessment-UK

Barbara Dodd, Sharon Crosbie, Beth McIntosh, Tania Teitzel, Anne Ozanne

Population: Ages 3 to 6 years

Purpose: Identifies children at risk for literacy problems

Description: This test has been developed to identify difficulties in the knowledge and manipulation of sound structure in young children. The assessment focuses on the child's ability to detect, isolate, manipulate, and convert sound units at the syllable, onset–rime, and phoneme levels, with six easy-to-administer subtests: Syllable Segmentation, Rhyme Awareness, Alliteration Awareness, Phoneme Isolation, Phoneme Segmentation, and Letter Knowledge.

Format: Examiner required; individual administration; untimed: 25 to 30 minutes

Scoring: Examiner evaluated

Cost: Complete Kit (manual, stimulus manual, 25 record forms, in a case) £92.00

Riley Articulation and Language Test: Revised

1971	Western Psychological Services

Glyndon D. Riley

Population: Grades K to 2

Purpose: Measures the language proficiency of young children; used to identify children most in need of speech therapy

Description: Oral-response screening test consisting of three subtests (Language Proficiency and Intelligibility, Articulation Function, and Language Function) measuring phonemic similarity, stimulability, number of defective sounds, error consistency, frequency of occurrence, and developmental expectancy. The test yields an objective articulation loss score and standardized language loss and language function scores.

Format: Examiner required; individual administration; untimed: 2 to 3 minutes

Scoring: Examiner evaluated

Cost: Kit (25 tests, manual) $58.00

Slosson Articulation, Language Test with Phonology (SALT-P)

| 1986 | Slosson Educational Publications, Inc. |

Wilma Jean Tade

Population: Ages 3 to 5 years

Purpose: Assesses articulation, phonology, and language in young children

Description: Indicates the communicative competency of a young child. Screening format utilizes structured conversation centering around stimulus pictures. The articulation section assesses 22 initial and 18 final consonants, 10 clusters/blends, plus 8 vowels and diphthongs. Phonological processes probed are initial and final consonant deletion, fronting, stopping, and cluster reduction. The language subscore reflects errors on 31 language behaviors normally acquired between ages 2½ to 6. Statistical section included in the manual.

Format: Examiner required; individual administration; untimed: 7 to 10 minutes

Scoring: Examiner evaluated

Cost: Complete Kit $95.25

Speech-Ease Screening Inventory (K–1)

| 1985 | PRO-ED, Inc. |

Teryl Pigott, Jane Barry, Barbara Hughes, Debra Eastin, Patricia Titus, Harriett Stensel, Kathleen Metcalf, Belinda Porter

Population: Grades K and 1

Purpose: Assesses the articulation and language

development of children; used to identify students needing speech–language services

Description: Multiple-item response test evaluating the speech and language development of children. The basic section assesses articulation, language association, auditory recall, expressive vocabulary, and concept development. An optional section includes additional auditory items, a section on similarities and differences, a language sample, and a section on linguistic relationships.

Format: Examiner required; individual administration; untimed: 7 to 10 minutes

Scoring: Examiner evaluated

Cost: Complete Kit (manual, 100 screening forms, 50 summary sheets—kindergarten, 50 summary sheets—first grade, 3 picture plates, storage box) $115.00

Structured Photographic Articulation and Phonological Test II featuring Dudsberry® (SPAT-D II)

| 2001 | Janelle Publications, Inc. |

Janet I. Dawson, Patricia Tattersall

Population: Ages 3 to 9 years

Purpose: Assesses phonological repertoire in a natural manner and provides a systematic means of assessing the child's articulation

Description: The second edition includes 40 full-color photographs that are used to assess 59 consonant singletons and 10 consonant blends, as well as seven phonological processes. The full-color photographs portray Dudsberry interacting with objects that contain the target phonemes. For optional assessment, eight photographs depicting the story of "Dudsberry's 1st Birthday" are included in the album to elicit phoneme production in connected speech. A color-coded response form allows for ease in recording. Errors can be transferred to the Consonant Classification Chart, enabling the examiner to immediately analyze articulation errors according to syllabic function and manner of articulation. Further, the child's consonant inventory, percentage of consonant correct (PCC), word shapes, and usage of seven common phonological processes can be evaluated. No whole word transcription is necessary.

Format: Examiner required; individual administration; untimed: 15 minutes

Scoring: Examiner evaluated; scoring software available

Cost: Complete Kit (manual, picture book, 30 response forms, storage box) $140.00; Software $75.00

Test of Articulation in Context (TAC)

1998   PRO-ED, Inc.

Teresa Lanphere

Population: Ages 3 to 12 years

Purpose: Assesses articulation and phonological skills in a natural context

Description: Each illustrated test board portrays a different scene, including a park, birthday party, classroom, and zoo. The format elicits all phonemes in initial, medial, and final positions, as well as blends.

Format: Examiner required; individual administration; untimed: 15 to 20 minutes

Scoring: Examiner evaluated

Cost: Complete Kit (manual, test boards, 25 response forms, canvas bag) $133.00

Test of Minimal Articulation Competence (T-MAC)

1981   Harcourt Assessment, Inc.

Wayne A. Secord

Population: Ages 3 years to adult

Purpose: Assesses the severity of articulation disorders; used to identify children needing therapy, monitors speech development in terms of research-based minimal expectations for age level, and targets the most trainable phonemes for remediation

Description: Multiple-item verbal-response test using one of the following procedures: picture identification, sentence reading, or sentence repetition. The test provides a flexible format for obtaining a diagnostic measure of articulation performance on 24 consonant phonemes; frequently occurring *s, r,* and *l* blends; 12 vowels; 4 diphthongs; and variations of vocalic *r.*

Format: Examiner required; individual administration; untimed: 10 to 20 minutes

Scoring: Examiner evaluated

Cost: Complete Program (manual, 25 protocols) $138.00

Test of Phonological Awareness–Second Edition: PLUS (TOPA-2+)

2004   PRO-ED, Inc.

Joseph K. Torgesen, Brian R. Bryant

Population: Ages 5 to 8 years

Purpose: Measures young children's awareness of the beginning and ending sounds in words and letter sounds

Description: The TOPA-2+ can be used to identify children in kindergarten who may profit from instructional activities to enhance their phonological awareness in preparation for reading instruction. There are two versions, a Kindergarten and an Early Elementary (for Grades 1 and 2). The kindergarten form uses two different item types to assess phonemic awareness: initial sound—same and initial sound—different. In addition, a letter-sounds subtest requires children to mark which letter, from a set of four, corresponds to a specific phoneme. The early elementary form uses ending sound—same and ending sound—different to assess phonemic awareness. The letter-sound test for this version requires children to spell simple pseudowords that are given as the names of "funny animals." The words vary from two to five phonemes in length, and they are all single syllable. A variety of standard scores is available.

Format: Examiner administered; individual or group administration; untimed: 30 to 45 minutes

Scoring: Examiner evaluated

Cost: Complete Kit (manual, 50 each K and EE summary forms, 25 each K and EE Student booklets, storage box) $210.00

Weiss Comprehensive Articulation Test (WCAT)

1980   PRO-ED, Inc.

Curtis E. Weiss

Population: All ages

Purpose: Determines articulation disorders or delays and identifies misarticulation patterns and other problems; used in articulation therapy

Description: Multiple-item criterion-referenced test in two forms: an easel-stand flipbook of 85 pictures for subjects who cannot read and a card with 38 sentences for those who can. With the pictures, the child supplies the missing word in a sentence spoken by the examiner; with the sentences, the child does the reading. Materials include the picture cards and forms.

Format: Examiner required; individual administration; untimed: 20 minutes

Scoring: Examiner evaluated

Cost: Complete Kit (manual, picture cards, sentence cards, 50 picture response forms, 50 sentence response forms) $125.00

Comprehensive Language

Adapted Sequenced Inventory of Communication Development (A-SICD) for Adolescents and Adults with Severe Handicaps

1989	Western Psychological Services

Sandra E. McClennen

Population: Adolescents, adults

Purpose: Evaluates the communication abilities of individuals with severe disabilities whose language skills are in the range of birth to 4 years; used for remedial programming by speech-language pathologists, audiologists, psychologists, and teachers

Description: Inventory with 76 items assessing and diagnosing language disorders in adolescents and adults. The receptive communication section (27 items) includes a processing profile for auditory perception and pragmatic, semantic, and syntactic language and a concepts profile for awareness, words, directions, questions, and attributes. The expressive communication section (31 items) includes a processing profile for pragmatic and semantic/syntactic language and imitation and a behavioral profile for imitating motor behavior, motor and/or vocal/verbal initiating behavior, and motor and/or vocal/verbal responding behavior. An observation/interview section (18 items) is also included. Approach is based on order of difficulty concept, and mode of expression is defined to recognize alternatives to vocal communication. The resulting Communication Profile provides guidelines for developing remedial programs for adolescents and adults who have little or no speech or who are understood only by those closest to them. Handicapping conditions represented in the norm group include severe hearing loss, legal blindness, epilepsy, spastic quadriplegia, and nonambulation. Adaptations are described for clients with cerebral palsy and other motor handicaps.

Format: Examiner required; individual administration; untimed: varies

Scoring: Examiner evaluated

Cost: Complete Kit (manuals, 50 receptive skills checklists and profiles, 50 expressive skills checklists and profiles, 50 assessment booklets, plastic carrying case) $396.00

Adolescent Language Screening Test (ALST)

1984	PRO-ED, Inc.

Denise L. Morgan, Arthur M. Guilford

Population: Ages 11 to 17 years

Purpose: Screens the dimensions of oral language use, content, and form

Description: Multiple-item thorough method of screening in seven subtests: Pragmatics, Receptive Vocabulary, Concepts, Expressive Vocabulary, Sentence Formulation, Morphology, and Phonology. The results provide the clinician with a solid foundation for recommending a total communication evaluation and outline the language dimensions on which extension testing should focus.

Format: Examiner required; individual administration; untimed: 15 minutes

Scoring: Examiner evaluated

Cost: Complete Kit (manual, picture book, 50 protocols, storage box) $140.00

Assessment of Communication and Interaction Skills, Version 4.0 (ACIS)

1998	Model of Human Occupation Clearinghouse

Kirsty Forsyth, Marcelle Salamy, Sandy Simon, Gary Kielhofner

Population: Children, adolescents, adults, older adults

Purpose: Gathers data on communication and interaction skills in a context of everyday activities

Description: Observational assessment that evaluates communication and interaction skills used to accomplish daily occupations. The 53-page manual includes reproducible assessment and data summary forms.

Format: Observation; untimed: 20 to 60 minutes

Scoring: Examiner evaluated

Cost: $35.00

Assessment of Language-Related Functional Activities (ALFA)

1999	PRO-ED, Inc.

Kathleen A. Baines, Ann W. Martin,
Heidi McMartin Heeringa

Population: Ages 20 years and older

Purpose: Assesses language-related functional activities

Description: The ALFA consists of 10 subtests: Telling Time, Counting Money, Addressing an Envelope, Solving Daily Math Problems, Writing a Check/Balancing a Checkbook, Understanding Medicine Labels, Using a Calendar, Reading Instructions, Using the Telephone, and Writing a Phone Message. The patient performs each functional activity, and the examiner records an objective, quantitative score. The subtests require use of all language modalities (auditory comprehension, verbal expression, reading, and writing), as well as cognitive and motor skills. The ALFA was standardized on 495 patients between the ages of 20 and 95 who had a history of neurological episodes, as well as on 150 normally functioning adults.

Format: Examiner required; individual administration; untimed: 30 to 90 minutes

Scoring: Examiner evaluated

Cost: Complete Kit (manual, picture book, 25 record booklets, materials kit, storage box) $159.00

Bankson Language Test– Second Edition (BLT-2)

1990	PRO-ED, Inc.

Nicholas W. Bankson

Population: Ages 3 years to 6 years 4 months

Purpose: Provides examiners with a measure of children's psycholinguistic skills

Description: The test is organized into three general categories that assess a variety of areas: Semantic Knowledge—body parts, nouns, verbs, categories, functions, prepositions, opposites; Morphological/Syntactical Rules—pronouns; verb usage/verb tense; verb usage (auxiliary, modal, copula); plurals; comparatives/superlatives; negation; questions; and Pragmatics—ritualizing, informing, controlling, imagining. The selection of subtests to be included in the BLT-2 was predicated on a review of those areas that language interventions frequently test and remediate in younger children. Test results may be reported in terms of standard scores and percentile ranks. Evidence of internal consistency reliability is provided in the test manual, and reliability coef-

ficients exceed .90. Support for content, concurrent, and construct validity also is provided.

Format: Examiner required; individual administration; untimed: 30 minutes

Scoring: Examiner evaluated

Cost: Complete Kit (manual, 25 profile/examiner's record booklets, 25 screen record forms, picture book, storage box) $143.00

Bracken Basic Concept Scale: Expressive

2006	Harcourt Assessment, Inc.

Bruce A. Bracken

Population: Ages 3 to 6 years

Purpose: Measures a child's acquisition of basic concepts and expressive language skills

Description: This latest version contains colorful artwork, new norms, and new items. Leading directly to IEP development and remediation, the test assesses a child's expressive knowledge. Contains a school readiness composite. Also available in Spanish.

Format: Examiner required; individual administration; untimed: 30 minutes

Scoring: Examiner evaluated; computer scoring available

Cost: Complete Kit (manual, stimulus manual, 25 forms) $225.00

CAT/5 Listening and Speaking Checklist

1993	CTB/McGraw-Hill

Population: Grades K to 12

Purpose: Assesses oral language proficiency in children and adolescents

Description: Oral response checklist that is teacher scored and individually administered to evaluate students' listening behavior, listening comprehension, critical listening, speaking behavior, and participation. The teacher uses one checklist per student to rate each student's ability based on classroom observation and experience. Students receive an overall rating, which classifies them as basic, proficient, or advanced.

Format: Examiner required; individually administered; untimed

Scoring: Examiner evaluated

Cost: Contact publisher

CELF®—Preschool–Second Edition (CELF-Preschool-2)

| 2004 | Harcourt Assessment, Inc. |

Elisabeth H. Wiig, Wayne A. Secord, Eleanor Semel

Population: Ages 3 to 6 years

Purpose: Measures a broad range of expressive and receptive language skills

Description: The second edition includes new features that comprehensively evaluate in an engaging approach. A variety of subtests, including a Preliteracy rating scale and Phonological Awareness subtest, provide in-depth assessment. The instrument also has a four-level process model.

Format: Examiner required; individual administration; untimed: 15 to 20 minutes

Scoring: Examiner evaluated; computer scoring available

Cost: Complete Kit (manual, 25 record forms, 2 stimulus books) $315.00

Clinical Evaluation of Language Fundamentals®– Fourth Edition (CELF®-4)

| 2003 | Harcourt Assessment, Inc. |

Eleanor Semel, Elisabeth H. Wiig, Wayne A. Secord

Population: Ages 5 to 21 years

Purpose: Yields detailed diagnostic information on language-processing and production skills to identify children with language disabilities

Description: This revision has two record forms that provide only the subtests needed for the student's age. The CELF-4 uses a four-level process model. Level 1 asks, "Is there a language disorder?" and yields a Core Language Score. Level 2 asks, "What is the nature of the disorder?" and comprises Receptive and Expressive Modalities; Language Strengths and Weaknesses; and Language Content, Language Structure, and Language and Memory. For Level 3, the question is, "What critical clinical skills or behaviors underlie the disorder?" and it comprises Phonological Awareness, Rapid Automatic Naming, Number Repetition, Familiar Sequences, Word Associations, and Working Memory Index. Then Level 4 asks, "How does the disorder affect classroom performance?" and comprises an Observational Rating Scale and a Pragmatics Profile. The Screening Test parallels the most discriminating items. Also available in Spanish.

Format: Examiner required; individual administration, untimed. 30 to 60 minutes, screening 15 minutes

Scoring: Examiner evaluated; computer scoring available

Cost: Complete Kit (2 manuals, 2 stimulus manuals, 10 record forms for Level 1 and Level 2, 50 observational forms, soft case) $499.00; Screening Kit (manual, stimulus book, 25 record forms) $225.00

Comprehensive Assessment of Spoken Language (CASL)

| 1999 | AGS Publishing/Pearson Assessments |

Elizabeth Carrow-Woolfolk

Population: Ages 3 to 21 years

Purpose: Assesses oral language skills

Description: Fifteen tests measure language-processing skills (comprehension, expression, and retrieval) in four language structure categories: Lexical/Semantic, Syntactic, Supralinguistic, and Pragmatic. In-depth assessment capabilities provide a precise picture of problems with language-processing skills and structural knowledge.

Format: Examiner required; individual administration; untimed: 30 to 45 minutes for core battery

Scoring: Examiner evaluated; computer scoring available

Cost: Complete Kit (3 test books, 12 each of 2 record forms, manual, norms book, carrying bag) $339.99

Early Language Milestone Scale– Second Edition (ELM Scale-2)

| 1993 | PRO-ED, Inc. |

James Coplan

Population: Ages birth to 36 months

Purpose: Assesses speech and language development

Description: The ELM Scale-2 is ideally suited to help clinicians implement the mandate to serve the developmental needs of children. The ELM Scale-2 also can be used with older children with developmental delays whose functional level falls within this range. The ELM Scale-2 consists of 43 items arranged in three divisions: Auditory Expressive (which is further subdivided into Content and Intelligibility), Auditory Receptive, and Visual. The scale may be used by examiners with varying levels of prior knowledge of early language development. It may be administered using either a pass–fail or a point-scoring method. The pass–fail method yields a global "pass" or "fail" rating for the test as a whole, whereas the point-scoring method yields percentile values, standard score equivalents, and age equivalents for each area of language function, as well as a Global Language score. The pass–fail method is preferred whenever large numbers of low-risk subjects must be evaluated. The point-scoring method is preferred whenever more detailed information is desired.

Format: Examiner required; individual administration; untimed: 1 to 10 minutes

Scoring: Examiner evaluated

Cost: Complete Kit (manual, object kit, 100 record forms, storage box) $160.00

Expression, Reception and Recall of Narrative Instrument (ERRNI)

2004	Harcourt Assessment-UK

Dorothy Bishop

Population: Ages 6 years to adult

Purpose: Assesses the ability to relate, comprehend, and remember a story after a delay

Description: Two parallel forms are each linked to a sequenced story of 15 scenes. Retell of The Beach Story or The Fish Story is recorded with and without visual cues and a series of comprehension questions are completed. Samples are then transcribed and analyzed. The parallel forms allow for retesting while minimizing practice effect. National UK norms are provided on how much relevant story content is provided, complexity of grammatical structure, comprehension of the pictured narrative, and forgetting. Detailed training examples are provided for transcriptions and coding.

Format: Examiner required; individual administration; untimed: 8 to 10 minutes

Scoring: Examiner evaluated

Cost: Complete Kit (manual, stimulus book, 25 each of Form A and Form B record forms, in a bag) £103.00

Fluharty Preschool Speech and Language Screening Test–Second Edition (FLUHARTY-2)

2000	PRO-ED, Inc.

Nancy Buono Fluharty

Population: Ages 3 to 6 years

Purpose: Measures early speech and language performance

Description: Contains five subtests: Articulation, Repeating Sentences, Responding to Directives and Answering Questions, Describing Actions, and Sequencing Events. The Fluharty-2 is a complete revision, normed on 705 children in 21 states. Standard scores are provided, as well as age equivalents, for the subtests and composites.

Format: Examiner required; individual administration; untimed: 45 minutes

Scoring: Examiner evaluated

Cost: Complete Kit (manual, picture book, 12 blocks, 25 record forms, storage box) $168.00

Fullerton Language Test of Adolescents–Second Edition (FLTA-2)

1986	PRO-ED, Inc.

Arden R. Thorum

Population: Ages 11 years to adult

Purpose: Measures receptive and expressive language skills to identify language impairment

Description: Standardized instrument contains eight subtests: Auditory Synthesis, Morphology Competency, Oral Commands, Convergent Production, Divergent Production, Syllabication, Grammatic Competency, and Idioms. The test diagnoses strengths and weaknesses and makes remediation suggestions.

Format: Examiner required; individual administration; untimed: 1 hour

Scoring: Examiner evaluated

Cost: Complete Kit (manual, stimulus items, protocols) $110.00

Functional Communication Profile–Revised (FCP-R)

2003	LinguiSystems, Inc.

Larry I. Kleiman

Population: Ages 3 years to adult

Purpose: Evaluates communication skills of those with developmental and acquired delays

Description: Assesses communication skills regardless of form of communication (sign, nonverbal, augmentative, etc.). Provides for evaluation in these 11 areas: Sensory, Attentiveness, Receptive Language, Expressive Language, Pragmatic/Social, Speech, Voice, Oral Language, Motor, Fluency, and Behavior. There is no scoring system, but the profile allows for variables in client ability, severity of impairment, mode of communication, degree of independence vs. assistance or prompting, and overall inventory of skills. The summary portion on the profile synthesizes client strengths and weaknesses, recommendations and strategies, and integration of objectives to help you prepare a complete, comprehensive report suitable for fulfillment of mandated Title 22 and educational federal or local reporting requirements.

Format: Examiner required; individual administration; untimed: 45 to 90 minutes

Scoring: Examiner evaluated

Cost: Manual and 15 Forms $41.95

HELP Test-Elementary

1996	LinguiSystems, Inc.

Andrea M. Lazzari

Population: Ages 6 to 11 years

Purpose: Assesses general language functioning for students with language disorders; yields information about students' semantic/syntactic skills in the familiar context of school-related language

Description: A total of 84 items in six subtests: Semantics, Specific Vocabulary, Word Order, General Vocabulary, Question Grammar, and Defining. Standard score, percentile rank, and age equivalency for each subtest and total test are provided.

Format: Examiner required; individual administration; untimed: 20 to 30 minutes

Scoring: Examiner evaluated

Cost: Complete Set (manual, stimuli book, 20 forms) $99.95

Illinois Test of Psycholinguistic Ability-Third Edition (ITPA-3)

2001	PRO-ED, Inc.

Donald D. Hammill, Nancy Mather, Rhia Roberts

Population: Ages 5 to 12 years

Purpose: Measures spoken and written language

Description: All of the subtests measure some aspect of language, including oral language, writing, reading, and spelling. The content in this edition is consistent with Charles Osgood's original Communication Model and also with the adaptations of that model made by Samuel Kirk, James McCarthy, and Winifred Kirk. The test can contribute to an accurate diagnosis of dyslexia and can identify children with general linguistic delays in the development of spoken and written language. There are 12 subtests: Spoken Analogies, Spoken Vocabulary, Morphological Closure, Syntactic Sentences, Sound Deletion, Rhyming Sequences, Sentence Sequencing, Written Vocabulary, Sight Decoding, Sound Decoding, Sight Spelling, and Sound Spelling. The subtests can be combined to form 10 composites: General Language, Spoken Language, Written Language, Semantics, Grammar, Phonology, Comprehension, Spelling, Sight-Symbol Processing, and Sound-Symbol Processing. Scores provided are standard scores, percentiles, and age equivalents.

Format: Examiner required; individual administration; untimed: 45 to 60 minutes

Scoring: Examiner evaluated; computer scoring available

Cost: Complete Kit (manual, 25 record booklets, 25 student response booklets, audiocassette, storage box) $179.00

Interaction Checklist for Augmentative Communication (INCH)

1991	PRO-ED, Inc.

Susan Oakander Bolton, Sallie E. Dashiell

Population: Children, adults

Purpose: Evaluates and remediates the interaction skills of nonspeaking individuals

Description: The INCH checklist evaluates responding to greetings from others, introducing self when appropriate, using AAC system without prompting, seeking help when needed, using pauses or spaces for greater clarity, and restating a message. Can be used as an initial and follow-up measure of communicative effectiveness with either an electronic or a manual device. Authors include suggestions for remediating interaction skills and for writing goals and objectives.

Format: Examiner required; individual administration; untimed

Scoring: Examiner evaluated

Cost: Manual and 25 Checklists $51.00

Kindergarten Language Screening Test–Second Edition (KLST-2)

1998	PRO-ED, Inc.

Sharon V. Gauthier, Charles L. Madison

Population: Ages 3 years 6 months to 6 years

Purpose: Measures receptive and expressive language competency and assesses language deficits that may cause kindergartners to fail academically

Description: Oral-response eight-item test identifying children for further diagnostic testing for language deficits that may accelerate academic failure. The child identifies name, age, colors, and body parts; demonstrates knowledge of number concepts; follows commands; repeats sentences; and engages in spontaneous speech. The test is based on the verbal language abilities considered average for children of kindergarten age.

Format: Examiner required; individual administration; untimed: 4 to 5 minutes

Scoring: Examiner evaluated

Cost: Complete Kit (manual, 50 profile/examiner record forms, picture book, picture cards, storage box) $130.00

Kohlman Evaluation of Living Skills (KELS)

1992	American Occupational Therapy Association, Inc.

Linda Kohlman Thomson

Population: Adults

Purpose: Measures ability to function in basic living skills

Description: Tests 17 basic living skills under five areas: Self-Care, Safety and Health, Money Management, Transportation and Telephone, and Work and Leisure. Used with persons who are elderly and with persons who have cognitive disabilities, in court for the determination of commitment, and in discharge planning at acute-care hospitals.

Format: Examiner required; individual administration; untimed: 30 to 45 minutes

Scoring: Examiner evaluated

Cost: Member Price $28.00; Nonmember Price $35.00

Language Processing Test–Elementary (LPT 3)

2005	LinguiSystems, Inc.

Gail J. Richard, Mary Anne Hanner

Population: Ages 5 to 11 years

Purpose: Measures language processing

Description: The third edition is normed on a population based on the 2000 U.S. Census. Oral-response verbal test with 84 items. The six subtests are Labeling and Stating Functions, Associations, Categorization, Similarities and Differences, Multiple Meanings, and Attributes. Assesses students' abilities to attach meaning to auditory stimuli by using a hierarchy of increased language complexity. Results are presented in standard scores and age equivalents. The tasks are based on A. R. Luria's Functional Organization of the Brain: when one part of the brain fails, another part should assume that function.

Format: Examiner required; individual administration; untimed: 35 minutes

Scoring: Examiner evaluated

Cost: Manual and 20 Test Forms $129.95

Oral and Written Language Scales (OWLS): Listening Comprehension (LC), Oral Expression (OE), and Written Expression (WE)

1995	AGS Publishing/Pearson Assessments

Elizabeth Carrow-Woolfolk

Population: Ages 3 to 21 years

Purpose: Assessment of receptive and expressive language

Description: OWLS consists of three scales: Listening Comprehension (LC), Oral Expression (OE), and Written Expression (WE). The scales were developed and normed as part of the same assessment. The oral language components (LC and OE) are packaged together with one manual. The WE scale is packaged separately with its own manual. The LC scale is designed to measure the understanding of spoken language. The OE scale is designed to measure the understanding and use of spoken language. The WE scale is designed to measure the ability to communicate meaningfully using written linguistic forms. Tasks in LC address the lexical (vocabulary), syntactic (grammar), and supralinguistic (higher order thinking) skills. Tasks in OE address lexical, syntactic, supralinguistic, and pragmatic (functional) language skills. Tasks address conventions (rules of spelling, capitalization, punctuation, etc.), linguistics (modifiers, phrases, verb forms, etc.), and content (ability to communicate meaningfully). Items are administered by age-appropriate item sets.

Format: Examiner required; individual administration; LC, 5 to 15 minutes; OE, 10 to 25 minutes; WE, 10 to 40 minutes

Scoring: Examiner interpretation; computer scoring is available for Macintosh and Windows formats

Cost: Complete Kit (Listening, Oral, and Written manuals, easels, 25 of each record forms) $339.99

Preschool Language Assessment Instrument–Second Edition (PLAI-2)

| 2003 | PRO-ED, Inc. |

Marion Blank, Susan A. Rose, Laura J. Berlin

Population: Ages 3 to 5 years

Purpose: Assesses children's abilities to meet the demands of classroom discourse

Description: The PLAI-2 provides norm referenced and informal assessment with six subtests: Matching, Analysis, Reordering, Reasoning, Receptive Mode, and Expressive Mode. The Discourse Ability Score provides an overall estimate of performance in percentiles, standard scores, and age equivalents. The informal assessment has two pragmatic measures: Adequacy of Response and Interfering Behaviors. The instrument serves as a guide for structuring teaching or therapy to match preschoolers' levels of functioning.

Format: Examiner required; individual administration; untimed: 30 minutes

Scoring: Examiner evaluated

Cost: Complete Kit (manual, picture book, 25 each record booklets for 3-year-olds and 4/5-year-olds, storage box) $197.00

Preschool Language Scale– Fourth Edition (PLS-4)

| 2002 | Harcourt Assessment, Inc. |

Irla Lee Zimmerman, Violette G. Steiner, Robert Evatt Pond

Population: Ages birth to 6 years

Purpose: Measures receptive and expressive language

Description: This newest edition provides developmental milestones, based on the latest research. The PLS-4 is designed to be fun for children and examiners. For children birth to 2 years 11 months, there are more items targeting interaction, attention, and vocal/gestural behaviors. For 5- and 6-year-olds, there are more items targeting early literacy and phonological awareness skills that tap school readiness. The test includes a reproducible Caregiver Questionnaire in which parents or caregivers share their knowledge of the child's typical communication at home. A screening instrument is for ages 3 to 6 years. Also available in Spanish.

Format: Examiner required; individual administration; untimed: 20 to 45 minutes

Scoring: Examiner evaluated

Cost: Complete Kit (manual, picture book, manipulatives, 15 record forms) $275.00; Screening Kit (manuals with stimulus pages, 25 record forms for 4 age groups) $125.00

Receptive-Expressive Emergent Language Scale– Second Edition (REEL-2)

| 1991 | PRO-ED, Inc. |

Kenneth R. Bzoch, Richard League

Population: Ages birth to 36 months

Purpose: Identifies language impairments for early childhood intervention program eligibility

Description: Designed for use with a broad range of infants and toddlers who are at risk in the new multidisciplinary programs developing under P.L. 99-457. The REEL-2 is a system of measurement and intervention planning based on neurolinguistic development and is designed to help public health nurses, pediatricians, and educators identify young children who have specific language problems based on specific language behaviors. These behaviors have been systematically selected based on extensive research, and all are age related. A supplementary subtest, Inventory of Vocabulary Words, is now included. Results are provided in standard scores, percentiles, and age equivalents.

Format: Examiner required; parent interview; untimed: 20 minutes

Scoring: Examiner evaluated

Cost: Complete Kit (examiner's manual, 25 profile/test forms, storage box) $100.00

Reynell Developmental Language Scales

1990 Western Psychological Services

Joan K. Reynell, Christian P. Gruber

Population: Ages 1 to 6 years

Purpose: Assesses two processes essential to language development: verbal comprehension and expressive language

Description: Battery of 134 items includes colorful test materials. Useful in evaluating language processes in young children, the test identifies the nature and extent of each child's language difficulty.

Format: Examiner required; individually administered; untimed: 30 minutes

Scoring: Examiner evaluated

Cost: Kit (set of stimulus materials, 10 test booklets, manual, carrying case) $549.00

Screening Kit of Language Development (SKOLD)

1983 Slosson Educational Publications, Inc.

Lynn S. Bliss, Doris V. Allen

Population: Ages 2 years 6 months to 4 years

Purpose: Assesses language disorders and delays in young children

Description: Oral-response 135-item test measuring language development in children speaking either Black English or Standard English. Picture stimuli are used to assess vocabulary, comprehension, story completion, individual and paired sentence repetition with pictures, individual sentence repetition without pictures, and comprehension of commands. The test consists of six subtests, three for Black English and three for Standard English, in each of the following age ranges: 30 to 36 months, 37 to 42 months, and 43 to 48 months. Norms are provided for speakers of Black English and Standard English. The manual includes guidelines for administration and scoring and the linguistic characteristics of Black English.

Format: Examiner required; individual administration; untimed: 15 minutes

Scoring: Examiner evaluated

Cost: Complete Kit (manual, stimulus materials, scoring guidelines, 25 of either Standard English or Black English scoring forms) $113.50

Sequenced Inventory of Communication Development– Revised (SICD-R)

1984 Western Psychological Services

Dona Lea Hendrick, Elizabeth M. Prather, Annette R. Tobin

Population: Developmental ages 4 through 48 months

Purpose: Evaluates communication abilities

Description: Measures receptive language with behavioral items that test sound and speech discrimination, awareness, and understanding and expressive language that includes three types of behavior (imitating, initiating, and responding), as well as two distinct areas of expressive measurement (length and grammatical and syntactic structures of verbal output and articulation). Provides a Receptive Communication Age and Expressive Communication Age. Helpful in developing IEPs.

Format: Examiner required; individual administration; untimed: 30 to 75 minutes

Scoring: Examiner evaluated

Cost: Kit (manuals, materials, 50 record booklets, carrying case) $435.00

Speech and Language Evaluation Scale (SLES)

1989 Hawthorne Educational Services, Inc.

Diane R. Fressola, Sandra C. Hoerchler

Population: Ages 4 years 5 months to 18 years

Purpose: Aids in the diagnosis of speech and language disorders

Description: The SLES is designed for in-school screening and referral of students with speech and language problems. The scale is designed to provide the clinician with input from classroom teachers, without requiring anecdotal reporting. The scale includes the most commonly recognized subscales of Speech (Articulation, Voice, and Fluency) and Language (Form, Content, and Pragmatics). A Windows Quick Score is available.

Format: Rating scale; untimed: 20 minutes

Scoring: Examiner evaluated; computer scoring available

Cost: Complete Kit (technical manual, intervention manual, 50 each of 3 forms) $135.00

Test for Auditory Comprehension of Language–Third Edition (TACL-3)

| 1999 | PRO-ED, Inc. |

Elizabeth Carrow-Woolfolk

Population: Ages 3 to 9 years

Purpose: Measures auditory comprehension of children

Description: Test consists of 142 items divided into three subtests (Vocabulary, Grammatical Morphemes, and Elaborated Phrases and Sentences) that assess a child's ability to understand English language forms. Ceiling rules for scoring are provided for each section. The Examiner's Manual includes a comprehensive discussion of the test's theoretical and research-based foundation, item development, standardization, administration and scoring procedures, norms tables, and guidelines.

Format: Examiner required; individual administration; untimed 15 to 25 minutes

Scoring: Examiner evaluated

Cost: Complete Kit (manual, picture book, 25 profile/examiner record booklets, storage box) $275.00

Test for Examining Expressive Morphology (TEEM)

| 1983 | PRO-ED, Inc. |

Kenneth G. Shipley, Terry A. Stone, Marlene B. Sue

Population: Ages 3 to 7 years

Purpose: Assesses the expressive morpheme development of children (language age 3 to 8 years, interest level 3 to 16 years), measures general language level, and monitors student progress

Description: Oral-response 54-item sentence-completion test assessing the allomorphic variations of six major morphemes: present progressives, plurals, possessives, past tenses, third-person singulars, and derived adjectives. The examiner presents each stimulus picture while reading the stimulus phrase, and the child completes the phrase while viewing the picture. Results identify specific morphemes and allomorphic variations requiring stimulation or instruction. The manual includes administration instructions and technical data.

Format: Examiner required; individual administration; untimed: 7 minutes

Scoring: Examiner evaluated

Cost: Test Kit (manual, 25 scoring forms, picture book) $71.00

Test of Adolescent and Adult Language–Fourth Edition (TOAL-4)

| 2007 | PRO-ED, Inc. |

Donald D. Hammill, Virginia L. Brown, Stephen C. Larsen, J. Lee Wiederholt

Population: Ages 12 years to 24 years 11 months

Purpose: Measures spoken and written language abilities

Description: The TOAL-4 has six subtests: Word Opposites, Word Derivations, Spoken Analogies, Word Similarities, Sentence Combining, and Orthographic Usage. These are combined into the following composites: Spoken Language, formed by combining the scaled scores of the subtests Word Opposites, Word Derivations, and Spoken Analogies; Written Language, formed by combining the scaled scores of the subtests Word Similarities, Sentence Combining, and Orthographic Usage; and General Language, formed by combining the scaled scores of all six subtests. Test results can be reported as percentile ranks and scaled scores. Features of the 4th edition, including the theoretical model on which the test was built, have been modified to better reflect the manner in which adolescents and adults actually use language, and the number of subtests has been reduced from eight to six, thereby considerably shortening the administration and scoring time.

Format: Examiner required; individual and group administration; untimed: 1 to 3 hours

Scoring: Examiner evaluated

Cost: Complete Kit (manual, 25 record booklets, 25 written language forms, storage box) $195.00

Test of Early Language Development–Third Edition (TELD-3)

| 1999 | PRO-ED, Inc. |

Wayne P. Hresko, D. Kim Reid, Donald D. Hammill

Population: Ages 2 to 7 years

Purpose: Measures content and form in the receptive and expressive language abilities of children; used to identify problems, document progress, conduct research, and guide instructional practices

Description: This edition is a major revision. Like the previous edition, the TELD-3 yields an overall Spoken Language score, but now it includes scores for Receptive Language and Expressive Language subtests. The TELD-3 was standardized on 2,127 children representing 35 states. Pictures are presented in color to make them more attractive to children. Standard scores (with a mean of 100 and a standard deviation of 15) and percentiles are provided for subtest and composite scores. Age-equivalent scores are also reported for the subtests. The test is quick and easy to administer and score. The attractive pictures and content, along with the untimed nature of the items, allow for optimal assessment. The kit now includes all the manipulatives the examiner needs.

Format: Examiner required; individual administration; untimed: 15 to 45 minutes

Scoring: Examiner evaluated

Cost: Complete Kit (manual, 25 each of Form A and Form B, picture book, manipulatives, storage box) $285.00

Test of Early Language Development–Third Edition: Spanish (TELD-3:S)

2007	PRO-ED, Inc.

Margarita Ramos, Jorge Ramos

Population: Ages 2 to 7 years

Purpose: Measures receptive and expressive language in Spanish-speaking children

Description: A translation and adaptation of the *Test of Early Language Development–Third Edition*. Scores are provided for Receptive, Expressive, and Overall Spoken Language. The TELD-3:S was normed on children residing in Chile, Costa Rica, Mexico, Spain, and the United States. The items were examined to ensure that little or no bias relative to gender, disability, race, socioeconomic level, ethnic group, and dialect variation existed. A chart is provided to ensure that appropriate vocabulary is used during administration. The manual is printed in English, except for the item instructions and the appendices used for scoring.

Format: Examiner required; individual administration; untimed: 20 minutes

Scoring: Examiner evaluated

Cost: Complete Kit (manual, picture book,

manipulatives, 25 response forms, 25 scoring forms, box) $145.00

Test of Language Competence–Expanded (TLC-Expanded)

1989	Harcourt Assessment, Inc.

Elisabeth H. Wiig, Wayne A. Secord

Population: Ages 5 to 18 years

Purpose: Measures metalinguistic higher-level language functions

Description: Multiple-item response test for diagnosing language disabilities by assessing language strategies rather than language skill. The Recreating Sentences subtest examines the ability to perceive the nature of a communication and recreate a semantically, syntactically, and pragmatically appropriate sentence. The Understanding Metaphoric Expressions subtest has students interpret an expression and select another one with the same meaning. The Understanding Ambiguous Sentences subtest evaluates the ability to recognize and interpret alternative meanings of lexical and structural ambiguities. The Making Inferences subtest has students identify permissible inferences based on causal relationships or chains. The test's features include norm-referenced scores, extension teaching and testing formats for each subtest, and Individualized Education Program guidelines. Two levels for different age groups.

Format: Examiner required; individual administration; untimed: less than an hour

Scoring: Examiner evaluated

Cost: Complete Kit (manuals, materials, 25 protocols for both levels, briefcase) $459.00

Test of Language Development–Intermediate: Third Edition (TOLD-I:3)

1997	PRO-ED, Inc.

Donald D. Hammill, Phyllis L. Newcomer

Population: Ages 8 to 12 years

Purpose: Assesses the expressive and receptive language abilities of children

Description: Different components of spoken language are measured in five subtests: Generals, Malapropisms with Picture Vocabulary, Sentence Combining, Word Ordering, and Grammatic Comprehension. The TOLD-I:3 was standardized on more than 700 children from 19 states.

Format: Examiner required; individual administration: untimed: 30 minutes to 1 hour

Scoring: Examiner evaluated; computer scoring available

Cost: Complete Kit (manual, picture book, 25 profile/examiner record forms, storage box) $185.00

Test of Language Development–Primary: Third Edition (TOLD-P:3)

| 1997 | PRO-ED, Inc. |

Phyllis L. Newcomer, Donald D. Hammill

Population: Ages 4 to 8 years

Purpose: Assesses the expressive and receptive language abilities of children

Description: Nine subtests measure different components of spoken language. Picture Vocabulary, Relational Vocabulary, and Oral Vocabulary assess the understanding and meaningful use of spoken words. Grammatic Understanding, Sentence Imitation, and Grammatic Completion assess differing aspects of grammar. Word Articulation, Phonemic Analysis, and Word Discrimination are supplemental subtests that measure the abilities to say words correctly and to distinguish between words that sound similar. The test was completely renormed in 1996 on more than 1,000 children from 30 states.

Format: Examiner required; individual administration; untimed: 30 minutes to 1 hour

Scoring: Examiner evaluated; computer scored

Cost: Complete Kit (manual, picture book, 25 profile/examiner record forms, storage box) $256.00

Test of Narrative Language (TNL)

| 2004 | PRO-ED, Inc. |

Ronald B. Gillam, Nils A. Pearson

Population: Ages 5 to 11 years

Purpose: Assesses receptive language by measuring the ability to answer literal and inferential comprehension questions

Description: The TNL utilizes three narrative formats that elicit scripts, personal narratives, and fictional narratives to assess how well children use their knowledge of the components of language as they engage in functional discourse. Three formats are used: no picture cues, sequence picture cues, and single picture cues. The examiner audiotapes the administration for later scoring. Raw scores are converted to standard scores and percentiles. The three formats yield scores for Narrative Comprehension, Oral Narration, and an overall Index of Narrative Language Ability.

Format: Examiner required; individual administration; untimed: 15 to 20 minutes

Scoring: Examiner evaluated

Cost: Complete Kit (manual, picture book, 25 record forms, storage box) $160

Test Of Problem Solving 3–Elementary (TOPS-3 Elementary)

| 2005 | LinguiSystems, Inc. |

Linda Bowers, Rosemary Huisingh, Carolyn LoGiudice

Population: Ages 6 to 12 years

Purpose: Measures language-based critical-thinking skills using logic and experience

Description: Addresses critical-thinking abilities based on students' language strategies in the following areas: making inferences, sequencing, negative questions, problem solving, predicting, and determining causes. Questions focus on a broad range of thinking skills, including clarifying, analyzing, generating solutions, evaluating, and affective thinking. The instrument guides professionals to confidently make placement decisions and write IEP goals. Responses receive 2, 1, or 0 points, depending on the appropriateness of the content, semantics, and linguistics. Separate scores are provided for each subtest and the total test.

Format: Examiner required; individual administration; untimed: 45 minutes

Scoring: Examiner evaluated

Cost: Complete Set (manual, stimuli book, 20 test forms, box) $139.95

Test of Semantic Skills–Intermediate (TOSS-I)

| 2004 | LinguiSystems, Inc. |

Rosemary Huisingh, Linda Bowers, Carolyn LoGiudice, Jane Orman

Population: Ages 9 to 13 years

Purpose: Assesses receptive and expressive language skills

Description: Measures skills in five areas: Labels, Categories, Attributes, Functions, and Definitions. Stimulus items are provided in the context of familiar, realistic, theme-based illustrations. Results provide standardized analysis of receptive, expressive, and overall semantic and vocabulary abilities.

Format: Examiner required; individual administration; untimed: 25 to 30 minutes

Scoring: Examiner evaluated

Cost: Test Kit (manual, picture stimuli book, 20 test forms) $129.95

Utah Test of Language Development–Third Edition (UTLD-3)

1989	PRO-ED, Inc.

Merlin J. Mecham

Population: Ages 3 to 9 years

Purpose: Identifies children with language-learning disabilities who may need further assistance

Description: Task-assessment oral-response 51-item test measuring the following factors: receptive semantic language, expressive semantic language, receptive sequential language, and expressive sequential language. Test items are arranged in developmental order.

Format: Examiner required; individual administration; untimed: 30 to 45 minutes

Scoring: Examiner evaluated

Cost: Complete Kit (manual, administration/picture book, 50 profile/examiner record forms, storage box) $140.00

Wiig Criterion-Referenced Inventory of Language (Wiig CRIL)

1990	Harcourt Assessment, Inc.

Elisabeth H. Wiig

Population: Ages 4 to 13 years

Purpose: Obtains information to plan and implement effective language intervention

Description: Language probe sets are organized into four modules: Semantics, Pragmatics, Morphology, and Syntax. The record form provides space for three administrations to determine progress over time. Can be used as follow-up for norm-referenced testing.

Format: Examiner required; individual administration; untimed

Scoring: Examiner evaluated

Cost: Complete Kit (guide, 4 stimulus manuals, 10 record forms of each form) $299.00

Woodcock Language Proficiency Battery–Revised (WLPB-R) English Form

1991	Riverside Publishing Company

Richard W. Woodcock

Population: Ages 2 to 90+ years

Purpose: Assesses language skills in English; used for purposes of eligibility and determination of language proficiency level

Description: Provides an overall measure of language proficiency in measures of oral language, reading, and written language. The subtests are Memory for Sentences, Picture Vocabulary, Oral Vocabulary, Listening Comprehension, Verbal Analogies, Letter–Word Identification, Passage Comprehension, Word Attack, Reading Vocabulary, Dictation, Writing Samples, Proofing, Writing Fluency; Punctuation and Capitalization, Spelling and Usage, and Handwriting. There are cluster scores for Oral Language, Reading, and Written Language. The tests are primarily measures of language skills predictive of success in situations characterized by cognitive-academic language proficiency (CALP) requirements. CALP levels from advanced to negligible are provided.

Format: Examiner required; individual administration; untimed: 20 to 60 minutes depending on number of subtests

Scoring: Examiner evaluated; computer software available

Cost: Complete Test (test book, audiocassette, 25 each of test records and response booklets, manual, norm tables) $381.50

Fluency and Voice

Computerized Scoring of Stuttering Severity (CSSS)

1996	PRO-ED, Inc.

Klaas Bakker, Glyndon D. Riley

Population: Children, adults

Purpose: Allows repeated measures of stuttering severity

Description: Designed for PC computers with Windows or DOS. Types of measurement include percentage of stuttered syllables, mean duration of the three longest stuttering events, mean duration of all stuttering events, fluent rate, and length of periods of fluent speech. These data are useful for tracking stuttering severity during treatment or in research over time. Results of CSSS scoring can be displayed as graphs to illustrate each measure to a client or an audience.

Format: Examiner required; individual administration; untimed: 5 to 20 minutes

Scoring: Computer evaluated; examiner interpretation

Cost: $92.00

Oral Speech Mechanism Screening Examination–Third Edition (OSMSE-3)

| 2000 | PRO-ED, Inc. |

Kenneth O. St. Louis, Dennis M. Ruscello

Population: Ages 5 to 78 years

Purpose: Evaluates speech, language, and other related skills; used for examining oral speech mechanisms in language and speech clients of all ages

Description: Provides an efficient, quick, and reliable method to examine the oral speech mechanism of all types of speech, language, and related disorders where oral structure and function is of concern. The third edition has a number of new features designed to make the instrument easier to administer and score. Included is a demonstration audiotape to assist in giving instructions, and an updated Examiner's Manual has 16 new photographs.

Format: Examiner required; individual administration; untimed: 5 to 10 minutes

Scoring: Examiner evaluated

Cost: Complete Kit (manual, 50 scoring forms, audiocassette, storage box) $101.00

Stuttering Prediction Instrument for Young Children (SPI)

| 1981 | PRO-ED, Inc. |

Glyndon D. Riley

Population: Ages 3 to 8 years

Purpose: Determines whether a child should be scheduled for therapy to treat stuttering

Description: Diagnostic test utilizing pictures, parent interview, observation, and taped recordings of the child's speech to assess the child's

history, reactions, part-word repetitions, prolongations, and frequency of stuttered words.

Format: Examiner required; individual administration; timed speech sample

Scoring: Examiner evaluated

Cost: Complete Kit (manual with picture plates and test forms, storage box) $105.00

Stuttering Severity Instrument for Children and Adults– Third Edition (SSI-3)

| 1994 | PRO-ED, Inc. |

Glyndon D. Riley

Population: Children, adults

Purpose: Measures the severity of stuttering and evaluates the effects of treatment

Description: The third edition of this widely used test includes the following features: new and updated procedures, new normative data, and expanded picture plates to simplify speaking samples. The SSI-3 can be used in conjunction with the *Stuttering Prediction Inventory*. Four major areas are evaluated: frequency (converted to scale scores 0 to 18); duration (converted to scale scores 0 to 18); physical concomitants (rated by degree of distractibility 0 to 20); and severity conversion tables for preschool, school-age, and adults.

Format: Examiner required; individual administration; untimed: 15 to 20 minutes

Scoring: Examiner evaluated

Cost: Complete Kit (manual, picture plates, 50 test record and frequency computation forms, storage box) $100.00

Test of Oral Structures and Functions (TOSF)

| 1986 | Slosson Educational Publications, Inc. |

Gary J. Vitali

Population: Ages 7 years to adult

Purpose: Assesses oral structures, nonverbal oral functioning, and verbal oral functioning; used by speech–language pathologists for screening, differential diagnosis, caseload management decisions, and pre- and posttreatment assessment

Description: Multiple-item paper–pencil and oral-response test assessing oral structures and motor integrity during verbal and nonverbal oral functioning and establishing the nature of structural, neurological, or functional disorders. The test is composed of five subtests: Speech Survey, Verbal Oral Functioning, Nonverbal Motor Functioning, Orofacial Structures, and History/Behavioral Survey. The Speech Survey targets articulation, rate/prosody, fluency, and voice during spontaneous or elicited speech. The Verbal Oral Functioning subtest assesses the integrity of oral–nasal resonance balance during imitated and spontaneous speech and articulatory precision and rate/prosody during tests that control for performance loading effects, syllable position effects, voicing, manner of articulation, and placement of articulation. The Nonverbal Motor Functioning subtest assesses volitional and automatic oral functioning during essentially static and sequenced activities controlled for general anatomic site of functioning. The Orofacial Structures subtest is an observational survey of intraoral and orofacial structures at rest.

Format: Examiner required; individual administration; untimed: 20 minutes

Scoring: Examiner evaluated

Cost: Complete Kit (manual, 25 test booklets, finger cots, tongue blades, balloons, oroscope penlight) $103.25

Verbal Motor Production Assessment for Children (VMPAC)

1999	Harcourt Assessment, Inc.

Deborah Hayden, Paula Square

Population: Ages 3 to 12 years

Purpose: Assesses the neuromotor integrity of the motor speech system

Description: Identifies children with motor issues that have negative effects on the development of normal speech control. Items are arranged from basic to complex to pinpoint where the child begins to have difficulty. A training video demonstrates administration and scoring. Three main areas are assessed: Global Motor Control, Focal Oromotor Control, and Sequencing, as well as two supplemental areas: Connected Speech and Language Control and Speech Characteristics.

Format: Examiner required; individual administration; untimed: 30 minutes

Scoring: Examiner evaluated

Cost: Complete Kit (manual, cards, 15 record forms, videotape) $122.00

Voice Assessment Protocol for Children and Adults (VAP)

1987	PRO-ED, Inc.

Rebekah H. Pindzola

Population: Ages 4 to 18 years

Purpose: Evaluates voice pitch, loudness, quality, breath features, and rate/rhythm

Description: Clinical tasks are guided step by step, and immediate interpretations of normalcy are facilitated by a grid-marking system. The VAP is equally applicable to functional and neurogenic voice disorders. The VAP includes a pitch level sample audiocassette for clinical use. By using these taped samples, musical instruments and sophisticated pitch determination equipment are not necessary for a voice assessment. The cassette contains whole notes of the musical scale between E2 and C6. The tape is arranged for clinical practicality. Each whole note and octave is identified, played on a piano, then followed by a vocal demonstration.

Format: Examiner required; individual administration; untimed

Scoring: Examiner evaluated

Cost: Complete Kit (manual, audiocassette, 25 protocols, storage box) $75.00

Pragmatics

Pragmatic Language Skills Inventory (PLSI)

2006	PRO-ED, Inc.

James E. Gilliam, Lynda Miller

Population: Ages 5 to 12

Purpose: Assesses pragmatic language abilities

Description: The PLSI has 45 items with three subscales: Personal Interaction Skills, Social Interaction Skills, and Classroom Interaction Skills. Cutoff scores are provided for determining whether the student exhibits characteristics of a pragmatic language disorder and should be referred for a more comprehensive language assessment.

Format: Rating scale; untimed: 5 to 10 minutes

Scoring: Examiner evaluated

Cost: Complete Kit (manual, 25 forms, storage box) $95.00

Test of Pragmatic Language– Second Edition (TOPL-2)

2007	PRO-ED, Inc.

Diana Phelps-Terasaki, Trisha Phelps-Gunn

Population: Ages 5 through 18 years

Purpose: Assesses the student's ability to effectively use pragmatic language

Description: The TOPL-2 expands the original test for a comprehensive analysis of social communication in context. Utilizing a short verbal prompt and a color picture aid, the student's response must resolve the social dilemma presented. Each of the 43 items establish a specific social context, such as classroom behavior problems, misunderstandings between peers or teachers, effective persuasion, and effective communicative repair, all of which yield an assessment of the student's ability to utilize and evaluate social language. This revision includes a Pragmatic Evaluation that focuses on the student's ability to monitor and appraise the effectiveness of the response to resolve the social problem situation. The pictorial prompts are in color in an easel-back book. Included in the manual is a comprehensive scoring guide with a clinical interpretive framework.

Format: Examiner required; individual administration; untimed: 40 to 60 minutes

Scoring: Examiner evaluated

Cost: Complete Kit (examiner's manual, picture book, 25 each profile/examiner record forms for ages 6 to 7 and 8 to 18, storage box) $215.00

Semantics

Joliet 3-Minute Preschool Speech and Language Screen

1993	Harcourt Assessment, Inc.

Mary C. Kinzler

Population: Ages 2 years 6 months and 4 years 6 months

Purpose: Identifies students' potential problems in grammar, semantics, and phonology

Description: Multiple-item individually administered oral-response test assessing receptive vocabulary, expressive syntax, voice, fluency, and phonological competence. Line drawings are used to elicit receptive vocabulary. Sentences are used to identify expressive syntax, morphology, and phonological competence.

Format: Examiner required; individual or group administration; untimed: 3 minutes

Scoring: Examiner evaluated

Cost: Test Kit (manuals, Apple II disk, vocabulary plates, scoring sheets, ring binder) $89.00

Joliet 3-Minute Speech and Language Screen (Revised)

1992	Harcourt Assessment, Inc.

Mary C. Kinzler, Constance Cowing Johnson

Population: K, Grades 2 and 5

Purpose: Identifies students' potential problems in grammar, semantics, and phonology

Description: Multiple-item individually administered oral-response test assessing receptive vocabulary, expressive syntax, voice, fluency, and phonological competence. Line drawings are used to elicit receptive vocabulary. Sentences are used to identify expressive syntax, morphology, and phonological competence.

Format: Examiner required; individual or group administration; untimed: 3 minutes

Scoring: Examiner evaluated

Cost: Test Kit (manuals, Apple II disk, vocabulary plates, scoring sheets, ring binder) $89.00

Pyramids and Palm Trees

1992	Harcourt Assessment, Inc.

David Howard, Karalyn Patterson

Population: Adults

Purpose: Determines the degree to which meaning from pictures and words can be accessed

Description: Information from the test will enable the examiner to establish whether difficulty in naming or pointing to a named picture is due to a difficulty in retrieving semantic information from pictures or words or in retrieving the appropriate spoken form of the word. Six different versions of the test are possible by using either pictures or written or spoken words to change the modality of stimulus or response items. The test is short and easily administered.

Format: Requires examiner; individual administration; untimed: 25 minutes

Scoring: Examiner evaluated

Cost: $158.00

Test of Adolescent/ Adult Word Finding (TAWF)

1990	PRO-ED, Inc.

Diane J. German

Population: Ages 12 to 80 years

Purpose: Identifies word-finding disorders

Description: Test with 107 items (or 40 in the brief test) with five naming sections: Picture Naming: Nouns; Picture Naming: Verbs; Sentence Completion Naming; Description Naming; and Category Naming. The TAWF includes a special sixth comprehension section that allows the examiner to determine if errors are a result of word-finding problems or are due to poor comprehension. The test provides formal and informal analyses of two dimensions of word finding: speed and accuracy. The formal analysis yields standard scores, percentile ranks, and grade standards for item response time. The informal analysis yields secondary characteristics (gestures and extra verbalization) and substitution types. Speed can be measured in actual or estimated item response time. The estimated response time can be done during testing and eliminates the need for a stopwatch or tape recorder.

Format: Examiner required; individual administration; untimed: 20 to 30 minutes

Scoring: Examiner evaluated

Cost: Complete Kit (examiner's manual, technical manual, test book, 25 response forms) $300.00

Test of Semantic Skills– Primary (TOSS-P)

2002	LinguiSystems, Inc.

Linda Bowers, Rosemary Huisingh, Carolyn LoGiudice, Jane Orman

Population: Ages 4 to 8 years

Purpose: Assesses receptive and expressive language skills

Description: Measures skills in five areas: Labels, Categories, Attributes, Functions, and Definitions. Stimulus items are provided in the context of familiar, realistic, theme-based illustrations. Results provide standardized analysis of receptive, expressive, and overall semantic and vocabulary abilities.

Format: Examiner required; individual administration; untimed: 25 to 30 minutes

Scoring: Examiner evaluated

Cost: Test Kit (manual, picture stimuli book, 20 test forms) $129.95

Test of Word Finding in Discourse (TWFD)

1991	PRO-ED, Inc.

Diane J. German

Population: Ages 6 years 6 months to 12 years 11 months

Purpose: Helps to answer questions related to word-finding difficulties

Description: In the TWFD, the child views three stimulus pictures contained in the manual and responds to standard auditory prompts. The elicited language sample is tape-recorded and then scored through a process of transcribing and segmenting the child's narrative. Scores obtained include the Productivity Index, a quantitative measure of how much language is produced in a child's discourse, and the Word Finding Behaviors Index, a frequency measure of specific word finding behaviors present in a child's discourse, such as repetitions, reformulations, substitutions, insertions, empty words, time fillers, and delays. Percentile ranks and standard scores can be obtained for both indexes.

Format: Examiner required; individual administration; untimed: 15 minutes

Scoring: Examiner evaluated

Cost: Complete Kit (manual, 25 record forms) $109.00

Test of Word Finding– Second Edition (TWF-2)

2000	PRO-ED, Inc.

Diane J. German

Population: Ages 4 to 12 years

Purpose: Diagnoses expressive language problems resulting from word retrieval difficulties

Description: Uses four naming sections to test a student's word-finding ability (Picture Naming Nouns, Sentence Completion Naming, Picture Naming Verbs, and Picture Naming Categories).

In addition, five supplemental analyses are provided as follow-up procedures to the TWF-2 word-finding measures. The examiner gains critical information from these analyses that will both enhance the interpretation of a student's test performance and help to formulate a word-finding intervention plan. The TWF-2 was normed on 1,836 students residing in 26 states from 1996 to 1999. Correlations between TWF-2 and other tests of vocabulary showed a considerable relationship.

Format: Examiner required; individual administration; untimed: 20 to 30 minutes

Scoring: Examiner evaluated

Cost: Complete Kit (manual, 2 picture books, 10 each of preprimary and primary, 10 intermediate profile/examiner record forms, storage box) $388.00

Test of Word Knowledge (TOWK)

1992	Harcourt Assessment, Inc.

Elisabeth H. Wiig, Wayne A. Secord

Population: Ages 5 to 18 years

Purpose: Evaluates deficits in semantic knowledge

Description: Designed for use as part of a total diagnostic language battery, the test helps evaluate the student's ability to understand and use words.

Format: Examiner required; individual administration; untimed

Scoring: Examiner evaluated

Cost: Complete Kit (manual, stimulus manual, 12 record forms) $195.00

WORD Test 2–Adolescent

2005	LinguiSystems, Inc.

Linda Bowers, Rosemary Huisingh, Carolyn LoGiudice, Jane Orman

Population: Ages 12 to 17 years

Purpose: Assesses ability to recognize and express critical semantic attributes of the lexicon

Description: Using vocabulary of the curriculum, the instrument has six subtests: Associations, Synonyms, Semantic Absurdities, Antonyms, Definitions, and Flexible Word Use. All items are presented in a conversational style with normal intonation and at a normal speaking rate. Concrete suggestions are made for remediation based on test performance. Results are reported as standard scores, percentile rank, and age equivalents for each subtest and for the total test.

Format: Examiner required; individual administration; untimed: 30 minutes

Scoring: Examiner evaluated

Cost: Manual and 20 Test Forms $129.95

WORD Test 2–Elementary

2004	LinguiSystems, Inc.

Linda Bowers, Rosemary Huisingh, Carolyn LoGiudice, Jane Orman

Population: Ages 7 to 11 years

Purpose: Assesses ability to recognize and express critical semantic attributes of the lexicon

Description: Using vocabulary of the curriculum, the instrument has six subtests: Associations, Synonyms, Semantic Absurdities, Antonyms, Definitions, and Flexible Word Use. All items are presented in a conversational style with normal intonation and at a normal speaking rate. Concrete suggestions are made for remediation based on test performance. Results are reported as standard scores, percentile ranks, and age equivalents for each subtest and for the total test.

Format: Examiner required; individual administration; untimed: 25 to 35 minutes

Scoring: Examiner evaluated

Cost: Manual and 20 Test Forms $129.95

Syntax

Language Sampling, Analysis, and Training–Third Edition (LSAT-3)

1998	PRO-ED, Inc.

Dorothy Tyack, Gail Portuff Venable

Population: Ages 2 years to adult

Purpose: Describes the procedures for analyzing the morphological and syntactical elements of sentences; also used as a resource for training children whose language delays are serious enough to warrant intervention

Description: Based on established linguistic and behavioral principles, this method is appropriate for both group or individual teaching. The child's speech sample demonstrates the rules that each child has acquired to form sentences. Analyzing the sample enables teachers and clinicians to write Individualized Education Programs that are precisely tailored to specific linguistic needs. The book contains four main chapters: Eliciting and Transcribing Language, Analyzing the Sample, Training Programs, and Measuring Change. Included with the handbook are the following worksheets: Transcription, Word/Morpheme Tally and Summary, Sequence of Language Acquisition, Baseline Analysis, Training Worksheet, and Score Sheet. Scored and unscored samples are provided for practice.

Format: Examiner required; individual administration; untimed

Scoring: Examiner evaluated

Cost: Complete Kit (manual, 25 analysis forms, 25 transcription sheets, storage box) $100.00

Vocabulary

Comprehensive Receptive and Expressive Vocabulary Test–Second Edition (CREVT-2)

2002	PRO-ED, Inc.

Gerald Wallace, Donald D. Hammill

Population: Ages 4 to 89 years

Purpose: Measures receptive and expressive oral vocabulary

Description: Receptive vocabulary is measured with the use of a picture book that has 10 color pictures for 61 items for the "point-to-the-picture-of-the-word-I-say" technique; 5 to 8 words are associated with each picture plate spread evenly across ability levels. On the Expressive Vocabulary subtest, the 25 words pertain to the same 10 common themes used in the Receptive Vocabulary subtest. The individual defines the word given. A combined score is provided on two equivalent forms.

Format: Examiner required; individual administration; untimed: 20 to 30 minutes

Scoring: Examiner evaluated

Cost: Complete Kit (manual, photo album, 25 each of Form A and B protocols, storage box) $243.00

Expressive Language Test

1998	LinguiSystems, Inc.

Rosemary Huisingh, Linda Bowers, Carolyn LoGiudice, Jane Orman

Population: Ages 5 to 11 years

Purpose: Assesses overall expressive language functioning

Description: An oral-response standardized test with eight subtests: Sequencing (13 items), Metalinguistics—Defining (15 items), Metalinguistics—Generating Examples (15 items), Grammar and Syntax (15 items), Concepts (15 items), Categorizing and Describing—Identifying Categories (10 items), Categorizing and Describing—Defining Categories (10 items), and Categorizing and Describing—Generating Examples (10 items).

Format: Examiner required; individual administration; untimed: 40 to 45 minutes

Scoring: Examiner evaluated

Cost: Test Kit (manual, sequencing cards, stimuli book, 20 forms) $102.95

Expressive One-Word Picture Vocabulary Test–2000 (EOWPVT-2000)

2000	Academic Therapy Publications

Rick Brownell

Population: Ages 2 to 18 years

Purpose: Provides assessment of English speaking vocabulary

Description: This 170-item test is co-normed with the *Receptive One-Word Picture Vocabulary Test–2000* on a representative national sample of over 2,000 individuals. New administration procedures permit examiners to cue examinees so that they will attend to the relevant aspects of each illustration. Record forms provide cues, acceptable alternate answers, and age-related start points. Newly rendered test plates provide full-color drawings; a number of test items are new to this edition. Raw scores are converted to standard scores, percentile ranks, and age equivalents.

Format: Examiner required; individual administration; untimed: 20 minutes

Scoring: Examiner evaluated

Cost: Test Kit (manual, test plates, 25 English forms, portfolio) $145.00

Expressive Vocabulary Test, Second Edition (EVT-2)

2006	AGS Publishing/Pearson Assessments

Kathleen T. Williams

Population: Ages 2 years 6 months to 90+ years

Purpose: Measures expressive vocabulary and word retrieval for Standard English

Description: The EVT-2 is comprised of 38 labeling items and 152 synonym items on two parallel forms. For the labeling items, the examiner points to a picture or a part of the body and asks a question. On the synonym items, the examiner presents a picture and stimulus word(s) within a carrier phrase. The examinee responds to each item with a one-word answer. All stimulus pictures are in full color and carefully balanced for gender and ethnic representation.

Format: Examiner required; individual administration; untimed: 10 to 20 minutes

Scoring: Examiner evaluated; computer scoring available

Cost: Complete Kit (easel, manual, 25 each Form A and Form B record forms, carrying case) $379.00

Peabody Picture Vocabulary Test, Fourth Edition (PPVT™-4)

2006	AGS Publishing/Pearson Assessments

Lloyd M. Dunn, Douglas M. Dunn

Population: Ages 2 years 6 months to 90+ years

Purpose: Measures receptive vocabulary for Standard American English

Description: The revised edition provides 228 words per alternate form with better representation of word types across all levels of difficulty. All items were evaluated for cultural sensitivity. New easy items were added to strengthen the floor of the test. Art is redesigned to be realistic. The Instrument was co-normed with the *Expressive Vocabulary Test, Second Edition*.

Format: Examiner required; individual administration; untimed: 10 to 15 minutes

Scoring: Examiner interpretation; computer scoring is available for Macintosh and Windows formats

Cost: Complete Kit (easels, manuals, 25 each of Forms A and B, carrying case) $379.00

Progressive Achievement Test (PAT): Listening Comprehension–Revised

1994	New Zealand Council for Educational Research

Neil Reid, Ian C. Johnstone, Warwick B. Elley

Population: Ages 7 to 14 years

Purpose: Assesses comprehension of orally presented material

Description: This test measures the child's ability to understand orally presented material of the kind commonly heard. Each stimulus passage contains approximately 100 to 300 words, depending on its type and placement in the test, and is typically followed by five or six multiple-choice items, each with four or five options. For the intermediate and secondary levels, the stimulus material is presented on audiocassette tape; the teacher reads from a script for the primary test. Recall and inferential questions are included at each class level.

Format: Examiner required; group administration; timed: 55 minutes

Scoring: Hand key

Cost: Manual $9.00; Booklet $1.80; 10 Answer Sheets $1.44; Key $.99

Receptive One-Word Picture Vocabulary Test–2000 (ROWPVT-2000)

2000	Academic Therapy Publications

Rick Brownell

Population: Ages 2 to 18 years

Purpose: Provides assessment of English hearing vocabulary

Description: This 170-item test provides a measure of receptive vocabulary. The test is co-normed with the *Expressive One-Word Picture Vocabulary Test–2000* on a representative national sample of over 2,000 individuals. Pronunciation guides are provided for the more difficult words. Record forms include detailed instructions for test administration. Newly rendered test plates provide full-color drawings; a number of test items are new to this edition. Raw scores are converted to standard scores, percentile ranks, and age equivalents.

Format: Examiner required; individual administration; untimed: 20 minutes

Scoring: Examiner evaluated

Cost: Test Kit (manual, test plates, 25 English record forms, in portfolio) $145.00

Structured Photographic Expressive Language Test–3 (SPELT-3)

2003	Janelle Publications, Inc.

Janet I. Dawson, Connie Stout, Julia Eyer

Population: Ages 4 to 9 years

Purpose: Measures expressive use of morphology and syntax

Description: New edition includes 54 new full-color photographs of everyday situations and objects aired with simple verbal questions and statements to elicit specific morphological and syntactic structures. It allows for analysis of specific language structures that may not occur in spontaneous language samples. Target structures include prepositions, articles, plurals, possessive nouns and pronouns, subject pronouns, auxiliary verbs, copulas, present participles, past tense, third person markers, as well as negative, conjoined sentence, "wh" question, interrogative reversal, infinitive phrase, propositional complement, relative clause, and front embedded clause. Standard scores and test-age equivalents are provided for females and males. A chapter on African American English and a scoring guide are included in the manual. Also available in Spanish.

Format: Examiner required; individual administration; untimed: 15 to 20 minutes

Scoring: Examiner evaluated

Cost: Complete Kit (manual, picture book, 50 response forms, storage box) $140.00

Structured Photographic Expressive Language Test–Preschool 2 (SPELT-P2)

1983   Janelle Publications, Inc.

Janet I. Dawson, Connie Stout, Julia Eyer, Pat Tattersall, Jan Fonkalsrud, Karen Croley

Population: Ages 3 to 5 years

Purpose: Measures abilities in expression of early developing morphological and syntactic features

Description: New edition includes 44 new full-color photographs of everyday situations and objects aired with simple verbal questions and statements to elicit specific morphological and syntactic structures. It allows for analysis of specific language structures that may not occur in spontaneous language samples. Target structures include prepositions, articles, plurals, possessive nouns and pronouns, subject pronouns, auxiliary verbs, copulas, present participles, past tense, third person markers, as well as negative, conjoined sentence, "wh" question, interrogative reversal, infinitive phrase, propositional complement, relative clause, and front embedded clause. Standard scores and test-age equivalents are provided for females and males. A chapter on African American English and a scoring guide are included in the manual. Also available in Spanish.

Format: Examiner required; individual administration; untimed: 15 to 20 minutes

Scoring: Examiner evaluated

Cost: Complete Kit (manual, picture book, 50 response forms) $140.00

Visual Processing

Aniselkonia Vision Test

Date not listed   Richmond Products, Inc.

Population: Ages 6 years to adult

Purpose: Identifies individuals with Aniselkonia vision defects

Description: Provides a series of plates to separate those with normal vision from those with Aniselkonia (one eye sees a larger size image than the other). PC version also calculates changes to eyewear prescription required to ameliorate affect.

Format: Examiner required; individual administration; untimed: 5 minutes

Scoring: Examiner evaluated

Cost: Book Version $220.00; PC Version $399.00

Basic Visual Motor Association Test (BVMAT)

1990   James Battle and Associates, Ltd.

James Battle

Population: Ages 6 to 15 years

Purpose: Measures visual motor skills; applicable for tutoring and remediation

Description: Multiple item paper–pencil test of visual integration, symbol integration, visual association, recall of visual symbols, and visual sequencing. Available in two forms: A and B (60 items each). Also available in large print and in French.

Format: Examiner required; individual or group administration; timed: 3 minutes

Scoring: Hand key; test scoring service available from publisher

Cost: Complete Battery (25 each Form A and B, manual) $50.00

Benton Visual Retention Test®, Fifth Edition

1991   Harcourt Assessment, Inc.

Abigail Benton Sivan

Population: Ages 8 years to adult

Purpose: Measures visual memory, visual perception, and visual attention

Description: Ten-item test of visual perception, visual memory, and visuo-constructive abilities. Items are designs that are shown to the subject one by one. The subject studies each design and reproduces it as exactly as possible by drawing it on plain paper. Materials include Design Cards and three alternate and equivalent forms. C, D, and E.

Format: Examiner required; individual administration; untimed: 15 minutes

Scoring: Examiner evaluated

Cost: Complete Set (manual, stimulus booklet— all 30 designs, scoring templates, 25 response-booklets record forms) $199.00

Comprehensive Test of Visual Functioning (CTVF)

1990   Slosson Educational Publishing, Inc.

Sue Larson, Evelyn Buethe, Gary J. Vitali

Population: Ages 8 years to adult

Purpose: Provides a profile of a person's ability in total visual processing

Description: The CTVF was designed to be a brief and meaningful assessment device to accurately detect and discriminate visual processing problems. The CTVF is an excellent complement to traditional assessments of IQ and standardized reading and neuropsychological evaluations. It is appropriate for multiple professions. No specific training is required. The CTVF may be used with populations manifesting visual-perceptual problems secondary to acute or chronic disorder processes.

Format: Examiner required; individual administration; untimed: 25 minutes

Scoring: Examiner evaluated

Cost: Complete Kit (manual, protocol, test booklets, cards) $136.50

DeGangi-Berk Test of Sensory Integration (TSI)

1983   Western Psychological Services

Georgia A. DeGangi, Ronald A. Berk

Population: Ages 3 to 5 years

Purpose: Measures overall sensory integration in preschool children; screens for young children with delays in sensory, motor, and perceptual skills in order to facilitate intervention programs

Description: Performance test with 36 items in three subdomains of sensory integration: postural control, bilateral motor integration, and reflex integration. The examiner rates the child's response to each item on a numerical scale, indicating abnormal to normal development.

Format: Examiner required; individual administration; untimed: 30 minutes

Scoring: Examiner required

Cost: Kit (test materials, 25 star design sheets, 25 protocol booklets, manual, carrying case) $192.50

Denver Eye Screening Test (DEST)

1973   Denver Developmental Materials, Inc.

William K. Frankenburg, J. Goldstein, A. Barker

Population: Ages 6 months to 7 years

Purpose: Helps evaluate eye problems and strabismus in children to determine if a child needs specialized testing

Description: Performance test in which the examiner shows seven picture cards and asks the child to name the picture at 15 feet. For children aged 6 months to 2 years 5 months, the examiner uses an "E" card and a spinning toy to attract the child's attention and examines his or her eyes to see if they track; first one eye is tested, then the other. Materials consist of picture cards, cord, toy, and "E" card. A flashlight is required. The alternate cover test and pupillary light reflex test are used to detect strabismus.

Format: Examiner required; individual administration; untimed: 10 minutes

Scoring: Examiner evaluated

Cost: Complete Kit (manuals, picture cards, manipulatives, 25 forms) $24.00

Developmental Test of Visual-Motor Integration–Third Edition (Beery VMI™)

1996	Pearson Assessments

Keith E. Beery, Norman A. Buktencia

Population: Ages 3 to 18 years

Purpose: Measures students' visual-motor skills by duplicating geometric figures

Description: Multiple-item paper–pencil test measuring the integration of visual perception and motor behavior. Test items, arranged in order of increasing difficulty, consist of geometric figures that the children are asked to copy. The Short Test Form (18 figures) is used with children ages 3 to 8. The Long Test Form (27 figures) is used with children ages 3 to 18 and adults with developmental delays. The manual includes directions for administration, scoring criteria, developmental comments, age norms, suggestions for teaching, percentiles, and standard score equivalents.

Format: Examiner required; individually administered; untimed: 10 to 15

Scoring: Examiner evaluated

Cost: Starter Kit (manual, 10 each of short form, long form, motor, visual) $106.65

Developmental Test of Visual Perception–Adolescent and Adult (DTVP-A)

2002	PRO-ED, Inc.

Cecil R. Reynolds, Nils A. Pearson, Judith K. Voress

Population: Ages 11 to 74 years

Purpose: Measures visual-perceptual and visual-motor abilities

Description: The DTVP-A is the latest version of Marianne Frostig's milestone test battery. The DTVP-A is an extension and redevelopment of this classic work, designed for use with adolescents and adults. The DTVP-A is especially useful in the evaluation of the neuropsychological integrity of TBI and stroke patients in which right hemisphere function may be at issue. There is sufficient floor to allow accurate assessment of individuals with severe TBI and other neurological impairment. The reliability of the various subtests and index scores indicates the DTVP-A will be sensitive to improvement over the course of treatment. The six subtests were built to conform to the visual perception constructs espoused by Marianne Frostig: Copying, Figure–Ground, Visual-Motor Search, Visual Closure, Visual-Motor Speed, and Form Constancy. There are three index scores: General Visual Perceptual, Motor-Reduced Visual Perception, and Visual-Motor Integration. Subtests were developed to be appropriate for adolescents and adults. Validity evidence shows that all DTVP-A subtests and indexes are useful for measuring visual-perceptual and visual-motor integration skills.

Format: Examiner required; individual administration; untimed: 25 minutes

Scoring: Examiner evaluated

Cost: Complete Kit (manual, picture book, 25 protocols, 25 response booklets, storage box) $200.00

Developmental Test of Visual Perception–Second Edition (DTVP-2)

1993	PRO-ED, Inc.

Donald D. Hammill, Nils A. Pearson, Judith K. Voress

Population: Ages 4 to 10 years

Purpose: Distinguishes between visual perception and visual motor problems

Description: Multiple-item instrument based on Marianne Frostig's milestone test battery yields scores for both pure visual perception with no motor response and visual-motor integration ability. The eight subtests are Eye–Hand Coordination, Copying, Spatial Relations, Position in Space, Figure–Ground, Visual Closure, Visual-Motor Speed, and Form Constancy. Standard scores, percentiles, and age equivalents are provided for each subtest, as well as the composites of General Visual Perception, Motor-Reduced Perception, and Visual-Motor Integration.

Format: Examiner required; individual administration; untimed: 35 minutes

Scoring: Examiner evaluated

Cost: Complete Kit (manual, picture book, 25 protocols, 25 scoring forms, storage box) $200.00

Dvorine Color Vision Test

Date not provided	Harcourt Assessment, Inc.

Israel Dvorine

Population: Adults

Purpose: Screens applicants for jobs that require color-discrimination abilities

Description: The test can ascertain type, as well as severity, of color blindness. Consists of a bound set of color plates that feature a number of designs made of colored dots against a background of contrasting dots. The figures are easily identified by persons with normal vision, but not by those with color blindness. There are two parts: nomenclature and tracing.

Format: Examiner required; individual administration; untimed: 2 minutes

Scoring: Examiner evaluated

Cost: Color Plates $390.00; 35 Record Forms $40.00

Farnsworth Color Deficiency Test (D-15)

1940	Richmond Products, Inc.

Population: Ages 5 years and older

Purpose: Diagnoses color deficiencies

Description: Measures color deficiencies as to color and depth of problem. This is a modification of the well known *Farnsworth-Munsell 100 Hue Test* intended for classification instead of in-depth study of color vision defects. The Farnsworth D-15 is called dichotomous because it was designed to separate subjects into one of two groups: (1) strongly color deficient or (2) mildly color deficient or color normal. This is accomplished by the arrangement of vivid (saturated) color discs. This makes the test fairly easy, and a nonperfect score is indicative of a strong color deficiency.

Format: Examiner required; individual administration; untimed: 10 to 15 minutes

Scoring: Hand key

Cost: $180.00

Full Range Test of Visual-Motor Integration (FRTVMI)

2005	PRO-ED, Inc.

Donald D. Hammill, Nils A. Pearson, Judith K. Voress, Cecil R. Reynolds

Population: Ages 5 to 74 years

Purpose: Assesses the ability to accurately relate visual stimuli to motor responses

Description: The test requires the person being tested to copy a series of increasingly complicated designs. Each item is rated 0, 1, 2, or

3. This range of points makes it possible for the examiner to distinguish readily among students with severe visual-motor problems and students with exceptional copying skills. Results are reported in standard scores, percentiles, and age equivalents.

Format: Examiner required; individual or group administration; untimed: 20 minutes

Scoring: Examiner evaluated

Cost: Complete Kit (manual, 50 protocols, storage box) $169.00

HRR Color Vision Test

2002	Richmond Products, Inc.

Population: Ages 4 to adult

Purpose: Identifies individuals with both congenital and acquired color vision defects

Description: Provides a screener series of plates to separate those with normal color vision from those with defective color vision. Further plates can be used to diagnose individuals with defective color vision in terms of the classification of defect (protan, deutan, or tritan) and severity defect.

Format: Examiner required; individual administration; untimed: 5 minutes

Scoring: Examiner evaluated

Cost: Standard Version $219.00

HRR Pseudoisochromatic Plates

2002	Richmond Products, Inc.

LeGrand Hardy, Gertrude Rand, M. Catherine Rittler

Population: Ages 3 years and older

Purpose: Screens for color perception deficiency

Description: Measures color deficiency separately for red, green, blue, and yellow. The HRR screener has three purposes: Screening test to separate those with defective color vision from those with normal color vision; a qualitative diagnostic test to classify the type of color defect, whether protan or deutan, tritan or tetartan; and a quantitative test to indicate the degree of the defect, whether mild, medium, or strong. There is growing evidence that adult acquired color deficiency, especially in the yellow and blue perception, can indicate medicinal toxicity and other problems. Included in the HRR are four demonstration plates, six screener plates, and the 14 diagnostic series.

Format: Examiner required; individual administration; untimed: 10 to 15 minutes

Scoring: Hand key

Cost: $219.00

Inventory of Perceptual Skills (IPS)

1983	Stoelting Company

Donald R. O'Dell

Population: Ages 5 to 10 years

Purpose: Assesses visual and auditory perceptual skills and provides the structure for individual remedial programs

Description: Oral-response and task-performance 79-item test assessing perceptual skills in the following areas: Visual Discrimination, Visual Memory, Object Recognition, Visual-Motor Coordination, Auditory Discrimination, Auditory Memory, Auditory Sequencing, and Auditory Blending. Once the subtests are scored and recorded on the student profile (included in the student record booklet), a graphic comparison can be made of all of the subtests. A score below the mean on any subtest indicates a weakness in that area. The test may be administered by teachers, aides, or specialists without special training. The teacher's manual contains many educational activities in visual and auditory perception. Games, exercises, and activities provide the teacher with a variety of approaches and materials to use with the student. The student workbook includes 18 exercises to improve the areas in need of remediation.

Format: Examiner required; individual administration; untimed: 15 minutes

Scoring: Examiner evaluated

Cost: Complete Set (manual, student workbook, 10 student record booklets, stimulus cards) $45.00

Jordan Left-Right Reversal Test–Revised (JLRRT)

1990	Academic Therapy Publications

Brian T. Jordan

Population: Ages 5 to 12 years

Purpose: Assesses the extent to which a child reverses letters, numbers, and words

Description: Multiple-item paper–pencil examination on two levels. Level I measures reversals of letters, numerals, and words. Level II reveals reversed lowercase letters within words and whole-word reversals within sentences. The manual includes detailed remediation exercises for reversal problems. The Laterality Checklist is an informal survey that determines whether a student prefers use of one side of his body and the Remedial Checklist provides a list of activities that can be used to develop laterality. Norm-referenced instrument provides developmental age and percentile ranks.

Format: Examiner required; individual and group administration; untimed: 20 minutes

Scoring: Examiner administered and interpreted

Cost: Test Kit (manual, protocols, checklists, in vinyl folder) $90.00

Kent Visual Perceptual Test (KVPT)

2000	Psychological Assessment Resources, Inc.

Lawrence E. Melamed

Population: Ages 5 to 11, 18 to 22, and 55 to 91

Purpose: Evaluate ability to discriminate, copy, or recall items

Description: The KVPT is a three-part test. The KVPT-D (Discrimination) requires the individual to select from a set of alternatives the item that matches a standard form. Stimuli are presented in a binder. The KVPT-C (Copy) consists of three increasingly difficult subtests requiring the individual to reproduce forms of the same type as the discrimination forms. The KVPT-M (Immediate Memory) requires the individual to locate a target form within a set of alternatives immediately following a brief exposure to the form. Stimuli are presented in a binder.

Format: Examiner required; individual administration; untimed: 25 to 30 minutes

Scoring: Examiner evaluated

Cost: Introductory Kit (manual, stimuli, 10 of each form) $216.00

Koppitz Developmental Scoring System for the Bender® Gestalt Test–Second Edition (KOPPITZ-2)

2007	PRO-ED, Inc.

Cecil R. Reynolds

Population: Ages 5 to 85 years

Purpose: Measures visual-motor integration

Description: The new KOPPITZ-2 has been expanded to cover a broad age range with additional designs and a revised scoring system to add reliability at all levels. For the first time, the instrument has been normed on a nationally stratified, census-matched sample of children and adults from throughout the United States. The KOPPITZ-2 is true to Koppitz's original conceptualization, but has been redeveloped to meet current psychometric standards. For older children and adults, both two- and three-dimensional drawings are now required that reveal subtle deficits in visual-motor processes. A chapter of the manual is devoted to the Koppitz Emotional Indicators and their proper use. A specialized scoring form is provided just for this purpose to make scoring objective and separate from the Developmental Scoring System. Detailed scoring guides and a clear template are provided. Provides standard scores and percentile ranks.

Format: Examiner required; individually administered; untimed: 5 to 10 minutes

Scoring: Examiner evaluated

Cost: Complete Kit with Bender® Cards (manual, cards, 25 each of record forms, scoring template, box) $209.00; Complete Kit Without Cards $169.00

Learning Efficiency Test-II (LET II)

1997	Academic Therapy Publications

Raymond E. Webster

Population: Ages 5 years to adult

Purpose: Used in education, rehabilitation, and cognitive assessment to measure information processing in auditory and visual modalities

Description: The LET-II provides a quick and reliable measure of visual and auditory information-processing characteristics and is useful in determining sequential processing deficits that may be related to learning problems in the classroom. The test yields information about a person's preferred modality for learning and provides valuable insights about the impact of interference on information storage and retrieval. The revised edition features an updated literature review, new case studies, expanded remediation strategies, and an improved record form and scoring system. The norms have been expanded to include adult values. Processing is assessed in two modalities (visual and auditory) and in three recall conditions (immediate recall, short-term recall, and long-term recall). The six subtest scores can be collapsed into Modality Scores and into a Global Memory Score; each score can be converted into standard scores and percentiles for comparison with other tests.

Format: Examiner required; individual administration; timed presentation, untimed response

Scoring: Examiner evaluated

Cost: Test Kit (manual, stimulus cards, 50 record forms, in vinyl folder) $92.00

McDowell Vision Screening Kit

1994	Western Psychological Services

P. Marlene McDowell, Richard L. McDowell

Population: Children

Purpose: Used for testing preschool and severely disabled children for vision problems

Description: This test assesses the functional vision of children previously considered untestable. It gives a behavioral assessment of visual performance in five areas: Distance Visual Acuity, Near Point Visual Acuity, Ocular Alignment and Motility, Color Perception, and Ocular Function. The kit contains all the toys, objects, and recording forms necessary for a comprehensive screening. The test requires no matching or verbal skills.

Format: Examiner required; individual administration; 10 to 20 minutes

Scoring: Examiner evaluated.

Cost: Kit (includes all test materials, 100 recording forms, manual) $54.00

Motor-Free Visual Perception Test-Third Edition (MVPT-3)

2003	Academic Therapy Publications

Ronald R. Colarusso, Donald D. Hammill

Population: Ages 4 to 94+ years

Purpose: Assesses visual perception without reliance on an individual's motor skills

Description: Measures skills without copying tasks. Contains many new, more difficult items at the upper end for older children and adults. Tasks include matching, figure–ground, closure, visual memory, and form discrimination. Stimuli are line drawings. Answers are presented in multiple-choice format. Responses may be given verbally or by pointing. Standard scores and percentiles are provided. Item response times may be interpreted in terms of functional behavioral categories. Clinical population comparisons are also provided.

Format: Examiner required; individual administration; untimed: 20 minutes

Scoring: Examiner evaluated

Cost: Test Kit (manual, test plates, 25 forms, portfolio) $120.00

Neitz Test of Color Vision

2000	Western Psychological Services

Jay Neitz, Phyllis Summerfelt, Maureen Neitz

Population: All ages

Purpose: Tests for color blindness

Description: The *Neitz Test of Color Vision* is a revolutionary new approach to testing for color-blindness. Accurate, quick, and inexpensive, the Neitz identifies the type and severity of color vision deficiency. It can be easily administered to people of any age, including very young children. Because it can be given to large groups at a very low cost, the Neitz makes routine screening—in school, military, and work settings—not only possible, but easy. The test includes nine items on a single sheet of paper, which is given to the examinee. Below each pattern are five smaller response options; the examinee simply marks the response that represents what he or she sees.

Format: Examiner required; individual and group administration; untimed: 5 minutes

Scoring: Examiner evaluated

Cost: Complete Kit (manual, scoring key, 10 of each version test sheets) $82.50

Ontario Society of Occupational Therapists–Perceptual Evaluation Kit (OSOT)

1991	Thomson Nelson

Marian Boys, Pat Fisher, Claire Holzberg

Population: Adults

Purpose: Assesses perceptual impairment; used for identification and monitoring of perceptual dysfunction

Description: Paper–pencil short-answer, oral response, show-and-tell, point-to test with 18 subtests: Scanning, Spatial Neglect, Motor Planning, Copying 2-D Designs, Copying 3-D Designs, Body Puzzle, Draw-a-Person, *r-l* Discrimination, Clock, Peg Board, Draw-a-House, Shape Recognition, Color Recognition, Size Recognition, *f-g* Discrimination, Proprioception, Stereognosis *r*, and Stereognosis *l*. Examiner must be a qualified occupational therapist. Also available with French manual.

Format: Examiner required; individual administration; timed and untimed

Scoring: Hand key

Cost: Kit $859.00

Perceptual Memory Task (PMT)

1985	McCarron-Dial Systems

Lawrence T. McCarron

Population: Ages 4 years and older

Purpose: Assesses individual learning style; used with special education and rehabilitation populations at any level of intellectual functioning and with physical, mental, emotional, or functional behavior disabilities

Description: Oral-response and show-and-tell 62-item test utilizing stimulus materials to assess fundamental information-processing skills essential for learning and performance, including perception and memory for spatial relationships; visual and auditory sequential memory, intermediate-term memory, and discrimination of detail. To test examinees with hearing or visual impairments (those with visual acuity of 20/400 or worse in either eye), supplementary procedures involving two alternate subtasks are provided. The instrument also assesses information-processing skills dependent on right and left cerebral functioning. Age-corrected norm tables are used to convert each subtest score to a standard score that can be profiled on the PMT Score Form to portray graphically the individual's relative strengths and/or weaknesses. Factor scores also may be determined and compared to indicate relative strengths and weaknesses in specific memory processes.

Format: Examiner required; individual administration; untimed

Scoring: Examiner evaluated; computer scoring available

Cost: Complete Set $470.00; PMT Computer Report $350.00

Perceptual-Motor Assessment for Children (P-MAC)

1988	McCarron-Dial Systems

Jack G. Dial, Lawrence T. McCarron, Garry Amann

Population: Ages 4 to 15 years

Purpose: Screens perceptual-motor skills; used by diagnosticians and classroom teachers to identify needs and provide educational management for special needs students

Description: Multiple-item oral-response point-to task-performance battery of perceptual-motor skills. The battery consists of selected subtests from the *McCarron Assessment of Neuromuscular*

Development (MAND), *Haptic Visual Discrimination Test* (HVDT), and *Perceptual Memory Task* (PMT). The P-MAC Computer Program provides scores for each area assessed. Four types of printed reports are offered: Educational Analysis Report, Classroom Report, Report of Trait Scores, and Comprehensive Evaluation Report. The computer program operates on Windows and Macintosh systems.

Format: Examiner required; individual administration; untimed

Scoring: Examiner evaluated; computer scored

Cost: Complete Set (assessment battery in single case, comprehensive manual, scoring forms, 5-volume set of Guides for Educational Management, computer program, operating manual) $2,075.00

School Nurse Vision Screening Kit

Various	Richmond Products, Inc.

Population: Ages 3 to 5 years

Purpose: Identifies children with vision problems for referral to eye care professionals

Description: This vision screening includes a textbook, vision testing devices for the recommended visual functions. Kit includes Lea Numbers™ for acuity testing at near and distance, plus tools for testing for ocular alignment, binocular vision, suppression, amblyopia, color vision, focal objects, and accommodation, plus occulders for monocular testing.

Format: Examiner required; individual administration; untimed: 15 minutes

Scoring: Examiner evaluated

Cost: $371.55

School Nurse Vision Screening Kit

Various	Richmond Products, Inc.

Population: Ages 6 years and older

Purpose: Identifies children with vision problems for referral to eye care professionals

Description: This vision screening includes a textbook and vision testing devices for the recommended visual functions. Kit includes Lea Numbers™ for acuity testing at near and distance, plus tools for testing for ocular alignment, binocular vision, suppression, amblyopia, color vision, focal objects, and accommodation, plus occulders for monocular testing.

Format: Examiner required; individual administration; untimed: 15 minutes

Scoring: Examiner evaluated

Cost: $366.80

Sensory Integration and Praxis Tests (SIPT)

1987	Western Psychological Services

A. Jean Ayres

Population: Ages 4 to 8 years

Purpose: Measures sensory integration processes that underlie learning problems and emotional disorders; used for analyzing sensory integrative dysfunction and planning treatment disorders

Description: Seventeen tests assessing aspects of sensory processing in the vestibular, proprioceptive, kinesthetic, tactile, and visual systems, as well as the behavior and learning disorders (including learning disabilities, emotional disorders, and minimal brain dysfunction) associated with inadequate integration of sensory input from these systems. The subtests are space Visualization, Figure–Ground Perception, Manual Form Perception, Kinesthesia, Finger Identification, Graphesthesia, Localization of Tactile Stimuli, Praxis on Verbal Command, Design Copying, Constructional Praxis, Postural Praxis, Oral Praxis, Sequencing Praxis, Bilateral Motor Coordination, Standing and Walking Balance, Motor Accuracy, and Postrotary Nystagmus. Computer scoring and interpretation are available. The ChromaGraph for SIPT provides an eight-color single-page visual summary of major testing and statistical results.

Format: Examiner required; individual administration; untimed

Scoring: Computer scored

Cost: Set (all test materials, 10 copies of each consumable test form, manual, carrying case) $929.50

Slosson Visual-Motor Performance Test (S-VMPT)

1962	Slosson Educational Publishing, Inc.

Richard L. Slosson, Charles L. Nicholson

Population: Ages 4 years to adult

Purpose: Measures visual-motor integration

Description: Individuals are asked to copy geometric figures, increasing in complexity, without the use of a ruler or other aid.

Format: Examiner required; group administration; untimed

Scoring: Examiner evaluated

Cost: Complete Kit $86.75

Slosson Visual Perceptual Skill Screener (SVPSS)

2006	Slosson Educational Publishing, Inc.

Bradley T. Erford

Population: Ages 5 to 10 years

Purpose: Measures ability to perceive visual information

Description: Three 20-item subtests (Visual Discrimination, Visual Figure–Ground, and Visual Closure) are helpful in diagnosing children with learning disabilities, visual-perceptual deficiencies, and visual processing disorders.

Format: Examiner required; group administration; untimed

Scoring: Examiner evaluated

Cost: Complete Kit $129.75

Standard Pseudoisochromatic Plates, Book 1

1978	Richmond Products, Inc.

H. Ichikawa

Population: Ages 6 years and older

Purpose: Screens for red and green color deficiencies

Description: A series of color plates designed to provide the most accurate discrimination of subjects with color deficiency from those without. The screening plates are accurate in the detection of even mild color defects. The diagnostic plates are effective for accurate classification of mild, moderate, and severe color defects. This series of pseudoisochromatic plates provides a rapid and easily administered test that lends itself especially well to mass screening.

Format: Requires examiner; administered individually; untimed: 8 to 10 minutes

Scoring: Hand key

Cost: $188.00

Standard Pseudoisochromatic Plates, Book 2

1983	Richmond Products, Inc.

H. Ichikawa

Population: Adults

Purpose: Screens for adult acquired color deficiency

Description: In this set of plates, emphasis is on the blue–yellow defect as this is often a presenting sign of various diseases. Plates for the acquired red–green defect, as well as two plates for scotopic vision, have been included to complete the series with appropriate plates to test all acquired color vision problems.

Format: Requires examiner; administered individually; untimed: 8 to 10 minutes

Scoring: Hand key

Cost: $188.00

Test of Handwriting Scale–Revised (THS-R)

2007	Academic Therapy Publications

Michael Milone

Population: Ages 6 to 18 years

Purpose: Assesses visual-motor integration seen in handwriting skills (manuscript or cursive)

Description: The THS-R measures neurosensory integration ability. Manuscript or cursive, uppercase and lowercase forms from the following are assessed: writing letters of the alphabet in alpha sequence from memory; writing letters of the alphabet out of alpha order from dictation; writing 8 numerals out of numerical order from dictation; copying 12 uppercase and 10 lowercase letters; copying 6 words and 2 sentences; and writing 6 words from dictation. Includes a CD tutorial.

Format: Examiner required; group administration; untimed: 30 to 40 minutes

Scoring: Examiner evaluated

Cost: Complete Test (manual, 15 each of cursive and manuscript booklets, 30 record forms) $120.00

Test of Pictures/Forms/Letters/Numbers Spatial Orientation and Sequencing Skills (TPFLNSOSS)

1991	Academic Therapy Publications

Morrison F. Gardner

Population: Ages 5 to 8 years

Purpose: Measures the ability to visually form letters and numbers in the correct direction and to visually perceive words with the letters in the correct sequence

Description: There are seven subtests: Spatial Relationships (Pictures and Forms), Reversed Letter and Number, Reversed Letter(s) in Words, Reversed Letters from Non-Reversed Letters and Numbers, and Letter Sequencing. No verbal responses are required; all responses are made in the test booklet.

Format: Examiner required; individual or group administration; untimed: 10 to 15 minutes

Scoring: Examiner evaluated

Cost: Complete Kit (manual, 25 test booklets) $55.00

Test of Visual-Motor Scale–Revised (TVMS-R)

1995	Academic Therapy Publications

Morrison F. Gardner

Population: Ages 3 to 13 years

Purpose: Measures visual-motor abilities

Description: The test contains 23 geometric forms that are scored based on eight classifications: closure, angles, intersecting lines, size, rotation or reversal, length of lines, overpenetration or underpenetration, and modification of form Norms for an individual's errors and accuracies are included. The TVMS-R was standardized on approximately 1,500 individuals.

Format: Examiner required; individual or group administration, untimed: 3 to 6 minutes

Scoring: Examiner evaluated; 15 to 20 minutes

Cost: Complete Test (manual, 15 test booklets, 15 scoring forms, protractor) $90.00

Test of Visual-Motor Scale–Revised Alternate Scoring Method [TVMS-R (ASM)]

1997	Academic Therapy Publications

Morrison F. Gardner

Population: Ages 3 to 13 years

Purpose: Measures visual-motor abilities

Description: The purpose of this method of scoring the geometric forms is to give examiners a more refined diagnosis of an individual's visual-motor strengths and weaknesses in eight categories. The Alternate Scoring Method is a 0, 1, 2, or 3.

Format: Examiner required; individual administration; untimed: 10 to 20 minutes

Scoring: Examiner evaluated

Cost: Complete Test (manual, 15 test booklets, 15 profile forms) $74.00

Test of Visual-Motor Skills: Upper Level [TVMS(UL)]

1992	Academic Therapy Publications

Morrison F. Gardner

Population: Ages 12 to 39 years

Purpose: Measures visual-motor abilities

Description: The test comprises 16 geometric figures arranged in increasing order of difficulty, each of which is to be copied. Each figure is scored for a variety of discrete errors (from a minimum of 9 to a maximum of 22 errors per figure). Standard scores are provided. A specific feature is having only one form per page. All 16 forms are in a single test booklet.

Format: Examiner required; individual or group administration; untimed: 5 to 10 minutes

Scoring: Examiner evaluated; 15 to 20 minutes

Cost: Complete Kit (manual, 25 test booklets, 25 scoring sheets, protractor) $70.00

Test of Visual-Perceptual Scale–Third Edition (TVPS-3)

2006	Academic Therapy Publications

Nancy A. Martin

Population: Ages 4 to 18 years

Purpose: Assesses visual-perceptual skills

Description: Black-and-white line drawings are presented in a multiple-choice format; responses are verbal (or by pointing). Tasks include Visual Discrimination, Visual Memory, Visual-Spatial Relationships, Form Constancy, Visual Sequential Memory, Figure–Ground, and Visual Closure. Raw scores are reported as scaled scores and percentile ranks for each subtest; Index (Basic Processes, Sequencing, and Complex Processes) and Overall score are reported as standard scores and percentile ranks. Age equivalents are provided.

Format: Examiner required; individual administration; untimed: 25 minutes

Scoring: Examiner evaluated

Cost: Complete Test (manual, test plates, 25 record forms) $150.00

Useful Field of View (UFOV)

| 1998 | Harcourt Assessment, Inc. |

Karlene Ball, Daniel Roenker

Population: Adults

Purpose: Predicts a driver's risk of accident involvement

Description: A computer-administered and scored test of visual attention that determines the size of a driver's perceptual window. Three parts measure components of an examinee's useful field of view: central vision and processing speed, divided attention, and selective attention. Rapidly presented target objects are viewed on a computer monitor, with the information displayed progressing from simple to complex. The software administers, scores, interprets responses, and prints a report that may be given to an examinee unedited. A risk level is assigned for each part.

Format: Computer administered; untimed: 15 minutes

Scoring: Computer scored

Cost: Complete Kit (manual, reference card, CD, 5 uses) $165.00

VCWS 205—Independent Perceptual Screening (Special Aptitude)

| 1982 | Valpar International Corporation |

Population: Ages 15 years and older

Purpose: Assesses worker qualification profile factors for job, curricula placement, and career planning

Description: Criterion-referenced work sample consisting of demonstrated performance of pin placement, pin assembly, six-part assembly, and three-dimensional assembly. Measures special aptitude, reasoning, general learning ability, form perception, motor coordination, and finger and manual dexterity. The test yields methods-time measurement percentage scores. Materials include assembly board, parts bin, and assorted assembly parts. This test is suitable for individuals with hearing, physical, or mental impairments. Signing for those with hearing impairments is necessary. Learning curve allows for multiple administrations as needed.

Format: Examiner required; individual administration; timed: 25 to 30 minutes

Scoring: Examiner evaluated

Cost: $695.00

Visual-Aural Digit Span Test (VADS)

| 1977 | Harcourt Assessment, Inc. |

Elizabeth M. Koppitz

Population: Ages 5 years 6 months to 12 years

Purpose: Diagnoses specific problems in reading recognition and spelling for children who can read and write digits; used to develop IEPs for children who are learning disabled

Description: Multiple-item test in which digit sequences on 26 test cards must be reproduced from memory, first orally, then in writing after being presented orally; and, finally, as a separate series, visually. The test measures auditory, visual, visual–auditory and auditory–visual integration; sequence and recall of digits; and organization of written material. There are 11 scores, which are interpreted individually. Also available in Spanish.

Format: Examiner required; suitable for group use; untimed: 10 minutes

Scoring: Examiner evaluated

Cost: Complete Kit (cards, directions, 100 scoring sheets) $80.00; Manual $107.00

Visual Skills Appraisal (VSA)

| 1984 | Academic Therapy Publications |

Regina G. Richards, Gary S. Oppenheim

Population: Ages 5 to 9 years

Purpose: Measures visual pursuit and tracking

Description: A screening tool to assist in the identification of visual inefficiencies that may affect school performance. Six subtests assess pursuit, scanning, alignment, and locating movements; eye–hand coordination; and fixation unity. The manual includes many visual skill training techniques that are keyed to each subtest.

Format: Examiner required; individual administration; untimed: 10 to 15 minutes

Scoring: Examiner evaluated

Cost: Test Kit (manual, stimulus cards, 25 each of 3 forms, red/green glasses, in vinyl folder) $85.00

Washer Visual Acuity Screening Technique (WVAST)

| 1984 | Scholastic Testing Service, Inc. |

Rhonda Wiczer Washer

Population: Mental age 2 years 6 months to adult

Purpose: Measures the visual abilities of individuals with severe mental challenges (mental age 2.6 years to adult), low-functioning, and very young children; used for screening groups of children to identify those with possible visual impairments

Description: Point-to vision test for screening both near- and far-point acuity. The testing procedure omits as many perceptual, motor, and verbal skills as possible. A conditioning process is outlined for familiarizing individuals with the symbols, matching skills, and eye occlusion used in the screening. Examiner must be certified for assessment.

Format: Examiner required; suitable for group use; untimed

Scoring: Examiner evaluated

Cost: Specimen Set $22.00

Wide Range Assessment of Visual Motor Ability (WRAVMA)

| 1995 | Psychological Assessment Resources, Inc. |

Wayne Adams, David Sheslow

Population: Ages 3 to 17 years

Purpose: Measures visual-motor integration

Description: Visual-motor integration is assessed by measuring its component parts: Visual-Motor, Visual-Spatial, and Fine-Motor abilities. These three areas can be measured individually or in combination. Each of the three subtests was

standardized nationally on the same stratified sample of over 2,600 children.

Format: Examiner required; suitable for group administration; untimed; 5 to 10 minutes per subtest

Scoring: Hand key; examiner evaluated

Cost: Kit (manual; 25 each of drawing forms, matching forms, and examiner forms; pegboard and pegs, pencils and markers; case) $285.00

Wilson Driver Selection Test

| 1986 | Martin M. Bruce, PhD |

Clark L. Wilson

Population: Adults

Purpose: Evaluates visual attention, depth visualization, eye-hand coordination, steadiness, and recognition of details; used by driver selection, evaluation companies, and schools to screen personnel in order to reduce the risk of operator-caused accidents

Description: Six-part paper-pencil nonverbal test measuring visual attention, depth perception, recognition of simple and complex details, eye hand coordination, and steadiness. The booklet includes norms for males and females, as well as items on the subject's accident record and personal history. Suitable for individuals with physical, hearing, or visual impairments.

Format: Examiner required; suitable for group use; timed: 26 minutes

Scoring: Hand key

Cost: Specimen Set $59.95

Business Instruments

The tests described in the Business Instruments section generally are used for personnel selection, evaluation, development, and promotion. In addition, the reader is encouraged to consult both the Psychology Instruments and the Education Instruments sections for other assessment tools that may be of value in the area of business.

General Aptitude

ACER Select

2003	Australian Council for Educational Research Limited

Population: Ages 15 years and older

Purpose: Assesses general intellectual ability

Description: A quick and easily administered test of verbal and numerical reasoning, suitable for recruitment for a variety of occupations. *ACER Select* is a major revision of the well established *ACER Higher and Advanced Tests*. Four test forms provide two levels of difficulty for verbal and numerical assessment. General Select (for technical, clerical and administrative, and customer service sales) is based on the level of the *ACER Higher Tests* ML/MQ/PL/PQ, and Professional Select (professional positions that require a high level of reasoning ability, such as managers, engineers, and marketing professionals) is based on the level of *ACER Advanced Tests* AL/AQ/BL/BQ. The four tests can be used individually or in combination to provide maximum flexibility in a range of recruitment scenarios.

Format: Examiner required; group administration; untimed: Verbal, 15 minutes; Numerical, 20 minutes

Scoring: Hand key; scoring service available

Cost: Starter Kit $129.95

ACER Test of Reasoning Ability (TORA)

1990	Australian Council for Educational Research Limited

Marion M. de Lemos

Population: Ages 15 years and older

Purpose: Assesses general intellectual ability

Description: A predominantly verbal test of general ability, based on the *ACER Test of Cognitive Ability* that has been converted to a multiple-choice format. The 70 items include content that involves numerical and verbal reasoning. Examples of the types of items are analogies, word meanings, numerically based problems, number series, and number matrices.

Format: Examiner required; individual and group administration; untimed: 45 minutes

Scoring: Hand key; scoring service available

Cost: Contact publisher

ACER Word Knowledge Test: Form F

1990	Australian Council for Educational Research Limited

Marion de Lemos

Population: Adults

Purpose: Measures verbal skills and general reasoning ability

Description: Tests of word knowledge have been found to correlate highly with other measures of verbal skills and general reasoning ability. Because they are relatively quick and easy to administer, they have been widely used as screening tests. This test enables the user to assess quickly student knowledge of word meanings. Students are required to select, from a list of five alternatives, the word or phrase that most closely approximates the meaning of each of the 72 items.

Format: Examiner required; group administration; untimed: 10 minutes

Scoring: Hand key; scoring service available

Cost: Contact publisher

Adaptability Test

| 1942 | Pearson Performance Solutions |

Joseph Tiffin, C. H. Lawshe

Population: Adults

Purpose: Measures mental adaptability and alertness; distinguishes between people who should be placed in jobs requiring more learning ability and those who should be in more simple or routine jobs

Description: Paper–pencil 35-item test consisting primarily of verbal items. The test predicts success in a variety of business and industrial situations. The test is available in two forms.

Format: Examiner required; suitable for group use; timed: 15 minutes

Scoring: Hand key

Cost: Contact publisher

Applied Technology Series (ATS) Diagrammatic Thinking (DTS6)

| 1988 | SHL People Performance |

Population: Adults

Purpose: Looks at the ability to follow a sequence of interdependent symbols arranged in a logical order

Description: This 36-item test is arranged in the form of simple flowcharts and involves keeping track of changes in shape, size, and color of objects. This aptitude to apply checks and follow sequences is likely to be relevant in following process control systems, in debugging software, and in systems design. Also available in French.

Format: Examiner required; individual administration; untimed: 20 minutes

Scoring: Hand key; machine scored; scoring service available

Cost: Contact publisher

Applied Technology Series (ATS) Fault Finding (FTS4)

| 1988 | SHL People Performance |

Population: Adults

Purpose: Assesses the ability to identify faults in logical systems

Description: This 36-item test requires no specialized knowledge of fault finding, but rather the ability to locate what element in an arrangement of color-coded symbols is not working as specified. This ability is appropriate in many applications including those of electronics fault finding, debugging of software, process control systems, and in systems design. Also available in French.

Format: Examiner required; individual administration; untimed: 20 minutes

Scoring: Hand key; machine scored; scoring service available

Cost: Contact publisher

Applied Technology Series (ATS) Spatial Checking (STS5)

| 1988 | SHL People Performance |

Population: Adults

Purpose: Measures the ability to locate differences between complex designs rotated and reversed in two or three dimensions

Description: This 40-item test measures the ability to locate differences between complex designs rotated and reversed in two or three dimensions. This ability is important in the checking and design of electronic systems, in engineering components, and in some applications of computer-aided design. Each item in this test involves identifying mismatches between master and copy designs. Also available in French.

Format: Examiner required; individual administration; untimed: 15 minutes

Scoring: Hand key; machine scored; scoring service available

Cost: Contact publisher

Barron Welsh Art Scale (BWAS)

| 1987 | Mind Garden, Inc. |

Frank Barron, George S. Welsh

Population: Adolescents, adults

Purpose: Measures creativity

Description: This 86-item abstract of the *Welsh Figure Preference Test* contains all items in the Art Scale and the Revised Art Scale. The BWAS has been used in many studies of creativity. It does not require respondents to read or write and may be administered in any language. High scorers on the scale manifest greater strength of primary processes in ego functioning, such as symbolization, condensation, and substitution. "Reality" is thereby transmuted into new forms and into creative individual visions. Secondary processes stress logic, planfulness, goal directedness, and adherence to form. The truly creative person has access to the primary, even primitive, functions of the ego, but not at the cost of abandoning logical reality. Whatever the ultimate nature of the configuration or style of personality captured in scores on the BWAS—and the search for such an absolute may be as futile and meaningless as a search for the philosopher's stone—there is no doubt about the convergence of our own studies, as well as those cited in the appended bibliography in showing that the measures do identify creative talent, and that they do this independently of intelligence, personal soundness, gender, age, and other powerful determinants that all too often limit the utility of our assessment tools.

Format: Self-administered; untimed

Scoring: Examiner evaluated

Cost: Manual/Sampler Set $30.00; 200 Uses $150.00

California Reasoning Appraisal (CRA)

1999	Insight Assessment

Population: Ages 18 years and older

Purpose: Measures reasoning skills that are essential to success at the professional and managerial levels

Description: The CRA has multiple-choice items intended for individuals with advanced reasoning skills (in the top 20% of the general population). Selected items on the CRA require analyzing and interpreting complex material; drawing correct inferences from diagrammatic and textual information; evaluating inferences which are provided; providing a cogent reason to support an evaluation; evaluating objections to stated inferences; providing justifications for these evaluations; and analyzing charts, graphs, and other quantitatively presented information. There is a long form with 78 items and a short form of 39 items. Online testing is available.

Format: Examiner required; group administration; timed and untimed: 1 to 2 hours

Scoring: Machine scored; scoring service available

Cost: Specimen Kit (manual, 1 protocol, 1 CapScore™ answer form) $25.00

Closure Flexibility (Concealed Figures)

1984	Pearson Performance Solutions

L. L. Thurstone, T. E. Jeffrey

Population: Adolescents, adults

Purpose: Measures the ability to hold a configuration in mind despite distracting irrelevancies, as indicated by identification of a given figure "hidden" or embedded in a larger more complex drawing; used for vocational counseling and selection of personnel

Description: Paper-pencil 49-item test measuring visual and space perception skills. Each item consists of a figure, presented on the left of the page, followed by a row of four more complex drawings. The subject must indicate whether the figure appears or does not appear in each of the drawings.

Format: Examiner required; suitable for group use; timed: 10 minutes

Scoring: Hand key

Cost: Contact publisher

Comprehensive Ability Battery (CAB)

1975	Institute for Personality and Ability Testing, Inc.

A. Ralph Hakstian, Raymond B. Cattell

Population: High school and older

Purpose: Measures various talents and basic skills; used for selection, training, needs analysis, and career counseling

Description: A group of short, timed standardized tests that measure 20 primary abilities and basic skills. Each test measures one ability factor and each factor contributes a measure of ability important in industrial settings and career and vocational counseling. The tests in the batteries may be used individually or in combination. There are five batteries that are in four forms. Percentile norms for males, females, or combined for each test at the high school level are available.

Format: Examiner required; group administration; timed: 5 to 7 minutes for each subtest

Scoring: Examiner evaluated

Cost: Specimen Set (1 each of four test booklets, answer and profile sheets, manual) $38.00

Cree Questionnaire

1995	Pearson Performance Solutions

Thelma Gwinn Thurstone, J. Mellinger

Population: Adults

Purpose: Evaluates an individual's overall creative potential and the extent to which his or her behavior resembles that of identified creative individuals; used for selection and placement of managerial and professional personnel and career counseling

Description: Paper–pencil 58-item test measuring the 10 factorially determined dimensions of the creative personality: dominance versus submission, independence versus conformity, autonomous versus structured work environment, pressured versus relaxed situation, high versus low energy level, fast versus slow reaction time, high versus low ideational spontaneity, high versus low theoretical interests, high versus low artistic interests, and high versus low mechanical interests.

Format: Self-administered; untimed: 15 minutes

Scoring: Hand key

Cost: Contact publisher

Critical Reasoning Test Battery (CRTB) Diagrammatic Series (DC3.1)

1991	SHL People Performance

Population: Ages 16 years to adult

Purpose: Measures critical-reasoning ability for thinking sequentially

Description: Paper–pencil 40-item test assessing the logical or analytical ability to follow a sequence of diagrams and select the next one in a series from five alternatives. The test is appropriate where logical or analytical reasoning is required, such as technical research or computer programming positions. Also available in French.

Format: Examiner required; individual administration; untimed: 20 minutes

Scoring: Hand key; machine scored; scoring service available

Cost: Contact publisher

Differential Aptitude Tests® for Personnel and Career Assessment

Date not provided	Harcourt Assessment, Inc.

George K. Bennett, Harold G. Seashore, Alexander G. Wesman

Population: Adults

Purpose: Identifies strengths and weaknesses

Description: Applicants are tested in eight key areas: Verbal Reasoning, Numerical Ability, Abstract Reasoning, Mechanical Reasoning, Space Relations, Spelling, Language Usage, and Clerical Speed and Accuracy. Each area is in a separate booklet.

Format: Examiner required; suitable for group use; can be taken online; untimed: 6 to 20 minutes per subtest

Scoring: Examiner evaluated

Cost: Examination Kit (manual, 1 of each subtest, directions) $70.00

Employee Aptitude Survey Test #1– Verbal Comprehension (EAS#1)

1984	Psychological Services, Inc.

G. Grimsley, F. L. Ruch, N. D. Warren, J. S. Ford

Population: Adults

Purpose: Measures ability to use and understand the relationships between words; used for selection and placement of executives, secretaries, professional personnel, and high-level office workers; also used in career counseling

Description: Paper–pencil 30-item multiple-choice test measuring word-relationship recognition, reading speed, and ability to understand instructions. Each item consists of a word followed by a list of four other words from which the examinee must select the one meaning the same or about the same as the first word. The test is available in two equivalent forms. Also available in German.

Format: Examiner required; suitable for group use; timed: 5 minutes

Scoring: Hand key; may be computer scored; scan scoring software available

Cost: Contact publisher

Employee Aptitude Survey Test #2– Numerical Ability (EAS#2)

1980	Psychological Services, Inc.

G. Grimsley, F. L. Ruch, N. D. Warren

Population: Adults

Purpose: Measures basic mathematical skill; used for selection and placement of executives, supervisors, engineers, accountants, sales people, and clerical workers; also used in career counseling

Description: Paper–pencil 75-item multiple-choice test arranged in three 25-item parts assessing addition, subtraction, multiplication, and division skills. Part I covers whole numbers, Part II covers decimal fractions, and Part III covers common fractions. The test is available in two equivalent forms. Also available in Spanish and German. Parts may be administered and timed separately.

Format: Examiner required; suitable for group use; timed: 10 minutes

Scoring: Hand key; may be computer scored; scan scoring software available

Cost: Contact publisher

Employee Aptitude Survey Test #3– Visual Pursuit (EAS#3)

1984	Psychological Services, Inc.

G. Grimsley, F. L. Ruch, N. D. Warren, J. S. Ford

Population: Adults

Purpose: Measures speed and accuracy in visually tracing lines through complex designs; used for selection and placement of drafters, design engineers, technicians, and other technical and production positions; also used in career counseling

Description: Paper–pencil 30-item multiple-choice test consisting of a maze of lines that weave their way from their starting points (numbered 1 to 30) on the right-hand side of the page to a column of boxes on the left. The task is to identify for each starting point the box on the left at which the line ends. Examinees are encouraged to trace with their eyes, not their pencils. The test is available in two equivalent forms. Also available in Spanish and French.

Format: Examiner required; suitable for group use; timed: 5 minutes

Scoring: Hand key; may be computer scored; scan scoring software available

Cost: Contact publisher

Employee Aptitude Survey Test #4– Visual Speed and Accuracy (EAS#4)

1980	Psychological Services, Inc.

G. Grimsley, F. L. Ruch, N. D. Warren

Population: Adults

Purpose: Measures ability to see details quickly and accurately; used to select bookkeepers, accountants, clerical and administrative personnel, and supervisors; also used in career planning

Description: Paper–pencil 150-item multiple-choice test in which each item consists of two series of numbers and symbols that the subject must compare and determine whether they are

the same or different. The test may be administered to applicants for sales, supervisory, and executive positions with the expectation that their scores will be above average. The test is available in two equivalent forms. Online form under development. Also available in Spanish.

Format: Examiner required; suitable for group use; timed: 5 minutes

Scoring: Hand key; may be computer scored; scan scoring software available

Cost: Contact publisher

Employee Aptitude Survey Test #5– Space Visualization (EAS#5)

1985	Psychological Services, Inc.

G. Grimsley, F. L. Ruch, N. D. Warren, J. S. Ford

Population: Adults

Purpose: Measures ability to visualize and manipulate objects in three dimensions by viewing a two-dimensional drawing; used to select employees for jobs requiring mechanical aptitude, like drafters, engineers, and personnel in technical and production positions

Description: Paper–pencil 50-item multiple-choice test consisting of 10 perspective line-drawings of stacks of blocks. The blocks are all the same size and rectangular in shape so that they appear to stack neatly and distinctly. Five of the blocks in each stack are lettered. The subjects must look at each lettered block and determine how many other blocks in the stack the lettered block touches. The test is available in two equivalent forms. Also available in Spanish.

Format: Examiner required; suitable for group use; timed: 5 minutes

Scoring: Hand key; may be computer scored; scan scoring software available

Cost: Contact publisher

Employee Aptitude Survey Test #6– Numerical Reasoning (EAS#6)

1985	Psychological Services, Inc.

G. Grimsley, F. L. Ruch, N. D. Warren, J. S. Ford

Population: Adults

Purpose: Measures the ability to analyze logical relationships and discover principles underlying such relationships, an important ingredient of "general intelligence"; used to select employees for professional, managerial, supervisory, and technical jobs

Description: Paper–pencil 20-item multiple-choice test in which each item consists of a series of seven numbers followed by a question mark where the next number of the series should be. Examinees must determine the pattern of each series and select (from five choices) the number that correctly fills the blank. Logic and deduction, rather than computation, are emphasized. The test is available in two equivalent forms. Online form under development. Also available in Spanish, German, and French.

Format: Examiner required; suitable for group use; timed: 5 minutes

Scoring: Hand key; may be computer scored; scan scoring software available

Cost: Contact publisher

Employee Aptitude Survey Test #7– Verbal Reasoning (EAS#7)

1985	Psychological Services, Inc.

G. Grimsley, F. L. Ruch, N. D. Warren, J. S. Ford

Population: Adults

Purpose: Measures ability to analyze information and make valid judgments about that information; also measures the ability to decide whether the available facts provide sufficient information to support a definite conclusion; used for employee selection

Description: Paper–pencil 30-item multiple-choice test consisting of six lists of facts (one-sentence statements) with five possible conclusions for each list of facts. The subject reads each list of facts and then looks at each conclusion and decides whether it is definitely true, definitely false, or unknown from the given facts. The test is available in two equivalent forms. Online form under development. Also available in Spanish and French.

Format: Examiner required; suitable for group use; timed: 5 minutes

Scoring: Hand key; may be computer scored; scan scoring software available

Cost: Contact publisher

Employee Aptitude Survey Test #8– Word Fluency (EAS#8)

1981	Psychological Services, Inc.

G. Grimsley, F. L. Ruch, N. D. Warren, J. S. Ford

Population: Adults

Purpose: Measures flexibility and ease in verbal communication; used to select sales representatives, journalists, field representatives, technical writers, receptionists, secretaries, and executives; also used in career counseling

Description: Open-ended paper–pencil test measuring word fluency by determining how many words beginning with one specific letter, given at the beginning of the test, a person can produce in a 5-minute test period (75 answer spaces are provided).

Format: Examiner required; suitable for group use; timed: 5 minutes

Scoring: Hand scored

Cost: Contact publisher

Employee Aptitude Survey Test #9– Manual Speed and Accuracy (EAS#9)

1984	Psychological Services, Inc.

G. Grimsley, F. L. Ruch, N. D. Warren, J. S. Ford

Population: Adults

Purpose: Measures ability to make fine-finger movements rapidly and accurately; used to select clerical workers, office machine operators, electronics and small parts assemblers, and employees for similar precision jobs involving repetitive tasks

Description: Multiple-item paper–pencil test consisting of a straightforward array of evenly spaced lines of 750 small circles. The applicant must place a pencil dot in as many of the circles as possible in five minutes. Also available in Spanish.

Format: Examiner required; suitable for group use; timed: 5 minutes

Scoring: Hand scored

Cost: Contact publisher

Employee Aptitude Survey Test #10– Symbolic Reasoning (EAS#10)

1985	Psychological Services, Inc.

G. Grimsley, F. L. Ruch, N. D. Warren, J. S. Ford

Population: Adults

Purpose: Measures ability to manipulate abstract symbols and use them to make valid decisions; used to evaluate candidates for positions requiring a high level of reasoning ability, such as troubleshooters, computer programmers, accountants, and engineers

Description: Paper–pencil 30-item multiple-choice test consisting of a list of abstract symbols (and their coded meanings) used to establish relationships in the pattern of "A" to "B" to "C." Given the statement, the examinee must decide whether a proposed relationship between "A" and "C" is true, false, or unknown from the given statement. The test is available in two equivalent forms. Online form under development. Also available in Spanish, German, and French.

Format: Examiner required; suitable for group use; timed: 5 minutes

Scoring: Hand key; may be computer scored; scan scoring software available

Cost: Contact publisher

IPI Employee Aptitude Series: Blocks
1986   Industrial Psychology International Ltd.

Population: Adults

Purpose: Measures aptitude to visualize objects on the basis of three-dimensional cues; used to screen applicants for mechanical and technical jobs

Description: Paper–pencil 32-item test of spatial relations and quantitative ability. The test does not require the ability to read. Also available in French and Spanish.

Format: Examiner required; suitable for group use; timed: 6 minutes

Scoring: Hand key

Cost: Introductory Kit (20 test booklets, manual) $33.00

IPI Employee Aptitude Series: Dexterity
1986   Industrial Psychology International Ltd.

Population: Adults

Purpose: Determines ability to rapidly perform routine motor tasks involving eye–hand coordination; used to screen applicants for mechanical and technical jobs

Description: Three 1-minute paper–pencil subtests (maze, checks, and dots) assess one's ability to perform routine motor tasks. The test does

not require the ability to read or write. Also available in French and Spanish.

Format: Examiner required; suitable for group use; timed: 3 minutes

Scoring: No key required

Cost: Introductory Kit (20 test booklets, manual) $33.00

IPI Employee Aptitude Series: Dimension
1986   Industrial Psychology International Ltd.

Population: Adults

Purpose: Evaluates ability to visualize objects drawn in their exact reverse; used to screen applicants for mechanical and technical jobs

Description: Paper–pencil 48-item test measuring spatial relations at a high level. The test does not require the ability to read or write. Also available in French and Spanish.

Format: Examiner required; suitable for group use; timed: 6 minutes

Scoring: Hand key

Cost: Introductory Kit (20 test booklets, scoring key, manual) $33.00

IPI Employee Aptitude Series: Fluency
1981   Industrial Psychology International Ltd.

Population: Adults

Purpose: Assesses aptitude to think of words rapidly and easily; used to screen applicants for clerical, sales, and supervisory jobs

Description: Three 2-minute paper–pencil subtest measuring the ability to write or talk without mentally blocking or searching for the right word. Also available in French and Spanish.

Format: Examiner required; suitable for group use; timed: 6 minutes

Scoring: No key required

Cost: Introductory Kit (20 test booklets, manual) $33.00

IPI Employee Aptitude Series: Judgment
1981   Industrial Psychology International Ltd.

Population: Adults

Purpose: Evaluates an individual's ability to

think logically and to deduce solutions to abstract problems; used to screen applicants for clerical, sales, and supervisory positions

Description: Paper-pencil 54-item test measuring aptitude to think logically, plan, and deal with abstract relations. Also available in French and Spanish.

Format: Examiner required; suitable for group use; timed: 6 minutes

Scoring: Hand key

Cost: Introductory Kit (20 test booklets, scoring key, manual) $33.00

IPI Employee Aptitude Series: Motor

1986	Industrial Psychology International Ltd.

Population: Adults

Purpose: Measures ability to coordinate eye and hand movements in a specific motor task; used to screen applicants for mechanical and technical jobs

Description: Three 2-minute trials of the same task that demonstrate manual dexterity and eye-hand coordination. The test requires a special motor apparatus for administration. Also available in French and Spanish.

Format: Examiner required; suitable for group use only if more than one apparatus is available; timed: 6 minutes

Scoring: No key required

Cost: Introductory Kit (20 test booklets, manual) $33.00; Motor Board $160.00

IPI Employee Aptitude Series: Numbers

1981	Industrial Psychology International Ltd.

Population: Adults

Purpose: Measures ability to perform numerical computations rapidly and accurately; used to screen applicants for clerical, administrative, mechanical, sales, technical, and supervisory positions

Description: Paper-pencil 54-item test measuring the ability to perform numerical computations and to understand mathematical concepts. This test is highly related to record keeping, typing, work planning, computational skills, and coding.

Format: Examiner required; suitable for group use; timed: 6 minutes

Scoring: Hand key

Cost: Introductory Kit (20 test booklets, scoring key, manual) $33.00

MD5 (Mental Ability Test)

Date not provided	Hogrefe Limited

D. Mackenzie Davey

Population: Adults

Purpose: Assesses a wide range of educational and ability levels of adults

Description: Paper-pencil 57-item test used with adults, including supervisors and managers, for measuring mental ability. The test involves finding missing letters, numbers, or words. Norms exist for several managerial groups, and the test is correlated with other mental ability tests.

Format: Examiner required; individual or group administration; can be computer administered; timed: 15 minutes

Scoring: Self-scored; computer scored; test scoring service available from publisher

Cost: Contact publisher

Multi-Craft Aptitude Test-Form A

2004, 2005	Ramsay Corporation

Roland T. Ramsay

Population: Adults

Purpose: Measures mechanical and electrical aptitude

Description: The paper-pencil test consists of 36 multiple-choice questions and is designed to measure the ability to learn and perform mechanical and electrical production and maintenance job activities.

Format: Examiner required; suitable for group use; timed: 20 minutes

Scoring: Examiner evaluated; scoring service available

Cost: Test Booklet $21.00 (minimum 20); Manual $24.95

Nonverbal Reasoning

1985	Pearson Performance Solutions

Raymond J. Corsini

Population: Adults

Purpose: Assesses capacity to reason logically as indicated by solutions to pictorial problems; used for job screening and selection and for vocational counseling

Description: Paper-pencil 44-item pictorial test.

The subject studies one picture and then selects from among four others the one that best compliments the first picture.

Format: Examiner required; suitable for group use; timed: 20 minutes

Scoring: Hand key

Cost: Contact publisher

Omnia 720 Composite®

Date not provided	Omnia Group, Incorporated

Population: Adults

Purpose: Measures job applicants' abilities

Description: A customized database is created using a site's top performers. Candidates are compared to this sample, showing each applicant's compatibility with the job. Also useful for promotions and department transfers.

Format: Self-administered online; untimed: 10 minutes

Scoring: Examiner evaluated; computer scored; scoring service available

Cost: Contact publisher

Omnia Profile®

1985	Omnia Group, Incorporated

J. B. Caswell, H. F. Livingstone

Population: Adults

Purpose: Measures preferred workplace behavior

Description: A simple, easy-to-complete adjective checklist includes two active behaviors and two passive behaviors. An eight-column graph indicates the subject's level of assertiveness, risk-avoidance, persuasion, analytical mindset, pace, patience, independence, and attention to detail. The report also notes energy, common sense, intensity, and stress measurements, as related to workplace behavior and career development.

Format: Self-administration; online available; untimed: 15 minutes

Scoring: Examiner evaluated; computer scored; scoring service by fax or mail

Cost: Contact publisher

Personnel Tests for Industry (PTI)

1969	Harcourt Assessment, Inc.

A. G. Wesman, J. E. Doppelt

Population: Adults

Purpose: Assesses general ability; used to se-lect workers for skilled positions in industrial settings

Description: Multiple-item paper–pencil multiple-choice tests covering two dimensions of general ability: verbal and numerical competence. Some items involve problem solving. Two equivalent forms and tapes for administering the test are available.

Format: Examiner required; suitable for group use; timed: verbal, 5 minutes; numerical, 20 minutes

Scoring: Examiner evaluated

Cost: Examination Kit (2 forms of each dimension, manual) $50.00

Personnel Tests for Industry— Oral Directions Test (PTI-ODT™)

1974 (Manual 1995)	Harcourt Assessment, Inc.

C. R. Langmuir

Population: Adults

Purpose: Assesses general mental ability and the ability to understand oral directions

Description: Recorded-format test measuring general mental ability of individuals with low ed-ucation levels or who speak English as a second language. Scores reflect minimal proficiency in conversational English and the ability to compre-hend oral directions. May be used to determine whether individuals can benefit from basic skills training, vocational training, training in conversational English, or educational remediation pro-grams. Two alternate forms.

Format: Examiner required; suitable for group use; untimed: approximately 15 minutes

Scoring: Examiner evaluated

Cost: Examination Kit (scripts, answer documents, manual) $50.00

Pictorial Reasoning Test (PRT)

1966	Pearson Performance Solutions

Robert N. McMurry, Phyllis D. Arnold

Population: Adolescents, adults

Purpose: Measures general reasoning ability of students, especially older nonreaders; used with individuals with a high school education or less, for predicting job success, and as a basic screening test for entry-level jobs

Description: Paper–pencil 80-item pictorial test measuring aspects of learning ability. The test is culturally unbiased and does not require previously learned reading skills.

Format: Examiner required; suitable for group use; timed: 15 minutes (may also be given untimed)

Scoring: Hand key

Cost: Contact publisher

Professional Employment Test
1986	Psychological Services, Inc.

Population: Adults

Purpose: Measures three cognitive abilities—verbal comprehension, quantitative problem solving, and reasoning—important for successful performance in many professional occupations; used to select professional, technical, and managerial personnel

Description: Paper–pencil multiple-choice test measuring the ability to understand and interpret complex information, determine the appropriate mathematical procedures to solve problems, and analyze and evaluate information to arrive at correct conclusions. The test includes 40 items of four item types: Reading Comprehension, Quantitative Problem Solving, Data Interpretation, and Reasoning. The test is available in two alternate forms and in a short form (20 questions). Online form is under development.

Format: Examiner required; suitable for group use; timed: regular form, 80 minutes; short form, 40 minutes

Scoring: Hand key; may be computer scored; scoring software available

Cost: Contact publisher

Security Aptitude Fitness Evaluation–Resistance (SAFE-R)
1987	Stoelting Company

John R. Taccarino

Population: Adults

Purpose: Measures honesty, dependability, socialization, substance, credibility, language, and numerical skills for employee selection

Description: Has 130 items in a multiple-choice format to assess numerical abilities, language abilities, and attitudes. Spanish version is available.

Format: Examiner required; suitable for group use; timed: 15 minutes and untimed: 20 minutes

Scoring: Computer scored; scoring service available

Cost: $225.00 to $375.00 depending on report format

Space Relations (Paper Puzzles)
1984	Pearson Performance Solutions

L. L. Thurstone, T. E. Jeffrey

Population: Adolescents, adults

Purpose: Assesses facility in visual–perceptual skills; used in vocational counseling or for selection for positions requiring mechanical ability and experience

Description: Paper–pencil 30-item test of the ability to visually select a combination of flat pieces that, together, cover a given two-dimensional space.

Format: Examiner required; suitable for group use; timed: 9 minutes

Scoring: Hand key

Cost: Contact publisher

Space Thinking (Flags)
1984	Pearson Performance Solutions

L. L. Thurstone, T. E. Jeffrey

Population: Adolescents, adults

Purpose: Assesses the ability to visualize a rigid configuration (a stable figure, drawing, or diagram) when it is moved into different positions; used for vocational counseling or selection for positions requiring mechanical ability or experience

Description: Paper–pencil 21-item test in which a solid object (flag) is pictured on the left and pictures of six positions into which the object has been moved are on the right. The examinee must identify whether each position represents the same or the opposite side of the object.

Format: Examiner required; suitable for group use; timed: 5 minutes

Scoring: Hand key

Cost: Contact publisher

Strategic Assessment of Readiness for Training (START)
1994	H & H Publishing Co., Inc.

Claire E. Weinstein, David R. Palmer

Population: Adults

Purpose: Diagnoses learning strengths and weaknesses in a work setting; used to increase a trainee's experience of the training experience; suitable for new employees and employees entering training programs

Description: Computer-administered or paper–

pencil multiple-choice test measuring anxiety, attitude, motivation, concentration, identifying important information, knowledge acquisition strategies, monitoring learning, and time management. A chart yielding total scale scores and average item scores is used as is a self-scored form or a computerized version. A Macintosh version is available.

Format: Self-administered; untimed: 20 to 30 minutes

Scoring: Computer scored; self-scored; also available on the Web

Cost: $5.95 each for 1 to 99; User's Manual $14.95

Technical Test Battery (TTB) Spatial Recognition (ST8.1)

1988	SHL People Performance

Population: Adults

Purpose: Measures basic spatial ability

Description: Test with 36 items measures the ability to recognize shapes in two dimensions.

Format: Examiner required; individual administration; untimed: 10 minutes

Scoring: Hand key; machine scored; scoring service available

Cost: Contact publisher

Technical Test Battery (TTB) Visual Estimation (ET3.1)

1992	SHL People Performance

Population: Adults

Purpose: Measures important elements of spatial perception

Description: Multiple-choice 36-item test involving the estimation of lengths, angles, and shapes. In each item, the respondent must select the two figures from a set of five that are identical in form, although in many cases they are rotated on the page.

Format: Examiner required; individual administration; untimed: 10 minutes

Scoring: Hand key; machine scored; scoring service available

Cost: Contact publisher

Test of Abstract Reasoning

2005	Australian Council for Educational Research Limited

Population: Adults

Purpose: Measures abstract reasoning

Description: A relatively language-free assessment, this can be used as a measure of general ability for selection into occupations with a moderate to high demand on reasoning and where the ability to think clearly to solve problems is important. With online administration, an instant report is generated. Also available in paper-pencil format. Available in a short (45 items) and a long (60 items) form. The short form is on an easier level and is designed for applicants with at least Year 11 and entering a variety of technical, clerical, and administrative positions. The long form is more challenging and is designed for applicants with at least Year 12 and entering roles requiring a high level of reasoning or increasing problem-solving demand over time.

Format: Examiner required; group administration; timed: short, 20 minutes; long, 25 minutes

Scoring: Examiner evaluated; online scoring

Cost: Specimen Set $36.00

Verbal Reasoning

1958	Pearson Performance Solutions

Raymond J. Corsini, Richard Renck

Population: Adults

Purpose: Assessing individual capacity to reason logically as indicated by solutions to verbal problems; used for job selection and vocational counseling

Description: Paper–pencil 36-item test of mental reasoning consisting of 12 statements with three questions each.

Format: Examiner required; suitable for group use; timed: 15 minutes

Scoring: Hand key

Cost: Contact publisher

Watson-Glaser Critical Thinking Appraisal®–Forms A & B

Date not provided	Harcourt Assessment, Inc.

Goodwin Watson, Edward M. Glaser

Population: Adults

Purpose: Predicts an employee's career path based on critical-thinking skills

Description: The 80-item test assesses five content areas: Inference, Recognition of Assumptions, Deduction, Interpretation, and Evaluation of Arguments. The manual offers percentile ranks corresponding to total scores for groups, including students, teachers, police officers, sales representatives, and state trooper applicants.

Format: Examiner required; suitable for group use; untimed: 40 to 60 minutes

Scoring: Examiner evaluated

Cost: Starter Kit for 10 Applicants (manual, answer documents, scoring key) $195.00

Wesman Personnel Classification Test (PCT)

1965	Harcourt Assessment, Inc.

A. G. Wesman,

Population: Adults

Purpose: Assesses general mental ability; used for selection of employees for sales, supervisory, and managerial positions

Description: Multiple-item paper-pencil test of two major aspects of mental ability: verbal and numerical. The verbal items are analogies. The numerical items test basic math skills and understanding of quantitative relationships. Three forms—A, B, and C—are available. The verbal part of Form C is somewhat more difficult than the verbal parts of Forms A and B.

Format: Examiner required; suitable for group use; timed: Verbal, 18 minutes; Numerical, 10 minutes

Scoring: Hand key

Cost: Examination Kit (1 booklet for each form, manual) $45.00

Wonderlic Personnel Test™ (WPT™)

1988	Wonderlic Personnel Test, Inc.

E. F. Wonderlic

Population: Adults

Purpose: Measures level of mental ability in business and industrial situations; used for selection and placement of business personnel and for vocational guidance

Description: Paper-pencil or computerized test with 50 items measuring general learning ability in verbal, spatial, and numerical reasoning. The test is used to predict an individual's ability to adjust to complex and rapidly changing job requirements and complete complex job training. Test items include analogies, analysis of geometric figures, arithmetic problems, disarranged sentences, sentence parallelism with proverbs, similarities, logic definitions, judgment, direction following, and others. Also available in Spanish, French, Mexican, Cuban, Puerto Rican, Canadian, Chinese, German, Japanese, Korean, Portuguese, Russian, Tagalog, and Vietnamese.

Format: Examiner required; suitable for group use; timed: 12 minutes; may also be administered untimed

Scoring: Hand key and test scoring available

Cost: Contact publisher

General Skills

ACER Applied Reading Test (ART)

1990	Australian Council for Educational Research Limited

Population: Ages 15 years and older

Purpose: Measures ability to read and understand technical reading material

Description: The instrument was designed for selection of apprentices, trainees, technical/trade personnel, and others who need to read and understand text. Six prose passages are presented in a reusable test booklet with four multiple-choice response alternatives for each of the items associated with each passage. The content of the passages deals with such topics as industrial safety and machine operation/maintenance, but attempts to avoid areas where knowledge, rather

reading ability, is rewarded. Two alternate forms of the ART are available; both have 32 questions.

Format: Examiner required; individual and group administration; timed: 30 minutes

Scoring: Hand key; scoring service available

Cost: Contact publisher

ACER Test of Employment Entry Mathematics (TEEM)

1992	Australian Council for Educational Research Limited

John Izard, Ian Woff, Brian Doig

Population: Ages 15 years and older

Purpose: Assesses basic mathematical ability

Description: Questions cover basic mathematical problems of a type that might be encountered in a technical or trade training course or on the Job In technical or trade positions. The test contains 32 items and is presented in a reusable multiple-choice test booklet with four response alternatives.

Format: Examiner required; individual and group administration; timed: 30 minutes

Scoring: Hand key; scoring service available

Cost: Contact publisher

Algebra—Form A

1992	Ramsay Corporation

Roland T. Ramsay

Population: Adults

Purpose: Measures knowledge of algebra

Description: A 30-item, paper–pencil test in multiple-choice format.

Format: Examiner required; suitable for group use, timed. 60 minutes

Scoring: Examiner evaluated; scoring service available

Cost: Test Booklet $12.00 (minimum 20); Manual $24.95

Applied Technology Series (ATS) Following Instructions (VTS1)

1988	SHL People Performance

Population: Adults

Purpose: Assesses the ability to follow simple technical instructions

Description: Test with 36 items measures the ability to follow written instructions. The topics covered are designed to be relevant in a technical environment and draw on the kind of materials often associated with equipment manuals or operating instructions. No prior knowledge of technical words is assumed. Also available in French.

Format: Examiner required; individual administration; untimed: 20 minutes

Scoring: Hand key; machine scored; scoring service available

Cost: Contact publisher

Applied Technology Series (ATS) Numerical Estimation (NTS2)

1988	SHL People Performance

Population: Adults

Purpose: Estimates answers to numerical calculations

Description: Test with 40 items measures the ability to estimate quickly the answers to numerical calculations. Fractions and percentages are included, as well as basic arithmetic. The task involves selecting an answer of an appropriate order of magnitude from a number of possible answers. Also available in French.

Format: Examiner required; individual administration; untimed: 10 minutes

Scoring: Hand key; machine scored; scoring service available

Cost: Contact publisher

Arithmetic—Form CO-O

1997	Ramsay Corporation

Roland T. Ramsay

Population: Adults

Purpose: Measures arithmetic skills

Description: Paper–pencil test in multiple-choice format. Evaluates the ability to perform basic computations at various levels.

Format: Examiner required; suitable for group use; timed: 24 minutes

Scoring: Examiner evaluated; scoring service available

Cost: Test Booklet $12.00 (minimum 20); Manual $24.95

Arithmetic—Form IHCR

1995	Ramsay Corporation

Roland T. Ramsay

Population: Adults

Purpose: Measures arithmetic skills

Description: Paper–pencil test in multiple-choice format. Evaluates the ability to perform basic computations at various levels.

Format: Examiner required; suitable for group use; timed: 24 minutes

Scoring: Examiner evaluated; scoring service available

Cost: Test Booklet $12.00 (minimum 20); Manual $24.95

Arithmetic—Form MCY

1997	Ramsay Corporation

Roland T. Ramsay

Population: Adults

Purpose: Measures arithmetic skills

Description: Paper–pencil test in multiple-choice format. Evaluates the ability to perform basic computations at various levels.

Format: Examiner required; suitable for group use; timed: 30 minutes

Scoring: Examiner evaluated; scoring service available

Cost: Test Booklet $12.00 (minimum 20); Manual $24.95

Arithmetic Test—Form A

1991	Ramsay Corporation

Roland T. Ramsay

Population: Adults

Purpose: Measures the ability of industrial workers to perform basic computations

Description: Paper–pencil 24-item multiple-choice test assessing the ability to perform computations involving addition, subtraction, multiplication, and division of whole numbers and fractions.

Format: Examiner required; suitable for group use; timed: 20 minutes

Scoring: Examiner evaluated; scoring service available

Cost: Test Booklets $6.95 (minimum 20); Manual $24.95

Arithmetic 2—Form I

1984	Ramsay Corporation

Roland T. Ramsay

Population: Adults

Purpose: Measures arithmetic skills

Description: Paper–pencil test in multiple-choice format. Evaluates the ability to perform basic computations at various levels.

Format: Examiner required; suitable for group use; timed: 20 minutes

Scoring: Examiner evaluated; scoring service available

Cost: Test Booklet $6.95 (minimum 20); Manual $24.95

Bruce Vocabulary Inventory

1974	Martin M. Bruce, PhD

Martin M. Bruce

Population: Adults

Purpose: Determines how a subject's vocabulary compares to the vocabulary of individuals employed in various business occupations

Description: Paper–pencil 100-item multiple-choice test in which the subject matches one of four alternative words with a key vocabulary word. Measures the ability to recognize and comprehend words. The subject's score can be compared to the scores of executives, middle managers, white-collar workers, engineers, blue-collar workers, and the total employed population. Suitable for individuals with physical, hearing, or visual impairments.

Format: Self-administered; untimed: 15 to 20 minutes

Scoring: Hand key

Cost: Specimen Set $39.00

CNC Mathematics Test–Form CNC

2000	Ramsay Corporation

Roland T. Ramsay

Population: Adults

Purpose: Measures knowledge of trigonometry

Description: This 35-item multiple-choice instrument tests knowledge of triangles, angles, pythagorean theorem, nomenclature, sine and cosine, tangent and cotangent, and miscellaneous.

Format: Examiner required; suitable for group use; untimed

Scoring: Self-scored, scoring service provided

Cost: Test Booklet $12.00 (minimum 20), Manual $24.95

Critical Reasoning Test Battery (CRTB) Interpreting Data (NC2.1)

1993	SHL People Performance

Population: Ages 16 years to adult

Purpose: Measures ability to make correct decisions or inferences from numerical data

Description: Paper–pencil 40-item test assessing the ability to interpret statistical and other numerical data, presented as tables or diagrams. Candidates must select the correct answer to a question from five alternatives. The test is appropriate for jobs involving analysis or decision making based on numerical facts. Also available in French.

Format: Examiner required; individual administration; untimed: 30 minutes

Scoring: Hand key; machine scored; scoring service available

Cost: Contact publisher

Critical Reasoning Test Battery (CRTB) Verbal Evaluation (VC1.1)

1993	SHL People Performance

Population: Ages 16 years to adult

Purpose: Measures ability to understand and evaluate the logic of arguments

Description: Sixty-item test measuring the ability to understand and evaluate the logic of various types of arguments. The candidate must decide if a statement is true or untrue, or whether there is insufficient information to judge. Also available in French.

Format: Examiner required; individual administration; untimed: 30 minutes

Scoring: Hand key; machine scored; scoring service available

Cost: Contact publisher

Customer Service Skills Inventory (CSSI™)

1995	Pearson Performance Solutions

Juan Sanchez, Scott Frazer

Population: Adults

Purpose: Determines whether an individual has critical customer service skills; used for selection and placement

Description: Multiple-choice 63-item inventory assessment measures skills, behavior, and traits indicative of success in service-oriented positions. The individual responds to situational type questions to determine whether applicants show a desire to help customers, understand and satisfy customer's needs, take responsibility for assisting customers, cooperate with coworkers, put forth extra job efforts, and keep a reasonable balance between customer requests and company interests.

Format: Examiner required; individual administration; untimed: 30 minutes

Scoring: Hand key; computer scored

Cost: Contact publisher

Experienced Worker Assessment Blueprints

Varies, customized	National Occupational Competency Testing Institute

Population: Adults

Purpose: Designed to measure knowledge of higher level concepts, theories, and applications in related occupations

Description: These tests are intended for evaluating individuals with a combination of education, training, and work experience. They can be used for education and business and industry applications. Tests are available in the following categories: Business, Computer, Construction, Consumer Economics, Culinary Arts, Drafting, Electrical/Electronics, Heating/Air Conditioning, and Machine Trades. Core competencies for each measure are available through the Web site. Customized assessments can be developed. Experienced worker assessments are designed for individuals who have 3 or more years of work experience in addition to training in the occupation.

Format: Examiner required; group administration; untimed

Scoring: Scoring service

Cost: Contact publisher

Farnsworth 100 Hue Color Discrimination Test

Not applicable	Richmond Products, Inc.

Population: Adults

Purpose: Identifies potential employees with less than optimal color hue discrimination capabilities for applications that require excellent color judgment

Description: Consists of 85 color discs of equal chroma but different hue. Arrangement by subject provides a score that determines ability to judge color and hue and thereby separates normal, superior, and deficient color discrimination.

Format: Examiner required; individual administration; untimed 15 to 30 minutes

Scoring: Examiner evaluated

Cost: $700.00

Flanagan Aptitude Classification Tests (FACT™)

1953	Pearson Performance Solutions

John C. Flanagan

Population: Adolescents, adults

Purpose: Assesses skills necessary for the successful completion of particular occupational tasks; used for vocational counseling, curriculum planning, and selection and placement of employees

Description: Battery of 16 multiple-item paper-pencil aptitude tests designed to help the subject to understand his or her abilities relative to others in the total population and in specific occupations. Each test is printed as a separate nonreusable booklet and may be administered individually or in combination. The FACT battery differs from the *Flanagan Industrial Tests* (FIT) battery in that the tests are generally of a lower level and have longer time limits.

Format: Self-administered; untimed: 2 to 40 minutes per test

Scoring: Hand key

Cost: Contact publisher

Flanagan Industrial Tests (FIT™)

1960	Pearson Performance Solutions

John C. Flanagan

Population: Adults

Purpose: Predicts success for given job elements in adults; used for employee screening, hiring, and placement in a wide variety of jobs

Description: Battery of 18 paper-pencil tests designed for use with adults in personnel selection programs. Each test is printed as a separate booklet and may be administered individually or in combination.

Format: Examiner required; suitable for group use; timed: 5 to 15 minutes per test

Scoring: Hand key

Cost: Contact publisher

General Aptitude Test Battery (GATB)

1986	Thomson Nelson

Population: Grades 9 and above

Purpose: Measures aptitudes for career counseling and employee selection

Description: Developed by the U.S. Department of Labor and Human Resources Development of Canada. This test measures nine different aptitudes. Includes 12 subtests taking approximately 50 minutes. Uses print, manual, and finger dexterity boards. Also available in French.

Format: Examiner required; suitable for group use; timed: 5 to 10 minutes per test

Scoring: Examiner evaluated; machine scored or computer scored; test scoring service available

Cost: Contact publisher

IPI Aptitude-Reading Comprehension

2000	Industrial Psychology International, Ltd.

Population: Adults

Purpose: Assesses literacy from functional to early college level

Description: Paper-pencil preemployment screening with 25 items, yielding raw score to grade-equivalent norms.

Format: Examiner required; suitable for group use; timed: 12 minutes

Scoring: Hand key

Cost: Introductory Kit $38.00; 20 Answer/Score Sheets $33.00; 10 Test Booklets $18.00

IPI Employee Aptitude Series: Applied Math

1995	Industrial Psychology International Ltd.

Population: Adolescents, adults

Purpose: Measures the ability to solve one- and two-step algebra problems; used for employee selection, promotion, and training

Description: Paper-pencil 18-item multiple-choice test. A fourth-grade reading level is required. Scores predict abstract and numeric estimation skills.

Format: Examiner required; suitable for group use; timed: 12 minutes

Scoring: Hand key

Cost: Introductory Kit (20 test booklets, scoring key, manual) $33.00

IPI Employee Aptitude Series: Memory

1984	Industrial Psychology International Ltd.

Population: Adults

Purpose: Determines ability to remember visual, verbal, and numerical information; used to screen applicants for clerical, sales, and supervisory jobs

Description: Three 2-minute paper-pencil subtests demonstrating aptitude to recognize and recall associations with names, faces, words, and numbers. Also available in French and Spanish.

Format: Examiner required; suitable for group use; timed: 6 minutes

Scoring: Hand key

Cost: Introductory Kit (20 test booklets, scoring key, manual) $47.00

IPI Employee Aptitude Series: Office Terms

| 1981 | Industrial Psychology International Ltd. |

Population: Adults

Purpose: Measures ability to understand special terminology used in business and industry; used to screen applicants for clerical, sales, and supervisory jobs

Description: Paper-pencil 54-item test measuring comprehension of information of an office or business nature. It also indicates overqualification for routine, repetitive assignments. Also available in French.

Format: Examiner required; suitable for group use; timed: 6 minutes

Scoring: Hand key

Cost: Introductory Kit (20 test booklets, scoring key, manual) $33.00

IPI Employee Aptitude Series: Parts

| 1984 | Industrial Psychology International Ltd. |

Population: Adults

Purpose: Assesses ability to see the whole in relation to its parts; used to screen applicants for clerical, mechanical, technical, sales, and supervisory positions

Description: Paper-pencil 48-item test measuring aptitude for visualizing size, shape, and spatial relations of objects in two and three dimensions. The test reveals one's sense of layout and organization. Also available in French and Spanish.

Format: Examiner required; suitable for group use; timed: 6 minutes

Scoring: Hand key

Cost: Introductory Kit (20 test booklets, scoring key, manual) $33.00

IPI Employee Aptitude Series: Perception

| 1981 | Industrial Psychology International Ltd. |

Population: Adults

Purpose: Measures ability to perceive differences in written words and numbers; used to screen applicants for clerical, sales, and supervisory jobs

Description: Paper-pencil 54-item test measuring the ability to rapidly scan and locate details in words and numbers and to recognize likenesses

and differences. Also available in French and Spanish.

Format: Examiner required; suitable for group use; timed: 6 minutes

Scoring: Hand key

Cost: Introductory Kit (20 test booklets, scoring key, manual) $33.00

IPI Employee Aptitude Series: Precision

| 1986 | Industrial Psychology International Ltd. |

Population: Adults

Purpose: Determines ability to perceive details in objects; used to screen applicants for technical and mechanical jobs requiring visual accuracy, such as inspector-related jobs

Description: Paper-pencil 48-item test using pictures to test the ability to perceive details in objects and rapidly recognize differences and likenesses. The test does not require the ability to read or write. Also available in French and Spanish.

Format: Examiner required; suitable for group use; timed: 6 minutes

Scoring: Hand key

Cost: Introductory Kit (20 test booklets, scoring key, manual) $33.00

Job Ready Assessments Blueprints

| Varies, customized | National Occupational Competency Testing Institute |

Population: Adolescents, adults

Purpose: Measures individual's knowledge of basic processes including the identification and use of terminology and tools

Description: The tests can be used in an educational setting to measure curriculum effectiveness, improve instructional methods, successfully link the world of education with the world of work, and enhance the transition between school and work. In the workplace, they can be used to assist in candidate selection. Tests are available in the following categories: Agriculture, Business, Computer, Construction, Consumer Economics, Culinary Arts, Drafting, Electrical/Electronics, Health Related, Machine Trades, and Maintenance Services. Job-ready assessments are designed to test individuals who have completed training or education in the occupation.

Format: Examiner required; group administration; untimed

Scoring: Scoring service

Cost: Contact publisher

Measurement, Reading, and Arithmetic—Form OE-C

2001	Ramsay Corporation

Roland T. Ramsay

Population: Adults

Purpose: Measures reading, arithmetic, and measurement skills for preemployment

Description: Paper–pencil 101-item multiple-choice test with three subtests: Reading, Measurement, and Arithmetic. Three subscores are yielded.

Format: Examiner required; suitable for group use; timed: 15 to 40 minutes per subtest

Scoring: Self-scored; scoring service available

Cost: Test Booklet $21.00 (minimum 20); Manual $24.95

Minnesota Job Description Questionnaire (MJDQ)

1986	Vocational Psychology Research

Population: Adults

Purpose: To measure the reinforcer (need-satisfier) characteristics of jobs along 21 reinforcer dimensions

Description: In typical applications, multiple raters are asked to rate a specific job. Composite scaling of the MJDQs completed by all raters results in an Occupational Reinforcer Pattern (ORP), which is the pattern of rated reinforcers or need-satisfiers on a given job. The MJDQ is the instrument used to create the ORPs in *Occupational Reinforcer Patterns* (1986) and can be used to create ORPs locally. The MJDQ can also be used to obtain an individual's perception of jobs. The MJDQ comes in two forms: Form E for employees and Form S for supervisors.

Format: Self-administered; untimed: 20 minutes

Scoring: Scoring service

Cost: Sample Set $7.50 (manual, Form S, Form E)

Occupational Vision Screening Kit

Varies	Richmond Products, Inc.

Population: Adults

Purpose: Identifies employees and prospective employees with vision problems for comparison to job-related vision requirements

Description: This vision screening includes a textbook and testing devices for a broad range of visual functions. Available as a kit or each test is available separately. Includes tests for visual acuity testing (distance and near), ocular alignment, binocular vision, suppression, basic color vision, focal objects, and accommodation. Text describes how each test is administered and scored. Optional test for Visual Field also available.

Format: Examiner required; individual administration; untimed: 15 to 30 minutes

Scoring: Examiner evaluated

Cost: Complete Kit (manual, vision tests) $362.00

Performance Skills Index™

Date not provided	LIMRA International

Population: Adults

Purpose: Measures ability to learn and remember information

Description: A multiple-choice test that consists of five sections: Vocabulary, Reading Comprehension, Math, Logic, and Reasoning. Identifies which candidates are likely to fail licensing exams and which ones will need extra help preparing for them.

Format: Online administration; untimed: 25 minutes

Scoring: Online scoring; results emailed

Cost: Contact publisher

Personal Work-Style Survey (PWS)

1995, 2003	APR Testing Services

Joel Peter Wiesen

Population: Adults

Purpose: Measures personal and interpersonal work styles

Description: The PWS is appropriate for use in an employee selection process in a variety of employment settings. The test yields scores in 10 domains, including Responsibility, Cautiousness, Originality, and Team Personal Relations. Items are forced-choice to make it difficult to fake.

Format: Examiner required; group administration; untimed: 30 minutes

Scoring: Scoring service

Cost: $60.00 per candidate for 1 to 9; $50.00 for 10+ candidates

Personnel Test Battery (PTB) Numerical Computation (NP2.1)

1993	SHL People Performance

Population: Adults

Purpose: Measures basic numbers skills

Description: Thirty-item multiple-choice test measuring the understanding of relationships between numbers and operations, as well as quick and accurate calculations. In each item, one number has been omitted from an equation. The examinee must select (from five choices) the number that will correctly complete the equation. Simple fractions and decimals are used, and some problems are expressed in numbers, but more complex notation or operations are deliberately omitted. The test is suitable for individuals with minimal educational qualifications. Also available in French.

Format: Examiner required; individual administration; untimed: 7 minutes

Scoring: Hand key; machine scored; scoring service available

Cost: Contact publisher

Personnel Test Battery (PTB) Numerical Reasoning (NP6.1, NP6.2)

1993	SHL People Performance

Population: Adults

Purpose: Assesses simple numerical reasoning skills

Description: Both tests have short written problems that involve using decimals, fractions, or graphs. Test content includes items based on subjects relevant to sales, clerical, and general staff. NP6.2 (24-items) has been developed in which aids to calculation are used and candidates are supplied with a calculator. NP6.1 (30-items) is completed without a calculator. Also available in French.

Format: Examiner required; individual administration; untimed: 15 minutes

Scoring: Hand key; machine scored; scoring service available

Cost: Contact publisher

Personnel Test Battery (PTB) Verbal Comprehension (VP5.1)

1993	SHL People Performance

Population: Adults

Purpose: Assesses an individual's knowledge of the meanings of words and the relationships between them; used where verbal communication skills are important

Description: Forty-item multiple-choice test requiring the candidate to identify the relationship (same or opposite) between one pair of words and to select (from five choices) the word that relates in the same way to a third given word. The vocabulary used is nonspecialist, everyday language. VP5.1 is more difficult than VP1.1 of the same battery. Also available in French.

Format: Examiner required; individual administration; untimed: 18 minutes

Scoring: Hand key; machine scored; scoring service available

Cost: Contact publisher

Position Analysis Questionnaire (PAQ)

1989	PAQ Services, Inc.

Ernest J. McCormick, P. R. Jeanneret, Robert C. Meacham

Population: Adults

Purpose: Analyzes jobs in terms of job elements that reflect directly or infer the basic human behaviors involved, regardless of their specific technological areas or functions; used with jobs at all levels

Description: Paper–pencil 187-item job-analysis rating scale in which the examiner indicates the degree of involvement of each of the elements listed using appropriate rating scales such as importance or frequency. The job elements are organized so that they provide a logical analysis of the job's structure. Six broad areas are assessed: information input, mental processes, work output, relationships with other persons, job context, and other job characteristics. Examples of specific job elements are the use of written materials, the level of decision making, the use of mechanical devices, working in a hazardous environment, and working at a specified pace. Analysis of the questionnaire is in terms of job dimensions.

Format: Self-administered; online administration; untimed

Scoring: Computer scored; scoring service available

Cost: $39.00

Position Classification Inventory (PCI)

| 1991 | Psychological Assessment Resources, Inc. |

Gary Gottfredson, John L. Holland

Population: Adults

Purpose: Used by human resources development and career counselors to classify positions or job classes

Description: Paper–pencil 84-item 3-point scale inventory. A Self-Directed Search summary code is produced. Materials used include a manual, reusable item booklet, and an answer/profile form.

Format: Self-administered; untimed: 10 minutes

Scoring: Examiner evaluated

Cost: Introductory Kit (manual, 25 reusable booklets, 25 forms) $90.00

Power and Performance Measures (PPM)

| 1996 | Hogrefe Limited |

James Barrett

Population: Adults

Purpose: Measures general abilities required by employees

Description: A total of 314 items within nine subtests: Applied Power, Processing Speed, Mechanical Understanding, Numerical Computation, Numerical Reasoning, Perceptual Reasoning, Spatial Ability, Verbal Comprehension, and Verbal Reasoning.

Format: Examiner required; suitable for group use; can be computer administered; timed

Scoring: Self-scored; computer scored; test scoring service available

Cost: Contact publisher

Press Test

| 1985 | Pearson Performance Solutions |

Melany E. Baehr, Raymond J. Corsini

Population: Adults

Purpose: Assesses adults' ability to work under pressure by comparing objective measures of reaction time under normal and high-pressure conditions; used for selection, career counseling

and placement of high-level personnel, where efficiency must be maintained

Description: Multiple-item paper–pencil test measuring speed of reaction to verbal stimuli, color stimuli, and color stimuli under distraction caused by interfering verbal stimuli. For valid results, stopwatch time limits and strict monitoring must be employed in the administration of the test, which is not designed to be completed in the allotted time. The test has been used to select high-level managers, professionals, and airline pilots.

Format: Examiner required; suitable for group use; timed: 10 to 12 minutes

Scoring: Hand key

Cost: Contact publisher

Purdue Pegboard Test

| 1992 | Pearson Performance Solutions |

Population: Adults

Purpose: Measures hand–finger–arm dexterity required for certain types of manual work; used in the selection of business and industrial personnel

Description: Multiple-operation manual test of gross and fine motor movements of hands, fingers, arms, and tips of fingers. The test measures the dexterity needed in assembly work, electronic production work, and similarly related jobs. Materials consist of a test board with two vertical rows of holes and four storage wells holding pegs, washers, and collars. The subject must complete as many assemblies as possible in the allotted time.

Format: Examiner required; suitable for group use; timed: 3 to 9 minutes

Scoring: Hand key

Cost: Contact publisher

Reading–Arithmetic Index (RAI™)

| 1995 | Pearson Performance Solutions |

Population: Adults

Purpose: Assesses reading and math proficiency levels

Description: The Reading Index contains 60 items that test applicants' ability to read and understand basic materials through Grade 9 level. The Arithmetic Index contains 54 items that test ability to add; subtract; multiply; divide; and use fractions, decimals, and percentages through Grade 8 level.

Format: Examiner required; suitable for group use; untimed: 35 minutes

Scoring: Hand key; computer scored

Cost: Contact publisher

Reading Test–Form A

| 1997, 2000 | Ramsay Corporation |

Roland T. Ramsay

Population: Adults

Purpose: Assesses the ability to read, comprehend, and answer written questions

Description: Paper–pencil 40-item multiple-choice test designed to measure an individual's ability to read, comprehend, and answer questions based on a printed passage. The topics of the passages are Plant Safety, Hydraulic Systems, Industrial Machines, Production Lubrication, and Computer Operation.

Format: Examiner required; suitable for group use; timed: 35 minutes

Scoring: Self-scored; scoring service available

Cost: Test Booklet $12.00 (minimum 20); Manual $24.95

Technical Test Battery (TTB) Numerical Computation (NT2.1)

| 1995 | SHL People Performance |

Population: Adults

Purpose: Measures basic ability to work with numbers in a technical setting

Description: Multiple-choice 36-item test assessing the understanding of mathematical relationships and operations and the ability to calculate quickly and accurately. In each item, one number or operation has been omitted from an equation. The examinee must select the missing element from five possible answers. Fractions, decimals, and percentages are included, but more complex notations or operations are omitted deliberately. The range extends from minimal educational qualifications to high school graduate level. Also available in French.

Format: Examiner required; individual administration; untimed: 18 minutes

Scoring: Hand key; machine scored; scoring service available

Cost: Contact publisher

Test of Basic Math (TBM)

| 1999, 2006 | APR Testing Services |

Joel Peter Wiesen

Population: Adults

Purpose: Measures job candidates' basic math skills

Description: Provides an objective measure of a candidate's abilities in six areas of basic math, including whole numbers, common fractions, and percentages.

Format: Computer administered; untimed: 30 minutes

Scoring: Online scoring report sent by email; examiner evaluated

Cost: 10-Candidate Package $300.00; Scoring Stencil $45.00

Test of Business English (TBE)

| 2004 | APR Testing Services |

Joel Peter Wiesen

Population: Adults

Purpose: Measures job candidates' written communication skills

Description: Provides an objective measure of a candidate's ability to read and write business English at a basic level. The test yields an overall score, as well as individual scores in four areas: Basic English Mechanics; Word Knowledge and Usage; Reading Comprehension and Paragraph Structure; and Spelling

Format: Computer administered; untimed: 30 minutes

Scoring: Online scoring; report sent by email

Cost: 1 Year License (unlimited use) $225.00; 3-Year License $540.00

Test of English for International Communication (TOEIC)

| Updated annually | Educational Testing Service |

Population: Adult nonnative speakers of English

Purpose: Measures English language proficiency required in business; used as a basis for employee selection and placement, for decisions concerning assignment, and to measure achievement in company-sponsored English-language programs

Description: Paper–pencil 200-item multiple-choice test of English language skills. Section I contains 100 listening comprehension items administered via audiotape. Section II contains 100 reading items. Total test scale scores range from

10 to 990; scale subscores for Sections I and II range from 5 to 495. The scores are correlated to direct measures of listening, speaking, reading, and writing, as well as to indirect measures. The test is used by multinational corporations, language schools, government agencies, public/private organizations for hiring, assignment to overseas posts, and assignment to/promotion within departments where English is desirable. Application to take the test is made through national/regional offices. A cassette player is required.

Format: Examiner required; suitable for group use; timed: 2 hours 30 minutes

Scoring: Hand key; may be computer scored

Cost: $65.00

Test of Practical Judgment–Revised

| 1999 | Institute of Psychological Research, Inc. |

Alfred J. Cardall

Population: Adults

Purpose: Determines employee ability to use practical judgment in solving problems; used to screen for management and sales positions

Description: Multiple-item paper–pencil multiple-choice test of judgment factors that may be used in conjunction with intelligence testing. The test also may be used for screening and for selection and placement of individuals whose work involves thinking, planning, or getting along with people. The test examines such factors as empathy, drive, and social maturity. Materials include five tests, a key, and a manual. Also available in French.

Format: Examiner required; suitable for group use; untimed: 30 minutes

Scoring: Hand key

Cost: Contact publisher

Thurstone Test of Mental Alertness (TMA™)

| 1959 | Pearson Performance Solutions |

L. L. Thurstone, Thelma Gwinn Thurstone

Population: Adults

Purpose: Measures an individual's capacity to acquire new knowledge and skills and to use what has been learned to solve problems; measures individual differences in ability to learn and perform mental tasks of varying types and complexity

Description: Test with 126 items measuring linguistic (vocabulary) and quantitative (arithmetic) factors. This test is available in two forms.

Format: Examiner required; suitable for group use; timed: 20 minutes

Scoring: Hand key; computer scored

Cost: Contact publisher

Understanding Communication

| 1984 | Pearson Performance Solutions |

Thelma Gwinn Thurstone

Population: Adults

Purpose: Measures comprehension of verbal material in short sentences and phrases; used for industrial screening and selection of clerical, first-line supervisors, or other positions that need to understand written material and communications

Description: Paper–pencil 40-item single-score test measuring verbal comprehension through the ability to identify the one of four words that will complete a given sentence.

Format: Examiner required; suitable for group use; timed: 15 minutes

Scoring: Hand key

Cost: Contact publisher

VCWS 2–Size Discrimination

| 1974 | Valpar International Corporation |

Population: Ages 15 years and older

Purpose: Assesses an individual's ability to perform tasks requiring visual size discrimination; provides insight into problem-solving abilities, work organization, ability to follow directions, and psychomotor coordination

Description: Manual assessment of an individual's ability to visually discriminate sizes. The individual must use his dominant hand to screw 49 hex nuts onto 32 bolt threads of various sizes. Both hands may be used to remove the nuts during disassembly. Performance indicates the ability to work successfully in occupations requiring visual size discrimination, eye–hand coordination, and bilateral dexterity. Work activities related to the test include examining and measuring for purposes of grading sorting, tools, and working within prescribed tolerances or standards. The work sample should not be used with individuals with severe impairment of the upper extremities. The work sample uses methods–time measurement and error scores to determine level of performance. Learning curve allows for multiple administrations as needed.

Format: Examiner required; individual administration; timed

Scoring: Examiner evaluated

Cost: $1,550.00

VCWS 3-Numerical Sorting

1974	Valpar International Corporation

Population: Ages 15 years and older

Purpose: Assesses an individual's ability to perform work tasks requiring sequential sorting of a combined numerical/alphabetical problem; provides insight into spatial and form perception, accuracy, and attention to detail in transferring data

Description: Manual assessment of the ability to sort, file, and categorize objects using a numerical code. The individual must transfer 42 of 56 numerically ordered white plastic chips inserted into correspondingly marked slots in Board I to the appropriate slots in Board II. After the chip placements on Board II are scored, the individual transfers the chips back to Board I. Work activities related to the work sample include examining, grading, and sorting; keeping records and receipts; recording or transmitting verbal or coded information; and posting verbal or numerical data on stock lists. The work sample should not be used with individuals with severe impairment of the upper extremities. The work sample uses methods time measurement and error scores to determine level of performance. Learning curve allows for multiple administrations as needed.

Format: Examiner required; individual administration; timed

Scoring: Examiner evaluated

Cost: $1,660.00

VCWS 6-Independent Problem Solving

1974	Valpar International Corporation

Population: Ages 15 years and older

Purpose: Assesses the ability to perform work tasks requiring visual comparison and proper selection of abstract designs

Description: Manual assessment of a person's ability to perform work tasks requiring a visual comparison of colored shapes. Work activities relating to the work sample are characterized by emphasis on decision-making and instruction-following abilities. The work sample should not

be used with individuals with severe impairment of the upper extremities or severe visual impairment. The work sample uses methods-time measurement and error scores to determine level of performance. Learning curve allows for multiple administrations as needed.

Format: Examiner required; individual administration; timed

Scoring: Examiner evaluated

Cost: $1,600.00

VCWS 10-Tri-Level Measurement

1974	Valpar International Corporation

Population: Ages 15 years and older

Purpose: Assesses an individual's ability to perform inspecting and measuring tasks ranging from the very simple to the very precise; measures ability to use independent judgment in following sequences of operations and selecting proper instruments

Description: Manual assessment of a person's ability to perform very simple to very precise inspection and measurement tasks. The individual must sort 61 incorrectly or correctly machined parts into nine inspection bins. The seven inspection tasks involved are visual and size discrimination; comparison (using jigs); and measurement with a ruler, micrometer, and vernier caliper. Performance indicates the ability to succeed in jobs requiring varying degrees of measurement and inspection skills and decision-making abilities. The work sample should not be administered to individuals with severe impairment of the upper extremities. Methods-time measurement and error scores are used to determine performance level. Learning curve allows for multiple administrations as needed.

Format: Examiner required; individual administration; untimed

Scoring: Examiner evaluated

Cost: $2,495.00

Wonderlic Basic Skills Test™ (WBST™)

1994	Wonderlic Personnel Test, Inc.

Eliot R. Long, Winifred L. Clonts, Victor S. Artese

Population: Ages 15 years and older

Purpose: Used in employment and job training to measure job-related math and verbal skills and for vocational guidance

Description: Multiple-choice paper–pencil test

with two subtests: Test of Verbal Skills (50 questions, 20 minutes) and Test of Quantitative Skills (45 questions, 20 minutes). JRT scale scores, scores by job requirements, and scores by grade level are yielded. Verbal forms VS1, VS2 and Quantitative forms QS1, QS2 are available. A sixth-grade reading level is required.

Format: Examiner required; individual administration; timed: 40 minutes

Scoring: Computer scored; test scoring service available from publisher

Cost: Contact publisher

Word Fluency

1961	Pearson Performance Solutions

Population: Adults

Purpose: Determines the speed of relevant verbal associations and an individual's ability to produce appropriate words rapidly; used for vocational counseling and personnel selection in fields requiring communication skills, such as supervision, management, and sales

Description: Paper–pencil 80-item test measuring verbal fluency.

Format: Examiner required; suitable for group use; timed: 10 minutes

Scoring: Hand key

Cost: Contact publisher

Work Keys Applied Mathematics Test

2000, 2001	ACT, Inc.

Population: Adolescents, adults

Purpose: Assesses mathematical problem solving

Description: Multiple-choice 30-item criterion-referenced test across five levels. A test form, formula sheet, answer folder, administrator's manual and video administrator's manual is used.

Format: Examiner required; individual or group administered; computer-administered available; timed: 45 minutes

Scoring: Machine scored; test scoring service available from publisher; computer scored

Cost: Contact publisher

Work Keys Applied Technology Test

2000, 2001	ACT, Inc.

Population: Adolescents, adults

Purpose: Used for program evaluation, skills

profile, and selection to assess technological problem solving

Description: Multiple-choice criterion-referenced test with 32 items across four levels, measures skills in applying the principles of mechanics, electricity, fluid, dynamics, and thermodynamics to workplace problems. A test booklet and answer folder, administrator's manual, and video administrator's manual are used.

Format: Examiner required; suitable for group administration; computer-administered available; timed: 45 minutes

Scoring: Machine scored; test scoring service available; computer scored

Cost: Contact publisher

Work Keys Listening Test

1992	ACT, Inc.

Population: Adolescents, adults

Purpose: Used in program evaluation, skills profiling, and selection to assess listening skills

Description: Six-prompt criterion-referenced test across five levels. An audiotape, answer folder, administrator's manual, and video administrator's manual are used.

Format: Examiner required; individual or group administered; timed: 45 minutes

Scoring: Holistic scoring by publisher only

Cost: Contact publisher

Work Keys Locating Information Test

2001	ACT, Inc.

Population: Adolescents, adults

Purpose: Used in program evaluation, skills profiling, and selection to assess locating information in business graphics and other materials

Description: Multiple-choice criterion-referenced test with 32 items across four levels. A test booklet, answer folder, administrator's manual, and videotape administrator's manual are used.

Format: Examiner required; individual or group administered; computer-administered available; timed: 45 minutes

Scoring: Machine scored; test scoring service available; computer scored

Cost: Contact publisher

Work Keys Observation Test

2001	ACT, Inc.

Population: Adolescents, adults

Purpose: Assesses observation skills in the workplace

Description: Multiple-choice criterion-referenced test with 32 items across four levels. A test booklet, answer folder, administrator's manual, and videotape administrator's manual are used.

Format: Examiner required; individual or group administered; timed: 60 minutes

Scoring: Machine scored; test scoring service available

Cost: Contact publisher

Work Keys Reading for Information Test

2001	ACT, Inc.

Population: Adolescents, adults

Purpose: Used in program evaluation, skills profiling, and selection to assess reading skills

Description: Multiple-choice criterion-referenced test with 30 items across five levels. A test booklet, answer folder, administrator's manual, and video administrator's manual are used.

Format: Examiner required; individual or group administered; computer-administered; timed: 60 minutes

Scoring: Machine scored; test scoring service available; computer-scored

Cost: Contact publisher

Work Keys Teamwork Test

2001	ACT, Inc.

Population: Adolescents, adults

Purpose: Assesses teamwork skills

Description: Multiple-choice 36-item criterion referenced test across four levels. A video, answer folder, administrator's manual, and video administrator's manual are used.

Format: Examiner required; individual administration; suitable for group use; timed: 60 minutes

Scoring: Machine scored; test scoring service available from publisher

Cost: Contact publisher

Work Keys Writing Test

1992	ACT, Inc.

Population: Adolescents, adults

Purpose: Used for program evaluation, skills profiling, and selection to assess business writing skills

Description: Six-prompt essay test across five levels. An audiotape, answer folder, administrator's manual, and video administrator's manual are used.

Format: Examiner required; suitable for group use; timed: 40 minutes

Scoring: Holistic scoring by publisher only

Cost: Contact publisher

Work Readiness Profile (WRP)

1995	Australian Council for Educational Research Limited

Helga Rowe

Population: Adolescents, adults

Purpose: Assesses major disability groups and rates their adaptive functioning

Description: Criterion-referenced tool designed to assist in the initial assessment of individuals with disabilities. This measure focuses on abilities, supports and empowerment, rather than on the level of disability. The multidimensional profile obtained focuses on the whole person and how he or she functions within the environment. It seeks to identify what people can do, rather than what they cannot do. Ratings are completed on 12 factors: Health, Hearing, Vision, Travel, Movement, Fine Motor Skills, Gross Motor Skills and Strength, Social and Interpersonal Skills, Work Adjustment, Communication Effectiveness, Abilities and Skills, and Literacy and Numeracy.

Format: Examiner required; individual and group administration; untimed

Scoring: Examiner evaluated

Cost: Contact publisher

Work Skills Series (WSS) Understanding Instructions (VWP1)

1988	SHL People Performance

Population: Adults

Purpose: Assesses the ability to follow and understand simple written instructions

Description: Test with 39 items measuring the ability to follow and apply instructions in practical and work-related situations. Candidates read a series of paragraphs outlining particular work procedures and are then tested on their understanding of these. The contents have been designed to look like those typically found in many technical, production, or manufacturing environments.

Format: Examiner required; individual administration; untimed: 12 minutes

Scoring: Hand key; machine scored; scoring service available

Cost: Contact publisher

Work Skills Series (WSS) Visual Checking (CWP3)

1990	SHL People Performance

Population: Adults

Purpose: Assesses the ability to check that one set of visual indicators corresponds with another

Description: Thirty-item test measuring the ability to check that one set of indicators corresponds to another set of indicators according to a number of simple rules. This skill is important whenever production or control equipment is used by semiskilled operators. Also available in French.

Format: Examiner required; individual administration; untimed: 7 minutes

Scoring: Hand key; machine scored; scoring service available

Cost: Contact publisher

Work Skills Series (WSS) Working with Numbers (NWP2)

1988	SHL People Performance

Population: Adults

Purpose: Assesses the ability to perform simple numerical computations, such as in stock control

Description: Test with 36 items measuring the ability to apply the basic rules of arithmetic to practical and work-related situations. The test content involves dealing quickly with stock levels and use of various types of mechanical components. This test is relevant to any job in industry or manufacturing where the appropriate application of basic arithmetical skills is important. Also available in French.

Format: Examiner required; individual administration; untimed: 10 minutes

Scoring: Hand key; machine scored; scoring service available

Cost: Contact publisher

Working: Assessing Skills, Habits, and Style

Date not provided	H & H Publishing Co., Inc.

Curtis Miles, Phyllis Grummon

Population: Adults

Purpose: Assesses workplace competencies

Description: A self-scoring assessment instrument designed to assess proficiency in nine competencies that go beyond academic and technical skills and knowledge. It provides information to the individual being assessed and gives teachers, trainers, and others a framework within which they can develop instructional activities.

Format: Self-administered; untimed: 20 to 30 minutes

Scoring: Computer scored; self-scored; also available on the Web

Cost: 1 to 99 $4.00 each

Workplace Skills Survey (WSS)

1998	Industrial Psychology International, Ltd.

Population: Ages 16 years and older

Purpose: Assesses nontechnical employability skills

Description: Used for preemployment and promotional screening. Contains 48 items within six skill areas: Teamwork, Communication, Adaptation to Change, Problem Solving, Work Ethics, and Technological Literacy. Yields stanine scores and *t*-scores.

Format: Requires examiner; individual or group administration; timed: 20 minutes

Scoring: Hand key

Cost: Introductory Kit $43.00; Answer/Score Sheets $32.00; 10 Test Booklets $18.00

Aptitude and Skills

Banking

Basic Banking Skills Battery (BBSB®)

1987	Pearson Performance Solutions

Population: Ages 16 years and older

Purpose: Measures potential for successful performance as a bank teller and customer service representative; used for employee selection and promotion

Description: Paper-pencil 317-item multiple-choice battery measuring potential in several key areas related to an applicant's ability to perform as a teller or a customer service representative. Scores are provided for 13 scales: Drive, School Achievement, Arithmetic Computation, Interpersonal Relations, Cognitive Skills, Error Recognition, Motor Ability, Math Ability, Name Comparison, Self Discipline, Leadership, Number Comparison, and Perceptual Skills. The battery yields a single score the Potential Estimate—for the bank teller and customer service positions. Form A combines the timed and untimed tests. A Short Form is comprised of the timed tests only

Format: Examiner required; suitable for group use; timed

Scoring: Computer scored

Cost: Contact publisher

Clerical

ACER Short Clerical Test (Forms C, D, and E)

2002	Australian Council for Educational Research Limited

Population: Ages 15 years and older

Purpose: Measures speed and accuracy in checking names and numbers and in basic arithmetic; used as a test of clerical aptitude in selecting employees for routine clerical jobs

Description: Multiple-item paper-pencil test measuring an individual's ability to perceive, remember, and check written or printed material (both verbal and numerical) and to perform arith-

metic operations. The test is available in three forms: Forms C and D are used for personnel selection and Form E for guidance and counseling in business training colleges.

Format: Examiner required; suitable for group use; timed: 5 minutes per part

Scoring: Hand key

Cost: Contact publisher

ACER Speed and Accuracy Test–Form A

1963	Australian Council for Educational Research Limited

Population: Ages 13 years 6 months and older

Purpose: Measures the checking skills of individuals; useful in the selection of clerical personnel

Description: Multiple-item paper-pencil test measuring the ability to perceive, retain, and check relatively familiar material in the form of printed numbers and names while working in a limited amount of time. The test contains two sections: name checking and number checking. Australian norms are available for school, university, adult, and some occupational groups.

Format: Examiner required; suitable for group use; timed: 6 minutes per part

Scoring: Hand key

Cost: Contact publisher

Administrative Series Modules

1975-1997	International Public Management Association for Human Resources

Population: Candidates for administrative positions

Purpose: Assesses skills needed in various administrative positions

Description: Designed in module format so that test users can select the modules that best suit their testing needs. Previous version listed as *Clerical Series Tests*. The individual modules are Grammar (15 minutes), Punctuation (11 minutes), Vocabulary (9 minutes), Spelling (6 minutes), Basic Filing Skills (18 minutes), Reasoning (9 minutes), Following Oral Instructions (33 minutes), Following Written Instructions (25 minutes), Forms, Completion/Listening (30 minutes), Data Proofing (13 minutes), Document Proofing—Part A (15 minutes), Document Proofing—Part B (20 minutes), Mathematical Reasoning (35 minutes), and Basic Math Calculations (20 minutes). Two combined modules are available: 1-A (Grammar, Punctuation, Vocabulary, Spelling, Basic Filing) and 1-B (Reasoning, Following Written Instructions, Basic Math Calculations).

Format: Examiner required; individual and group administration

Scoring: Examiner evaluated; machine scoring for all modules except Forms and both Document Proofing modules

Cost: Contact publisher

Checking Accuracy-Form A

1999	Ramsay Corporation

Roland T. Ramsay

Population: Adults

Purpose: Measures the ability to make accurate readings of identification numbers, names, and tables

Description: Paper-pencil test in multiple-choice format. Total score provided.

Format: Examiner required; suitable for group use; timed: 24 minutes

Scoring: Examiner evaluated; scoring service available

Cost: Test Booklet $12.00 (minimum 20); Manual $24.95

Clerical Abilities Battery (CAB)

1987	Harcourt Assessment, Inc.

Population: Adults

Purpose: Assesses clerical skills

Description: Contains seven subtests that measure clerical tasks of filing, copying information, comparing information, using tables, proofreading, addition and subtraction, and reasoning with numbers.

Format: Examiner required; suitable for group use; timed: 5 to 20 minutes

Scoring: Hand key

Cost: Examination Kit (one booklet for each subtest and manual) $63.00

Clerical Skills Series-Revised

1990	Martin M. Bruce, PhD

Martin M. Bruce

Population: Adults

Purpose: Assesses the language, physical coor-

dination, and mathematical abilities necessary for various clerical jobs; used for screening prospective employees, measuring student skills, and evaluating current employees

Description: Ten-category paper-pencil test series covering alphabetizing, filing, arithmetic, clerical speed and accuracy, coding, eye-hand accuracy, grammar and punctuation, spelling, vocabulary, and word fluency. The series consists of 10 short tests, 6 of which are timed. Suitable for individuals with physical, hearing, or visual impairments.

Format: Examiner required for timed items; suitable for group use; timed: 2 to 8 minutes per section

Scoring: Hand key

Cost: Specimen Set (total series) $65.00

General Clerical Test-Revised

Date not provided	Harcourt Assessment, Inc.

Population: Adults

Purpose: Assesses clerical aptitude; used for selecting applicants and evaluating clerical employees for promotion

Description: Multiple-item paper-pencil test of three types of abilities needed for clerical jobs: clerical speed and accuracy, numerical ability, and verbal ability. The clerical subtest involves finding errors by comparing copy with the original and using an alphabetical file. The numerical subtest requires the applicant to solve arithmetic problems, find numerical errors, and solve numerical word problems. The verbal subtest involves correcting spelling errors, answering questions about reading passages, understanding word meanings, and correcting grammatical errors. Separate booklets for the clerical and numerical subtests combined and the verbal subtest only are available for use where one ability is of consideration.

Format: Self-administered; timed: 46 minutes

Scoring: Hand key

Cost: Examination Kit (1 copy of each test booklet, manual, answer key) $57.00

Hay Aptitude Test Battery™

1984	Wonderlic Personnel Test, Inc.

Edward N. Hay

Population: Adults

Purpose: Identifies job applicants with the greatest aptitude for handling alphabetical and numerical clerical detail; used to select personnel for office and clerical positions, and trainee positions requiring innate perceptual skills

Description: Four paper-pencil tests assessing clerical and numerical aptitude: Warm-Up, Number Perception Test, Name Finding Test, and Number Series Completion Test. The Warm-Up Test, which is not scored, is designed to prepare the examinee for testing. The Number Perception Test (4 minutes) assesses numerical accuracy. Applicants must identify exact pairs of numbers from groups of similar pairs. Results do not necessarily indicate general mental ability. The Name Finding Test (4 minutes) screens the applicant's short-term memory and word accuracy. The examinee must read words and retain them long enough to verify them. The Number Series Completion Test (4 minutes) assesses numerical reasoning abilities. Also available in Spanish and French.

Format: Examiner required; suitable for group use; timed: 13 minutes total

Scoring: Hand key

Cost: Contact publisher

IPI Job-Field Series: Clerical Staff

1997	Industrial Psychology International Ltd.

Population: Ages 16 years and older

Purpose: Assesses skills and personality of applicants for supervisory positions in an office setting; used to screen for the positions of administrator, controller, department head, and vice president

Description: Multiple-item paper-pencil battery of seven aptitude and two personality tests. The tests are Judgment, Parts, Fluency, Office Terms, Numbers, NPF, CPF, Perception, and Memory. For individual test descriptions, see the *IPI Employee Aptitude Series*. Also available in French and Spanish.

Format: Examiner required; suitable for group use; timed: 82 minutes

Scoring: Hand keys

Cost: Starter Kit (test materials for 5 applicants, scoring keys, manuals) $80.00; Test Package $14.00/applicant

Learning Business Procedures Test (LBPT)

2004	APR Testing Services

Joel Peter Wiesen

Population: Candidates for higher level administrative positions

Purpose: Assesses ability to learn and apply written business procedures

Description: The LBPT is for jobs that involve complicated office procedures. The test presents a candidate with a complicated business procedure in the form of written instructions and data tables. The candidate must apply the procedure to various situations. Meant for a variety of work settings, the test is appropriate for employees who must implement specific and detailed written procedures on a regular basis.

Format: Self-administered; untimed: 35 minutes

Scoring: Online scoring; reports sent by email

Cost: 10 Candidate Packages $325.00

Minnesota Clerical Test (MCT)

1979	Harcourt Assessment, Inc.

D. M. Andrew, D. G. Peterson, H. P. Longstaff

Population: Adults

Purpose: Measures ability to see differences or errors in pairs of names and pairs of numbers; used to select clerical applicants

Description: Multiple item paper-pencil test of speed and accuracy of visual perception. Items are pairs of names and numbers. The applicant checks each pair that is identical. The test predicts performance in numerous jobs, including adding-machine operators, clerical employees, key machine operators, and filing and cataloging personnel. Materials include optional tapes for test administration.

Format: Examiner required; suitable for group use; timed: 15 minutes

Scoring: Hand key

Cost: Examination Kit (test booklet, manual) $32.00; Scoring Key $38.00

Office Arithmetic Test–Form CA

1990, 2005	Ramsay Corporation

Roland T. Ramsay

Population: Adults

Purpose: Assesses math skills necessary for the position of office clerk; used for hiring

Description: Paper-pencil 40-item multiple-choice test assessing addition and subtraction of 1-, 2-, and 3-digit whole numbers and decimals; multiplication and division of 1- and 2-digit whole numbers and decimals; and reading simple charts and tables. Materials include reusable booklet, answer sheet, and manual with key.

Format: Examiner required; suitable for group use; timed: 30 minutes

Scoring: Examiner evaluated; scoring service available

Cost: Test Booklet $12.00 (minimum 20); Manual $24.95

Office Proficiency Assessment & Certification® (OPAC®)

Date not provided	Pearson Performance Solutions

Population: Adults

Purpose: Assesses general office and basic software skills

Description: Consists of four modules: Keyboarding and Word-Processing, Language Arts and Records Management, Financial Record Keeping and Applications, and 10-Key and Data Entry. They may be used independently of each other.

Format: Computer administered; time set by administrator

Scoring: Computer scored

Cost: Contact publisher

Office Reading Test–Form G

1990	Ramsay Corporation

Roland T. Ramsay

Population: Adults

Purpose: Assesses reading skills necessary for office workers; used for hiring

Description: Paper–pencil 40-item multiple-choice test based on five written passages: Operating the Copier, Travel Arrangements, Operating a Computer, The Business Letter, and Telephone Procedures. Materials include reusable booklet, answer sheet, and manual with key.

Format: Examiner required; suitable for group use; timed: 30 minutes

Scoring: Examiner evaluated; scoring service available

Cost: Test Booklet $12.00 (minimum 20); Manual $24.95

Office Skills Assessment Battery (OSAB®)

Date not provided	Pearson Performance Solutions

Population: Adults

Purpose: Assesses the attitudes and skills needed to be productive, dependable office employees

Description: A brief, yet comprehensive questionnaire. One section, the Attitudes Inventory, addresses interest, motivation, and knowledge related to office work; a second section, the Skills Inventory, measures clerical and language skills.

Format: Self- or computer administered; untimed: 15 minutes

Scoring: Telephone scoring available; computer scoring; scannable form

Cost: Contact publisher

Office Skills Tests (OST™)

1977	Pearson Performance Solutions

Population: Adults

Purpose: Assesses clerical ability of job applicants; used for employee selection and placement

Description: Twelve tests suitable for screening clerks, accounting clerks, typists, secretaries/stenographers, library assistants, and other office personnel. The tests are Checking, Coding, Filing, Forms Completion, Grammar, Numerical Skills, Oral Directions, Punctuation, Reading Comprehension, Spelling, Typing, and Vocabulary. Each test is available in two forms (A and B). Norms are provided for timed and untimed administration.

Format: Examiner required; suitable for group use; untimed: 3 to 10 minutes per test

Scoring: Hand key; computer scored

Cost: Contact publisher

Perceptual Speed (Identical Forms)

1984	Pearson Performance Solutions

L. L. Thurstone, T. E. Jeffrey

Population: Adults

Purpose: Measures ability to identify rapidly the similarities and differences in visual configurations; used to select clerical personnel or workers in occupations that require rapid perception of inaccuracies in written materials and diagrams

Description: Paper–pencil 140-item test of perceptual skill. The subject selects the figure among five choices that appears to be most similar to the illustration.

Format: Examiner required; suitable for group use; timed: 5 minutes

Scoring: Hand key

Cost: Contact publisher

Personnel Test Battery (PTB)
Audio Checking (CP8.1)

1991   SHL People Performance

Population: Adults

Purpose: Assesses an individual's ability to receive and check information that is presented orally; used to select clerical staff who must process information presented orally as in telesales or airline and hotel bookings

Description: Multiple-choice 60-item test in which the task is to listen to a string of numbers or letters presented on an audiotape and select the identical string from the five choices presented in the question booklet. There are three subtests covering letters, numbers, and letters and numbers mixed. The test is suitable for individuals with minimal educational qualifications. Also available in French.

Format: Examiner required; individual administration; untimed: 10 minutes

Scoring: Hand key; machine scored; scoring service available

Cost: Contact publisher

Personnel Test Battery (PTB)
Basic Checking (CP7.1)

1991   SHL People Performance

Population: Adults

Purpose: Measures speed and accuracy in checking a variety of materials at a very basic level; used for selection of clerical and general staff concerned with simple routine checking

Description: Multiple-choice 40-item test consisting of two subtests. One involves checking a list of numbers, and the other involves checking a list of letters. In each list, a series of strings of numbers or letters is presented. These are compared with another page from which the identical string must be selected (from five choices). The test is suitable for individuals with minimal educational qualifications. Also available in French.

Format: Examiner required; individual administration; untimed: 5 minutes

Scoring: Hand key; machine scored; scoring service available

Cost: Contact publisher

Personnel Test Battery (PTB)
Classification (CP4.1)

1993   SHL People Performance

Population: Adults

Purpose: Measures the ability to perceive and classify material in accordance with a set of instructions; appropriate when data handling, filing, or the following of instructions are important skills

Description: Sixty-item test representing a clerical task in which a number of sales order forms must be filed. The candidate classifies each order and then records the order in coded form. Some orders ("account sales") must be filed alphabetically, and others ("cash sales") must be classified under seven categories of goods purchased. Also available in French.

Format: Examiner required; individual administration; untimed: 7 minutes

Scoring: Hand key; machine scored; scoring service available

Cost: Contact publisher

Personnel Test Battery (PTB)
Clerical Checking (CP3.1)

1993   SHL People Performance

Population: Adults

Purpose: Measures ability to perceive and check a variety of material quickly and accurately

Description: Forty item proofreading test in which two lists of information about hotels are presented; one list is handwritten and the other is printed. The material contained in the lists includes names, numbers, and symbols. The candidates must compare the two lists and note any errors in accordance with a given code (designed to represent an actual clerical task). Also available in French.

Format: Examiner required; individual administration; untimed: 7 minutes

Scoring: Hand key; machine scored; scoring service available

Cost: Contact publisher

Personnel Test Battery (PTB)
Text Checking (CP9.1)

1993   SHL People Performance

Population: Adults

Purpose: Measures proofreading speed and accuracy

Description: Fifty-item test that assesses speed and accuracy in proofreading, an important skill in the production of all kinds of documents. The test requires detailed proofreading from one set of text to another, with candidates required to specify the exact nature of errors identified. Also available in French.

Format: Examiner required; individual administration; untimed: 10 minutes

Scoring: Hand key; machine scored; scoring service available

Cost: Contact publisher

PSI Basic Skills Tests for Business, Industry, and Government: Classifying (BST #11)

1981	Psychological Services, Inc.

W. W. Ruch, A. N. Shub, S. M. Moinat, D. A. Dye

Population: Adults

Purpose: Measures ability to place information into appropriate categories; used to select customer service, clerical, and administrative personnel

Description: Multiple-choice 48-item test presenting four sets of data. Each set contains 12 items that must be properly categorized. The test is available in two equivalent paper–pencil forms and in computerized form. Transported validity study is available.

Format: Examiner required for paper–pencil forms; suitable for group use; timed: 5 minutes

Scoring: Hand key; may be computer scored; scoring software available

Cost: Contact publisher

PSI Basic Skills Tests for Business, Industry, and Government: Coding (BST #12)

1981	Psychological Services, Inc.

W. W. Ruch, A. N. Shub, S. M. Moinat, D. A. Dye

Population: Adults

Purpose: Measures ability to code information according to a prescribed system; used to select customer service, clerical, and administrative personnel

Description: Multiple-choice 72-item test in which the subjects are given systems for coding information (each system codes four categories of related information). For each test item, the subject must code the given information into categories. The test is available in two equivalent

paper–pencil forms and in computerized form. Transported validity study is available.

Format: Examiner required for paper–pencil forms; suitable for group use; timed: 5 minutes

Scoring: Hand key; may be computer scored; scoring software available

Cost: Contact publisher

PSI Basic Skills Tests for Business, Industry, and Government: Computation (BST #4)

1981	Psychological Services, Inc.

W. W. Ruch, A. N. Shub, S. M. Moinat, D. A. Dye

Population: Adults

Purpose: Measures ability to solve arithmetic problems; used to select customer service, clerical, and administrative personnel

Description: Multiple-choice 40-item test measuring the ability to add, subtract, multiply, and divide, using whole numbers, fractions, and decimals. The test is available in two equivalent paper–pencil forms and in computerized form. Transported validity study is available.

Format: Examiner required for paper–pencil forms; suitable for group use; timed: 5 minutes

Scoring: Hand key; may be computer scored; scoring software available

Cost: Contact publisher

PSI Basic Skills Tests for Business, Industry, and Government: Decision Making (BST #6)

1981	Psychological Services, Inc.

W. W. Ruch, A. N. Shub, S. M. Moinat, D. A. Dye

Population: Adults

Purpose: Measures ability to read a set of procedures and apply them to new situations by determining the appropriate action; used to select customer service, clerical, and administrative personnel

Description: Paper–pencil 20-item multiple-choice test in which sets of procedures (related to clerical or office duties) and a set of action codes for implementing the procedures are described. The examinee is presented with a number of problems in which he must decide the course of action for each item and mark the appropriate action code. The test is available in two equivalent forms. Transported validity study is available.

Format: Examiner required; suitable for group use; timed: 5 minutes

Scoring: Hand key; may be computer scored; scoring software available

Cost: Contact publisher

PSI Basic Skills Tests for Business, Industry, and Government: Filing Names (BST #13)

1981	Psychological Services, Inc.

W. W. Ruch, A. N. Shub, S. M. Moinat, D. A. Dye

Population: Adults

Purpose: Measures ability to file simple entries alphabetically; used to select customer service, clerical, and administrative personnel

Description: Multiple-choice 50-item test in which the subject is presented with a name, followed by a list of four other names (arranged alphabetically). The subject "files" the given name at the beginning, between two of the names, or at the end of the list. The test is available in two equivalent paper-pencil forms and in computerized form. Transported validity study is available.

Format: Examiner required for paper-pencil forms; suitable for group use; timed: 90 seconds

Scoring: Hand key; may be computer scored, scoring software available

Cost: Contact publisher

PSI Basic Skills Tests for Business, Industry, and Government: Filing Numbers (BST #14)

1981	Psychological Services, Inc.

W. W. Ruch, A. N. Shub, S. M. Moinat, D. A. Dye

Population: Adults

Purpose: Measures ability to file numbers in numerical order; used to select customer service, clerical, and administrative personnel

Description: Multiple-choice test in which each of the 75 items consists of a six-digit number to be filed numerically in a list of four other six-digit numbers (already arranged in numerical order). The test is available in two equivalent

paper-pencil forms and in computerized form. Transported validity study is available.

Format: Examiner required for paper-pencil forms; suitable for group use; timed: 2 minutes

Scoring: Hand key; may be computer scored; scoring software available

Cost: Contact publisher

PSI Basic Skills Tests for Business, Industry, and Government: Following Oral Directions (BST #7)

1981	Psychological Services, Inc.

W. W. Ruch, A. N. Shub, S. M. Moinat, D. A. Dye

Population: Adults

Purpose: Measures ability to listen to information and instructions presented orally and answer questions about what is heard; used to select customer service, clerical, and administrative personnel

Description: Paper-pencil 24-item multiple-choice test in which the subjects listen to a 6½-minute prerecorded cassette tape and then answer questions about the content of the tape. The tape is played only once (no rewinding or stopping of the tape is allowed), and subjects are encouraged to take written notes during the playing of the tape. The tape is a recording of conversations that take place in an employment setting.

Format: Examiner required; suitable for group use; timed: 5 minutes

Scoring: Hand key; may be computer scored; scoring software available

Cost: Contact publisher

PSI Basic Skills Tests for Business, Industry, and Government: Following Written Directions (BST #8)

1981	Psychological Services, Inc.

W. W. Ruch, A. N. Shub, S. M. Moinat, D. A. Dye

Population: Adults

Purpose: Measures ability to read, understand, and apply sets of written instructions; used to select customer service, clerical, and administrative personnel

Description: Multiple-choice 36-item test requiring examinees to read sets of rules and apply them to a number of case examples. The test is available in two equivalent paper-pencil forms and in computerized form. Transported validity study is available.

Format: Examiner required for paper-pencil forms; suitable for group use; timed: 5 minutes

Scoring: Hand key; may be computer scored; scoring software available

Cost: Contact publisher

PSI Basic Skills Tests for Business, Industry, and Government: Forms Checking (BST #9)

1981 Psychological Services, Inc.

W. W. Ruch, A. N. Shub, S. M. Moinat, D. A. Dye

Population: Adults

Purpose: Measures ability to verify the accuracy of completed forms; used to select customer service, clerical, and administrative personnel

Description: True-false 42-item test in which the examinee verifies the accuracy of information in clerical forms filled out using information in written paragraphs. The examinee must check a number of the entries on each form against the information in the paragraphs to determine whether the entries are correct or incorrect. The test is available in two equivalent paper-pencil forms and in computerized form. Transported validity study is available.

Format: Examiner required for paper-pencil forms; suitable for group use; timed: 5 minutes

Scoring: Hand key; may be computer scored; scoring software available

Cost: Contact publisher

PSI Basic Skills Tests for Business, Industry, and Government: Language Skills (BST #1)

1981 Psychological Services, Inc.

W. W. Ruch, A. N. Shub, S. M. Moinat, D. A. Dye

Population: Adults

Purpose: Measures language skills used in proofing written material

Description: Multiple-choice 25-item test in which the examinee reads a sentence, part of which is underlined, and determines whether the underlined portion contains errors in spelling, punctuation, capitalization, grammar, or usage. The test is available in two equivalent

paper-pencil forms and in computerized form. Transported validity study is available.

Format: Examiner required for paper-pencil forms; suitable for group use; timed: 10 minutes

Scoring: Hand key; may be computer scored; scoring software available

Cost: Contact publisher

PSI Basic Skills Tests for Business, Industry, and Government: Problem Solving (BST #5)

1981 Psychological Services, Inc.

W. W. Ruch, A. N. Shub, S. M. Moinat, D. A. Dye

Population: Adults

Purpose: Measures ability to solve written math problems

Description: Multiple-choice 25-item test in which the examinee reads a word problem and applies the appropriate arithmetic operations to solve the problem. The test is available in two equivalent paper-pencil forms and in computerized form. Transported validity study is available.

Format: Examiner required for paper-pencil forms; suitable for group use; timed: 5 minutes

Scoring: Hand key; may be computer scored; scoring software available

Cost: Contact publisher

PSI Basic Skills Tests for Business, Industry, and Government: Reading Comprehension (BST #2)

1981 Psychological Services, Inc.

W. W. Ruch, A. N. Shub, S. M. Moinat, D. A. Dye

Population: Adults

Purpose: Measures basic reading comprehension; used to select clerical and administrative personnel

Description: Paper-pencil 23-item multiple-choice test measuring the ability to read short passages and answer literal and inferential questions about them.

Format: Examiner required for paper-pencil forms; suitable for group use; timed: 10 minutes

Scoring: Hand key; may be computer scored; scoring software available

Cost: Contact publisher

PSI Basic Skills Tests for Business, Industry, and Government: Reasoning (BST #10)

| 1981 | Psychological Services, Inc. |

W. W. Ruch, A. N. Shub, S. M. Moinat, D. A. Dye

Population: Adults

Purpose: Measures ability to analyze a list of facts and draw valid and logical conclusions from that information; used to select clerical and administrative personnel

Description: Multiple-choice 30-item test consisting of six lists of facts (one-sentence statements), with five possible conclusions for each list of facts. The examinee must read each list of facts and decide whether each conclusion is definitely true, definitely false, or unknown based on the given facts. The test is available in two equivalent paper–pencil forms and in computerized form. Transported validity study is available.

Format: Examiner required for paper–pencil forms; suitable for group use; timed: 5 minutes

Scoring: Hand key; may be computer scored; scoring software available

Cost: Contact publisher

PSI Basic Skills Tests for Business, Industry, and Government: Visual Speed and Accuracy (BST #15)

| 1981 | Psychological Services, Inc. |

W. W. Ruch, A. N. Shub, S. M. Moinat, D. A. Dye

Population: Adults

Purpose: Measures ability to see details quickly and accurately; used to select clerical and administrative personnel

Description: Multiple-choice 150-item test in which each test item consists of two series of numbers and symbols. The examinee compares the numbers or symbols and determines whether they are the same or different. The test is available in two equivalent paper–pencil forms and in computerized form. Transported validity study is available.

Format: Examiner required for paper–pencil forms; suitable for group use; timed: 5 minutes

Scoring: Hand key; may be computer scored; scoring software available

Cost: Contact publisher

PSI Basic Skills Tests for Business, Industry, and Government: Vocabulary (BST #3)

| 1981 | Psychological Services, Inc. |

W. W. Ruch, A. N. Shub, S. M. Moinat, D. A. Dye

Population: Adults

Purpose: Measures the ability to identify the correct synonym for the word underlined in each sentence; used to select clerical and office workers

Description: Multiple-choice 45-item test in which each item consists of a sentence with one word underlined, followed by four words. The examinee must select the word meaning the same or about the same as the word that is underlined in the sentence. The test is available in two equivalent paper–pencil forms and in computerized form. Transported validity study is available.

Format: Examiner required for paper–pencil forms; suitable for group use; timed: 5 minutes

Scoring: Hand key; may be computer scored; scoring software available

Cost: Contact publisher

Short Employment Tests® (SET®)

| 1951 | (Manual 1993) Harcourt Assessment, Inc. |

G. K. Bennett, Marjorie Gelink

Population: Adults

Purpose: Measures verbal, numerical, and clerical skills; used to select qualified individuals for a variety of administrative and entry-level positions

Description: Three 5-minute subtests: Verbal, Numerical, and Clerical Aptitude. May be used as a complete battery to produce a total score or as individual tests. Available in four forms.

Format: Examiner required; suitable for group use; timed: 5 minutes per subtest

Scoring: Hand key

Cost: Examination Kit (booklet for each of 3 tests, manual) Form 1 $50.00; Forms 2, 3, and 4 $55.00

Short Tests of Clerical Ability (STCA™)

| 1959 | Pearson Performance Solutions |

Population: Adults

Purpose: Assesses aptitudes and abilities important to the successful completion of typical office tasks; used for selection and placement in office personnel

Description: Multiple-item paper–pencil battery consisting of seven tests. The battery includes Arithmetic Skills, Business Vocabulary, Checking Accuracy, Coding, Oral and Written Directions, Filing, and Language (grammar and mechanics).

Format: Examiner required; suitable for group use; untimed: 3 to 6 minutes per subtest

Scoring: Hand key

Cost: Contact publisher

SkillCheck® Professional Plus

Date not provided	Pearson Performance Solutions

Population: Adults

Purpose: Assesses software knowledge or keyboard skills

Description: Measures competency on a variety of Windows-based software programs. This unique program offers more than 100 interactive questions covering all levels and functions of a software program. Organizations may choose the basic, standard, or advanced tests or create their own instrument.

Format: Computer administered; time set by administrator

Scoring: Computer scoring

Cost: Contact publisher

VCWS 5–Clerical Comprehension and Aptitude

1974	Valpar International Corporation

Population: Ages 15 years and older

Purpose: Assesses basic clerical aptitude (the ability to perform a variety of answering, mail sorting, alphabetical filing, bookkeeping, and typing tasks) and ability to communicate effectively both verbally and in writing

Description: Work sample featuring three separate sections that assess an individual's ability to perform a variety of clerical tasks and his or her ability to learn the tasks. The exercises begin with mail sorting and simultaneous phone answering. A tape plays a series of phone conversations at prerecorded intervals requiring the individual to stop the mail sorting in order to take the phone message. The individual also must complete an alphabetical filing task. In the second section, the individual must use a 10-key adding machine to perform three exercises emphasizing accurate recording of numerical data and basic math skills. In the typing section, the typewriter has been modified to measure a person's typing coordi-

nation skills. Learning curve allows for multiple administrations as needed, except for the bookkeeping exercise.

Format: Examiner required; individual administration; timed

Scoring: Examiner evaluated

Cost: $2,865.00

Wonderlic Interactive Skills Evaluations (WISE) Keyboard and Office Skills

Date not provided	Wonderlic Personnel Test, Inc.

Population: Adults

Purpose: Measures office skills; used for preemployment and skills assessment

Description: WISE provides online typing tests that measure standard typing skills, as well as those in specialty areas. Also measures numeric and alphanumeric data-entry skills in common formats. Test results are sent via email. The following skills are available: general typing test, legal typing test, medical typing test, alphanumeric data entry, and numeric data entry.

Format: Online administration

Scoring: Online scoring

Cost: Contact publisher

Wonderlic Interactive Skills Evaluations (WISE) Software Skills

Date not provided	Wonderlic Personnel Test, Inc.

Population: Adults

Purpose: Measures knowledge and skills for Microsoft® software applications; used in preemployment and skills assessment

Description: WISE offers Standard and Expert level evaluations. All questions are presented as interactive simulations with realistic interfaces that respond just like the actual software. WISE reports provide percentile scores for beginning, intermediate, and advanced items and look at individual productivity by measuring the response times. Results are received by email.

Format: Online administration; untimed: Standard, 20 to 35 minutes; Expert, 30 to 45 minutes

Scoring: Online scoring

Cost: Contact publisher

Computer

Computer Operator Aptitude Battery (COAB)

1973	Pearson Performance Solutions

Population: Adults

Purpose: Helps predict job performance of computer operators; used by data processing managers and personnel directors to select applicants for computer operator positions

Description: Paper–pencil test predicting success as a computer operator. The test consists of three separately timed subtests: Sequence Recognition, Format Checking, and Logical Thinking.

Format: Examiner required; suitable for group use; timed: 45 minutes

Scoring: Hand key

Cost: Contact publisher

Computer Programmer Aptitude Battery (CPAB™)

1964	Pearson Performance Solutions

Population: Adults

Purpose: Measures potential for success in the computer programming field; used by data processing managers and personnel directors to identify people with the aptitude for computer programming

Description: Five separately timed paper–pencil subtests measuring verbal meaning, reasoning, letter series, number ability, and diagramming (problem analysis and logical solution). The test is available in a short version, which includes reasoning and diagramming.

Format: Examiner required; suitable for group use; timed: 1 hour 19 minutes

Scoring: Hand key

Cost: Contact publisher

Information Technology Test Series (ITTS) Diagramming (DIT5)

1988	SHL People Performance

Population: Adults

Purpose: Measures logical analysis through the ability to follow complex instructions; appropriate for technical occupations and jobs involving systems design, flow charting, and similar skills

Description: Fifty-item multiple-choice test consisting of a series of abstract designs in logical sequences. Respondents must select, from five choices, the design that completes the logical sequence. Candidates must think logically and flexibly. Also available in French.

Format: Examiner required; individual administration; untimed: 20 minutes

Scoring: Hand key; machine scored; scoring service available

Cost: Contact publisher

Information Technology Test Series (ITTS) Spatial Reasoning (SIT7)

1988	SHL People Performance

Population: Adults

Purpose: Measures ability to visualize and manipulate shapes in three dimensions when given a two-dimensional drawing

Description: Forty-item multiple-choice test consisting of a series of folded-out cubes and perspective drawings of assembled cubes. The respondents must identify the assembled cubes that could be made from the folded-out cube, each face of which has a different pattern. The test discriminates at a high level and would be relevant for engineers, designers, architects, and information technology staff. Also available in French.

Format: Examiner required; individual administration; untimed: 20 minutes

Scoring: Hand key; machine scored; scoring service available

Cost: Contact publisher

Language-Free Programmer/ Analyst Aptitude Test (LPAT)

1999	APR Testing Services

Joel Peter Wiesen, Charles Halbfinger

Population: Adults

Purpose: Measures the aptitude to be a computer programmer/analyst; can be given to a person with no computer training or background; designed for use in personal selection for trainee and entry-level positions

Description: Objective multiple-item, paper–pencil test to measure aptitude and potential rather than knowledge of specific computer language syntax or commands. A "miniature training and evaluation" approach is used for several questions in which the candidates are given information and then asked to apply that information. The test questions resemble tasks done by applications and database programmers. There are three main test areas: reasoning and problem solving, numerical and logical analysis, and understanding and analyzing written documentation. There are nine question types providing nine diagnostic scores and an overall score. Available with paper answer sheet for group administration.

Format: Self-administered; untimed: 2 hours

Scoring: Online scoring; results sent by email

Cost: Single Candidate Package (test booklet, online scoring) $90.00; 3 Candidates $180.00; 10 Candidates $455.00

PLC Test-Form PLC

2005	Ramsay Corporation

Roland T. Ramsay

Population: Adults

Purpose: Measures knowledge and skill in the area of programmable logic controllers

Description: This multiple-choice paper–pencil test has 50 items in the following subareas: Ladder Logic; I/O Devices; and Programs/Software, Systems, and Troubleshooting.

Format: Examiner required; suitable for group use; untimed

Scoring: Self-scored; scoring service available

Cost: Test Booklet $21.00 (minimum 20); Manual $24.95

Technology and Internet Assessment (TIA)

Date not provided	H & H Publishing Co., Inc.

Michael R. Ealy

Population: Adolescents, adults

Purpose: Designed to determine strengths and weaknesses related to a basic understanding of computer, Internet, and information technology skills

Description: Focuses on eight areas that present barriers for individuals seeking employment and for those striving to succeed in our educational system. The results can be used to provide baseline information for academic instructors and counselors, workplace trainers, and social service professionals. The TIA is administered via

the Web. Immediately upon completion, a two-page report is displayed listing the percentile scores for each scale, along with suggestions for improving each area.

Format: Self-administered online; untimed: 20 to 30 minutes

Scoring: Scored on the Web

Cost: 1-99 Administrations $3.00 each

Customer Service

Assessment of Service Readiness (ASR)

1993	Life Office Management Association

Population: Adults

Purpose: Assesses entry-level customer service skills; used for selection and development of employees in insurance/financial services

Description: The system has two parts. The first consists of videotaped situations that present job candidates with difficult customer service scenarios. Candidates indicate how they would handle or resolve the situations by responding to a series of paper–pencil questions. The second part is a background information inventory that asks questions about experiences, interests, and activities that lead to the development of customer service skill.

Format: Examiner required; suitable for group use; timed: 90 minutes

Scoring: Computer scored

Cost: Contact publisher

Customer Service Applicant Inventory (CSAI™)

Date not provided	Pearson Performance Solutions

Population: Adults

Purpose: Evaluates skills and attitudes considered necessary for service-oriented employees

Description: Measures customer service, teamwork, communication, stress tolerance, honesty, drug avoidance, safety, training readiness, applied math, employability index, validity/candidness, and validity/accuracy to identify people who can effectively handle concerns, establish rapport with other employees, and work effectively in group or individual situations.

Format: Self-administration; untimed: 50 minutes

Scoring: Computer scored

Cost: Contact publisher

Customer Service Profile (CSP™)

Date not provided	Pearson Performance Solutions

Population: Adults

Purpose: Evaluates applicants' attitudes

Description: The CSP dimensions help to identify people who can effectively establish rapport with customers, sell promotional items, and display pride and enthusiasm on the job. Significant Behavioral Indicators are included in a report that provides narrative evaluation of details on an individual's strengths and weaknesses.

Format: Self-administration; untimed: 20 minutes

Scoring: Computer scored; telephone scoring available

Cost: Contact publisher

Customer Service Stimulator (CSS)

Updated yearly	Management & Personnel Systems, Inc.

Population: Adults

Purpose: Identifies people who have a customer service orientation and can project responsiveness and sensitivity in dealing with customers

Description: The CSS comes in a booklet format. Candidates are placed in a hypothetical organization and told that they are monitoring the phone calls received by a new Customer Service Representative. Actual dialogue is given for five job-related customer inquiries/complaints. For each situation, candidates must evaluate the dialogue and indicate what they would say or do. The questions are designed to determine the candidate's level of understanding and course of action in dealing with the situations. Because the test has a national database, the scores can be compared to other supervisors on a national level. The factors measured are Leadership/Decision Making and Team Relations. The SupSim has explicit scoring criteria for each problem. Results are provided in the form of a rank-ordered list of candidates and an individual bar-chart profile. The factors measured are Customer Service Orientation and Interpersonal Sensitivity.

Format: Self-administered; timed: 90 minutes

Scoring: Scoring service

Cost: $90 each candidate

LOMASelect REPeValuator

2003	Life Office Management Association

Population: Adults

Purpose: Measures call center skills

Description: Using a 30-minute, Web-delivered simulation, the system imitates chat and voice-over-Internet interactions for a company that sells and services a leading product to businesses and consumers. Candidates assume the role of a customer contact representative during a variety of situations including product/service inquiry, technical support, account, inquiry, order status, and service termination. The system measures an applicant's skills in key contact center competencies, such as problem solving, keyboarding, communication, servicing customers, and soft selling. The system automatically calculates the results and generates reports. A separate module is also available that tests a candidate's ability to cross-sell and up-sell. Also available in Spanish.

Format: Self-administered online

Scoring: Online scoring

Cost: Contact publisher

LOMASelect Service Index

2003	Life Office Management Association

Population: Adults

Purpose: Measures call center fit

Description: This system helps to gather systematic information about the applicant's preferences corresponding with those most likely to lead to successful long-term employment in call center positions. Benefits include knowing the candidate wants to do the job, improving company customer service and overall performance, and reducing turnover. Also available in Spanish.

Format: Self-administered online

Scoring: Online scoring

Cost: Contact publisher

Electrical

ElecTest Form A-C

1997, 2001	Ramsay Corporation

Roland T. Ramsay

Population: Adults

Purpose: Assesses the ability to answer electrical/electronics questions; used for hiring and promotion for trade/craft jobs

Description: Paper–pencil 60-item multiple-choice test. The categories are Power Distribution, Construction and Installation, Motors, Digital and Analog Electronics, Schematics, Print Reading and Control Circuits, AC/DC Theory and Electrical Maintenance, Computers/PLC, Test Instruments, Power Supplies, and Mechanical and Hand and Power Tools.

Format: Examiner required; suitable for group use; untimed: approximately 60 minutes

Scoring: Self-scored; scoring service available

Cost: Test Booklet $21.00 (minimum 20); Manual $24.95

Electrical & Electronics Test (EET)

Date not provided	Hogrefe Limited

John D. Morgan

Population: Adolescents, adults

Purpose: Assesses knowledge and ability in electrical and electronics fields

Description: Thirty-item paper–pencil test for determining knowledge of fundamental laws, symbols, and definitions related to electricity and electronics. The test emphasizes the ability to use knowledge in practical situations.

Format: Examiner required; suitable for group use; timed: 15 minutes

Scoring: Hand key; test scoring service available

Cost: Contact publisher

Electrical Aptitude Test–Form EA-R-C

2003	Ramsay Corporation

Roland T. Ramsay

Population: Adults

Purpose: Measures electrical aptitude

Description: Paper–pencil test with 36 items in multiple-choice format measures areas of Mathematics, Electrical Concepts, Process Flow, Signal Flow, Electrical Schematics, and Electrical Sequences. Online administration available.

Format: Examiner required; suitable for group use; timed: 18 minutes

Scoring: Examiner evaluated; scoring service available; online scoring

Cost: Test Booklet $21.00 (minimum 20); Manual $24.95

Electrical Maintenance Trainee–Form UKE-IC

1998, 2001	Ramsay Corporation

Roland T. Ramsay

Population: Adults

Purpose: Measures electrical knowledge and skills

Description: Using 60 items, skills are assessed in these 11 areas: Motors; Digital and Analog Electronics; Schematics and Electrical Print Reading; Control; Power Supplies; Basic AC/DC Theory; Construction, Installation, and Distribution; Test Instruments; Computers and PLC; Mechanical, Equipment Operation, and Hand and Power Tools; and Electrical Maintenance.

Format: Examiner required; suitable for group use; untimed: approximately 60 minutes

Scoring: Self-scored; scoring service available

Cost: Test Booklet $20.00 (minimum 20); Manual $24.95

Electrical Repair Apprentice Battery–Form CEB-C

1996, 2001	Ramsay Corporation

Roland T. Ramsay

Population: Adults

Purpose: Measures basic electrical skills and knowledge

Description: A basic skills test battery assessing Reading, Arithmetic, Electrical Print Reading, Troubleshooting and Problem Solving, and Basic Electricity. These five tests are more demanding of job knowledge than a basic skills battery, but less demanding than the Electrical Maintenance Trainee Test.

Format: Examiner required; suitable for group use; timed: ranges from 24 to 45 minutes per subtest

Scoring: Self-scored; scoring service available

Cost: Test Booklet $11.00 (minimum 20); Manual $24.95

Electrician (Chemical)–Form AIE-C

2001, 2005	Ramsay Corporation

Roland T. Ramsay

Population: Adults

Purpose: Measures knowledge and skill in the electrical area

Description: Used in selecting chemical electricians who have knowledge or experience in the following areas: Motors and Electrical Maintenance; Electronics, Instrumentation, and Test Instruments, Schematics and Electrical Print Reading; Control Circuits; Power Supplies and Power Distribution; Basic AC/DC Theory; Mechanical and Hand and Power Tools; and Construction and Installation, and Mobile Equipment. There are 60 multiple-choice items.

Format: Examiner required; suitable for group use; untimed

Scoring: Self-scored; scoring service available

Cost: Test Booklet $21.00 (minimum 20); Manual $24.95

Electronics and Instrumentation Technician Test–Form A2

1991	Ramsay Corporation

Roland T. Ramsay

Population: Adults

Purpose: Measures knowledge and skill in the area of electronics and instrumentation

Description: This multiple-choice paper–pencil test has 184 items. Categories tested include Motors, Digital Electronics, Schematics and Print Reading, Analog Electronics, Radio Controls, Power Rectifiers, Basic AC/DC Theory, Power Distribution, Test Instruments, Mechanical, and Computers and PLC.

Format: Examiner required; suitable for group use; untimed

Scoring: Self-scored; scoring service available

Cost: Test Booklet $25.00 (minimum 20); Manual $24.95

ElectronTest Form H-C

1998, 2005	Ramsay Corporation

Roland T. Ramsay

Population: Adults

Purpose: Measures knowledge and skill in the area of electronics

Description: A 60-item paper–pencil multiple-choice test assessing AC/DC theory, Digital Electronics and Analog Electronics, Print Reading, Power Supplies, Regulators, Test Instruments, Motors, Electronic Equipment, Radio Theory, Power Distribution, Computers and PLC, and Mechanical.

Format: Examiner required; suitable for group use; untimed: approximately 60 minutes

Scoring: Self-scored; scoring service available

Cost: Test Booklet $20.00 (minimum 20); Manual $24.95

Instrument Technician–Form IPO

1989	Ramsay Corporation

Roland T. Ramsay

Population: Adults

Purpose: Measures technical knowledge of instrumentation

Description: The test for Level I has 100 items in 11 categories: Mathematics, Digital Electronics, Analog Electronics, Electrical Print Reading, Process Control, Power Supplies, Basic AC/DC Theory, Test Instruments, Mechanical, Computers and PLC, and Chemical Processes. The more advanced Level II has 122 items in the same categories.

Format: Examiner required; suitable for group use; untimed: 120 minutes

Scoring: Self-scored; scoring service available

Cost: Test Booklet $25.00 (minimum 20); Manual $24.95

Maintenance Electrician– Forms BTA-C, BTB-C

2000, 2005	Ramsay Corporation

Roland T. Ramsay

Population: Adults

Purpose: Measures electrical knowledge and skills

Description: Forms A and B have 60 items in seven categories: Motors; Digital and Analog Electronics; Schematics, Print Reading, Control Circuits; Power Supplies, Power Distribution, Construction, and Installation; Basic AC/DC Theory, Electrical Maintenance, and Troubleshooting; Test Instruments, Computers, and PLC; and Mechanical Maintenance.

Format: Examiner required; suitable for group use; untimed: 60 minutes

Scoring: Self-scored; scoring service available

Cost: Test Booklet $21.00 (minimum 20); Manual $24.95

Reading Electrical Prints and Drawings–Form A

2005	Ramsay Corporation

Roland T. Ramsay

Population: Adults

Purpose: Measures ability to read electrical drawings and schematics

Description: This multiple-choice paper–pencil test has 38 items in the following subareas: Drawings and Schematics, Basic Electrical Symbols, and Wiring Diagrams.

Format: Examiner required; suitable for group use; timed: 35 minutes

Scoring: Self-scored; scoring service available

Cost: Test Booklet $12.00 (minimum 20); Manual $24.95

Reading–Form IHER

1995	Ramsay Corporation

Roland T. Ramsay

Population: Adults

Purpose: Assesses the ability to read, comprehend, and answer written questions

Description: Paper–pencil 40-item multiple-choice test designed to measure an individual's ability to read, comprehend, and answer questions based on a printed passage.

Format: Examiner required; suitable for group use; timed: 40 minutes

Scoring: Self-scored; scoring service available

Cost: Test Booklet $12.00 (minimum 20)

VCWS 12–Soldering and Inspection (Electronic)

1974	Valpar International Corporation

Population: Ages 15 years and older

Purpose: Assesses an individual's ability to acquire and apply basic soldering techniques to tasks requiring varying degrees of precision; provides insight into the ability to follow sequential instructions and acquire new tool use skills

Description: The examinee uses wire cutters, wire strippers, needlenose pliers, a soldering iron, and a solder to perform exercises involving the use of the tools in precision solder tasks. Exercises include work with both wires and circuit board assemblies. Performance indicates the individual's ability to become a successful worker in jobs related to electronic assembly and soldering. Learning curve allows for multiple administrations as needed.

Format: Examiner required; individual administration; timed

Scoring: Examiner evaluated

Cost: $2,195.00

VCWS 15–Electrical Circuitry and Print Reading

1974	Valpar International Corporation

Population: Ages 15 years and older

Purpose: Assesses the ability to understand, comprehend, and apply the principles and functions of electrical circuitry through the modality of electronic components; provides insight into potential without basing performance exclusively on prior knowledge

Description: The examinee performs various exercises in three areas: testing for circuit continuity using probes; testing and repairing circuits using probes, wires, and pliers; and reading an electrical schematic print and inserting wires, diodes, and two types of resistors as specified by the print. The examinee is given trays containing various electrical components and appropriate tools. The various electrical circuits to be tested range from simple to complex. The examinee tests each circuit; records malfunctions; and, if necessary, repairs nonfunctioning circuits. No previous experience with electrical or electronic principles is required. Results indicate potential for success in an entry-level position in fields that require electrical circuitry and print reading skills. The work sample uses methods–time measurement and error scores to determine level of performance. Learning curve allows for multiple administrations as needed.

Format: Examiner required; individual administration; timed

Scoring: Examiner evaluated

Cost: $2,195.00

Factory

Combined Basic Skills–Form BWC-R

2003	Ramsay Corporation

Roland T. Ramsay

Population: Adults

Purpose: Measures skills in literacy performance required in manufacturing processing

Description: Paper–pencil test in multiple-choice format with 52 items for operating technicians. A score is provided for each section (Reading, Arithmetic, Inspection and Measurement, and Process Monitoring and Problem Solving Skills).

Format: Examiner required; suitable for group use; timed: ranges from 8 to 14 minutes per subtest

Scoring: Examiner evaluated; scoring service available

Cost: Test Booklet $15.00 (minimum 20); Manual $24.95

Industrial Assessment Blueprints

Varies, customized	National Occupational Competency Testing Institute

Population: Adults

Purpose: Measures knowledge of competencies related specifically to industrial occupations

Description: Intended for evaluating individuals with a combination of education, training, and work experience. Tests are available in a variety of job titles.

Format: Examiner required; group administration; untimed

Scoring: Scoring service

Cost: Contact publisher

Reading–Form WH

1994	Ramsay Corporation

Roland T. Ramsay

Population: Adults

Purpose: Assesses the ability to read, comprehend, and answer written questions

Description: Paper–pencil 40-item multiple-choice test designed to measure an individual's ability to read, comprehend, and answer questions based on a printed passage.

Format: Examiner required; suitable for group use; timed: 40 minutes

Scoring: Self-scored; scoring service available

Cost: Test Booklet $12.00 (minimum 20)

VCWS 8–Simulated Assembly

1974	Valpar International Corporation

Population: Ages 15 years and older

Purpose: Assesses an individual's ability to work at an assembly task requiring repetitive physical manipulation and evaluates bilateral use of the upper extremities; determines standing and sitting tolerance

Description: Manual assessment of an individual's ability to work at conveyor-assembly jobs. The individual stands or sits in front of two parts bins, one containing metal pins and the other containing black washers and white caps. The individual must place the pin, then the washer, and then the cap on the assembly board, which rotates automatically at a constant speed. Correct assemblies are counted automatically, and all assemblies are recycled to the parts bins automatically. Work activities relating to the work sample including placing materials in or on automatic machines; following simple instructions; and starting, stopping, and observing the functions of machines and equipment. Methods–time measurement standards are used to determine performance level. Learning curve allows for multiple administrations as needed.

Format: Examiner required; individual administration; timed

Scoring: Examiner evaluated

Cost: $2,995.00

VCWS 19–Dynamic Physical Capacities

1982	Valpar International Corporation

Population: Ages 15 years and older

Purpose: Assesses the Physical Demands factors of the *Dictionary of Occupational Titles*; evaluates an individual's endurance and strength; may be used in postinjury cases

Description: Objective measure of functional capacity in terms of strength. The exercise measures each of the strength levels represented in the Physical Demands factor: sedentary, light, medium, heavy, and very heavy. The examinee, who assumes the role of a shipping and receiving clerk, handles materials varying in weight from 5 pounds to 115 pounds. The examinee begins with exercises on the sedentary level and gradually moves through the range of strengths until his or her capacity is reached. The work sample may be discontinued at any time. The work sample should be administered only to individuals who are able to walk, are free of visual handicaps, and who have use of their upper extremities. The work sample uses methods–time measurement and error scores to determine level of performance. Learning curve allows for multiple administrations as needed.

Format: Examiner required; individual administration; timed

Scoring: Examiner evaluated

Cost: $5,795.00

Food Industry

Reading-Form A-FI

| 2002 | Ramsay Corporation |

Roland T. Ramsay

Population: Adults

Purpose: Assesses the ability to read, comprehend, and answer written questions

Description: Paper–pencil 40-item multiple-choice test designed to measure an individual's ability to read, comprehend, and answer questions based on a printed passage.

Format: Examiner required; suitable for group use; timed: 40 minutes

Scoring: Self-scored; scoring service available

Cost: Test Booklet $12.00 (minimum 20)

Health Services

Healthcare Employee Productivity Report™

| Date not provided | Pearson Performance Solutions |

Population: Adults

Purpose: Identifies those applicants who have the potential to become highly productive staff members

Description: Helps measure five dimensions correlated with workplace productivity: Conscientiousness, Reliability, Punctuality, Responsibility, and Consistency. Designed and statistically validated to assist employers in documenting compliance with applicable employment laws.

Format: Examiner required; suitable for group use; timed: 15 minutes

Scoring: Hand key; scoring service available

Cost: Contact publisher

Health Science Reasoning Test (HSRT)

| 2006 | Insight Assessment |

Noreen C. Facione, Peter A. Facione

Population: Adults

Purpose: Measures critical-thinking and reasoning skills

Description: The HSRT is designed as a 33-item multiple-choice format test. Items present necessary informational content in text-based and diagrammatic formats. Questions invite test takers to draw inferences, to make interpretations, to analyze information, to draw warranted inferences, to identify claims and reasons, and to evaluate the quality of arguments. Subscale scores are reported by the classical categories of Inductive Reasoning and Deductive Reasoning and by the contemporary categories of Analysis, Inference, and Evaluation. Test items are set in clinical and professional practice contexts and supply the necessary content for applying one's thinking skills. Students are neither advantaged nor disadvantaged based on specific subject-matter factual content knowledge or specialized experience. Success on this testing tool depends on the correct application of their thinking skills, not on memorized information. The HSRT is designed for undergraduate and graduate professional school students in nursing, pharmacy, dentistry, optometry, occupational therapy, social work, physical therapy, medical technology, and the health sciences.

Format: Examiner required; individual administration; timed and untimed: 40 to 50 minutes

Scoring: Scoring service available from publisher; online scoring available

Cost: Specimen Kit (manual, 1 protocol, 1 CapScore™ answer form) $140.00

IPI Job-Field Series: Medical Office Assistant

| 1997 | Industrial Psychology International, Ltd. |

Population: Ages 16 years and older

Purpose: Assesses skills and personality of applicants for optometric assistant positions

Description: Used to screen individuals who will act as a support person for optometrists, work with the practitioner and patients, and perform reception and secretarial duties. Multiple-item paper–pencil battery of five aptitude and two personality tests. The tests are Numbers, NPF, CPF, Office Terms, Judgment, Perception, and Fluency. For individual test descriptions, see the *IPI Employee Aptitude Series*. Also available in French and Spanish.

Format: Examiner required; suitable for group use; timed: 50 minutes

Scoring: Hand key

Cost: Starter Kit (test materials for 5 applicants, scoring keys, manuals) $80.00; Test Package $14.00/applicant

Quality Healthcare Employee Inventory (QHEI™)

Date not provided	Pearson Performance Solutions

Population: Adults

Purpose: Helps to select applicants who exhibit favorable attitudes necessary for quality patient care

Description: The assessment provides Healthcare Service Index and health-care–specific norms and covers virtually all health-care employees.

Format: Self-administered; computer administered; untimed: 40 minutes

Scoring: Telephone and fax scoring; software scoring available; scannable forms

Cost: Contact publisher

Reading Form HC-1

1992	Ramsay Corporation

Roland T. Ramsay

Population: Adults

Purpose: Assesses the ability to read, comprehend, and answer written questions

Description: Paper–pencil 40-item multiple-choice test designed to measure an individual's ability to read, comprehend, and answer questions based on a printed passage.

Format: Examiner required, suitable for group use; timed: 30 minutes

Scoring: Self-scored; scoring service available

Cost: Test Booklet $12.00 (minimum 20)

Preference. Potential estimate scores for the positions of claims examiner, customer service representative, and correspondence representative are yielded. Standard scores for each of the 11 measures are also profiled.

Format: Self-administered; computer administered; timed

Scoring: Computer scored

Cost: Contact publisher

LOMASelect-Entry Level

2000	Life Office Management Association

Population: Adults

Purpose: Assesses general abilities and soft personal attributes in preemployment testing

Description: This preemployment screening can be utilized by any business in the insurance/financial services industry. Seven tests yield background information inventory and situational judgment inventory. The seven tests are Reading Comprehension, Language Usage, Following Policies, Procedures, Quantitative Reasoning, Proofing, and Checking. Forms available are support and professional. This test is PC or Web based. The system provides information on key developmental needs and strengths.

Format: Computer administered; online administration available; untimed

Scoring: Computer scored

Cost: Contact publisher

Insurance

Insurance Selection Inventory (ISI)

1986	Pearson Performance Solutions

Population: Ages 16 years and older

Purpose: Evaluates potential for success as a claims examiner, customer service representative, and correspondence representative; used for employee selection and promotion

Description: Paper–pencil 275 item multiple-choice test measuring 11 basic functions necessary to succeed in key insurance positions: Number Comparison, Verbal Reasoning, Applied Arithmetic, Arithmetic Computation, Error Recognition, Drive, Interpersonal Skills, Cognitive Skills, Self-Discipline, Writing Skills, and Work

Mechanical

ACER Mechanical Comprehension Test

1989	Australian Council for Educational Research Limited

Population: Ages 13 years 6 months and older

Purpose: Measures mechanical aptitude; used for employee selection and placement for positions requiring some degree of mechanical aptitude

Description: Paper–pencil 45-item multiple-choice test consisting of problems in the form of diagrams that illustrate various mechanical principles and mechanisms. Australian norms are provided for various age groups, university and technical college groups, and national service trainees and applicants for apprenticeships. Materials include a reusable booklet, separate answer sheet, scoring key, manual, and specimen set.

Format: Examiner required; suitable for group use; timed: 30 minutes

Scoring: Hand key; may be computer scored

Cost: Contact publisher

ACER Mechanical Reasoning Test (Revised Edition)

1997	Australian Council for Educational Research Limited

Population: Ages 15 years and older

Purpose: Measures basic mechanical reasoning abilities; used for employee selection and placement for positions requiring some degree of mechanical aptitude

Description: Multiple-item paper–pencil multiple-choice test consisting of problems in the form of diagrams that illustrate various mechanical principles and mechanisms. This test is a shortened version of the *ACER Mechanical Comprehension Test* and contains some different items and less verbal content. Australian norms are provided for apprenticeship applicants for a variety of trades and for apprentices beginning training. Materials include a reusable booklet, answer sheet, score key, manual, and specimen set.

Format: Examiner required; suitable for group use; timed: 20 minutes

Scoring: Hand key; may be machine scored

Cost: Contact publisher

Air Conditioning Specialist–Form SWA-C

1992, 2002	Ramsay Corporation

Roland T. Ramsay

Population: Adults

Purpose: Measures knowledge and skill in the area of air conditioning

Description: This multiple-choice paper–pencil test has 60 items. Categories tested include Print Reading, Electrical, and Test Equipment; Controls; Welding, Piping, and Plumbing; Mechanical Maintenance and Machines and Equipment; Heating and Ventilation and Combustion; and Air Conditioning and Refrigeration.

Format: Examiner required; suitable for group use; untimed

Scoring: Self-scored; scoring service available

Cost: Test Booklet $21.00 (minimum 20); Manual $24.95

Applied Technology Series (ATS) Mechanical Comprehension (MTS3)

1988	SHL People Performance

Population: Adults

Purpose: Assesses the understanding of basic mechanical principles

Description: Test with 36 items assesses the understanding of basic mechanical principles and their application to such devices as pulleys, gears, and simple structures. The task involves selecting the answer to a short written question from a number of alternatives, which is supported by a realistic technical drawing. Also available in French.

Format: Examiner required; individual administration; untimed: 15 minutes

Scoring: Hand key; machine scored; scoring service available

Cost: Contact publisher

Auto Technician–Form AM-1R

2000, 2003	Ramsay Corporation

Roland T. Ramsay

Population: Adults

Purpose: Measures knowledge and skill in the area of auto repair

Description: This multiple-choice paper–pencil test has 60 items. Categories tested include Electrical and Electronic Systems; Accessories, Mechanical Maintenance, and Equipment Installation; Prints, Schematics, and Diagrams; Welding, Tools, Materials, and Equipment; Power Transmission and Lubrication; Fuel Systems and Internal Combustion Engines; Cooling and Heating Systems, Inspection, Record Keeping, Mathematics, and Environmental Concerns; and Shop Machines.

Format: Examiner required; suitable for group use; untimed

Scoring: Self-scored; scoring service available

Cost: Test Booklet $21.00 (minimum 20); Manual $24.95

Bennett Hand-Tool Dexterity Test

Date not provided	Harcourt Assessment, Inc.

George K. Bennett

Population: Adults

Purpose: Measures basic hand-tool skills required for a job

Description: The test measures key skills by having the examinee disassemble 12 fasteners in a directed order; reassemble the nuts, washers, and bolts on the opposite side; and use wrenches, screwdrivers, and other tools. Score is determined by speed. No reading is required. Included in the Technical Manual are percentile ranks for maintenance mechanics, technical trainees, physically injured workers, special education and vocational training students, and trainees with mental or emotional disabilities.

Format: Examiner required; individual administration; timed: 10 minutes

Scoring: Examiner evaluated

Cost: Complete Set (all equipment and manual for 1 applicant) $390.00

BldqTest-Form MBI-C

1998	Ramsay Corporation

Roland T. Ramsay

Population: Adults

Purpose: Measures building maintenance knowledge and skill

Description: Uses 60 items to measure the following nine areas: Electrical, Print Reading, Plumbing, HVAC, General Repairs, Carpentry, Painting, Masonry, and Clerical Records.

Format: Examiner required; suitable for group use; untimed. approximately 60 minutes

Scoring: Self-scored; scoring service available

Cost: Test Booklets $20.00 (minimum 20); Manual $24.95

C, B, and A Maintenance Mechanics–Forms CI-C, BI-C, and AI-C

1999, 2005	Ramsay Corporation

Roland T. Ramsay

Population: Adults

Purpose: Measures mechanical knowledge and skills

Description: There are three forms of the instrument, each containing 60 items. Each version measures four to five categories of the following skills: Welding, Plumbing, HVAC, Electrical, Pneumatics, Lubrication, Shop, Tools, Machines, Rigging, Mechanical, and Print Reading. Each version has a differing number of items for each skill measured.

Format: Examiner required; suitable for group use; untimed: approximately 60 minutes

Scoring: Self-scored; scoring service available

Cost: Test Booklets $20.00 (minimum 20); Manual $24.95

Cellular Technician–Form TBS

1996	Ramsay Corporation

Roland T. Ramsay

Population: Adults

Purpose: Measures knowledge and skill in the telecommunications area

Description: This multiple-choice paper–pencil test has 120 items. Categories tested include: Mathematics; Schematics and Print Reading; Power Supplies; Basic AC/DC Theory; Test Instruments; Mechanical; Computers; Radios; and Telecommunications.

Format: Examiner required; suitable for group use; untimed

Scoring: Self-scored; scoring service provided

Cost: Test Booklet $25.00 (minimum 20); Manual $24.95

Chemical Reading Form CH

1985	Ramsay Corporation

Roland T. Ramsay

Population: Adults

Purpose: Measures ability to read a passage and answer questions about what is read

Description: A 40-item reading test that contains passages related to chemicals. Answers are in multiple-choice format.

Format: Examiner required; suitable for group use; timed: 40 minutes

Scoring: Examiner evaluated; scoring service available

Cost: Test Booklet $12.00 (minimum 20)

ChemTest-Form AC

2001	Ramsay Corporation

Roland T. Ramsay

Population: Adults

Purpose: Measures knowledge and skill in the area of chemistry

Description: This multiple-choice paper–pencil

test has 43 items. Categories tested include Physical Knowledge; Acids, Bases, and Salts; Compounds; Elements; Mechanical Principles; Gases and Fluids; and Miscellaneous. Also available in Spanish.

Format: Examiner required; suitable for group use; untimed

Scoring: Self-scored; scoring service available

Cost: Test Booklet $21.00 (minimum 20); Manual $24.95

Closure Speed (Gestalt Completion)

1984	Pearson Performance Solutions

L. L. Thurstone, T. E. Jeffrey

Population: Adolescents, adults

Purpose: Measures the ability to hold a configuration in mind despite distracting irrelevancies as indicated by identification of a given figure "hidden" or embedded in a larger more complex drawing; used for vocational counseling and selection of personnel.

Description: Paper–pencil 24-item test in which each item consists of an incomplete picture drawn in black on a white background. The subject must identify and briefly describe the subject of the picture.

Format: Examiner required; suitable for group use; timed: 3 minutes

Scoring: Hand key

Cost: Contact publisher

CNC Operator–Form CNC-2

2000	Ramsay Corporation

Roland T. Ramsay

Population: Adults

Purpose: Measures knowledge and skill in CNC operation

Description: Has 101 multiple-choice items in seven categories: General Knowledge, Coordinate Systems, Interpolation, Program Structure, Tool Compensation, M-Codes, and Operations.

Format: Examiner required; suitable for group use; untimed: 2 hours

Scoring: Self-scored; scoring service available

Cost: Test Booklet $25.00 (minimum 20); Manual $24.95

Combined Basic Skills–Form LCS-C

1998, 2002	Ramsay Corporation

Roland T. Ramsay

Population: Adults

Purpose: Measures basic skills for manufacturing and processing skills

Description: Enables a quick evaluation of literacy and performance skills. A total of 52 items measure reading, arithmetic, inspection and measurement, and process monitoring and problem solving in a multiple-choice format. Spanish version also available.

Format: Examiner required; suitable for group use; online administration available; timed: ranges from 8 to 16 minutes per subtest

Scoring: Self-scored

Cost: Test Booklet $15.00 (minimum 20); Manual $24.95

Combustion Control Technician–Form MCT

1992	Ramsay Corporation

Roland T. Ramsay

Population: Adults

Purpose: Measures knowledge and skill for combustion control technicians

Description: This multiple-choice paper–pencil test has 134 items. Categories tested include Electrical; Digital Electronics; Basic AC/DC Theory; Test Instruments; Mechanical; Computers and PLC; Control Concepts; Electronic Equipment; Combustion; and Analog Electronics.

Format: Examiner required; suitable for group use; untimed

Scoring: Self-scored; scoring service available

Cost: Test Booklet $25.00 (minimum 20); Manual $24.95

Crawford Small Parts Dexterity Test (CPSDT)

1981	Harcourt Assessment, Inc.

John Crawford

Population: Adolescents, adults

Purpose: Measures fine-motor dexterity and eye–hand coordination; used for selecting applicants for such jobs as engravers, watch repairers, and telephone installers

Description: Two-part performance measure of dexterity. Part 1 measures dexterity in using tweezers to assemble pins and collars. Part 2 measures dexterity in screwing small screws with a screwdriver after placing them in threaded holes. The test may be administered in two ways. In the work-limit method, the subject completes the task and the total time is the score. Using the time-limit procedure, the score is the amount of work completed during a specified time. Materials include an assembly plate, pins, collars, and screws.

Format: Examiner required; suitable for group use; timed: 10 to 15 minutes

Scoring: Examiner evaluated

Cost: Complete Set (manual, board and plate, tools, spare parts) $535.00

Drafter (CAD Operator)–Form DDC

2005	Ramsay Corporation

Roland T. Ramsay

Population: Adults

Purpose: Measures ability to draft and perform CAD operations

Description: The instrument contains 30 items in a multiple-choice format. Categories tested include print reading and computer aided design.

Format: Examiner required; suitable for group use; timed: 30 minutes

Scoring: Examiner evaluated; scoring service available

Cost: Test Booklet $21.00 (minimum 20); Manual $24.95

Hydraulics–Form HMD

1999	Ramsay Corporation

Roland T. Ramsay

Population: Adults

Purpose: Measures knowledge and skill in the area of hydraulics

Description: This multiple-choice paper–pencil test has 60 items. Categories tested include Basic Knowledge, Maintenance, and Troubleshooting.

Format: Examiner required; suitable for group use; untimed

Scoring: Self-scored; scoring service available

Cost: Test Booklet $12.00 (minimum 20); Manual $24.95

Inspection and Measurement–Form LCI-C

1997	Ramsay Corporation

Roland T. Ramsay

Population: Adults

Purpose: Measures ability to measure, inspect, and follow directions

Description: The instrument is paper–pencil in a multiple-choice format. Included are exercises in measuring objects, reading dials, determining differences, and arranging items numerically and alphanumerically. Alternate form available.

Format: Examiner required; suitable for group use; timed: 15 minutes

Scoring: Examiner evaluated; scoring service available

Cost: Test Booklet $12.00 (minimum 20); Manual $24.95

Instrument Technician–Form HIT

2001	Ramsay Corporation

Roland T. Ramsay

Population: Adults

Purpose: Measures knowledge and skill in the instrument technician area

Description: This multiple-choice paper–pencil test has 121 items. Categories tested include Mathematics; Digital and Analog Electronics; Schematics and Electrical Print Reading; Process Control; Power Supplies; Basic AC/DC Theory; Test Instruments; Mechanical; Computers and PLC; and Chemical Processes.

Format: Examiner required; suitable for group use; untimed

Scoring: Self-scored; scoring service available

Cost: Test Booklet $25.00 (minimum 20); Manual $24.95

Intuitive Mechanics (Weights and Pulleys)

1984	Pearson Performance Solutions

L. L. Thurstone, T. E. Jeffrey

Population: Ages 16 years and older

Purpose: Measures ability to understand mechanical relationships and to visualize internal movement in a mechanical system; used for vocational counseling or for selection in positions requiring mechanical interest and experience

Description: Paper–pencil 32-item test in which each item is a drawing that represents a system of weights and pulleys. For each system, the examinee must determine whether the system is stable (will not produce movement) or unstable (will produce movement).

Format: Examiner required; suitable for group use; timed: 3 minutes

Scoring: Hand key

Cost: Contact publisher

IPI Employee Aptitude Series: Tools
1986   **Industrial Psychology International Ltd.**

Population: Adults

Purpose: Measures ability to recognize simple tools and mechanical equipment; used to screen applicants for mechanical and technical jobs

Description: Paper-pencil 48-item test measuring the ability to recognize pictures of common tools, equipment, and machines used in factory and mechanical areas. The test does not require the ability to read or write. Also available in French and Spanish.

Format: Examiner required; suitable for group use; timed: 6 minutes

Scoring: Hand key

Cost: Introductory Kit (20 test booklets, scoring key, manual) $33.00

Ironworker–Form A
1987   **Ramsay Corporation**

Roland T. Ramsay

Population: Adults

Purpose: Measures knowledge and skill in the ironworking area

Description: This multiple-choice paper-pencil test has 124 items. Categories tested include Rigging; Welding, Burning, and Heat-Treating; Layout, Cutting, Burning, Assembly, and Fabrication; Mechanical Principles and Repair; Tools, Materials, and Equipment; Mobile Equipment Operation; Shop Machines (Operations, Maintenance, and Use); Steel, Metals, and Materials; Power Transmission; Print Reading; and Lubrication.

Format: Examiner required; suitable for group use; untimed

Scoring: Self-scored; scoring service available

Cost: Test Booklet $25.00 (minimum 20); Manual $24.95

Machinist–Forms AC and AC-SF
1998, 2000   **Ramsay Corporation**

Roland T. Ramsay

Population: Adults

Purpose: Assesses knowledge and skill in machine shop practices

Description: Form AC contains 60 items measuring knowledge in the following areas: Heat Treating; Layout; Cutting and Assembly; Print Reading; Steel, Metals, and Materials; Rigging; Mechanical Principles and Repair; Machine Tools; Tools, Material, and Equipment; and Machine Shop Lubrication. Form AC-SF contains 45 items and is a shortened version for Form AC.

Format: Examiner required; suitable for group use; untimed: Form AC, approximately 60 minutes; Form AC-SF, approximately 45 minutes

Scoring: Self-scored; scoring service available

Cost: Test Booklet $20.00 (minimum 20); Manual $24.95

MainTest–Forms NL-1R, B, and C
1999, 2004   **Ramsay Corporation**

Roland T. Ramsay

Population: Adults

Purpose: Assesses maintenance ability for trade and craft jobs; used for hiring and promotion

Description: Paper-pencil 153-item multiple-choice test. Use Form NL-1R or alternate Forms B and C. Measures knowledge and skill in 21 maintenance areas.

Format: Examiner required; suitable for group use; untimed: approximately 2 hours 30 minutes

Scoring: Scoring service provided

Cost: Test Booklets $60.00 (minimum 10)

Measurement–Form A-C or B-C
2000   **Ramsay Corporation**

Roland T. Ramsay

Population: Adults

Purpose: Assesses an individual's ability to measure accurately with a ruler; used to predict job performance in areas such as maintenance, machine operation, and quality control

Description: Paper-pencil 20-item multiple-choice test designed to assess an individual's ability to measure accurately with a scale in rule dimensions of wholes, halves, quarters, eighths, and sixteenths.

Format: Examiner required; suitable for group use; timed: 15 minutes

Scoring: Self-scored

Cost: Test Booklet $12.00 (minimum 20); Manual $24.95

Mechanical Aptitudes

1947	Pearson Performance Solutions

Population: Grades 10 and above

Purpose: Evaluates an individual's mechanical aptitude; used for employee selection and placement

Description: Three-part paper–pencil aptitude test measuring mechanical knowledge, space relations, and shop arithmetic. The Mechanical Knowledge subtest consists of 46 pictures of common tools and measures general mechanical background. The Space Relations subtest (40 items) measures the ability to visualize and mentally manipulate objects in space. The Shop Arithmetic subtest (24 problems) measures application of quantitative reasoning and fundamental math operations.

Format: Examiner required; suitable for group use; timed: 35 minutes

Scoring: Hand key

Cost: Contact publisher

Mechanical Aptitude Test–Form MAT-AR2-C

2002, 2004	Ramsay Corporation

Roland T. Ramsay

Population: Adults

Purpose: Measures mechanical aptitude

Description: Paper–pencil test with 36 items in multiple-choice format measures aptitude to learn and perform production and maintenance job activities. Used for preemployment selection and predicting success in employee training programs. Online administration available.

Format: Examiner required; suitable for group use; timed: 20 minutes

Scoring: Examiner evaluated; scoring service available; online scoring

Cost: Test Booklet $21.00 (minimum 20); Manual $24.95

Mechanical Maintenance Trainee–Form UKM-IC

1998, 2005	Ramsay Corporation

Roland T. Ramsay

Population: Adults

Purpose: Measures mechanical knowledge and skills

Description: Sixty-item test assessing skills in 12 areas: Hydraulics; Pneumatics; Print Reading; Welding; Power Transmission; Lubrication; Pumps; Piping; Rigging; Maintenance; Shop Machines; and Tools, Material, and Equipment.

Format: Examiner required; suitable for group use; untimed: approximately 60 minutes

Scoring: Self-scored; scoring service available

Cost: Test Booklet $21.00 (minimum 20); Manual $24.95

Mechanical Movements

1984	Pearson Performance Solutions

L. L. Thurstone, T. E. Jeffrey

Population: Adolescents, adults

Purpose: Determines degree of mechanical interest and experience; used for vocational counseling and to select persons for mechanical occupations in industry

Description: Paper–pencil 37-item multiple-choice measure of mechanical comprehension indicating the ability to visualize a mechanical system in which there is internal movement or displacement of the parts.

Format: Examiner required; suitable for group use; timed: 14 minutes

Scoring: Hand key

Cost: Contact publisher

Mechanical Repair Apprentice Battery–Form CMB-C

1990, 2001	Ramsay Corporation

Roland T. Ramsay

Population: Adults

Purpose: Measures basic mechanical skills and knowledge

Description: A basic skills test battery measuring five areas: Reading, Arithmetic, Measurement, Reading Prints and Drawings, and Basic Mechanical Knowledge. The reading items are directly related to mechanical repair. These tests, in multiple-choice format, are more demanding of job knowledge than is a basic skills battery, but less demanding than the *Mechanical Maintenance Trainee Test*.

Format: Examiner required; suitable for group use; untimed: ranges from 15 to 20 minutes per subtest

Scoring: Self-scored; scoring service available

Cost: Test Booklet per Area $11.00 (minimum 20); Manual $24.95

Mechanical Technician A, B, C–Form MTA-XC, Form MTB-XC, Form MTC-XC

2003	Ramsay Corporation

Roland T. Ramsay

Population: Adults

Purpose: Measures knowledge and skill in the mechanical area

Description: Each level progresses in complexity, with Mechanical Technician A being the most advanced. Categories measured are Hydraulics and Pneumatics; Print Reading; Power Transmission and Lubrication; Mechanical Maintenance Principles; and Pumps and Piping. The B and C version of the test also includes Burning, Fabricating, Welding, and Rigging, as well as Shop Equipment and Tools. Alternate forms available for each level.

Format: Examiner required; suitable for group use; untimed

Scoring: Self-scored; scoring service available

Cost: Test Booklet $21.00 (minimum 20); Manual $24.95

MecTest–Form AU-C

1998, 2000	Ramsay Corporation

Roland T. Ramsay

Population: Adults

Purpose: Assesses mechanical ability for trade and craft jobs; used for hiring and promotion

Description: Sixty-item multiple-choice test. Assesses skills in eight areas: Hydraulics and Pneumatics; Print Reading; Welding and Rigging; Power Transmission; Lubrication; Pumps and Piping; Mechanical Maintenance; and Shop Machines, Tools, and Equipment. Also available in Spanish.

Format: Examiner required; suitable for group use; untimed: approximately 60 minutes

Scoring: Self-scored; scoring service available

Cost: Test Booklet $21.00 (minimum 20); Manual $24.95

Millwright Test–Form MWB-1C

2000	Ramsay Corporation

Roland T. Ramsay

Population: Adults

Purpose: Measures millwright knowledge and skill

Description: Contains 60 items. Measures knowledge in seven categories: Hydraulics and Pneumatics; Burning and Fabrication and Print Reading; Power Transmission and Lubrication; Pumps and Piping; Rigging; Mechanical/Maintenance; and Shop Equipment and Tools, Materials, and Equipment.

Format: Examiner required; suitable for group use; untimed: approximately 60 minutes

Scoring: Self-scored

Cost: Test Booklet $21.00 (minimum 20); Manual $24.95

Minnesota Paper Form Board Test–Revised

1941 (Manual 1995)	Harcourt Assessment, Inc.

Rensis Likert, W. H. Quasha

Population: Adolescents, adults

Purpose: Measures ability to visualize and manipulate objects in space; used to select applicants for jobs requiring mechanical-spatial ability

Description: Multiple-item paper–pencil test of spatial perception. The applicant is required to visualize the assembly of two-dimensional geometric shapes into a whole design. The test is related to both mechanical and artistic ability. Two equivalent forms, AA and BB (hand scoring) and MA and MB (machine scoring), are available. Also available in French-Canadian.

Format: Examiner required; suitable for group use; timed: 20 minutes

Scoring: Hand key; may be machine scored locally

Cost: Examination Kit (manual, test booklets for each form) $60.00

Minnesota Rate of Manipulation Tests

1969	AGS Publishing/Pearson Assessments

Population: Adults

Purpose: Measures finger–hand–arm dexterity; used for employee selection for jobs requiring manual dexterity and in vocational and rehabilitation training programs

Description: Five-test battery measuring manual dexterity. The five tests are The Placing Test, The Turning Test, The Displacing Test, The One-Hand Turning and Placing Test, and The Two-Hand Turning and Placing Test. Materials consist of two test boards with holes and blocks. Each block is painted orange on the upper half and yellow on the lower half. The blocks are manipulated in prescribed ways. Specific tests assess movements with the preferred hand and with both hands. The five tests may be administered separately. All tests are repeated for four complete trials. The Displacing and Turning tests are suitable for use with individuals who are blind.

Format: Self-administered; timed: 10 minutes for each test

Scoring: Examiner interpreted

Cost: Complete Kit (manual, protocols, test boards, blocks, carrying case) $353.95

Mobile Equipment Mechanic–Form A

1980–1989	Ramsay Corporation

Roland T. Ramsay

Population: Adults

Purpose: Measures knowledge and skill in the area of mobile equipment maintenance

Description: This multiple-choice paper–pencil test has 120 items. Categories tested include Electrical Systems; Pneumatics; Print Reading; Welding; Power Transmission; Lubrication; Pumps; Piping; Rigging; Mechanical Maintenance; Shop Machines; Tools, Materials, and Equipment; Internal Combustion Engines; and Hydraulics.

Format: Examiner required; suitable for group use; untimed

Scoring: Self-scored; scoring service available

Cost: Test Booklet $25.00 (minimum 20); Manual $24.95

Mobile Equipment Operator–Form A

1997–2005	Ramsay Corporation

Roland T. Ramsay

Population: Adults

Purpose: Measures knowledge and skill in the area of mobile equipment operation

Description: This multiple-choice paper–pencil test has 50 items. Categories tested include Operation; Material Handling; Cleaning and Lubrication; Inspection; Piling; Loading and Unloading; Traveling; Hooks; Slings; Forklifts; Signals; and Booms of Cranes.

Format: Examiner required; suitable for group use; untimed

Scoring: Self-scored; scoring service available

Cost: Test Booklet $12.00 (minimum 20); Manual $24.95

Multi-Craft Test–Form MC-C

2000	Ramsay Corporation

Roland T. Ramsay

Population: Adults

Purpose: Measures maintenance knowledge and skill

Description: Test with 60 items in seven categories: Hydraulics and Pneumatics; Welding and Rigging; Power Transmission, Lubrication, Mechanical/Maintenance, Shop Machines, and Tools and Equipment; Pumps, Piping, and Combustion; Motors, Control Circuits, Schematics, and Print Reading; Digital Electronics, Power Supplies, Computers, and PLC and Test Instruments; and Basic AC/DC Theory, Power Distribution, and Electrical Maintenance.

Format: Examiner required; suitable for group use; untimed: 60 minutes

Scoring: Self-scored; scoring service available

Cost: Test Booklet $21.00 (minimum 20); Manual $24.95

Multi-Craft Trainee Test Form A

2004	Ramsay Corporation

Roland T. Ramsay

Population: Adults

Purpose: Measures knowledge and skill in the mechanical and electrical area

Description: This multiple-choice paper–pencil test has 60 items in seven subareas: Hydraulics and Pneumatics; Welding, Cutting, and Rigging; Power Transmission, Lubrication, Mechanical Maintenance, and Shop Machines, and Tools and Equipment; Pumps, Piping, and Combustion; Motors, Control Circuits, and Schematics and Print Reading; Digital and Analog Electronics, Power Supplies, Computers, and PLC, and Test Instruments; and Basic AC/DC Theory, Power Distribution, and Electrical Maintenance.

Format: Examiner required; suitable for group use; untimed

Scoring: Self-scored; scoring service available

Cost: Test Booklet $21.00 (minimum 20); Manual $24.95

OSHA Safety Violations Test–Form A

1999	Ramsay Corporation

Roland T. Ramsay

Population: Adults

Purpose: Measures knowledge and skill in the

area of OSHA safety and violations of OSHA safety

Description: This multiple-choice paper–pencil test has 100 items in the following subareas: Scaffolding, Fall Protection, Hazard Communication, Lockout/Tagout, Machine Guarding, Power Press, Mechanical Power, Electrical, Excavation, and Machine Guarding (Abrasive Wheels).

Format: Examiner required; suitable for group use; untimed

Scoring: Self-scored; scoring service available

Cost: Test Booklet $12.00 (minimum 20); Manual $24.95

Pennsylvania Bi-Manual Worksample
1969   AGS Publishing/Pearson Assessments

John R. Roberts

Population: Ages 16 years and older

Purpose: Measures manual dexterity and eye–hand coordination; used for employee placement

Description: Multiple-operation manual dexterity test utilizing an 8 × 24 inch board containing 100 holes arranged in 10 rows and a set of nuts and bolts to test finger dexterity of both hands, whole movement of both arms, eye–hand coordination, and bi-manual coordination. The employee grasps a nut between the thumb and index finger of the other hand, turns the bolt into the nut, and places both in a hole in the board. Twenty practice motions are allowed, and 80 motions are timed. Disassembly reverses the process and involves timing 100 motions. A special supplement contains directions for administration to employees who are blind.

Format: Examiner required; suitable for small-group use; untimed: 12 minutes

Scoring: Examiner interpreted

Cost: Complete Kit (manual, protocols, board, bolts, nuts, carrying case) $199.95

PipeTest–BJP-IC
1998, 2005   Ramsay Corporation

Roland T. Ramsay

Population: Adults

Purpose: Measures plumbing and pipefitting knowledge and skills

Description: The test contains 60 multiple-choice items in 10 categories: Piping, Plumbing, and Combustion; Pumps; Hydraulics; Pneumat-

ics; Burning, Soldering, and Fabrication; Print Reading; Rigging; Mathematics and Layout; Mechanical Maintenance; and Tools, Materials, and Equipment.

Format: Examiner required; suitable for group use; untimed: approximately 60 minutes

Scoring: Self-scored; scoring service available

Cost: Test Booklet $21.00 (minimum 20); Manual $24.95

Precision Measurement–Form A
1998   Ramsay Corporation

Roland T. Ramsay

Population: Adults

Purpose: Measures ability to measure, inspect, and follow directions

Description: This multiple-choice paper–pencil test has 60 items in the following subareas: (a) Layout, Calculations, Figures, and Formulas and (b) Precision Measurement.

Format: Examiner required; suitable for group use; untimed

Scoring: Self-scored; scoring service available

Cost: Test Booklet $12.00 (minimum 20); Manual $24.95

PrinTest–Form A-C or B-C
1998 (A-C); 2001 (B-C)   Ramsay Corporation

Roland T. Ramsay

Population: Adults

Purpose: Assesses ability to read mechanical prints and drawings; used for hiring and promotion

Description: Paper–pencil 33-item multiple-choice test assessing ability to read mechanical prints and drawings. Form A-C (fractions) and Form B-C (decimals) both measure skills in views and surfaces; simple drawings; intermediate drawings; and complex drawings.

Format: Examiner required; suitable for group use; timed: 35 minutes

Scoring: Self-scored; scoring service available

Cost: Test Booklet $21.00 (minimum 20); Manual $24.95

Process Flow–Form WLP
1997   Ramsay Corporation

Roland T. Ramsay

Population: Adults

Purpose: Measures ability to read and analyze processing diagrams and flowcharts

Description: The instrument is paper–pencil in a multiple-choice format. Developed to measure the ability to follow the flow of liquid or material through a chemical or industrial process, including reading gauges.

Format: Examiner required; suitable for group use; timed: 20 minutes

Scoring: Examiner evaluated; scoring service available

Cost: Test Booklet $12.00 (minimum 20); Manual $24.95

Refrigeration Mechanic–Form RV-5

2005	Ramsay Corporation

Roland T. Ramsay

Population: Adults

Purpose: Measures knowledge and skill in refrigeration

Description: This multiple-choice paper–pencil test has 121 items in the following subareas: Print Reading; Lubrication; Welding, Burning, and Heat-Treating; Mechanical; Pneumatics; Shop Machines and Equipment; and HVAC and Refrigeration.

Format: Examiner required; suitable for group use; untimed

Scoring: Self-scored; scoring service available

Cost: Test Booklet $25.00 (minimum 20); Manual $24.95

Senior Maintenance Technician Pipefitter–Form SCP-1

1993	Ramsay Corporation

Roland T. Ramsay

Population: Adults

Purpose: Measures pipefitting knowledge and skill

Description: This multiple-choice paper–pencil test has 121 items in the following subareas: Piping and Plumbing; Pumps; Pneumatics; Burning, Soldering, and Fabrication; Print Reading; Rigging; Mathematics; Mechanical Maintenance; and Tools, Materials, and Equipment.

Format: Examiner required; suitable for group use; untimed

Scoring: Self-scored; scoring service available

Cost: Test Booklet $25.00 (minimum 20); Manual $24.95

Sheet Metal Worker–Form ASM

2001	Ramsay Corporation

Roland T. Ramsay

Population: Adults

Purpose: Measures knowledge and skill of sheet metal worker abilities

Description: This multiple-choice paper–pencil test has 113 items in the following subareas: Layout and Fabrication; Hand and Power Tools; Fasteners; Ladders and Scaffolds; Metals; Rigging; Mathematics; Mechanical Principles and Repair; Print Reading; and Welding, Cutting, and Burning.

Format: Examiner required; suitable for group use; untimed

Scoring: Self-scored; scoring service available

Cost: Test Booklet $25.00 (minimum 20); Manual $24.95

Stromberg Dexterity Test (SDT)

1981	Harcourt Assessment, Inc.

E. L. Stromberg

Population: Adults

Purpose: Measures manipulative skill in sorting by color and sequence; used to select applicants for jobs requiring manual speed and accuracy; also used for assessing manual dexterity of individuals with disabilities in vocational training programs

Description: Two-trial performance test of manual dexterity in which the applicant is asked to discriminate and sort biscuit-sized discs and to move and place them as fast as possible. The score is the number of seconds required to complete the two trials. Materials include assembly board and discs.

Format: Examiner required; individual administration; timed: 5 to 10 minutes

Scoring: Score obtained by timing

Cost: Complete Set (all necessary equipment, manual, carrying case) $700.00

Technical Test Battery (TTB) Mechanical Comprehension (MT4.1)

1992	SHL People Performance

Population: Adults

Purpose: Measures understanding of basic mechanical principles

Description: Multiple-choice test with 36 items

measuring knowledge of the classic mechanical elements, such as gears, pulleys, and levers, and a wide range of domestic and leisure applications of physics and mechanics, from electric ovens to billiard balls. Each item consists of a three-choice question about a technical drawing. The drawings are presented in technical workshop style without demanding any specific preknowledge to interpret them.

Format: Examiner required; individual administration; untimed: 18 minutes

Scoring: Hand key; machine scored; scoring service available

Cost: Contact publisher

Test of Mechanical Concepts
1975	Pearson Performance Solutions

Population: Adults

Purpose: Measures an individual's ability to visualize and understand basic mechanical and spatial interrelationships; used for employee selection and screening for such jobs as assembler, maintenance mechanic, machinist, and factory production worker

Description: Paper-pencil 78-item test consisting of three subtests measuring separate skills or abilities necessary for jobs requiring mechanical ability. The Mechanical Interrelationships subtest consists of 24 drawings depicting mechanical movements and interrelationships. The Mechanical Tools and Devices subtest consists of 30 items measuring knowledge of common mechanical tools and devices. The Spatial Relations subtest consists of 24 items measuring the ability to visualize and manipulate objects in space. The test is available in two forms.

Format: Examiner required; suitable for group use; untimed: 35 to 45 minutes

Scoring: Hand key

Cost: Contact publisher

Tool Knowledge and Use Test-Form JLR
1994	Ramsay Corporation

Roland T. Ramsay

Population: Adults

Purpose: Assesses knowledge of tools and their uses; used for hiring for trade and craft jobs

Description: Paper-pencil 70-item multiple-choice test.

Format: Examiner required; suitable for group use; untimed: approximately 60 minutes

Scoring: Self-scored; scoring service available

Cost: Test Booklet $25.00 (minimum 20); Manual $24.95

VCWS 1-Small Tools (Mechanical)
1974	Valpar International Corporation

Population: Ages 15 years and older

Purpose: Assesses an individual's understanding of small tools and ability to work with them

Description: The design of the test challenges the individual to demonstrate skill in working in small, confined spaces while using the fingers and hands to manipulate tools to perform the assigned task. The individual works through a small hole in the work sample in order to simulate working conditions in which an individual is unable to view the work he or she is doing. The individual completes five panels. In each panel, the individual uses a different set of tools to insert fasteners such as screws, bolts, and hitch pin clips. Performance indicates the ability to complete successfully jobs requiring various degrees of ability in using small tools. The work sample uses methods-time measurement and error scores to determine level of performance. Learning curve allows for multiple administrations as needed.

Format: Examiner required; individual administration; timed: 90 minutes

Scoring: Examiner evaluated

Cost: $1,895.00

VCWS 11-Eye-Hand-Foot Coordination
1974	Valpar International Corporation

Population: Ages 15 years and older

Purpose: Assesses eye, hand, and foot coordination; provides insight into individual concentration, learning, planning, spatial discrimination, and reaction to immediate positive and negative feedback

Description: Manual assessment of an individual's ability to use his or her eyes, hands, and feet simultaneously in a coordinated manner. The examinee sits in front of the work sample and maneuvers nine steel balls, one at a time, through a maze containing 13 holes into which the steel balls may drop, thus ending the examinee's attempt to make it to the end of the maze with that particular ball. In order to move the ball, the examinee tilts the maze left and right with his or her hands, forward and backward with his or her feet, and traces the track of the ball with his or her eyes. Learning curve allows for multiple administrations as needed.

Format: Examiner required; individual administration; timed

Scoring: Examiner evaluated

Cost: $1,895.00

Vibration Analysis–Form A

1999	Ramsay Corporation

Roland T. Ramsay

Population: Adults

Purpose: Measures knowledge and skill in the area of vibration analysis

Description: This multiple-choice paper–pencil test has 32 items.

Format: Examiner required; suitable for group use; untimed

Scoring: Self-scored; scoring service available

Cost: Test Booklet $12.00 (minimum 20)

Welder–Form BJW-1

1991	Ramsay Corporation

Roland T. Ramsay

Population: Adults

Purpose: Measures welding knowledge and skill

Description: This multiple-choice paper–pencil test has 121 items in the following subareas: Print Reading; Welding Processes; Types of Joints; Welding Positions; Filler Metals; Processes Related to Welding; Welding Metals; Welding Defects; Repair Welding and Surfacing; and Tools, Machines, and Equipment.

Format: Examiner required; suitable for group use; untimed

Scoring: Self-scored; scoring service available

Cost: Test Booklet $25.00 (minimum 20); Manual $24.95

WeldTest–Form AC

1998	Ramsay Corporation

Roland T. Ramsay

Population: Adults

Purpose: Assesses welding ability for trade and craft jobs; used for hiring and promotion

Description: Multiple-choice 60-item test that measures skills in six areas: Print Reading; Weld-

ing, Cutting Torch, and Arc Air Cutting; Welder Maintenance Operations; Tools, Machines, Materials, and Equipment; Mobile Equipment and Rigging; and Production Welding Calculations.

Format: Examiner required; suitable for group use; untimed: approximately 60 minutes

Scoring: Self-scored; scoring service available

Cost: Test Booklet $21.00 (minimum 20); Manual $24.95

Wiesen Test of Mechanical Aptitude (WTMA)–PAR Edition

1999	Psychological Assessment Resources, Inc.

Joel P. Wiesen

Population: Ages 18 years and older

Purpose: Measures mechanical aptitudes for employment

Description: Sixty items, consisting of eight mechanical/physical principals classified into three types. Sixth-grade reading level is required.

Format: Self-administered; timed: 30 minutes

Scoring: Examiner evaluated

Cost: Introductory Kit (manual, 10 reusable booklets, 25 forms, scoring key) $222.00

Work Skills Series (WSS) Index

1991	SHL People Performance

Population: Adults

Purpose: Measures the ability to manipulate small objects requiring fine finger dexterity

Description: The candidate is required to insert thin steel rods into small holes and secure them with the aid of a screwdriver. The working area is restricted and both hands need to be used to complete the task.

Format: Examiner required; individual administration; untimed: 10 minutes

Scoring: Hand score

Cost: Contact publisher

Work Skills Series (WSS) Mandex

1991	SHL People Performance

Population: Adults

Purpose: Measures ability to manipulate and construct components using medium finger and hand dexterity

Description: The candidate is presented with a preassembled structure (mounted on one end of a wood base) consisting of six steel plates joined together by an assortment of nuts, bolts, washers, and spacers. Using this as a model, the task is to build an identical structure on the other end of the base using a set of plates and related materials provided. No tools are necessary. Scoring is achieved by awarding points for the correct selection and positioning of plates. The number of nuts, bolts, washers, and spacers used is also taken into account.

Format: Examiner required; individual administration; untimed: 15 minutes

Scoring: Hand score

Cost: Contact publisher

Municipal Services

A-4 Police Officer Video Test

| 1999 | International Public Management Association for Human Resources |

Population: Adults

Purpose: Candidates for entry-level police officer positions

Description: Designed as an entry-level 90-item test to assess both cognitive and noncognitive competencies that new police officers need to perform successfully on the job. Administered via videotaped scenarios as an alternative to traditional multiple-choice tests; all instructions, as well as countdown timer, are included on the video to facilitate test administration in three knowledge areas: Ability to Observe, Listen to, and Remember Information; Ability to Use Situational Judgment and Interpersonal Skills; and Ability to Learn and Apply Police Information.

Format: Examiner required; individual and group administration; timed: 2 hours 35 minutes

Scoring: Examiner evaluated; machine scoring

Cost: Contact publisher

B-3R, B-4R, B-5, and B-5a Firefighter Tests

| 1994-2001 | International Public Management Association for Human Resources |

Population: Adults

Purpose: Candidates for entry-level firefighter positions

Description: Designed to assess critical abilities necessary for the successful job performance of entry-level firefighters. B-3R and B-4R have scores in 10 knowledge areas: Reading Comprehension, Interpreting Tables, Situational Judgment, Logical Reasoning, Reading Gauges, Applying Basic Math Rules, Mechanical Aptitude, Spatial Sense, Map Reading, and Vocabulary. These are parallel forms. B-5 and B-5a have scores in five knowledge areas: Ability to Learn, Remember, and Apply Information; Reading Comprehension; Interests (B-5 only); Situational Judgment; and Logical and Mathematical Reasoning Ability. B-5 assesses a wider range of characteristics than typical entry-level firefighter tests do and includes a noncognitive component that measures personal traits.

Format: Examiner required; individual or group administration; timed: B-3R, B-4R, 120 minutes; B-5, 140 minutes; B-5a, 125 minutes

Scoring: Examiner evaluated; machine scoring

Cost: Contact publisher

C-1 and C-2 Correctional Officer Tests

| 1991-1995 | International Public Management Association for Human Resources |

Population: Candidates for entry-level positions

Purpose: Assesses skills needed for entry-level correctional officers

Description: Measures four knowledge areas with 90 items: Reading Comprehension, Counting Accuracy, Inductive Reasoning, and Deductive Reasoning. There are two forms available.

Format: Examiner required; individual and group administration; timed: 2 hours

Scoring: Examiner evaluated; machine scoring

Cost: Contact publisher (administration fee is waived if ordered with another product)

C-BDQ Correctional Officer Background Data Questionnaire

| 1995 | International Public Management Association for Human Resources |

Population: Candidates for entry-level positions

Purpose: Assesses background and personal characteristics

Description: Measures seven biodata subtypes: Unscored Demographic Information, Background, Lifestyle, Interest, Personality, Ability, and Opinion-Based.

Format: Examiner required; individual and group administration; timed: 1 hour

Scoring: Scoring service

Cost: Contact publisher

Correctional Officers' Interest Blank (COIB)

| 1982 | Mind Garden, Inc. |

Harrison G. Gough

Population: Adults

Purpose: Recommended for research and application in the development of selection techniques for correctional officers

Description: Forty questions about interests and attitudes that have been found to have a good potential for predicting performance of correctional officers. Scoring information is only by special license.

Format: Self-administered; untimed: 10 minutes

Scoring: Hand key through special permission

Cost: Manual/Sampler Set $30.00; 200 Uses $150.00

D-1, D-2, and D-3 Police Officer Tests

| 1999-2006 | International Public Management Association for Human Resources |

Population: Adults

Purpose: Candidates for entry-level police officer positions

Description: Designed to assess with 100 items the basic abilities identified as being important for successful performance as a police officer in five job dimensions: Observation and Memory [Wanted Posters], Ability to Learn Police Material, Police Interest Questionnaire [Noncognitive], Verbal and Reading Comprehension (all but D-1), and Situational Judgment and Problem Solving. D-1, D-2, D-3 are comparable forms; no prior training or experience as a police officer is assumed of candidates taking any of the three forms. Test Information Packets are available for candidate study purposes.

Format: Examiner required; individual or group administration; timed: 2 hours 30 minutes (includes 325 minutes for information packet)

Scoring: Examiner evaluated; machine scoring

Cost: Contact publisher

801 Public Safety Telecommunicator First-Line Supervisor Test

| 2002-2006 | International Public Management Association for Human Resources |

Population: Candidates for promotion

Purpose: Assesses qualification for promotion to first-line supervisor

Description: Measures six knowledge areas: Communication Center Operation, Concepts of Supervision, Concepts of Evaluating Subordinate Performance, Concepts of Training, Concepts of Writing and Reviewing Reports and Paperwork, and Concepts of Administration. A reading list is provided to help candidates prepare for the test.

Format: Examiner required; individual and group administration; timed: 2 hours 30 minutes

Scoring: Examiner evaluated; machine scored

Cost: Contact publisher

Firefighter Learning Simulation (FLS)

| 1998 | Psychological Services, Inc. |

Population: Adults

Purpose: Measures the ability to learn information similar to material presented in the fire academy; used to select applicants for entry-level firefighter positions or training programs

Description: Multiple-choice 65-item test based on material presented in a Firefighter Learning Simulation Training Manual that is distributed to examinees in advance of the testing session. Examinee must answer the questions only on the basis of information contained in the Training Manual. May be used in conjunction with *PSI Firefighter Selection Test* and/or *Work Orientation Survey for Firefighters*.

Format: Examiner required; suitable for group use; untimed: 90 minutes

Scoring: Hand key; may be computer scored; scoring service available from publisher

Cost: Contact publisher

Firefighter Selection Test

| 1983 | Psychological Services, Inc. |

Population: Adults

Purpose: Measures three abilities important for learning and performing the job of firefighter: mechanical comprehension, reading comprehension, and report interpretation; used to select applicants for entry-level firefighter positions or training programs

Description: Paper–pencil 100-item multiple-choice test measuring the understanding of mechanical principles relevant to the firefighting job (39 items), the ability to read and interpret a passage (51 items), and the ability to read and interpret charts and reports (10 items). The items consist of drawings and passages based on firefighter training materials and sample charts and reports presenting fire department data. May be used with the *PSI Firefighter Learning Simulation, Work Orientation Survey for Firefighters,* or both.

Format: Examiner required; suitable for group use; timed: 2 hours 30 minutes

Scoring: Hand key; may be computer scored; scoring service available from publisher

Cost: Contact publisher

Hilson Background Investigation Inventory-Revised (HBIR)

2004   Institute for Personality and Ability Testing, Inc.

Robin E. Inwald

Population: Adults

Purpose: Screens public safety and security applicants

Description: Aids in identifying candidates with antisocial and behavior patterns and/or job-related difficulties. For use with Public Safety/ Security officer preemployment screening and background investigations. The revised version includes 309 true-false questions from which both raw scores and *t*-scores are derived. A fifth-grade reading level is required. Also available in Spanish.

Format: Self-administered; untimed: 45 minutes

Scoring: Examiner evaluated; computer scoring available

Cost: $31.00 to $35.00 depending on scoring method

Inwald Personality Inventory (IPI)

1980   Institute for Personality and Ability Testing, Inc.

Robin E. Inwald

Population: Adults

Purpose: Assesses behavior patterns and characteristics of police, security, firefighter, and correction officer candidates; used for preemployment screening

Description: Paper-pencil 310-item true-false instrument consisting of a validity measure and 25 scales assessing specific external behavior, attitudes and temperament, internalized conflict measures, and interpersonal conflict measures: Guardedness, Alcohol, Drugs, Driving Violations, Job Difficulties, Trouble with the Law and Society, Absence Abuse, Substance Abuse, Antisocial At-

titudes, Hyperactivity, Rigid Type, Type "A" Illness Concerns, Treatment Programs, Anxiety, Phobic Personality, Obsessive Personality, Depression, Loner Type, Unusual Experience/Thoughts, Lack of Assertiveness, Interpersonal Difficulties, Undue Suspiciousness, Family Conflicts, Sexual Concerns, and Spouse/Mate Conflicts. The test yields raw scores and *t*-scores. Also available in Spanish and French.

Format: Self-administered; untimed: 30 to 45 minutes

Scoring: Computer scored; scoring service available

Cost: $16.00 to $20.00 depending on scoring method

Inwald Survey 5-Revised (IS5-R)

2001   Institute for Personality and Ability Testing, Inc.

Robin E. Inwald

Population: Adults

Purpose: Used for preemployment screening

Description: Total of 192 items for police applicants. Screens work ethic, domestic violence, social initiative, work adjustment, and frustration/anger. Also available in Spanish.

Format: Examiner required; suitable for group use; untimed: 20 minutes

Scoring: Computer scored; scoring service available

Cost: $16.00 to $20.00 depending on scoring method

National Municipal Fire Fighter Examination (NMFE)

1994, 1995, 1999   APR Testing Services

Joel Peter Wiesen

Population: Adults

Purpose: Measures job-related cognitive ability of candidates for firefighter

Description: The NMFE measures mechanical ability, reasoning and problem solving, reading ability, math ability, special ability, EMS (optional), and paramedic math (optional). Test services include candidate orientation booklets, written test booklets, on-site administration, computerized scoring, and computerized score reporting.

Format: Examiner required; group administration; untimed: 2 hours

Scoring: Examiner evaluated after computer scoring

Cost: Base price for one-time use for 50 candidates $1,400.00

901 Correctional Facility
First-Line Supervisor Test

2002–2006	International Public Management Association for Human Resources

Population: Candidates for promotion

Purpose: Assesses qualification for promotion to the correctional facility first-line supervisory position

Description: Measures six knowledge areas: Concepts of Supervision, Correctional Facility Operation, Concepts for Writing and Reviewing Reports and Paperwork, Concepts of Evaluating Subordinate Performance, Concepts of Training, and Concepts of Administration. A reading list is available to help candidates prepare for the test.

Format: Examiner required; individual and group administration; timed: 2 hours 30 minutes

Scoring: Examiner evaluated; machine scoring

Cost: Contact publisher

P-1SV and P-2SV Police Officer Tests

2003, 2006	International Public Management Association for Human Resources

Population: Adults

Purpose: Candidates for entry-level police officer positions

Description: Developed to assess the competencies that new police officers need to perform successfully on the job in five knowledge areas: Ability to Learn and Apply Police Information, Ability to Observe and Remember Details, Verbal Ability, Ability to Follow Directions, and Ability to Use Judgment and Logic. There are two forms available with 100 items each. A Test Information Packet is available for candidate study purposes.

Format: Examiner required; individual administration; timed: 2 hours 10 minutes (includes 25 minutes for information packet)

Scoring: Examiner evaluated; machine scoring

Cost: Contact publisher

P-BDQ Police Officer Background
Data Questionnaire

1999–2000	International Public Management Association for Human Resources

Population: Candidates for entry-level police officer positions

Purpose: Assesses backgrounds and personal characteristics

Description: Measures five biodata subtypes in 50 items: Background, Lifestyle, Interest, Personality, and Ability.

Format: Examiner required; individual and group administration; timed: 30 minutes

Scoring: Scoring service

Cost: Contact publisher

P-Det 2.0 Police Detective Test

2004–2006	International Public Management Association for Human Resources

Population: Candidates for promotion

Purpose: Measures qualification for promotion to police detective

Description: Measures three knowledge areas: Police Investigation Procedures, Laws Related to Police Work, and Concepts for Writing and Completing Reports/Records and Paperwork. A reading list is available to help candidates prepare for the test.

Format: Examiner required; individual and group administration; timed: 2 hours

Scoring: Examiner evaluated; machine scoring

Cost: Contact publisher

PL-1 Police Administrator
Test (Lieutenant)

1998–2006	International Public Management Association for Human Resources

Population: Candidates for promotion

Purpose: Assesses skills suitable to assist police departments in promoting to a higher rank

Description: Measures four knowledge areas: Police Procedures: Patrol and Investigation, Laws Related to Police Work, Concepts of Supervision, and Concepts of Administration. A reading list is available to help candidates prepare for the test.

Format: Examiner required; individual and group administration; timed: 2 hours 30 minutes

Scoring: Examiner evaluated; machine scored

Cost: Contact publisher

Police Candidate Background
Self-Report (PCBS)

2001	APR Testing Services

Joel Peter Wiesen

Population: Police officer candidates

Purpose: Provides a system for collection of background information from job candidates; can improve and simplify the work of the background investigator

Description: Collects background information to be used in assessment of appropriateness of hire. Paper–pencil multiple-item fill-in-the-blank test. Collects both factual data and opinions. The subjects covered include basic identification information, military experience, work experience, education, illegal behaviors, weapon ownership and use, finances, hobbies/interests, group memberships, self-evaluation, illegal drug use, alcohol use, work-style preferences, interpersonal behavior, and family. Test yields scores in 10 areas. Provides two score reports; one consists of a listing of red flags, and the other consists of scores in each of 10 areas (reported as high, medium, or low).

Format: May be given on a take-home basis; self-administered; untimed: 2 hours

Scoring: Examiner evaluated after computer scoring

Cost: Police Service Specimen Set (test, sample reports) $75.00; Psychologist's Specimen Set (test, sample reports, manual) $75.00; Per Candidate $23.00 to $28.00 depending on number tested

Police Selection Test

1995	Psychological Services, Inc.

Population: Adults

Purpose: Measures five abilities important in learning and performing the job of police officer: reading comprehension, quantitative problem solving, data interpretation, writing skills, and reasoning; used to select applicants for entry-level police positions

Description: Paper–pencil 100-item multiple-choice test measuring the ability to read and interpret a passage (19 items), the ability to analyze logical numerical relationships (20 items), the ability to interpret data and other information (23 items), the ability to express information in writing (15 items), and the ability to analyze information and make valid judgments based on available facts (23 items). The test consists of passages, tables, forms, and maps based on police officer training material. Study guide available.

Format: Examiner required; suitable for group use; timed: 2 hours

Scoring: Hand key; may be computer scored; scoring service available

Cost: Contact publisher

PSACS Public Safety Assessment Center System for Police Sergeant

2005	International Public Management Association for Human Resources

Population: Candidates for promotion

Purpose: Assesses potential for the position of police sergeant

Description: Measures seven competencies: Problem Identification and Analysis, Decision Making/Decisiveness, Oral Communication, Written Communication, Interpersonal and Community Relations, Planning and Supervising, and Applied Technical Knowledge.

Format: Examiner required; individual and group administration; timed: 2 days

Scoring: Examiner evaluated

Cost: Contact publisher (administration fee is waived if ordered with another product)

PST-100SV and PST-80SV Public Safety Telecommunicator Test

1995	International Public Management Association for Human Resources

Population: Adults

Purpose: Candidates for entry-level public safety communicator positions

Description: Designed to assess critical abilities required for entry-level public safety telecommunicator positions in five knowledge areas: Listening Skills, Reading Comprehension, Ability to Learn and Apply Information, Reasoning Ability, and Ability to Use Situational Judgment. The two versions contain exactly the same questions with the exception of the Listening Skills subtest, which has an audio component; the PST-80SV version of the exam is available for those jurisdictions that do not have the audio equipment needed to administer the Listening Skills subtest. The PST-100SV has 100 items, while the PST-80SV has 80 items.

Format: Examiner required; individual or group administration; untimed: 2 hours 24 minutes (100 items) or 2 hours (80 items)

Scoring: Examiner evaluated; machine scored

Cost: Contact publisher

PSUP 1.1, 2.1, and 3.1 Police Supervisor (Corporal/Sergeant)

2003 2006	International Public Management Association for Human Resources

Population: Adults

Purpose: Candidates for promotion to the police supervisor or corporal/sergeant position

Description: Designed as a promotional test for first-line police supervisor. PSUP 1.1, PSUP 2.1, PSUP 3.1 are comparable forms; reading lists are available to help candidates prepare for the tests. Tests five knowledge areas: Laws Related to Police Work, Police Field Operations, Investigative Procedures, Supervisory Principles and Concepts and Reports, and Records and Paperwork.

Format: Examiner required; individual or group administration; 2 hours 30 minutes

Scoring: Examiner evaluated; machine scoring

Cost: Contact publisher

Report Completion Exercise for Firefighter, Police Officer, and Correctional Officer

2005	International Public Management Association for Human Resources

Population: Candidates for entry-level positions

Purpose: Assesses observation, listening, and written communication skills

Description: Three separate instruments designed to measure the abilities of candidates for public service positions.

Format: Examiner required; individual and group administration; timed: varies depending on position

Scoring: Departments develop scoring criteria

Cost: Contact publisher (administration fee is waived if ordered with another product)

701 and 702 Fire Supervisor Tests

2001–2006	International Public Management Association for Human Resources

Population: Candidates for promotion

Purpose: Assesses knowledge for qualification for fire supervisor or lieutenant position

Description: Measures nine knowledge areas with 100 items: Fire Behavior and Fire Service, Firefighting Tactics and Procedures, Rescue and Safety, Firefighting Equipment and Apparatus,

Building Construction, Supervisory Practices, Fire Prevention and Fire Safety, Hazardous Materials, and Emergency Medical Care (Test 701 only). There are two forms available. A reading list is provided to help candidates prepare for the test.

Format: Examiner required; individual and group administration; timed: 2 hours

Scoring: Examiner evaluated; machine scoring

Cost: Contact publisher (administration fee is waived if ordered with another product)

Sales

Career Profile+™ (CP+)

1992	LIMRA International

Population: Adults

Purpose: Evaluates the career experience and expectations of individuals considering an insurance or financial services sales career; used for employee screening and selection

Description: Multiple-choice online or paper-pencil questionnaire assessing career information related to future success as an insurance salesperson. Each candidate is rated on four key personality characteristics: persuasiveness, energy, achievement drive, and initiative and persistence. Validated for use in the United States, Canada, and the Caribbean.

Format: Online administration; untimed

Scoring: Computer scored; online scoring; results emailed

Cost: Contact publisher

Client Relations

1998	Performance Programs, Inc.

Clark L. Wilson

Population: Consultants and client service representatives

Purpose: Measures the strengths and soft spots of the internal or external consultant or representative in responding to a client's needs

Description: Contains 55 questions with three open-ended questions. Also available in Spanish.

Format: Self-administered; untimed

Scoring: Online scoring service

Cost: $260.00 up to 15 surveys

Customer Contact Styles Questionnaire (CCSQ5.2 or CCSQ7.2)

1998   SHL People Performance

Population: Adults; front-line staff

Purpose: Selection and development of sales, customer service, and call center staff

Description: Assesses 16 dimensions of work style. There are 136 items in three categories: Relationships With People, Thinking Styles, and Emotions and Drives. Also available in French.

Format: Examiner required; individual administration; untimed: 25 minutes

Scoring: Hand key; machine scored; scoring service available

Cost: Contact publisher

Hilson Personnel Profile/Success Quotient–Sales Version (HPP/SQ-S)

1995   Institute for Personality and Ability Testing, Inc.

Robin E. Inwald

Population: Adults

Purpose: Screens job applicants in sales positions

Description: Paper–pencil 160-item true–false test used for prescreening of job applicants for sales positions. Assesses Achievement History, Social Ability, and Sales Interest. Materials used are a test booklet, answer sheets, and scoring program. Also available in Spanish.

Format: Examiner required; suitable for groups; untimed: 30 minutes

Scoring: Computer scored; scoring service available

Cost: $16.00 to $20.00 depending on scoring method

MarketMatch™

Date not provided   LIMRA International

Population: Adults

Purpose: Rates the match between a candidate's natural market and an office's target market

Description: Managers use MarketMatch to describe their office's typical prospects and clients on 10 key dimensions, including annual household income, occupation, relationship to the candidate, and ability to provide referrals. Candidates collect information from possible sales prospects on the same dimensions and MarketMatch scores the match on each dimension. Potential prospects are ranked on their approachability and their match to an office's target market.

Format: Online administration; untimed: 20 minutes

Scoring: Online scoring; results emailed

Cost: Contact publisher

Sales Achievement Predictor (SalesAP)

1995   Western Psychological Services

Jotham Friedland, Sander Marcus, Harvey Mandel

Population: Ages 14 years and older

Purpose: Measures traits that are critical to success in sales and related fields

Description: Composed of 140 items, the on-line or paper–pencil answer test can be scored on the computer, via fax or mail. An interpretive report is received that gives the applicant one of three clear-cut ratings: Highly recommended for sales, recommended with areas that could be improved, or not recommended for sales. Validity scales identify applicants who are exaggerating strengths or minimizing weaknesses; the scores of those applicants are automatically adjusted. In addition, the report includes recommendations for training and motivation.

Format: Self-administered; untimed

Scoring: Computer scored; scoring service available

Cost: Kit (manual, 2 mail-in answer sheets) $165.00

Sales Aptitude Test

1993   Pearson Performance Solutions

Population: Adults

Purpose: Measures behavioral and personality characteristics indicative of success in sales positions; used for sales selection programs

Description: Multiple-choice 86-item test measures eight traits important to sales success: ego strength, persuasiveness, sociability, entrepreneurship, achievement motivation, energy, self-confidence, and empathy.

Format: Examiner required; suitable for group use; untimed: 30 minutes

Scoring: Hand key; computer scored

Cost: Contact publisher

Sales Attitude Checklist (SACL™)

1992	Pearson Performance Solutions

Erwin K. Taylor

Population: Adults

Purpose: Measures attitudes and behaviors involved in sales and selling; used for sales selection programs

Description: Paper–pencil 31-item test assessing basic attitudes toward selling and habits in the selling situation.

Format: Examiner required; suitable for group use; untimed: 10 to 15 minutes

Scoring: Hand key

Cost: Contact publisher

Sales Comprehension Test

1998	Martin M. Bruce, PhD

Martin M. Bruce

Population: Adults

Purpose: Measures sales ability and potential based on the understanding of the principles of selling; used for evaluating prospective sales people, vocational counseling, and training projects for salespersons

Description: Paper–pencil 30-item multiple-choice test. Available in Spanish, Italian, Dutch, and German. Also available in French from the Institute of Psychological Research, Inc.

Format: Self-administered; untimed: 15 to 20 minutes

Scoring: Hand key

Cost: Specimen Set $56.95

Sales Motivation Inventory, Revised

1985	Martin M. Bruce, PhD

Martin M. Bruce

Population: Adults

Purpose: Assesses interest in and motivation for sales work, both commission and wholesale-retail

Description: Paper–pencil 75-item test measuring sales motivation and drive. Consists of multiple-choice triads. Available also in French. Suitable for individuals with physical, hearing, or visual impairments.

Format: Self-administered; untimed: 20 to 30 minutes

Scoring: Hand key

Cost: Specimen Set $52.50

Sales Professional Assessment Inventory (SPAI-II™)

Date not provided	Pearson Performance Solutions

Population: Adults

Purpose: Assesses potential for success in sales positions; used for selection and screening of candidates for direct sales to business and retail sales of consumer durable goods or special services

Description: Paper–pencil 210-item multiple-choice test with 12 diagnostic scales yielding scores in Sales and Work Experience, Sales Interest, Sales Responsibility, Sales Orientation, Energy Level, Self Development, Sales Skills, Sales Understanding, Customer Service, Business Ethics, and Job Stability. Two validity scales—Candidness and Accuracy—are provided. A Sales Potential Index that is a composite of the 12 diagnostic scales is provided for decision-making purposes. In addition to scores, the SPAI-II generates positive indicators, training needs, and follow-up interview questions, based on examinee responses to individual items.

Format: Examiner required; suitable for group use; untimed: 60 minutes

Scoring: Computer scored; test scoring service available

Cost: Contact publisher

Sales Sentence Completion Blank, Revised

1982	Martin M. Bruce, PhD

Martin M. Bruce

Population: Adults

Purpose: Aids in evaluating and selecting sales personnel by providing insight into how the applicant thinks and his or her social attitudes and general personality

Description: Paper–pencil 40-item test consisting of sentence fragments to be completed by the subject. The examiner assesses the responses by scoring them on a 7-point scale. Responses are a projection of the subject's attitudes about life, self, and others. Suitable for individuals with physical, hearing, or visual impairments.

Format: Self-administered; untimed: 20 to 35 minutes

Scoring: Hand key

Cost: Specimen Set $28.50

Sales Skills–Form A-C

2000	Ramsay Corporation

Roland T. Ramsay

Population: Adults

Purpose: Measures sales knowledge

Description: The test contains 48 multiple-choice items in 12 categories: Prospecting Skills, Interpersonal Skills, Communication/Expressiveness Skills, Persistence, Product Knowledge, Confidence, Listening Skills, Closing Skills, Follow-Up Skills, Negotiating Skills, Honesty, and Motivation.

Format: Examiner required; suitable for group use; untimed: approximately 60 minutes

Scoring: Self-scored; scoring service available

Cost: Test Booklet $13.00 (minimum 20); Manual $24.95

Selling Judgment Test

1959	Martin M. Bruce, PhD

Martin M. Bruce

Population: Adolescents, adults

Purpose: Measures sales comprehension; used by sales trainers to develop discussion topics

Description: Paper–pencil five-item multiple-choice test assessing sales competence in the retail and wholesale fields. The items in this test are taken from the *Sales Comprehension Test* and were chosen by the Associated Merchandising Corporation as particularly pertinent to the department retail store field. The test is used primarily for training and discussion purposes. The *Sales Comprehension Test* is more appropriate for assessment purposes. Suitable for individuals with physical, hearing, or visual impairments.

Format: Self-administered; untimed: 3 minutes

Scoring: Examiner evaluated

Cost: 20 Forms $17.50

SellingStyles Questionnaire™

Date not provided	LIMRA International

Population: Adults

Purpose: Identifies candidates who can successfully sell products

Description: The scale helps to explain how candidates put their sales personality into action and provides information about how they will behave in each step of the sales process, including prospecting, handling objections, and closing sales. Each candidate report includes interview questions for potential problem areas and tips for evaluating candidate responses. Three fundamental selling styles are identified: Dynamic, Analytic, Interpersonal.

Format: Online administration; untimed

Scoring: Online scoring; results posted online

Cost: Contact publisher

ServiceFirst™

Date not provided	LIMRA International

Population: Adults

Purpose: Determines which candidates will provide appropriate service

Description: A multiple-choice test that asks candidates to share their attitudes on a wide variety of issues and describe how they would act in specific situations. Each candidate report provides an overall rating of the candidate's customer service potential. Four areas are reported: Active, Polite, Helpful, and Personalized.

Format: Online administration; untimed

Scoring: Online scoring; results emailed

Cost: Contact publisher

Telemarketing Applicant Inventory (TMAI)

Date not provided	Pearson Performance Solutions

Population: Adults

Purpose: Measures an applicant's potential for success in telephone sales and service positions

Description: The TMAI helps measure sales interest and skills, sales responsibility, productivity, confidence and influence, interpersonal orientation, stress tolerance, job stability, job simulation rating, communicator competence, applied verbal reasoning, validity/candidness, and validity/accuracy.

Format: Self-administration; untimed

Scoring: Computer scored; telephone and fax scoring available

Cost: Contact publisher

Test of Sales Aptitude, Revised

1983	Martin M. Bruce, PhD

Martin M. Bruce

Population: Adults

Purpose: Evaluates an individual's aptitude for selling; used as an aid in vocational guidance and in the selection and training of sales personnel

Description: Paper–pencil 50-item test measuring the subject's knowledge and understanding of the principles of selling a wide variety of goods ranging from heavy industrial capital items to door-to-door housewares. Norms are available to compare the subject's score with salespeople, men, women, and selected special sales groups. The subject reads the directions and completes the test. Suitable for individuals with physical, hearing, or visual impairments.

Format: Self-administered; untimed: 20 to 30 minutes

Scoring: Hand key

Cost: Specimen Set $52.50

Technical

Laboratory Technician–Form LW

1992	Ramsay Corporation

Roland T. Ramsay

Population: Adults

Purpose: Measures laboratory knowledge and skill

Description: This multiple-choice paper–pencil test has 101 items. Categories tested include Chemical Processes, Mathematics, Inspection, and Metallurgy.

Format: Examiner required; suitable for group use; untimed

Scoring: Self-scored; scoring service available

Cost: Test Booklet $25.00 (minimum 20); Manual $24.95

VCWS 16–Drafting

1974	Valpar International Corporation

Population: Ages 15 years and older

Purpose: Assesses an individual's potential to compete in an entry-level position requiring basic drafting and print reading skills; provides insight into the ability to visualize abstract problems and to acquire new tool-use skills

Description: Manual assessment of the potential to compete in an entry-level position requiring basic drafting skills. The examinee performs a series of exercises measuring his or her ability to measure objects accurately in inches and centimeters; learn the use of drafting tools such as a T square, compass, circle template, and triangles; and read blueprints. The examinee must produce three view drawings of three wooden blocks. Each subtest screens the examinee in terms of his or her ability to cope successfully with the next subtest. The test is designed to accommodate a range of needs within the drafting industry from minimal expertise to sophisticated high-level performance.

Format: Examiner required; individual administration; timed

Scoring: Examiner evaluated

Cost: $1,795.00

Attitudes

Abridged Job Descriptive Index (AJDI)

1997	Bowling Green State University

*Jeffrey M. Stanton, Evan F. Sinar,
William K. Balzer, Amanda L. Julian,
Paul Thoreson, Shahnaz Aziz,
Patricia L. Smith*

Population: Ages 17 years and older

Purpose: Measures job satisfaction

Description: There are 25 items in five categories: Work on Present Job (5 items), Present Pay (5 items), Opportunities for Promotion (5 items), Supervision (5 items), and Coworkers (5 items). Scores range from 0 to 15 on each scale.

Format: Self-administered; untimed: 10 minutes

Scoring: Hand key; may be computer scored; may be machine scored

Cost: $1.00 per scale

Applicant Potential Inventory (API™)

Date not provided	Pearson Performance Solutions

Population: Adults

Purpose: Evaluates attitudes that can improve employee productivity

Description: The API assessment evolved from the *Personnel Selection Inventory* instrument.

Each version of the API may contain the following scales: Honesty, Drug Avoidance, Employee Relations, Work Values, Supervision Attitudes, Tenure, Safety, Customer Service, Validity/Candidness, and Validity/Accuracy. Results in an Employability Index.

Format: Self-administered; untimed: 15 minutes

Scoring: Software scoring; computer scoring via telephone and fax; scoring service available

Cost: Contact publisher

Assessment of Personal Goals (APG)

| 2004 | Mind Garden, Inc. |

Martin E. Ford, Charles W. Nichols

Population: Adults

Purpose: Measures personal goals and teaches how to use the power of that knowledge

Description: Provides how to gain insight into personal goals that can increase a client's motivation, effectiveness, and satisfaction, as well as his or her overall sense of meaning and purpose in life.

Format: Self-administered; untimed: 60 minutes

Scoring: Examiner evaluated; online scoring available

Cost: Booklet $20.00; 200 Uses $150.00

Attentional and Interpersonal Style (TAIS) Inventory

| 1976 | Enhanced Performance Systems, Inc. |

Robert M. Nideffer

Population: Ages 13 years and older

Purpose: Identifies root cause of a performance problem

Description: The TAIS measures three basic performance building blocks—Leadership, Emotional Control, and Performance Under Pressure—using 144 items in a self-report questionnaire. The scores provide the information on which to build a highly individualized or situation-specific program to enhance or develop performance skills. Various reports can be generated online to assess abilities in a specific performance context, such as sales, leadership, or two-person interaction. TAIS scores are interpreted in the context of the demands of the workplace in question.

Format: Self-administered; untimed: 20 to 30 minutes

Scoring: Computer scored; scoring service available

Cost: Contact publisher

Business Practices Index™

| Date not provided | LIMRA International |

Population: Adults

Purpose: Assesses the likelihood that candidates will be conscientious, responsible, and ethical

Description: The index asks candidates to share their attitudes on a wide range of issues, such as rule breaking, misrepresenting company products or services, disciplining irresponsible behavior, personal honesty, and workplace theft. Reports clearly tell managers whether individuals are likely to engage in inappropriate behaviors and identify candidates who have extremely positive and potentially biased views of themselves.

Format: Online administration; untimed: 20 minutes

Scoring: Online scoring; results emailed

Cost: Contact publisher

Campbell Organizational Survey (COS)

| 1995 | Pearson Performance Solutions |

David P. Campbell

Population: Adults

Purpose: Assesses employee attitudes of organizations

Description: Paper–pencil 67-item test with 17 scales, plus an overall index. A sixth-grade reading level is required. Examiner must have taken psychology courses. Also available in Spanish and French.

Format: Self-administered; untimed

Scoring: Computer scored; test scoring service available

Cost: Contact publisher

Career Attitudes and Strategies Inventory (CASI™)

| 1994 | Psychological Assessment Resources, Inc. |

John L. Holland, Gary D. Gottfredson

Population: Adults

Purpose: Assesses an employee's current work situation that includes common attitudes, as well as strategies for coping with job, family, coworkers, and supervisors; used for career counseling

Description: Multiple-choice and true–false test

with 130 items on nine scales: Geographical Barriers, Job Satisfaction, Work Involvement, Skill Development, Dominant Style, Career Worries, Interpersonal Abuse, Family Commitment, and Risk-Taking Style. Materials used include a manual, inventory booklet, hand-scorable answer sheet, and interpretive summary booklet.

Format: Self-administered; untimed

Scoring: Self-scored

Cost: Introductory Kit (manual, 25 of each booklet) $124.00

Career Survival: Strategic Job and Role Planning

1995	Wiley

Edgar H. Schein

Population: Adults

Purpose: Identifies the key elements of an individual's job now and in the future and how to set appropriate priorities

Description: Helps managers, employers, and human resource specialists answer such questions as these: What does the job currently involve? How will the job itself change over the next few years? How will the environment around the job change? Do these changes mean that the job may require a different person? *Career Survival* helps organizations more accurately forecast their needs and helps individual employees effectively structure their priorities and future plans.

Format: Self administration; untimed

Scoring: Self-scoring

Cost: $18.00

Career Values Card Sort

2005	Career Trainer

Richard L. Knowdell

Population: Adults

Purpose: Prioritizes career values to assist in career planning

Description: A simple tool that allows clients to prioritize their values with 41 variables of work satisfaction—such as time freedom, precision work, power, technical competence, and public contact—listed and described. The individual sorts them based on a 5-point Likert scale (*always, often, sometimes, seldom,* and *never values*). An effective tool for job seekers and those fine-tuning their present jobs. The kit includes guidelines for counselors and group facilitators, an overview of values and their role in career decision making,

explicit instructions for the individual user, and supplementary activities for further clarification of career values.

Format: Examiner required; individual or group administration; untimed: 15 to 20 minutes

Scoring: Examiner evaluated

Cost: Cards and Manual $8.00

Change Readiness Assessment

2001	Performance Programs, Inc.

Paul M. Connolly

Population: Adults

Purpose: Measures employees' willingness to change

Description: How quickly and thoroughly an enterprise can respond to change in the fast-paced environment has an impact on people and their working relationships. This 41-question survey features 36 standardized questionnaire items, up to five customized questions, up to five demographic categories for reporting, and three open-ended questions. Online administration is available. Norms are available.

Format: Self administered; untimed

Scoring: Scoring service available

Cost: Contact publisher

Cross-Cultural Adaptability Inventory™ (CCAI™)

1995	Pearson Performance Solutions

Colleen Kelley, Judith Meyers

Population: Adults

Purpose: A culture general test used to assess an individual's ability to adapt to other cultures

Description: Paper–pencil 50-item test that measures an individual's cultural adaptability.

Format: Self-administered; untimed

Scoring: Self-scored

Cost: Contact publisher

CultureFit®

Date not provided	LIMRA International

Population: Adults

Purpose: Identifies candidates who are more likely to succeed because they fit the work culture

Description: Key members of an organization set the unique culture profile by rating 28 key work values, then job candidates rate the same values to describe the environment they would like to work in.

Format: Online administration; untimed: 20 minutes

Scoring: Online scoring; results emailed

Cost: Contact publisher

Dealing with Conflict

1999	HRD Press

Alexander Hiam

Population: Adults

Purpose: Measures how individuals deal with conflict through five styles: Accommodate, Avoid, Comprise, Compete, and Collaborate for any occupational setting where conflict can arise

Description: This assessment uses a forced choice format between pairs of statements. One or more dominant styles are identified, as well as one or more secondary styles. The questionnaire booklet provides information on interpreting results and how to select the most ideal conflict style for a given situation. The overall emphasis is on building and improving skills in collaboration. There is a Leader's Guide that outlines a half-day conflict styles workshop. There is also a 360-degree feedback form that provides information from coworkers on how they perceive others' conflict style. Also available in Spanish.

Format: Self-administered; untimed: 10 minutes

Scoring: Examiner evaluated

Cost: $7.50 each; Leader's Guide $49.95

Diagnosing Organizational Culture

1992	Wiley

Roger Harrison, Herb Stakes

Population: Adults

Purpose: Designed to help identify the shared values and beliefs that constitute an organization's culture

Description: Organizations can use this instrument for team building, organizational development, productivity improvement, and human resources development. It defines four cultures basic to most organizations: Power, Role, Achievement, and Support.

Format: Self-administration; untimed

Scoring: Self-scored

Cost: $18.00

Diversity Awareness Profile (DAP)

1991	Wiley

K. Stinson

Population: Adults

Purpose: Helps people become more aware of their behaviors, evaluate their own behaviors, and modify behaviors to be empowering and respectful to all people

Description: The DAP is based on the belief that if people discriminate, judge, or isolate others, it is unintentional. These self-scoring instruments are based on information gathered in a series of focus groups and one-on-one interviews. The groups included older workers, women, people with disabilities, African Americans, Native Americans, Hispanics, and other groups that experience discrimination.

Format: Self-administration; untimed

Scoring: Self-scored

Cost: $10.00

Employee Reliability Inventory® (ERI®)

Date not provided	Wonderlic Personnel Test, Inc.

Population: Adults

Purpose: Helps to determine which individuals are most likely to become valued employees

Description: Inventory measures whether an individual is low-risk or high-risk on seven scales: Long-Term Commitment, Safety, Trustworthiness, Conscientious Job Performance, Freedom from Alcohol/Substance Abuse, Courtesy, and Emotional Maturity. Follow-up questions consistent with EEOC guidelines are provided for any areas of concern. These can be used during interviews and reference checks to help clarify an individual's results.

Format: Self-administered via paper–pencil, computer, or online

Scoring: Online scoring; fax scoring; computer scoring

Cost: Contact publisher

Employee Safety Inventory (ESI®)

1988	Pearson Performance Solutions

Population: Adults

Purpose: Assesses attitudes toward on-the-job safety; used for screening, placement, and training of job applicants and current employees

Description: Paper–pencil multiple-choice and short-answer test yielding scores in four areas (Risk Avoidance, Stress Tolerance, Safety Control, and Validity). Scores on a supplemental scale (Driver Attitudes) and a composite are also available. Materials include test booklet, interpretation guide, and administrator's guide. Must purchase a minimum of 25 booklets.

Format: Examiner required; suitable for group use; untimed

Scoring: Computer scored; test scoring service available

Cost: Contact publisher

Epstein Creativity Competencies Inventory–Individuals

2003   Personal Strengths Publishing

Robert E. Epstein

Population: Adults

Purpose: Measures creativity

Description: Measures four core skills sets that individuals need in order to be able to express their creative potential

Format: Rating scale, untimed

Scoring: Scoring service available from publisher

Cost: $10.00

Expectations Edition® Strength Deployment Inventory

2005   Personal Strengths Publishing

Elias H. Porter

Population: Adolescents, adults

Purpose: Clarifies expectations in relationships

Description: Comparing *Strength Deployment Inventory* results to *Expectations Editions* results suggests way that people may be able to borrow or change expectations to be more effective and have a higher level of satisfaction in a relationship.

Format: Requires facilitation; individual or group administration; untimed: 20 to 40 minutes

Scoring: Self-scored; examiner evaluated; online scoring available

Cost: $4.75

Feedback Edition of the Strength Deployment Inventory

2005   Personal Strengths Publishing

Elias H. Porter

Population: Adults

Purpose: Elicits feedback to describe how a person uses his or her personal strengths in relationships

Description: Used in team building, organizational development, career development, and relationship counseling. There are 20 items: 10 measure a significant other's perceptions of an individual's strength deployment when things are going well, and 10 measure strength deployment in the face of conflict. Uses self-ratings and ratings of a significant other person. For use in conjunction with the *Strength Deployment Inventory*.

Format: Requires facilitation; individual or group administration; untimed: 20 to 40 minutes

Scoring: Self-scored; examiner evaluated

Cost: $4.75

Feedback Portrait of Overdone Strengths

1997   Personal Strengths Publishing

Population: Adults

Purpose: Elicits feedback to describe how a person may overdo or misapply his or her personal strengths

Description: Used in leadership development, career development, and relationship counseling. A Q-Sort of 40 overdone personal strengths providing a profile of top and least overdone per feedback giver. Used with *Strength Deployment Inventory* and *Portrait of Personal Strengths*, and *Portrait of Overdone Strengths*.

Format: Requires facilitation; individual or group administration; untimed: 20 to 40 minutes

Scoring: Examiner evaluated

Cost: $5.75

Feedback Portrait of Personal Strengths

1997   Personal Strengths Publishing

Population: Adults

Purpose: Elicits feedback to describe how a person uses his or her personal strengths in relationships

Description: Used in team building, leadership training, career development, and relationship counseling. A Q-Sort of 40 personal strengths providing a profile of a significant other person's perceptions of an individual's use of personal strengths. Used with *Portrait of Personal Strengths* and *Strength Deployment Inventory*.

Format: Requires facilitation; individual or group administration; untimed: 20 to 40 minutes

Scoring: Examiner evaluated

Cost: $5.75

Full Engagement Inventory– Self Assessment Version

Updated yearly	Performance Programs, Inc. for the Human Performance Institute

Jim Loehr, Paul M. Connolly, Wendy Alfus Rothman

Population: Ages 21 years and older

Purpose: Measures an individual's views of overall engagement in work and life; used for business training and development, career counseling, and work–life balance counseling

Description: The instrument has 149 items and a 7-point agreement scale. Sixteen-page reports available instantaneously online. Report assesses overall engagement in life and work and provides norms. Provides ideas for specific actions that equip the individual to achieve full engagement.

Format: Self-administered; online only; untimed

Scoring: Immediate online scoring service

Cost: $49.00

Full Engagement Inventory 360 Multirater Feedback Version

Updated yearly	Performance Programs, Inc. for the Human Performance Institute

Jim Loehr, Paul M. Connolly, Wendy Alfus Rothman

Population: Ages 21 years and older

Purpose: Measures self and others' views of an individual's overall engagement in work and life; used for business training and development, career counseling, and work–life balance counseling

Description: The instrument has 99 items and a 7-point agreement scale (extent). Online only. Forty-page reports provided through organization offering training. Learn about overall engagement in work and life. Individuals learn how they scored on 16 personal energy measures. See how others score on these measures through normative data. Learn about level of negative stress or imbalance compared to others. Get specific actions for achieving a more fully engaged life at work and home. Make important decisions about where to place efforts through new energy management practices, further training, reading, or counseling. Also available in Danish, Slovenian, Mexican Spanish, and South American Spanish. Includes optional family and children's feedback.

Format: Self-administered; untimed

Scoring: Online scoring service

Cost: Embedded in training

Global Assessment Inventory

2007 Performance Programs, Inc. for Prudential Financial

Population: Adults

Purpose: Identifies areas of potential misunderstanding or conflict when working across cultures for individuals who need to interact with individuals from other cultures for business purposes by telephone or through short-term (less than 3 months) assignments

Description: Based on the research from the *Overseas Assignment Inventory* (OAI), this new inventory is designed to assess challenges an individual is likely to face in working with individuals from other cultures.

Format: Online survey; untimed

Scoring: Online scoring service

Cost: $50.00

Insight Inventory Form B

1988	HRD Press

Patrick Handley

Population: Adults

Purpose: Measures four primary behavioral styles relevant to occupational settings

Description: This is a self-scoring assessment that uses ratings of 32 common adjectives to produce normative scores on Getting Your Way, Responding to People, Pacing Activity, and Dealing with Detail. Participants develop important behavior skills, including how to flex their style to manage conflict and to facilitate teamwork. The instrument's clarity and uncomplicated format allows for integration into existing training or use as the centerpiece of a workshop to improve communication. A comprehensive Trainer's Guide provides information on the research and validity of the instrument, as well as several training outlines for a variety of purposes, including team building, stress management, improving communication, and lessening interpersonal conflict. Also available in Spanish, Dutch, and French.

Format: Self-administered; group setting; online available; untimed: 15 minutes

Scoring: Self-scored; online scoring

Cost: $15.95 each

Job Descriptive Index, Revised (JDI REV)

1997	Bowling Green State University

Patricia C. Smith, Lorne M. Kendall, Charles L. Hulin

Population: Ages 17 to 100 years

Purpose: Assesses an individual's job satisfaction

Description: Paper-pencil 72-item test consisting of five scales: Satisfaction with Work (18 items), Pay (9 items), Promotions (9 items), Supervision (18 items), and Coworkers (18 items). Items are answered in yes-no format. The test yields five scores per scale. A scoring service is available by special arrangement with the publisher. A second-grade reading level is required. The Job in General (JIG) test may be administered as a follow-up. Suitable for use with individuals who have hearing or physical impairments. Also available in French, Spanish, Chinese, and other languages.

Format: Self-administered; untimed: 15 minutes

Scoring: Hand key; may be computer/machine scored

Cost: $1.00 per scale

Job in General (JIG)

1985	Bowling Green State University

Gail H. Ironson, Patricia C. Smith, Michael T. Brannick

Population: Adults

Purpose: Assesses overall job satisfaction

Description: Paper-pencil 18-item yes-no test assessing workers' job satisfaction. The test is to be administered following the *Job Descriptive Index* (JDI), which measures five specific areas of job satisfaction. A scoring service is available by special arrangement with the publisher. A second-grade reading level is required. Suitable for use with individuals with hearing or physical impairments.

Format: Self-administered; untimed: 1 minute

Scoring: Hand key; may be computer or machine scored

Cost: 100 Questionnaires $20.00; included with *Job Descriptive Index* at no charge

Job Stress Survey (JSS)

1999, 2000	Psychological Assessment Resources, Inc.

Charles D. Spielberger, Peter R. Vagg

Population: Adults

Purpose: Identifies major sources of stress in the workplace

Description: Thirty job-related stressor events are presented in three scales: Job Stress Index, Job Stress Severity, Job Stress Frequency, and the following subscales: Job Pressure Index, Job Pressure Severity, Job Pressure Frequency, Lack of Organizational Support Index, and Lack of Organizational Support Frequency. A sixth-grade reading level is required.

Format: Self-administered; untimed: 10 to 15 minutes

Scoring: Evaluator evaluated; computer scoring available

Cost: Introductory Kit (manual, 25 test booklets, 25 profile forms, 3.5 program disk with 5 bonus uses of Windows Scoring Program) $142.00

Kolb Learning Style Inventory– Version 3.1 (LSI-3.1)

2005	Hay Group

David A. Kolb

Population: Adults

Purpose: Identifies preferred learning styles and explores the opportunities different styles present for problem solving, teamwork, conflict resolution, career choice, and communication

Description: Online and paper-pencil 12-item test. Results are plotted onto two graphs: Cycle of Learning and Learning Type Grid. A Facilitator's Guide is available. The LSI is also available in paper only in French and Spanish.

Format: Self-administered; untimed: 20 to 30 minutes

Scoring: Self-scored

Cost: $15.00 per Online Assessment; $90.00 (10 booklets); $50.00 Facilitator's Guide

Miner Sentence Completion Scale: Form H

1989	Organizational Measurement Systems Press

John B. Miner

Population: Adults

Purpose: Measures an individual's hierarchic (bureaucratic) motivation; used for employee counseling and development and organizational assessment

Description: Multiple-item paper–pencil free-response or multiple-choice sentence completion test measuring an individual's motivation in terms of motivational patterns that fit the hierarchic (bureaucratic) organizational form. Both forms (free-response version or multiple-choice version offering six alternatives for each stem) measure the following subscales: Authority Figures, Competitive Games, Competitive Situations, Assertive Role, Imposing Wishes, Standing Out from the Group, and Routine Administrative Functions. The basic scoring guide (for use with the free-response version) discusses categorizing the responses, the subscales, supervisory jobs, total scores, and the sample scoring sheet.

Format: Examiner required; suitable for group use; untimed

Scoring: Examiner evaluated

Cost: 50 Scales (specify free-response or multiple-choice version) $30.00; 64-Page Basic Scoring Guide (includes supplementary scoring guides) $10.00

Miner Sentence Completion Scale: Form P

1981	Organizational Measurement Systems Press

John B. Miner

Population: Adults

Purpose: Measures an individual's professional (specialized) motivation; used for employee counseling and development and organizational assessment

Description: Multiple-item paper–pencil free-response sentence completion test measuring motivation in terms of motivational patterns that fit the professional (specialized) organizational form. The test measures the following subscales: Acquiring Knowledge, Independent Action, Accepting Status, Providing Help, and Professional Commitment. Each test item consists of a sentence stem that individuals complete in their own words. The scoring guide discusses categorizing the responses, the subscales, actual scoring, reliability, normative data, use of Form P, and bibliographic notes.

Format: Examiner required; suitable for group use; untimed

Scoring: Examiner evaluated

Cost: 50 Scales $30.00; Scoring Guide $10.00

Miner Sentence Completion Scale: Form T

1984	Organizational Measurement Systems Press

John B. Miner

Population: Adults

Purpose: Measures an individual's task (entrepreneurial) motivation; used for employee counseling and development and organizational assessment

Description: Multiple-item paper–pencil free-response sentence-completion test measuring an individual's motivation in terms of patterns that fit the task (entrepreneurial) organizational form. The test measures the following subscales: Self-Achievement, Avoiding Risks, Feedback of Results, Personal Innovation, and Planning for the Future. These subscales are generally parallel to the five aspects of David McClelland's achievement situation. Each test item consists of a sentence stem that individuals complete in their own words. The scoring guide discusses categorizing the responses, the subscales, actual scoring, reliability, normative data, the use of the MSCS-Form T, and bibliographic notes.

Format: Examiner required; suitable for group use; untimed

Scoring: Examiner evaluated

Cost: 50 Scales $30.00; Scoring Guide $10.00

Minnesota Satisfactoriness Scales (MSS)

1970	Vocational Psychology Research

Population: Supervisors

Purpose: Measures an employee's satisfactoriness on a job

Description: The MSS is usually completed by the employee's supervisor, who evaluates the employee on 28 items describing the employee's behavior on the job. The MSS provides scores on five scales: Performance, Conformance, Dependability, Personal Adjustment, and General Satisfactoriness. The MSS can be used to evaluate the effectiveness of job placement or the success of specific training programs.

Format: Self-administered; untimed: 5 minutes

Scoring: Hand scored; scoring service available

Cost: Sample Set $3.75 (manual, 1 copy of scale)

Mirror Edition of the Personal Values Inventory

1997	Personal Strengths Publishing

Elias H. Porter

Population: Adolescents, adults

Purpose: Elicits feedback to describe how a person uses his or her personal strengths in relationships; used in team building, career development, and relationship counseling

Description: Of the 20 items, 10 measure a significant other's perception of an individual's use of his or her strengths, and 10 measure an individual's response to conflict. For use in conjunction with the *Personal Values Inventory*. Requires a sixth-grade reading level.

Format: Requires facilitation; individual or group administration; untimed: 20 to 40 minutes

Scoring: Self-scored; examiner evaluated

Cost: $4.75

Motivated Skills Card Sort

2005	Career Trainer

Richard L. Knowdell

Population: Adults

Purpose: Measures transferable skills for career planning

Description: Based on experience, feedback, and instinct, the client uses the cards to assess proficiency and motivation in 48 transferable skills areas. Complete instructional manual includes counselor guidelines, an overview of achievement, and its role in career decision making.

Format: Examiner required; individual or group administration; untimed: 30 to 45 minutes

Scoring: Examiner evaluated

Cost: Complete Kit (cards, category cards, blank cards, summary sheet, manual) $12.00

Motivation Questionnaire (MQ)

1992	SHL People Performance

Population: Adult professionals

Purpose: Selection and development of staff motivation

Description: Measures 18 dimensions of motivation with 144 items in four categories: Energy and Dynamism, Synergy, Intrinsic, and Extrinsic. Also available in French.

Format: Examiner required; individual administration; computer and online administration available; untimed: 35 minutes

Scoring: Hand key; machine scored; scoring service available; online scoring

Cost: Contact publisher

Occupational Interests Card Sort

2001	Career Trainer

Richard L. Knowdell

Population: Adults

Purpose: Measures occupational and career interests

Description: Clarifies the high-appeal jobs and fields; the degree of readiness, skills, and knowledge needed; and competency-building steps for entry or progress. There are 110 occupational cards that the examinee rank-orders as *definitely interested, probably interested, indifferent, probably disinterested,* or *definitely disinterested.*

Format: Examiner required; individual or group administration; untimed: 15 to 20 minutes

Scoring: Examiner evaluated

Cost: Complete Kit (cards, category cards, summary sheet, manual) $18.00

Occupational Stress Inventory Revised™ (OSI-R™)

1998	Psychological Assessment Resources, Inc.

Samuel H. Osipow, Arnold Spokane

Population: Adults

Purpose: Measures dimensions of occupational adjustment of individuals employed primarily in technical, professional, and managerial positions in school, service, and manufacturing settings

Description: Paper–pencil 140-item test measuring three dimensions of occupational adjustment: occupational stress, psychological strain, and coping resources. The instrument consists of three separate questionnaires. The Occupational Roles Questionnaire (ORQ; six scales with 10 items each) analyzes stress due to occupational roles. The Personal Strain Questionnaire (PSQ; four scales with 10 items each) measures psychological strain as reflected in behaviors and attitudes. The Personal Resources Questionnaire (PRQ; four scales with 10 items each) analyzes effective coping via personal resources. The profile form is used to convert raw scores to *t*-scores. The questionnaires may be administered together or separately.

Format: Self-administered; untimed: 20 to 40 minutes

Scoring: Self-scored

Cost: Introductory Kit (manual, 25 reusable booklets, 50 of each form) $178.00

Organizational Assessment Survey

| 1985 | MetriTech, Inc. |

Larry A. Braskamp, Martin L. Maehr

Population: Adults

Purpose: Assesses organizational culture and employee commitment, assesses worker motivation by determining personal values and incentives, and evaluates the opportunities for fulfillment that individuals perceive in their present jobs

Description: A total of 200 Likert-scale items measuring four aspects of the worker, job, and organization: Accomplishment, Recognition, Power, and Affiliation. Both group and individual reports are available. Individual reports provide employees feedback about their incentives, personal values, and job opportunities. A second type of individual report provides supervisors with insights into their own management style and the impact their styles have on the people they supervise. The group report provides feedback on organizational culture, degree of employee commitment, and areas of job satisfaction.

Format: Self-administered; untimed: 1 hour

Scoring: Computer scored through publisher

Cost: Introductory Kit (test materials, manual, processing of 2 reports) $49.50

Organizational Survey System (OSS™)

| Date not provided | Pearson Performance Solutions |

Melany E. Baehr

Population: Adults

Purpose: Provides feedback on the functioning of an organization

Description: Helps gather information about an organization from employees working in healthcare or business/industry settings. Nine occupation-specific versions are available. Surveys are completed anonymously on work premises or at home and returned for processing. The survey can be modified to meet the workplace requirements.

Format: Self-administration; untimed: 45 minutes

Scoring: Scoring service

Cost: Contact publisher

Overseas Assignment Inventory (OAI)

| 2007 | Performance Programs, Inc. for Prudential Financial |

Population: Employees and partners relocating from one country to another for a long-term (1 year or more) business assignment

Purpose: Provides predeparture coaching for relocating an employee and spouse; identifies areas that might make cultural adaptation problematic, including the need for premature repatriation

Description: Originally developed in the early 1970s for the Peace Corps and the U.S. Navy, the OAI is the oldest and most well validated assessment for cultural adaptation. It has been used since then by many major corporations as a foundation for predeparture coaching, as well as for career planning. This 2007 revision maintains much of the original work, but incorporates new items and scales based on current research. Takes about 25 minutes to complete.

Format: Online survey; untimed

Scoring: Online scoring service

Cost: $225.00

Personal Values Inventory (PVI)

| 1997 | Personal Strengths Publishing |

Elias H. Porter

Population: Adolescents, adults

Purpose: Measures personal style of approaching tasks, conflicts, decision making, and relationships; used in team building, career development, and relationship counseling

Description: There are 20 items, 10 measuring motivational values when things are going well and 10 measuring predictable progressive responses to conflict. Requires a sixth-grade reading level.

Format: Requires facilitation; individual or group administration, untimed. 20 to 40 minutes

Scoring: Self scored; examiner evaluated

Cost: $10.50

Personal Values Questionnaire (PVQ)

1993	Hay Group

Population: Adults

Purpose: Provides an analysis of personal values versus job requirements

Description: A total of 36 items measure the degree to which a person values Achievement, Affiliation, and Power—the three social motives that drive human behavior.

Format: Self-administered; online administration available; untimed: 20 minutes

Scoring: Self-scored

Cost: $69.00 per Package of 10 Booklets, $10.00 each online

Portrait of Overdone Strengths

1996	Personal Strengths Publishing

Elias H. Porter

Population: Adults

Purpose: Demonstrates how a person may overdo or misapply personal strengths, thereby contributing to unwarranted conflict in relationships; used in team building, leadership training, and relationship counseling

Description: A Q-Sort of 40 overdone personal strengths. A profile provides most and least overdone strengths. For use in conjunction with the *Strength Deployment Inventory*.

Format: Requires facilitation; individual or group administration; untimed: 20 to 40 minutes

Scoring: Self-scored; examiner evaluated

Cost: $5.75

Portrait of Personal Strengths

1996	Personal Strengths Publishing

Elias H. Porter

Population: Adults

Purpose: Helps people to see how well they use their strengths when things are going well in a relationship

Description: Used for team building, leadership training, and relationship counseling. This is a Q-Sort of 40 personal strengths providing a profile of top 6 strengths and 6 least deployed strengths. A feedback edition is available. For use in conjunction with the *Strength Deployment Inventory*.

Format: Requires facilitation; individual or group administration; untimed: 20 to 40 minutes

Scoring: Self-scored; examiner evaluated

Cost: $5.75

Retirement Activities Kit

2001	Career Trainer

Richard L. Knowdell

Population: Adults

Purpose: Measures activities of interest for those approaching retirement

Description: An easy-to-use and approachable tool to aid in the transition from formal employment to a meaningful retirement lifestyle. Forty-eight common pastimes—from cultural events to meditation, from entertaining to group leadership—are listed and described. Cards can be used to determine current frequency, as well as preferred activity patterns. The manual provides explicit instructions for using the card sort, an overview of the concepts and issues of retiring, and activities for dealing with aging and retirement.

Format: Examiner required; individual or group administration; untimed: 15 to 20 minutes

Scoring: Examiner evaluated

Cost: Complete Kit (cards, category cards, blank cards, summary sheet, manual) $12.00

Retirement Descriptive Index (RDI)

1975	Bowling Green State University

Patricia C. Smith, Lorne M. Kendall, Charles L. Hulin

Population: Adults

Purpose: Assesses satisfaction with activities, finances, people, and health; used with retired persons and other nonworking adults

Description: Paper–pencil 63-item test consisting of four scales measuring satisfaction: Activities and Work (18 items), Financial Situation (9 items), People You Associate With (18 items), and Health (18 items). The items follow a yes-no format. The test yields scores for each of the four scales. A scoring service is available by special arrangement with the publisher. A second-grade reading level is required.

Format: Self-administered; untimed: 10 minutes

Scoring: Hand key; may be computer or machine scored

Cost: 100 Booklets $50.00

Strength Deployment Inventory (SDI)

2006	Personal Strengths Publishing

Elias H. Porter

Population: Adults

Purpose: Assesses personal strengths when things are going well and when there is conflict

Description: In a total of 20 items, 10 measure motivational values when things are going well, and 10 measure conflict sequence. Seven motivational values and 13 conflict sequences are the result. The motivational values are Altruistic–Nurturing, Assertive–Directing, Analytic–Autonomizing, Flexible–Cohering, Assertive–Nurturing, Judicious–Competing, and Cautious–Supporting. The items are written at a high school reading level.

Format: Requires facilitation; individual or group administration; untimed: 20 to 40 minutes

Scoring: Self scored; examiner evaluated

Cost: $10.50

Stress in General (SIG)

1995	Bowling Green State University

Jeffrey M. Stanton, William K. Balzer, Patricia C. Smith, Luis F. Parra

Population: Ages 15 years and older

Purpose: Self-report measure of work-related stress

Description: There are 15 items in two categories: Pressure Scale (7 items) and Threat Scale (8 items).

Format: Self-administered; untimed: 5 minutes

Scoring: Hand key; may be computer scored; may be machine scored

Cost: $.10 per scale

SureHire

1997	Psychological Services, Inc.

S. W. Stang, M. L. Holcom, W. W. Ruch

Population: Adults

Purpose: Measures problem-solving abilities and work attitudes; used to select personnel for convenience store, fast-food, and retail industries

Description: Multiple-choice 50-item test, divided into two sections: Problem Solving (math and reading questions) and Work Orientation (questions about work situations and preferences). With Problem Solving, the examinee must read a statement and choose the answer he or she believes is correct. With Work Orientation, the examinee chooses the answer that most closely describes his or her views.

Format: Examiner required; suitable for group use; untimed: 25 minutes

Scoring: Self-scoring carbon form; fax-back scoring available

Cost: Contact publisher

Survey of Work Values (SWV)

1976	Bowling Green State University

Steven Wollack, James G. Goodale, Jan P. Wijting, Patricia C. Smith

Population: Adults

Purpose: Assesses an individual's work values

Description: Paper–pencil 72-item test in which examinees use a 5-point scale (*strongly agree* to *strongly disagree*) to rate statements. The test contains six scales consisting of nine items each: Pride in Work, Social Status of Job, Attitude Toward Earnings, Activity Preference, Upward Striving, and Job Involvement. The test can be scored to measure two factors: Intrinsic Values and Extrinsic Values. The test yields scores for each of the scales and factors. A scoring service is available by special arrangement with the publisher. A fifth-grade reading level is required. Suitable for use with individuals with hearing or physical impairments.

Format: Self-administered; untimed: 10 minutes

Scoring: Hand key; may be computer or machine scored

Cost: 100 Booklets $21.00; 100 Answer Sheets $10.00

ViewPoint

1998	Psychological Services, Inc.

Wade M. Gibson, Melvin L. Holcom, Susan W. Stang, William W. Ruch

Population: Adults

Purpose: Assesses work dimensions that are of concern to most employers

Description: Applications include job candidate preemployment screening. The *ViewPoint* has seven primary scales: Conscientiousness, Trustworthiness, Managing Work Pressure, Getting Along with Others, Drug/Alcohol Avoidance, Safety Orientation, and Service Orientation. The *ViewPoint* scales are published in five different combinations, providing employers the flexibility to focus on core work attitudes. Each of the five forms also includes the Carelessness and Faking scales.

Format: Examiner required; individual or group administration; untimed: 10 to 30 minutes

Scoring: Hand key; may be computer scored

Cost: Contact publisher

Work Aspect Preference Scale (WAPS)

1999	Australian Council for Educational Research Limited

R. Pryor

Population: Grades 10 and above

Purpose: Measures work qualities that individuals consider important; used in career counseling, vocational rehabilitation, the study of personal and work values, and research on career development and worker satisfaction

Description: Paper–pencil or computer-administered 52-item inventory assessing an individual's work values along 13 scales: Altruism, Coworkers, Creativity, Detachment, Independence, Life Style, Management, Money, Physical Activity, Prestige, Security, Self-Development, and Surroundings. Computer scoring converts raw scores on each scale to percentiles and ranks the scales in order of raw score and percentile. The computer-administered and scored version required an Apple II+, IIe, or IIc computer with 48K; an 80-column printer; and a single or dual disk drive.

Format: Examiner required; suitable for group use; untimed: 10 to 20 minutes

Scoring: Hand key; may be machine scored; may be computer scored

Cost: Contact publisher

Work Motivation Inventory

1986	MetriTech, Inc.

Larry A. Braskamp, Martin L. Maehr

Population: Adults

Purpose: Measures individual work motivation factors; used for employee selection/promotion and career counseling

Description: Paper–pencil or computer-adminis-

tered 77-item multiple-choice test measuring four basic work motivation factors: Accomplishment, Recognition, Power, and Affiliation. The information obtained from the test helps predict job success and aids in understanding burnout and stress. Responses to the paper–pencil version may be entered into a computer for scoring and analysis. The computer version, which operates on IBM PC systems, administers and scores the test and generates reports. This test is an adaptation of the *Organizational Assessment Survey*.

Format: Self-administered; untimed: 15 minutes

Scoring: Computer scored

Cost: Narrative Report Kit (test materials, manual, processing of 5 reports) $34.00

Work Orientation Survey for Firefighters

1997	Psychological Services, Inc.

Population: Adults

Purpose: Measures work attitudes reflecting the degree to which an examinee can be expected to be reliable, dependable, and conscientious, used to select applicants for entry-level firefighter position or training programs

Description: Multiple-choice 87-item survey questions; examinee is to select the answer that most closely describes his or her views. Measures six work dimensions, including Conscientiousness, Trustworthiness, Managing Work Pressure, Getting Along with Others, Drug/Alcohol Avoidance, and Safety Orientation. May be used in conjunction with the *PSI Firefighter Selection Test* and/or *Firefighter Learning Simulation*.

Format: Examiner required; suitable for group use; untimed: 15 to 20 minutes

Scoring: Scoring service available from publisher

Cost: Contact publisher

Work Potential Profile (WPP)

1997	Australian Council for Educational Research Limited

Helga Rowe

Population: Adolescents, adults

Purpose: Describes psychological barriers to gaining employment

Description: Criterion-referenced tool for the initial assessment of long-term unemployed persons and persons who are having difficulty finding employment. It can serve the collection and management of information in areas of support needs, strengths and weaknesses for employment, occupational planning, and the individual's developmental and current intervention or training needs. The WPP Questionnaire contains 171 items.

Format: Self-administered; untimed

Scoring: Hand key

Cost: Contact publisher

Work Styles Questionnaire (WSQ or WSQn)

1988 | **SHL People Performance**

Population: Adults in production and operations

Purpose: Measures 17 dimensions of work styles

Description: Intended for manufacturing, retail, service, and similar jobs. A total of 162 items in four categories: Relationships With People, Thinking Style, Emotions, and Energies. Also available in French.

Format: Examiner required; individual administration; untimed: 30 minutes

Scoring: Hand key; machine scored; scoring service available

Cost: Contact publisher

Emotional Intelligence

Benchmark of Organizational Emotional Intelligence (BOEI™)

2002 | **Multi-Health Systems, Inc.**

Steve Stein

Population: Ages 18 years and older

Purpose: Measures the level of emotional intelligence in organizations as a whole and its parts

Description: Items (143) are categorized into one of the following key areas: Job Happiness, Compensation, Work/Life Stress Management, Organizational Cohesiveness, Supervisory Leadership, Diversity and Anger Management, Organizational Responsiveness, Positive Impression, and Negative Impression. Requires a ninth-grade reading level. To administer the BOEI, one organizational report and an individual report for everyone in the organization is required.

Format: Self-administered online; untimed: 30 minutes

Scoring: Online scoring

Cost: Organizational Report Kit (manual, report) $330.00; Individual Reports $12.00 each

Emotional Competence Inventory (ECI)–360°

2002 | **Hay Group**

Daniel Goleman, Richard Boyatzis

Population: Adults

Purpose: Measures emotional intelligence for

organizational improvement and management development

Description: This 72-item multirater assessment provides individual feedback reports. Workforce composites are available. Requires that the examiner be accredited through the Hay Group. Also available in Spanish, Italian, German, Japanese, Chinese, French (Canadian and Parisian), and Portuguese.

Format: Examiner required; individual or group administration; timed: 45 to 60 minutes

Scoring: Examiner evaluated; computer scored

Cost: Accreditation Fee $3,000.00; Test $150.00 for online per participant

Emotional Judgment Inventory (EJI)

2002 | **Institute for Personality and Ability Testing, Inc.**

Scott Bedwell

Population: Ages 16 years and older

Purpose: Measures emotional intelligence to provide insight into an applicant's tendency to recognize and effectively use emotional information; used for selection, promotion, and professional development

Description: Using a 7-point scale ranging from *absolutely disagree* to *absolutely agree*, the instrument has 80 items. Scores provide seven dimensions of emotional intelligence: Being Aware of Emotions, Identifying Own Emotions, Identifying Others' Emotions, Managing Own Emotions, Managing Others' Emotions, Using Emotions in

Problem Solving, and Expressing Emotions Adaptively. Can be administered paper–pencil, computer, or online. The report contains results for an impression management scale and each of the seven scales.

Format: Self-administered; untimed: 15 minutes

Scoring: Scoring service available; examiner evaluated; online scoring

Cost: Introductory Kit $41.00

Emotional Quotient Inventory: Short™ Development Edition (EQ-iS™)

Date not provided	Multi-Health Systems, Inc.

Reuven Bar-On

Population: Ages 16 years and older

Purpose: Measures emotional intelligence

Description: The instrument covers the same main scales as the original EQ-i, but does not probe further to the subscale level. The following key areas are measured in 51 items: Intrapersonal, Interpersonal, Stress Management, Adaptability, General Mood, Positive Impression (validity), and Inconsistency Index (validity). Online administration is available. Requires a sixth-grade reading level.

Format: Self-administered; untimed: 10 to 15 minutes

Scoring: Hand scored; online; software; scoring service

Cost: Complete Kit (manual, 10 complete assessment sets) $144.00

Emotional Quotient 360™ Assessment (EQ-360™)

2002	Multi-Health Systems, Inc.

Reuven Bar-On, Rich Handley

Population: Ages 16 years and older

Purpose: Measures emotional intelligence from a multirater perspective

Description: Independent observer ratings are compared with the results of a self-assessment that is completed by the subject of focus. What emerges is a more complete 360-degree profile in which external impressions of a person's EQ are combined with the person's self-rating. The EQ-360 is ideal for use in corporate environments, where the nature of human interactions relating to leadership, team, and organizational development is a key component.

Format: Self-administered; untimed: 20 minutes

Scoring: Scoring service available; online scoring

Cost: Online Complete Kit for 3 to 10 Raters (manual, 1 feedback report) $205.00

Mayer-Salovey-Caruso Emotional Intelligence Test (MECEIT™)

Date not provided	Multi-Health Systems, Inc.

John D. Mayer, Peter Salovey, David R. Caruso

Population: Ages 17 years and older

Purpose: Measures capacity for reasoning with emotional information

Description: Uses a variety of interesting and creative tasks to make the test ideal for situations in which respondents may want to create a positive impression. The following key areas are measured: Perceiving Emotions, Facilitating Thought, Understanding Emotions, and Managing Emotions. Requires an eighth-grade reading level. Online administration is available.

Format: Self-administered; untimed: 10 to 15 minutes

Scoring: Hand scored; online; software; scoring service

Cost: Manual $51.00; 3 Reusable Item Booklets $48.00; Online Report Kit $60.00

Personnel Reaction Blank (PRB)

2004	Institute for Personality and Ability Testing, Inc.

Harrison G. Gough, Richard D. Arvey, Pamela Bradley

Population: Ages 15 years and older

Purpose: Measures personality-based integrity; used for selection and placement

Description: The instrument has 84 items providing scores in prosocial background, compliance with social norms, sense of well-being, conventional occupational preferences, and an overall composite of the four subscales. Part I has 30 items with three response options (Like, Indifferent, Dislike), and Part II has 54 items with true–false response options. The report is generated online. If administered paper–pencil, then the administration inputs the responses. The report produces a narrative statement for each score that describes typical behavior of low scorers and high scorers.

Format: Examiner required; group administration; online administration; untimed: 15 minutes

Scoring: Online scoring

Cost: Report costs based on quantity (e.g., 1–9

$30.00 each); Manual $38.00; 10 Test Booklets $20.00

WPQei Emotional Intelligence Questionnaire

| 1998 | Hogrefe Limited |

Allan Cameron

Population: Adults

Purpose: Measures emotional intelligence

Description: This measure, which incorporates much of the latest thinking on the measurement of personality, is based on a conceptual model of emotional intelligence that has seven compo-nents: Self-Awareness, Empathy, Intuition, Emotions, Motivation, Social Skills, and Innovation. The WPQei gives a score on each of seven competencies together with an overall score for emotional intelligence. A PC-generated narrative report then reports in more detail on each of these areas. Where necessary, the report advises on areas for development and identifies respondents' preferred team role using the Belbin model.

Format: Examiner required; suitable for group administration; can be computer administered; untimed

Scoring: Self-scored; computer scored; test scoring service available from publisher

Cost: Contact publisher

Interests

Career Directions Inventory® (CDI®)

| Date not provided | Wonderlic Personnel Test, Inc. |

Population: Adults

Purpose: Measures interests then links them to career and education resources

Description: The inventory consists of 100 groups of activities from which an individual must choose those most/least likely will participate. Generates a 25-page report with graphic presentation of scores and profiles, Basic Interest Scale profile, profile on seven general occupational themes, special clusters survey covering 22 broad areas, comparisons to more than 100 educational/occupational groups, and encourages consideration of all occupations.

Format: Self-administered online

Scoring: Online scoring

Cost: Contact publisher

World of Work Inventory (WOWI)

| 2001 | World of Work, Inc. |

Robert E. Ripley, Karen Hudson, Gregory P. M. Neidert, Nancy L. Ortman

Population: Ages 13 to 65+ years

Purpose: Measures work-related temperaments, interests, and aptitudes; used for career counseling, vocational rehabilitation, employee selection and development, and adult/career education classes

Description: The short form is administered as a 330-item online or paper–pencil inventory. The 98 multiple-choice items assess verbal, numerical, abstractions, spatial-form, mechanical-electrical, and clerical areas. The 232 rating items (3-point Likert) assess 12 job-related temperament factors and career interests in activities related to 17 professional and industrial career areas. The WOWI paper–pencil long form is comprised of 516 items. Results for all forms are provided in profile, summary, and interpretative report formats. Available in a variety of reading levels. Keyedv to *Dictionary of Occupational Titles* career families and the *O*NET Dictionary of Occupational Titles*.

Format: Self-administered; untimed: online, 1 hour; short form, 1½ hours; long form, 2½ hours

Scoring: Online scoring instantly, machine scored, computer scored, test scoring service available

Cost: Online Site License $189.00; Reusable Test Booklet $7.00; Interpretation Manual $19.95; Each report priced separately

Management

Advanced Managerial Tests (AMT) Numerical Analysis (NMT4)

1995 | SHL People Performance

Population: Adults

Purpose: Assesses numerical skills of managers, professional staff, and work-experienced graduates across a range of functions

Description: Thirty-item test measuring the ability to interpret and utilize complex business-related numerical information. The test consists of a number of charts, tables, and graphs relating to one business organization. Candidates are required to interpret the data and combine the information from different sources in order to answer the questions. Calculators may be used. This test would be used in assessing a manager's ability to identify trends across a wide range of data or combine statistics from different departments to establish new information.

Format: Examiner required; individual administration; untimed: 35 minutes

Scoring: Hand key; machine scored; scoring service available

Cost: Contact publisher

Advanced Managerial Tests (AMT) Numerical Reasoning (NMT2)

1995 | SHL People Performance

Population: Adults

Purpose: Assesses verbal skills of managers, professional staff, and work experienced graduates across a range of functions

Description: Test with 35 items measuring the ability to understand the relationship between pieces of numerical information and to complete the relevant operations needed to solve specific problems. The test consists of a series of short problems set in a range of business contexts. Candidates are required to use the information given and, with the aid of a calculator, reach appropriate solutions. Problem types range from arithmetic to proportions, ratios, and probabilities. The main use of this test would be to establish a manager's competence in handling basic business data.

Format: Examiner required; individual administration; untimed: 20 minutes

Scoring: Hand key; machine scored; scoring service available

Cost: Contact publisher

Advanced Managerial Tests (AMT) Verbal Analysis (VMT3)

1995 | SHL People Performance

Population: Adults

Purpose: Assesses numerical skills of managers, professional staff, and work-experienced graduates across a range of functions

Description: Test with 35 items measuring the ability to interpret high-level written information in a variety of ways. The test consists of a series of passages of complex information. The questions asked address a broad range of verbal analysis skills such as summarizing, drawing appropriate inferences, and logical reasoning. This test would assess a manager's ability to interpret complex reports and documents.

Format: Examiner required; individual administration; untimed: 35 minutes

Scoring: Hand key; machine scored; scoring service available

Cost: Contact publisher

Advanced Managerial Tests (AMT) Verbal Application (VMT1)

1995 | SHL People Performance

Population: Adults

Purpose: Assesses verbal skills of managers, professional staff, and work-experienced graduates across a range of functions

Description: Test with 35 items measuring the ability to understand the meaning of words, logic within sentences, and the use of grammar. The test consists of short sentences from which two or three words have been omitted. Candidates are required to select the correct combination of words to complete the sentences. One use of this test would be to assess a candidate's ability to understand, complete, or correct high-level written text.

Format: Examiner required; individual administration; untimed: 20 minutes

Scoring: Hand key; machine scored; scoring service available

Cost: Contact publisher

Assessment Inventory for Management (AIM)

1991	LIMRA International

Population: Adults

Purpose: Identifies candidates with the greatest potential for success at all levels of field sales management for the insurance and financial services industry

Description: The AIM identifies strengths and developmental opportunities for 12 key behavioral competencies that are essential prerequisites for performing management tasks, including interpersonal, leadership, and organizational. The AIM provides each candidate with a list of training exercises, training courses, and other developmental ideas to groom promising candidates for field management. Copies of the Management Selection Interview Guide (one for inexperienced candidates and one for experienced candidates) are included with every AIM feedback report. The guides help the interviewer understand the candidate's background and match the candidate's experiences to the job requirements.

Format: Self-administered online; untimed: 45 minutes

Scoring: Online scoring

Cost: Contact publisher

ASSET: A Supervisory Selection and Development Tool

1990	Life Office Management Association

Population: Adults

Purpose: Provides a valid selection system to identify supervisory potential for the insurance and financial services industry

Description: The system consists of two paper-pencil test batteries. Battery 1 provides developmental data in addition to selection information. Battery 2 provides selection information only. A three-test supplement, which can be used with either battery, tests for basic skills. Training is available for those planning to implement the ASSET tests.

Format: Examiner required; suitable for group use; timed

Scoring: Hand key

Cost: Contact publisher

Campbell-Hallam™ Team Leader Profile (TLP™)

Date not provided	Pearson Performance Solutions

Population: Adults

Purpose: Provides multisource feedback on group leadership skills

Description: The TLP survey helps provide objective information on the team leader's strengths and weaknesses based on the perceptions of the leader and selected observers such as direct reports, peers, and managers. The normative sample includes 2,500 team members who rated 500 team leaders in more than 100 different organizations.

Format: Self-administered; untimed: 20 minutes

Scoring: Scoring service

Cost: Contact publisher

Coaching Skills Inventory– Second Edition (CSI): Observer

1999	Wiley

Dennis C. Kinlaw

Population: Adults

Purpose: Helps managers to develop skills in counseling, mentoring, tutoring, and confronting

Description: Measures participants' coaching skills and helps them to create action plans for improvement. They measure the coaching skills used by superior leaders: Contact and Core Skills, Counseling, Mentoring, Tutoring, and Confronting and Challenging.

Format: Self-administration; untimed

Scoring: Peer scored

Cost: $7.00

Coaching Skills Inventory– Second Edition (CSI): Self

1999	Wiley

Dennis C. Kinlaw

Population: Adults

Purpose: Helps managers to develop skills in counseling, mentoring, tutoring, and confronting

Description: Measures participants' coaching skills and helps them to create action plans for improvement. Measures the coaching skills used by superior leaders: Contact and Core Skills, Counseling, Mentoring, Tutoring, and Confronting and Challenging.

Format: Self-administration; untimed

Scoring: Self-scored

Cost: $12.00

Critical Thinking Test (CTT)
Numerical Critical Reasoning (NCT1)

1988	SHL People Performance

Population: Adults

Purpose: Assesses numerical critical-reasoning skills in managers

Description: Forty-item multiple-choice test measuring understanding and reasoning of numerical data, rather than pure computation. Candidates are required to make decisions or inferences from numerical data presented in a variety of formats. The use of calculators is permitted. The format has clear relevance to management decision making based on numerical and statistical data. Also available in French.

Format: Examiner required; individual administration; untimed: 35 minutes

Scoring: Hand key; machine scored; scoring service available

Cost: Contact publisher

Critical Thinking Test (CTT)
Verbal Critical Reasoning (VCT1)

1988	SHL People Performance

Population: Adults

Purpose: Assesses verbal critical-reasoning skills in managers

Description: Multiple-choice 52-item test measuring the ability to evaluate the logic of various kinds of argument within a realistic context. Candidates are given passages of information followed by series of statements. The candidates must decide whether a given statement is true or untrue, or whether there is insufficient information to make the judgment. The test clearly relates to a key element in managerial or senior specialist jobs in which decisions or inferences must be made or evaluated either on paper or in meetings. Also available in French.

Format: Examiner required; individual administration; untimed: 25 minutes

Scoring: Hand key; machine scored; scoring service available

Cost: Contact publisher

Developing the Leader Within (DLW)

1995	Mind Garden, Inc.

Linda Phillips-Jones

Population: Adults

Purpose: Assesses leadership skills levels; used in psychology and in leadership development

Description: Likert-scale test with 45 items covering Developing Within, Helping Others Excel, Improving Critical Processes, and Showing Commitment to the Team. Uses 360-degree feedback.

Format: Self-administered; untimed: 15 minutes

Scoring: Computer scored

Cost: Multirater $80.00; Single Version $20.00

Epstein Creativity Competencies
Inventory–Managers

2003	Personal Strengths Publishing

Robert E. Epstein

Population: Adults

Purpose: Measures creativity

Description: Measures eight skill sets that managers, teachers, and other leaders need to be able to help other people to express creativity

Format: Rating scale; untimed

Scoring: Scoring service available from publisher

Cost: $10.00

Executive Leadership

1998	Performance Programs, Inc.

Clark L. Wilson, Paul M. Connolly

Population: Senior executive staff

Purpose: Measures the skills and attributes that contribute to the success of leadership

Description: Provides validated 360-degree feedback from multiple levels on key executive competencies, including vision, organizational and marketplace awareness, and executive energy. Contains 84 questionnaire items and three open-ended questions. Inquire about translations (10 languages). Validity and reliability program in place since 1985. Renormed in 2006.

Format: Self-administered; untimed

Scoring: Online scoring service

Cost: $425.00 for up to 15 surveys

Executive Profile Survey (EPS)

1978	Institute for Personality and Ability Testing, Inc.

Virgil R. Lang

Population: Adults

Purpose: Helps to determine if an individual has the attributes for success by measuring behavioral characteristics

Description: Eighty-one items plus 13 short paragraphs are rated on a 7-point scale to measure self-attitudes, values, and beliefs of individuals in comparison with over 2,000 top-level executives. Based on a 15-year study of the "executive personality," the EPS measures the 11 personality-profile dimensions most important in business, management, and executive settings. The profile dimensions include ambitious, assertive, enthusiastic, creative, spontaneous, self-focused, considerate, open-minded, relaxed, practical, and systematic traits of the individual. The survey also provides two validity scales. Norms, reliability, validity, and developmental background are explained.

Format: Self-administered; untimed: 1 hour

Scoring: Computer scored; scoring service available

Cost: Introductory Kit $34.00

Experience and Background Inventory (EBI)

1996	Pearson Performance Solutions

Melany E. Baehr, Ernest C. Froemel

Population: Adults

Purpose: Evaluates an individual's past performance and experience on nine factorially determined dimensions of quantified personal background data; used for selection, promotion, and career counseling of higher-level managerial and professional personnel

Description: Paper–pencil 55-item multiple-choice inventory assessing the following background areas: School Achievement, Choice of a College Major, Aspiration Level, Drive/Career Progress, Leadership and Group Participation, Vocational Satisfaction, Financial Responsibility, General Responsibility, and Relaxation Pursuits. Different combinations of factors have been validated for selection and evaluation of potential for successful performance in higher-level managerial and professional positions.

Format: Self-administered; untimed: 20 minutes

Scoring: Hand key

Cost: Contact publisher

General Management In-Basket (GMIB)

Updated yearly	Management & Personnel Systems, Inc.

Population: Adults

Purpose: Assesses management skills

Description: The GMIB consists of 15 carefully selected problems (Leadership, Decision Making, Performance, Delegation, Conflict, and Organization) that have been proven to separate effective managers from those who are destined for less than excellence. The instrument is used for any management job in either the private or public sector. There are multiple versions of the test, each with multiple parallel forms. The problems are presented in memos and letters. Each involves a managerial issue or problem. Candidates must provide a written analysis of the management issues involved in each and explain the actions they would take. They must also write memos and letters, as though they were on the job. Because the test has a national database, the scores can be compared to other managers on a national level. The GMIB has explicit scoring criteria for each problem. Results are provided in the form of a rank-ordered list of candidates and an individual bar-chart profile. A short form is also available.

Format: Self-administered; timed: 2 hours 45 minutes to 3 hours

Scoring: Scoring service

Cost: $325 per candidate (long form); $255 per candidate (short form)

Hilson Job Analysis Questionnaire–Revised (HJAQ-R)

2002	Institute for Personality and Ability Testing, Inc.

Robin E. Inwald

Population: Adults

Purpose: Assesses job-related personality characteristics

Description: The HJAQ-R includes 134 true–false questions. It is administered to a group and a composite score is derived. A fifth-grade reading level is required. Also available in Spanish.

Format: Self-administered; untimed: 15 minutes

Scoring: Examiner evaluated; computer scoring available; scoring service available

Cost: $16.00 to $20.00 depending on scoring method

Hilson Management Inventory (HMI)

1997	Institute for Personality and Ability Testing, Inc.

Robin E. Inwald

Population: Adults

Purpose: Screens individuals for managerial and executive positions

Description: Measures leadership, work ethic, drive, and social skills. Used for preemployment screening or promotion of job candidates. A 263-item true-false test. Available in Spanish. Test is a composite of the HPP/SQ and the HMS.

Format: Examiner required; suitable for groups; untimed: 30 minutes

Scoring: Computer scored; scoring service available

Cost: $26.00 to $30.00 depending on scoring method

Hilson Management Survey (HMS)

1995	Institute for Personality and Ability Testing, Inc.

Robin E. Inwald

Population: Adults

Purpose: Assesses work-related behavioral characteristics

Description: Paper-pencil 103 item true-false test with a profile graph within a computer-generated report. A test book and scorable answer sheets are used. A fifth-grade reading level is required. Also available in Spanish.

Format: Examiner required; suitable for groups; untimed: 30 minutes

Scoring: Computer scored; scoring service

Cost: $16.00 to $20.00 depending on scoring method

Influence Strategies Exercise (ISE)

1993	Hay Group

Population: Adults

Purpose: Tool for identifying and developing influence techniques

Description: Consists of 54 items dealing with nine influence strategies: empowerment, interpersonal awareness, bargaining, relationship building, organizational awareness, common vision, impact management, logical persuasion, and coercion. At least three people per participant provide feedback. There are no right or wrong styles; all nine influence techniques can make communication more efficient and effective. Used at all levels within organizations.

Format: Self-administration; untimed: 30 minutes

Scoring: Self-scored

Cost: 10 Participant Questionnaires and Interpretative Notes $79.00; 10 Employee Questionnaires $29.00

Inventory of Management Competencies (IMC)

1994	SHL People Performance

Population: Managers (all levels)

Purpose: Measures managerial competencies

Description: Assesses 16 generic management competencies using 40 questions. One test is for self-assessment, and two to six tests are for 360-degree feedback. A two-page color profile and optional expert narrative report are provided. Also available in French.

Format: Examiner required; individual administration; computer and online administration available; untimed: 20 minutes

Scoring: Hand key; machine scored; scoring service available; online scoring

Cost: Contact publisher

IPI Job-Field Series: Production/Mechanical

1997	Industrial Psychology International Ltd.

Population: Adults

Purpose: Assesses skills and personality for supervisory positions in a factory setting; used to evaluate the achievement and personality of maintenance and production people, supervisors, and superintendents

Description: Multiple-item paper-pencil battery of seven aptitude and two personality tests. The tests are Motor, Precision, Blocks, Dexterity, Dimension, Parts, Neurotic Personality Factor, Numbers, and Contact Personality Factor. For individual test descriptions, see the *IPI Employee Aptitude Series*. Also available in French and Spanish.

Format: Examiner required; suitable for group use; timed 128 minutes

Scoring: Hand key

Cost: Starter Kit (test materials for 5 applicants, scoring keys, manuals) $80.00; Test Package $14.00 per applicant

IPI Job-Field Series: Sales Personnel

1997	Industrial Psychology International Ltd.

Population: Adults

Purpose: Assesses skills and personality of applicants for supervisory positions in various sales fields; used to screen for advertising, credit, merchandise, service, and store sales supervisor positions

Description: Multiple-item paper–pencil battery of seven aptitude and two personality tests. The tests are Fluency, Sales Terms, Memory, Judgment, Contact Personality Factor, Parts, Numbers, Neurotic Personality Factor, and Perception. For individual test descriptions, see the *IPI Employee Aptitude Series*. Also available in French and Spanish.

Format: Self-administered; timed: 82 minutes

Scoring: Hand key

Cost: Starter Kit (test materials for 5 applicants, scoring keys, manuals) $80.00; Test Package $14.00 per applicant

Leadership Competencies for Managers–Version D

1998, 2006	Performance Programs, Inc.

Clark L. Wilson

Population: Middle- to senior-level managers

Purpose: Measures the skills essential to both the management and leadership roles

Description: A multiple-rater assessment that provides feedback on leadership skills. Contains 59 questions plus 3 open-ended questions. Reliability and validity program in place since 1985. Renormed in 2006.

Format: Self-administered; untimed

Scoring: Online scoring service

Cost: $260.00 for up to 15 surveys

Leadership in Health Services

2000	Performance Programs, Inc.

Clark L. Wilson, Richard Dowall

Population: Executives in health services industry

Purpose: Measures leadership skills needed to lead the organization in competing successfully in the changing health-care environment

Description: A multiple-rater assessment that provides feedback on leadership skills. Contains 106 questions plus 3 open-ended questions. Developed in conjunction with physicians and physician administrators. Inquire about Portuguese translation. Reliability and validity program in place since 2000. Renormed in 2006.

Format: Self-administered; untimed

Scoring: Online scoring service

Cost: $260.00 for up to 15 surveys

Leadership Opinion Questionnaire (LOQ)

1989	Pearson Performance Solutions

Edwin A Fleishman

Population: Adults

Purpose: Measures leadership style; used in a variety of industrial and organizational settings for selection, appraisal, counseling, and training of employees

Description: Paper–pencil or computerized 40-item test measuring two aspects of leadership: consideration (how likely an individual's job relationship with subordinates is characterized by mutual trust, respect, and consideration) and structure (how likely an individual is to define and structure personal and subordinate's roles toward goal attainment).

Format: Self-administered; untimed: 10 to 15 minutes

Scoring: Hand key; computer scored

Cost: Contact publisher

Leadership Practices

1996	Performance Programs, Inc.

Clark L. Wilson

Population: Midlevel leadership staff

Purpose: Measures the skills and personal attributes that will move the organization toward positive change

Description: A multiple-rater assessment that provides the midlevel organizational leader with feedback on leadership skills. Contains 77 questions, plus 8 questions on sources of influence, plus 3 open-ended questions. Reliability and validity program in place since 2000. Renormed in 2006. Inquire about Arabic, Spanish, and Portuguese translations.

Format: Self-administered; untimed

Scoring: Online scoring service

Cost: $260.00 for up to 15 surveys

Leadership Practices Inventory–Third Edition (LPI)

2003	Wiley

James M. Kouzes, Barry Z. Posner

Population: Managers, supervisors

Purpose: Helps managers to set goals, create solid action plans, cultivate innovative thinking, improve interpersonal skills, and take other positive steps to develop essential leadership traits

Description: Includes 10-point Likert scale, scoring software, participant workbooks, tools needed to obtain complete 360-degree feedback, and 3-month follow-up program to track progress. The self-inventory evaluates performance and effectiveness as a leader. The observer provides a balanced picture of how others perceive leadership traits and allows for constructive discussion of ways to improve.

Format: Self-administered; untimed: 2 to 4 hours

Scoring: Self-scored; computer scored

Cost: Facilitator's Package (1 each of guide and book) $70.00

Management and Supervisory Skills-Form A-C

2000	Ramsay Corporation

Roland T. Ramsay

Population: Adults

Purpose: Measures knowledge of management and supervisory skills

Description: In 40 items, the following five skills are measured: Planning, Organizing, Communicating, Motivating, and Managing.

Format: Examiner required; suitable for group use; untimed: approximately 60 minutes

Scoring: Self-scored; scoring service available

Cost: Test Booklet $13.00 (minimum 20); Manual $24.95

Management Aptitude Test (MAT™)

Date not provided	Pearson Performance Solutions

Population: Adults

Purpose: Assesses a leadership candidate's critical-thinking ability and business knowledge

Description: Measures problem solving, planning and organizing, communication, supervisory skills, administrative skills, and business control to provide a Manager Potential Index. Candidates are asked to respond to situational questions.

Format: Self-administration; untimed: 90 minutes

Scoring: Software scoring; computer scoring via telephone

Cost: Contact publisher

Management Development Questionnaire (MDQ)

1996	Hogrefe Limited

Allan Cameron

Population: Adults

Purpose: Assists managers and supervisors to identify strengths and weaknesses in their management style

Description: The MDQ can be used as a candidate self-perception inventory in a recruitment environment alongside personality assessment instruments to provide a candidate's perception of his or her managerial ability. The MDQ provides tailored reports of candidate profiles. It works by applying a set of decision rules to the candidate's sten scores. Depending on the sten scores, certain statements give the meaning and potential implications of the scores.

Format: Examiner required; suitable for group use; can be computer administered; untimed

Scoring: Self-scored; computer scored; machine scored; test scoring service available

Cost: Contact publisher

Management Practices

1993	Performance Programs, Inc.

Clark L. Wilson

Population: Managers and supervisors at all levels

Purpose: Measures strengths and weaknesses in key management behaviors; provides feedback to managers to enhance their skills

Description: A multiple-rater assessment that provides managers with feedback on their management skills and practices. Contains 100 questions plus 3 open-ended questions. Reliability and validity program in place since 2000. Renormed in 2006. Inquire about translations (six languages).

Format: Self-administered; untimed

Scoring: Online scoring service

Cost: $260.00 for up to 15 surveys

Management Readiness Profile (MRP™)

1988	Pearson Performance Solutions

Population: Adults

Purpose: Evaluates job applicants or employees for managerial interests and basic management orientation

Description: Paper–pencil 188-item multiple-choice test with seven subtests: Management Interests, Leadership, Energy and Drive, Practical Thinking, Management Responsibility, Sociability, and Candidates. Subscale scores and a composite Management Readiness Index are generated.

Format: Self-administration; untimed: 20 minutes

Scoring: Computer scored

Cost: Contact publisher

Management Report & Briefing (MRB)

Updated yearly   Management & Personnel Systems, Inc.

Population: Adults

Purpose: Measures ability to evaluate and analyze information, sort through what is pertinent, and write effective reports

Description: The MRB provides information on the management and goal attainment of a hypothetical program (or department). Candidates are given two hours to evaluate the information and write a report with recommendations. The test requires candidates to evaluate a wealth of information, including before and after data, budget allocations, and statements contained in various memos and letters. Candidates must identify problems and critical issues and write a report that analyzes the information and makes recommendations for action by higher management. An optional oral report may also be utilized. Results are reported in the form of a rank-ordered list of the candidates. In addition, the MRB uses a behavioral checklist approach to provide performance feedback for candidates on each of the factors (problem analysis, judgment and decision making, and written communications) measured.

Format: Self-administered; untimed

Scoring: Scoring service

Cost: $180 each candidate

Management Success Profile (MSP™)

Date not provided   Pearson Performance Solutions

Population: Adults

Purpose: Evaluates skills and attitudes that are critical to management success

Description: Identifies those candidates who will follow company procedures and make ethical business decisions. The following areas are assessed: Work Background, Leadership, Coaching, Adaptability, Management Responsibility, Practical Thinking, Customer Service Orientation, Productivity, Job Commitment, Business Ethics, Validity/Accuracy, and Validity/Candidness.

Format: Self-administration; untimed: 45 minutes

Scoring: Software scoring; computer scoring via telephone and fax

Cost: Contact publisher

Managerial Assessment of Proficiency (MAP)

2000   HRD Press

Scott Parry

Population: Adults

Purpose: Measures 12 fundamental management competencies for management training

Description: Multiple-choice and true–false versions of MAP link sets of test questions to video scenes of a group of managers working through a series of issues and problems during the course of a workday. Scores are provided as percentile ranking in each competency as compared to a norm composed of over 80,000 managers who have completed this assessment. Competencies include Setting Goals and Standards, Time Management, Planning and Scheduling, Work, Listening and Organizing, Giving Clear Information, Getting Unbiased Information, Training/Coaching/Delegating, Appraising People, Disciplining and Counseling, Problem Solving, Decision Making, and Analytical Thinking. Participants also receive a composite profile of all scores combined, a score on their theory X/Y behavior, and scores on their communication style and personal style. The report produces scores plus narrative directing development. Managers receive a comprehensive participant booklet with exercises and interpretation that can cover up to two full days of assessment debriefing and development planning. There is also an Instructor's Guide for facilitators. Organizations can use MAP through a limited pilot license or a full organization license. Also available in Spanish, Chinese, and Filipino.

Format: Examiner required; untimed: 3 hours

Scoring: Online or computer scoring; test scoring service available from publisher

Cost: $400.00 per assessment, licensing reduces per participant cost

Managerial Style Questionnaire (MSQ)

1994   Hay Group

Population: Adults

Purpose: Identifies a manager's style and the

impact of managerial style on performance, productivity, and profits

Description: This questionnaire consists of 36 Items that measure six managerial styles: Coercive, Democratic, Authoritative, Coaching, Pacesetting, and Affiliative. Identifies which style or styles a manager relies on most and when those styles are most and least effective. Also available in Spanish and French.

Format: Self-administered; untimed: 30 minutes

Scoring: Self-scored

Cost: $79.00 for 10 participant questionnaires and interpretative notes; Trainer's Guide $25.00

Multi-Factor Leadership Questionnaire for Research (MLQ)

1995	Mind Garden, Inc.

Bernard M. Bass, Bruce J. Avolio

Population: Adults

Purpose: Assessment of leadership and management abilities

Description: The MLQ provides the best relationship of survey data to organizational outcome. The multirater report brings home the relationship between the leader's perceptions and those of the raters. The new report shows how best to use the MLQ data, explains Full Range Leadership, and provides tips for improving leadership. The 45-item MLQ contains 12 scales: Idealized Attributes, Idealized Behaviors, Inspirational Motivation, Intellectual Stimulation, Individualized Consideration, Contingent Reward, Management-by-Exception (Active), Management-by-Exception (Passive), Laissez-Faire, Extra Effort, Effectiveness, and Satisfaction. The narrative report is available both with and without group data.

Format: Self administered; untimed

Scoring: Examiner evaluated; computer scored; online service available; test scoring service available

Cost: Manual/Sampler Set $40.00; Permission Set of 200 $150.00

Occupational Personality Questionnaire (OPQ32)

1999	SHL People Performance

Population: Managers and other professionals

Purpose: Assessment and development of behavior at work

Description: A total of 230 items in three categories: Relationships With People, Thinking

Style, and Feelings and Emotions. Describes 32 dimensions of preferred/typical style of behavior at work. Provides a variety of expert reports on assessment and development. Also available in French.

Format: Examiner required; individual administration; computer and online administration available; untimed: 35 minutes

Scoring: Hand key; machine scored; scoring service available; online scoring

Cost: Contact publisher

Organizational Description Questionnaire (ODQ)

1992	Mind Garden, Inc.

Bernard M. Bass, Bruce J. Avolio

Population: Adults

Purpose: Explore the relationship between leaders of an organization

Description: Brief paper–pencil 28-item questionnaire and resulting report. Measures how often each member of the organization perceives the culture of his or her unit, department, or organization to be using a full range of specific leadership factors. The ODQ places the organization on a 9-point scale spanning cultures such as Bureaucratic, Coasting, and Highly Developed. Online administration and scoring available.

Format: Self-administered; untimed

Scoring: Examiner evaluated

Cost: 100 forms $200.00

Peer Relations

1994	Performance Programs, Inc.

Population: Management-level professionals

Purpose: Measures management skills with the focus on the horizontal relationship between professional or technical specialists and their internal clients

Description: A multiple-rater assessment that helps independent contributors in professional roles learn about their strengths and weaknesses. Evaluates the specialist's management expertise, which is as important as technical expertise on the job. Contains 80 questions with 3 open-ended questions. Inquire about Spanish translation. Reliability and validity program in place since 2000. Renormed in 2006.

Format: Self-administered; untimed

Scoring: Online scoring service

Cost: $260.00 for up to 15 surveys

Performance Skills Leader (PS Leader)

1996	HRD Press

Population: Adults

Purpose: Measures 24 leadership competencies grouped in five areas of focus: Strategic, Business, Workforce, Interpersonal, and Personal for management/leadership training

Description: A research-based 82-item assessment that gives leaders an objective analysis of their leadership effectiveness. *PS Leader* is specifically designed for 360-degree feedback. The assessment helps leaders to identify development priorities and determine their known and unknown strengths by comparing their own self-perceptions to those of their supervisor, direct reports, and peers. Available for online administration or with paper–pencil questionnaires. Reports are computer processed and returned to the designated individual. An Administrator's Guide is available that outlines how to deliver a half-day or full-day session helping managers interpret their results and plan for development. Resources are available for calculating return on investment when using *PS Leader* for pre- and posttesting.

Format: Self-administered; untimed

Scoring: Online scoring; scoring service available from publisher

Cost: $125.00 per complete 360 assessment cycle

Perspectives on Management Competencies

1998	SHL People Performance

Population: Managers (all levels)

Purpose: An in-depth assessment of management competencies

Description: A total of 144 items. One test is for self-assessment; two to six tests provide 360-degree assessment. Thirty-six key management competencies are viewed from multiple perspectives. Multiple reports and detailed behavioral feedback are available. Also available in French.

Format: Examiner required; individual administration; untimed: 18 minutes

Scoring: Hand key; machine scored; scoring service available

Cost: Contact publisher

Reading–Form A (Supervisory Reading)

1992	Ramsay Corporation

Roland T. Ramsay

Population: Adults

Purpose: Assesses the ability to read, comprehend, and answer written questions

Description: Paper–pencil 40-item multiple-choice test designed to measure an individual's ability to read, comprehend, and answer questions based on a printed passage.

Format: Examiner required; suitable for group use; timed: 30 minutes

Scoring: Self-scored; scoring service available

Cost: Test Booklet $12.00 (minimum 20)

Retail Management Assessment Inventory (RMAI)

1989	Pearson Performance Solutions

Population: Adults

Purpose: Selects and screens applicants for the position of unit manager in retail or restaurant outlets

Description: Multi-item multiple-choice paper-pen test comprised of 10 subtests: Background and Work Experience, Management and Leadership Interests, Management Responsibility, Understanding Management Procedures and Practices, Customer Service, Applied Management Computations, Energy Level, Job Stability, Business Ethics, and Management Orientation. Scores are provided for each subtest and for an overall Management Potential Index. In addition to scores, the RMAI generates positive indicators, training needs, and follow-up interview questions. Three scoring options are available.

Format: Examiner required; suitable for group use; untimed: 75 minutes

Scoring: Computer scored

Cost: Contact publisher

Sales Management Practices

1994	Performance Programs, Inc.

Clark L. Wilson

Population: Managers, supervisors

Purpose: Provides feedback on management skills and practices

Description: Contains 145 questions with 3 open-ended questions completed by multiraters.

Format: Self-administered; untimed

Scoring: Online scoring service

Cost: $260.00 for up to 15 surveys

Strategic Leadership Type Indicator (SLTI)

2003	HRD Press

Alexander Hiam

Population: Adults

Purpose: Measures the appropriate use of four management styles: Relate, Coach, Delegate, and Instruct

Description: Participants rank four alternative management strategies for each of 16 case descriptions. This instrument determines a manager's ability to appropriately use strategies according to the motivation and capability levels of the employee. Managers determine their primary and secondary strategic styles and receive a score on their flexibility to use each of the styles when the circumstances dictate. The questionnaire booklet is self-scoring and includes a series of exercises that teach when and how to use the four primary styles appropriately. There is a Leader Guide for facilitating a workshop with the assessment. There are also one and two day workshops available.

Format: Self-administered; individual or group setting; untimed: 20 minutes

Scoring: Self-scored

Cost: $14.95 each

Supervisory Practices Test, Revised

2006	Martin M. Bruce, PhD

Martin M. Bruce

Population: Adults

Purpose: Evaluates supervisory ability and potential in a business-world setting; used for personnel selection, evaluation, and training

Description: Paper–pencil 50-item multiple-choice test indicating the extent to which the subject is able to choose a desirable course of action (as compared with the perceptions and attitudes of managers and subordinates) when presented with a business decision. Minority group data are available. Suitable for individuals with physical, hearing, or visual impairments. Also available in French, Spanish, and German.

Format: Self-administered; untimed: 20 minutes

Scoring: Hand key

Cost: Specimen Set $58.95

Supervisory Simulator (SupSim)

Updated yearly	Management & Personnel Systems, Inc.

Population: Adults

Purpose: Identifies skills needed to be a successful first-level supervisor

Description: The test comes in a booklet format and consists of five realistic problem situations involving members of the work team. Each problem is one that is commonly encountered by first-level supervisors, forepersons, or team leaders. Candidates must respond in narrative fashion to questions that are posed about each situation, indicating what they would do or say. Because the test has a national database, the scores can be compared to other supervisors on a national level. The factors measured are Leadership/Decision Making and Team Relations. The SupSim has explicit scoring criteria for each problem. Results are provided in the form of a rank-ordered list of candidates and an individual bar-chart profile.

Format: Self-administered; timed: 75 minutes

Scoring: Scoring service

Cost: $235 each candidate

System for Testing and Evaluation of Potential (LH-STEP™)

Date not provided	Pearson Performance Solutions

Population: Adults

Purpose: Helps add insight to hiring, training, and promotion decisions to enhance the quality of management teams

Description: First, members of a staff complete a questionnaire to create a profile of the job functions most critical to the position needing to be filled. This description is matched to a national databank of job profiles to develop a clear definition of the skills, abilities, and attitudes of job applicants. The second phase consists of a battery measuring up to 50 skills, abilities, and attributes for six key areas that is administered to candidates. The third step compares an individual with the critical job functions defined in the first step. Helps to reduce turnover.

Format: Self-administration; untimed: 2 hours 30 minutes

Scoring: Scoring service

Cost: Contact publisher

Working with Others

2000	Performance Programs, Inc.

Clark L. Wilson

Population: Candidates for supervisory roles, coworkers

Purpose: Screens to identify candidates for promotion or to coach and counsel those who have recently been promoted

Description: Multilevel survey of organizational skills for people entering supervisory positions.

Contains 60 questions with 3 open-ended questions. Also available in Spanish.

Format: Self-administered; untimed

Scoring: Online scoring service

Cost: $260.00 for up to 15 surveys

Personality

Adult Personality Inventory

| 1982 | MetriTech, Inc. |

Samuel E. Krug

Population: Adults

Purpose: Assesses personality characteristics, interpersonal style, and career preferences for personnel evaluation, career planning, rehabilitation counseling, and family therapy

Description: Series of computer-administered multiple-item multiple-choice paper–pencil subtests yielding scores in three areas: Personality Characteristics (extroverted, adjusted, tough-minded, independent, disciplined, creative, and enterprising), Interpersonal Style (caring, adapting, withdrawn, submissive, hostile, rebellious, sociable, and assertive), and Career Orientation (practical, scientific, aesthetic, social, competitive, and structured). Four validity scales (Good Impression, Bad Impression, Infrequency, and Uncertainty) complete the test profile. Reports available through mail-in service or through on-site software programs (MS/PC DOS on IBM systems).

Format: Self-administered; untimed: 30 to 60 minutes

Scoring: Computer scored

Cost: Narrative Report Kit (test material, manual, processing of 5 reports) $49.00

Adult Personality Inventory (API)

| 1982 | Institute for Personality and Ability Testing, Inc. |

Samuel E. Krug

Population: Ages 16 years to adult

Purpose: Analyzes and reports individual differences in seven personality characteristics, eight interpersonal styles, and six career/lifestyle factors; used for selection, placement, and individual counseling

Description: Using 324 items, 21 scales (Extroverted, Tough-Minded, Disciplined, Enterprising, Adapting, Submissive, Rebellious, Assertive, Scientific, Social, Structured, Adjusted, Independent, Creative, Caring, Withdrawn, Hostile, Sociable, Practical, Aesthetic, and Competitive) are reported with four validity scales (Good Impression, Bad Impression, Infrequency, and Uncertainty). The report of the scores has three parts. Part 1 deals with patterns that characterize broad segments of behavior, including overall adjustment, cognitive style, and achievement orientation. Part 2 focuses on how the individual relates to other people by evaluating eight styles and providing a chart of the scores, plus a narrative summary. Part 3 examines occupational and lifestyle preferences from the perspective of six orientations that are present to some extent in all of us. Standard scores for men and women are provided. Requires a fourth-grade reading level.

Format: Self-administered; untimed: 1 hour

Scoring: Scoring service available from publisher

Cost: Introductory Kit $29.00

Assessment & Development Profile (ADP)

| Date not provided | Winslow Research Institute |

Population: Adults

Purpose: Measures personality, behavior, and attitudes

Description: This comprehensive assessment program measures 33 personality traits of coaching program participants. Presents suggestions for self-improvement. The reports enhance the probability that clients will achieve and maintain optimum career performance and personal happiness. The characteristics are measured in 726 questions and grouped by the following: Interpersonal, Organizational, Dedication, and Self-Control.

Format: Self-administered; untimed: 3 hours

Scoring: Completed online; scoring service

Cost: Contact publisher

Bass Orientation Inventory (ORI)

| 1977 | Mind Garden, Inc. |

Bernard M. Bass

Population: Adults

Purpose: Measures three types of orientation; used for personnel assessment, college vocational counseling, and group research

Description: Paper–pencil 27-item forced-choice test of three types of orientation toward satisfaction and rewards: Self-Orientation, Interaction-Orientation, and Task-Orientation. Results help to predict an individual's success and performance in various types of work. The inventory is based on Bass's theory of interpersonal behavior in organizations.

Format: Self-administered; untimed: 10 to 15 minutes

Scoring: Examiner evaluated

Cost: Sampler Set $30.00; Permission Set for Up to 200 Uses $150.00

Business Judgment Test, Revised

| 1999 | Martin M. Bruce, PhD |

Martin M. Bruce

Population: Adults

Purpose: Evaluates the subject's sense of "social intelligence" in business-related situations; used for employee selection and training

Description: Paper–pencil 25-item multiple-choice test in which the subject selects one of four ways to complete a stem statement, allowing the examiner to gauge the subject's sense of socially accepted and desirable ways to behave in business relationships. The score suggests the degree to which the subject agrees with the general opinion of businesspeople as to the proper way to handle various relationships. Also available in French.

Format: Self-administered; untimed: 10 to 15 minutes

Scoring: Hand key

Cost: Specimen Set $55.50

Career Anchors: Self Assessment

| 2006 | Wiley |

Edgar H. Schein

Population: Adults

Purpose: Helps people to define dominant themes and patterns in their lives, to understand their own approach to work and a career, to find reasons for choices they make, and to take steps to fulfill their self-image

Description: Helps people to uncover their real values and to use them to make better career choices. The instrument includes the orientations inventory, the career anchor interview, and conceptual material. The Trainer's Manual provides facilitation instructions for a 2-hour workshop and an extended workshop of 4 hours or more. A lecture on the concept of career anchors is included.

Format: Self-administration; untimed

Scoring: Self-scoring

Cost: $15.00

Comprehensive Personality Profile® (CPP®)

| 1980 | Wonderlic Personnel Test, Inc. |

Larry L. Craft

Population: Ages 18 years and older

Purpose: Used in preemployment selection to measure personality and assess job compatibility

Description: Paper–pencil 88-item test with seven primary scales, 10 secondary scales, and sales training reports. A ninth-grade reading level is required. Also available in Spanish and French.

Format: Self-administered; untimed

Scoring: Computer scored; test scoring service available from publisher

Cost: Contact publisher

Core Values Index™ (CVI)

| 1999 | Taylor Protocols |

Lynn E. Taylor

Population: Ages 11 years and older

Purpose: Measures the innate unchanging core values of the nature of each person

Description: A one-page assessment with 144 values loaded into 36 boxes with force preference of two in each box. Nine subtests, each utilizing the same 144 values in a different fashion. Results are reported for Personal Values Index, Ideal Profile, Core Values Business Optimization Protocol, Conflict Resolution Protocol, Mentoring Protocol, and 720 Degree Review. A tool for personal/professional development, business reorganization, productivity optimization, reduction in employee turnover, prescreening for employment, and matching Ideal Profile with individual profiles to create best job fit. Also available in Spanish and Malaysian.

Format: Self-administered online; timed: 10 minutes

Scoring: Online scoring; results sent by e-mail

Cost: Contact publisher

DISCstyles

2006	HRD Press

Population: Adults

Purpose: Determines primary and secondary behavioral styles: Dominant, Interactive, Steady, or Compliant

Description: A behavioral style assessment of 30 items including use of work, home, and social settings that produces a profile using the most widely used behavioral standard in the training industry. Helps participants to better understand others by understanding the chemistry between their own styles and differing styles. The skills learned enable participants to enhance relationships and improve their success in any interpersonal settings. The online version provides a personal Web account that enables users to get unlimited 360-degree feedback on their behavioral styles. Participants learn their behavioral style tendencies, what motivates them, their communication preferences, and how to become more adaptable. Items require a high school reading level.

Format: Self-administered; group setting; untimed: 15 minutes

Scoring: Computer scored; online scoring

Cost: Online $59.95; Paper–Pencil 5 Pack $75.00

Emo Questionnaire

1995	Pearson Performance Solutions

George O. Baehr, Melany E. Baehr

Population: Adults

Purpose: Determines an individual's personal-emotional adjustment; used to evaluate the potential of sales, managerial, and professional personnel and to screen applicants for jobs requiring efficient performance under pressure

Description: Paper–pencil 140-item examination measuring 10 traditional psychodiagnostic categories (Rationalization, Inferiority Feelings, Hostility, Depression, Fear and Anxiety, Organic Reaction, Projection, Unreality, Sex Problems, and Withdrawal) and three composite adjustment

factors (Internal, External, and Somatic). The results reflect both the individual's internal psychodynamics and his or her relationship with the external environment. In combination with other instruments, the test has been validated for selection of salespersons, police and security guards, and transit operators. In hospital settings, it is useful as a diagnosis of emotional health and to chart the course of psychotherapy. Basic reading skills are required.

Format: Examiner required; suitable for group use; untimed: 20 minutes

Scoring: Hand key

Cost: Contact publisher

Employee Reliability Inventory Screening System (ERI®)

1986	Bay State Psychological Associates, Inc.

Gerald L. Borofsky

Population: Adults

Purpose: Assesses dimensions of behavior; used to help screen job applicants

Description: The ERI is an 81-item true–false test designed to screen for unreliable and unproductive behavior. The seven areas measured are Freedom from Disruptive Alcohol and Substance Use, Courteous Job Performance, Emotional Maturity, Conscientiousness, Trustworthiness, Long Term Job Commitment, and Safe Job Performance. Scores are reported as work ready, not work ready, and special needs. Also available in Chinese, Hindi, Spanish, and French. A sixth-grade reading level is required. Also available in large print, on audiocassette, and in Braille.

Format: Self-administered; untimed

Scoring: Hand scored; phone; Web; computer

Cost: Contact publisher

Employee Wellness Evaluation (EWE™)

1994	Change Companies

Population: Adults

Purpose: Screens for common problems seen among employee populations

Description: It covers indications of alcohol abuse, depression, stress, anger, workplace conflicts, and job–family tensions. Designed to be administered prior to face-to-face counseling by an EAP professional.

Format: Rating scale; untimed

Scoring: Examiner evaluated

Cost: Guide $15.00; 25 Forms $52.50

Employment Productivity Index (EPI)

| Date not provided | Pearson Performance Solutions |

Population: Job applicants

Purpose: Assesses personality trait combinations that lead to productive and responsible work behavior; used to identify applicants who will remain on the job, have low absentee rates, and obey company rules, particularly those prohibiting alcohol and drugs

Description: Multiple-item paper–pencil survey consisting of four scales measuring personality traits that lead to productive employment: Dependability, Interpersonal Cooperation, Drug Avoidance, and Validity. A Composite Productivity Index is provided. In addition, a test analysis report includes a Significant Behavioral Indicators section highlighting specific responses that may be useful in making decisions about borderline candidates. The EPI-3S version includes a safety scale measuring safety consciousness and identifying applicants at risk for on-the-job accidents.

Format: Self-administered; untimed: 30 minutes

Scoring: Operator-assisted telephone; computer scored

Cost: Contact publisher

Entrepreneurial Quotient™ (EQ™)

| 1984 | Wonderlic Personnel Test, Inc. |

Edward J. Fasiska

Population: Adults

Purpose: Assesses adaptability, management, and personality traits to measure entrepreneurial potential

Description: Paper–pencil 100-item multiple-choice test that measures Risk Tolerance, Creativity, Strategic Thinking, Planning, Goal Orientation, Intuition, Adaptability, and Time Management. The following reports are yielded: four summary scales, adaptability, managerial traits, personality traits, and EQ index.

Format: Self-administered; untimed

Scoring: Computer scored

Cost: Contact publisher

Gordon Personal Profile–Inventory (GPP-I™)

| 1978 (Manual 1993) | Harcourt Assessment, Inc. |

Leonard V. Gordon

Population: Adults

Purpose: Provides measurement of factors in the personality domain

Description: Eight factors provide coverage of five personality traits (Extraversion, Agreeableness, Conscientiousness, Emotional Stability, and Openness). Respondents select one item in each group of four as being most like themselves and one as being least like themselves. Also available in French from the Institute of Psychological Research, Inc.

Format: Examiner required; suitable for group use; untimed: 20 to 30 minutes

Scoring: Hand key or machine scorable

Cost: Starter Kit (25 hand-scorable booklets, 25 machine-scorable booklets, interpretive guide, scoring key, inventory, manual) $300.00

Hilson Attitude Survey–Revised (HAS-R)

| 2006 | Institute for Personality and Ability Testing, Inc. |

Robin E. Inwald

Population: Adolescents, adults

Purpose: Measures individual reliability and integrity

Description: Used for preemployment screening and counseling. The HAS-R includes true false questions from which both raw scores and t-scores are derived. The instrument is the short form of the IS5-R. A fifth-grade reading level is required. Also available in Spanish.

Format: Self-administered; untimed

Scoring: Examiner evaluated; computer scoring available

Cost: $16.00 to $20.00 depending on scoring method

Hilson Life Adjustment Profile (HLAP)

| 1993 | Institute for Personality and Ability Testing, Inc. |

Robin E. Inwald

Population: Ages 18 years and older

Purpose: Measures emotional adjustment

Description: A total of 144 items for preemployment screening of high-risk occupations. Screens for emotional adjustment, functioning level, and psychopathology. Also available in Spanish.

Format: Examiner required; suitable for group administration; untimed: 15 minutes

Scoring: Computer scored; scoring service available

Cost: $16.00 to $20.00 depending on scoring method

Hilson Personnel Profile/ Success Quotient (HPP/SQ)

1988	Institute for Personality and Ability Testing, Inc.

Robin E. Inwald

Population: Ages 15 years and older

Purpose: Assesses behavioral patterns and characteristics related to success in the working world; measures individual strengths and positive features; used for preemployment screening and in-house staff training programs

Description: Paper–pencil 15-item behaviorally oriented true–false instrument consisting of one validity measure and five scales: Candor, Achievement History, Social Ability, "Winner's" Image, and Initiative. Content areas for the SA scale include Extroversion, Popularity, and Sensitivity. Areas covered by the WI scale include Competitive Drive, Self-Worth, and Family Achievement. For the IN scale, four content areas are included: Drive, Preparation Style, Goal Orientation, and Anxiety about Organization. A narrative report and two profile graphs of six scales and nine scale content areas are provided with raw scores and *t*-scores. Local/Specific job category norms are also available. A fifth-grade reading level is required. Also available in Spanish.

Format: Self-administered; untimed: 20 minutes

Scoring: Computer scored

Cost: $16.00 to $20.00 depending on scoring method

Hilson Safety/Security Risk Inventory (HSRI)

1993	Institute for Personality and Ability Testing, Inc.

Robin E. Inwald

Population: Adults

Purpose: Measures characteristics associated with antisocial/violent behavioral tendencies

Description: The HSRI contains 178 true–false items from which both raw scores and *t*-scores are derived. The instrument is designed to aid in the assessment of individuals who will be working in positions where personal/mechanical safety practices are required. It can be administered prior to a conditional job offer. A fifth-grade reading level is required. Also available in Spanish.

Format: Self-administered; untimed: 30 minutes

Scoring: Examiner evaluated; computer scoring available

Cost: $16.00 to $20.00 depending on scoring method

Hogan Development Survey (HDS)

1997	Hogan Assessment Systems, Inc.

Robert Hogan, Joyce Hogan

Population: Working adults

Purpose: Assesses common dysfunctional personality tendencies in the normal range that impede careers

Description: An inventory designed to measure career derailing tendencies. The inventory contains 11 scales: Excitable, Skeptical, Cautious, Reserved, Leisurely, Bold, Mischievous, Colorful, Imaginative, Diligent, and Dutiful. The HDS is used for employee development because early detection of these tendencies can be followed by coaching feedback. Reports for career management, leadership challenges, and coaching are available. Assessments and reports are also produced in UK English, Spanish, German, French, and more than 15 other languages.

Format: Online administration; untimed: 15 minutes

Scoring: Computer scored

Cost: Contact publisher; reports vary

Hogan Personality Inventory (HPI)

1995	Hogan Assessment Systems, Inc.

Robert Hogan, Joyce Hogan

Population: Working adults

Purpose: Assesses normal personality based on the Five-Factor Model

Description: An inventory designed to measure normal personality for employee selection and development. The inventory contains seven primary scales: Adjustment, Ambition, Sociability, Prudence, Interpersonal Sensitivity, Inquisitive, and Learning Approach. Together, these scales provide a comprehensive evaluation of a person's strengths and shortcomings with regard to occupational goals and job performance. Reports for employee selection and interviewing, career development, leadership potential, and coaching are available. Assessments and reports are also produced in UK English, Spanish, German, French, and more than 15 other languages.

Format: Online administration; untimed: 20 minutes

Scoring: Computer scored

Cost: Contact publisher; reports vary

InQ–Your Thinking Profile

2005   INQ Educational Materials, Inc.

Allen Harrison, Robert Bramson, Susan Bramson, Nicholas Parlette

Population: Adults

Purpose: Identifies one's preferred mode of thinking. Used in training, team building, and sales

Description: The Inquiry Mode Questionnaire is a set of statements with 18 forced, multiple-choice items yielding scores in five categories: Analyst, Synthesist, Pragmatist, Idealist, and Realist. The InQ measures the extent to which a person uses each of these styles, highlighting the strengths and limitations of each. Also available in Spanish

Format: Examiner required; suitable for group use; untimed: 15 to 20 minutes

Scoring: Self-scored

Cost: 10 Tests $69.95

Inwald Survey 2 (IS2)

1994   Institute for Personality and Ability Testing, Inc.

Robin E. Inwald

Population: Adults

Purpose: Assesses violence-related behavior characteristics; used for preemployment and promotional screening for job applicants

Description: Paper-pencil 110-item true false test with a profile graph and computer-generated report. A test book and scannable answer sheets are used. Scales include denial of shortcomings—validity scale, risk-taking tendencies, lack of temper control, reckless driving/safety patterns, firearms interest, work difficulties, lack of social sensitivity, lack of leadership interest; attitudes—antisocial behaviors; and behavior patterns—integrity concerns. A fifth-grade reading level is required. A computer version is available using software for IBM compatibles. Also available in Spanish.

Format: Examiner required; suitable for group use; untimed: 15 minutes

Scoring: Computer scored; scoring service available

Cost: $16.00 to $20.00 depending on scoring method

Inwald Survey 3 (IS3)

Date not provided   Institute for Personality and Ability Testing, Inc.

Robin E. Inwald

Population: Adults

Purpose: Measures antisocial tendencies

Description: Used for preemployment screening and counseling. The IS3 includes 128 true-false questions from which both raw scores and t-scores are derived. The IS3 is the short form of the antisocial scales from the Inwald Personality Inventory. A fifth-grade reading level is required. Online administration is available.

Format: Self-administered; untimed: 30 minutes

Scoring: Examiner evaluated; computer scoring available

Cost: $16.00 to $20.00 depending on scoring method

IPI Employee Aptitude Series CPF

1992   Industrial Psychology International Ltd.

Population: Adults

Purpose: Measures extroversion versus introversion; used for screening, placement, and promotion of employees

Description: Paper-pencil 40-item personality test determines contact versus noncontact factor to determine Contact Personality Factor. Also available in French and Spanish.

Format: Examiner required; suitable for group use; untimed: 5 to 10 minutes

Scoring: Hand key

Cost: Introductory Kit (20 test booklets, scoring key, manual) $33.00

IPI Employee Aptitude Series NPF

1992   Industrial Psychology International Ltd.

Population: Adults

Purpose: Measures emotional balance, stability, and stress tolerance; used to screen applicants for a variety of positions and to place and promote employees

Description: Paper-pencil 40-item test measuring an individual's general stability and emotional balance. Also available in French and Spanish.

Format: Examiner required; suitable for group use; untimed: 5 to 10 minutes

Scoring: Hand key

Cost: Introductory Kit (20 test booklets, scoring key, manual) $33.00

Job and Vocational Attitudes Assessment (JAVAA)

| 1994 | Change Companies |

Population: Adults

Purpose: Provides information for return to work after treatment for substance use disorders

Description: The JAVAA consists of two instruments for making return to work evaluations that can be used independently or as paired assessments to compare clinician and employee perspectives. The I form is a semistructured interview covering key factors, and the Q form is a self-administered questionnaire covering the same content areas. JAVAA content includes measures of attitudes, work relationships, recovery strategy, insight, emotional well-being, anger resolution, and support systems.

Format: Examiner required; self-administered; untimed

Scoring: Examiner evaluated

Cost: Package of 25 Forms (specify I or Q) $62.50; 25 × 3 Summary Forms $37.50

Kirton Adaption-Innovation Inventory (KAI)

| 1985 | Occupational Research Centre |

Michael J. Kirton

Population: Adolescents, adults

Purpose: Evaluates an individual's cognitive style preference in creativity, problem solving, and decision making; used in personality and occupational psychology and in business management for training and team building

Description: Paper–pencil 33-item test containing three subtests: Sufficiency, Efficiency Preference, and Rule/Group Conformity Preference. Scores are yielded for each subtest. The preferred cognitive style measured is unrelated to an individual's capacity; however, it is strongly related to a critical cluster of personality traits. Also available in Italian, Dutch, French, and Slovak/Czech.

Format: Examiner required; individual or group administration; untimed: 20 minutes

Scoring: Examiner evaluated by certified practitioner

Cost: $335.00 for 50 + KAI booklets; discounts for larger orders

Minnesota Importance Questionnaire (MIQ)

| 1975 | Vocational Psychology Research |

Population: Adults

Purpose: Measures an individual's vocational needs and values, which are important aspects of the work personality

Description: The MIQ is designed to measure the following six vocational values (and the 20 vocational needs from which the values derive): Achievement, Altruism, Comfort, Safety, Status, and Autonomy. The MIQ currently permits the comparison of the vocational needs of individuals with estimates of reinforcers present in 185 occupations representative of the major fields and levels of the world of work. There are two equivalent forms of the MIQ: The Paired form and the Ranked form. The Paired form is more suitable for individual clients. The Ranked form may be more suitable in group settings. Also available in a Spanish language edition.

Format: Self-administered; untimed: Paired form, 30 to 40 minutes; Ranked form, 15 to 25 minutes

Scoring: Scoring service

Cost: Sample Set $11.00 (manual, 1 booklet, 1 answer sheet for both Paired and Ranked forms)

Minnesota Satisfaction Questionnaire (MSQ)

| 1963, 1967, 1977 | Vocational Psychology Research |

Population: Adults

Purpose: Measures an employee's satisfaction with his or her job

Description: Three forms are available: two long forms and a short form. The MSQ provides more specific information on the aspects of a job that an individual finds rewarding than do more general measures of job satisfaction. The MSQ is useful in exploring client vocational needs, in counseling follow-up studies, and in generating information about the reinforcers in jobs. All three forms are gender neutral. Instructions for the administration of the MSQ are given in the booklet. It is strongly recommended that the long form be used, as it provides much more information. The long form has 20 scales, with five items each.

Format: Self-administered; untimed: long form, 15 to 20 minutes; short form, 5 minutes

Scoring: Hand scored; computer scoring service available

Cost: Sample Set $6.60 (manual, both versions of long form, 1 short form)

Motives, Values, Preferences Inventory

| 1996 | Hogan Assessment Systems, Inc. |

Joyce Hogan, Robert Hogan

Population: Adults

Purpose: Assesses core values and interests organizing research from Spanger to present

Description: To identify a person's core values and interests, the inventory contains 10 scales for Aesthetic, Affiliation, Altruistic, Commercial, Hedonistic, Power, Recognition, Scientific, Security, and Tradition. The information provided by the MVPI can be used to understand how a person's values fit with the job and the organization. It can also help diagnose compatibility of team members and be used as a foundation to inform team building. Reports for career planning, career coaching, and leadership values are available. Assessments and reports are also produced in UK English, Spanish, German, French, and more than 15 other languages.

Format: Online administration; untimed: 20 minutes

Scoring: Computer scored

Cost: Contact publisher; reports vary

MPQ 14.2

| 1997 | Hogrefe Limited |

Allan Cameron

Population: Adults

Purpose: Identifies key personality traits likely to have a high impact on behavior and success at work and to highlight individual strengths, weaknesses, and competence

Description: The MPQ is a multiple-choice questionnaire available in three forms. MPQ Factor Version 14.2 is the full questionnaire covering all the factors and dimensions measured by the instrument. MPQ Factor Version 5 is a shorter questionnaire that looks at the Big Five factors only. It has been specially designed for those who do not need the full set of information, but who need a simple, cost-effective global measure. MPQ 7 is a unique questionnaire variant that looks carefully at creativity. MPQ Questionnaires are all untimed.

The longest of the questionnaires is MPQ 14.2, which contains 120 multiple-choice items. It is, however, generally completed in under 25 minutes. The other questionnaires require less time.

Format: Examiner required; suitable for group administration; can be computer administered; untimed

Scoring: Self-scored; computer scored; machine scored; test scoring service available

Cost: Contact publisher

Occupational Personality Questionnaire (OPQ Concept)

| 1987 | SHL People Performance |

Population: Adults

Purpose: Assesses personality traits used in personnel selection, placement, counseling, and development

Description: Multiple choice 248 item paper-pencil or computer-administered questionnaire measuring 30 work-related personality traits covering relationships with people (persuasive, outgoing, and democratic), thinking style (practical, conceptual, and conscientious), and feelings and emotions (worrying, critical, and competitive), along with others. Application is expanded by using in conjunction with Hurmis EXPERT Software to produce a 25-page Interpretive report.

Format: Examiner required; individual administration, computer and online administration available; untimed: 35 minutes

Scoring: Hand key; machine scored; scoring service available; online scoring

Cost: Contact publisher

PASAT 2000 Effective Sales & Customer Service Predictor

| 1998 | Hogrefe Limited |

Steven Poppleton, Peter Jones

Population: Adults

Purpose: Measures those personality attributes that have a direct bearing on success in a sales environment

Description: The PASAT 2000 has eight main scales: Social Adjustment, Motivational Adjustment, Emotional Adjustment, Adaptability, Conscientiousness, Social Control, Emotional Stability, and Self-Assurance. In addition, the PASAT 2000 has three further scales designed to detect attempts to present false impressions: Attentive Distortion, Adaptive Distortion, and Social

Distortion. Respondents use a 5-point scale to indicate the degree to which they have/have not used the behaviors described by each questionnaire item. The value of each item response is cumulated for each of the instrument's scales to produce a scale score that is then converted into a stanine score.

Format: Examiner required; suitable for group administration; can be computer administered; untimed

Scoring: Self-scored; computer scored; test scoring service available

Cost: Contact publisher

People Smarts–Behavioral Profiles: Observer Assessment

1994	Wiley

Tony Alessandra, Michael J. O'Connor, Janice Van Dyke

Population: Adults

Purpose: Helps people to define their own styles; provides a picture of how others perceive an individual's interactions

Description: Used together with the *Behavioral Profiles: Self Assessment,* this instrument provides valuable information for personal growth. Participants can recognize differences between the way they think they are and the way they are actually perceived by others. This evaluation provides tangible goals for improving versatility and enhancing relationships.

Format: Self-administration; untimed

Scoring: Self-scoring

Cost: $8.00

People Smarts–Behavioral Profiles: Self Assessment

1994	Wiley

Tony Alessandra, Michael J. O'Connor, Janice Van Dyke

Population: Adults

Purpose: Helps people define their own styles; determines how a person believes he or she interacts with others

Description: Used together with the *Behavioral Profiles: Observer Assessment,* this instrument provides valuable information for personal growth. Participants can recognize differences between the way they think they are and the way they are actually perceived by others. This evalu-

ation provides tangible goals for improving versatility and enhancing relationships.

Format: Self-administration; untimed

Scoring: Self-scoring

Cost: $8.00

Personal Characteristics Inventory™ (PCI™)

Date not provided	Wonderlic Personnel Test, Inc.

Murray Barrick, Michael Mount

Population: Adults

Purpose: Measures personality traits for preemployment screening

Description: The PCI focuses on job–person compatibility by identifying a job applicant's standing on the Big Five personality dimensions, success scales, occupational scores, and 12 other subscales (e.g., sociability, cooperation).

Format: Self-administered via paper–pencil, computer, or online

Scoring: Online scoring, fax scoring, computer scoring

Cost: Contact publisher

Personal Dynamics Profile (PDP)

Date not provided	Winslow Research Institute

Population: Adults

Purpose: Measures behavioral characteristics relevant to career success and personal contentment

Description: The information provides objective feedback to enable participants in Personal Coaching to attain a maximum return on their investment. The characteristics are divided into interpersonal organizational, dedication, and self-control. There are 260 questions.

Format: Self-administered; untimed: less than 1 hour

Scoring: Completed online; scoring service

Cost: Contact publisher

Personal Success Profile (PSP)

Date not provided	Winslow Research Institute

Population: Adults

Purpose: Measures behavioral characteristics relevant to career success and personal contentment

Description: Innovative assessment program designed for those new to the personality assessment process and those experiencing time and/or financial restraints. This assessment is easy to understand and all individuals can benefit, regardless of their education, sophistication, or experience. The 11 characteristics measured in 130 questions are grouped by competitiveness, self-control, and dedication.

Format: Self-administered; untimed: less than 30 minutes

Scoring: Completed online; scoring service

Cost: Contact publisher

Personnel Selection Inventory (PSI™)

1988	Pearson Performance Solutions

Population: Job applicants

Purpose: Assesses personality trait combinations that lead to honest, productive, and service-oriented employees; designed to reduce absenteeism, shrinkage, turnover, on-the-job accidents, and substance abuse; meets both human resource and loss-prevention needs

Description: Multiple-item paper–pencil survey. Eight versions of the PSI are available to meet various companies' screening needs. The forms range from PSI-1, which assesses honesty only, to PSI-7ST, which assesses a wide range of attributes. The various forms contain combinations of the following scales: Honesty, Supervision Attitudes, Employee/Customer Relations, Drug Avoidance, Work Values, Safety, Emotional Stability, Nonviolence, and Tenure. A distortion and an accuracy scale are included. Some versions contain a detailed personal and behavioral history section that aids in making decisions about borderline candidates. Industry-specific norms are available for some PSI versions. A seventh-grade reading level is required.

Format: Self-administered; untimed: 30 to 40 minutes

Scoring: Computer scored

Cost: Contact publisher

Social Skills Inventory (SSI)

2003	Mind Garden, Inc.

Ronald E. Riggio

Population: Adolescents, adults

Purpose: Measures verbal and nonverbal social competence and emotional intelligence

Description: The instrument is useful in individual and couples counseling, management and leadership training, and health psychology. The following areas are measured: assesses communication skills as they relate to overall social competence; clients respond to items using a 5-point scale, indicating the extent to which the description of the item applies to them; scores are reported for each of the scales and a combined score is given to indicate global social intelligence; 90 items can be completed in 30 to 40 minutes; efficient to score; and requires an eighth-grade reading level. The SSI assesses skills in these key areas: Emotional Expressivity, Emotional Sensitivity, Emotional Control, Social Expressivity, Social Sensitivity, and Social Control.

Format: Self-administered; untimed

Scoring: Examiner evaluated; scoring service available; online administration available

Cost: Manual/Sampler Set $40.00; Permission Set of 200 $150.00

Survey of Interpersonal Values (SIV)

1960	Pearson Performance Solutions

Leonard V. Gordon

Population: Grades 10 and above

Purpose: Measures individuals' values by assessing what they consider important in relationships with others; used to measure values associated with adjustment and performance for selection, placement, employment counseling, and research purposes

Description: Paper–pencil 30-item Inventory assessing interpersonal values. Each item consists of a triad of value statements. For each triad, examinees must indicate most and least important values. Six values are measured: support, conformity, recognition, independence, benevolence, and leadership. Also available in French from the Institute of Psychological Research, Inc.

Format: Self-administered; untimed: 15 minutes

Scoring: Hand key

Cost: Contact publisher

Survey of Personal Values

1965	Pearson Performance Solutions

Leonard V. Gordon

Population: Grades 10 and above

Purpose: Measures the critical values that help an individual determine coping ability with everyday problems; used for employee screening and placement, vocational guidance, and counseling

Description: Paper–pencil 30-item inventory assessing personal values. Each item consists of a triad of value statements. For each triad, examinees must indicate most and least important values. Six values are measured: Practical Mindedness, Achievement, Variety, Decisiveness, Orderliness, and Goal Orientation.

Format: Self-administered; untimed: 15 minutes

Scoring: Hand key

Cost: Contact publisher

Thurstone Temperament Schedule (TTS™)

1991	Pearson Performance Solutions

L. L. Thurstone, Thelma Gwinn Thurstone

Population: Adults

Purpose: Evaluates permanent aspects of personality and how normal, well-adjusted people differ from one another; used by managers to determine employee suitability for particular jobs

Description: Paper–pencil or computerized 120-item inventory assessing seven areas of temperament: Active, Vigorous, Impulsive, Dominant, Stable, Sociable, and Reflective. The inventory is limited to use by individuals with advanced training in personality instruments.

Format: Self-administered; untimed: 15 to 20 minutes

Scoring: Hand key; computer scored

Cost: Contact publisher

TotalView

2000	HRD Press

David Bartram, Patricia Lindley

Population: Adults

Purpose: Measures abilities, interests, personality traits, and working characteristics for comparison to job-specific benchmarks for selection, training/coaching, and succession planning

Description: A battery of six subtests that provides scores in eight scales and 11 subscales. Items are presented in stens for comparison with unique, optimal job-related benchmark ranges. TotalView produces scores in Abilities: General Abilities, Working with Words, Working with Numbers, and Working with Shapes. Interest scales include Working with People, Working with Data, and Working with Things. Personality scales include Independence (with subscales Competitiveness and Assertiveness), Conscientiousness (with subscales Conventional and Organized), Extroversion (with subscales Outgoing and Group Oriented), and Emotional Stability (with subscales

Poised and Relaxed). There is also a social desirability scale to detect persons who may not be answering questions truthfully. *TotalView* also measures the following working characteristics: Compensation Preference, Focus on Work, Tolerance for Risk, Preference for Change, and Perception of the World. An overall suitability score is produced from a quantitative evaluation of the level of match between the test takers profile and the job-related benchmark. Narrative accompanies the score chart and provides an assessment of the person's personality and interviewing questions to probe scores outside the optimal scoring ranges. Also available in French.

Format: Examiner required for paper–pencil; self-administered online; timed and untimed

Scoring: Examiner evaluated; scoring service available

Cost: $136.00; quantity discounts available

Trait Evaluation Index

1967	Martin M. Bruce, PhD

Alan R. Nelson

Population: Adults

Purpose: Assesses adult personality traits; used for job placement and career counseling

Description: Paper–pencil 125-item two-choice test measuring 24 personality dimensions, including Social Orientation, Elation, Self-Control, Sincerity, Compliance, Ambition, Dynamism, Caution, Propriety, and Intellectual Orientation. Materials consist of a test manual, keys, answer sheets, and academic and industrial-business profile sheets. Also available in German.

Format: Self-administered; untimed: 30 to 40 minutes

Scoring: Hand key

Cost: Specimen Set $75.50

Values Scale–Second Edition

1985	CPP, Inc.

Donald E. Super, Dorothy D. Nevill

Population: Adults

Purpose: Measures intrinsic and extrinsic life–career values

Description: Paper–pencil 106-item inventory measuring intrinsic and extrinsic life–career values and many cultural perspectives of adults. Items are rated on a 4-point scale ranging from *little or no importance* to *very important*. The 21 scales are Ability Utilization, Achievement, Advancement, Aesthetics, Altruism, Authority, Autonomy, Creativity, Economic Rewards, Lifestyle, Personal Development, Physical Activity, Prestige, Risk, Social Interaction, Social Relations, Variety, Working Conditions, Cultural Identity, Physical Prowess, and Economic Security. The scale was developed as part of the international Work Importance Study and has international norms. The profile available through the computer scoring service plots the 21 scales.

Format: Examiner required; suitable for group use; untimed: 30 to 45 minutes

Scoring: Hand scored; computer scoring service available

Cost: Preview Kit (booklet, answer sheet, manual) $78.50

Wonderlic Productivity Index™ (WPI™)

Date not provided	Wonderlic Personnel Test, Inc.

Murray Barrick, Michael Mount

Population: Adults

Purpose: Measures personality as it relates to productive behavior in the workplace

Description: The WPI is a short assessment for entry-level positions. An individual's willingness to perform productively and cooperatively on the job and avoid engaging in counterproductive behavior is measured. A one-page report provides graphical scores on the following productivity indicators and risk factors: Personal Productivity Score, Work Effort and Persistence, Service and Support, Counterproductive Work Behavior, and Turnover. Accuracy index scales measure the reliability and accuracy of candidate responses.

Format: Self-administered via paper–pencil or online

Scoring: Fax-back scoring; online scoring

Cost: Contact publisher

Work Profile Questionnaire (WPQ)

1998	Hogrefe Limited

Allan Cameron

Population: Adults

Purpose: Measures work preferences and identifies situations in which the individual is most likely to flourish and be effective

Description: The WPQ profile report looks at these strengths and preferences and reports them under five broad headings: Communication Style, Emotions, Drive and Determination, Relationships with People, and Thinking Style. The main section of the WPQ report is written in the second person so that, if required, the report can be presented to and discussed with an applicant as part of the interview process. For each of the five domains analyzed by the WPQ, four probing questions are given: two designed to examine personality strengths associated with that trait, and two to assist the interviewer to probe the extent of any weaknesses. Report gives information for two areas: Relationships and Accomplishing Tasks.

Format: Examiner required; suitable for group administration; can be computer administered; untimed

Scoring: Self-scored; computer scored; test scoring service available

Cost: Contact publisher

Team Skills

Campbell-Hallam™ Team Development Survey (TDS™)

1994	Pearson Performance Solutions

David P. Campbell, Glenn Hallam

Population: Adults

Purpose: Assesses perceptions of team effectiveness; used for identifying team strengths and weaknesses

Description: Paper–pencil 72-item test with 18 dimensions, plus an overall index. A sixth-grade reading level is required. Examiner must have taken psychology coursework.

Format: Self-administered; untimed

Scoring: Computer scored; test scoring service available from publisher

Cost: Contact publisher

Group Environment Scale (GES)

2002	Mind Garden, Inc.

Rudolf H. Moos

Population: Adults

Purpose: Facilitates group counseling and team building

Description: The 90 items of the GES are grouped into 10 subscales with three dimensions. Three subscales (Cohesion, Leader Support, Expressiveness) tap the degree of commitment, concern, and friendship group members show for one another; the amount of help, concern, and friendship the leaders shows for team members; and the amount that freedom of action and expression of feelings is encouraged in the group. Personal growth is measured by Independence (assesses how much the group encourages independent action and expression among members); Task Orientation (reflects how much emphasis is placed on completing concrete, practical tasks and on decision making and training); Self-Discovery (measures how much the group encourages members' discussion of personal problems); and Anger and Aggression (assesses the extent that there is open expression of anger and disagreement in the group). Three dimensions (Order and Organization, Leader Control, Innovation) measure the degree of importance of clear organization; structure and rules in the group, as well as the extent to which the leader directs the group, makes decisions, and enforces rules; and finally, how much the group promotes diversity and change in its own functions and activities.

Format: Self-administered; untimed

Scoring: Examiner evaluated

Cost: Manual/Sampler Set $40.00; Permission Set of 200 Uses $150.00

Lake St. Clair Incident

1988	Western Psychological Services

Albert A. Canfield

Population: Adults

Purpose: Examines individual and group decision-making processes; used to improve decision making, communication skills, and teamwork

Description: Multiple-item paper–pencil test requiring a team of three to seven individuals to work together to solve a hypothetical problem situation involving cold weather and cold water survival. Participants are provided with considerable information on the subject, maps, charts, drawings, and a list of 15 items available for them to use in their struggle for survival. The team must reach a decision on what action to take and the relative importance of the 15 items. Three different decision-making processes are required:

independent, consultive, and participative/consensual. Scoring procedure uses Coast Guard officer decisions and rankings as "expert" opinions. Scores are provided for three types of decision-making processes.

Format: Self-administered (teams must cooperate to get team performance scores); suitable for group use; untimed: 1½ to 2 hours

Scoring: Self-scored

Cost: Kit (10 booklets, manual) $46.95

Mentoring/Coaching Skills Assessment

1998	Mind Garden, Inc.

Linda Phillips-Jones

Population: Adults

Purpose: Assessment feedback report designed to improve mentoring and mentee skills

Description: The mentor version, for managers and leaders, includes a survey for the mentor and three for their colleagues to rate skills in the areas of Quality and Frequency of mentoring skills. The profile provides an objective assessment of the mentor in nine areas and includes personalized tips to improve mentoring skills. The mentee version includes a survey for the mentee and three for their colleagues to rate skills in the areas of Quality and Frequency of skills. The profile provides an objective assessment of nine areas and includes personalized tips.

Format: Individual administration; untimed

Scoring: Computer scored; test scoring service available from publisher; online service available

Cost: Mentor or Mentee Version $60.00

MTR-i

2000	Hogrefe Limited

Steve Myers

Population: Adults

Purpose: Measures the contribution being made by an individual to the team and profiles an individual's work persona

Description: The test measures how Jungian function-attitudes are currently being used, by trying to measure how people see themselves affecting the inner or outer worlds. MTR-i team roles change from situation to situation, in accord with the demands of the environment. By using the MTR-i with the Myers Briggs Type Indicator, individuals can derive a comparison between innate preference and how the Jungian function-attitudes are being used in daily work life. The MTR-i can be applied in guidance, development, and training. MTR-i reports eight distinct team roles.

Format: Examiner required; individual or group administration; can be computer administered; untimed

Scoring: Self-scored

Cost: Contact publisher

Multi-Factor Leadership Questionnaire for Teams (MLQT)

1996	Mind Garden, Inc.

Bernard M. Bass, Bruce J. Avolio

Population: Adults

Purpose: Assessment of the leadership style of the team

Description: Paper–pencil full-range assessment of the leadership style of the team. The report shows how best to use the MLQT data, explains Full Range Leadership, and provides tips for improving team leadership. The 53-item MLQT contains 12 scales: Idealized Attributes, Idealized Behaviors, Inspirational Leadership, Intellectual Stimulation, Individualized Consideration, Contingent Reward, Management-by-Exception (Active), Management-by-Exception (Passive), Laissez-Faire, Extra Effort, Effectiveness, and Satisfaction.

Format: Self-administered; suitable for groups (paper–pencil); untimed

Scoring: Examiner evaluated; computer scored; test scoring service available from publisher; online service available

Cost: Web-Based Team Report $100.00

My Team Mates

1998	Performance Programs, Inc.

Clark L. Wilson

Population: Work groups and intact teams

Purpose: Shows the aggregate evaluation of the team by all members

Description: A multiple-rater assessment, *My Team Mates* is used to assess each member's group skills by his or her other team colleagues. The Feedback Report compares the Self assessment to the Mates assessment of an individual's skills. Inquire about Spanish and Portuguese translations. Reliability and validity program in place since 2000. Renormed in 2006.

Format: Self-administered; untimed

Scoring: Online scoring service

Cost: $260.00 up to 15 surveys

Our Team

1993	Performance Programs, Inc.

Clark L. Wilson

Population: Work groups and intact teams

Purpose: Assesses the self-management processes of the team as a unit

Description: Each team member completes the survey and judges how well the team is functioning. The report shows how closely the team member's individual evaluation coincides with the average of the other members. Has 71 questions plus 3 open-ended questions. Reliability and validity program in place since 1998. Renormed in 2006.

Format: Self-administered; untimed

Scoring: Online scoring service

Cost: $260 up to 15 surveys

Personality Poker

Date not provided	Hogrefe & Huber Publishers

S. Hugentobler, B. Oettli, D. Ruckstuhl

Population: Adults

Purpose: Promotes personal and team growth

Description: Allows individuals to gain a broadened perspective on how they view themselves and how they are perceived by work colleagues. It can be utilized in management teams, project groups, company department, in-house training groups, and training courses. It is ideal for testing out individual strengths and encouraging a feedback culture. This is a straightforward but subtly provoking card game.

Format: Group administration; untimed

Scoring: Examiner evaluated

Cost: Complete Kit (228 cards, evaluation sheets, manual) $178.00

Project Leadership Practices

1995	Performance Programs, Inc.

Clark L. Wilson, Paul M. Connolly, David Gillespie

Population: Project manager, project leaders

Purpose: Identifies the skills that are important for overall project effectiveness

Description: A multiple-rater assessment that will help a project leader be more effective in directing team efforts. Contains 90 questions plus 3 open-ended questions. Reliability and validity program in place since 1995. Renormed in 2006.

Format: Self-administered; untimed

Scoring: Scoring service

Cost: $260 up to 15 surveys

Team Skills–Form A-C

1998	Ramsay Corporation

Roland T. Ramsay

Population: Adults

Purpose: Measures team building knowledge and skills

Description: This 35-item multiple-choice test measures seven categories, including Conflict Resolution, Group Dynamics, Team Decision Making, Productivity and Motivation, Communication Skills, Leader and Member Skills, and Interpersonal Skills. Written at an eighth-grade reading level.

Format: Examiner required; suitable for group use; untimed: approximately 60 minutes

Scoring: Self-scored; scoring service available

Cost: Test Booklet $13.00 (minimum 20); Manual $24.95

Teamwork–KSA Test

1995	Pearson Performance Solutions

Michael J. Stevens, Michael A. Campion

Population: Adults

Purpose: Assesses individuals who work well in a team-oriented work environment

Description: Multiple-choice 35-item test measures the essential knowledge, skills, and abili-

ties that individuals must have to work effectively in teams. Three interpersonal skills areas (conflict resolution skills, collaborative problem-solving skills, and interpersonal communicative skills) and two self-management areas (team goal setting and performance management, team planning and task coordination) are measured.

Format: Examiner required; suitable for group use; untimed: 30 to 40 minutes

Scoring: Hand key; computer scored

Cost: Contact publisher

Work Team Simulator (WTS)

Updated yearly	Management & Personnel Systems, Inc.

Population: Adults

Purpose: Identifies individual contributors who seek an empowered work environment

Description: The WTS consists of five realistic problem situations involving interactions among the employees and/or their supervisor in a hypothetical organization. The test comes in booklet format and poses specific questions about each situation. Candidates must describe what they would actually say or do in dealing with each problem or situation. Because the test has a national database, the scores can be compared to other supervisors on a national level. The factors measured are Leadership/Decision Making and Team Relations. The WTS has explicit scoring criteria for each problem. Results are provided in the form of a rank-ordered list of candidates and an individual bar-chart profile. The factors measured are Group Decision Making and Team Relations.

Format: Self-administered; timed: 75 minutes

Scoring: Scoring service

Cost: $150 each candidate

Work Environment

Business Culture and Climate Survey

2000	Performance Programs, Inc.

Paul M. Connolly

Population: Employees of organizations

Purpose: Measures how employees feel about the practices and values of an organization and how those practices influence employee behaviors

Description: This 75-question employee survey reflects the culture-related topics requested most often by organizations in the author's consulting practice. The first 70 items are standardized. Norms are available for many items. The client chooses the last five questions. Up to five demographic categories available for reports.

Format: Online survey; untimed

Scoring: Scoring service available

Cost: Contact publisher

Employee–Management Relations Survey

2001 **Performance Programs, Inc.**

Population: Adults

Purpose: Measures overall opinions and feelings toward management at a company

Description: This survey helps to diagnose improvement opportunities so they can be addressed through training, structure, communications, and other interventions. The 45 questions reflect the topics most requested. The first 40 questionnaire items are standardized, and the last 5 are chosen by the site. Online administration is available.

Format: Self-administered; untimed

Scoring: Scoring service available

Cost: Contact publisher

Employee Opinion Survey

2000 **Performance Programs, Inc.**

Population: Adults

Purpose: Measures a broad range of employee-organizational issues

Description: With 65 standardized questionnaire items, the survey measures the following topics: commitment, satisfaction, communications, their jobs, organization's culture, and organizational leadership. In addition, up to five customized questions and two open-ended questions can be added. Online administration is available.

Format: Self-administered; untimed

Scoring: Scoring service available

Cost: Contact publisher

Oliver Organization Description Questionnaire (OODQ)

1981 **Organizational Measurement Systems Press**

John E. Oliver

Population: Adults

Purpose: Evaluates the organizational form of a particular organization

Description: Multiple-item paper–pencil questionnaire measuring the extent to which four organizational forms exist within a particular organization. The forms are hierarchic (bureaucratic), professional (specialized), task (entrepreneurial),

and group (socio-technical). The scoring guide discusses the form of the instrument, the four domains, scoring, potential uses of the scores, development of the instrument, interpretation of individual scores, and interpretation of organization scores.

Format: Examiner required; suitable for group use; untimed

Scoring: Examiner evaluated

Cost: 50 Questionnaires $30.00; Scoring Guide $5.00

Productivity Environmental Preference Survey (PEPS)

1975-2003 **Price Systems, Inc.**

Rita Dunn, Kenneth Dunn, Gary E. Price

Population: Adults

Purpose: Assesses the manner in which adults prefer to function, learn, concentrate, and perform in their occupational or educational activities; used for employee placement, counseling, and office design and layout

Description: Paper–pencil or computer-administered 100-item Likert-scale inventory measuring the following environmental factors related to educational or occupational activities: immediate environment (sound, temperature, light, and design), emotionality (motivation, responsibility, persistence, and structure), sociological needs (self-oriented, peer-oriented, authority-oriented, and combined ways), and physical needs (perceptual preferences, time of day, intake, and mobility). Test items consist of statements about the ways people like to work or study. Respondents are asked to indicate whether they agree or disagree with each statement.

Format: Self-administered, untimed. 20 to 30 minutes

Scoring: Computer scored

Cost: Specimen Set (manual, answer sheet) $11.00; Diskette (100 administrations per licensing agreement) $395.00; Each 100 Additional Administrations $60.00; NCS Scanner Program $495.00; 100 Answer Sheets for NCS Scanner Program $60.00

Work Environment Scale (WES)

1974 **CPP, Inc.**

Rudolf H. Moos, Paul M. Insel

Population: Adults

Purpose: Evaluates the social climate of work

units; used to assess correlates of productivity worker satisfaction, quality assurance programs, work stressors, individual adaptation, and supervisory methods

Description: Paper–pencil 90-item measure of 10 dimensions of work social environments: Involvement, Peer Cohesion, Supervisor Support, Autonomy, Task Orientation, Work Pressure, Clarity, Control, Innovation, and Physical Comfort. These dimensions are grouped into three sets: relationships, personal growth, and system maintenance and change. Three forms are available: the Real Form (Form R), which measures perceptions of existing work environments; the Ideal Form (Form I), which measures conceptions of ideal work environments; and the Expectations Form (Form E), which measures expectations about work settings. Forms I and E are not published, although items and instructions will be provided upon request.

Format: Self-administered; untimed: 20 minutes

Scoring: Self-scored; hand scored

Cost: Preview Kit (Form R booklet, answer sheet, scoring keys, manual) $88.75; Self-Scored Preview Kit (booklet, answer sheet, interpretive form) $8.75

Indexes

Index of Publishers Not in the Sixth Edition

Ablin Press Distributors; no longer publishing

Accrediting Association of Bible Colleges; no response

ADECCA Educational Alternatives; no response

American Association for Active Lifestyles and Fitness; no response

Assessment Systems Corporation; instrument no longer available

Associated Consultants in Education; no longer publishing

Ball Foundation; no response

Behavioral-Developmental Initiatives; no updates received

Ber-Sil Company; no information found

Brandt Management Group; no information found

Camelot Unlimited; no information found

Center for Management Effectiveness, Inc.; no information found

Center for Rehabilitation Effectiveness; no response

Center for the Study of Aging and Human Development; no response

Center for the Study of Ethical Development; no response

Central Wisconsin Center for the Developmentally Disabled; no information found

CFKR Career Materials; no response

Chronicle Guidance Publications, Inc.; no response

CogniSyst, Inc.; no response

Consulting Resource Group International, Inc.; no response

CPS, Inc.; no information found

Creative Learning Press, Inc.; no response

Dallas Educational Services; no longer publishing

EdITS/Educational and Industrial Testing Service; no response

Educational Activities, Inc.; no information found

Heinemann; no tests on Web site

Hilson Research, Inc.; sold to Institute for Personality and Ability Training, Inc.

International Society for General Semantics; no response

International Training Consultants, Inc.; no response

Key Education, Inc.; mail returned

Donald L. Kirkpatrick, PhD; no information found

Life Advance, Inc.; no response

Lippincott Williams & Wilkins; no longer publishing

Massachusetts School of Professional Psychology; no information found

Kenneth M. Matthews, EdD; no response

McGraw-Hill Companies; no information found

Miller & Tyler, Ltd.; no response

Modern Learning Press, Inc.; now with EPS

James H. Morrison; no information found

Moving Boundaries; no response

Norland Software; no information found

Northwest Publications; no response

Nova Media, Inc.; no information found

Pain Resource Center; mail returned

Personnel Decisions International; no response

I. Pilowsky; mail returned

Pinkerton Services Group; no response

Program Development Associates; no longer publishing tests

Psychological and Educational Publications, Inc.; now part of Academic Therapy

Psychological Corporation, The; now part of Harcourt Assessment

Psychological Test Specialists; no information found

Psychology Press; no information found

Psychology Press, Inc.; no response

Psychometric Affiliates; no information found

Psychometric Software, Inc.; no response

Donald K. Pumroy; no information found

Risk & Needs Assessment, Inc.; now part of Behavior Data Systems

Index of Tests Not in the Sixth Edition

Index of Test Publishers

Academic Communication Associates
4001 Avendia de la Plata #102
Oceanside, CA 92052
888/758-9558; FAX 760/722-1625
www.acadcom.com

Academic Therapy Publications
20 Commercial Blvd.
Novato, CA 94949
800/422-7249; FAX 888/287-9975
www.academictherapy.com

ACT, Inc.
PO Box 168
2255 N. Dubuque Rd.
Iowa City, IA 52243-0168
800/498-6065; FAX 319/337-1598
www.act.org

ADE Incorporated
PO Box 660
Clarkston, MI 48347
248/625-7200; FAX 248/625-1839
www.adeincorp.com

AGS Publishing/Pearson Assessments
PO Box 1416
Minneapolis, MN 55437
800/627 7271; FAX 800/632 9011
www.ags.pearsonassessments.com and www.
speechandlanguage.com

American Association of Teachers of German
112 Haddontowne Ct. #104
Cherry Hill, NJ 08034
856/795-5553; FAX 856/795 9398
www.aatg.org

American Dental Association
211 E. Chicago Ave., Sixth Fl.
Chicago, IL 60611
312/440-7465; FAX 312/587-4105
www.ada.org/prof/ed/index.asp

American Occupational Therapy Association, Inc.
4720 Montgomery Ln.
Bethesda, MD 20814-3425
888/466-8878; FAX 301/652-7711
www.aota.org

American Psychiatric Publishing, Inc.
1100 Wilson Blvd., Ste. 1825
Arlington, VA 22209-3901
800/368-5777; FAX 703/907-1091
www.appi.org

Andrews University Press
Sutherland House
Berrien Springs, MI 49104-1700
269/471-3435; FAX 269/471-6224
www.universitypress.andrews.edu

APR Testing Services
27 Judith Rd.

Newton, MA 02459
617/244-7405; FAX 617/244-8904
www.aprtestingservices.com

ASEBA® Research Center for Children, Youth, and
Families
University of Vermont
One S. Prospect St.
Burlington, VT 05401-3456
802/264-6432; FAX 802/264-6433
www.ASEBA.org

Assessment-Intervention Resources
2285 Elysium Ave.
Eugene, OR 97401
541/338-8736; FAX 541/338-8736
www.assessment-intervention.com

Assessment Resource Center
2800 Maguire Blvd.
Columbia, MO 65211
800/366-8232; FAX 573/882 8937
http://arc.missouri.edu

Association of Schools and Colleges of Optometry
Optometry Admission
6110 Executive Blvd.
Rockville, MD 20852
301/231-5944; FAX 301/770-1828
www.opted.org/info_oat.ctm

ASVAB Career Exploration
www.asvabprogram.com

Australian Council for Educational Research Limited
19 Prospect Hill Rd.
Private Bag 55
Camberwell, Victoria 3124 Australia
61-3-9277, FAX 61-3-9277
www.acer.edu.au

Ballard & Tighe Publishers
480 Atlas St.
Brea, CA 92821
800/321-4332; FAX 714/255 9828
www.ballard-tighe.com

Donna Bardis
6512 Carrietowne St.
Toledo, OH 43615
419/517-3279

Battle, James, and Associates Limited
10240 124th St. #207
Edmonton, Alberta T5N 3W6 Canada
780/488-1362; FAX 780/482-3332
www.jamesbattle.com

Bay State Psychological Associates, Inc.
225 Friend St.
Boston, MA 02114
800/438-2772; FAX 617/367-5888
www.eri.com

Behavior Data Systems, Ltd.
    4105 N. 20th St.
    Phoenix, AZ 85016
    800/231-2401; FAX 602/266-8227
    www.bdsltd.com

Behavior Science Systems, Inc.
    PO Box 19512
    Minneapolis, MN 55419-9998
    612/850-8700; FAX 360/351-1374
    www.childdevelopmentreview.com

Bowling Green State University
    JDI Office
    Bowling Green, OH 43403
    419/372-8247; FAX 419/372-6013
    www.bgsu.edu/departments/psych/JDI

BrainTrain
    727 Twin Ridge Ln.
    Richmond, VA 23235
    804/320-0105; FAX 804/320-0242
    www.braintrain.com

Brigham Young University
    Foreign Language Testing
    3060 JKHB
    Provo, UT 84602
    801/422-3511; FAX 801/378-4649
    http://creativeworks.byu.edu/htrsc

Brookes Publishing Company, Inc.
    PO Box 10624
    Baltimore, MD 21285-0624
    800/638-3775; FAX 410/337-8539
    www.brookespublishing.com

Brougham Press
    PO Box 2702
    Olathe, KS 66063-0702
    800/360-6244; FAX 913/782-1116
    www.workingmagic.com

Martin M. Bruce, PhD
    22516 Caravelle Cr.
    Boca Raton, FL 33433
    561/393-2428; FAX 561/362-6185

Arnold R. Bruhn and Associates
    The Topaz House
    4400 East West Hwy.
    Bethesda, MD 20814
    301/654-2017; FAX 301/654-4072
    www.arbruhn.com

Canadian Test Centre
    Educational Assessment Services
    85 Citizen Court, Suites 7 & 8
    Markham, Ontario L6G 1A8 Canada
    800/668-1006; FAX 905/513-6639
    www.canadiantestcentre.com

Career Trainer
    10725 Ellis Ave., #D
    Fountain Valley, CA 92708
    800/888-4945; FAX 714/965-7697
    www.careertrainer.com

Carousel House
    212C Arguello Blvd.

San Francisco, CA 94118
    800/526-4824; FAX 415/379-3735
    www.carouselhouse.com

CASAS
    5151 Murphy Canyon Rd., Ste. 220
    San Diego, CA 92123-4339
    800/255-1036; FAX 858/292-2910
    www.casas.org

Center for Applied Linguistics
    4646 40th St. NW
    Washington, DC 20016-1859
    800/551-3709; FAX 202/362-3740
    www.cal.org

Center for the Study of Higher Education
    The University of Memphis
    308 Browning Hall
    Memphis, TN 38152
    901/678-2775; FAX 901/678-4291
    http://coe.memphis.edu/CSHE/CCSEQ.asp

Central Institute for the Deaf Publications
    4560 Clayton Ave.
    St. Louis, MO 63110
    314/977-0133; FAX 314/977-0016
    www.cid.edu

Change Companies
    5221 Sigstrom Dr.
    Carson City, NV 89706
    888/889-8866; FAX 775/885-0643
    www.changecompanies.net

Checkmate Plus, Ltd.
    PO Box 696
    Department D
    Stony Brook, NY 11790-0696
    800/779-4292; FAX 631-360-3432
    www.checkmateplus.com

College Board
    45 Columbus Ave.
    New York, NY 10023-6992
    212/713-8193; FAX 212/713-8063
    www.collegeboard.com

CPP, Inc.
    1055 Joaquin Rd., Second Fl.
    Mountain View, CA 94043
    800/624-1765; FAX 650/969-8608
    www.cpp.com

Critical Thinking Company
    PO Box 448
    Pacific Grove, CA 93950
    800/458-4849; FAX 831/393-3277
    www.criticalthinking.com

CTB/McGraw-Hill
    160 Spear St.
    San Francisco, CA 94002
    415/268-5367; FAX 415/268-5374
    www.ctb.com

Curriculum Associates®, Inc.
    153 Rangeway Rd.
    North Billerica, MA 01862

800/225-0248; FAX 800/366-1158
www.curriculumassociates.com

Dansk psykologisk Forlag
Kongevejen155
DK-2830 Virum Denmark
45 3538 1655; FAX 45 33538
www.dpf.dk

Denver Developmental Materials, Inc.
PO Box 371075
Denver, CO 80237
800/419-4729; FAX 303/355-5622
www.denverii.com

Development Associates, Inc.
22300 Wilson Blvd.
Arlington, VA 22201-5426
703/276-0677; FAX 703/276 0432
www.devassoc.com

Developmental Therapy Institute, Inc.
PO Box 5153
Athens, GA 30604-5153
706/369-5689; FAX 706/369-5690
www.developmentaltherapyinstitute.org

Ed & Psych Associates
210 West Hamilton St.
State College, PA 16801
814/235-9115; FAX 814-235-9115

Education Associates, Inc.
340 Crab Orchard Rd.
Frankfort, KY 40604
800/626-2950; FAX 502-227-8608
www.educationassociates.com

Educational & Psychological Consultants, Inc.
1715 West Worley St.
Columbia, MO 65203
573/446-6232; FAX 573/446-8532
www.epc-psi.com

Educational Assessment Service, Inc.
W6050 Apple Rd.
Watertown, WI 53098
800/795 7466; FAX 920/261-6622
www.sylviarimm.com

Educational Records Bureau
220 E. 42nd St.
New York, NY 10017
800/989-3721; FAX 212/370-4096
www.erbtest.org

Educational Testing Service
Rosedale Rd.
Princeton, NJ 08541
609/921-9000; FAX 609/734-5410
www.ets.org

Educators Publishing Service, Inc.
PO Box 9031
Cambridge, MA 02139-9031
800/225-5750; FAX 617/547-0412
www.epsbooks.com

Elbern Publications
PO Box 09497

Columbus, OH 43209
614/231-1950; FAX 614/237-2637

Ellsworth & Vandermeer Press, Ltd.
PO Box 68164
Nashville, TN 37206
615/776-4121; FAX 615/776-4119
www.pedstest.com

Meryl E. Englander
3508 William Court
Bloomington, IN 47401
812/336-2746

English Language Institute, University of Michigan
McKinley Towne Centre
401 E. Liberty St., Ste. 350
Ann Arbor, MI 48104-2298
734/615-5606; FAX 734/615-6586
www.lsa.umich.edu/eli/testing/publications

Enhanced Performance Systems, Inc.
18829 Bernardo Trl.
San Diego, CA 92128
858/613-0625
www.enhanced-performance.com

Functional Resources
3905 Huntington Dr.
Amarillo, TX 79019
806/353 1114; FAX 806/353 1114
www.winfssi.com

GIA Publications, Inc.
7404 S. Mason Ave.
Chicago, IL 60638
800/442-1358; FAX 708/496-3828
www.giamusic.com

Gordon Systems, Inc.
PO Box 746
DeWitt, NY 13214
800/550-2343; FAX 315/446-2012
www.gsi-add.com

Guilford Publications, Inc.
Department 5X
72 Spring St.
New York, NY 10012
800/365-7006; FAX 212/966-6708
www.GUILFORD.com

H & H Publishing Company, Inc.
1231 Kapp Dr.
Clearwater, FL 33765
800/366-4079; FAX 727/442-2195
www.hhpublishing.com

Harcourt Assessment, Inc.
School and Developmental Psychology
19500 Bulverde Rd.
San Antonio, TX 78259
800/211-8378; FAX 800/232-1223
www.harcourtassessment.com

Harcourt Assessment-UK
Proctor House
1 Proctor St.
London WC1V 6EU United Kingdom

44 20 7911; FAX 44 20 7911
www.harcourt-uk.com

Hawthorne Educational Services, Inc.
800 Gray Oak Dr.
Columbia, MO 65201
800/542-1673; FAX 800/442-9509
www.hes-inc.com

Hay Group
116 Huntington Ave.
Boston, MA 02116
800/729-8074; FAX 617/927-5008
www.hayresourcesdirect.haygroup.com

Hester Evaluation Systems, Inc.
2410 SW Granthurst St.
Topeka, KS 66611
800/832-3825; FAX 785/357-4041
www.hestertesting.com

High/Scope Educational Research Foundation
600 N. River St.
Ypsilanti, MI 48198
734/485-2000; FAX 734/485-4467
www.highscope.org

Joseph A. Hirsch, PhD, PsyD
55 Perry St. #4D
New York, NY 10014-3278
917/865-5066; FAX 212/644-3119
www.nyneuropscholigist.com

Hodder Murray
338 Euston Rd.
London NW1 3BH United Kingdom
207/873-6239; FAX 207/873-6325
www.hoddertests.co.uk

Hogan Assessment Systems, Inc.
PO Box 521176
2622 E. 21st St.
Tulsa, OK 74152
800/756-0632; FAX 918/749-0635
www.hoganassessments.com

Hogrefe & Huber Publishers
875 Massachusetts Ave.
Cambridge, MA 02139
866/823-4726; FAX 617/354-6875
www.hhpub.com

Hogrefe Limited
Burgner House
4630 Kingsgate
Oxford Business Park
Oxford OX4 2SU United Kingdom
44-1865; FAX 44-1865
www.hogrefe.co.uk

Home Inventory LLC
Distribution Center
2627 Winsor Dr.
Eau Claire, WI 54703
715/835-4393
www.ualr.edu/crtldept/home4.htm

HRD Press
22 Amherst Rd.
Amherst, MA 01002-9709

800/822-2801; FAX 413/253-3490
www.hrdpress.com

Industrial Psychology International, Ltd.
4106 Fieldstone Rd.
Champaign, IL 61821
800/747-1119; FAX 217/398-5798
www.metritech.com

InQ Educational Materials, Inc.
PO Box 13306, Montclair Station
Oakland, CA 94661-0306
888/339-2323; FAX 510/339-6729
www.INQ-hpa.com

Insight Assessment
217 La Cruz Ave.
Milbrae, CA 94030
650/697-5628; FAX 650/692-0141
www.insightassessment.com

Institute for Matching Person & Technology, Inc.
486 Lake Rd.
Webster, NY 14580
585/671-3461; FAX 585/671-3461
www.members.aol.com/IMPT97/MPT.html

Institute for Personality and Ability Testing, Inc.
1801 Woodfield Dr.
Savoy, IL 61874
800/225-4728; FAX 217/352-9674
www.ipat.com

Institute of Psychological Research, Inc.
34 Fleury St. West
West Montreal, Quebec, H3L 1S9 Canada
514/382-3000; FAX 514/382-3007
www.i-r-p.ca/English/

International Public Management Association for Human Resources
1617 Duke St.
Alexandria, VA 22314
800/381-8378; FAX 703/684-0948
www.ipma-hr.org

Janelle Publications, Inc.
PO Box 811
1189 Twombley Rd.
DeKalb, IL 60115
800/888-8834; FAX 815/756-4799
www.janellepublications.com

JIST Publishing
8902 Otis Ave.
Indianapolis, IN 46216-1033
877/454-7877; FAX 317/713-1609
www.jist.com

Kaplan Early Learning Company
1310 Lewisville-Clemons Rd.
Lewisville, NC 27023
800/334-2014; FAX 336/712-3243
www.kaplanco.com

Kindergarten Interventions and Diagnostic Services, Inc.
1156 Point Vista Rd.
Hickory Creek, TX 75065
800/594-4649; FAX 940/497-2127
www.kidsinc.com

Life Innovations, Inc.
  PO Box 190
  Minneapolis, MN 55440-0190
  800/331-1661; FAX 651/636-1668
  www.prepare-enrich.com

Life Office Management Association
  2300 Windy Rdg. Pkwy. #600
  Atlanta, GA 30339
  770/984-6450; FAX 770/984-3758
  www.loma.org

LIMRA International
  PO Box 208
  300 Day Hill Rd.
  Windsor, CT 06095
  800/235-4672; FAX 800/846-0923
  www.limra.com

LinguiSystems, Inc.
  PO Box 747
  East Moline, IL 61244
  800/776-4332; FAX 800/577-4555
  www.linguisystems.com

Management & Personnel Systems, Inc.
  2707 N. Main St., Ste. 2
  Walnut Creek, CA 94597
  800/576-7455; FAX 925/977-8200
  www.mps-corp.com

McCarron-Dial Systems
  PO Box 45628
  Dallas, TX 75245
  214/634-2863; FAX 214-634-9970
  www.mccarrondial.com

Albert Mehrabian, PhD
  1130 Alta Mesa Rd.
  Monterey, CA 93940
  888/363-1732
  www.kaaj.com/psych

MetriTech, Inc.
  PO Box 6479
  Champaign, IL 61821-6479
  800/747-4868; FAX 217/398-5798
  www.metritech.com

Mind Garden, Inc.
  855 Oak Grove Ave., Ste. 215
  Menlo Park, CA 94025
  650/322-6300; FAX 650/322-6398
  www.mindgarden.com

Model of Human Occupation Clearinghouse
  1919 W. Taylor St., MC811
  Chicago, IL 60612
  312/413-7469; FAX 312-413-0256
  www.moho.uic.edu

Moreno Educational Company
  PO Box 19329
  San Diego, CA 92159
  619/461-0565; FAX 619/469-1073
  www.morenoed.com

Multi-Health Systems, Inc.
  PO Box 950
  North Tonawanda, NY 14120-0950

800/456-3003; FAX 888/540-4484
www.mhs.com

National Career Assessment Services, Inc.
  PO Box 277
  Adel, IA 50003
  800/314-8972; FAX 515/993-5422
  www.ncasi.com; www.kuder.com

National Occupational Competency Testing Institute
  500 N. Bronson St.
  Big Rapids, MI 49307
  800/334-6283; FAX 231/796-4699
  www.whitenergroup.com

National Reading Styles Institute, Inc.
  PO Box 737
  179 Lafayette Dr.
  Syosset, NY 11791
  800/331-3117; FAX 516/921-5591
  www.nrsi.com

National Spanish Exam
  2051 Mt. Zion Dr.
  Golden, CO 80401
  303/278-1021; FAX 303/278-6400
  www.2nse.org

National Study of School Evaluation
  1699 E. Woodfield Rd.
  Schaumburg, IL 60173
  800/843-6773; FAX 847/995-9088
  www.nsse.org

NeuropsychWorks, Inc.
  8536 Carter Farm Rd.
  Summerfield, NC 27358
  336/664-9351; FAX 336/644-9351
  www.neuropsychworks.com

New Zealand Council for Educational Research
  Education House West
  178-182 Willis St.
  PO Box 3237
  Wellington 6000 New Zealand
  64-4-802-1488; FAX 64-4-384-7933
  www.nzcer.org.nz

Nichols and Molinder Assessments
  437 Bowes Dr.
  Tacoma, WA 98466
  253/565-4539; FAX 253/565-0164
  www.nicholsandmolinder.com

Occupational Research Centre
  Cornerways Cardigan St.
  Newmarket, Suffolk CB8 UK
  44 1638 662
  www.kaicentre.com

OMNIA Group, Incorporated
  601 S. Blvd., 4th Fl.
  Tampa, FL 33606
  800/525-7117; FAX 813/254-8558
  www.omniagroup.com

Organizational Measurement Systems Press
  PO Box 70586
  34199 Country View Dr.

Eugene, OR 97401
541/484-2715; FAX 541/465-1602

Pain Assessment Resources
6490 S. McCarran Blvd., Ste. 52
Reno, NV 89509
800/782-1501; FAX 775/828-4275
www.painassessmentresources.com

PAQ Services, Inc.
11 Bellwether Way, Ste. 107
Bellingham, WA 98225
800/292-2198; FAX 877/395-0236
www.paq.com

Pearson Assessments
5601 Green Valley Dr.
Bloomington, MN 55437
952/681-3364; FAX 952/681-3259
www.pearsonassessments.com

Pearson Early Learning
145 Mt. Zion Rd.
Lebanon, IN 46052
800/321-3106; FAX 800/393-3156
www.pearsonearlylearning.com

Pearson Performance Solutions
One N. Dearborn, Ste. 1600
Chicago, IL 60602
800/922-7343; FAX 312/242-4400
www.pearsonps.com

Penn State Gerontology Center
Pennsylvania State University
135 E. Nittany, Ste. 405
State College, PA 16801-5363
814/865-1710; FAX 814/863-9423
http://geron.psu.edu

Performance Programs, Inc.
PO Box 630
Old Saybrook, CT 06475
800/565-4223 or 860/388-9777;
FAX 860/388-6862
www.PerformancePrograms.com

Personal Strengths Publishing
PO Box 2605
Carlsbad, CA 92018
800/624-7347; FAX 760/602-0087
www.PersonalStrengths.com

PESCO International
21 Paulding St.
Pleasantville, NY 10570
800/431-2016; FAX 914/769-2970
www.pesco.org

Piney Mountain Press, Inc.
PO Box 333
Cleveland, GA 30528
800/255-3127; FAX 800/905-3127
www.pineymountain.com

Price Systems, Inc.
PO Box 1818
Lawrence, KS 66044

800/574-4441; FAX 785/843-0101
www.learningstyle.com

PRO-ED, Inc.
8700 Shoal Creek Blvd.
Austin, TX 78757
800/897-3202; FAX 512/451-8542
www.proedinc.com

Prufrock Press, Inc.
PO Box 8813
Waco, TX 76714
800/998-2208; FAX 800/240-0333
www.prufrock.com

Psycho-Educational Services
5114 Balcones Woods Dr.
Austin, TX 78759
512/335-1591; FAX 512/335-1889
www.psycho-educational.com

Psychological Assessment Resources, Inc.
16204 N. Florida Ave.
Lutz, FL 33549
800/331-8378; FAX 800/727-9329
www.parinc.com

Psychological Growth Associates, Inc.
Products Division
3813 Tiffany Dr.
Lawrence, KS 66049
785/749-2190; FAX 785/749-2190
www.nvo.com/tcs

Psychological Publications, Inc.
PO Box 3577
Thousand Oaks, CA 91359-0577
800/345-8378; FAX 805/527-9266
www.TJTA.com

Psychological Services Bureau, Inc.
2774 Hydraulic Rd.
Charlottesville, VA 22901
877/932-8378; FAX 800/257-0527
www.psbtests.com

Psychological Services, Inc.
Test Publication Division
2950 N. Hollywood Way
Burbank, CA 91505
800/367-1565; FAX 818/847-8701
www.PSIonline.com

Ramsay Corporation
Boyce Station Offices
1050 Boyce Rd.
Pittsburgh, PA 15241-3907
412/257-0732; FAX 412/257-9929
www.ramsaycorp.com

Renaissance Learning, Inc.
PO Box 8036
Wisconsin Rapids, WI 54495-8036
800/200-4848; FAX 715/424-4242
www.renlearn.com

Richmond Products, Inc.
4400 Silver Ave. SE
Albuquerque, NM 87108

505/275-2406; FAX 810/885-8319
www.richmondproducts.com

Riverside Publishing Company
135 Spring Lake Dr.
Itasca, IL 60143
800/323-9540; FAX 630/467-7192
www.riverpub.com

Rocky Mountain Behavioral Science Institute, Inc.
305 W. Magnolia St.
Fort Collins, CO 80521
800/447-6354; FAX 970/221-0595
www.rmbsi.com

Rohner Research Publications
255 Codfish Falls Rd.
Storrs, CT 06268
860/486-0073; FAX 860/486-3915
www.cspar.uconn.edu

SASSI Institute
Rt. 2, Box 134
Springville, IN 47462
800/726-0526; FAX 800/546-7995
www.sassi.com

Nina G., Schneider, PhD
VA Greater LA Healthcare System
Box 51667, Mail Code: 166747
Los Angeles, CA 00005 1667
310/268-3059; FAX 310/268-4125
www.proqolid.org

Scholastic Testing Service, Inc.
480 Meyer Rd.
Bensenville, IL 00106 1617
800/642-6787; FAX 866/766-8054
www.ststesting.com

Sensonics, Inc.
PO Box 112
Haddon Heights, NJ 08035
800/547-8838; FAX 856/547-5665
www.smelltest.com

SHL People Performance
200 S. Wacker Dr.
Chicago, IL 60606
312/655-8420; FAX 312/655-8421
www.shl.com

Sidran Foundation
200 E. Joppa Rd., Ste. 207
Twoson, MD 21286-3107
410/825-8888; FAX 410/337-0747
www.sidran.org

Sigma Assessment Systems, Inc.
PO Box 610984
1110 Military St.
Port Huron, MI 48061-0984
800/265-1285; FAX 800/361-9411
www.sigmaassessmentsystems.com

Slosson Educational Publications, Inc.
PO Box 280
East Aurora, NY 14052

888/756-7766; FAX 800/655-3840
www.slosson.com

Sopris West Educational Services
4039 Speciality Pl.
Longmont, CO 80504
800/547-6747; FAX 888/819-7767
www.sopriswest.com

Stoelting Company
620 Wheat Ln.
Wood Dale, IL 60191
630/860-9700; FAX 630/860-9775
www.stoeltingco.com/tests

Taylor Protocols
16040 Christensen Rd., Ste. 315
Tukwila, WA 98115
877/355-8229; FAX 206/283-0844
www.taylorprotocols.com

Teachers College Press
1234 Amsterdam Ave.
New York, NY 10027
800/575-6566; FAX 212/678-4149
www.teacherscollegepress.com

Thomson Nelson
1120 Birchmount Rd.
Toronto, ON M1K 5G4
800/268-2222; FAX 800/430-4445
www.assess.nelson.com

Touchstone Applied Science Associates, Inc.
PO Box 382
4 Hardscrabble Hts.
Brewster, NY 10509
800/800-2598; FAX 845/777-8115
www.tasaliteracy.com

Trust Tutoring
8115 Fenton St.
Silver Spring, MD 20910
800/301-3131; FAX 301/589-0733
http://trusttutoring.com

Universal Attention Disorders, Inc.
4281 Katella Ave. #215
Los Alamitos, CA 90720
800/729-2886; FAX 800/452-6919
www.tovatest.com

Valpar International Corporation
2450 W. Ruthrauff Rd., Ste. 180
Tucson, AZ 85705
800/633-3321; FAX 262/797-8488
www.Valparint.com

Variety Child Learning Center
47 Humphrey Dr.
Syosset, NY 11791
800/933-8779; FAX 516/921-8130
www.vclc.org

Village Publishing
73 Valley Dr.
Furlong, PA 18925
215/794-0202; FAX 215/794-3386
www.vp411.com

Vocational Psychology Research
  University of Minnesota
  N620 Elliot Hall
  75 E. River Rd.
  Minneapolis, MN 55455-0344
  612/625-1367; FAX 612/626-0345
  www.psych.umn.edu/psylabs/vpr

Vocational Research Institute
  1528 Walnut St., Ste. 1502
  Philadelphia, PA 19102
  800/874-5387; FAX 215/875-0198
  www.vri.org

VORT Corporation
  PO Box 60132
  Palo Alto, CA 94306
  888/757-8678; FAX 650/327-0747
  www.vort.com

Western Psychological Services
  12031 Wilshire Blvd.
  Los Angeles, CA 90025-1251
  800/648-8857; FAX 310/478-7838
  www.wpspublish.com

Wiley
  989 Market St.
  San Francisco, CA 94103
  800/569-0443; FAX 415/433-0499
  www.wiley.com

Winslow Research Institute
  1933 Windward Pt.
  Discovery Bay, CA 95414
  925/516-8686; FAX 925/516-7015
  www.WinslowResearch.com

Wonderlic Personnel Test, Inc.
  1795 N. Butterfield Rd.
  Libertyville, IL 60048
  800/323-3742; FAX 847/680-9492
  www.wonderlic.com

World of Work, Inc.
  410 W. 1st St.
  Tempe, AZ 85281
  800/272-9694; FAX 480/966-6200
  www.wowi.com

Index of Test Authors

Index of Test Titles

About the Editor

Taddy Maddox joined PRO-ED in 1994 after completing her doctorate in special education at the University of Texas at Austin. Previously she worked as an educational diagnostician in Texas public schools for 15 years. Prior to that, Dr. Maddox was a special education teacher in self-contained and resource settings. In January 2006, she retired from direct employment at PRO-ED.

Since joining PRO-ED, Dr. Maddox has worked on the development of many test instruments and is co-author on the *Basic School Skills Instrument* and *Developmental Assessment of Young Children*. She was also the editor of the Fourth and Fifth Editions of *Tests*. In addition, she has been active in professional organizations as an officer and committee member.